Bootstrap methods and their application

Cambridge Series on Statistical and Probabilistic Mathematics

Editorial Board:
R. Gill (Utrecht)
B.D. Ripley (Oxford)
S. Ross (Berkeley)
M. Stein (Chicago)
D. Williams (Bath)

This series of high quality upper-division textbooks and expository mono-
graphs covers all areas of stochastic applicable mathematics. The topics
range from pure and applied statistics to probability theory, operations research, mathematical programming, and optimzation. The books contain
clear presentations of new developments in the field and also of the state of
the art in classical methods. While emphasizing rigorous treatment of theoretical methods, the books contain important applications and discussions
of new techniques made possible be advances in computational methods.

Bootstrap methods and their application

A. C. Davison

Professor of Statistics, Department of Mathematics,
Swiss Federal Institute of Technology, Lausanne

D. V. Hinkley

Professor of Statistics, Department of Statistics and Applied Probability,
University of California, Santa Barbara

CAMBRIDGE
UNIVERSITY PRESS

PUBLISHED BY THE PRESS SYNDICATE OF THE UNIVERSITY OF CAMBRIDGE
The Pitt Building, Trumpington Street, Cambridge CB2 1RP, United Kingdom

CAMBRIDGE UNIVERSITY PRESS
The Edinburgh Building, Cambridge CB2 2RU, United Kingdom
40 West 20th Street, New York, NY 10011-4211, USA
10 Stamford Road, Oakleigh, Melbourne 3166, Australia

© Cambridge University Press 1997

First published 1997

Printed in the United States of America

Typeset in TEX Monotype Times

A catalogue record for this book is available from the British Library

Library of Congress Cataloguing in Publication data

Davison, A. C. (Anthony Christopher)
Bootstrap methods and their application / A.C. Davison,
D.V. Hinkley.
p. cm.
Includes bibliographical references and index.
ISBN 0 521 57391 2 (hb).   ISBN 0 521 57471 4 (pb)
1. Bootstrap (Statistics) I. Hinkley, D. V. II. Title.
QA276.8.D38   1997
519.5′44–dc21   96-30064   CIP

ISBN 0 521 57391 2 hardback
ISBN 0 521 57471 4 paperback

Contents

Preface

The publication in 1979 of Bradley Efron's first article on bootstrap methods was a major event in Statistics, at once synthesizing some of the earlier resampling ideas and establishing a new framework for simulation-based statistical analysis. The idea of replacing complicated and often inaccurate approximations to biases, variances, and other measures of uncertainty by computer simulations caught the imagination of both theoretical researchers and users of statistical methods. Theoreticians sharpened their pencils and set about establishing mathematical conditions under which the idea could work. Once they had overcome their initial skepticism, applied workers sat down at their terminals and began to amass empirical evidence that the bootstrap often did work better than traditional methods. The early trickle of papers quickly became a torrent, with new additions to the literature appearing every month, and it was hard to see when would be a good moment to try to chart the waters. Then the organizers of COMPSTAT '92 invited us to present a course on the topic, and shortly afterwards we began to write this book.

We decided to try to write a balanced account of resampling methods, to include basic aspects of the theory which underpinned the methods, and to show as many applications as we could in order to illustrate the full potential of the methods — warts and all. We quickly realized that in order for us and others to understand and use the bootstrap, we would need suitable software, and producing it led us further towards a practically oriented treatment. Our view was cemented by two further developments: the appearance of two excellent books, one by Peter Hall on the asymptotic theory and the other on basic methods by Bradley Efron and Robert Tibshirani; and the chance to give further courses that included practicals. Our experience has been that hands-on computing is essential in coming to grips with resampling ideas, so we have included practicals in this book, as well as more theoretical problems.

As the book expanded, we realized that a fully comprehensive treatment was beyond us, and that certain topics could be given only a cursory treatment because too little is known about them. So it is that the reader will find only brief accounts of bootstrap methods for hierarchical data, missing data problems, model selection, robust estimation, nonparametric regression, and complex data. But we do try to point the more ambitious reader in the right direction.

No project of this size is produced in a vacuum. The majority of work on the book was completed while we were at the University of Oxford, and we are very grateful to colleagues and students there, who have helped shape our work in various ways. The experience of trying to teach these methods in Oxford and elsewhere — at the Université de Toulouse I, Université de Neuchâtel, Università degli Studi di Padova, Queensland University of Technology, Universidade de São Paulo, and University of Umeå — has been vital, and we are grateful to participants in these courses for prompting us to think more deeply about the material. Readers will be grateful to these people also, for unwittingly debugging some of the problems and practicals. We are also grateful to the organizers of COMPSTAT '92 and CLAPEM V for inviting us to give short courses on our work.

While writing this book we have asked many people for access to data, copies of their programs, papers or reprints; some have then been rewarded by our bombarding them with questions, to which the answers have invariably been courteous and informative. We cannot name all those who have helped in this way, but D. R. Brillinger, P. Hall, M. P. Jones, B. D. Ripley, H. O'R. Sternberg and G. A. Young have been especially generous. S. Hutchinson and B. D. Ripley have helped considerably with computing matters.

We are grateful to the mostly anonymous reviewers who commented on an early draft of the book, and to R. Gatto and G. A. Young, who later read various parts in detail. At Cambridge University Press, A. Woollatt and D. Tranah have helped greatly in producing the final version, and their patience has been commendable.

We are particularly indebted to two people. V. Ventura read large portions of the book, and helped with various aspects of the computation. A. J. Canty has turned our version of the bootstrap library functions into reliable working code, checked the book for mistakes, and has made numerous suggestions that have improved it enormously. Both of them have contributed greatly — though of course we take responsibility for any errors that remain in the book. We hope that readers will tell us about them, and we will do our best to correct any future versions of the book; see its WWW page, at URL

`http://dmawww.epfl.ch/davison.mosaic/BMA/`

The book could not have been completed without grants from the UK Engineering and Physical Sciences Research Council, which in addition to providing funding for equipment and research assistantships, supported the work of A. C. Davison through the award of an Advanced Research Fellowship. We also acknowledge support from the US National Science Foundation.

We must also mention the Friday evening sustenance provided at the Eagle and Child, the Lamb and Flag, and the Royal Oak. The projects of many authors have flourished in these amiable establishments.

Finally, we thank our families, friends and colleagues for their patience while this project absorbed our time and energy. Particular thanks are due to Claire Cullen Davison for keeping the Davison family going during the writing of this book.

A. C. Davison and D. V. Hinkley
Lausanne and Santa Barbara
May 1997

1

Introduction

The explicit recognition of uncertainty is central to the statistical sciences. Notions such as prior information, probability models, likelihood, standard errors and confidence limits are all intended to formalize uncertainty and thereby make allowance for it. In simple situations, the uncertainty of an estimate may be gauged by analytical calculation based on an assumed probability model for the available data. But in more complicated problems this approach can be tedious and difficult, and its results are potentially misleading if inappropriate assumptions or simplifications have been made.

For illustration, consider Table 1.1, which is taken from a larger tabulation (Table 7.4) of the numbers of AIDS reports in England and Wales from mid-1983 to the end of 1992. Reports are cross-classified by diagnosis period and length of reporting delay, in three-month intervals. A blank in the table corresponds to an unknown (as yet unreported) entry. The problem was to predict the states of the epidemic in 1991 and 1992, which depend heavily on the values missing at the bottom right of the table.

The data support the assumption that the reporting delay does not depend on the diagnosis period. In this case a simple model is that the number of reports in row j and column k of the table has a Poisson distribution with mean $\mu_{jk} = \exp(\alpha_j + \beta_k)$. If all the cells of the table are regarded as independent, then the total number of unreported diagnoses in period j has a Poisson distribution with mean

$$\sum_k \mu_{jk} = \exp(\alpha_j) \sum_k \exp(\beta_k),$$

where the sum is over columns with blanks in row j. The eventual total of as yet unreported diagnoses from period j can be estimated by replacing α_j and β_k by estimates derived from the incomplete table, and thence we obtain the predicted total for period j. Such predictions are shown by the solid line in

Diagnosis period		Reporting delay interval (quarters):									Total reports to end of 1992
Year	Quarter	0†	1	2	3	4	5	6	⋯	≥14	
1988	1	31	80	16	9	3	2	8	⋯	6	174
	2	26	99	27	9	8	11	3	⋯	3	211
	3	31	95	35	13	18	4	6	⋯	3	224
	4	36	77	20	26	11	3	8	⋯	2	205
1989	1	32	92	32	10	12	19	12	⋯	2	224
	2	15	92	14	27	22	21	12	⋯	1	219
	3	34	104	29	31	18	8	6	⋯		253
	4	38	101	34	18	9	15	6	⋯		233
1990	1	31	124	47	24	11	15	8	⋯		281
	2	32	132	36	10	9	7	6	⋯		245
	3	49	107	51	17	15	8	9	⋯		260
	4	44	153	41	16	11	6	5	⋯		285
1991	1	41	137	29	33	7	11	6	⋯		271
	2	56	124	39	14	12	7	10			263
	3	53	175	35	17	13	11				306
	4	63	135	24	23	12					258
1992	1	71	161	48	25						310
	2	95	178	39							318
	3	76	181								273
	4	67									133

Table 1.1 Numbers of AIDS reports in England and Wales to the end of 1992 (De Angelis and Gilks, 1994) extracted from Table 7.4. A † indicates a reporting delay less than one month.

Figure 1.1, together with the observed total reports to the end of 1992. How good are these predictions?

It would be tedious but possible to put pen to paper and estimate the prediction uncertainty through calculations based on the Poisson model. But in fact the data are much more variable than that model would suggest, and by failing to take this into account we would believe that the predictions are more accurate than they really are. Furthermore, a better approach would be to use a semiparametric model to smooth out the evident variability of the increase in diagnoses from quarter to quarter; the corresponding prediction is the dotted line in Figure 1.1. Analytical calculations for this model would be very unpleasant, and a more flexible line of attack is needed. While more than one approach is possible, the one that we shall develop based on computer simulation is both flexible and straightforward.

Purpose of the Book

Our central goal is to describe how the computer can be harnessed to obtain reliable standard errors, confidence intervals, and other measures of uncertainty for a wide range of problems. The key idea is to resample from the original data — either directly or via a fitted model — to create replicate datasets, from

Figure 1.1 Predicted
quarterly diagnoses
from a parametric
model (solid) and a
semiparametric model
(dots) fitted to the
AIDS data, together
with the actual totals to
the end of 1992 (+).

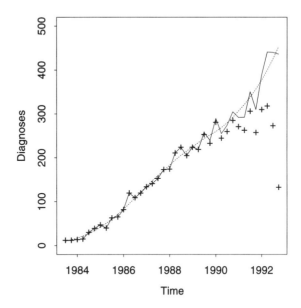

which the variability of the quantities of interest can be assessed without long-winded and error-prone analytical calculation. Because this approach involves repeating the original data analysis procedure with many replicate sets of data, these are sometimes called *computer-intensive methods*. Another name for them is *bootstrap methods*, because to use the data to generate more data seems analogous to a trick used by the fictional Baron Munchausen, who when he found himself at the bottom of a lake got out by pulling himself up by his bootstraps. In the simplest nonparametric problems we do literally sample from the data, and a common initial reaction is that this is a fraud. In fact it is not. It turns out that a wide range of statistical problems can be tackled this way, liberating the investigator from the need to oversimplify complex problems. The approach can also be applied in simple problems, to check the adequacy of standard measures of uncertainty, to relax assumptions, and to give quick approximate solutions. An example of this is random sampling to estimate the permutation distribution of a nonparametric test statistic.

It is of course true that in many applications we can be fairly confident in a particular parametric model and the standard analysis based on that model. Even so, it can still be helpful to see what can be inferred without particular parametric model assumptions. This is in the spirit of *robustness of validity* of the statistical analysis performed. Nonparametric bootstrap analysis allows us to do this.

| 3 | 5 | 7 | 18 | 43 | 85 | 91 | 98 | 100 | 130 | 230 | 487 |

Table 1.2 Service hours between failures of the air-conditioning equipment in a Boeing 720 jet aircraft (Proschan, 1963).

Despite its scope and usefulness, resampling must be carefully applied. Unless certain basic ideas are understood, it is all too easy to produce a solution to the wrong problem, or a bad solution to the right one. Bootstrap methods are intended to help avoid tedious calculations based on questionable assumptions, and this they do. But they cannot replace clear critical thought about the problem, appropriate design of the investigation and data analysis, and incisive presentation of conclusions.

In this book we describe how resampling methods can be used, and evaluate their performance, in a wide range of contexts. Our focus is on the methods and their practical application rather than on the underlying theory, accounts of which are available elsewhere. This book is intended to be useful to the many investigators who want to know how and when the methods can safely be applied, and how to tell when things have gone wrong. The mathematical level of the book reflects this: we have aimed for a clear account of the key ideas without an overload of technical detail.

Examples

Bootstrap methods can be applied both when there is a well-defined probability model for data and when there is not. In our initial development of the methods we shall make frequent use of two simple examples, one of each type, to illustrate the main points.

Example 1.1 (Air-conditioning data)   Table 1.2 gives $n = 12$ times between failures of air-conditioning equipment, for which we wish to estimate the underlying mean or its reciprocal, the failure rate. A simple model for this problem is that the times are sampled from an exponential distribution.

The dotted line in the left panel of Figure 1.2 is the cumulative distribution function (CDF)

$$F_\mu(y) = \begin{cases} 0, & y \le 0, \\ 1 - \exp(-y/\mu), & y > 0, \end{cases}$$

for the fitted exponential distribution with mean μ set equal to the sample average, $\bar{y} = 108.083$. The solid line on the same plot is the nonparametric equivalent, the empirical distribution function (EDF) for the data, which places equal probabilities $n^{-1} = 0.08\dot{3}$ at each sample value. Comparison of the two curves suggests that the exponential model fits reasonably well. An alternative view of this is shown in the right panel of the figure, which is an exponential

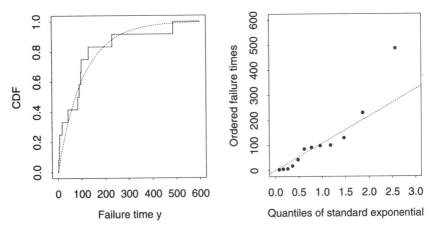

Figure 1.2 Summary displays for the air-conditioning data. The left panel shows the EDF for the data, $\hat{F}$ (solid), and the CDF of a fitted exponential distribution (dots). The right panel shows a plot of the ordered failure times against exponential quantiles, with the fitted exponential model shown as the dotted line.

Q-Q plot — a plot of ordered data values $y_{(j)}$ against the standard exponential quantiles

$$F_\mu^{-1}\left(\frac{j}{n+1}\right)\Bigg|_{\mu=1} = -\log\left(1-\frac{j}{n+1}\right).$$

Although these plots suggest reasonable agreement with the exponential model, the sample is rather too small to have much confidence in this. In the data source the more general gamma model with mean μ and index κ is used; its density is

$$f_{\mu,\kappa}(y) = \frac{1}{\Gamma(\kappa)}\left(\frac{\kappa}{\mu}\right)^\kappa y^{\kappa-1}\exp(-\kappa y/\mu), \qquad y>0, \quad \mu,\kappa>0. \tag{1.1}$$

For our sample the estimated index is $\hat{\kappa} = 0.71$, which does not differ significantly ($P = 0.29$) from the value $\kappa = 1$ that corresponds to the exponential model. Our reason for mentioning this will become apparent in Chapter 2.

Basic properties of the estimator $T = \bar{Y}$ for μ are easy to obtain theoretically under the exponential model. For example, it is easy to show that T is unbiased and has variance μ^2/n. Approximate confidence intervals for μ can be calculated using these properties in conjunction with a normal approximation for the distribution of T, although this does not work very well: we can tell this because $\bar{Y}/\mu$ has an exact gamma distribution, which leads to exact confidence limits. Things are more complicated under the more general gamma model, because the index κ is only estimated, and so in a traditional approach we would use approximations — such as a normal approximation for the distribution of T, or a chi-squared approximation for the log likelihood ratio statistic.

The parametric simulation methods of Section 2.2 can be used alongside these approximations, to diagnose problems with them, or to replace them entirely.

■

Example 1.2 (City population data)   Table 1.3 reports $n = 49$ data pairs, each corresponding to a city in the United States of America, the pair being the 1920 and 1930 populations of the city, which we denote by u and x. The data are plotted in Figure 1.3. Interest here is in the ratio of means, because this would enable us to estimate the total population of the USA in 1930 from the 1920 figure. If the cities form a random sample with (U, X) denoting the pair of population values for a randomly selected city, then the total 1930 population is the product of the total 1920 population and the ratio of expectations $\theta = \mathrm{E}(X)/\mathrm{E}(U)$. This ratio is the parameter of interest.

In this case there is no obvious parametric model for the joint distribution of (U, X), so it is natural to estimate θ by its empirical analog, $T = \bar{X}/\bar{U}$, the ratio of sample averages. We are then concerned with the uncertainty in T. If we had a plausible parametric model — for example, that the pair (U, X) has a bivariate lognormal distribution — then theoretical calculations like those in Example 1.1 would lead to bias and variance estimates for use in a normal approximation, which in turn would provide approximate confidence intervals for θ. Without such a model we must use nonparametric analysis. It is still possible to estimate the bias and variance of T, as we shall see, and this makes normal approximation still feasible, as well as more complex approaches to setting confidence intervals.   ■

Example 1.1 is special in that an exact distribution is available for the statistic of interest and can be used to calculate confidence limits, at least under the exponential model. But for parametric models in general this will not be true. In Section 2.2 we shall show how to use parametric simulation to obtain approximate distributions, either by approximating moments for use in normal approximations, or — when these are inaccurate — directly.

In Example 1.2 we make no assumptions about the form of the data disribution. But still, as we shall show in Section 2.3, simulation can be used to obtain properties of T, even to approximate its distribution. Much of Chapter 2 is devoted to this.

Layout of the Book

Chapter 2 describes the properties of resampling methods for use with single samples from parametric and nonparametric models, discusses practical matters such as the numbers of replicate datasets required, and outlines delta methods for variance approximation based on different forms of jackknife. It

Table 1.3 Populations
in thousands of $n = 49$
large US cities in 1920
(u) and in 1930 (x)
(Cochran, 1977, p. 152).

u	x	u	x	u	x
138	143	76	80	67	67
93	104	381	464	120	115
61	69	387	459	172	183
179	260	78	106	66	86
48	75	60	57	46	65
37	63	507	634	121	113
29	50	50	64	44	58
23	48	77	89	64	63
30	111	64	77	56	142
2	50	40	60	40	64
38	52	136	139	116	130
46	53	243	291	87	105
71	79	256	288	43	61
25	57	94	85	43	50
298	317	36	46	161	232
74	93	45	53	36	54
50	58				

Figure 1.3 Populations
of 49 large United
States cities (in 1000s)
in 1920 and 1930.

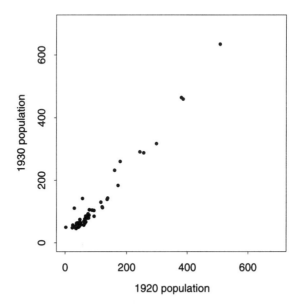

also contains a basic discussion of confidence intervals and of the ideas that underlie bootstrap methods.

Chapter 3 outlines how the basic ideas are extended to several samples, semiparametric and smooth models, simple cases where data have hierarchical structure or are sampled from a finite population, and to situations where data are incomplete because censored or missing. It goes on to discuss how the simulation output itself may be used to detect problems — so-called bootstrap diagnostics — and how it may be useful to bootstrap the bootstrap.

In Chapter 4 we review the basic principles of significance testing, and then describe Monte Carlo tests, including those using Markov Chain simulation, and parametric bootstrap tests. This is followed by discussion of nonparametric permutation tests, and the more general methods of semi- and nonparametric bootstrap tests. A double bootstrap method is detailed for improved approximation of P-values.

Confidence intervals are the subject of Chapter 5. After outlining basic ideas, we describe how to construct simple confidence intervals based on simulations, and then go on to more complex methods, such as the studentized bootstrap, percentile methods, the double bootstrap and test inversion. The main methods are compared empirically in Section 5.7, then there are brief accounts of confidence regions for multivariate parameters, and of prediction intervals.

The three subsequent chapters deal with more complex problems. Chapter 6 describes how the basic resampling methods may be applied in linear regression problems, including tests for coefficients, prediction analysis, and variable selection. Chapter 7 deals with more complex regression situations: generalized linear models, other nonlinear models, semi- and nonparametric regression, survival analysis, and classification error. Chapter 8 details methods appropriate for time series, spatial data, and point processes.

Chapter 9 describes how variance reduction techniques such as balanced simulation, control variates, and importance sampling can be adapted to yield improved simulations, with the aim of reducing the amount of simulation needed for an answer of given accuracy. It also shows how saddlepoint methods can sometimes be used to avoid simulation entirely.

Chapter 10 describes various semiparametric versions of the likelihood function, the ideas underlying which are closely related to resampling methods. It also briefly outlines a Bayesian version of the bootstrap.

Chapters 2–10 contain problems intended to reinforce the reader's understanding of both methods and theory, and in some cases problems develop topics that could not be included in the text. Some of these demand a knowledge of moments and cumulants, basic facts about which are sketched in the Appendix.

The book also contains practicals that apply resampling routines written in the S language to sets of data. The practicals are intended to reinforce the ideas in each chapter, to supplement the more theoretical problems, and to give examples on which readers can base analyses of their own data.

It would be possible to give different sorts of course based on this book. One would be a "theoretical" course based on the problems and another an "applied" course based on the practicals; we prefer to blend the two.

Although a library of routines for use with the statistical package SPlus is bundled with it, most of the book can be read without reference to particular software packages. Apart from the practicals, the exception to this is Chapter 11, which is a short introduction to the main resampling routines, arranged roughly in the order with which the corresponding ideas appear in earlier chapters. Readers intending to use the bundled routines will find it useful to work through the relevant sections of Chapter 11 before attempting the practicals.

Notation

Although we believe that our notation is largely standard, there are not enough letters in the English and Greek alphabets for us to be entirely consistent. Greek letters such as θ, β and ν generally denote parameters or other unknowns, while α is used for error rates in connection with significance tests and confidence sets. English letters X, Y, Z, and so forth are used for random variables, which take values x, y, z. Thus the estimator T has observed value t, which may be an estimate of the unknown parameter θ. The letter V is used for a variance estimate, and the letter p for a probability, except for regression models, where p is the number of covariates. Script letters such as $\mathcal{N}$ are used to denote sets.

Probability, expectation, variance and covariance are denoted $\Pr(\cdot)$, $E(\cdot)$, $\text{var}(\cdot)$ and $\text{cov}(\cdot, \cdot)$, while the joint cumulant of Y_1, $Y_1 Y_2$ and Y_3 is denoted $\text{cum}(Y_1, Y_1 Y_2, Y_3)$. We use $I\{A\}$ to denote the indicator random variable, which takes values one if the event A is true and zero otherwise. A related function is the Heaviside function

$$H(u) = \begin{cases} 0, & u < 0, \\ 1, & u \geq 0. \end{cases}$$

We use $\#\{A\}$ to denote the number of elements in the set A, and $\#\{A_r\}$ for the number of events A_r that occur in a sequence $A_1, A_2, \ldots$. We use $\doteq$ to mean "is approximately equal to", usually corresponding to asymptotic equivalence as sample sizes tend to infinity, $\sim$ to mean "is distributed as" or "is distributed according to", $\dot\sim$ to mean "is distributed approximately as", $\overset{iid}{\sim}$ to mean "is a sample of independent identically distributed random variables from", while $\equiv$ has its usual meaning of "is equivalent to".

The data values in a sample of size n are typically denoted by $y_1, \ldots, y_n$, the observed values of the random variables $Y_1, \ldots, Y_n$; their average is $\bar{y} = n^{-1} \sum y_j$.

We mostly reserve Z for random variables that are standard normal, at least approximately, and use Q for random variables with other (approximately) known distributions. As usual $N(\mu, \sigma^2)$ represents the normal distribution with mean μ and variance σ^2, while z_α is often the α quantile of the standard normal distribution, whose cumulative distribution function is $\Phi(\cdot)$.

The letter R is reserved for the number of replicate simulations. Simulated copies of a statistic T are denoted T_r^*, $r = 1, \ldots, R$, whose ordered values are $T_{(1)}^* \leq \cdots \leq T_{(R)}^*$. Expectation, variance and probability calculated with respect to the simulation distribution are written $\Pr^*(\cdot)$, $E^*(\cdot)$ and $\text{var}^*(\cdot)$.

Where possible we avoid boldface type, and rely on the context to make it plain when we are dealing with vectors or matrices; a^T denotes the matrix transpose of a vector or matrix a.

We use PDF, CDF, and EDF as shorthand for "probability density function", "cumulative distribution function", and "empirical distribution function". The letters F and G are used for CDFs, and f and g are generally used for the corresponding PDFs. An exception to this is that f_{rj}^* denotes the frequency with which y_j appears in the rth resample.

We use MLE as shorthand for "maximum likelihood estimate" or sometimes "maximum likelihood estimation".

The end of each example is marked ■, and the end of each algorithm is marked •.

2

The Basic Bootstraps

2.1 Introduction

In this chapter we discuss techniques which are applicable to a single, homogeneous sample of data, denoted by $y_1, \ldots, y_n$. The sample values are thought of as the outcomes of independent and identically distributed random variables $Y_1, \ldots, Y_n$ whose *probability density function* (PDF) and *cumulative distribution function* (CDF) we shall denote by f and F, respectively. The sample is to be used to make inferences about a population characteristic, generically denoted by θ, using a statistic T whose value in the sample is t. We assume for the moment that the choice of T has been made and that it is an estimate for θ, which we take to be a scalar.

Our attention is focused on questions concerning the probability distribution of T. For example, what are its bias, its standard error, or its quantiles? What are likely values under a certain null hypothesis of interest? How do we calculate confidence limits for θ using T?

There are two situations to distinguish, the parametric and the nonparametric. When there is a particular mathematical model, with adjustable constants or parameters ψ that fully determine f, such a model is called *parametric* and statistical methods based on this model are parametric methods. In this case the parameter of interest θ is a component of or function of ψ. When no such mathematical model is used, the statistical analysis is *nonparametric*, and uses only the fact that the random variables Y_j are independent and identically distributed. Even if there is a plausible parametric model, a nonparametric analysis can still be useful to assess the robustness of conclusions drawn from a parametric analysis.

An important role is played in nonparametric analysis by the *empirical distribution* which puts equal probabilities n^{-1} at each sample value y_j. The corresponding estimate of F is the *empirical distribution function* (EDF) $\hat{F}$, which is defined as the sample proportion

$$\hat{F}(y) = \frac{\#\{y_j \leq y\}}{n}.$$

$\#\{A\}$ means the number of times the event A occurs.

More formally

$$\hat{F}(y) = \frac{1}{n} \sum_{j=1}^{n} H(y - y_j), \qquad (2.1)$$

where $H(u)$ is the unit step function which jumps from 0 to 1 at $u = 0$. Notice that the values of the EDF are fixed $(0, \frac{1}{n}, \frac{2}{n}, \ldots, \frac{n}{n})$, so the EDF is equivalent to its points of increase, the ordered values $y_{(1)} \leq \cdots \leq y_{(n)}$ of the data. An example of the EDF was shown in the left panel of Figure 1.2.

When there are repeat values in the sample, as would often occur with discrete data, the EDF assigns probabilities proportional to the sample frequencies at each distinct observed value y. The formal definition (2.1) still applies.

The EDF plays the role of fitted model when no mathematical form is assumed for F, analogous to a parametric CDF with parameters replaced by their estimates.

2.1.1 Statistical functions

Many simple statistics can be thought of in terms of properties of the EDF. For example, the sample average $\bar{y} = n^{-1} \sum y_j$ is the mean of the EDF; see Example 2.1 below. More generally, the statistic of interest t will be a symmetric function of $y_1, \ldots, y_n$, meaning that t is unaffected by reordering the data. This implies that t depends only on the ordered values $y_{(1)} \leq \cdots \leq y_{(n)}$, or equivalently on the EDF $\hat{F}$. Often this can be expressed simply as $t = t(\hat{F})$, where $t(\cdot)$ is a *statistical function* — essentially just a mathematical expression of the algorithm for computing t from $\hat{F}$. Such a statistical function is of central importance in the nonparametric case because it also defines the parameter of interest θ through the "algorithm" $\theta = t(F)$. This corresponds to the qualitative idea that θ is a characteristic of the population described by F. Simple examples of such functions are the mean and variance of Y, which are respectively defined as

$$t(F) = \int y \, dF(y), \qquad t(F) = \int y^2 \, dF(y) - \left\{ \int y \, dF(y) \right\}^2. \qquad (2.2)$$

The same definition of θ applies in parametric problems, although then θ is more usually defined explicitly as one of the model parameters ψ.

The relationship between the estimate t and $\hat{F}$ can usually be expressed as $t = t(\hat{F})$, corresponding to the relation $\theta = t(F)$ between the characteristic of interest and the underlying distribution. The statistical function $t(\cdot)$ defines both the parameter and its estimate, but we shall use $t(\cdot)$ to represent the function, and t to represent the estimate of θ based on the observed data $y_1, \ldots, y_n$.

Example 2.1 (Average) The sample average, $\bar{y}$, estimates the population mean

$$\mu = \int y \, dF(y).$$

To show that $\bar{y} = t(\hat{F})$, we substitute for $\hat{F}$ in the defining function at (2.2) to obtain

$$t(\hat{F}) = \int y \, d\hat{F}(y) = \int y \, d\left(\frac{1}{n}\sum_{j=1}^{n} H(y - y_j)\right) = \frac{1}{n}\sum_{j=1}^{n}\int y \, dH(y - y_j)$$

$$= \frac{1}{n}\sum_{j=1}^{n} y_j = \bar{y},$$

because $\int a(y) \, dH(y - x) = a(x)$ for any continuous function $a(\cdot)$. ∎

Example 2.2 (City population data) For the problem outlined in Example 1.2, the parameter of interest is the ratio of means $\theta = E(X)/E(U)$. In this case F is the bivariate CDF of $Y = (U, X)$, and the bivariate EDF $\hat{F}$ puts probability n^{-1} at each of the data pairs (u_j, x_j). The statistical function version of θ simply uses the definition of mean for both numerator and denominator, so that

$$t(F) = \frac{\int x \, dF(u, x)}{\int u \, dF(u, x)}.$$

The corresponding estimate of θ is

$$t = t(\hat{F}) = \frac{\int x \, d\hat{F}(u, x)}{\int u \, d\hat{F}(u, x)} = \frac{\bar{x}}{\bar{u}},$$

with $\bar{x} = n^{-1}\sum x_j$ and $\bar{u} = n^{-1}\sum u_j$. ∎

It is quite straightforward to show that (2.1) implies convergence of $\hat{F}$ to F as $n \to \infty$ (Problem 2.1). Then if $t(\cdot)$ is continuous in an appropriate sense, the definition $T = t(\cdot)$ implies that T converges to θ as $n \to \infty$, which is the property of consistency.

Not all estimates are exactly of the form $t(\hat{F})$. For example, if $t(F) = \text{var}(Y)$ then the usual unbiased sample variance is $nt(\hat{F})/(n-1)$. Also the sample median is not exactly $\hat{F}^{-1}(\frac{1}{2})$. Such small discrepancies are fairly unimportant as far as applying the bootstrap techniques discussed in this book. In a very formal development we could write $T = t_n(\hat{F})$ and require that $t_n \to t$ as $n \to \infty$, possibly even that $t_n - t = O(n^{-1})$. But such formality would be excessive here, and we shall assume in general discussion that $T = t(\hat{F})$. (One case that does

A quantity A_n is said to be $O(n^d)$ if $\lim_{n \to \infty} n^{-d} A_n = a$ for some finite a, and $o(n^d)$ if $\lim_{n \to \infty} n^{-d} A_n = 0$.

require special treatment is nonparametric density estimation, which we discuss in Example 5.13.)

The representation $\theta = t(F)$ defines the parameter and its estimator T in a robust way, without any assumption about F, other than that θ exists. This guarantees that T estimates the right thing, no matter what F is. Thus the sample average $\bar{y}$ is the only statistic that is generally valid as an estimate of the population mean μ: only if Y is symmetrically distributed about μ will statistics such as trimmed averages also estimate μ. This property, which guarantees that the correct characteristic of the underlying distribution is estimated, whatever that distribution is, is sometimes called *robustness of specification*.

2.1.2 Objectives

Much of statistical theory is devoted to calculating approximate distributions for particular statistics T, on which to base inferences about their estimands θ. Suppose, for example, that we want to calculate a $(1 - 2\alpha)$ confidence interval for θ. It may be possible to show that T is approximately normal with mean $\theta + \beta$ and variance v; here β is the bias of T. If β and v are both known, then we can write

$$\Pr(T \leq t \mid F) \doteq \Phi\left(\frac{t - (\theta + \beta)}{v^{1/2}}\right), \qquad (2.3)$$

$\doteq$ means "is approximately equal to".

where $\Phi(\cdot)$ is the standard normal integral. If the α quantile of the standard normal distribution is $z_\alpha = \Phi^{-1}(\alpha)$, then an approximate $(1 - 2\alpha)$ confidence interval for θ has limits

$$t - \beta - v^{1/2}z_{1-\alpha}, \quad t - \beta - v^{1/2}z_\alpha, \qquad (2.4)$$

as follows from

$$\Pr(\beta + v^{1/2}z_\alpha \leq T - \theta \leq \beta + v^{1/2}z_{1-\alpha}) \doteq 1 - 2\alpha.$$

There is a catch, however, which is that in practice the bias β and variance v will not be known. So to use the normal approximation we must replace β and v with estimates. To see how to do this, note that we can express β and v as

$$\beta = b(F) = \mathrm{E}(T \mid F) - t(F), \quad v = v(F) = \mathrm{var}(T \mid F), \qquad (2.5)$$

thereby stressing their dependence on the underlying distribution. We use expressions such as $\mathrm{E}(T \mid F)$ to mean that the random variables from which T is calculated have distribution F; here a pedantic equivalent would be $\mathrm{E}\{t(\hat{F}) \mid Y_1, \ldots, Y_n \overset{iid}{\sim} F\}$. Suppose that F is estimated by $\hat{F}$, which might be the empirical distribution function, or a fitted parametric distribution. Then estimates of bias and variance are obtained simply by substituting $\hat{F}$ for F in

(2.5), that is

$$B = b(\hat{F}) = \mathrm{E}(T \mid \hat{F}) - t(\hat{F}), \quad V = v(\hat{F}) = \mathrm{var}(T \mid \hat{F}). \tag{2.6}$$

These estimates B and V are used in place of β and v in equations such as (2.4).

Example 2.3 (Air-conditioning data) Under the exponential model for the data in Example 1.1, the mean failure time μ is estimated by the average $T = \bar{Y}$, which has a gamma distribution with mean μ and shape parameter $\kappa = n$. Therefore the bias and variance of T are $b(F) = 0$ and $v(F) = \mu^2/n$, and these are estimated by 0 and $\bar{y}^2/n$. Since $n = 12$, $\bar{y} = 108.083$, and $z_{0.025} = -1.96$, a 95% confidence interval for μ based on the normal approximation (2.3) is $\bar{y} \pm 1.96 n^{-1/2} \bar{y} = (46.93, 169.24)$. ∎

Estimates such as those in (2.6) are bootstrap estimates. Here they have been used in conjunction with a normal approximation, which sometimes will be adequate. However, the bootstrap approach of substituting estimates can be applied more ambitiously to improve upon the normal approximation and other first-order theoretical approximations. The elaboration of the bootstrap approach is the purpose of this book.

2.2 Parametric Simulation

In the previous section we pointed out that theoretical properties of T might be hard to determine with sufficient accuracy. We now describe the sound practical alternative of repeated simulation of data sets from a fitted parametric model, and empirical calculation of relevant properties of T.

Suppose that we have a particular parametric model for the distribution of the data $y_1, \ldots, y_n$. We shall use $F_\psi(y)$ and $f_\psi(y)$ to denote the CDF and PDF respectively. When ψ is estimated by $\hat{\psi}$ — often but not invariably its maximum likelihood estimate — its substitution in the model gives the *fitted model*, with CDF $\hat{F}(y) = F_{\hat{\psi}}(y)$, which can be used to calculate properties of T, sometimes exactly. We shall use Y^* to denote the random variable distributed according to the fitted model $\hat{F}$, and the superscript $*$ will be used with E, var and so forth when these moments are calculated according to the fitted distribution. Occasionally it will also be useful to write $\hat{\psi} = \psi^*$ to emphasize that this is the parameter value for the simulation model.

Example 2.4 (Air-conditioning data) We have already calculated the mean and variance under the fitted exponential model for the estimator $T = \bar{Y}$ of Example 1.1. Our sample estimate for the mean μ is $t = \bar{y}$. So here Y^* is exponential with mean $\bar{y}$. In the notation just introduced, we have by theoretical calculation with this exponential distribution that

$$E^*(\bar{Y}^*) = \bar{y}, \qquad \text{var}^*(\bar{Y}^*) = \bar{y}^2/n.$$

Note that the estimated bias of $\bar{Y}$ is zero, being the difference between $E^*(\bar{Y}^*)$ and the value $\mu^* = \bar{y}$ for the mean of the fitted distribution. These moments were used to calculate an approximate normal confidence interval in Example 2.3.

If, however, we wished to calculate the bias and variance of $T = \log \bar{Y}$ under the fitted model, i.e. $E^*(\log \bar{Y}^*) - \log \bar{y}$ and $\text{var}^*(\log \bar{Y}^*)$, exact calculation is more difficult. The delta method of Section 2.7.1 would give approximate values $-(2n)^{-1}$ and n^{-1}. But more accurate approximations can be obtained using simulated samples of Y^*s.

Similar results and comments would apply if instead we chose to use the more general gamma model (1.1) for this example. Then Y^* would be a gamma random variable with mean $\bar{y}$ and index $\hat{\kappa}$.   ∎

2.2.1 Moment estimates

So now suppose that theoretical calculation with the fitted model is too complex. Approximations may not be available, or they may be untrustworthy, perhaps because the sample size is small. The alternative is to estimate the properties we require from simulated datasets. We write such a dataset as $Y_1^*, \ldots, Y_n^*$ where the Y_j^* are independently sampled from the fitted distribution $\hat{F}$. When the statistic of interest is calculated from a simulated dataset, we denote it by T^*. From R repetitions of the data simulation we obtain $T_1^*, \ldots, T_R^*$. Properties of $T - \theta$ are then estimated from $T_1^*, \ldots, T_R^*$. For example, the estimator of the bias $b(F) = E(T \mid F) - \theta$ of T is

$$B = b(\hat{F}) = E(T \mid \hat{F}) - t = E^*(T^*) - t,$$

and this in turn is estimated by

$$B_R = R^{-1} \sum_{r=1}^{R} T_r^* - t = \bar{T}^* - t. \tag{2.7}$$

Note that in the simulation t is the parameter value for the model, so that $T^* - t$ is the simulation analogue of $T - \theta$. The corresponding estimator of the variance of T is

$$V_R = \frac{1}{R-1} \sum_{r=1}^{R} (T_r^* - \bar{T}^*)^2, \tag{2.8}$$

with similar estimators for other moments.

These empirical approximations are justified by the law of large numbers. For example, B_R converges to B, the exact value under the fitted model, as R

Figure 2.1 Empirical
biases and variances of
$\bar{Y}^{*}$ for the
air-conditioning data
from four repetitions of
parametric simulation.
Each line shows how the
estimated bias and
variance for $R = 10$
initial simulations
change when further
simulations are
successively added. Note
how the variability
decreases as the
simulation size
increases, and how the
simulated values
converge to the exact
values under the fitted
exponential model,
given by the horizontal
dotted lines.

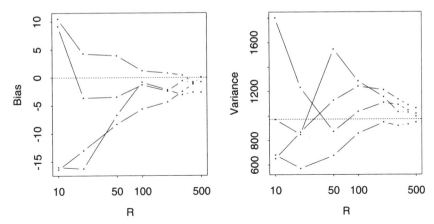

increases. We usually drop the subscript R from B_R, V_R, and so forth unless
we are explicitly discussing the effect of R. How to choose R will be illustrated
in the examples that follow, and discussed in Section 2.5.2.

It is important to recognize that we are not estimating absolute properties of
T, but rather of T relative to θ. Usually this involves the estimation error $T - \theta$,
but we should not ignore the possibility that T/θ (equivalently $\log T - \log \theta$)
or some other relevant measure of estimation error might be more appropriate,
depending upon the context. Bootstrap simulation methods will apply to any
such measure.

Example 2.5 (Air-conditioning data) Consider Example 1.1 again. As we
have seen, simulation is unnecessary in practice for this problem because the
moments are easy to calculate theoretically, but the example is useful for
illustration. Here the fitted model is an exponential distribution for the failure
times, with mean estimated by the sample average $\bar{y} = 108.083$. All simulated
failure times Y^{*} are generated from this distribution.

Figure 2.1 shows the results from several simulations, four for each of
eight values of R, in each of which the empirical biases and variances of
$T^{*} = \bar{Y}^{*}$ have been calculated according to (2.7) and (2.8). On both panels the
"correct" values, namely zero and $\bar{y}^2/n = (108.083)^2/12 = 973.5$, are indicated
by horizontal dotted lines.

Evidently the larger is R, the closer is the simulation calculation to the right
answer. How large a value of R is needed? Figure 2.1 suggests that for some
purposes $R = 100$ or 200 will be adequate, but that $R = 10$ will not be large
enough. In this problem the accuracy of the empirical approximations is quite
easy to determine from the fact that $n\bar{Y}/\mu$ has a gamma distribution with

index n. The simulation variances of B_R and V_R are

$$\frac{t^2}{nR}, \quad \frac{t^4}{n^2}\left(\frac{2}{R-1} + \frac{6}{nR}\right),$$

and we can use these to say how large R should be in order that the simulated values have a specified accuracy. For example, the coefficients of variation of V_R at $R = 100$ and 1000 are respectively 0.16 and 0.05. However, for a complicated problem where simulation was really necessary, such calculations could not be done, and general rules are needed to suggest how large R should be. These are discussed in Section 2.5.2. ∎

2.2.2 Distribution and quantile estimates

The simulation estimates of bias and variance will sometimes be of interest in their own right, but more usually would be used with normal approximations for T, particularly for large samples. For situations like those in Examples 1.1 and 1.2, however, the normal approximation is intrinsically inaccurate. This can be seen from a normal Q-Q plot of the simulated values $t_1^*, \ldots, t_R^*$, that is, a plot of the ordered values $t_{(1)}^* < \cdots < t_{(R)}^*$ against expected normal order statistics. It is the empirical distribution of these simulated values which can provide a more accurate distributional approximation, as we shall now see.

If as is often the case we are approximating the distribution of $T - \theta$ by that of $T^* - t$, then cumulative probabilities are estimated simply by the empirical distribution function of the simulated values $t^* - t$. More formally, if $G(u) = \Pr(T - \theta \le u)$, then the simulation estimate of $G(u)$ is

$$\hat{G}_R(u) = \frac{\#\{t_r^* - t \le u\}}{R} = \frac{1}{R}\sum_{r=1}^{R} I\{t_r^* - t \le u\},$$

where $I\{A\}$ is the indicator of the event A, equal to 1 if A is true and 0 otherwise. As R increases, so this estimate will converge to $\hat{G}(u)$, the exact CDF of $T^* - t$ under sampling from the fitted model. Just as with the moment approximations discussed earlier, so the approximation $\hat{G}_R$ to G contains two sources of error, i.e. that between $\hat{G}$ and G due to data variability and that between $\hat{G}_R$ and $\hat{G}$ due to finite simulation.

We are often interested in quantiles of the distribution of $T - \theta$, and these are approximated using ordered values of $t^* - t$. The underlying result used here is that if $X_1, \ldots, X_N$ are independently distributed with CDF K and if $X_{(j)}$ denotes the jth ordered value, then

$$\mathrm{E}(X_{(j)}) \doteq K^{-1}\left(\frac{j}{N+1}\right).$$

This implies that a sensible estimate of $K^{-1}(p)$ is $X_{((N+1)p)}$, assuming that

$(N + 1)p$ is an integer. So we estimate the p quantile of $T - \theta$ by the $(R+1)p$th ordered value of $t^* - t$, that is $t^*_{((R+1)p)} - t$. We assume that R is chosen so that $(R + 1)p$ is an integer.

The simulation approximation $\hat{G}_R$ and the corresponding quantiles are in principle better than results obtained by normal approximation, provided that R is large enough, because they avoid the supposition that the distribution of $T^* - t$ has a particular form.

Example 2.6 (Air-conditioning data) The simulation experiments described in Example 2.5 can be used to study the simulation approximations to the distribution and quantiles of $\bar{Y} - \mu$. First, Figure 2.2 shows normal Q-Q plots of t^* values for $R = 99$ (top left panel) and $R = 999$ (top right panel). Clearly a normal approximation would not be accurate in the tails, and this is already fairly clear with $R = 99$. For reference, the lower half of Figure 2.2 shows corresponding Q-Q plots with exact gamma quantiles.

The nonnormality of T^* is also reasonably clear on histograms of t^* values, shown in Figure 2.3, at least at the larger value $R = 999$. Corresponding density estimate plots provide smoother displays of the same information.

We look next at the estimated quantiles of $\bar{Y} - \mu$. The p quantile is approximated by $\bar{y}^*_{((R+1)p)} - \bar{y}$ for $p = 0.05$ and 0.95. The values of R are $19, 39, 99, 199, \ldots, 999$, chosen to ensure that $(R + 1)p$ is an integer throughout. Thus at $R = 19$ the 0.05 quantile is approximated by $\bar{y}^*_{(1)} - \bar{y}$ and so forth. In order to display the magnitude of simulation error, we ran four independent simulations at $R = 19, 39, 99, \ldots, 999$. The results are plotted in Figure 2.4. Also shown by dotted lines are the exact quantiles under the model, which the simulations approach as R increases. There is large variability in the approximate quantiles for R less than 100 and it appears that 500 or more simulations are required to get accurate results.

The same simulations can be used in other ways. For example, we might want to know about $\log \bar{Y} - \log \mu$, in which case the empirical properties of $\log \bar{y}^* - \log \bar{y}$ are relevant. ∎

The illustration used here is very simple, but essentially the same methods can be used in arbitrarily complicated parametric problems. For example, distributions of likelihood ratio statistics can be approximated when large-sample approximations are inaccurate or fail entirely. In Chapters 4 and 5 respectively we show how parametric bootstrap methods can be used to calculate significance tests and confidence sets.

It is sometimes useful to be able to look at the density of T, for example to see if it is multimodal, skewed, or otherwise differs appreciably from normality. A rough idea of the density $g(u)$ of $U = T - \theta$, say, can be had from a histogram of the values of $t^* - t$. A somewhat better picture is offered by a kernel density

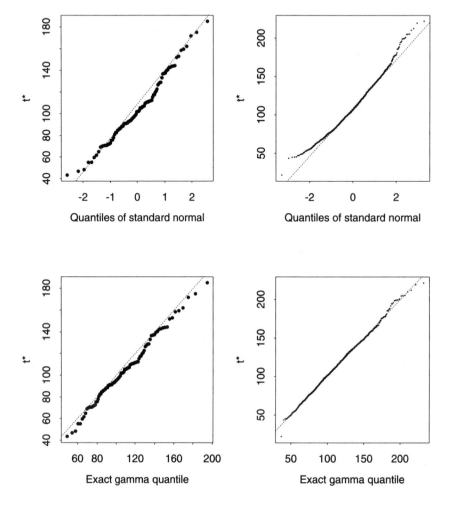

Figure 2.2 Normal (upper) and gamma (lower) Q-Q plots of t^* values based on $R = 99$ (left) and $R = 999$ (right) simulations from the fitted exponential model for the air-conditioning data.

estimate, defined by

$$\hat{g}_h(u) = \frac{1}{Rh} \sum_{r=1}^{R} w \left\{ \frac{u - (t_r^* - t)}{h} \right\}, \qquad (2.9)$$

where w is a symmetric PDF with zero mean and h is a positive bandwidth that determines the smoothness of $\hat{g}_h$. The estimate $\hat{g}_h$ is non-negative and has unit integral. It is insensitive to the choice of $w(\cdot)$, for which we use the standard normal density. The choice of h is more important. The key is to produce a smooth result, while not flattening out significant modes. If the choice of h is quite large, as it may be if $R \leq 100$, then one should rescale the density

Figure 2.3 Histograms
of t^* values based on
$R = 99$ (left) and
$R = 999$ (right)
simulations from the
fitted exponential model
for the air-conditioning
data.

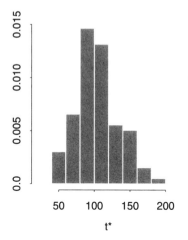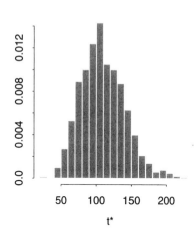

Figure 2.4 Empirical
quantiles ($p = 0.05, 0.95$)
of $T^* - t$ under
resampling from the
fitted exponential model
for the air-conditioning
data. The horizontal
dotted lines are the
exact quantiles under
the model.

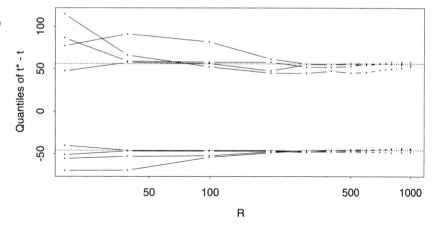

estimate to make its mean and variance agree with the estimated mean b_R and
variance v_R of $T - \theta$; see Problem 3.8.

As a general rule, good estimates of density require at least $R = 1000$:
density estimation is usually harder than probability or quantile estimation.

Note that the same methods of estimating density, distribution function and
quantiles can be applied to any transformation of T. We shall discuss this
further in Section 2.5.

2.3 Nonparametric Simulation

Suppose that we have no parametric model, but that it is sensible to assume that $Y_1, \ldots, Y_n$ are independent and identically distributed according to an unknown distribution function F. We use the EDF $\hat{F}$ to estimate the unknown CDF F. We shall use $\hat{F}$ just as we would a parametric model: theoretical calculation if possible, otherwise simulation of datasets and empirical calculation of required properties. In only very simple cases are exact theoretical calculations possible, but we shall see in Section 9.5 that good theoretical approximations can be obtained in many problems involving sample moments.

Example 2.7 (Average)   In the case of the average, exact moments under sampling from the EDF are easily found. For example,

$$\mathrm{E}^*(\bar{Y}^*) = \mathrm{E}^*(Y^*) = \sum_{j=1}^{n} \frac{1}{n} y_j = \bar{y}$$

and similarly

$$
\begin{aligned}
\mathrm{var}^*(\bar{Y}^*) = \frac{1}{n}\mathrm{var}^*(Y^*) &= \frac{1}{n}\mathrm{E}^*\{Y^* - \mathrm{E}^*(Y^*)\}^2 = \frac{1}{n} \times \sum_{j=1}^{n} \frac{1}{n}(y_j - \bar{y})^2 \\
&= \frac{(n-1)}{n} \times \frac{1}{n(n-1)} \sum_{j=1}^{n}(y_j - \bar{y})^2.
\end{aligned}
$$

Apart from the factor $(n-1)/n$, this is the usual result for the estimated variance of $\bar{Y}$.   ∎

Other simple statistics such as the sample variance and sample median are also easy to handle (Problems 2.3, 2.4).

To apply simulation with the EDF is very straightforward. Because the EDF puts equal probabilities on the original data values $y_1, \ldots, y_n$, each Y^* is independently sampled at random from those data values. Therefore the simulated sample $Y_1^*, \ldots, Y_n^*$ is a random sample taken with replacement from the data. This simplicity is special to the case of a homogeneous sample, but many extensions are straightforward. This resampling procedure is called the *nonparametric bootstrap*.

Example 2.8 (City population data)   Here we look at the ratio estimate for the problem described in Example 1.2. For convenience we consider a subset of the data in Table 1.3, comprising the first ten pairs. This is an application with no obvious parametric model, so nonparametric simulation makes good sense. Table 2.1 shows the data and the first simulated sample, which has been drawn by randomly selecting subscript j^* from the set $\{1, \ldots, n\}$ with equal probability and taking $(u^*, x^*) = (u_{j^*}, x_{j^*})$. In this sample $j^* = 1$ never occurs

Table 2.1 The dataset for ratio estimation, and one synthetic sample. The values j^* are chosen randomly with equal probability from $\{1,\dots,n\}$ with replacement; the simulated pairs are (u_{j^*}, x_{j^*}).

j	1	2	3	4	5	6	7	8	9	10
u	138	93	61	179	48	37	29	23	30	2
x	143	104	69	260	75	63	50	48	111	50
j^*	6	7	2	2	3	3	10	7	2	9
u^*	37	29	93	93	61	61	2	29	93	30
x^*	63	50	104	104	69	69	50	50	104	111

Table 2.2 Frequencies with which each original data pair appears in each of $R = 9$ nonparametric bootstrap samples for the data on US cities.

j	1	2	3	4	5	6	7	8	9	10
u	138	93	61	179	48	37	29	23	30	2
x	143	104	69	260	75	63	50	48	111	50

	Numbers of times each pair sampled										Statistic
Data	1	1	1	1	1	1	1	1	1	1	$t = 1.520$
Replicate r											
1		3	2			1	2		1	1	$t_1^* = 1.466$
2	1		1		2	2	1		2	1	$t_2^* = 1.761$
3	1	1		1		1		4		2	$t_3^* = 1.951$
4		1	2		1	1	2	2		1	$t_4^* = 1.542$
5	3			1	3		1	1	1		$t_5^* = 1.371$
6	1	1	2			1		1	1	3	$t_6^* = 1.686$
7	1	1	2	2	2		1			1	$t_7^* = 1.378$
8	2		1		3	1	1	1	1		$t_8^* = 1.420$
9		1	1	1	2	1			2	1	$t_9^* = 1.660$

and $j^* = 2$ occurs three times, so that the first data pair is never selected, the second is selected three times, and so forth.

Table 2.2 shows the same simulated sample, plus eight more, expressed in terms of the frequencies of original data pairs. The ratio t^* for each simulated sample is recorded in the last column of the table. After the R sets of calculations, the bias and variance estimates are calculated according to (2.7) and (2.8). The results are, for the $R = 9$ replicates shown,

$$b = 1.582 - 1.520 = 0.062, \quad v = 0.03907.$$

A simple approximate distribution for $T - \theta$ is $N(b, v)$. With the results so far, this is $N(0.062, 0.0391)$, but this is unlikely to be accurate enough and a larger value of R should be used. In a simulation with $R = 999$ we obtained $b = 1.5755 - 1.5203 = 0.0552$ and $v = 0.0601$. The latter is appreciably bigger than the value 0.0325 given by the delta method variance estimate

$$v_L = n^{-2} \sum_{j=1}^{n} (x_j - t u_j)^2 / \bar{u}^2,$$

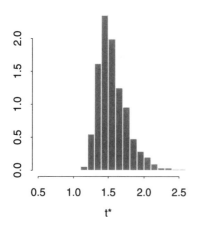 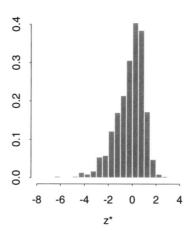

Figure 2.5 City population data. Histograms of t^* and z^* under nonparametric resampling for sample of size $n = 10$, $R = 999$ simulations. Note the skewness of both t^* and z^*.

which is based on an expansion that is explained in Section 2.7.2; see also Problem 2.9. The discrepancy between v and v_L is due partly to a few extreme values of t^*, an issue we discuss in Section 2.3.2.

The left panel of Figure 2.5 shows a histogram of t^*, whose skewness is evident: use of a normal approximation here would be very inaccurate.

We can use the same simulations to estimate distributions of related statistics, such as transformed estimates or studentized estimates. The right panel of Figure 2.5 shows a histogram of studentized values $z^* = (t^* - t)/v_L^{*1/2}$, where v_L^* is the delta method variance estimate based on a simulated sample. That is,

$$v_L^* = n^{-2} \sum_{j=1}^{n} (x_j^* - t^* u_j^*)^2 / \bar{u}^{*2}.$$

The corresponding theoretical approximation for Z is the $N(0, 1)$ distribution, which we would judge also inaccurate in view of the strong skewness in the histogram. We shall discuss the rationale for the use of z^* in Section 2.4.

One natural question to ask here is what effect the small sample size has on the accuracy of normal approximations. This can be answered in part by plotting density estimates. The left panel of Figure 2.6 shows three estimated densities for $T^* - t$ with our sample of $n = 10$, a kernel density estimate based on our simulations, the $N(b, v)$ approximation with moments computed from the same simulations, and the $N(0, v_L)$ approximation. The right panel shows corresponding density approximations for the full data with $n = 49$; the empirical bias and variance of T are $b = 0.00118$ and $v = 0.001290$, and the

Figure 2.6 Density
estimates for $T^* - t$
based on 999
nonparametric
simulations for the city
population data. The
left panel is for the
sample of size $n = 10$ in
Table 2.1, and the right
panel shows the
corresponding estimates
for the entire dataset of
size $n = 49$. Each plot
shows a kernel density
estimate (solid), the
$N(b,v)$ approximation
(dashes), with these
moments computed
from the same
simulations, and the
$N(0,v_L)$ approximation
(dots).

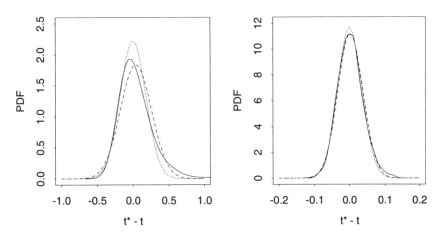

delta method variance approximation is $v_L = 0.001166$. At the larger sample size the normal approximations seem very accurate. ∎

2.3.1 Comparison with parametric methods

A natural question to ask is how well the nonparametric resampling methods might compare to parametric methods, when the latter are appropriate. Equally important is the question as to which parametric model would produce results like those for nonparametric resampling: this is another way of asking just what the nonparametric bootstrap does. Some insight into these questions can be gained by revisiting Example 1.1.

Example 2.9 (Air-conditioning data)   We now look at the results of applying nonparametric resampling to the air-conditioning data. One might naively expect to obtain results similar to those in Example 2.5, where exponential resampling was used, since we found in Example 1.1 that the data appear compatible with an exponential model.

Figure 2.7 is the nonparametric analogue of Figure 2.4, and shows quantiles of $T^* - t$. It appears that $R = 500$ or so is needed to get reliable quantile estimates; $R = 100$ is enough for the corresponding plot for bias and variance. Under nonparametric resampling there is no reason why the quantiles should approach the theoretical quantiles under the exponential model, and it seems that they do not do so. This suggestion is confirmed by the Q-Q plots in Figure 2.8. The first panel compares the ordered values of t^* from $R = 999$ nonparametric simulations with theoretical quantiles under the fitted exponential model, and the second panel compares the t^* with theoretical quantiles

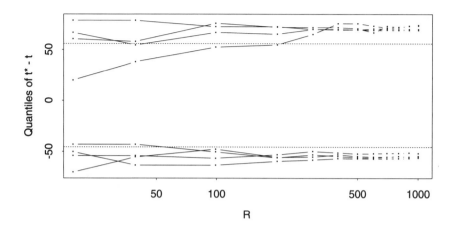

Figure 2.7 Empirical quantiles ($p = 0.05, 0.95$) of $T^* - t$ under nonparametric resampling from the air-conditioning data. The horizontal lines are the exact quantiles based on the fitted exponential model.

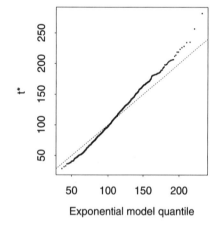 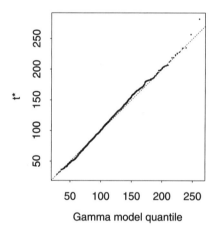

Figure 2.8 Q-Q plots of $\bar{y}^*$ under nonparametric resampling from the air-conditioning data, first against theoretical quantiles under fitted exponential model (left panel) and then against theoretical quantiles under fitted gamma model (right panel).

under the best-fitting gamma model with index $\hat{\kappa} = 0.71$. The agreement in the second panel is strikingly good. On reflection this is natural, because the EDF is closer to the larger gamma model than to the exponential model. ■

2.3.2 Effects of discreteness

For intrinsically continuous data, a major difference between parametric and nonparametric resampling lies in the discreteness of the latter. Under nonparametric resampling, T^* and related quantities will have discrete distributions, even though they may be approximating continuous distributions. This makes results somewhat "fuzzy" compared to their parametric counterparts.

Example 2.10 (Air-conditioning data) For the nonparametric simulation discussed in the previous example, the right panels of Figure 2.9 show the scatter plots of sample standard deviation versus sample average for $R = 99$ and $R = 999$ simulated datasets. Corresponding plots for the exponential simulation are shown in the left panels. The qualitative feature to be read from any one of these plots is that data standard deviation is proportional to data average. The discreteness of the nonparametric model (the EDF) adds noise whose peculiar banded structure is evident at $R = 999$, although the qualitative structure is still apparent. ∎

For a statistic that is symmetric in the data values, there are up to

$$m_n = \binom{2n-1}{n-1} = \frac{(2n-1)!}{n!(n-1)!}$$

possible values of t^*, depending upon the smoothness of the statistical function $t(\cdot)$. Even for moderately small samples the support of the distribution of T^* will often be fairly dense: values of m_n for $n = 7$ and 11 are 1716 and 352716 (Problem 2.5). It would therefore usually be harmless to think of there being a PDF for T^*, and to approximate it, either using simulation results as in Figure 2.6 or theoretically (Section 9.5). There are exceptions, however, most notably when T is a sample quantile. The case of the sample median is discussed in Example 2.16; see also Problem 2.4 and Example 2.15.

For many practical applications of the simulation results, the effects of discreteness are likely to be fairly minimal. However, one possible problem is that outliers are more likely to occur in the simulation output. For example, in Example 2.8 there were three outliers in the simulation, and these inflated the estimate v^* of the variance of T^*. Such outliers should be evident on a normal Q-Q plot (or comparable relevant plot), and when found they should be omitted. More generally, a statistic that depends heavily on a few quantiles can be sensitive to the repeated values that occur under nonparametric sampling, and it can be useful to smooth the original data when dealing with such statistics; see Section 3.4.

2.4 Simple Confidence Intervals

The major application for distributions and quantiles of an estimator T is in the calculation of confidence limits. There are several ways of using bootstrap simulation results in this context, most of which will be explored in Chapter 5. Here we describe briefly two basic methods.

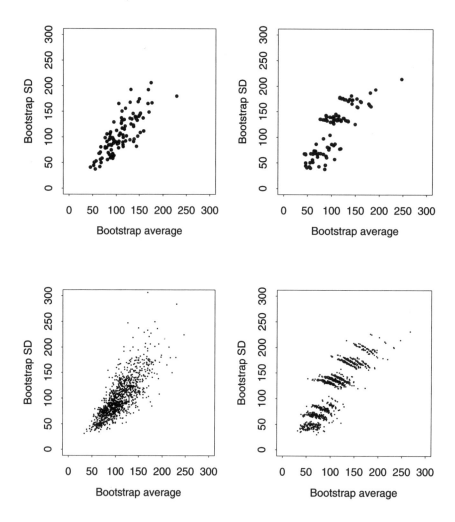

Figure 2.9 Scatter plots of sample standard deviation versus sample average for samples generated by parametric simulation from the fitted exponential model (left panels) and by nonparametric resampling (right panels). Top line is for $R = 99$ and bottom line is for $R = 999$.

The simplest approach is to use a normal approximation to the distribution of T. As outlined in Section 2.1.2, this means estimating the limits (2.4), which require only bootstrap estimates of bias and variance. As we have seen in previous sections, a normal approximation will not always suffice. Then if we use the bootstrap estimates of quantiles for $T - \theta$ as described in Section 2.2.2, an equitailed $(1 - 2\alpha)$ confidence interval will have limits

$$t - (t^*_{((R+1)(1-\alpha))} - t), \quad t - (t^*_{((R+1)\alpha)} - t). \tag{2.10}$$

This is based on the probability implication

$$\mathrm{Pr}(a < T - \theta < b) = 1 - 2\alpha \quad \Rightarrow \quad \mathrm{Pr}(T - b \le \theta \le T - a) = 1 - 2\alpha.$$

We shall refer to the limits (2.10) as the *basic bootstrap confidence limits*. Their accuracy depends upon R, of course, and one would typically take $R \geq 1000$ to be safe. But accuracy also depends upon the extent to which the distribution of $T^* - t$ agrees with that of $T - \theta$. Complete agreement will occur if $T - \theta$ has a distribution not depending on any unknowns. This special property is enjoyed by quantities called *pivots*, which we discuss in more detail in Section 2.5.1.

If, as is usually the case, the distribution of $T - \theta$ does depend on unknowns, then we can try alternative expressions contrasting T and θ, such as differences of transformed quantities, or studentized comparisons. For the latter, we define the studentized version of $T - \theta$ as

$$Z = \frac{T - \theta}{V^{1/2}}, \qquad (2.11)$$

where V is an estimate of $\mathrm{var}(T \mid F)$: we give a fairly general form for V in Section 2.7.2. The idea is to mimic the Student-t statistic, which has this form, and which eliminates the unknown standard deviation when making inference about a normal mean. Throughout this book we shall use Z to denote a studentized statistic.

Recall that the Student-t $(1 - 2\alpha)$ confidence interval for a normal mean μ has limits

$$\bar{y} - v^{1/2} t_{n-1}(1 - \alpha), \quad \bar{y} - v^{1/2} t_{n-1}(\alpha),$$

where v is the estimated variance of the mean and $t_{n-1}(\alpha)$, $t_{n-1}(1 - \alpha)$ are quantiles of the Student-t distribution with $n - 1$ degrees of freedom, the distribution of the pivot Z. More generally, when Z is defined by (2.11), the $(1 - 2\alpha)$ confidence interval limits for θ have the analogous form

$$t - v^{1/2} z_{1-\alpha}, \quad t - v^{1/2} z_{\alpha},$$

where z_p denotes the p quantile of Z. One simple approximation, which can often be justified for large sample size n, is to take Z as being $N(0, 1)$. The result would be no different in practical terms from using a normal approximation for $T - \theta$, and we know that this is often inadequate. It is more accurate to estimate the quantiles of Z from replicates of the *studentized bootstrap statistic*, $Z^* = (T^* - t)/V^{*1/2}$, where T^* and V^* are based on a simulated random sample, $Y_1^*, \ldots, Y_n^*$.

If the model is parametric, the Y_j^* are generated from the fitted parametric distribution, and if the model is nonparametric, they are generated from the EDF $\hat{F}$, as outlined in Section 2.3. In either case we use the $(R + 1)\alpha$th order statistic of the simulated values $z_1^*, \ldots, z_R^*$, namely $z_{((R+1)\alpha)}^*$, to estimate z_α. Then the *studentized bootstrap* confidence interval for θ has limits

$$t - v^{1/2} z_{((R+1)(1-\alpha))}^*, \quad t - v^{1/2} z_{((R+1)\alpha)}^*. \qquad (2.12)$$

This studentized bootstrap method is most likely to be of use in nonparametric problems. One reason for this is that with parametric models we can sometimes find "exact" solutions (as with the exponential model for Example 1.1), and otherwise we have available methods based on the likelihood function. This does not necessarily rule out the use of parametric simulation, of course, for approximating the distribution of the quantity used as basis for the confidence interval.

Example 2.11 (Air-conditioning data)   Under the exponential model for the data of Example 1.1, we have $T = \bar{Y}$, and since $\mathrm{var}(T \mid F_\mu) = \mu^2/n$, we would take $V = \bar{Y}^2/n$. This gives

$$Z = (T - \mu)/V^{1/2} = n^{1/2}(1 - \mu/\bar{Y}),$$

which is an exact pivot because $Q = \bar{Y}/\mu$ has the gamma distribution with index n and unit mean. Simulation to construct confidence intervals is unnecessary because the quantiles of the gamma distribution are available from tables. Parametric simulation would be based on $Q^* = \bar{Y}^*/t$, where $\bar{Y}^*$ is the average of a random sample $Y_1^*, \ldots, Y_n^*$ from the exponential distribution with mean t. Since Q^* has the same distribution as Q, the only error incurred by simulation would be due to the randomness of the simulated quantiles. For example, the estimates of the 0.025 and 0.975 quantiles of Q based on $R = 999$ simulations are 0.504 and 1.608, compared to the exact values 0.517 and 1.640; these lead to estimated and exact 95% confidence intervals $(67.2, 214.6)$ and $(65.9, 209.2)$ respectively. We shall discuss these intervals more fully in Chapter 5.   ∎

Example 2.12 (City population data)   For the sample of $n = 10$ pairs analysed in Example 2.8, our estimate of the ratio θ is $t = \bar{x}/\bar{u} = 1.52$. The 0.025 and 0.975 quantiles of the 999 values of t^* are 1.236 and 2.059, so the 95% basic bootstrap confidence interval (2.10) for θ is $(0.981, 1.804)$.

To apply the studentized interval, we use the delta method approximation to the variance of T, which is (Problem 2.9)

$$v_L = n^{-2} \sum_{j=1}^{n} (x_j - t u_j)^2/\bar{u}^2,$$

and base confidence intervals for θ on $(T - \theta)/v_L^{1/2}$, using simulated values of $z^* = (t^* - t)/v_L^{*1/2}$. The simulated values in the right panel of Figure 2.5 show that the density of the studentized bootstrap statistic Z^* is not close to normal. The 0.025 and 0.975 quantiles of the 499 simulated z^* values are -3.063 and 1.447, and since $v_L = 0.0325$, an approximate 95% equitailed confidence interval based on (2.12) is $(1.260, 2.072)$. This is quite different from the interval above.

The usefulness of these confidence intervals will depend on how well $\hat{F}$

estimates F and the extent to which the distributions of $T - \theta$ and of Z depend on F. We cannot judge the former, but we can check the latter using the methods outlined in Section 3.9.2; see Examples 3.20 and 9.11. ∎

2.5 Reducing Error

The error in resampling methods is generally a combination of statistical error and simulation error. The first of these is due to the difference between F and $\hat{F}$, and the magnitude of the resulting error will depend upon the choice of T. The simulation error is wholly due to use of empirical estimates of properties under sampling from $\hat{F}$, rather than exact properties.

Figure 2.7 illustrates these two sources of error in quantile estimation. The decreasing simulation error shows as reduced scatter of the quantile estimates for increased R. Statistical error due to an inappropriate model for T is reflected by the difference between the simulated nonparametric quantiles for large R and the dotted lines that indicate the quantiles under the exponential model. The further statistical error due to the difference between $\hat{F}$ and F cannot be illustrated, because we do not know the true model underlying the data. However, other samples of the same size from that model would yield different estimates of the true quantiles, quite apart from the variability of the quantile estimates obtained from each specific dataset by simulation.

2.5.1 Statistical error

The basic bootstrap idea is to approximate a quantity $c(F)$ — such as $\mathrm{var}(T \mid F)$ — by the estimate $c(\hat{F})$, where $\hat{F}$ is either a parametric or a nonparametric estimate of F based on data $y_1, \ldots, y_n$. The statistical error is then the difference between $c(\hat{F})$ and $c(F)$, and as far as possible we wish to minimize this or remove it entirely. This is sometimes possible by careful choice of $c(\cdot)$. For example, in Example 1.1 with the exponential model, we have seen that working with T/θ removes statistical error completely.

For both confidence interval and significance test calculation, we usually have a choice as to what T is and how to use it. Significance testing raises special issues, because we then have to deal with a null hypothesis sampling distribution, so here it is best to focus on confidence interval calculation. For simplicity we also assume that estimate T is decided upon. Then the quantity $c(F)$ will be a quantile or a moment of some quantity $Q = q(\hat{F}, F)$ derived from T, such as $h(T) - h(\theta)$ or $(T - \theta)/V^{1/2}$ where V is an estimated variance, or something more complicated such as a likelihood ratio. The statistical problem is to choose among these possible quantities so that the resulting Q is as nearly pivotal as possible, that is it has (at least approximately) the same distribution under sampling from both F and $\hat{F}$.

Provided that Q is a monotone function of θ, it will be straightforward to obtain confidence limits. For example, if $Q = h(T) - h(\theta)$ with $h(t)$ increasing in t, and if a_α is an approximate lower α quantile of $h(T) - h(\theta)$, then

$$1 - \alpha \doteq \Pr\{h(T) - h(\theta) \geq a_\alpha\} = \Pr\left[\theta \leq h^{-1}\{h(T) - a_\alpha\}\right], \qquad (2.13)$$

where $h^{-1}(\cdot)$ is the inverse transformation. So $h^{-1}\{h(T) - a_\alpha\}$ is an upper $(1 - \alpha)$ confidence limit for θ.

Parametric problems

In parametric problems $\hat{F} \equiv F_{\hat{\psi}}$ and $F \equiv F_\psi$ have the same form, differing only in parameter values. The notion of a pivot is quite simple here, meaning constant behaviour under all values of the model parameters. More formally, we define a *pivot* as a function $Q = q(T, \theta)$ whose distribution does or not a particular quantity Q is exactly or nearly pivotal, by examining its behaviour under the model form with varying parameter values. For example, in the context of Example 1.1 not depend on the value of ψ: for all q, In general Q may also depend on other statistics, as when Q is the studentized form of T.

$$\Pr\{q(T, \theta) \leq q \mid \psi\}$$

is independent of ψ.

One can check, sometimes theoretically and always empirically, whether, we could simultaneously examine properties of $T - \theta$, $\log T - \log \theta$ and the studentized version of the former, by simulation under several exponential models close to the fitted model. This might result in plots of variance or selected quantiles versus parameter values, from which we could diagnose the nonpivotal behaviour of $T - \theta$ and the pivotal behaviour of $\log T - \log \theta$.

A special role for transformation $h(T)$ arises because sometimes it is relatively easy to choose $h(\cdot)$ so that the variance of T is approximately or exactly independent of θ, and this stability is the primary feature of stability of distribution. Suppose that T has variance $v(\theta)$. Then provided the function $h(\cdot)$ is well behaved at θ, Taylor series expansion as described in Section 2.7.1 leads to

$$\text{var}\{h(T)\} \doteq \left\{\dot{h}(\theta)\right\}^2 v(\theta), \qquad$$ $\dot{h}(\theta)$ is the first derivative $dh(\theta)/d\theta$.

which in turn implies that the variance is made approximately constant (equal to 1) if

$$h(t) = \int^t \frac{du}{\{v(u)\}^{1/2}}. \qquad (2.14)$$

This is known as the *variance-stabilizing transformation*. Any constant multiple of $h(T)$ will be equally effective: often in one-sample problems where $v(\theta) = n^{-1}\sigma^2(\theta)$ equation (2.14) would be applied with $\sigma(u)$ in place of $\{v(u)\}^{1/2}$, in which case $h(\cdot)$ is independent of n and $\text{var}(T) \doteq n^{-1}$.

For a problem where $v(\theta)$ varies strongly with θ, use of this transformation

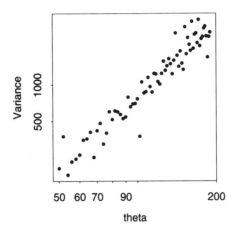

Figure 2.10 Log-log plot of estimated variance of $\bar{Y}$ against θ for the air-conditioning data with an exponential model. The plot suggests strongly that $\text{var}(\bar{Y} \mid \theta) \propto \theta^2$.

in conjunction with (2.13) will typically give more accurate confidence limits than would be obtained using direct approximations of quantiles for $T - \theta$.

If such use of the transformation is appropriate, it will sometimes be clear from theoretical considerations, as in the exponential case. Otherwise the transformation would have to be identified from a scatter plot of simulation-estimated variance of T versus θ for a range of values of θ.

Example 2.13 (Air-conditioning data)   Figure 2.10 shows a log-log plot of the empirical variances of $t^* = \bar{y}^*$ based on $R = 50$ simulations for each of a range of values of θ. That is, for each value of θ we generate R values t_r^* corresponding to samples $y_{r1}^*, \ldots, y_{rn}^*$ from the exponential distribution with mean θ, and then plot $\log\left\{(R-1)^{-1} \sum (t_r^* - \bar{t}^*)^2\right\}$ against $\log \theta$. The linearity and slope of the plot confirm that $\text{var}(T \mid F) \propto \theta^2$, where $\theta = \text{E}(T \mid F)$.   ∎

Nonparametric problems

In nonparametric problems the situation is more complicated. It is now unlikely (but not strictly impossible) that any quantity can be exactly pivotal. Also we cannot simulate data from a distribution with the same form as F, because that form is unknown. However, we can simulate data from distributions near to and similar to $\hat{F}$, and this may be enough since F is near $\hat{F}$. A rough idea of what is possible can be had from Example 2.10. In the right-hand panels of Figure 2.9 we plotted sample standard deviation versus sample average for a series of nonparametrically resampled datasets. If the EDFs of those datasets are thought of as models near both $\hat{F}$ and F, then although the pattern is obscured by the banding, the plots suggest that the true model has standard deviation proportional to its mean — which is indeed the case for the most likely true model. There are conceptual difficulties with this argument, but there is little question that the implication drawn is correct, namely that $\log \bar{Y}$ will have approximately the same variance under sampling from both F and $\hat{F}$.

A more thorough discussion of these ideas for nonparametric problems will be given in Section 3.9.2.

A major focus of research on resampling methods has been the reduction of statistical error. This is reflected particularly in the development of accurate confidence limit methods, which are described in Chapter 5. In general it is best to remove as much of the statistical error as possible in the choice of procedure. However, it is possible to reduce statistical error by a bootstrap technique described in Section 3.9.1.

2.5.2 Simulation error

Simulation error arises when Monte Carlo simulations are performed and properties of statistics are approximated by their empirical properties in these simulations. For example, we approximate the estimate $B = E^*(T^* \mid \hat{F}) - t$ of bias $\beta = E(T) - \theta$ by the average $B_R = R^{-1} \sum (T_r^* - t) = \bar{T}^* - t$, using the independent replications $T_1^*, \ldots, T_R^*$, each based on a random sample from our data EDF $\hat{F}$. The Monte Carlo variability in $R^{-1} \sum T_r^*$ can only be removed entirely by an infinite simulation, which seems both impossible and unnecessary in practice. The practical question is, how large does R need to be to achieve reasonable accuracy, relative to the statistical accuracy of the quantity (bias, variance, etc.) being approximated by simulation? While it is not possible to give a completely general and firm answer, we can get a fairly good sense of what is required by considering the bias, variance and quantile estimates in simple cases. This we now do.

Suppose that we have a sample $y_1, \ldots, y_n$ from the $N(\mu, \sigma^2)$ distribution, and that the parameter of interest $\theta = \mu$ is estimated by the sample average $t = \bar{y}$. Suppose that we use nonparametric simulation to approximate the bias, variance and the p quantile a_p of $T - \theta = \bar{Y} - \mu$. Then the first step, as described in Section 2.3, is to take R independent replicate samples from $y_1, \ldots, y_n$, and calculate their means $\bar{Y}_1^*, \ldots, \bar{Y}_R^*$. From these we calculate the bias, variance and quantile estimators as described earlier. Of course the problem is so simple that we know the real answers, namely 0, $n^{-1}\sigma^2$ and $n^{-1/2}\sigma z_p$, where z_p is the p quantile of the standard normal distribution. So the corresponding (infinite simulation) estimates of bias and variance are 0 and $n^{-1}\hat{\sigma}^2$, where $\hat{\sigma}^2 = n^{-1} \sum (y_j - \bar{y})^2$. The corresponding estimate $\hat{a}_p$ of the p quantile a_p is approximately $n^{-1/2}\hat{\sigma} z_p$ under nonparametric resampling, ignoring $O(n^{-1})$ terms. We now compare the finite-simulation approximations to these estimates.

First consider the bias estimator

$$B_R = R^{-1} \sum \bar{Y}_r^* - \bar{Y}.$$

Conditional on the particular sample $y_1, \ldots, y_n$, or equivalently its EDF $\hat{F}$, the mean and variance of the bias estimator across all possible simulations are

$$\mathrm{E}^* \left(R^{-1} \sum \bar{Y}_r^* - \bar{y} \right) = 0, \qquad \mathrm{var}^* \left(R^{-1} \sum \bar{Y}_r^* - \bar{y} \right) = \frac{\hat{\sigma}^2}{Rn}, \qquad (2.15)$$

because $\mathrm{E}^*(\bar{Y}_r^*) = \bar{y}$ and $\mathrm{var}^*(\bar{Y}_r^*) = n^{-1}\hat{\sigma}^2$. The unconditional variance of B_R, taking into account the variability between different samples from the underlying distribution, is

$$\mathrm{var} \left(R^{-1} \sum \bar{Y}_r^* - \bar{Y} \right) = \mathrm{var}_Y \left\{ \mathrm{E}^* \left(R^{-1} \sum \bar{Y}_r^* - \bar{Y} \right) \right\}$$
$$+ \mathrm{E}_Y \left\{ \mathrm{var}^* \left(R^{-1} \sum \bar{Y}_r^* - \bar{Y} \right) \right\},$$

where $\mathrm{E}_Y(\cdot)$ and $\mathrm{var}_Y(\cdot)$ denote the mean and variance taken with respect to the joint distribution of $Y_1, \ldots, Y_n$. From (2.15) this gives

$$\mathrm{var}(B_R) = \mathrm{var}_Y(0) + \mathrm{E}_Y \left(\frac{\hat{\sigma}^2}{nR} \right) = \frac{\sigma^2}{n} \times \frac{n-1}{nR}. \qquad (2.16)$$

This result does not depend on normality of the data. A similar expression holds for any smooth statistic T with a linear approximation (Section 2.7.2), except for an $O(n^{-2})$ term.

Next consider the variance estimator $V_R = (R-1)^{-1} \sum (\bar{Y}_r^* - \bar{Y}_\cdot^*)^2$, where $\bar{Y}_\cdot^* = R^{-1} \sum \bar{Y}_r^*$. The mean and variance of V_R across all possible simulations, conditional on the data, are

$$\mathrm{E}^*(V_R) = \frac{\hat{\sigma}^2}{n}, \qquad \mathrm{var}^*(V_R) \doteq \left(\frac{\hat{\sigma}^2}{n} \right)^2 \frac{2}{R} \left(1 + \tfrac{1}{2}\hat{\gamma}_2 \right),$$

where $\hat{\gamma}_2$ is the standardized fourth cumulant — the standardized kurtosis — of the data (Appendix A). Note that $\hat{\gamma}_2$ would be zero for a parametric simulation but not for our nonparametric simulation, although in general $\hat{\gamma}_2 = O(n^{-1})$ because the data are normally distributed. The unconditional variance of V_R, averaging over all possible datasets, is

$$\mathrm{var}(V_R) \doteq \mathrm{var}_Y \left(\frac{\hat{\sigma}^2}{n} \right) + \mathrm{E}_Y \left\{ \left(\frac{\hat{\sigma}^2}{n} \right)^2 \frac{2}{R} \left(1 + \tfrac{1}{2}\hat{\gamma}_2 \right) \right\}$$

which reduces to

$$\mathrm{var}(V_R) \doteq \frac{2\sigma^4}{n^3} + \frac{2}{R} \left(\frac{2\sigma^4}{n^3} + \frac{\sigma^4}{n^2} \right). \qquad (2.17)$$

The first term on the right of (2.17) is due to data variation, the second to simulation variation. The implication is that to make the simulation variance as small as 10% of that due to data variation, one must take $R = 10n$.

The corresponding result for general data distributions would include an additional term from the kurtosis of the Y_j. A similar result holds for a general smooth statistic T.

Finally consider the estimator of the p quantile a_p for $\bar{Y} - \mu$, which is $\hat{a}_{p,R} = \bar{Y}^*_{((R+1)p)} - \bar{y}$ with $\bar{Y}^*_{((R+1)p)}$ the $(R+1)p$th order statistic of the simulated values $\bar{Y}^*_1, \ldots, \bar{Y}^*_R$. The general calculation of simulation properties of $\hat{a}_{p,R}$ is complicated, so we make the simplifying assumption that the $N(\bar{y}, n^{-1}\hat{\sigma}^2)$ approximation for $\bar{Y}^*$ is exact. With this assumption, standard properties of order statistics give

$$\mathrm{E}^*(\hat{a}_{p,R}) \doteq \hat{a}_p = n^{-1/2}\hat{\sigma}z_p,$$

and

$$\mathrm{var}^*(\hat{a}_{p,R}) \doteq \frac{p(1-p)}{Rg^2(\hat{a}_p)} = \frac{2\pi p(1-p)\hat{\sigma}^2 \exp(z_p^2)}{nR}, \qquad (2.18)$$

where $g(\cdot)$ is the density of $\bar{Y}^* - \bar{Y}$ conditional on $\hat{F}$, here taken to be the $N(0, n^{-1}\hat{\sigma}^2)$ density. (Note that the middle term of (2.18) applies for any T and any data distribution, with $g(\cdot)$ the density of $T - \theta$.) The unconditional variance of $\hat{a}_{p,R}$ over all datasets can then be reduced to

$$\mathrm{var}(\hat{a}_{p,R}) \doteq \frac{\sigma^2}{n}\left\{\frac{z_p^2}{2n} + \frac{2\pi p(1-p)\exp(z_p^2)}{R}\right\}. \qquad (2.19)$$

The implication of (2.19) is that the variance inflation due to simulation is approximately

$$\frac{4\pi np(1-p)\exp(z_p^2)}{z_p^2 R} = \frac{nd(p)}{R},$$

say. Some values of $d(p)$ are as follows.

p or $1-p$	0.01	0.025	0.05	0.10	0.25
$d(p)$	5.15	3.72	3.30	3.56	8.16

So to make the variance inflation factor 10% for the 0.025 quantile, for example, we would need $R \doteq 40n$. Equation (2.19) may not be useful in the centre of the distribution, where $d(p)$ is very large because z_p is small.

Example 2.14 (Air-conditioning data)   To see how well this discussion applies in practice, we look briefly at results for the data in Example 1.1. The statistic of interest is $T = \log \bar{Y}$, which estimates $\theta = \log \mu$. The true model for Y is taken to be the gamma distribution with index $\kappa = 0.71$ and mean $\mu = 108.083$; these are the data estimates. Effects due to simulation error are approximated

Table 2.3 Components of variance ($\times 10^{-3}$) in bootstrap estimation of p quantile for $\log \bar{Y} - \log \mu$, due to data variation and simulation variation, based on nonparametric simulation applied to the data of Example 1.1.

Source	Type	p					
		0.01	0.99	0.05	0.95	0.10	0.90
Data	actual	31.0	6.9	14.0	3.6	8.3	2.2
	theoretical	26.6	26.6	13.3	13.3	8.1	8.1
Simulation, $R = 100$	actual	53.6	9.4	8.5	3.2	3.8	2.6
	theoretical	32.9	32.9	10.5	10.5	6.9	6.9
Simulation, $R = 500$	actual	4.3	2.4	2.0	0.6	1.2	0.4
	theoretical	6.6	6.6	2.1	2.1	1.4	1.4
Simulation, $R = 1000$	actual	2.2	0.8	1.5	0.1	0.8	0.2
	theoretical	3.3	3.3	1.0	1.0	0.7	0.7

by taking sets of R simulations from one long nonparametric simulation of 9999 datasets. Table 2.3 shows the actual components of variation due to simulation and data variation, together with the theoretical components in (2.19), for estimates of quantiles of $\log \bar{Y} - \log \mu$. On the whole the theory gives a fairly accurate prediction of performance. ∎

It is not necessarily best to choose R solely on the basis of the variance inflation factor. For example, if we had been discussing the studentized statistic Z defined by (2.11) and its quantiles, then the component of variation due to data variance would be approximately zero to the accuracy used in (2.18), based on the $N(0,1)$ approximation. So the variance inflation factor would be enormous. What really counts is the effect of the simulation on the final result, say the length and coverage of the confidence interval. This presents a much more delicate question (Problem 5.5).

Another way to estimate quantiles for $T - \theta$ is by normal approximation with bootstrap estimates of bias and variance. Similar calculations of simulation error are possible; see Problem 2.7. In general the normal approximation is suspect, although its applicability can be assessed by a normal Q-Q plot of the simulated t^* values.

2.6 Statistical Issues

2.6.1 When does the bootstrap work?

Consistency

There are two senses in which resampling methods might "work". First, do they give reliable results when used with the sort of data encountered in practice? This question is crucial in applications, and is a major focus of this book. It leads one to consider how the resamples themselves can be used to tell when and how a bootstrap calculation might fail, and ideally how it should be amended to yield useful answers. This topic of bootstrap diagnostics is discussed more fully in Section 3.10.

A second question is: under what idealized conditions will a resampling procedure produce results that are in some sense mathematically correct? Answers to questions of this sort involve an asymptotic framework in which the sample size $n \to \infty$. Although such asymptotics are ultimately intended to guide practical work, they often act only as a backstop, by removing from consideration procedures that do not have appropriate large-sample properties, and are usually not subtle enough to discriminate among competing procedures according to their finite-sample characteristics. Nevertheless it is essential to appreciate when a naive application of the bootstrap will fail.

To put the theoretical basis for the bootstrap in simple terms, suppose that we have a random sample $y_1, \ldots, y_n$, or equivalently its EDF $\hat{F}$, from which we wish to estimate properties of a standardized quantity $Q = q(Y_1, \ldots, Y_n; F)$. For example, we might take

$$Q(Y_1, \ldots, Y_n; F) = n^{1/2}\left\{ \bar{Y} - \int y\,dF(y) \right\} = n^{1/2}(\bar{Y} - \theta),$$

say, and want to estimate the distribution function

$$G_{F,n}(q) = \Pr\left\{ Q(Y_1, \ldots, Y_n; F) \le q \mid F \right\}, \qquad (2.20)$$

where the conditioning on F indicates that $Y_1, \ldots, Y_n$ is a random sample from F. The bootstrap estimate of (2.20) is

$$G_{\hat{F},n}(q) = \Pr\left\{ Q(Y_1^*, \ldots, Y_n^*; \hat{F}) \le q \mid \hat{F} \right\} \qquad (2.21)$$

where in this case $Q(Y_1^*, \ldots, Y_n^*; \hat{F}) = n^{1/2}(\bar{Y}^* - \bar{y})$. In order for $G_{\hat{F},n}$ to approach $G_{F,n}$ as $n \to \infty$, three conditions must hold. Suppose that the true distribution F is surrounded by a neighbourhood $\mathcal{N}$ in a suitable space of distributions, and that as $n \to \infty$, $\hat{F}$ eventually falls into $\mathcal{N}$ with probability one. Then the conditions are:

1 for any $A \in \mathcal{N}$, $G_{A,n}$ must converge weakly to a limit $G_{A,\infty}$;
2 this convergence must be uniform on $\mathcal{N}$; and
3 the function mapping A to $G_{A,\infty}$ must be continuous.

Here weak convergence of $G_{A,n}$ to $G_{A,\infty}$ means that as $n \to \infty$,

$$\int h(u)\,dG_{A,n}(u) \quad \to \quad \int h(u)\,dG_{A,\infty}(u)$$

for all integrable functions $h(\cdot)$. Under these conditions the bootstrap is *consistent*, meaning that for any q and $\varepsilon > 0$, $\Pr\{|G_{\hat{F},n}(q) - G_{F,\infty}(q)| > \varepsilon\} \to 0$ as $n \to \infty$.

The first condition ensures that there is a limit for $G_{F,n}$ to converge to, and would be needed even in the happy situation where $\hat{F}$ equalled F for every $n \geq n'$, for some n'. Now as n increases, $\hat{F}$ changes, so the second and third conditions are needed to ensure that $G_{\hat{F},n}$ approaches $G_{F,\infty}$ along every possible sequence of $\hat{F}$s. If any one of these conditions fails, the bootstrap can fail.

Example 2.15 (Sample maximum) Suppose that $Y_1, \ldots, Y_n$ is a random sample from the uniform distribution on $(0, \theta)$. Then the maximum likelihood estimate of θ is the largest sample value, $T = Y_{(n)}$, where $Y_{(1)} \leq \cdots \leq Y_{(n)}$ are the sample order statistics. Consider nonparametric resampling. The limiting distribution of $Q = n(\theta - T)/\theta$ is standard exponential, and this suggests that we take our standardized quantity to be $Q^* = n(t - T^*)/t$, where t is the observed value of T, and T^* is the maximum of a bootstrap sample of size n taken from $y_1, \ldots, y_n$. As $n \to \infty$, however,

$$\Pr(Q^* = 0 \mid \hat{F}) = \Pr(T^* = t \mid \hat{F}) = 1 - (1 - n^{-1})^n \to 1 - e^{-1},$$

and consequently the limiting distribution of Q^* cannot be standard exponential. The problem here is that the second condition fails: the distributional convergence is not uniform on useful neighbourhoods of F. Any fixed order statistic $Y_{(k)}$ suffers from the same difficulty, but a statistic like a sample quantile, where we would take $k \doteq pn$ for some fixed $0 < p < 1$, does not. ∎

Asymptotic accuracy

Here and below we say $X_n = O_p(n^d)$ when $\Pr(n^{-d}|X_n| \geq \epsilon) \to p$ for some constant p as $n \to \infty$, and $X_n = o_p(n^d)$ when $\Pr(n^{-d}|X_n| \geq \epsilon) \to 0$ as $n \to \infty$, for any $\epsilon > 0$.

Consistency is a weak property, for example guaranteeing only that the true probability coverage of a nominal $(1 - 2\alpha)$ confidence interval is $1 - 2\alpha + o_p(1)$. Standard normal approximation methods are consistent in this sense. Once consistency is established, meaning that the resampling method is "valid", we need to know whether the method is "good" relative to other possible methods. This involves looking at the rate of convergence to nominal properties. For example, does the coverage of the confidence interval deviate from $(1 - 2\alpha)$ by $O_p(n^{-1/2})$ or by $O_p(n^{-1})$? Some insight into this can be obtained by expansion methods, as we now outline. More detailed calculations are made in Section 5.4.

Suppose that the problem is one where the limiting distribution of Q is standard normal, and where an *Edgeworth expansion* applies. Then the distribution of Q can be written in the form

$$\Pr(Q \leq q \mid F) = \Phi(q) + n^{-1/2}a(q)\phi(q) + O(n^{-1}), \tag{2.22}$$

where $\Phi(\cdot)$ and $\phi(\cdot)$ are the CDF and PDF of the standard normal distribution, and $a(\cdot)$ is an even quadratic polynomial. For a wide range of problems it can be shown that the corresponding approximation for the bootstrap version of Q is

$$\Pr(Q^* \leq q \mid \hat{F}) = \Phi(q) + n^{-1/2}\hat{a}(q)\phi(q) + O_p(n^{-1}), \tag{2.23}$$

where $\hat{a}(\cdot)$ is obtained by replacing unknowns in $a(\cdot)$ by estimates. Now typically $\hat{a}(q) = a(q) + O_p(n^{-1/2})$, so

$$\Pr(Q^* \leq q \mid \hat{F}) - \Pr(Q \leq q \mid F) = O_p(n^{-1}). \qquad (2.24)$$

Thus the estimated distribution for Q differs from the true distribution by a term that is $O_p(n^{-1})$, provided that Q is constructed in such a way that it is asymptotically pivotal. A similar argument will typically hold when Q has a different limiting distribution, provided it does not depend on unknowns.

Suppose that we choose not to standardize Q, so that its limiting distribution is normal with variance v. An Edgeworth expansion still applies, now with form

$$\Pr(Q \leq q \mid F) = \Phi\left(\frac{q}{v^{1/2}}\right) + n^{-1/2} a'\left(\frac{q}{v^{1/2}}\right) \phi\left(\frac{q}{v^{1/2}}\right) + O(n^{-1}), \qquad (2.25)$$

where $a'(\cdot)$ is a quadratic polynomial that is different from $a(\cdot)$. The corresponding expansion for Q^* is

$$\Pr(Q^* \leq q \mid \hat{F}) = \Phi\left(\frac{q}{\hat{v}^{1/2}}\right) + n^{-1/2} a'\left(\frac{q}{\hat{v}^{1/2}}\right) \phi\left(\frac{q}{\hat{v}^{1/2}}\right) + O_p(n^{-1}). \qquad (2.26)$$

Typically $\hat{v} = v + O_p(n^{-1/2})$, which would imply that

$$\Pr(Q^* \leq q \mid \hat{F}) - \Pr(Q \leq q \mid F) = O_p(n^{-1/2}), \qquad (2.27)$$

because the leading terms on the right-hand sides of (2.25) and (2.26) are different.

The difference between (2.24) and (2.27) explains our insistence on working with approximate pivots whenever possible: use of a pivot will mean that a bootstrap distribution function is an order of magnitude closer to its target. It also gives a cogent theoretical motivation for using the bootstrap to set confidence intervals, as we now outline.

We can obtain the α quantile of the distribution of Q by inverting (2.22), giving the *Cornish–Fisher expansion*

$$q_\alpha = z_\alpha + n^{-1/2} a''(z_\alpha) + O(n^{-1}),$$

where z_α is the α quantile of the standard normal distribution, and $a''(\cdot)$ is a further polynomial. The corresponding bootstrap quantile has the property that $q_\alpha^* - q_\alpha = O_p(n^{-1})$. For simplicity take $Q = (T - \theta)/V^{1/2}$, where V estimates the variance of T. Then an exact one-sided confidence interval for θ based on Q would be $I_\alpha = [T - V^{1/2} q_\alpha, \infty)$, and this contains the true θ with probability α. The corresponding bootstrap interval is $I_\alpha^* = [T - V^{1/2} q_\alpha^*, \infty)$, where q_α^* is the α quantile of the distribution of Q^* — which would often be estimated by simulation, as we have seen. Since $q_\alpha^* - q_\alpha = O_p(n^{-1})$, we have

$$\Pr(\theta \in I_\alpha) = \alpha, \quad \Pr(\theta \in I_\alpha^*) = \alpha + O(n^{-1}),$$

so that the actual probability that I_α^* contains θ differs from the nominal probability by only $O(n^{-1})$. In contrast, intervals based on inverting (2.25) will contain θ with probability $\alpha + O(n^{-1/2})$. This interval is in principle no more accurate than using the interval $[T - V^{1/2}z_\alpha, \infty)$ obtained by assuming that the distribution of Q is standard normal. Thus one-sided confidence intervals based on quantiles of Q^* have an asymptotic advantage over the use of a normal approximation. Similar comments apply to two-sided intervals.

The practical usefulness of such results will depend on the numerical value of the difference (2.24) at the values of q of interest, and it will always be wise to try to decrease this statistical error, as outlined in Section 2.5.1.

The results above based on Edgeworth expansions apply to many common statistics: smooth functions of sample moments, such as means, variances, and higher moments, eigenvalues and eigenvectors of covariance matrices; smooth functions of solutions to smooth estimating equations, such as most maximum likelihood estimators, estimators in linear and generalized linear models, and some robust estimators; and to many statistics calculated from time series.

2.6.2 Rough statistics: unsmooth and unstable

What typically validates the bootstrap is the existence of an Edgeworth expansion for the statistic of interest, as would be the case when that statistic is a differentiable function of sample moments. Some statistics, such as sample quantiles, depend on the sample in an unsmooth or unstable way such that standard expansion theory does not apply. Often the nonparametric resampling method will still be valid, in the sense that it is consistent, but for finite samples it may not work very well. Part of the reason for this is that the set of possible values for T^* may be very small, and very vulnerable to unusual data points. A case in point is that of sample quantiles, the most familiar of which — the sample median — is discussed in the next example. Example 2.15 gives a case where naive resampling fails completely.

Example 2.16 (Sample median) Suppose that the sample size is odd, $n = 2m + 1$, so that the sample median is $\tilde{y} = y_{(m+1)}$. In large samples the median is approximately normally distributed about the population median μ, but standard nonparametric methods of variance estimation (jackknife and delta method) do not work here (Example 2.19, Problem 2.17). Nonparametric resampling does work to some extent, provided the sample size is quite large and the data are not too dirty. Crucially, bootstrap confidence limits work quite well.

Note first that the bootstrap statistic $\tilde{Y}^*$ is concentrated on the sample values $y_{(k)}$, which makes the estimated distribution of the median very discrete and very vulnerable to unusual observations. Problem 2.4 shows that the exact

	Normal		t_3		Cauchy	
	11	21	11	21	11	21
Theoretical	14.3	7.5	16.8	8.8	22.4	11.7
Empirical	13.9	7.3	19.1	9.5	38.3	14.6
Mean bootstrap	17.2	8.8	25.9	11.4	14000	22.8
Effective df	4.3	5.4	3.2	4.9	0.002	0.5

Table 2.4 Theoretical, empirical and mean bootstrap estimates of variance ($\times 10^{-2}$) of sample median, based on 10000 datasets of sizes $n = 11, 21$. The effective degrees of freedom of bootstrap variances uses a χ^2 approximation to their distribution.

distribution of $\tilde{Y}^*$ is

$$\Pr(\tilde{Y}^* = y_{(k)}) = \sum_{j=0}^{m} \binom{n}{j} p_{k-1}^j (1 - p_{k-1})^{n-j} - \sum_{j=0}^{m} \binom{n}{j} p_k^j (1 - p_k)^{n-j}, \quad (2.28)$$

for $k = 1, \ldots, n$ where $p_k = k/n$; simulation is not needed in this case. The moments of this bootstrap distribution, including its mean and variance, converge to the correct values as n increases. However, the convergence can be very slow. To illustrate this, Table 2.4 compares the average bootstrap variance with the empirical variance of the median for data samples of sizes $n = 11$ and 21 from the standard normal distribution, the Student-t distribution with three degrees of freedom, and the Cauchy distribution; also shown are the theoretical variance approximations, which are incalculable when the true distribution F is unknown. We see that the bootstrap variance can be very poor for $n = 11$ when distributions are long-tailed. The value 1.4×10^4 for average bootstrap variance with Cauchy data is not a mistake: the bootstrap variance exceeds 100 for about 1% of datasets: for some samples the bootstrap variance is huge. The situation stabilizes when n reaches 40 or more.

The gross discreteness of $\tilde{y}^*$ could also affect the simple confidence limit method described in Section 2.4. But provided the inequalities used to justify (2.10) are taken to be $\leq$ and $\geq$ rather than $<$ and $>$, the method works well. For example, for Cauchy samples of size $n = 11$ the coverage of the 90% basic bootstrap confidence interval (2.10) is 90.8% in 1000 samples; see Problem 2.4. We suggest adopting the same practice for all problems where t^* is supported on a small number of values. ∎

The statistic T will certainly behave wildly under resampling when $t(F)$ does not exist, as happens for the mean when F is a Cauchy distribution. Quite naturally over repeated samples the bootstrap will produce silly and useless results in such cases. There are two points to make here. First, if data are taken from a real population, then such mathematical difficulties cannot arise. Secondly, the standard approaches to data analysis include careful screening of data for outliers, nonnormality, and so forth, which leads either to deletion of disruptive data elements or to sensible and reliable choices of estimators

T. In short, the mathematical pathology of nonexistence is unlikely to be a practical problem.

2.6.3 Conditional properties

Resampling calculations are based on the observed data, and in that sense resampling methods are conditional on the data. This is especially so in the nonparametric case, where nothing but data is used. Because of this, the question is sometimes asked: "Are resampling methods therefore conditional in the inferential sense?" The short answer is: "No, at least not in any useful way — unless the relevant conditioning can be made explicit."

Conditional inference arises in parametric inference when the sufficient statistic includes an *ancillary statistic A* whose distribution is free of parameters. Then we argue that inferences about parameters (e.g. confidence intervals) should be based on sampling distributions conditional on the observed value of A; this brings inference more into line with Bayesian inference. Two examples are the configuration of residuals in location models, and the values of explanatory variables in regression models. The first cannot be accommodated in nonparametric bootstrap analysis because the effect depends upon the unknown F. The second can be accommodated (Chapter 6) because the effect does not depend upon the stochastic part of the model. It is certainly true that the bootstrap distribution of T^* will *reflect* ancillary features of the data, as in the case of the sample median (Example 2.16), but the reflection is pale to the point of uselessness.

There are situations where it is possible explicitly to condition the resampling so as to provide conditional inference. Largely these situations are those where there is an experimental ancillary statistic, as in regression. One other situation is discussed in Example 5.17.

2.6.4 When might the bootstrap fail?

Incomplete data

So far we have assumed that F is the distribution of interest and that the sample $y_1, \ldots, y_n$ drawn from F has nothing removed before we see it. This might be important in several ways, not least in guaranteeing statistical consistency of our estimator T. But in some applications the observation that we get may not always be y itself. For example, with survival data the *y*s might be censored, meaning that we may only learn that y was greater than some cut-off c because observation of the subject ceased before the event which determines y. Or, with multiple measurements on a series of patients it may be that for some patients certain measurements could not be made because the patient did not consent, or the doctor forgot.

Under certain circumstances the resampling methods we have described will work, but in general it would be unwise to assume this without careful thought. Alternative methods will be described in Section 3.6.

Dependent data

In general the nonparametric resampling method that we have described will not work for dependent data. This can be illustrated quite easily in the case where the data $y_1, \ldots, y_n$ form one realization of a correlated time series. For example, consider the sample average $\bar{y}$ and suppose that the data come from a stationary series $\{Y_j\}$ whose marginal variance is $\sigma^2 = \mathrm{var}(Y_j)$ and whose autocorrelations are $\rho_h = \mathrm{corr}(Y_j, Y_{j+h})$ for $h = 1, 2, \ldots$ In Example 2.7 we showed that the nonparametric bootstrap estimate of the variance of $\bar{Y}$ is approximately s^2/n, and for large n this will approach σ^2/n. But the actual variance of $\bar{Y}$ is

$$\mathrm{var}(\bar{Y}) = \frac{\sigma^2}{n} \sum_{h=-(n-1)}^{n-1} \left(1 - \frac{|h|}{n}\right) \rho_h.$$

The sum here would often differ considerably from one, and then the bootstrap estimate of variance would be badly wrong.

Similar problems arise with other forms of dependent data. The essence of the problem is that simple bootstrap sampling imposes mutual independence on the Y_j, effectively assuming that their joint CDF is $F(y_1) \times \cdots \times F(y_n)$ and thus sampling from its estimate $\hat{F}(y_1^*) \times \cdots \times \hat{F}(y_n^*)$. This is incorrect for dependent data. The difficulty is that there is no obvious way to estimate a general joint density for $Y_1, \ldots, Y_n$ given one realization. We shall explore this important subject further in Chapter 8.

Weakly dependent data occur in the altogether different context of finite population sampling. Here the basic nonparametric resampling methods work reasonably well. More will be said about this in Section 3.7.

Dirty data

What if simulated resampling is used when there are outliers in the data? There is no substitute for careful data scrutiny in this or any other statistical context, and if obvious outliers are found, they should be removed or corrected. When there is a fitted parametric model, it provides a benchmark for plots of residuals and the panoply of statistical diagnostics, and this helps to detect poor model fit. When there is no parametric model, F is estimated by the EDF, and the benchmark is swept away because the data and the model are one and the same. It is then vital to look closely at the simulation output, in order to see whether the conclusions depend crucially on particular observations. We return to this question of sensitivity analysis in Section 3.10.

2.7 Nonparametric Approximations for Variance and Bias

2.7.1 Delta methods

In parametric analysis it is often possible to represent estimators T in terms of fundamental statistics $U_1, \ldots, U_m$, such as sample moments, for which exact or approximate distributional calculations are relatively easy. Then we can take advantage of the delta method to obtain distributional approximations for T itself.

Consider first the case of a scalar estimator T which is a function of the scalar statistic U based on a sample of size n, say $T = g(U)$. Suppose that it is known that

$$U \dot\sim N\left(\zeta, n^{-1}\sigma^2(\zeta)\right).$$

Two formal expressions are $U = \zeta + o_p(1)$ and $U = \zeta + n^{-1/2}\sigma(\zeta)Z + O_p(n^{-1})$, where Z is a $N(0,1)$ variable. The first of these corresponds to a statement of the consistency property of U, and the second amplifies this to state both the rate of convergence and the normal approximation in an alternative form.

Now consider $T = g(U)$, where $g(\cdot)$ is a smooth function. We shall see below that provided that $\dot g(\zeta) \neq 0$,

$$T \dot\sim N\left(\theta, n^{-1}\{\dot g(\zeta)\}^2\sigma^2(\zeta)\right),$$

where $\theta = g(\zeta)$; the dot indicates differentation with respect to ζ. This result is what is usually meant by the *delta method result*, the principal feature being the *delta method variance approximation*

$$\text{var}\{g(U)\} \doteq \{\dot g(\zeta)\}^2 \text{var}(U). \tag{2.29}$$

To see why (2.29) should be true, note that if $g(\cdot)$ is smooth then T is consistent for $\theta = g(\zeta)$, since

$$g(U) = g(\zeta + o_p(1)) = g(\zeta) + o_p(1).$$

Further, by Taylor series expansion we can write

$$T = g(U) = g(\zeta) + (U - \zeta)\dot g(\zeta) + \tfrac{1}{2}(U - \zeta)^2\ddot g(\zeta) + o_p(n^{-1}), \tag{2.30}$$

since the remainder is proportional to $(U - \zeta)^3$. A truncated version of the series expansion is

$$T = g(U) = g(\zeta) + (U - \zeta)\dot g(\zeta) + o_p(n^{-1/2}). \tag{2.31}$$

From the latter, we can see that the normal approximation for U implies that

$$T = g(\zeta) + n^{-1/2}\dot g(\zeta)\sigma(\zeta)Z + o_p(n^{-1/2}),$$

which in turn entails (2.29).

Nothing has yet been said about the bias of T, which would usually be hidden in the $O_p(n^{-1})$ term. If we take the larger expansion (2.30), ignore the remainder term, and take expectations, we obtain

$$E(T) \doteq g(\zeta) + \dot{g}(\zeta)E(U - \zeta) + \frac{1}{2n}\ddot{g}(\zeta)\sigma^2(\zeta);$$

or, if U is unbiased for ζ,

$$E(T) \doteq \theta + \frac{1}{2n}\ddot{g}(\zeta)\sigma^2(\zeta).$$

These results extend quite easily to the case of vector U and vector T, as outlined in Problem 2.9. The extension includes the case where U is the set of observed frequencies $f_1, \ldots, f_m$ when Y is discrete with probabilities $\pi_1, \ldots, \pi_m$ on m possible values. Then the analogue of (2.31) is

$$T \doteq g(\pi_1, \ldots, \pi_m) + \sum_{j=1}^{m} \left(\frac{f_j}{n} - \pi_j \right) \frac{\partial g(\pi_1, \ldots, \pi_m)}{\partial \pi_j}. \qquad (2.32)$$

In this case the normal approximation for $f_1, \ldots, f_m$ is easy to derive, but is singular because of the constraint $\sum f_j = n \sum \pi_j = n$. In effect (2.32) provides a version of the nonparametric delta method, restricted to discrete data problems. In the next subsection we extend the expansion method to the general nonparametric case.

2.7.2 Influence function and nonparametric delta method

There is a simple variance approximation for many statistics T with the representation $t(\hat{F})$. The key idea is an extension of the Taylor series expansion to statistical functions, which allows us to extend (2.32) to continuous distributions. The linear form of the expansion is

$$t(G) \doteq t(F) + \int L_t(y; F)\, dG(y), \qquad (2.33)$$

where L_t, the first derivative of $t(\cdot)$ at F, is defined by

$$L_t(y; F) = \lim_{\varepsilon \to 0} \frac{t\{(1 - \varepsilon)F + \varepsilon H_y\} - t(F)}{\varepsilon} = \left. \frac{\partial t\{(1 - \varepsilon)F + \varepsilon H_y\}}{\partial \varepsilon} \right|_{\varepsilon=0}, \qquad (2.34)$$

with $H_y(u) \equiv H(u - y)$ the Heaviside or unit step function jumping from 0 to 1 at $u = y$. In this form the derivative satisfies $\int L_t(y; F)\, dF(y) = 0$, as seen on setting $G = F$ in (2.33). Often the function $L_t(y) = L_t(y; F)$ is called the *influence function* of T and its empirical approximation $l(y) = L_t(y; \hat{F})$ is called the *empirical influence function*. The particular values $l_j = l(y_j)$ are called the *empirical influence values*.

The *nonparametric delta method* comes from applying the first-order approximation (2.33) with $G = \hat{F}$,

$$t(\hat{F}) \doteq t(F) + \int L_t(y; F) d\hat{F}(y) = t(F) + \frac{1}{n} \sum_{j=1}^{n} L_t(y_j; F). \tag{2.35}$$

The right-hand side of (2.35) is also known as the *linear approximation*. We apply the central limit theorem to the sum on the right-hand side of (2.35) and obtain

$$T - \theta \;\overset{\cdot}{\sim}\; N(0, v_L(F))$$

because $\int L_t(y; F) dF(y) = 0$, where

$$v_L(F) = n^{-1} \text{var}\{L_t(Y)\} = n^{-1} \int L_t^2(y) \, dF(y).$$

In practice $v_L(F)$ is approximated by substituting $\hat{F}$ for F in the result, that is by using the sample version

$$v_L = v_L(\hat{F}) = n^{-2} \sum_{j=1}^{n} l_j^2, \tag{2.36}$$

which is known as the *nonparametric delta method variance estimate*. Note that (2.35) implies that

$$\int L_t(y; \hat{F}) d\hat{F}(y) = n^{-1} \sum l_j \equiv 0.$$

In some cases it may be difficult to evaluate the derivative (2.34) theoretically. Then a numerical approximation to the derivative can be made, that is

$$L_t(y; F) \doteq \frac{t\{(1 - \varepsilon)F + \varepsilon H_y\} - t(F)}{\varepsilon} \tag{2.37}$$

with a small value of ε such as $(100n)^{-1}$. The same method can be used for empirical influence values $l_j \equiv L_t(y_j; \hat{F})$. Alternative approximations to the empirical influence values l_j, which are all that are needed in (2.36), are described in the following sections.

Example 2.17 (Average) Let $t = \bar{y}$, corresponding to the statistical function $t(F) = \int y dF(y)$. To apply (2.34) we write

$$t\{(1 - \varepsilon)F + \varepsilon H_y\} = (1 - \varepsilon)\mu + \varepsilon y,$$

and differentiate to obtain

$$L_t(y) = \left. \frac{\partial\{(1 - \varepsilon)\mu + \varepsilon y\}}{\partial \varepsilon} \right|_{\varepsilon=0} = y - \mu.$$

The empirical influence function is therefore $l(y) = y - \bar{y}$, with $l_j = y_j - \bar{y}$. Thus the delta method variance approximation (2.36) is $v_L = (n - 1)s^2/n^2$, where s^2

is the unbiased sample variance of the y_j. This differs by the factor $(n-1)/n$ from the more usual nonparametric variance estimate for $\bar{y}$.   ∎

The mean is an example of a linear statistic, whose general form is $\int a(y)\,dF(y)$. As the terminology suggests, linear statistics have zero derivatives beyond the first; they have influence function $a(y) - \mathrm{E}\{a(Y)\}$. This applies to all moments about zero; see Problem 2.10.

Complicated statistics which are functions of simple statistics can be dealt with using the chain rule. So if $t(F) = a\{t_1(F), \ldots, t_m(F)\}$, then

$$L_t(y) = \sum_{i=1}^{m} \frac{\partial a}{\partial t_i} L_{t_i}(y). \tag{2.38}$$

This can also be used to find the influence function for a transformed statistic, given the influence function for the statistic itself.

Example 2.18 (Correlation)   The sample correlation is the sample version of the product moment correlation, which for the pair $Y = (U, X)$ can be defined in terms of $\mu_{rs} = \mathrm{E}(U^r X^s)$ by

$$\rho \equiv \rho(F) = \frac{\mu_{11} - \mu_{10}\mu_{01}}{\{(\mu_{20} - \mu_{10}^2)(\mu_{02} - \mu_{01}^2)\}^{1/2}}. \tag{2.39}$$

The influence functions of means are given in Example 2.17. For second moments we have $L_{\mu_{rs}}(u, x) = u^r x^s - \mu_{rs}$, when $r + s = 2$, because the μ_{rs} are linear statistics (Problem 2.10). The partial derivatives of $\rho(\cdot)$ with respect to the μs are straightforward, and (2.38) leads to the influence function for the correlation coefficient,

$$L_\rho(u, x) = u_s x_s - \tfrac{1}{2}\rho(u_s^2 + x_s^2), \tag{2.40}$$

where $u_s = (u - \mu_{10})/(\mu_{20} - \mu_{10}^2)^{1/2}$, and $x_s = (x - \mu_{01})/(\mu_{02} - \mu_{01}^2)^{1/2}$ are standardized variates.

If we wanted to work with the standard transformation $\zeta = \tfrac{1}{2}\log\left(\frac{1+\rho}{1-\rho}\right)$, whose derivative is $(1 - \rho^2)^{-1}$, then another application of (2.38) shows that the influence function would be

$$L_\zeta(u, x) = \frac{1}{1 - \rho^2}\left\{u_s x_s - \tfrac{1}{2}\rho(u_s^2 + x_s^2)\right\}.$$

   ∎

Example 2.19 (Quantile)   The p quantile q_p of a distribution F with density f is defined as the solution to the equation $F\{q_p(F)\} = p$. If we set $F_\varepsilon(x) = (1 - \varepsilon)F(x) + \varepsilon H(x - y)$, we have

$$p = F_\varepsilon\{q_p(F_\varepsilon)\} = (1 - \varepsilon)F\{q_p(F_\varepsilon)\} + \varepsilon H\{q_p(F_\varepsilon) - y\}.$$

Table 2.5 Exact empirical influence values and their regression estimates for the ratio applied to the city population data with $n = 10$.

Case	1	2	3	4	5	6	7	8	9	10
Exact	−1.04	−0.58	−0.37	−0.19	0.03	0.11	0.09	0.20	1.02	0.73
Regression	−1.11	−0.65	−0.44	−0.38	−0.04	0.12	0.13	0.27	1.16	0.94

Figure 2.11 Empirical influence values for city population example. The left panel shows the l_j for the $n = 10$ cases; the line has slope $t = 1.52$. The right panels show 999 values of t_r^* plotted against jittered values of $n^{-1} f_{rj}^*$ for $j = 1, 2, 9, 4$ (clockwise from top left); the lines have slope l_j and pass through t when $f^* = 0$.

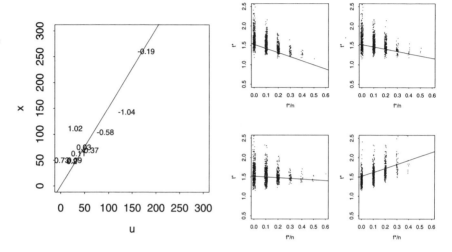

On differentiating this with respect to ε and setting $\varepsilon = 0$, we find that

$$L_{q_p}(y; F) = -\frac{H(q_p - y) - p}{f(q_p)} = \begin{cases} \frac{p-1}{f(q_p)}, & y \le q_p, \\ \frac{p}{f(q_p)}, & y > q_p. \end{cases}$$

Evidently this has mean zero.

The approximate variance of $q_p(\hat{F})$ is

$$v_L(F) = n^{-1} \int L_{q_p}^2(y; F)\, dF(y) = \frac{p(1-p)}{n f(q_p)^2},$$

the empirical version of which requires an estimate of $f(q_p)$. But since nonparametric density estimates converge much more slowly than estimates of means, variances, and so forth, estimation of variance for quantile estimates is harder and requires much larger samples. ∎

Example 2.20 (City population data) For the ratio estimate $t = \bar{x}/\bar{u}$, calculations in Problem 2.16 lead to empirical influence values $l_j = (x_j - t u_j)/\bar{u}$. Numerical values for the city population data of size 10 are given in Table 2.5; the regression estimates are discussed in Example 2.23. The variance estimate is $v_L = n^{-2} \sum l_j^2 = 0.18^2$.

The l_j are plotted in the left panel of Figure 2.11. Values of $y_j = (u_j, x_j)$ close to the line $x = tu$ have little effect on the ratio t. Changing the data by giving more weight to those y_j with negative influence values, for which (u_j, x_j) lies below the line, would result in smaller values of t than that actually observed, and conversely. We discuss the right panels in Example 2.23. ∎

In some applications the estimator T will be defined by an estimating equation, the simplest form being $\sum c(y_j, t) = 0$ such that $\int c(y, \theta) dF(y) = 0$. Then the influence function for scalar t is (Problem 2.12)

$$L_t(y) = \frac{c(y, \theta)}{\mathrm{E}\{-\dot{c}(Y, \theta)\}},$$

where $\dot{c} \equiv \partial c / \partial \theta$. The corresponding empirical influence values are therefore

$$l_j = \frac{-nc(y_j, t)}{\sum \dot{c}(y_j, t)},$$

and the nonparametric delta method variance estimate is

$$v_L = \frac{\sum \{c(y_j, t)\}^2}{\{\sum \dot{c}(y_j, t)\}^2}.$$

A simple illustration is Example 2.20, where t is determined by the estimating function $c(y, \theta) = x - \theta u$.

For some purposes it is useful to go beyond the first derivative term in the expansion of $t(\hat{F})$ and obtain the quadratic approximation

$$t(\hat{F}) \doteq t(F) + \int L_t(y; F) \, d\hat{F}(y) + \tfrac{1}{2} \int \int Q_t(y, z; F) \, d\hat{F}(y) d\hat{F}(z), \qquad (2.41)$$

where the second derivative $Q_t(y, z; F)$ is defined by

$$Q_t(y, z; F) = \frac{\partial^2 t\{(1 - \varepsilon_1 - \varepsilon_2)F + \varepsilon_1 H_y + \varepsilon_2 H_z\}}{\partial \varepsilon_1 \partial \varepsilon_2} \bigg|_{\varepsilon_1 = \varepsilon_2 = 0}$$

This derivative satisfies $\int Q_t(x, y; F) dF(x) = \int Q_t(x, y; F) dF(y) = 0$, but in general $\int Q_t(x, x; F) dF(x) \neq 0$. The values $q_{jk} = Q_t(y_j, y_k; \hat{F})$ are empirical second derivatives of $t(\cdot)$ analogous to the empirical influence values l_j. In principle (2.41) will be more accurate than (2.35).

2.7.3 Jackknife estimates

Another approach to approximating the influence function, but only at the sample values $y_1, \ldots, y_n$ themselves, is the *jackknife*. Here l_j is approximated by

$$l_{jack,j} = (n - 1)(t - t_{-j}), \qquad (2.42)$$

where t_{-j} is the estimate calculated with y_j omitted from the data. In effect this corresponds to numerical approximation (2.37) using $\varepsilon = -(n - 1)^{-1}$; see Problem 2.18.

The jackknife approximations to the bias and variance of T are

$$b_{jack} = -\frac{1}{n} \sum_{j=1}^{n} l_{jack,j}, \qquad v_{jack} = \frac{1}{n(n-1)} \left(\sum l_{jack,j}^2 - nb_{jack}^2 \right). \qquad (2.43)$$

It is reasonably straightforward to apply (2.33) with $\hat{F}_{-j}$ and $\hat{F}$ in place of G and F, respectively, to show that

$$l_{jack,j} \doteq l_j;$$

see Problem 2.15.

Example 2.21 (Average) For the sample average $t = \bar{y}$ and the case deletion values are $t_{-j} = (n\bar{y} - y_j)/(n-1)$ and so $l_{jack,j} \doteq y_j - \bar{y}$. This is the same as the empirical influence function because t is linear. The variance approximation in (2.43) reduces to $\{n(n-1)\}^{-1} \sum (y_j - \bar{y})^2$ because $b_{jack} \equiv 0$; the denominator $n - 1$ in the formula for v_{jack} was chosen to ensure that this happens. ∎

One application of (2.43) is to show that in large samples the jackknife bias approximation gives

$$b_{jack} \doteq \mathrm{E}^*(T^*) - t \doteq \tfrac{1}{2}n^{-2} \sum_{j=1}^{n} q_{jj};$$

see Problem 2.15.

So far we have seen two ways to approximate the bias and variance of T using approximations to the influence function, namely the nonparametric delta method and the jackknife method. One can generalize the basic approximation by using alternative numerical derivatives in these two methods.

2.7.4 Empirical influence values via regression

The approximation (2.35) can also be applied to the bootstrap estimate T^*. If the EDF of the bootstrap sample is denoted by $\hat{F}^*$, then the analogue of (2.35) is

$$t(\hat{F}^*) \doteq t(\hat{F}) + \frac{1}{n} \sum_{j=1}^{n} L_t(y_j^*; \hat{F}),$$

or in simpler notation

$$t^* \doteq t + \frac{1}{n} \sum_{j=1}^{n} f_j^* l_j = t_L^*, \qquad (2.44)$$

say, where f_j^* is the number of times that y_i^* equals y_j, for $j = 1, \ldots, n$. The linear approximation (2.44) will be used several times in future chapters.

Under the nonparametric bootstrap the joint distribution of the f_j^* is multinomial (Problem 2.19). It is easy to see that $\mathrm{var}(T^*) \doteq n^{-2} \sum l_j^2 = v_L$, showing

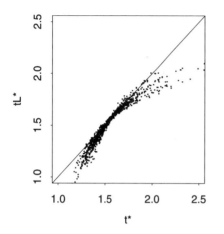
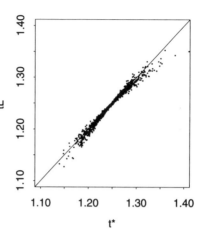

Figure 2.12 Plots of linear approximation t_L^* against t^* for the ratio applied to the city population data, with $n = 10$ (left panel), and $n = 49$ (right panel).

that the bootstrap estimate of variance should be similar to the nonparametric delta method approximation.

Example 2.22 (City population data)   The right panels of Figure 2.11 show how 999 resampled values of t^* depend on $n^{-1}f_j^*$ for four values of j, for the data with $n = 10$. The lines with slope l_j summarize fairly well how t^* depends on f_j^*, but the correspondence is not ideal.

A different way to see this is to plot t^* against the corresponding t_L^*. Figure 2.12 shows this for 499 replicates. The line shows where the values for an exactly linear statistic would fall. The linear approximation is poor for $n = 10$, but it is more accurate for the full dataset, where $n = 49$. In Section 3.10 we outline how such plots may be used to find a suitable scale on which to set confidence limits.   ∎

Expression (2.44) suggests a way to approximate the l_js using the results of a bootstrap simulation. Suppose that we have simulated R samples from $\hat{F}$ as described in Section 2.3. Define f_{rj}^* to be the frequency with which the data value y_j occurs in the rth bootstrap sample. Then (2.44) implies that

$$t_r^* \doteq t + \frac{1}{n}\sum_{j=1}^{n} f_{rj}^* l_j, \quad r = 1,\dots,R.$$

This can be viewed as a linear regression equation for "responses" t_r^* with "covariate values" $n^{-1}f_{rj}^*$ and "coefficients" l_j. We should, however, adjust for the facts that $E^*(T^*) \neq t$ in general, that $\sum_j l_j = 0$, and that $\sum_j f_{rj}^* = n$. For the first of these we add a general intercept term, or equivalently replace t with $\bar{t}^*$.

For the second two we drop the term $f^*_{rn}l_n$, resulting in the regression equation

$$t^*_r - \bar{t}^* = \frac{1}{n}\sum_{j=1}^{n-1} f^*_{rj}l_j, \quad r = 1,\dots,R. \tag{2.45}$$

So the vector $\hat{l} = (\hat{l}_1,\dots,\hat{l}_{n-1})^T$ of approximate values of the l_j is obtained with the least-squares regression formula

$$\hat{l} \doteq (F^{*T}F^*)^{-1}F^{*T}d^*, \tag{2.46}$$

where F^* is the $R \times (n-1)$ matrix with (r, j) element $n^{-1}f^*_{rj}$, and the rth row of the $R \times 1$ vector d^* is $t^*_r - \bar{t}^*$. In fact (2.45) is related to an alternative, orthogonal expansion of T in which the "remainder" term is uncorrelated with the "linear" piece.

The several different versions of influence produce different estimates of $\text{var}(T)$. In general v_L is an underestimate, whereas use of the jackknife values or the regression estimates of the ls will typically produce an overestimate. We illustrate this in Section 2.7.5.

Example 2.23 (City population data) For the previous example of the ratio estimator, Table 2.5 gives regression estimates of empirical influence values, obtained from $R = 1000$ samples. The exact estimate v_L for $\text{var}(T)$ is 0.036, compared to the value 0.043 obtained from the regression estimates. The bootstrap variance is 0.042. For $n = 49$ the corresponding values are 0.00119, 0.00125 and 0.00125.

Our experience is that R must be in the hundreds to give a good regression approximation to the empirical influence values. ■

2.7.5 Variance estimates

In previous sections we have outlined the merits of studentized quantities

$$Z = \frac{T - \theta}{V^{1/2}} = \frac{t(\hat{F}) - t(F)}{v(\hat{F})^{1/2}}, \tag{2.47}$$

where $V = v(\hat{F})$ is an estimate of $\text{var}(T \mid \hat{F})$. One general way to obtain a value for V is to set

$$v = (M-1)^{-1}\sum_{m=1}^{M}(t^*_m - \bar{t}^*)^2,$$

where $t^*_1,\dots,t^*_M$ are calculated by bootstrap sampling from $\hat{F}$. Typically we would take M in the range 50–200. Note that resampling is needed to produce a standard error for the original value t of T.

Now suppose that we wish to estimate the quantiles of Z, using empirical quantiles of bootstrap simulations

$$z_r^* = \frac{t_r^* - t}{v_r^{*1/2}} = \frac{t^*(\hat{F}_r^*) - t(\hat{F})}{v(\hat{F}_r^*)^{1/2}}, \quad r = 1,\dots,R. \tag{2.48}$$

Since M bootstrap samples from $\hat{F}$ were needed to obtain v, M bootstrap samples from $\hat{F}_r^*$ are needed to produce v_r^*. Thus with $R = 999$ and $M = 50$, we would require $R(M+1) = 50\,949$ samples in all, which seems prohibitively large for many applications. This suggests that we should replace $v^{1/2}$ with a standard error that involves no resampling, as follows.

When a linear approximation (2.44) applies, we have seen that $\text{var}(T^* \mid \hat{F})$ can be estimated by $v_L = n^{-2} \sum l_j^2$, where the $l_j = L_t(y_j; \hat{F})$ are the empirical influence values for t based on the EDF $\hat{F}$ of $y_1,\dots,y_n$. The corresponding variance estimate for $\text{var}(T^* \mid \hat{F}_r^*)$ is $v_{Lr}^* = n^{-2} \sum L_t^2(y_j^*; \hat{F}_r^*)$, based on the empirical influence values for t_r^* at the EDF $\hat{F}_r^*$ of $y_{r1}^*,\dots,y_{rn}^*$. Although this requires no further simulation, the $L_t(y_j^*; \hat{F}_r^*)$ must be calculated for each of the R samples. If an analytical expression is known for the empirical influence values, it will typically be straightforward to calculate the v_{Lr}^*. If not, numerical differentiation can be used, though this is more time-consuming. If neither of these is feasible, we can use the further approximation

$$v_{Lr}^* \doteq \frac{1}{n^2} \sum_{j=1}^n \left\{ L_t(y_{rj}^*; \hat{F}) - n^{-1} \sum_{k=1}^n L_t(y_{rk}^*; \hat{F}) \right\}^2, \tag{2.49}$$

which is exact for a linear statistic. In effect this uses the usual formula, with l_j replaced by $L_t(y_{rj}^*; \hat{F}) - n^{-1} \sum L_t(y_{rk}^*; \hat{F})$ in the rth resample. However, the right-hand side of (2.49) can badly underestimate v_{Lr}^* if the statistic is not close to linear. An improved approximation is outlined in Problem 2.20.

Example 2.24 (City population data) Figure 2.13 compares the variance approximations for $n = 10$. The top left panel shows v^* with $M = 50$ plotted against the values

$$v_L^* = n^{-2} \sum_{j=1}^n (x_j^* - t^* u_j^*)^2 / \bar{u}^{*2}$$

for $R = 200$ bootstrap samples. The top right panel shows the values of the approximate variance on the right of (2.49), also plotted against v_L^*. The lower panels show Q-Q plots of the corresponding z^* values, with $(t^* - t)/v_L^{*1/2}$ on the horizontal axis. Plainly v_L^* underestimates v^*, though not so severely as to have a big effect on the studentized bootstrap statistic. But the right of (2.49) underestimates v_L^* to an extent that greatly changes the distribution of the corresponding studentized bootstrap statistics.

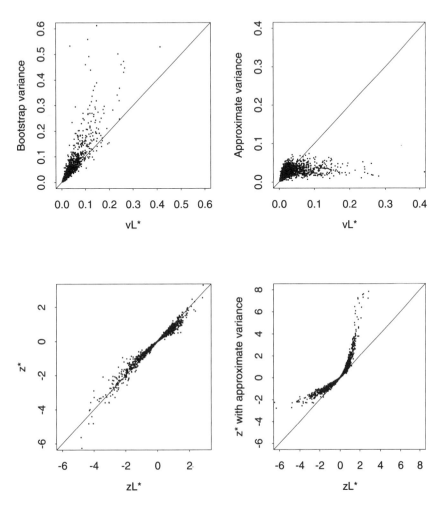

Figure 2.13 Variance approximations for the city population data, $n = 10$. The top panels compare the bootstrap variance v^* calculated with $M = 50$ and the right of (2.49) with v_L^* for $R = 200$ samples. The bottom panels compare the corresponding studentized bootstrap statistics.

The right-hand panels of the corresponding plots for the full data show more nearly linear relationships, so it appears that (2.49) is a better approximation at sample size $n = 49$. In practice the sample size cannot be increased, and it is necessary to seek a transformation of t to attain approximate linearity. The transformation outlined in Example 3.25 greatly increases the accuracy of (2.49), even with $n = 10$.   ∎

2.8 Subsampling Methods

Before and after the development of nonparametric bootstrap methods, other methods based on subsamples were developed to deal with special problems.

We briefly review three such methods here. The first two are in principle superior to resampling for certain applications, although their competitive merits in practice are largely untested. The third method provides an alternative to the nonparametric delta method for variance approximation.

2.8.1 Jackknife methods

In Section 2.7.3 we mentioned briefly the jacknife method in connection with estimating the variance of T, using the values t_{-j} of t obtained when each case· is deleted in turn. Generalized versions of the jackknife have also been proposed for estimating the distribution of $T - \theta$, as alternatives to the bootstrap. For this to work, the jackknife must be generalized to multiple case deletion. For example, suppose that we delete d observations rather than one, there being $N = \binom{n}{d}$ ways of doing this; this is the same thing as taking all subsets of size $n - d$. The full set of group-deletion estimates is $t_1^{\dagger}, \ldots, t_N^{\dagger}$, say. The empirical distribution of $t^{\dagger} - t$ will approximate the distribution of $T - \theta$ only if we renormalize to remove the discrepancy in sample sizes, $n - d$ versus n. So if $T - \theta = O_p(n^{-a})$, we take the empirical distribution of

$$z^{\dagger} = (n - d)^a(t^{\dagger} - t) \tag{2.50}$$

as the delete-d jackknife approximation to the distribution of $Z = n^a(T - \theta)$. In practice we would not use all N subsamples of size $n - d$, but rather R random subsamples, just as with ordinary resampling.

In principle this method will apply much more generally than bootstrap resampling. But to work in practice it is necessary to know a and to choose d so that $n - d \to \infty$ and $d/n \to 1$ as n increases. Therefore the method will work only in rather special circumstances.

Note that if $n - d$ is small relative to n, then the method is not very different from a generalized bootstrap that takes samples of size $n - d$ rather than n.

Example 2.25 (Sample maximum) We referred earlier to the failure of the bootstrap when applied to the largest order statistic $t = y_{(n)}$, which estimates the upper limit of a distribution on $[0, \theta]$. The jackknife method applies here with $a = 1$, as $n(\theta - T)$ is approximately exponential with mean θ for uniformly distributed ys. However, empirical evidence suggests that the jackknife method requires a very large sample size in order to give good results. For example, if we take samples of $n = 100$ uniform variables, for values of d in the range 80–95 the distribution of $(n - d)(t - T^{\dagger})$ is close to exponential, but the mean is wrong by a factor that can vary from 0.6 to 2.   ∎

2.8.2 All-subsamples method

A different type of subsampling consists of taking all $N = 2^n - 1$ non-empty subsets of the data. This can be applied to a limited type of problem, including M-estimation where mean μ is estimated by the solution t to the estimating equation $\sum c(y_j - t) = 0$. If the ordered estimates from subsets are denoted by $t^\dagger_{(1)}, \ldots, t^\dagger_{(N)}$, then remarkably μ is equally likely to be in any of the $N + 1$ intervals

$$(-\infty, t^\dagger_{(1)}), [t^\dagger_{(1)}, t^\dagger_{(2)}), \ldots, [t^\dagger_{(N)}, \infty).$$

Hence confidence intervals for μ can be determined. In practice one would take a random selection of R such subsets, and attach equal probability $(R + 1)^{-1}$ to the $R + 1$ intervals defined by the R $t^\dagger$ values. It is unclear how efficient this method is, and to what extent it can be generalized to other estimation problems.

2.8.3 Half-sampling methods

The jackknife method for estimating $\mathrm{var}(T)$ can be extended to deal with estimates based on many samples, but in one special circumstance there is another, simpler subsampling method. Originally this was proposed for sample-survey data consisting of stratified samples of size 2. To fix ideas, suppose that we have samples of size 2 from each of m strata, and that we estimate the population mean μ by the weighted average $t = \sum_{i=1}^{m} w_i \bar{y}_i$; these weights reflect stratum sizes. The usual estimate for $\mathrm{var}(T)$ is $v = \sum w_i^2 s_i^2$ with s_i^2 the sample variance for the ith stratum. The half-sampling method is designed to reproduce this variance estimate using only subsample values of t, just as the jackknife does. Then the method can be applied to more complex problems.

In the present context there are $N = 2^m$ half-samples formed by taking one element from each stratum sample. If $t^\dagger$ denotes the estimator calculated on such a half-sample, then clearly $t^\dagger - t$ equals $\frac{1}{2} \sum w_i(y_{i1} - y_{i2})c_i^\dagger$, where $c_i^\dagger = \pm 1$ according to which of y_{i1} and y_{i2} is in the half-sample. Direct calculation shows that for a random half-sample $\mathrm{E}(T^\dagger - T)^2 = \frac{1}{2}\mathrm{var}(T)$, so that an unbiased estimate of $\mathrm{var}(T)$ is obtained by doubling the average of $(t^\dagger - t)^2$ over all N half-samples: this average equals the usual estimate given earlier. But it is unnecessary to use all N half-samples. If, say, we use R half-samples, then we require that

$$\frac{1}{R} \sum_{r=1}^{R} (t^\dagger_r - t)^2 = \frac{1}{2} \sum_{i=1}^{m} w_i^2 s_i^2.$$

From the earlier representation for $t^\dagger - t$ we see that this implies that

$$\frac{1}{R}\sum_{r=1}^{R}\left\{\frac{1}{4}\sum_{i=1}^{m}w_i^2(y_{i1}-y_{i2})^2 + \frac{1}{4}\sum_{i=1}^{m}\sum_{j=1}^{m}c_{r,i}^\dagger c_{r,j}^\dagger(y_{i1}-y_{i2})(y_{j1}-y_{j2})\right\}$$

equals

$$\frac{1}{4}\sum_{i=1}^{m}w_i^2(y_{i1}-y_{i2})^2.$$

For this to hold for all data values we must have $\sum_{r=1}^{R}c_{r,i}^\dagger c_{r,j}^\dagger = 0$ for all $i \neq j$. This is a standard problem arising in factorial design, and is solved by what are known as Plackett-Burman designs. If the rth half-sample coefficients $c_{r,i}^\dagger$ form the rth row of the $R \times m$ matrix $C^\dagger$, and if every observation occurs in exactly $\frac{1}{2}R$ half-samples, then $C^{\dagger T}C^\dagger = mI_{m\times m}$. In general the ith column of $C^\dagger$ can be expressed as $(c_{1,i}, \ldots, c_{R-1,i}, -1)$ with the first $R-1$ elements obtained by $i-1$ cyclic shifts of $c_{1,1}, \ldots, c_{R-1,1}$. For example, one solution for $m = 7$ with $R = 8$ is

$$C^\dagger = \begin{pmatrix} +1 & -1 & -1 & +1 & -1 & +1 & +1 \\ +1 & +1 & -1 & -1 & +1 & -1 & +1 \\ +1 & +1 & +1 & -1 & -1 & +1 & -1 \\ -1 & +1 & +1 & +1 & -1 & -1 & -1 \\ +1 & -1 & +1 & +1 & +1 & -1 & -1 \\ -1 & +1 & -1 & +1 & +1 & +1 & -1 \\ -1 & -1 & +1 & -1 & +1 & +1 & +1 \\ -1 & -1 & -1 & -1 & -1 & -1 & -1 \end{pmatrix}.$$

This solution requires that R be the first multiple of 4 greater than or equal to m. The half-sample designs for $m = 4, 5, 6, 7$ are the first m columns of this $C^\dagger$ matrix.

In practice it would be common to double the half-sampling design by adding its complement $-C^\dagger$, which adds further balance.

It is fairly clear that the half-sampling method extends to stratum sample sizes k larger than 2. The basic idea can be seen clearly for linear statistics of the form

$$t = \mu + \sum_{i=1}^{m}k^{-1}\sum_{j=1}^{k}a_i(y_{ij}) = \mu + \sum_{i=1}^{m}k^{-1}\sum_{j=1}^{k}a_{ij},$$

say. Suppose that in the rth subsample we take one observation from each stratum, as specified by the zero–one indicator $c_{r,ij}^\dagger$. Then

$$t_r^\dagger - t = \sum\sum c_{r,ij}^\dagger(a_{ij}-\bar{a}_i),$$

which is a linear regression model without error in which the $a_{ij} - \bar{a}_i$ are coefficients and the $c_{r,ij}^\dagger$ are covariate values to be determined. If the $a_{ij} - \bar{a}_i$

can be calculated, then the usual estimate of var(T) can be calculated. The choice of $c_{r,ij}^{\dagger}$ values corresponds to selection of a fractional factorial design, with only main effects to be calculated, and this is solved by a Plackett-Burman design. Once the subsampling design is obtained, the estimate of var(T) is a formula in the subsample values $t_r^{\dagger}$. The same formula works for any statistic that is approximately linear.

The same principles apply for unequal stratum sizes, although then the solution is more complicated and makes use of orthogonal arrays.

2.9 Bibliographic Notes

There are two key aspects to the methods described in this chapter. The first is that in order for statistical inference to proceed, an unknown distribution F must be replaced by an estimate. In a parametric model, the estimate is a parametric distribution $F_{\hat{\psi}}$, whereas in a nonparametric situation the estimate is the empirical distribution function or some modification of it (Section 3.3). Although the use of the EDF to estimate F may seem novel at first sight, it is a natural development of replacing F by a parametric estimate. We have seen that in essence the EDF will produce results similar to those for the "nearest" parametric model.

The second aspect is the use of simulation to estimate quantities of interest. The widespread availability of fast cheap computers has made this a practical alternative to analytical calculation in many problems, because computer time is increasingly plentiful relative to the number of hours in a researcher's day. Theoretical approximations based on large samples can be time-consuming to obtain for each new problem, and there may be doubt about their reliability in small samples. Contrariwise, simulations are tailored to the problem at hand and a large enough simulation makes the numerical error negligible relative to the statistical error due to the inescapable uncertainty about F.

Monte Carlo methods of inference had already been used for many years when Efron (1979) made the connection to standard methods of parametric inference, drew the attention of statisticians to their potential for nonparametric inference, and originated the term "bootstrap". This work and subsequent developments such as his 1982 monograph made strong connections with the jackknife, which had been introduced by Quenouille (1949) and Tukey (1958), and with other subsampling methods (Hartigan, 1969, 1971, 1975; McCarthy, 1969). Miller (1974) gives a good review of jackknife methods; see also Gray and Schucany (1972).

Young and Daniels (1990) discuss the bias in the nonparametric bootstrap introduced by using the empirical distribution function in place of the true distribution.

Hall (1988a, 1992a) strongly advocates the use of the studentized bootstrap statistic for confidence intervals and significance tests, and makes the connection to Edgeworth expansions for smooth statistics. The empirical choice of scale for resampling calculations is discussed by Chapman and Hinkley (1986) and Tibshirani (1988).

Hall (1986) analyses the effect of discreteness on confidence intervals. Efron (1987) discusses the numbers of simulations needed for bias and quantile estimation, while Diaconis and Holmes (1994) describe how simulation can be avoided completely by complete enumeration of bootstrap samples; see also the bibliographic notes for Chapter 9.

Bickel and Freedman (1981) were among the first to discuss the conditions under which the bootstrap is consistent. Their work was followed by Bretagnolle (1983) and others, and there is a growing theoretical literature on modifications to ensure that the bootstrap is consistent for different classes of awkward statistics. The main modifications are smoothing of the data (Section 3.4), which can improve matters for nonsmooth statistics such as quantiles (De Angelis and Young, 1992), subsampling (Politis and Romano, 1994b), and reweighting (Barbe and Bertail, 1995). Hall (1992a) is a key reference to Edgeworth expansion theory for the bootstrap, while Mammen (1992) describes simulations intended to help show when the bootstrap works, and gives theoretical results for various situations. Shao and Tu (1995) give an extensive theoretical overview of the bootstrap and jackknife.

Athreya (1987) has shown that the bootstrap can fail for long-tailed distributions. Some other examples of failure are discussed by Bickel, Götze and van Zwet (1996).

The use of linear approximations and influence functions in the context of robust statistical inference is discussed by Hampel et al. (1986). Fernholtz (1983) describes the expansion theory that underlies the use of these approximation methods. An alternative and orthogonal expansion, similar to that used in Section 2.7.4, is discussed by Efron and Stein (1981) and Efron (1982). Tail-specific approximations are described by Hesterberg (1995a).

The use of multiple-deletion jackknife methods is discussed by Hinkley (1977), Shao and Wu (1989), Wu (1990), and Politis and Romano (1994b), the last with numerous theoretical examples. The method based on all non-empty subsamples is due to Hartigan (1969), and is nicely put into context in Chapter 9 of Efron (1982). Half-sample methods for survey sampling were developed by McCarthy (1969) and extended by Wu (1991). The relevant factorial designs for half-sampling were developed by Plackett and Burman (1946).

2.10 Problems

1   Let $\hat{F}$ denote the EDF (2.1). Show that $\mathrm{E}\{\hat{F}(y)\} = F(y)$ and that $\mathrm{var}\{\hat{F}(y)\} = F(y)\{1 - F(y)\}/n$. Hence deduce that provided $0 < F(y) < 1$, $\hat{F}(y)$ has a limiting

normal distribution for large n, and that $\Pr(|\hat{F}(y) - F(y)| \leq \epsilon) \to 1$ as $n \to \infty$ for any positive ϵ. (In fact the much stronger property $\sup_{-\infty < y < +\infty} |\hat{F}(y) - F(y)| \to 0$ holds with probability one.)
(Section 2.1)

2   Suppose that $Y_1, \ldots, Y_n$ are independent exponential with mean μ; their average is $\bar{Y} = n^{-1} \sum Y_j$.
(a) Show that $\bar{Y}$ has the gamma density (1.1) with $\kappa = n$, so its mean and variance are μ and μ^2/n.
(b) Show that $\log \bar{Y}$ is approximately normal with mean $\log \mu$ and variance n^{-1}.
(c) Compare the normal approximations for $\bar{Y}$ and for $\log \bar{Y}$ in calculating 95% confidence intervals for μ. Use the exact confidence interval based on (a) as the baseline for the comparison, which can be illustrated with the data of Example 1.1.
(Sections 2.1, 2.5.1)

3   Under nonparametric simulation from a random sample $y_1, \ldots, y_n$ in which $T = n^{-1} \sum (Y_j - \bar{Y})^2$ takes value t, show that

$$\mathrm{E}^*(T^*) = (n-1)t/n, \quad \mathrm{var}^*(T^*) = (n-1)^2 \left[m_4/n + (3-n)t^2/\{n(n-1)\}\right]/n^2,$$

where $m_4 = n^{-1} \sum_j (y_j - \bar{y})^4$.
(Section 2.3; Appendix A)

4   Let t be the median of a random sample of size $n = 2m+1$ with ordered values $y_{(1)} < \cdots < y_{(n)}$; $t = y_{(m+1)}$.
(a) Show that $T^* > y_{(l)}$ if and only if fewer than $m+1$ of the Y_j^* are less than or equal to $y_{(l)}$.
(b) Hence show that

$$\Pr{}^*(T^* > y_{(l)}) = \sum_{j=0}^{m} \binom{n}{j} \left(\frac{l}{n}\right)^j \left(1 - \frac{l}{n}\right)^{n-j}.$$

This specifies the exact resampling density (2.28) of the sample median. (The result can be used to prove that the bootstrap estimate of $\mathrm{var}(T)$ is consistent as $n \to \infty$.)
(c) Use the resampling distribution to show that for $n = 11$

$$\Pr{}^*(T^* \leq y_{(3)}) = \Pr{}^*(T^* \geq y_{(9)}) = 0.051,$$

and apply (2.10) to deduce that the basic bootstrap 90% confidence interval for the population median θ is $(2y_{(6)} - y_{(9)}, 2y_{(6)} - y_{(3)})$.
(d) Examine the coverage of the confidence interval in (c) for samples from normal and Cauchy distributions.
(Sections 2.3, 2.4; Efron, 1979, 1982)

5   Consider nonparametric simulation of $\bar{Y}^*$ based on distinct linearly independent observations $y_1, \ldots, y_n$.
(a) Show that there are $m_n = \binom{2n-1}{n-1}$ ways that $n-1$ red balls can be put in a line with n white balls. Explain the connection to the number of distinct values taken by $\bar{Y}^*$.
(b) Suppose that the value $\bar{y}^*$ taken by $\bar{Y}^*$ is $n^{-1} \sum f_j^* y_j$, where f_j^* can be one of $0, \ldots, n$, and $\sum_j f_j^* = n$. Find $\Pr(\bar{Y}^* = \bar{y})$, and deduce that the most likely value of $\bar{Y}^*$ is $\bar{y}$, with probability $p_n = n!/n^n$.
(c) Use Stirling's approximation, i.e. $n! \sim (2\pi)^{1/2} e^{-n} n^{n+1/2}$ as $n \to \infty$, to find approximate formulae for m_n and p_n.
(d) For the correlation coefficient T calculated from distinct pairs $(u_1, x_1), \ldots, (u_n, x_n)$,

show that T^* is indeterminate with probability $n^{-(n-1)}$. What is the probability that $|T^*| = 1$? Discuss the implications of this when $n < 10$.
(Section 2.3; Hall, 1992a, Appendix I)

6   Suppose that $Y_1, \ldots, Y_n$ are independently distributed with a two-parameter density $f_{\theta,\lambda}(y)$. What simulation experiment would you perform to check whether or not $Q = q(Y_1, \ldots, Y_n; \theta)$ is a pivot?
If f is the gamma density (1.1), let $\hat{\mu}$ be the MLE of μ, let

$$\ell_p(\mu) = \max_{\kappa} \sum_{j=1}^{n} \log f_{\mu,\kappa}(y_j)$$

be the profile log likelihood for μ and let $Q = 2\{\ell_p(\hat{\mu}) - \ell_p(\mu)\}$. In theory Q should be approximately a χ_1^2 variable for large n. Use simulation to examine whether or not Q is approximately pivotal for $n = 10$ when κ is in the range $(0.5, 2)$.
(Section 2.5.1)

7   The bootstrap normal approximation for $T - \theta$ is $N(b_R, v_R)$, so that the p quantile a_p for $T - \theta$ can be approximated by $\hat{a}_p = b_R + z_p v_R^{1/2}$. Show that the simulation variance of this estimate is

$$\text{var}(\hat{a}_p) \doteq \frac{v_\infty}{R} \left\{ 1 + z_p \frac{\hat{\kappa}_3}{v_\infty^{3/2}} + \tfrac{1}{4} z_p^2 \left(2 + \frac{\hat{\kappa}_4}{v_\infty^2} \right) \right\},$$

where $\hat{\kappa}_3$ and $\hat{\kappa}_4$ are the third and fourth cumulants of T^* under bootstrap resampling. If T is asymptotically normal, $\hat{\kappa}_3/v_\infty^{3/2} = O(n^{-1/2})$ and $\hat{\kappa}_4/v_\infty^2 = O(n^{-1})$. Compare this variance to that of the bootstrap quantile estimate $T^*_{((R+1)(1-\alpha))} - t$ in the special case $T = \bar{Y}$.
(Sections 2.2.1, 2.5.2; Appendix A)

8   Suppose that estimator T has expectation equal to $\theta(1 + \gamma)$, so that the bias is $\theta\gamma$. The bias factor γ can be estimated by $C = E^*(T^*)/T - 1$. Show that in the case of the variance estimate $T = n^{-1} \sum (Y_j - \bar{Y})^2$, C is exactly equal to γ. If C were approximated from R resamples, what would be the simulation variance of the approximation?
(Section 2.5)

9   Suppose that the random variables $U = (U_1, \ldots, U_m)$ have means $\zeta_1, \ldots, \zeta_m$ and covariances $\text{cov}(U_k, U_l) = n^{-1}\omega_{kl}(\zeta)$, and that $T_1 = g_1(U), \ldots, T_q = g_q(U)$. Show that

$$E(T_i) \doteq g_i(\zeta) + \tfrac{1}{2} n^{-1} \sum_{k,l=1}^{m} \omega_{kl}(\zeta) \frac{\partial^2 g_i(\zeta)}{\partial \zeta_k \partial \zeta_l},$$

$$\text{cov}(T_i, T_j) \doteq n^{-1} \sum_{k,l=1}^{m} \omega_{kl}(\zeta) \frac{\partial g_i(\zeta)}{\partial \zeta_k} \frac{\partial g_j(\zeta)}{\partial \zeta_l}.$$

How are these estimated in practice?
Show that

$$n^{-2} \sum_{j=1}^{n} \frac{(x_j - t u_j)^2}{\bar{u}^2}$$

is a variance estimate for $t = \bar{x}/\bar{u}$, based on independent pairs $(u_1, x_1), \ldots, (u_n, x_n)$.
(Section 2.7.1)

10 (a) Show that the influence function for a linear statistic $t(F) = \int a(x)\,dF(x)$ is $a(y) - t(F)$. Hence obtain the influence functions for a sample moment $\mu_r = \int x^r\,dF(x)$, for the variance $\mu_2(F) - \{\mu_1(F)\}^2$, and for the correlation coefficient (Example 2.18).
(b) Show that the influence function for $\{t(F) - \theta\}/v(F)^{1/2}$ evaluated at $\theta = t(F)$ is $v(F)^{-1/2}L_t(y;F)$. Hence obtain the empirical influence values l_j for the studentized quantity $\{t(\hat{F}) - t(F)\}/v_L(\hat{F})^{1/2}$, and show that they have the properties $\sum l_j = 0$ and $n^{-2}\sum l_j^2 = 1$.
(Section 2.7.2; Hinkley and Wei, 1984)

11 The pairs $(U_1, X_1),\ldots,(U_n, X_n)$ are independent bivariate normal with correlation θ. Use the influence function of Example 2.18 to show that the sample correlation T has approximate variance $n^{-1}(1 - \theta^2)^2$. Then apply the delta method to show that $\frac{1}{2}\log\left(\frac{1+T}{1-T}\right)$, called Fisher's z-transform, has approximate variance n^{-1}.
(Section 2.7.1; Appendix A)

12 Suppose that a parameter $\theta = t(F)$ is determined implicitly through the estimating equation

$$\int u(y;\theta)\,dF(y) = 0.$$

(a) Write the estimating equation as

$$\int u\{y;t(F)\}\,dF(y) = 0,$$

replace F by $(1-\varepsilon)F + \varepsilon H_y$, and differentiate with respect to ε to show that the influence function for $t(\cdot)$ is

$\dot{u}(x;\theta) = \partial u(x;\theta)/\partial\theta$

$$L_t(y;F) = \frac{u(y;\theta)}{-\int \dot{u}(x;\theta)\,dF(x)}.$$

Hence show that with $\hat{\theta} = t(\hat{F})$ the jth empirical influence value is

$$l_j = \frac{u(y_j;\hat{\theta})}{-n^{-1}\sum_{k=1}^n \dot{u}(y_k;\hat{\theta})}.$$

(b) Let $\hat{\psi}$ be the maximum likelihood estimator of the (possibly vector) parameter of a regular parametric model $f_\psi(y)$ based on a random sample $y_1,\ldots,y_n$. Show that the jth empirical influence value for $\hat{\psi}$ at y_j may be written as $nI^{-1}S_j$, where

$$I = -\sum_{j=1}^n \frac{\partial^2 \log f_{\hat{\psi}}(y_j)}{\partial\psi\partial\psi^T}, \quad S_j = \frac{\partial \log f_{\hat{\psi}}(y_j)}{\partial\psi}.$$

Hence show that the nonparametric delta method variance estimate for $\hat{\psi}$ is the so-called *sandwich estimator*

$$I^{-1}\left(\sum_{j=1}^n S_j S_j^T\right) I^{-1}.$$

Compare this to the usual parametric approximation when $y_1,\ldots,y_n$ is a random sample from the exponential distribution with mean ψ.
(Section 2.7.2; Royall, 1986)

13   The α trimmed average is defined by

$$t(F) = \frac{1}{1 - 2\alpha} \int_\alpha^{1-\alpha} F^{-1}(u)\, du$$

computed at the EDF $\hat{F}$. Express $t(\hat{F})$ in terms of order statistics, assuming that $n\alpha$ is an integer. How would you extend this to deal with non-integer values of $n\alpha$? Suppose that F is a distribution symmetric about its mean, μ. By rewriting $t(F)$ as

$$\frac{1}{1 - 2\alpha} \int_{q_\alpha(F)}^{q_{1-\alpha}(F)} u\, dF(u),$$

where $q_\alpha(F)$ is the α quantile of F, use the result of Example 2.19 to show that the influence function of $t(F)$ is

$$L_t(y; F) = \begin{cases} \{q_{1-\alpha}(F) - \mu\}(1 - 2\alpha)^{-1}, & y < q_\alpha(F), \\ (y - \mu)(1 - 2\alpha)^{-1}, & q_\alpha(F) \leq y < q_{1-\alpha}(F), \\ \{q_\alpha(F) - \mu\}(1 - 2\alpha)^{-1}, & q_{1-\alpha}(F) \leq y. \end{cases}$$

Hence show that the variance of $t(\hat{F})$ is approximately

$$\frac{1}{n(1 - 2\alpha)^2} \left[\int_{q_\alpha(F)}^{q_{1-\alpha}(F)} (y - \mu)^2\, dF(y) + \alpha \{q_\alpha(F) - \mu\}^2 + \alpha \{q_{1-\alpha}(F) - \mu\}^2 \right].$$

Evaluate this at $F = \hat{F}$.
(Section 2.7.2)

14   Let Y have a p-dimensional multivariate distribution with mean vector μ and covariance matrix Ω. Suppose that Ω has eigenvalues $\lambda_1 \geq \cdots \geq \lambda_p$ and corresponding orthogonal eigenvectors e_j, where $e_j^T e_j = 1$. Let $F_\varepsilon = (1 - \varepsilon)F + \varepsilon H_y$. Show that the influence function for Ω is

$$L_\Omega(y; F) = (y - \mu)(y - \mu)^T - \Omega,$$

and by considering the identities

$$\Omega(F_\varepsilon)e_j(F_\varepsilon) = \lambda_j(F_\varepsilon)e_j(F_\varepsilon), \qquad e_j(F_\varepsilon)^T e_j(F_\varepsilon) = 1,$$

or otherwise, show that the influence function for λ_j is $\{e_j^T(y - \mu)\}^2 - \lambda_j$.
(Section 2.7.2)

15   Consider the biased sample variance $t = n^{-1} \sum (y_j - \bar{y})^2$.
(a) Show that the empirical influence values and second derivatives are

$$l_j = (y_j - \bar{y})^2 - t, \qquad q_{jk} = -2(y_j - \bar{y})(y_k - \bar{y}).$$

(b) Show that the exact case-deletion values of t are

$$t_{-j} = t + \frac{1}{n-1} \left\{ t - \frac{n}{n-1}(y_j - \bar{y})^2 \right\}.$$

Compare these with the result of the general approximation

$$t - t_{-j} \doteq (n-1)^{-1} l_j - \tfrac{1}{2}(n-1)^{-2} q_{jj},$$

which is obtained from (2.41) by substituting $\hat{F}$ for F and $\hat{F}_{-j}$ for $\hat{F}$.
(c) Calculate jackknife estimates of the bias and variance of T. Are these sensible estimates?
(Section 2.7.3; Appendix A)

16 The empirical influence values l_j can also be defined in terms of distributions supported on the data values. Suppose that the support of F is restricted to $y_1, \ldots, y_n$, with probabilities $p = (p_1, \ldots, p_n)$ on those values. For such distributions $t(F)$ can be re-expressed as $t(p)$.
(a) Show that

$$l_j = \left. \frac{d}{d\varepsilon} t\{(1-\varepsilon)\hat{p} + \varepsilon 1_j\} \right|_{\varepsilon=0},$$

where $\hat{p} = (\frac{1}{n}, \ldots, \frac{1}{n})$ and 1_j is the vector with 1 in the jth position and 0 elsewhere. Hence or otherwise show that

$$l_j = \dot{t}_j(\hat{p}) - n^{-1} \sum_{k=1}^{n} \dot{t}_k(\hat{p}),$$

where $\dot{t}_j(p) = \partial t(p)/\partial p_j$.
(b) Apply this result to derive the empirical influence values $l_j = (x_j - tu_j)/\bar{u}$ for the estimate $t = \sum p_j x_j / \sum p_j u_j$ of the ratio of two means.
(c) The empirical second derivatives q_{ij} can be defined similarly. Show that

$$q_{ij} = \left. \frac{\partial^2}{\partial \varepsilon_1 \partial \varepsilon_2} t\{(1-\varepsilon_1-\varepsilon_2)\hat{p} + \varepsilon_1 1_i + \varepsilon_2 1_j\} \right|_{\varepsilon_1=\varepsilon_2=0}.$$

Hence deduce that

$$q_{ij} = \ddot{t}_{ij}(\hat{p}) - n^{-1} \sum_{k=1}^{n} \ddot{t}_{ik}(\hat{p}) - n^{-1} \sum_{k=1}^{n} \ddot{t}_{jk}(\hat{p}) + n^{-2} \sum_{k,l=1}^{n} \ddot{t}_{kl}(\hat{p}).$$

(Section 2.7.2)

17 Suppose that $t = \frac{1}{2}(y_{(m)} + y_{(m+1)})$ is the median of a sample of even size $n = 2m$ from a distribution with continuous CDF F and PDF f whose median is μ. Show that the case-deletion values t_{-j} are either $y_{(m)}$ or $y_{(m+1)}$, and that the jackknife variance estimate is

$$v_{jack} = \frac{n-1}{4} \left(y_{(m+1)} - y_{(m)} \right)^2.$$

By writing $Y_{(j)} = F^{-1}\{1 - \exp(-E_{(j)})\}$, where $E_{(j)}$ is the jth order statistic of a random sample $E_1, \ldots, E_n$ from the standard exponential distribution, and recalling properties of exponential order statistics, show that

$$n V_{jack} \overset{.}{\sim} \frac{1}{4f^2(\mu)} \left(\tfrac{1}{2}\chi_2^2 \right)^2$$

as $n \to \infty$. This confirms that the jackknife variance estimate is not consistent.
(Section 2.7.3)

18 A generalized form of jackknife can be defined by estimating the influence function at y_j by

$$\frac{t\{(1-\varepsilon)\hat{F} + \varepsilon H_{y_j}\} - t(\hat{F})}{\varepsilon}$$

for some value ε. Discuss the effects of (a) $\varepsilon \to 0$, (b) $\varepsilon = -(n-1)^{-1}$, (c) $\varepsilon = (n+1)^{-1}$, which respectively give the *infinitesimal jackknife*, the *ordinary jackknife*, and the *positive jackknife*.

Show that in (b) and (c) the squared distance $(d\hat{F} - d\hat{F}_\varepsilon)^T(d\hat{F} - d\hat{F}_\varepsilon)$ from $\hat{F}$ to $\hat{F}_\varepsilon = (1 - \varepsilon)\hat{F} + \varepsilon H_{y_j}$ is of order $O(n^{-2})$, but that if $\hat{F}^*$ is generated by bootstrap sampling, $E^*\left\{(d\hat{F}^* - d\hat{F})^T(d\hat{F}^* - d\hat{F})\right\} = O(n^{-1})$. Hence discuss the results you would expect from the *butcher knife*, which uses $\varepsilon = n^{-1/2}$. How would you calculate it?
(Section 2.7.3; Efron, 1982; Hesterberg, 1995a)

19 The cumulant generating function of a multinomial random variable $(f_1^*, \ldots, f_n^*)$ with denominator n and probability vector $(\pi_1, \ldots, \pi_n)$ is

$$K(\xi) = n \log\left\{\sum_{j=1}^{n} \pi_j \exp(\xi_j)\right\},$$

where $\xi = (\xi_1, \ldots, \xi_n)$.
(a) Show that with $\pi_j \equiv n^{-1}$, the first four cumulants of the f_j^* are

$$
\begin{aligned}
E^*(f_i^*) &= 1, \\
\text{cov}^*(f_i^*, f_j^*) &= \delta_{ij} - n^{-1}, \\
\text{cum}^*(f_i^*, f_j^*, f_k^*) &= n^{-2}\{n^2\delta_{ijk} - n\delta_{ik}[3] + 2\}, \\
\text{cum}^*(f_i^*, f_j^*, f_k^*, f_l^*) &= n^{-3}\{n^3\delta_{ijkl} - n^2(\delta_{ik}\delta_{jl}[3] + \delta_{jkl}[4]) + 2n\delta_{il}[6] - 6\},
\end{aligned}
$$

where $\delta_{ij} = 1$ when $i = j$ and zero otherwise, and so on, and $\delta_{ik}[3] = \delta_{ik} + \delta_{ij} + \delta_{jk}$, and so forth.
(b) Now consider $t_Q^* = t + n^{-1}\sum f_j^* l_j + \frac{1}{2}n^{-2}\sum f_j^* f_k^* q_{jk}$. Show that $E^*(t_Q^*) = t + \frac{1}{2}n^{-2}\sum q_{jj}$ and that t_Q^* has variance

$$\frac{1}{n^2}\sum l_j^2 + \frac{1}{n^3}\sum l_j q_{jj} + \frac{1}{4}\frac{1}{n^4}\left\{\sum q_{jj}^2 - \frac{1}{n}\left(\sum q_{jj}\right)^2 + 2\frac{n-1}{n}\sum\sum q_{ij}^2\right\}. \quad (2.51)$$

(Section 2.7.2; Appendix A; Davison, Hinkley and Schechtman, 1986; McCullagh, 1987)

20 Show that the difference between the second derivative $Q_t(x, y)$ and the first derivative of $L_t(x)$ is equal to $L_t(y)$. Hence show that the empirical influence value can be written as

$$l_j \doteq L_t(y_j) + n^{-1}\sum_{k=1}^{n}\{Q_t(y_j, y_k) - L_t(y_k)\}.$$

Use the resampling version of this result to discuss the accuracy of approximation (2.49) for v_L^*.
(Sections 2.7.2, 2.7.5)

2.11 Practicals

1 Consider parametric simulation to estimate the distribution of the ratio when a bivariate lognormal distribution is fitted to the data in Table 2.1:

```
m1 <- mean(log(city$u)); m2 <- mean(log(city$x))
s1 <- sqrt(var(log(city$u))); s2 <- sqrt(var(log(city$x)))
rho <- cor(log(city))[1,2]
city.mle <- c(m1, m2, s1, s2, rho)
```

```
city.sim <- function(city, mle)
{  n <- nrow(city)
   z1 <- rnorm(n); z2 <- rnorm(n)
   z2 <- mle[5]*z1+sqrt(1-mle[5]^2)*z2
   data.frame(u=exp(mle[1]+mle[3]*z1), x=exp(mle[2]+mle[4]*z2)) }
city.fun <- function(data, i=1:nrow(data))
{  d <- data[i,]
   tstar <- sum(d$x)/sum(d$u)
   ubar <- mean(d$u)
   c(tstar,  sum((d$x-tstar*d$u)^2/(nrow(d)*ubar)^2))   }
city.para <- boot(city,city.fun,R=999,
                  sim="parametric",ran.gen=city.sim,mle=city.mle)
```

Are histograms of t^* and z^* similar to those for nonparametric simulation, shown in Figure 2.5?

```
tstar <- city.para$t[,1]
zstar <- (tstar-city.para$t0[1])/sqrt(city.para$t[,2])
split.screen(c(1,2))
screen(1); hist(tstar)
screen(2); hist(zstar)
screen(1); qqnorm(tstar,pch=".")
screen(2); qqnorm(zstar,pch="."); abline(0,1,lty=2)
```

Use (2.10) and (2.12) to give 95% confidence intervals for the true ratio under this model:

```
city.para$t0[1] - sort(tstar-city.para$t0[1])[c(975,25)]
city.para$t0[1] - sqrt(city.para$t0[2])*sort(zstar)[c(975,25)]
```

Compare these intervals with those given in Example 2.12.
Repeat this with $R = 199$ and $R = 399$.
(Sections 2.2, 2.3, 2.4)

2   co.transfer contains data on the carbon monoxide transfer factor for seven smokers with chickenpox, measured on admission to hospital and after a stay of one week. The aim is to estimate the average change in the factor.
To display the data:

```
attach(co.transfer)
plot(0.5*(entry+week),week-entry)
t.test(week-entry)
```

Are the differences normal? Is the Student-t confidence interval reliable?
For a bootstrap approach:

```
co.fun <- function(data, i)
{  d <- data[i,]
   y <- d$week-d$entry
   c(mean(y), var(y)/nrow(d)) }
co.boot <- boot(co.transfer, co.fun, R=999)
```

Compare the variance of the bootstrap estimate t^* with the estimated variance of t, in co.boot$t0[2]. Compare normal-based and studentized bootstrap 95% confidence intervals.
To display the bootstrap output:

```
split.screen(c(1,2))
screen(1); split.screen(c(2,1))
screen(3); qqnorm(co.boot$t[,1],ylab="t*",pch=".")
abline(co.boot$t0[1],sqrt(co.boot$t0[2]),lty=2)
screen(2)
plot(co.boot$t[,1],sqrt(co.boot$t[,2]),xlab="t*",ylab="SE*",pch=".")
screen(4); z <- (co.boot$t[,1]-co.boot$t0[1])/sqrt(co.boot$t[,2])
qqnorm(z); abline(0,1,lty=2)
```

What is going on here? Is the normal interval useful? What difference does dropping the simulation outliers make to the studentized bootstrap confidence interval?
(Sections 2.3, 2.4; Hand *et al.*, 1994, p. 228)

3   cd4 contains the CD4 counts in hundreds for 20 HIV-positive patients at baseline and after one year of treatment with an experimental anti-viral drug. We attempt to set a confidence interval for the correlation between the baseline and later counts, using the nonparametric bootstrap.

```
corr.fun <- function(d, w = rep(1, nrow(d))/nrow(d))
{ w <- w/sum(w)
  n <- nrow(d)
  m1 <- sum(d[, 1] * w)
  m2 <- sum(d[, 2] * w)
  v1 <- sum(d[, 1]^2 * w) - m1^2
  v2 <- sum(d[, 2]^2 * w) - m2^2
  rho <- (sum(d[, 1] * d[, 2] * w) - m1 * m2)/sqrt(v1 * v2)
  i <- rep(1:n,round(n*w))
  us <- (d[i, 1] - m1)/sqrt(v1)
  xs <- (d[i, 2] - m2)/sqrt(v2)
  L <- us * xs - 0.5 * rho * (us^2 + xs^2)
  c(rho, sum(L^2)/n^2)  }
cd4.boot <- boot(cd4, corr.fun, R=999, stype="w")
```

Is the variance independent of t? Is z^* pivotal? Should we transform the correlation coefficient?

```
t0 <- cd4.boot$t0[1]
tstar <- cd4.boot$t[,1]
vL <- cd4.boot$t[,2]
zstar <- (tstar-t0)/sqrt(vL)
fisher <- function( r ) 0.5*log( (1+r)/(1-r) )
split.screen(c(1,2))
screen(1); plot(tstar,vL)
screen(2); plot(fisher(tstar),vL/(1-tstar^2)^2)
```

For a studentized bootstrap confidence interval on transformed scale:

```
zstar <- (fisher(tstar)-fisher(t0))/sqrt(vL/(1-tstar^2)^2)
v0 <- cd4.boot$t0[2]/(1-t0^2)^2
fisher(t0) - sqrt(v0)*sort(zstar)[c(975,25)]
```

What are these on the correlation scale? How do they compare to intervals obtained without the transformation?
If there are simulation outliers, delete them and recalculate the intervals.
(Sections 2.3, 2.4, 2.5; DiCiccio and Efron, 1996)

4   How many simulations are required for quantile estimation? To get some idea, we make four replicate plots with 39, 99, 399 and 999 simulations.

```
split.screen(c(4,4))
quantiles <- matrix(NA,16,4)
n <- c(39,99,399,999)
p <- c(0.025,0.05,0.95,0.975)
for (i in 1:4)
{ y <- rnorm(999)
  for (j in 1:4) {
    quantiles[(j-1)*4+i,] <- quantile(y[1:n[j]], probs=p)
    screen((i-1)*4+j)
    qqnorm(y[1:n[j]],ylab="y",main=paste("R = ",n[j]))
    abline(h=quantile(y[1:n[j]],p),lty=2)  }  }
```

Repeat the loop a few times. How large a simulation is required to get reasonable estimates of the 0.05 and 0.95 quantiles? Of the 0.025 and 0.975 quantiles? (Section 2.5.2)

5   Following on from Practical 2.3, we compare variance approximations for the correlation in cd4:

```
L.inf <- empinf(data=cd4,statistic=corr.fun)
L.jack <- empinf(data=cd4,statistic=corr.fun,type="jack")
L.reg <- empinf(boot.out=cd4.boot,type="reg")
split.screen(c(1,2))
screen(1); plot(L.inf,L.jack); screen(2); plot(L.inf,L.reg)
v.inf <- sum(L.inf^2)/nrow(cd4)^2
v.jack <- var(L.jack)/nrow(cd4)
v.reg <- sum(L.reg^2)/nrow(cd4)^2
v.boot <- var(cd4.boot$t[,1])
c(v.inf,v.reg,v.jack,v.boot)
```

Discuss the different variance approximations in relation to the values of the influence values. Compare with results for the transformed correlation coefficient. To see the accuracy of the linear approximation:

```
close.screen(all=T);plot(tstar,linear.approx(cd4.boot,L.reg))
```

Find the correlation between t^* and its linear approximation. Make the corresponding plots for the other empirical influence values. Are the plots better on the transformed scale?
(Section 2.7)

3

Further Ideas

3.1 Introduction

In the previous chapter we laid out the basic elements of resampling or bootstrap methods, in the context of the analysis of a single homogeneous sample of data. This chapter deals with how those ideas are extended to some more complex situations, and then turns to uses for variations and elaborations of simple bootstrap schemes.

In Section 3.2 we describe how to construct resampling algorithms for several independent samples, and then in Section 3.3 we discuss briefly the use of partial modelling, either qualitative or semiparametric, a topic explored more fully in the later chapters on regression models (Chapters 6 and 7). Section 3.4 examines when it is worthwhile to modify the statistic by using a smoothed empirical distribution function. In Sections 3.5 and 3.6 we turn to situations where data are censored or missing and therefore are incomplete. One relatively simple situation where the standard bootstrap must be modified to succeed is finite population sampling, which we consider in Section 3.7. In Section 3.8 we deal with simple situations of hierarchical variation. Section 3.9 is an account of nested bootstrapping, where we outline how to overcome some of the shortcomings of a single bootstrap calculation by a further level of simulation. Section 3.10 describes bootstrap diagnostics, which are concerned with the assessment of sensitivity of resampling analysis to individual observations, as well as the use of bootstrap output to suggest modifications to the calculations. Finally, Section 3.11 describes the use of nested bootstrapping in selecting an estimator from the data.

3.2 Several Samples

Suppose that we are interested in a parameter that depends on the populations $F_1,\ldots,F_k$, and that the data consist of independent random samples from these populations. The ith sample is $y_{i1},\ldots,y_{in_i}$ and arises from population F_i, for $i = 1,\ldots,k$. If there is no further information about the populations, the nonparametric estimate of F_i is the EDF of the ith sample,

Recall that the Heaviside function $H(u)$ jumps from 0 to 1 at $u = 0$.

$$\hat{F}_i(y) = \frac{1}{n_i} \sum_{j=1}^{n_i} H(y - y_{ij}).$$

Since each of the k populations is separate, nonparametric simulation from their respective EDFs $\hat{F}_1,\ldots,\hat{F}_k$ leads to datasets

$$y_{11}^*,\ldots,y_{1n_1}^*, \quad y_{21}^*,\ldots,y_{2n_2}^*, \quad \cdots \quad y_{k1}^*,\ldots,y_{kn_k}^*,$$

where $y_{i1}^*,\ldots,y_{in_i}^*$ is generated by sampling n_i times with equal probabilities, n_i^{-1}, from the ith original sample, independently of all other simulated samples. This amounts to stratified sampling in which each of the original samples corresponds to a stratum, and n_i observations are taken with equal probability from the ith stratum. With this extension of the resampling algorithm, we proceed as outlined in Chapter 2. For example, if $v = v(\hat{F}_1,\ldots,\hat{F}_k)$ is an estimated variance for t, confidence intervals for θ could be based on simulated values of $z^* = (t^* - t)/v^{*1/2}$ just as described in Section 2.4, where now t^* and v^* are formed from samples generated by the simulation algorithm described above.

Example 3.1 (Difference of population means) Suppose we are interested in the difference of two population means, $\theta = t(F_1, F_2) = \int y\, dF_1(y) - \int y\, dF_2(y)$. The corresponding estimate of $t(F_1, F_2)$ based on independent samples from the two distributions is the difference of the two sample averages,

$$t(\hat{F}_1, \hat{F}_2) = \int y\, d\hat{F}_1(y) - \int y\, d\hat{F}_2(y) = \bar{y}_1 - \bar{y}_2,$$

for which the usual unbiased estimate of variance is

$$v = \frac{1}{n_1(n_1 - 1)} \sum_{j=1}^{n_1} (y_{1j} - \bar{y}_1)^2 + \frac{1}{n_2(n_2 - 1)} \sum_{j=1}^{n_2} (y_{2j} - \bar{y}_2)^2.$$

This differs slightly from the delta method variance approximation, which we describe in Section 3.2.1.

A simulated value of T would be $t^* = \bar{y}_1^* - \bar{y}_2^*$, where $\bar{y}_1^*$ is the average of n_1 observations generated with equal probability from the first sample, $y_{11},\ldots,y_{1n_1}$, and $\bar{y}_2^*$ is the average of n_2 observations generated with equal

			Series				
1	2	3	4	5	6	7	8
76	87	105	95	76	78	82	84
82	95	83	90	76	78	79	86
83	98	76	76	78	78	81	85
54	100	75	76	79	86	79	82
35	109	51	87	72	87	77	77
46	109	76	79	68	81	79	76
87	100	93	77	75	73	79	77
68	81	75	71	78	67	78	80
	75	62			75	79	83
	68				82	82	81
	67				83	76	78
						73	78
						64	78

Table 3.1 Eight series of measurements of the acceleration due to gravity, g, given as deviations from $980\,000 \times 10^{-3}$ cm s^{-2}, in units of cm s$^{-2} \times 10^{-3}$. (Cressie, 1982)

probability from the second sample, $y_{21}, \ldots, y_{2n_2}$. The corresponding unbiased estimate of variance for t^* based on these samples would be

$$ v^* = \frac{1}{n_1(n_1 - 1)} \sum_{j=1}^{n_1} (y_{1j}^* - \bar{y}_1^*)^2 + \frac{1}{n_2(n_2 - 1)} \sum_{j=1}^{n_2} (y_{2j}^* - \bar{y}_2^*)^2. $$

∎

Example 3.2 (Gravity data)　　Between May 1934 and July 1935, a series of experiments to determine the acceleration due to gravity, g, was performed at the National Bureau of Standards in Washington DC. The experiments, made with a reversible pendulum, led to eight successive series of measurements. The data are given in Table 3.1. Figure 3.1 suggests that the variance decreases from one series to the next, that there is a possible change in location, and that mild outliers may be present.

　　The measurements for the later series seem more reliable, and although we would wish to estimate g from all the data, it seems inappropriate to pool the series. We suppose that each of the series is taken from a separate population, $F_1, \ldots, F_8$, but that each population has mean g; for a check on this see Example 4.14. Then the appropriate form of estimator is a weighted combination

$$ T = \frac{\sum_{i=1}^{8} \mu(\hat{F}_i)/\sigma^2(\hat{F}_i)}{\sum_{i=1}^{8} 1/\sigma^2(\hat{F}_i)}, $$

where $\hat{F}_i$ is the EDF of the ith series, $\mu(\hat{F}_i)$ is an estimate of g from $\hat{F}_i$, and

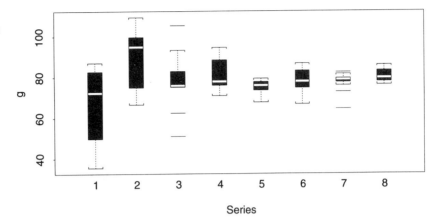

Figure 3.1 Gravity series box plots, showing a reduction in variance, a shift in location, and possible outliers.

$\sigma^2(\hat{F}_i)$ is an estimated variance for $\mu(\hat{F}_i)$. The estimated variance of T is

$$V = \left\{\sum_{i=1}^{8} 1/\sigma^2(\hat{F}_i)\right\}^{-1}.$$

If the data were thought to be normally distributed with mean g but different variances, we would take

$$\mu(\hat{F}_i) = \bar{y}_i, \qquad \sigma^2(\hat{F}_i) = \{n_i(n_i - 1)\}^{-1}\sum_{j}(y_{ij} - \bar{y}_i)^2$$

to be the average of the ith series and its estimated variance. The resulting estimator T is then an empirical version of the optimal weighted average. For our data $t = 78.54$ with standard error $v^{1/2} = 0.59$.

Figure 3.2 shows summary plots for $R = 999$ nonparametric simulations from this model. The top panels show normal plots for the replicates t_r^* and for the corresponding studentized bootstrap statistics $z_r^* = (t_r^* - t)/v_r^{*1/2}$. Both are more dispersed than normal. There is one large negative value of z^*, and the lower panels show why: on the left we see that the v_r^* for the smallest value of t_r^* is very small, which inflates the corresponding z^*. We would certainly omit this value on the grounds that it is a simulation outlier.

The average and variance of the t_r^* are 78.51 and 0.371, so the bias estimate for t is $78.51 - 78.54 \doteq -0.03$, and a 95% confidence interval for g based on a normal approximation is $(77.37, 79.76)$. The $0.025 \times (R + 1)$ and $0.975 \times (R + 1)$ order statistics of the z_r^* are -3.03 and 2.50, so the 95% studentized bootstrap confidence interval for g is $(77.07, 80.32)$, slightly wider than that based on the normal approximation, as the top right panel of Figure 3.2 would suggest.

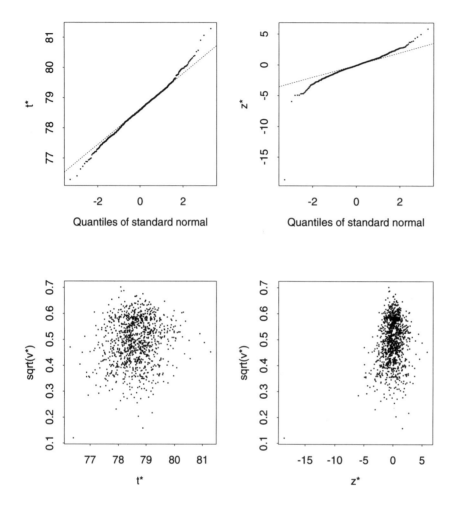

Figure 3.2 Summary plots for 999 nonparametric simulations of the weighted average t for the gravity data and its estimated variance v. The top panels show normal quantile plots of t^* and the studentized bootstrap statistic $z^* = (t^* - t)/v^{*1/2}$. The line on the top left has intercept t and slope $v^{1/2}$, and on the top right the line has intercept zero and unit slope. The bottom panels show that the smallest t^* also has the smallest v^*, leading to an outlying value of z^*.

Apart from the resampling algorithm, this mimics exactly the studentized bootstrap procedure described in Section 2.4.   ∎

Other, constrained resampling plans may be suggested by stronger assumptions about the populations, as discussed in Section 3.3. The advantage of the resampling plan described here is that it is robust.

3.2.1 Influence functions and variance approximations

The discussion in Section 2.7.2 generalizes quite easily to the case of multiple independent samples, with separate influence functions corresponding to each population represented. When T has the representation $t(\hat{F}_1, \ldots, \hat{F}_k)$, the analogue of the linear approximation (2.35) is

$$t(\hat{F}_1, \ldots, \hat{F}_k) \doteq t(F_1, \ldots, F_k) + \sum_{i=1}^{k} \frac{1}{n_i} \sum_{j=1}^{n_i} L_{t,i}(y_{ij}; F), \qquad (3.1)$$

where the influence functions $L_{t,i}$ are defined by

$$L_{t,i}(y; F) = \left. \frac{\partial t\left(F_1, \ldots, (1-\varepsilon)F_i + \varepsilon H_y, \ldots, F_k\right)}{\partial \varepsilon} \right|_{\varepsilon=0}, \qquad (3.2)$$

and for brevity we write $F = (F_1, \ldots, F_k)$. As in the single sample case, the influence functions have mean zero, $\mathrm{E}\{L_{t,i}(y; F)\} = 0$ for each i. Then the immediate consequence of (3.1) is the nonparametric delta method approximation

$$T - \theta \;\; \dot{\sim} \;\; N(0, v_L),$$

for large n_i, where the variance approximation v_L is given by the variance of the second term on the right-hand side of (3.1), that is

$$v_L = \sum_{i=1}^{k} \frac{1}{n_i} \mathrm{var}\{L_{t,i}(Y; F) \mid F\}. \qquad (3.3)$$

By analogy with the single sample case, empirical influence values are obtained by substituting the EDFs $\hat{F} = (\hat{F}_1, \ldots, \hat{F}_k)$ for the CDFs F in (3.2) to give

$$l_{ij} = L_{t,i}(y_j; \hat{F}).$$

These values satisfy $\sum_{j=1}^{n_i} l_{ij} = 0$ for each i. Substitution of empirical variances of the empirical influence values in (3.3) gives the variance approximation

$$v_L = \sum_{i=1}^{k} \frac{1}{n_i^2} \sum_{j=1}^{n_i} l_{ij}^2, \qquad (3.4)$$

which generalizes (2.36).

Example 3.3 (Difference of population means)   For the difference between sample averages in Example 3.1, the first influence function is

$$L_{t,1}(y, F) = \left. \frac{\partial}{\partial \varepsilon} \left[\int x_1 \{(1-\varepsilon)dF_1(x_1) + \varepsilon dH_y(x_1)\} - \int x_2 dF_2(x_2) \right] \right|_{\varepsilon=0} = y - \mu_1$$

just as in Example 2.17. Similarly $L_{t,2}(y, F) = -(y - \mu_2)$. In this case the linear approximation (3.1) is exact. The variance approximation formula (3.3) gives

$$v_L = \frac{1}{n_1} \mathrm{var}(Y_1) + \frac{1}{n_2} \mathrm{var}(Y_2),$$

and the empirical version (3.4) is

$$v_L = \frac{1}{n_1^2} \sum_{j=1}^{n_1} (y_{1j} - \bar{y}_1)^2 + \frac{1}{n_2^2} \sum_{j=1}^{n_2} (y_{2j} - \bar{y}_2)^2.$$

As usual this differs slightly from the unbiased variance approximation.

Note that if we could assume that the two population variances were equal, then it would be appropriate to replace v_L by

$$\left(\frac{1}{n_1} + \frac{1}{n_2} \right) \frac{1}{n_1 + n_2} \left\{ \sum (y_{1j} - \bar{y}_1)^2 + \sum (y_{2j} - \bar{y}_2)^2 \right\},$$

similar to the usual "pooled variance" formula.   ∎

The various comments made about calculation in Section 2.7 apply here with obvious modifications. Thus the empirical influence values can be approximated accurately by numerical differentiation, which here means

$$l_{ij} \doteq \frac{t(\hat{F}_1, \ldots, (1 - \varepsilon)\hat{F}_i + \varepsilon H_{y_j}, \ldots, \hat{F}_k) - t}{\varepsilon}$$

for small ε. We can also use the generalization of (2.44), namely

$$t^* \doteq t + \sum_{i=1}^{k} \frac{1}{n_i} \sum_{j=1}^{n_i} f_{ij}^* l_{ij}, \tag{3.5}$$

where f_{ij}^* denotes the frequency of data value y_{ij} in the bootstrap sample. Then given simulated values $t_1^*, \ldots, t_R^*$ we can approximate the l_{ij} by regression, generalizing the method outlined in Section 2.7.4. Alternative ways to calculate the l_{ij} and v_L are described in Problems 3.6 and 3.7.

The multisample analogue of the jackknife method of Section 2.7.3 involves the case deletion estimates

$$l_{jack,ij} = (n_i - 1)(t - t_{-ij}),$$

where t_{-ij} is the estimate obtained by omitting the jth case in the ith sample. Then

$$v_{jack} = \sum_{i=1}^{k} \frac{1}{n_i(n_i - 1)} \sum_{j=1}^{n_i} (l_{jack,ij} - \bar{l}_{jack,i})^2.$$

One can also generalize the discussion of bias approximation in Section 2.7.3. However, the extension of the quadratic approximation (2.41) is not straightforward, because there are "cross-population" terms.

The same approximation (3.1) could be used even when the samples, and hence the $\hat{F}_i$s, are correlated. But this would have to be taken into account in (3.3), which as stated assumes mutual independence of the samples. In general it would be safer to incorporate dependence through the use of appropriate multivariate EDFs.

3.3 Semiparametric Models

In a semiparametric model, some aspects of the data distribution are specified in terms of a small number of parameters, but other aspects are left arbitrary. A simple example would be the characterization $Y = \mu + \sigma\varepsilon$, with no assumption on the distribution of ε except that it has centre and scale zero and one. Usually a semiparametric model is useful only when we have nonhomogeneous data, with only the differences characterized by parameters, common elements being nonparametric.

In the context of Section 3.2, and especially Example 3.2, we might for example be fairly sure that the distributions F_i differ only in scale or, more cautiously, scale and location. That is, Y_{ij} might be expressed as

$$Y_{ij} = \mu_i + \sigma_i \varepsilon_{ij},$$

where the ε_{ij} are sampled from a common distribution with CDF F_0, say. The normal distribution is a parametric model of this form. The form can be checked to some extent by plotting standardized residuals such as

$$e_{ij} = \frac{y_{ij} - \hat{\mu}_i}{\hat{\sigma}_i},$$

for appropriate estimates $\hat{\mu}_i$ and $\hat{\sigma}_i$, to verify homogeneity across samples. The common F_0 will be estimated by the EDF of all $\sum n_i$ of the e_{ij}s, or better by the EDF of the standardized residuals $e_{ij}/(1 - n_i^{-1})^{1/2}$. The resampling algorithm will then be

$$Y_{ij}^* = \hat{\mu}_i + \hat{\sigma}_i \varepsilon_{ij}^*, \quad j = 1, \ldots, n_i, i = 1, \ldots, k,$$

where the ε_{ij}^*s are randomly sampled from the EDF, i.e. randomly sampled with replacement from the standardized e_{ij}s; see Problem 3.1.

In another context, with positive data such as lifetimes, it might be appropriate to think of distributions as differing only by multiplicative effects, i.e. $Y_{ij} = \mu_i \varepsilon_{ij}$, where the ε_{ij} are randomly sampled from some baseline distribution with unit mean. The exponential distribution is a parametric model of this form. The principle here would be essentially the same: estimate the ε_{ij} by residuals such as $e_{ij} = y_{ij}/\hat{\mu}_i$, then define $Y_{ij}^* = \hat{\mu}_i \varepsilon_{ij}^*$ with the ε_{ij}^* randomly sampled with replacement from the e_{ij}s.

Similar ideas apply in regression situations. The parametric part of the model concerns the systematic relationship between the response y and explanatory variables x, e.g. through the mean, and the nonparametric part concerns the random variation. We consider this in detail in Chapters 6 and 7.

Resampling plans such as those just outlined will give more accurate answers when their assumptions about the relationships between F_i are correct, but they are not robust to failure of these assumptions. Some pooling of information across samples may be essential in order to avoid difficulties when the samples are small, but otherwise it is usually unnecessary.

If we widen the meaning of semiparametric to include any partial modelling, then features less tangible than parameters come into play. The following two examples illustrate this.

Example 3.4 (Symmetric distribution)   Suppose that with our simple random sample it was appropriate to assume that the distribution was symmetric about its mean or median. Using this assumption could be critical to correct statistical analysis; see Example 3.26. Without a parametric model it is hard to see a clear choice for $\hat{F}$. But we can argue as follows: under F the distributions of $Y - \mu$ and $-(Y - \mu)$ are the same, so under $\hat{F}$ the distributions of $Y^* - \hat{\mu}$ and $-(Y^* - \hat{\mu})$ should be the same. This will be true if we symmetrize the EDF about $\hat{\mu}$, meaning that we take $\hat{F}$ to be the EDF of $y_1, \ldots, y_n, 2\hat{\mu} - y_1, \ldots, 2\hat{\mu} - y_n$. A robust choice for $\hat{\mu}$ would be the median. (For discrete distributions we could equivalently average sample proportions for appropriate pairs of data values.) The mean, median and other symmetrically defined location estimates of the resulting estimated distribution are all equal.   ∎

Example 3.5 (Equal marginal distributions)   Suppose that Y is bivariate, say $Y = (U, X)$, and that it is appropriate from the context to assume that U and X have the same marginal distribution. Then $\hat{F}$ can be forced to have the same margins by defining it as the EDF of the $2n$ pairs $(u_1, x_1), \ldots, (u_n, x_n), (x_1, u_1), \ldots, (x_n, u_n)$.   ∎

In both of these examples the resulting estimate will be more efficient than the EDF. This may be less important than producing a model which satisfies the practical assumptions and makes intuitive sense.

Example 3.6 (Mixed discrete–continuous distributions)   There will be situations where the raw EDF is not suitable for resampling because it is not a credible model. Such a situation arises in classification, where we have a binary response y and covariates x which are used to predict y. If the observed covariate values $x_1, \ldots, x_n$ are distinct, then the conditional probabilities $\pi(x) = \Pr(Y = 1 \mid x)$ estimated from the EDF are all 0 or 1. This is clearly not credible, so the EDF should not be used as a resampling model if the focus of interest is a property that depends critically on the conditional probabilities $\pi(x)$. A natural modification of the EDF is to keep the marginal EDF of x, but to replace the 0–1 values of the conditional distribution by a smooth estimate of $\pi(x)$. This is discussed further in Example 7.9.   ∎

3.4 Smooth Estimates of *F*

For nonparametric situations we have so far mostly assumed that the EDF $\hat{F}$ is a suitable estimate of F. But $\hat{F}$ is discrete, and it is natural to ask if a smooth estimate of F might be better. The most likely situation for improvement is where the effects of discreteness (Section 2.3.2) are severe, as in the case of the sample median (Example 2.16) or other sample quantiles.

When it is reasonable to suppose that F has a continuous PDF, one possibility is to use kernel density estimation. For scalar y we take

$$\hat{f}_h(y) = \frac{1}{nh} \sum_{j=1}^{n} w \left(\frac{y - y_j}{h} \right), \tag{3.6}$$

where $w(\cdot)$ is a continuous and symmetric PDF with mean zero and unit variance, and do calculations or simulations based on the corresponding CDF $\hat{F}_h$, rather than on the EDF $\hat{F}$. This corresponds to simulation by setting

$$Y_j^* = y_{I_j^*} + h\varepsilon_j, \quad j = 1,\ldots,n,$$

where the I_j^* are independent and uniformly distributed on the integers $1,\ldots,n$ and the ε_j are a random sample from $w(\cdot)$, independent of the I_j^*. This is the *smoothed bootstrap*. Note that $h = 0$ recovers the EDF.

The variance of an observation generated from (3.6) is $n^{-1} \sum(y_j - \bar{y})^2 + h^2$, and it may be preferable for the samples to have the same variance as for the unsmoothed bootstrap. This is implemented via the *shrunk smoothed bootstrap*, under which h smooths between $\hat{F}$ and a model in which data are generated from density $w(\cdot)$ centred at the mean and rescaled to have the variance of $\hat{F}$; see Problem 3.8.

Having decided which smoothed bootstrap is to be used, we estimate the required property of F, $a(F)$, by $a(\hat{F}_h)$ rather than $a(\hat{F})$. So if T is an estimator of $\theta = t(F)$, and we intend to estimate $a(F) = \text{var}(T \mid F)$ by simulation, we would obtain values $t_1^*,\ldots,t_R^*$ calculated from samples generated from $\hat{F}_h$, and then estimate $a(F)$ by $(R-1)^{-1} \sum(t_r^* - \bar{t}^*)^2$. Notice that it is $a(F)$, not $t(F)$, that is estimated using smoothing.

To see when $a(\hat{F}_h)$ is better than $a(\hat{F})$, suppose that $a(F)$ has linear approximation (2.35). Then

$$a(\hat{F}_h) - a(F) = n^{-1} \sum_{j=1}^{n} \int L_a(Y_j + h\varepsilon_j; F) w(\varepsilon_j)\, d\varepsilon_j + \cdots$$

$$= n^{-1} \sum_{j=1}^{n} L_a(Y_j; F) + \tfrac{1}{2} h^2 n^{-1} \sum_{j=1}^{n} L_a''(Y_j; F) + \cdots$$

for large n and small h, where $L_a''(u; \hat{F}) = \partial^2 L_a(u; \hat{F})/\partial u^2$. It follows that the

n	Usual	Smoothed, h			
	$h = 0$	0.1	0.25	0.5	1.0
20	18.9	18.6	16.6	11.9	6.6
80	11.4	11.2	10.4	8.5	6.4

Table 3.2 Root mean squared error ($\times 10^{-2}$) for estimation of $n^{1/2}$ times the standard deviation of the transformed correlation coefficient for bivariate normal data with correlation 0.7, for usual and smoothed bootstraps with $R = 200$ and smoothing parameter h.

mean squared error of $a(\hat{F}_h)$, $MSE(h) = E[\{a(\hat{F}_h) - a(F)\}^2]$, roughly equals

$$n^{-1}\int L_a(y;F)^2\,dF(y) + h^2 n^{-1}\int L_a(y;F)L_a''(y;F)\,dF(y) + \tfrac{1}{4}h^4\left\{\int L_a''(y;F)\,dF(y)\right\}^2. \tag{3.7}$$

Smoothing is not beneficial if the coefficient of h^2 is positive, but if it is negative (3.7) can be reduced by choosing a positive value of h that trades off the last two terms. The leading term in (3.7) is unaffected by the choice of h, which suggests that in large samples any effect of smoothing will be minor for such statistics.

Example 3.7 (Sample correlation)   To illustrate the discussion above, we take $a(F)$ to be the scaled standard deviation of $T = \tfrac{1}{2}\log\{(1+C)/(1-C)\}$, where C is the correlation coefficient for bivariate normal data. We extend (3.6) to bivariate y by taking $w(\cdot)$ to be the bivariate normal density with mean zero and variance matrix equal to the sample variance matrix. For each of 200 samples, we applied the smoothed bootstrap with different values of h and $R = 200$ to estimate $a(F)$.

Table 3.2 shows results for two sample sizes. For $n = 20$ there is a reduction in root mean squared error by a factor of about three, whereas for $n = 80$ the factor is about two. Results for the shrunk smoothed bootstrap are the same, because of the scale invariance of C and the form of $w(\cdot)$.   ∎

Smoothing is potentially more valuable when the quantity of interest depends on the local behaviour of F, as in the case of a sample quantile.

Example 3.8 (Sample median)   Suppose that $t(\hat{F})$ is the sample median, and that we wish to estimate its variance $a(F)$. In Example 2.16 we saw that the discreteness of the median posed problems for the ordinary, unsmoothed, bootstrap. Does smoothing improve matters?

Under regularity conditions on F and h, detailed calculations show that the mean squared error of $na(\hat{F}_h)$ is proportional to

$$(nh)^{-1}c_1 + h^4 c_2, \tag{3.8}$$

where c_1 and c_2 depend on F and $w(\cdot)$ but not on n. Provided that c_1 and c_2 are non-zero, (3.8) is minimized at $h \propto n^{-1/5}$, and (3.8) is then of order $n^{-4/5}$,

Table 3.3 Root mean squared error for estimation of n times the variance of the median of samples of size n from the t_3 and exponential densities, for usual, smoothed and shrunk smoothed bootstraps with $R = 200$ and smoothing parameter h.

	n	Usual $h = 0$	Smoothed, h				Shrunk smoothed, h			
			0.1	0.25	0.5	1.0	0.1	0.25	0.5	1.0
t_3	11	2.27	2.08	2.17	3.59	10.63	2.06	2.00	2.72	4.91
	81	0.97	0.76	0.77	1.81	6.07	0.75	0.67	1.17	2.30
Exp	11	1.32	1.15	1.02	1.18	7.53	1.13	0.92	0.76	0.93
	81	0.57	0.48	0.37	0.41	1.11	0.47	0.34	0.27	0.27

whereas it is $O(n^{-1/2})$ in the unsmoothed case. Thus there are advantages to smoothing here, at least in large samples. Similar results hold for other quantiles.

Table 3.3 shows results of simulation experiments where 1000 samples were taken from the exponential and t_3 distributions. For each sample smoothed and shrunk smoothed bootstraps were performed with $R = 200$ and several values of h. Unlike in Table 3.2, the advantage due to smoothing increases with n, and the shrunk smoothed bootstrap improves on the smoothed bootstrap, particularly at larger values of h.

As predicted by the theory, as n increases the root mean squared error decreases more rapidly for smoothed than for unsmoothed bootstraps; it decreases fastest for shrunk smoothing. For the t_3 data the root mean squared error is not much reduced. For the exponential data smoothing was performed on the log scale, leading to reduction in root mean squared error by a factor two or so. Too large a value of h can lead to large increases in root mean squared error, but choice of h is less critical for shrunk smoothing. Overall, a small amount of shrunk smoothing seems worthwhile here, provided the data are well-behaved. But similar experiments with Cauchy data gave very poor results made worse by smoothing, so one must be sure that the data are not pathological. Furthermore, the gains in precision are not large enough to be critical, at least for these sample sizes.

∎

The discussion above begs the important question of how to choose the smoothing parameter for use with a particular dataset. One possibility is to treat the problem as one of choosing among possible estimators $a(\hat{F}_h)$ and use the nested bootstrap, as in Example 3.26. However, the use of an estimated h is not sure to give improvement. When the rate of decrease of the optimal value of h is known, another possibility is to use subsampling, as in Example 8.6.

3.5 Censoring

3.5.1 Censored data

Censoring is present when data contain a lower or upper bound for an observation rather than the value itself. Such data often arise in medical and industrial reliability studies. In the medical context, the variable of interest might represent the time to death of a patient from a specific disease, with an indicator of whether the time recorded is exact or a lower bound due to the patient being lost to follow-up or to death from other causes.

The commonest form of censoring is *right-censoring*, in which case the value observed is $Y = \min(Y^0, C)$, where C is a censoring value, and Y^0 is a non-negative failure time, which is known only if $Y^0 \leq C$. The data themselves are pairs (Y, D), where D is a censoring indicator, which equals one if Y^0 is observed and equals zero if C is observed. Interest is usually focused on the distribution F^0 of Y^0, which is obscured if there is censoring.

The *survivor function* and the *cumulative hazard function* are central to the study of survival data. The survivor function corresponding to $F^0(y)$ is $\Pr(Y^0 > y) = 1 - F^0(y)$, and the cumulative hazard function is $A^0(y) = -\log\{1 - F^0(y)\}$. The cumulative hazard function may be written as $\int_0^y dA^0(u)$, where for continuous y the *hazard function* $dA^0(y)/dy$ measures the instantaneous rate of failure at time y, conditional on survival to that point. A constant hazard λ leads to an exponential distribution of failure times with survivor and cumulative hazard functions $\exp(-\lambda y)$ and λy; departures from these simple forms are often of interest.

The simplest model for censoring is *random censorship*, under which C is a random variable with distribution function G, independent of Y^0. In this case the observed variable Y has survivor function

$$\Pr(Y > y) = \{1 - F^0(y)\}\{1 - G(y)\}.$$

Other forms of censoring also arise, and these are often more realistic for applications.

Suppose that the data available are a homogeneous random sample (y_1, d_1), $\ldots, (y_n, d_n)$, and that censoring occurs at random. Let $y_1 < \cdots < y_n$, so there are no tied observations. A standard estimate of the failure-time survivor function, the *product-limit* or *Kaplan–Meier* estimate, may then be written as

$$1 - \hat{F}^0(y) = \prod_{j: y_j \leq y} \left(\frac{n - j}{n + 1 - j} \right)^{d_j}. \tag{3.9}$$

If there is no censoring, all the d_j equal one, and $\hat{F}^0(y)$ reduces to the EDF of $y_1, \ldots, y_n$ (Problem 3.9). The product-limit estimate changes only at successive failures, by an amount that depends on the number of censored observations between them. Ties between censored and uncensored data are resolved by assuming that censoring happens instantaneously after a failure might have occurred; the estimate is unaffected by other ties. A standard error for $1-\hat{F}^0(y)$ is given by *Greenwood's formula*,

$$\left\{1-\hat{F}^0(y)\right\} \left\{ \sum_{j:y_j \leq y} \frac{d_j}{(n-j)(n-j+1)} \right\}^{1/2}. \tag{3.10}$$

In setting confidence intervals this is usually applied on a transformed scale. Both (3.9) and (3.10) are unreliable where the numbers at risk of failure are small.

Since $1 - d_j$ is an indicator of censoring, the product-limit estimate of the censoring survivor function $1 - G$ is

$$1 - \hat{G}(y) = \prod_{j:y_j \leq y} \left(\frac{n-j}{n+1-j} \right)^{1-d_j}. \tag{3.11}$$

The cumulative hazard function may be estimated by the *Nelson–Aalen* estimate

$H(u)$ is the Heaviside function, which equals zero if $u < 0$ and equals one otherwise.

$$\hat{A}^0(y) = \sum_{j:y_j \leq y} \frac{d_j}{\sum_{k=1}^n H(y_j - y_k)}. \tag{3.12}$$

Since $y_1 < \cdots < y_n$, the increase in $\hat{A}^0$ at y_j is $d\hat{A}^0(y_j) = d_j/(n-j+1)$. The interpretation of (3.12) is that at each failure the hazard function is estimated by the number observed to fail, divided by the number of individuals at risk (i.e. available to fail) immediately before that time. In large samples the increments of $\hat{A}^0$, the $d\hat{A}^0(y_j)$, are approximately independent binomial variables with denominators $(n + 1 - j)$ and probabilities $d_j/(n - j + 1)$. The product-limit estimate may be expressed as

$$1 - \hat{F}_0(y) = \prod_{j:y_j \leq y} \left\{1 - d\hat{A}^0(y_j)\right\} \tag{3.13}$$

in terms of the components of (3.12).

Example 3.9 (AML data)   Table 3.4 contains data from a clinical trial conducted at Stanford University to assess the efficacy of maintenance chemotherapy for the remission of acute myelogeneous leukaemia (AML). After reaching a state of remission through treatment by chemotherapy, patients were divided randomly into two groups, one receiving maintenance chemotherapy and the other not. The objective of the study was to see if maintenance chemotherapy lengthened the time of remission, when the symptoms recur. The data in the table were gathered for preliminary analysis before the study ended.

Group 1	9	13	≥13	18	23	≥28	31	34	≥45	48	≥161	
Group 2	5	5	8	8	12	≥16	23	27	30	33	43	45

Table 3.4 Remission times (weeks) for two groups of patients with acute myelogeneous leukaemia (AML), one receiving maintenance chemotherapy (Group 1) and the other not (Miller, 1981, p. 49). ≥ indicates right-censoring.

The left panel of Figure 3.3 shows the estimated survivor functions for the times of remission. A plus on one of the lines indicates a censored observation. There is some suggestion that maintenance prolongs the time to remission, but the samples are small and the evidence is not overwhelming. The right panel shows the estimated survivor functions for the censoring times. Only one observation in the non-maintained group is censored, but the censoring distributions seem similar for both groups.

The estimated probabilities that remission will last beyond 20 weeks are respectively 0.71 and 0.59 for the groups, with standard errors from (3.10) both equal to 0.14. ∎

3.5.2 Resampling plans

Cases

When the data are a homogeneous sample subject to random censorship, the most direct way to bootstrap is to set $Y^* = \min(Y^{0*}, C^*)$, where Y^{0*} and C^* are independently generated from $\hat{F}^0$ and $\hat{G}$ respectively. This implies that

$$\Pr(Y^* > y) = \{1 - \hat{G}(y)\}\{1 - \hat{F}^0(y)\} = \prod_{j:y_j \leq y} \left(\frac{n-j}{n+1-j}\right),$$

which corresponds to the EDF that places mass n^{-1} on each of the n cases (y_j, d_j). That is, ordinary bootstrap sampling under the random censorship model is equivalent to resampling cases from the original data.

Conditional bootstrap

A second sampling scheme starts from the premise that since the censoring variable C is unrelated to Y^0, knowledge of the quantities $C_1, \ldots, C_n$ alone would tell us nothing about F^0. They would in effect be ancillary statistics. This suggests that simulations should be conditional on the pattern of censorship, so far as practicable. To allow for the censoring pattern, we argue that although the only values of c_j known exactly are those y_j with $d_j = 0$, the observed values of the remaining observations are lower bounds for the censoring variables, because $c_j > y_j$ when $d_j = 1$. This suggests the following algorithm.

Figure 3.3
Product-limit survivor
function estimates for
two groups of patients
with AML, one
receiving maintenance
chemotherapy (solid)
and the other not (dots).
The left panel shows
estimates for the time to
remission, and the right
panel shows the
estimates for the time to
censoring. In the left
panel, + indicates times
of censored
observations; in the
right panel + indicates
times of uncensored
observations.

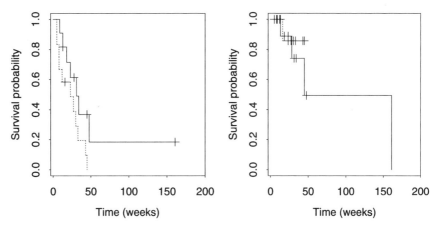

Algorithm 3.1 (Conditional bootstrap for censored data)

For $r = 1, \ldots, R$,

1. generate $Y_1^{0*}, \ldots, Y_n^{0*}$ independently from $\hat{F}^0$;
2. for $j = 1, \ldots, n$, make simulated censoring variables by setting $C_j^* = y_j$ if $d_j = 0$, and if $d_j = 1$, generating C_j^* from $\{\hat{G}(y) - \hat{G}(y_j)\}/\{1 - \hat{G}(y_j)\}$, which is the estimated distribution of C_j conditional on $C_j > y_j$; then
3. set $Y_j^* = \min(Y_j^{0*}, C_j^*)$, for $j = 1, \ldots, n$. •

If the largest observation is censored, it is given a notional failure time to the right of the observed value, and conversely if the largest observation is uncensored, it is given a notional censoring time to the right of the observed value. This ensures that the observation can appear in bootstrap resamples.

Both the above sampling plans can accommodate more complicated patterns of censoring, provided it is uninformative. For example, it might be decided at the start of a reliability experiment on independent and identical components that if they have not already failed, items will be censored at fixed times $c_1, \ldots, c_n$. In this situation an appropriate resampling plan is to generate failure times Y_j^{0*} from $\hat{F}^0$, and then to take $Y_j^* = \min(Y_j^{0*}, c_j)$, for $j = 1, \ldots, n$. This amounts to having separate censoring distributions for each item, with the jth putting mass one at c_j. Or in a medical study the jth individual might be subject to random censoring up to a time c_j^∞, corresponding to a fixed calendar date for the end of the study. In this situation, $Y_j = \min(Y_j^0, C_j, c_j^\infty)$, with the indicator D_j equalling zero, one, or two according to whether C_j, Y_j^0, or c_j^∞ was observed. Then an appropriate conditional sampling plan would generate

Y_j^{0*} and C_j^* as in the conditional plan above, but take $Y_j^* = \min(Y_j^{0*}, C_j^*, c_j^\infty)$, and make D_j^* accordingly.

Weird bootstrap

The sampling plans outlined above mimic how the data are thought to arise, by generating individual failure and censoring times. When interest is focused on the survival or hazard functions, a third and quite different approach uses direct simulation from the Nelson–Aalen estimate (3.12) of the cumulative hazard. The idea is to treat the numbers of failures at each observed failure time as independent binomial variables with denominators equal to the numbers of individuals at risk, and means equal to the numbers that actually failed. Thus when $y_1 < \cdots < y_n$, we take the simulated number to fail at time y_j, N_j^*, to be binomial with denominator $n - j + 1$ and probability of failure $d_j/(n - j + 1)$. A simulated Nelson–Aalen estimate is then

$$\hat{A}^{0*}(y) = \sum_{j=1}^{n} \frac{N_j^*}{\sum_{k=1}^{n} H(y_j - y_k)}, \tag{3.14}$$

which can be used to estimate the uncertainty of the original estimate $\hat{A}^0(y)$. In this *weird bootstrap* the failures at different times are unrelated, the number at risk does not depend on previous failures, there are no individuals whose simulated failure times underlie $\hat{A}^{0*}(y)$, and no explicit assumption is made about the censoring mechanism. Indeed, under this scheme the censored individuals are held fixed, but the number of failures is a sum of binomial variables (Problem 3.10).

The simulated survivor function corresponding to (3.14) is obtained by substituting

$$dA^{0*}(y_j) = \frac{N_j^*}{\sum_{k=1}^{n} H(y_j - y_k)}$$

into (3.13) in place of $d\hat{A}^0(y_j)$.

Example 3.10 (AML data) Figure 3.3 suggests that the censoring distributions for both groups of data in Table 3.4 are similar, but that the survival distributions themselves are not. To compare the resampling schemes described above, we consider estimates of two parameters, the probability of remission beyond 20 weeks and the median survival time, both for Group 1. These estimates are $1 - \hat{F}^0(20) = 0.71$ and $\inf\{t : \hat{F}^0(t) \geq \frac{1}{2}\} = 31$.

Table 3.5 compares results from 499 simulations using the ordinary, conditional, and weird bootstraps. For the survival probabilities, the ordinary and conditional bootstraps give similar results, and both standard errors are similar to that from Greenwood's formula; the weird bootstrap probabilities are significantly higher and are less variable. The schemes give infinite estimates

Table 3.5 Results for 499 replicates of censored data bootstraps of Group 1 of the AML data: average (standard deviation) for estimated probability of remission beyond 20 weeks, average (standard deviation) for estimated median survival time, and the number of resamples in which case 3 occurs 0, 1, 2 and 3 or more times.

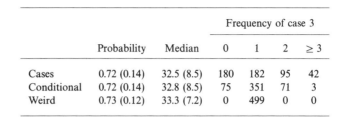

			Frequency of case 3			
	Probability	Median	0	1	2	≥ 3
Cases	0.72 (0.14)	32.5 (8.5)	180	182	95	42
Conditional	0.72 (0.14)	32.8 (8.5)	75	351	71	3
Weird	0.73 (0.12)	33.3 (7.2)	0	499	0	0

Figure 3.4 Comparison of distributions of differences in median survival times for censored data bootstraps applied to the AML data. The dotted line is the line $x = y$.

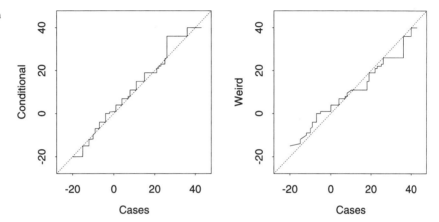

of the median 21, 19, and 2 times respectively. The weird bootstrap results for the median are less variable than the others.

The last columns of the table show the numbers of samples in which the smallest censored observation appears 0, 1, 2, and 3 or more times. Under the conditional scheme the observation appears more often than under the ordinary bootstrap, and under the weird bootstrap it occurs once in each resample.

Figure 3.4 compares the distributions of the difference of median survival times between the two groups, under the three schemes. Results for the conditional and ordinary bootstraps are similar, but the weird bootstrap again gives results that are less variable than the others.

This set of data gives an extreme test of methods for censored data, because quantiles of the product-limit estimate are very discrete.

The weird bootstrap also gave results less variable than the other schemes for a larger set of data. In general it seems that case resampling and conditional resampling give quite similar and reliable results, both differing from the weird bootstrap. ∎

3.6 Missing Data

The expression "missing data" relates to datasets of a standard form for which some entries are missing or incomplete. This happens in a variety of different ways. For example, censored data as described in Section 3.5 are incomplete when the censoring value c is reported instead of y^0. Or in a factorial experiment a few factor combinations may not have been used. In such cases estimates and inferences would take a simple form if the dataset were "complete". But because part of the standard form is missing, we have two problems: how to estimate the quantities of interest, and how to make inferences about them. We have already discussed ways of dealing with censored data. Now we examine situations where each response has several components, some of which are missing for some cases.

Suppose, then, that the fictional or potential complete data are y^0s and that corresponding observed data are ys, with some components taking the value NA to represent "not available".

Parametric problems

For parametric problems the situation is relatively straightforward, at least in principle. First, in defining estimators there is a general framework within which complete-data MLE methods can be applied using the iterative EM algorithm, which essentially works by estimating missing values. Formulae exist for computing approximate standard errors of estimators, but simulation will often be required to obtain accurate answers. One extra component that must be specified is the mechanism which takes complete data y^0 into observed data y, i.e. $f(y \mid y^0)$. The methodology is simplest when data are missing at random.

The corresponding Bayesian methodology is also relatively straightforward in principle, and numerous general algorithms exist for using complete-data forms of posterior distribution. Such algorithms, although they involve simulation, are somewhat removed from the general context of bootstrap methods and will not be discussed here.

The EM or expectation maximization algorithm is widely used in incomplete data problems.

Nonparametric problems

Nonparametric analysis is somewhat more complicated, in part because of the difficulty of defining appropriate estimators. The following artificial example illustrates some of the key ideas.

Example 3.11 (Mean with missing data) Suppose that responses y^0 had been obtained from n randomly chosen individuals, but that m randomly selected values were then lost. So the observed data are

$$y_1, \ldots, y_n = y_1^0, \ldots, y_{n-m}^0, NA, \ldots, NA.$$

To estimate the population mean μ we should of course use the average response $\bar{y} = (n - m)^{-1} \sum_{j=1}^{n-m} y_j$, whose variance we would estimate by

$$v = (n - m)^{-2} \sum_{j=1}^{n-m} (y_j - \bar{y})^2.$$

But think of this as a prototype missing data problem, to which resampling methods are to be applied. Consider the following two approaches:

1   First estimate μ by $t = \bar{y}$, the average of the non-missing data. Then

    (*a*) simulate samples $y_1^*, \ldots, y_n^*$ by sampling with replacement from the n observations $y_1, \ldots, y_{n-m}, NA, \ldots, NA$; then

    (*b*) calculate t^* as the average of non-missing values.

2   First estimate the missing values $y_{n-m+1}^0, \ldots, y_n^0$ by $\hat{y}_j^0 = \bar{y}$ for $j = n - m + 1$, $\ldots, n$ and estimate μ as the mean of $y_1^0, \ldots, y_{n-m}^0, \hat{y}_{n-m+1}^0, \ldots, \hat{y}_n^0$. Then

    (*a*) sample with replacement from $y_1^0, \ldots, y_{n-m}^0, \hat{y}_{n-m+1}^0, \ldots, \hat{y}_n^0$ to get $y_1^{*0}, \ldots, y_n^{*0}$;

    (*b*) duplicate the data-loss procedure by replacing a randomly chosen m of the y_j^{*0} with NA; finally

    (*c*) duplicate the data estimation of μ to get t^*.

In the first approach, we choose the form of t to take account of the missing data. Then in the resampling we get a random number of missing values, M^* say, whose mean is m. The effect of this is to make the variance of T^* somewhat larger than the variance of T: specifically

$$\text{var}^*(T^*) = (n - m)v\,\text{E}^* \left(\frac{1}{n - M^*} \right) > v.$$

Assuming that we discard all resamples with $m^* = n$ (all data missing), the bootstrap variance will overestimate $\text{var}(T)$ by a factor which ranges from 15% for $n = 10, m = 5$ to 4% for $n = 30, m = 15$.

In the second approach, the first step was to fix the data so that the complete-data estimation formula $\hat{\mu} = n^{-1} \sum_{j=1}^{n} y_j^0$ for t could be used. Then we attempted to simulate data according to the two steps in the original data-generation process. Unfortunately the EDF of $y_1^0, \ldots, y_{n-m}^0, \hat{y}_{n-m+1}^0, \ldots, \hat{y}_n^0$ is an underdispersed estimate of the true CDF F. Even though the estimate t is not affected in this particularly simple problem, the bootstrap distribution certainly is. This is illustrated by the bootstrap variance

$$\text{var}^*(T^*) = \left(\frac{n - m}{n} \right) v.$$

Both approaches can be repaired. In the first, we can stratify the sampling with complete and incomplete data as strata. In the second approach, we can add variability to the estimates of missing values. This device, called *multiple* *imputation*, replaces the single estimate $\hat{y}_j^0 = \bar{y}$ by the set $\hat{y}_j^0 + e_1, \ldots, \hat{y}_j + e_{n-m}$, where $e_k = y_k - \bar{y}$ for $k = 1, \ldots, n - m$. Where the estimate $\hat{y}_j$ was previously given weight 1, the $n - m$ imputed values for the jth case are now given equal weights $(n - m)^{-1}$. The implication is that $\hat{F}$ is modified to equal n^{-1} on each complete-data value, and $n^{-1} \times (n - m)^{-1}$ on the $m(n - m)$ values $\hat{y}_j^0 + e_k$. In this simple case $\hat{y}_j^0 + e_k = y_k$, so $\hat{F}$ reduces to the EDF of the non-missing data $y_1, \ldots, y_{n-m}$, as a consequence of which $t(\hat{F}) = \bar{y}$ and the bootstrap distribution of T^* is correct.   ∎

This example suggests two lessons. First, if the complete-data estimator can be modified to work for incomplete data, then resampling cases will work reasonably well provided the proportion of missing data is small: stratified resampling would reduce variation in the amount of missingness. Secondly, the complete-data estimator and full simulation of data observation (including the data-loss step) cannot be based on single imputation estimation of missing values, but may work if we use multiple imputation appropriately.

One further point concerns the data-loss mechanism, which in the example we assumed to be completely random. If data loss is dependent upon the response value y, then resampling cases should still be valid: this is somewhat similar to the censored-data problem. But the other approach via multiple imputation will become complicated because of the difficulty of defining appropriate multiple imputations.

Example 3.12 (Bivariate missing data)   A more realistic example concerns the estimation of bivariate correlation when some cases are incomplete. Suppose that Y is bivariate with components U and X. The parameter of interest is $\theta = \text{corr}(U, X)$. A random sample of n cases is taken, such that m cases have x missing, but no cases have both u and x missing or just u missing. If it is safe to assume that X has a linear regression on U, then we can use fitted regression to make single imputations of missing values. That is, we estimate each missing x_j by

$$\hat{x}_j = \bar{x} + b(u_j - \bar{u}),$$

where $\bar{x}$, $\bar{u}$ and b are the averages and the slope of linear regression of x on u from the $n - m$ complete pairs.

It is easy to see that it would be wrong to substitute these single imputations in the usual formula for sample correlation. The result would be biased away from zero if $b \neq 0$. Only if we can modify the sample correlation formula to remove this effect will it be sensible to use simple resampling of cases.

The other strategy is to begin with multiple imputation to obtain a suitable bivariate $\hat{F}$, next estimate θ with the usual sample correlation $t(\hat{F})$, and then resample appropriately. Multiple imputation uses the regression residuals from

Figure 3.5 Scatter plot
of bivariate sample and
multiple imputation
values. Left panel shows
observed pairs (○) and
cases where only u is
observed (•). Right
panel shows observed
pairs (○) and multiple
imputation values (+).
Dotted line is
imputation regression
line obtained from
observed pairs.

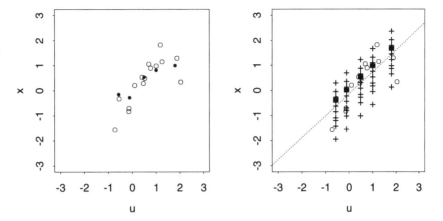

complete pairs,

$$e_j = x_j - \hat{x}_j = x_j - \{\bar{x} + b(u_j - \bar{u})\},$$

for $j = 1, \ldots, n-m$. Then each missing x_j is $\hat{x}_j$ plus a randomly selected e_j. Our estimate $\hat{F}$ is the bivariate distribution which puts weight n^{-1} on each complete pair, and weight $n^{-1} \times (n-m)^{-1}$ on each of the $n-m$ multiple imputations for each incomplete case. There are two strong, implicit assumptions being made here. First, as throughout our discussion, it is assumed that values are missing at random. Secondly, homogeneity of conditional variances is being assumed, so that pooling of residuals makes sense.

As an illustration, the left panel of Figure 3.5 shows a scatter plot for a sample of $n = 20$ where $m = 5$ cases have x components missing. Complete cases appear as open circles, and incomplete cases as filled circles — only the u components are observed. In the right panel, the dotted line is the imputation line which gives $\hat{x}_j$ for $j = 16, \ldots, 20$, and the multiple imputation values are plotted with symbol +. The multiple imputation EDF will put probability $\frac{1}{20}$ on each open circle, and probability $\frac{1}{20 \times 15}$ on each +.

The results in Table 3.6 illustrate the effectiveness of the multiple imputation EDF. The table shows simulation averages and standard deviations for estimates of correlation θ and $\sigma_X^2 = \text{var}(X)$ using the standard complete-data forms of the estimators, when half of the x values are missing in a sample of size $n = 20$ from the bivariate normal distribution. In this problem there would be little gain from using incomplete cases, but in more complex situations there might be so few complete cases that multiple imputation would be highly effective or even essential.

	Full data estimates	Observed data estimates		
		Complete case only	Single imputation	Multiple imputation
$\hat{\sigma}_x^2$	1.00 (0.33)	1.01 (0.49)	0.79 (0.44)	0.96 (0.46)
$\hat{\theta}$	0.69 (0.13)	0.68 (0.20)	0.79 (0.18)	0.70 (0.19)

Table 3.6 Average (standard deviation) of estimators for variance σ_x^2 and correlation θ from bivariate normal data (u, x) with sample size $n = 20$ and $m = 10$ x values missing at random. True values $\sigma_x^2 = 1$ and $\theta = 0.7$. Results from 1000 simulated datasets.

Having set up an appropriate multiple imputation EDF $\hat{F}$, resampling proceeds in an obvious way, first creating a full set of n pairs by random sampling from $\hat{F}$, and then selecting m cases randomly without replacement for which the x values are "lost". The first stage is equivalent to random sampling with replacement from $n - m$ copies of the complete data plus all $m \times (n - m)$ possible multiple imputation values. ∎

3.7 Finite Population Sampling

Basics

The simplest form of finite population sampling is when a sample $y_1, \ldots, y_n$ is taken randomly without replacement from a population $\mathscr{Y}$ with values $\mathscr{Y}_1, \ldots, \mathscr{Y}_N$, with $N > n$ known. The statistic $t(y_1, \ldots, y_n)$ is used to estimate the corresponding population quantity $\theta = t(\mathscr{Y}_1, \ldots, \mathscr{Y}_N)$. The data are one of the $\binom{N}{n}$ possible samples $Y_1, \ldots, Y_n$ from the population, and the without-replacement sampling means that the Y_j are exchangeable but not independent; the sampling fraction is defined to be $f = n/N$. If $n \ll N$, f is very small and correlation among the $Y_1, \ldots, Y_n$ will have little effect, but in practice f often lies in the range 0.1–0.5 and cannot be ignored. Dependence among the Y_j complicates inference for θ, as the following example indicates.

Example 3.13 (Sample average) Suppose that the y_j are scalar and that we want a confidence interval for the population average $\theta = N^{-1} \sum \mathscr{Y}_j$. Although the sample average $\bar{Y} = n^{-1} \sum Y_j$ is an unbiased estimator of θ, when sampling with and without replacement we find

$$\text{var}(\bar{Y}) = \begin{cases} n^{-1}\gamma, & \text{with replacement,} \\ (1 - f)n^{-1}\gamma, & \text{without replacement,} \end{cases} \tag{3.15}$$

where $\gamma = (N - 1)^{-1} \sum (\mathscr{Y}_j - \bar{\mathscr{Y}})^2$. The sample variance $c = (n - 1)^{-1} \sum (y_j - \bar{y})^2$ is an unbiased estimate of γ, and the usual standard error for $\bar{y}$ under without-replacement sampling is obtained from the second line of (3.15) by replacing γ with c. Normal approximation to the distribution of $\bar{Y}$ then gives approximate $(1 - 2\alpha)$ confidence limits $\bar{y} \pm (1 - f)^{1/2} c^{1/2} n^{-1/2} z_\alpha$ for θ, where z_α is the α

quantile of the standard normal distribution. Such confidence intervals are a factor $(1-f)^{1/2}$ shorter than for sampling with replacement.

The lack of independence affects possible resampling plans, as is seen by applying the ordinary bootstrap to $\bar{Y}$. Suppose that $Y_1^*,\ldots,Y_n^*$ is a random sample taken with replacement from $y_1,\ldots,y_n$. Their average $\bar{Y}^*$ has variance $\text{var}^*(\bar{Y}^*) = n^{-2}\sum(y_j-\bar{y})^2$, and this has expected value $n^{-2}(n-1)\gamma$ over possible samples $y_1,\ldots,y_n$. This only matches the second line of (3.15) if $f = n^{-1}$. Thus for the larger values of f generally met in practice, ordinary bootstrap standard errors for $\bar{y}$ are too large and the confidence intervals for θ are systematically too wide. ∎

Modified sample size

The key difficulty with the ordinary bootstrap is that it involves with-replacement samples of size n and so does not capture the effect of the sampling fraction, which is to shrink the variance of an estimator. One way to deal with this is to take resamples of size n', resampling with or without replacement. The value of n' is chosen so that the estimator variance is matched, at least approximately.

For with-replacement resamples the average $\bar{Y}^*$ of $Y_1^*,\ldots,Y_{n'}^*$ has variance $\text{var}^*(\bar{Y}^*) = (n-1)c/(n'n)$, which is only an unbiased estimate of $(1-f)\gamma/n$ when $n' = (n-1)/(1-f)$; this usually exceeds n.

For without-replacement resampling, a similar argument implies that we should take $n' = fn$. One obvious difficulty with this is that if $f \ll 1$, the resample size is much smaller than n, and then the resampled statistics may be much less stable than those based on samples of size n. This suggests that we mirror the dependence induced by sampling without replacement but try to match the original sample size, by resampling as follows. Suppose first that $m = nf$ and $k = n/m$ are both integers, and that to form our resample we concatenate k without-replacement samples of size m taken independently from $y_1,\ldots,y_n$. Then our resample has size $n' = mk$, and the same sampling fraction as the original data. This is known as the *mirror-match bootstrap*. When m and k are not integers we choose m to be the positive integer closest to nf and take k so that $km \le n \le (k+1)m$. We then select randomly either k or $k+1$ without-replacement samples from $y_1,\ldots,y_n$ with probabilities chosen to match the original sampling fraction. If randomization is used it is important that it be incorporated correctly into the resampling scheme (Problem 3.15).

Population and superpopulation bootstraps

Suppose for the moment that N/n is an integer, k. Then one obvious idea is to form a fake population $\mathcal{Y}^*$ of size N by concatenating k copies of $y_1,\ldots,y_n$. The natural next step — which mimics how the data were sampled — is to generate a bootstrap replicate of $y_1,\ldots,y_n$ by taking a sample of size n without replacement from $\mathcal{Y}^*$. So the bootstrap sample, $Y_1^*,\ldots,Y_n^*$, is one of the $\binom{N}{n}$ possible without-replacement samples from $\mathscr{Y}^*$, and the corresponding bootstrap value is $T^* = t(Y_1^*, \ldots, Y_n^*)$.

If N/n is not an integer, we write $N = kn + l$, where $0 < l < n$, and form $\mathscr{Y}^*$ by taking k copies of $y_1, \ldots, y_n$ and adding to them a sample of size l taken without replacement from $y_1, \ldots, y_n$. Bootstrap samples are formed as when $N = kn$, but a different $\mathscr{Y}^*$ is used for each. We call this the *population bootstrap*. Under a superpopulation model, the members of the population $\mathscr{Y}$ are themselves a random sample from an underlying distribution, $\mathscr{P}$. The nonparametric maximum likelihood estimate of $\mathscr{P}$ is the EDF of the sample, which suggests the following resampling plan.

Algorithm 3.2 (Superpopulation bootstrap)

For $r = 1, \ldots, R$,

1 generate a replicate population $\mathscr{Y}^* = (\mathscr{Y}_1^*, \ldots, \mathscr{Y}_N^*)$ by sampling N times with replacement from $y_1, \ldots, y_n$; then

2 generate a bootstrap sample $Y_1^*, \ldots, Y_n^*$ by sampling n times without replacement from $\mathscr{Y}^*$, and set $T_r^* = t(Y_1^*, \ldots, Y_n^*)$.

                                                                                     ●

As one would expect, this gives results similar to the population bootstrap.

Example 3.14 (Sample average)   Suppose that $y_1, \ldots, y_n$ are scalars, that $N = kn$, and that interest focuses on $\theta = N^{-1} \sum \mathscr{Y}_j$, as in Example 3.13. Then under the population bootstrap,

$$\text{var}^*(\bar{Y}^*) = \frac{N(n-1)}{(N-1)n} \times (1-f)n^{-1}c,$$

and this is the correct formula apart from the first factor on the right, which is typically close to one. Under the superpopulation bootstrap a straightforward calculation establishes that the mean variance of $\bar{Y}^*$ is $(n-1)/n \times (1-f)n^{-1}c$ (Problem 3.12).

These sampling schemes make almost the right allowance for the sampling fraction, at least for the average.

For the mirror-match scheme we suppose that $n = km$ for integer m, and write $\bar{Y}^* = n^{-1} \sum_{i=1}^{k} \sum_{j=1}^{m} Y_{ij}^*$, where $(Y_{i1}^*, \ldots, Y_{im}^*)$ is the ith without-replacement resample, independent of the other without-replacement resamples. Then we can use (3.15) to establish that $\text{var}^*(\bar{Y}^*) = (km)^{-1}(1 - m/n)m^{-1}c$. Because our assumptions imply that $f = m/n$, this is an unbiased estimate of $\text{var}(\bar{Y})$, but it would be biased if $m \neq nf$.   ■

Studentized confidence intervals

Suppose that $v = v(y_1, \ldots, y_n)$ is an estimated variance for the statistic $t = t(y_1, \ldots, y_n)$, based on the without-replacement sample $y_1, \ldots, y_n$, and that some bootstrap scheme is used to form replicates t_r^* and v_r^* of t and v, for $r = 1, \ldots, R$. Then the studentized bootstrap can be used to form confidence intervals for θ, based on the values of $z_r^* = (t_r^* - t)/v_r^{*1/2}$. As outlined in Section 2.4, a $(1 - 2\alpha)$ confidence interval has limits

$$t - v^{1/2} z_{((R+1)(1-\alpha))}^*, \quad t - v^{1/2} z_{((R+1)\alpha)}^*,$$

where $z_{((R+1)p)}^*$ is the empirical p quantile of the z_r^*. If the population or superpopulation bootstraps are used, and $N, n \to \infty$ in such a way that $f = n/N \to \pi$, where $0 < \pi < 1$, these intervals can be shown to have the same good properties as when the $y_1, \ldots, y_n$ are a random sample from an infinite population; see Section 5.4.1.

Example 3.15 (City population data) For a numerical assessment of the schemes outlined above, we consider again the data in Example 1.2, on 1920 and 1930 populations (in thousands) of $N = 49$ US cities. Table 2.1 contains populations $y_j = (u_j, x_j)$ for a sample of $n = 10$ cities taken without replacement from the 49, and we use them to estimate the mean 1930 population $\theta = N^{-1} \sum_{j=1}^{N} x_j$ for the 49 cities.

Two standard estimators of θ are the ratio and regression estimators. The ratio estimate and its estimated variance are given by

$$t_{rat} = \bar{u}_N \times \frac{\sum_{j=1}^{n} x_j}{\sum_{j=1}^{n} u_j}, \quad v_{rat} = \frac{(1-f)}{n(n-1)} \sum_{j=1}^{n} \left(x_j - \frac{u_j t_{rat}}{\bar{u}_N}\right)^2, \quad \bar{u}_N = \frac{1}{N} \sum_{j=1}^{N} u_j. \tag{3.16}$$

For our data $t_{rat} = 156.8$ and $v_{rat} = 10.85^2$. The regression estimate is based on the straight-line regression $x = \hat{\beta}_0 + \hat{\beta}_1 u$ fit to the data $(u_1, x_1), \ldots, (u_n, x_n)$, using least squares estimates $\hat{\beta}_0$ and $\hat{\beta}_1$. The regression estimate of θ and its estimated variance are

$$t_{reg} = \hat{\beta}_0 + \hat{\beta}_1 \bar{u}_N, \quad v_{reg} = \frac{(1-f)}{n(n-2)} \sum_{j=1}^{n} (x_j - \hat{\beta}_0 - \hat{\beta}_1 u_j)^2; \tag{3.17}$$

for our data $t_{reg} = 138.3$ and $v_{reg} = 8.32^2$.

Table 3.7 contains 95% confidence intervals for θ based on normal approximations to t_{rat} and t_{reg}, and on the studentized bootstrap applied to (3.16) and (3.17). Normal approximations to the distributions of t_{rat} and t_{reg} are poor, and intervals based on them are considerably shorter than the other intervals. The population and superpopulation bootstraps give rather similar intervals.

The sampling fraction is $f = 10/49$, so the estimate of the distribution of T^* using modified sample size and without-replacement resampling uses

Scheme	Ratio		Regression	
Normal	137.8	174.7	123.7	152.0
Modified size, $n' = 2$	58.9	298.6	—	—
Modified size, $n' = 11$	111.9	196.2	114.0	258.2
Mirror-match, $m = 2$	115.6	196.0	112.8	258.7
Population	118.9	193.3	116.1	240.7
Superpopulation	120.3	195.9	114.0	255.4

Table 3.7 City population data: 95% confidence limits for the mean population per city in 1930 based on the ratio and regression estimates, using normal approximation and various resampling methods with $R = 999$.

	Coverage			Length	
	Lower	Upper	Overall	Average	SD
Normal	7	89	82	23	8.2
Modified size, $n' = 2$	1	98	98	151	142
Modified size, $n' = 11$	2	91	89	34	19
Mirror-match, $m = 2$	3	91	88	33	19
Population	2	91	89	36	21
Superpopulation	1	92	91	41	24

Table 3.8 City population data. Empirical coverages (%) and average and standard deviation of length of 90% confidence intervals based on the ratio estimate of the 1930 total, based on 1000 samples of size 10 from the population of size 49. The nominal lower, upper and overall coverages are 5, 95 and 90.

samples of size $nf \doteq 2$. Not surprisingly, without-replacement resamples of size $n' = 2$ from 10 observations give a very poor idea of what happens when samples of size 10 are taken without replacement from 49 observations, and the corresponding confidence interval is very wide. Studentized bootstrap confidence limits cannot be based on t_{reg}, because with $n' = 2$ we have $v_{reg}^* \equiv 0$. For with-replacement resampling, we take $(n-1)/(1-f) \doteq n' = 11$, giving intervals quite close to those for the mirror-match, population and superpopulation bootstraps.

Figure 3.6 shows why the upper endpoints of the ratio and regression confidence intervals differ so much. The variance estimate v_{reg}^* is unstable because of resamples in which case 4 does not appear and case 9 appears just once or not at all; then z_{reg}^* takes large negative values. The right panel of the figure explains this: the regression slope changes markedly when case 4 is deleted. Exclusion of case 9 further reduces the regression sum of squares and hence v_{reg}^*. The ratio estimate is much less sensitive to case 4. If we insisted on using t_{reg}, one solution would be to exclude from the simulation samples in which case 4 does not appear. Then the 0.025 and 0.975 quantiles of z_{reg}^* using the population bootstrap are -1.30 and 3.06, and the corresponding confidence interval is $[112.9, 149.1]$.

Figure 3.6 Population bootstrap results for regression estimator based on city data with $n = 10$. The left panel shows values of z^*_{reg} and $v^{*1/2}_{reg}$ for resamples in which case 4 appears at least once (dots), and in which case 4 does not appear and case 9 appears zero times (0), once (1), or more times (+); the dotted line shows $v^{*1/2}_{reg}$. The right panel shows the sample and the regression lines fitted to the data with case 4 (dashes) and without it (dots); the vertical line shows the value $\bar{u}$ at which θ is estimated.

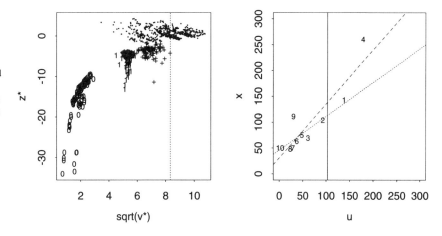

To compare the performances of the various methods in setting confidence intervals, we conducted a numerical experiment in which 1000 samples of size $n = 10$ were taken without replacement from the population of size $N = 49$. For each sample we calculated 90% confidence intervals $[L, U]$ for θ using $R = 999$ bootstrap samples. Table 3.8 contains the empirical values of $\Pr(\theta \leq L)$, $\Pr(\theta \leq U)$, and $\Pr(L < \theta \leq U)$. The normal intervals are short and their coverages are much too small, while the modified intervals with $n' = 2$ have the opposite problem. Coverages for the modified sample size with $n' = 11$ and for the population and superpopulation bootstrap are close to their nominal levels, though their endpoints seem to be slightly too far left. The 80% and 95% intervals and those for the regression estimator have similar properties. In line with other studies in the literature, we conclude that the population and superpopulation bootstraps are the best of those considered here.   ∎

Stratified sampling

In most applications the population is divided into k strata, the ith of which contains N_i individuals from which a sample of size n_i is taken without replacement, independent of other strata. The ith sampling fraction is $f_i = n_i/N_i$ and the proportion of the population in the ith stratum is $w_i = N_i/N$, where $N = N_1 + \cdots + N_k$. The estimate of θ and its standard error are found by combining quantities from each stratum.

Two different setups can be envisaged for mathematical discussion. In the first — the "small-k" case — there is a small number of large strata: the asymptotic regime takes k fixed and $n_i, N_i \rightarrow \infty$ with $f_i \rightarrow \pi_i$, where $0 < \pi_i < 1$.

Apart from there being k strata, the same ideas and results will apply as above, with the chosen resampling scheme applied separately in each stratum. The second setup — the "large-k" case — is where there are many small strata; in mathematical terms we suppose that $k \to \infty$ but that N_i and n_i are bounded. This situation is more complicated, because biases from each stratum can combine in such a way that a bootstrap fails completely.

Example 3.16 (Average)   Suppose that the population $\mathscr{Y}$ comprises k strata, and that the jth item in the ith stratum is labelled $\mathscr{Y}_{ij}$; the average for that stratum is $\bar{\mathscr{Y}}_i$. Then the population average is $\theta = \sum_i w_i \bar{\mathscr{Y}}_i$, which is estimated by $T = \sum_i w_i \bar{Y}_i$, where $\bar{Y}_i$ is the average of the sample $Y_{i1}, \ldots, Y_{in_i}$ from the ith stratum. The variance of T is

$$v = \sum_{i=1}^{k} w_i^2 (1 - f_i) \times \frac{1}{N_i - 1} \sum_{j=1}^{N_i} (\mathscr{Y}_{ij} - \bar{\mathscr{Y}}_i)^2, \tag{3.18}$$

an unbiased estimate of which is

$$V = \sum_{i=1}^{k} w_i^2 (1 - f_i) \times \frac{1}{n_i - 1} \sum_{j=1}^{n_i} (Y_{ij} - \bar{Y}_i)^2. \tag{3.19}$$

Suppose for sake of simplicity that each N_i/n_i is an integer, and that the population bootstrap is applied to each stratum independently. Then the variance of the bootstrap version of T is

$$\mathrm{var}^*(T^*) = \sum_{i=1}^{k} w_i^2 (1 - f_i) \times \frac{N_i(n_i - 1)}{(N_i - 1)n_i} \times \frac{1}{n_i - 1} \sum_{j=1}^{n_i} (y_{ij} - \bar{y}_i)^2, \tag{3.20}$$

the mean of which is obtained by replacing the last term on the right by $(N_i - 1)^{-1} \sum_j (\mathscr{Y}_{ij} - \bar{\mathscr{Y}}_i)^2$. If k is fixed and $n_i, N_i \to \infty$ while $f_i \to \pi_i$, (3.20) will converge to v, but this will not be the case if n_i, N_i are bounded and $k \to \infty$. The bootstrap bias estimate also may fail for the same reason (Problem 3.12). ∎

For setting confidence intervals using the studentized bootstrap the key issue is not the performance of bias and variance estimates, but the extent to which the distribution of the resampled quantity $Z^* = (T^* - t)/V^{*1/2}$ matches that of $Z = (T - \theta)/V^{1/2}$. Detailed calculations show that when the population and superpopulation bootstraps are used, Z and Z^* have the same limiting distribution under both asymptotic regimes, and that under the fixed-k setup the approximation is better than that using the other resampling plans.

Example 3.17 (Stratified ratio)   For empirical comparison of the more promising of these finite population resampling schemes with stratified data, we generated a population with N pairs (u, x) divided into strata of sizes $N_1, \ldots, N_k$

Table 3.9 Empirical coverages (%) of nominal 90% confidence intervals using the ratio estimate for a population average, based on 1000 stratified samples from populations with k strata of size N, from each of which a sample of size $n = N/3$ was taken without replacement. The nominal lower (L), upper (U) and overall (O) coverages are 5, 95 and 90.

	$k = 20, N = 18$			$k = 5, N = 72$			$k = 3, N = 18$		
	L	U	O	L	U	O	L	U	O
Normal	5	93	88	4	94	90	7	93	86
Modified size	6	94	89	4	94	90	6	96	90
Mirror-match	9	92	83	8	90	82	6	94	88
Population	6	95	89	5	95	90	6	95	89
Superpopulation	3	97	95	2	98	96	3	98	96

according to the ordered values of u. The aim was to form 90% confidence intervals for

$$\theta = N^{-1} \sum_{i=1}^{k} \sum_{j=1}^{N_i} x_{ij},$$

where x_{ij} is the value of x for the jth element of stratum i.

We took independent samples (u_{ij}, x_{ij}) of sizes n_i without replacement from the ith stratum, and used these to form the ratio estimate of θ and its estimated variance, given by

$$t = \sum_{i=1}^{k} w_i \bar{u}_i \times t_i, \quad v = \sum_{i=1}^{k} w_i^2 (1 - f_i) \times \frac{1}{n_i(n_i - 1)} \sum_{j=1}^{n_i} (x_{ij} - t_i u_{ij})^2,$$

where

$$t_i = \frac{\sum_{j=1}^{n_i} x_{ij}}{\sum_{j=1}^{n_i} u_{ij}}, \quad \bar{u}_i = \frac{1}{N_i} \sum_{j=1}^{N_i} u_{ij}, \quad w_i = \frac{N_i}{N}, \quad i = 1, \ldots, k;$$

these extend (3.16) to stratified sampling. We used bootstrap resamples with $R = 199$ to compute studentized bootstrap confidence intervals for θ based on 1000 different samples from simulated datasets. Table 3.9 shows the empirical coverages of these confidence intervals in three situations, a "large-k" case with $k = 20$, $N_i \equiv 18$ and $n_i \equiv 6$, a "small-k" case with $k = 5$, $N_i \equiv 72$ and $n_i \equiv 24$, and a "small-k" case with $k = 3$, $N_i \equiv 18$ and $n_i \equiv 6$. The modified sampling method used sampling with replacement, giving samples of size $n' = 7$ when $n = 6$ and size $n' = 34$ when $n = 24$, while the corresponding values of m for the mirror-match method were 3 and 8. Throughout $f_i \equiv \frac{1}{3}$.

In all three cases the coverages for normal, population and modified sample size intervals are close to nominal, while the mirror-match method does poorly. The superpopulation method also does poorly, perhaps because it was applied to separate strata rather than used to construct a new population to be stratified at each replicate. Similar results were obtained for nominal 80% and 95% confidence limits. Overall the population bootstrap and modified sample

size methods do best in this limited comparison, and coverage is not improved
by using the more complicated mirror-match method.   ■

3.8 Hierarchical Data

In some studies the variation in responses may be hierarchical or multi-
level, as happens in repeated-measures experiments and the classical split-plot
experiment. Depending upon the nature of the parameter being estimated, it
may be important to take careful account of the two (or more) sources of
variation when setting up a resampling scheme. In principle there should be
no difficulty with parametric resampling: having fitted the model parameters,
resample data will be generated according to a completely defined model.
Nonparametric resampling is not straightforward: certainly it will not make
sense to use simple nonparametric resampling, which treats all observations as
independent. Here we discuss some of the basic points about nonparametric
resampling in a relatively simple context.

Perhaps the most basic problem involving hierarchical variation can be
formulated as follows. For each of a groups we obtain b responses y_{ij} such
that

$$y_{ij} = x_i + z_{ij}, \quad i = 1, \ldots, a, \ j = 1, \ldots, b, \qquad (3.21)$$

where the x_is are randomly sampled from F_x and independently the z_{ij}s
are randomly sampled from F_z, with $E(Z) = 0$ to force uniqueness of the
model. Thus there is homogeneity of variation in Z between groups, and the
structure is additive. The feature of this model that complicates resampling is
the correlation between observations within a group,

$$\text{var}(Y_{ij}) = \sigma_x^2 + \sigma_z^2, \quad \text{cov}(Y_{ij}, Y_{ik}) = \sigma_x^2, \quad j \neq k. \qquad (3.22)$$

For data having this nested structure, one might be interested in parameters of
F_x or F_z or some combination of both. For example, when testing for presence
of variation in X the usual statistic of interest is the ratio of between-group
and within-group sums of squares.

How should one resample nonparametrically for such a data structure? There
are two simple strategies, for both of which the first stage is to randomly sample
groups with replacement. At the second stage we randomly sample within the
groups selected at the first stage, either without replacement (Strategy 1) or
with replacement (Strategy 2). Note that Strategy 1 keeps selected groups intact.
To see which strategy is likely to work better, we look at the second moments
of resampled data y_{ij}^* to see how well they match (3.22). Consider selecting
$y_{i1}^*, \ldots, y_{ib}^*$. At the first stage we select a random integer I^* from $\{1, 2, \ldots, a\}$.
At the second stage, we select random integers $j_1^*, \ldots, j_b^*$ from $\{1, 2, \ldots, b\}$,
either without replacement (Strategy 1) or with replacement (Strategy 2): the

sampling without replacement is equivalent to keeping the I^*th group intact. Under both strategies

$$E^*(Y_{ij}^* \mid I^* = i^*) = \bar{y}_{i^*},$$

and

$$E^*(Y_{ij}^{*2} \mid I^* = i^*) = \frac{1}{b} \sum_{l=1}^{b} y_{i^*l}^2.$$

However,

$$E^*(Y_{ij}^* Y_{ik}^* \mid I^* = i^*) = \begin{cases} \frac{1}{b(b-1)} \sum_{1 \le l \ne m \le b} y_{i^*l} y_{i^*m}, & \text{Strategy 1}, \\ \frac{1}{b^2} \sum_{l,m=1}^{b} y_{i^*l} y_{i^*m}, & \text{Strategy 2}. \end{cases}$$

Therefore

$$E^*(Y_{ij}^*) = \bar{y}_{..}, \quad \mathrm{var}^*(Y_{ij}^*) = \frac{SS_B}{a} + \frac{SS_W}{ab}, \tag{3.23}$$

and

$$\mathrm{cov}^*(Y_{ij}^*, Y_{ik}^*) = \begin{cases} \frac{SS_B}{a} - \frac{SS_W}{ab(b-1)}, & \text{Strategy 1}, \\ \frac{SS_B}{a}, & \text{Strategy 2}, \end{cases} \tag{3.24}$$

where $\bar{y} = a^{-1} \sum \bar{y}_i$, $SS_B = \sum_{i=1}^{a} (\bar{y}_i - \bar{y}_.)^2$ and $SS_W = \sum_{i=1}^{a} \sum_{j=1}^{b} (y_{ij} - \bar{y}_i)^2$. To see how well the resampling variation mimics (3.22), we calculate expectations of (3.23) and (3.24), using

$$E(SS_B) = (a-1) \left(\sigma_x^2 + \frac{\sigma_z^2}{b} \right), \quad E(SS_W) = a(b-1)\sigma_z^2.$$

This gives

$$E\left\{ \mathrm{var}^*(Y_{ij}^*) \right\} = \frac{a-1}{a} \sigma_x^2 + \frac{ab-1}{ab} \sigma_z^2,$$

and

$$E\left\{ \mathrm{cov}^*(Y_{ij}^*, Y_{ik}^*) \right\} = \begin{cases} \frac{a-1}{a} \sigma_x^2 - \frac{1}{ab} \sigma_z^2, & \text{Strategy 1}, \\ \frac{a-1}{a} \sigma_x^2 + \frac{a-1}{ab} \sigma_z^2, & \text{Strategy 2}. \end{cases}$$

On balance, therefore, Strategy 1 more closely mimics the variation properties of the data, and so is the preferable strategy. Resampling should work well so long as a is moderately large, say at least 10, just as resampling homogeneous data works well if n is moderately large. Of course both strategies would work well if both a and b were very large, but this is rarely the case.

An application of these results is given in Example 6.9.

The preceding discussion would apply to balanced data structures, but not to more complex situations, for which a more general approach is required. A direct, model-based approach would involve resampling from suitable estimates of the two (or more) data distributions, generalizing the resampling from $\hat{F}$ in Chapter 2. Here we outline how this might work for the data structure (3.21).

Estimates of the two CDFs F_x and F_z can be formed by first estimating the xs and zs, and then using their EDFs. A naive version of this, which parallels standard linear model theory, is to define

$$\hat{x}_i = \bar{y}_{i\cdot}, \quad \hat{z}_{ij} = y_{ij} - \bar{y}_{i\cdot}. \tag{3.25}$$

The resulting way to obtain a resampled dataset is to

1   choose $x_1^*, \ldots, x_a^*$ by randomly sampling with replacement from $\hat{x}_1, \ldots, \hat{x}_a$; then

2   choose $z_{11}^*, \ldots, z_{ab}^*$ by randomly sampling ab times with replacement from $\hat{z}_{11}, \ldots, \hat{z}_{ab}$; and finally

3   set $y_{ij}^* = x_i^* + z_{ij}^*$, $\quad i = 1, \ldots, a, \ j = 1, \ldots, b$.

Straightforward calculations (Problem 3.17) show that this approach has the same second-moment properties of Y_{ij}^* as Strategy 2 earlier, shown in (3.23) and (3.24), which are not satisfactory. Somewhat predictably, Strategy 1 is mimicked by choosing $z_{i1}^*, \ldots, z_{ib}^*$ randomly with replacement from one group of residuals $\hat{z}_{k1}, \ldots, \hat{z}_{kb}$ — either a randomly selected group or the group corresponding to x_i^* (Problem 3.17).

What has gone wrong here is that the estimates $\hat{x}_i$ in (3.25) have excess variation, namely $a^{-1} SS_B \doteq \sigma_x^2 + b^{-1}\sigma_z^2$, relative to σ_x^2. The estimates $\hat{z}_{ij}$ defined in (3.25) will be satisfactory provided b is reasonably large, although in principle they should be standardized to

$$\hat{z}_{ij} = \frac{y_{ij} - \bar{y}_{i\cdot}}{(1 - b^{-1})^{1/2}}. \tag{3.26}$$

The excess variation in $\hat{x}_i$ can be corrected by using the shrinkage estimate

$$\hat{x}_i = c\bar{y}_{\cdot\cdot} + (1 - c)\bar{y}_{i\cdot},$$

where c is given by

$$(1 - c)^2 = \frac{a}{a - 1} - \frac{SS_W}{b(b - 1)SS_B},$$

or 1 if the right-hand side is negative. A straightforward calculation shows that this choice for c makes the variance of the $\hat{x}_i$ equal to the components of variance estimator of σ_x^2; see Problem 3.18. Note that the wisdom of matching first and second moments may depend upon θ being a function of such moments.

3.9 Bootstrapping the Bootstrap

3.9.1 Bias correction of bootstrap calculations

As with most statistical methods, the bootstrap does not provide exact answers. For example, the basic confidence interval methods outlined in Section 2.4 do not have coverage exactly equal to the target, or nominal, coverage. Similarly the bias and variance estimates B and V of Section 2.2.1 are typically biased. In many cases the discrepancies involved are not practically important, or there is some specific remedy — as with the improved confidence limit methods of Chapter 5. Nevertheless it is useful to have available a general technique for making a bias correction to a bootstrap calculation. That technique is the bootstrap itself. Here we describe how to apply the bootstrap to improve estimation of the bias of an estimator in the simple situation of a single random sample.

In the notation of Chapter 2, the estimator $T = t(\hat{F})$ has bias

$$\beta = b(F) = \mathrm{E}(T) - \theta = \mathrm{E}\{t(\hat{F}) \mid F\} - t(F).$$

The bootstrap estimate of this bias is

$$B = b(\hat{F}) = \mathrm{E}^*(T^*) - T = \mathrm{E}^*\{t(\hat{F}^*) \mid \hat{F}\} - t(\hat{F}), \qquad (3.27)$$

where $\hat{F}^*$ denotes either the EDF of the bootstrap sample $Y_1^*, \ldots, Y_n^*$ drawn from $\hat{F}$ or the parametric model fitted to that sample. Thus the calculation applies to both parametric and nonparametric situations. There is both random variation and systematic bias in B in general: it is the bias with which we are concerned here.

As with T itself, so with B: the bias can be estimated using the bootstrap. If we write $\gamma = c(F) = \mathrm{E}(B \mid F) - b(F)$, then the simple bootstrap estimate according to the general principle laid out in Chapter 2 is $C = c(\hat{F})$. From the definition of $c(F)$ this implies

$$C = \mathrm{E}^*(B^* \mid \hat{F}) - B,$$

the bootstrap estimate of the bias of B. To see just what C involves, we use the definition of B in (3.27) to obtain

$$C = \mathrm{E}^*[\mathrm{E}^{**}\{t(\hat{F}^{**}) \mid \hat{F}^*\} - t(\hat{F}^*) \mid \hat{F}] - [\mathrm{E}^*\{t(\hat{F}^*) \mid \hat{F}\} - t(\hat{F})]; \qquad (3.28)$$

or more simply, after combining terms,

$$C = \mathrm{E}^*\{\mathrm{E}^{**}(T^{**})\} - 2\mathrm{E}^*(T^* \mid \hat{F}) + T. \qquad (3.29)$$

Here $\hat{F}^{**}$ denotes the EDF of a sample drawn from $\hat{F}^*$, or from the parametric model fitted to that sample; T^{**} is the estimate computed with that sample; and E^{**} denotes expectation over the the distribution of that sample conditional on $\hat{F}^*$. There are two levels of bootstrapping in this procedure, which is therefore called the *nested* or *double bootstrap*. In principle a nested bootstrap might involve more than two levels, but in practice the computational burden would ordinarily be too great for more than two levels to be worthwhile, and we shall assume that a nested bootstrap has just two levels.

The adjusted estimate of the bias of T is

$$B_{adj} = B - C.$$

Since typically bias is of order n^{-1}, the adjustment C is typically of order n^{-2}. The following example gives a simple illustration of the adjustment.

Example 3.18 (Sample variance)   Suppose that $T = n^{-1} \sum (Y_j - \bar{Y})^2$ is used to estimate $\mathrm{var}(Y) = \sigma^2$. Since $\mathrm{E}\{\sum (Y_j - \bar{Y})^2\} = (n-1)\sigma^2$, the bias of T is easily seen to be $\beta = -n^{-1}\sigma^2$, which the bootstrap estimates by $B = -n^{-1}T$. The bias of this bias estimate is $\mathrm{E}(B) - \beta = n^{-2}\sigma^2$, which the bootstrap estimates by $C = n^{-2}T$. Therefore the adjusted bias estimate is

$$B - C = -n^{-1}T - n^{-2}T.$$

That this is an improvement can be checked by showing that it has expectation $\beta(1 + n^{-2})$, whereas B has expectation $\beta(1 + n^{-1})$.   ∎

In most applications bootstrap calculations are approximated by simulation. So, as explained in Chapter 2, for most estimators T we would approximate the bias B by $R^{-1} \sum t_r^* - t$ using the resampled values $t_1^*, \ldots, t_R^*$ and the data value t of the estimator. Likewise the expectations involved in the bias adjustment C will usually be approximated by simulation. The calculation is as follows.

Algorithm 3.3 (Double bootstrap for bias adjustment)

For $r = 1, \ldots, R$,

   1 generate the rth original bootstrap sample $y_1^*, \ldots, y_n^*$ and then t_r^* by
      • sampling at random from $y_1, \ldots, y_n$ (nonparametric case) or
      • sampling parametrically from the fitted model (parametric case);

   2 obtain M second-level bootstrap samples $y_1^{**}, \ldots, y_n^{**}$, either
      • sampling with replacement from $y_1^*, \ldots, y_n^*$ (nonparametric case)
      or
      • sampling from the model fitted to $y_1^*, \ldots, y_n^*$ (parametric case);

   3 evaluate the estimator T for each of the M second-level samples to give $t_{r1}^{**}, \ldots, t_{rM}^{**}$.

Then approximate the bias adjustment C in (3.29) by

$$C = \frac{1}{RM} \sum_{r=1}^{R} \sum_{m=1}^{M} t_{rm}^{**} - \frac{2}{R} \sum_{r=1}^{R} t_r^* + t. \qquad (3.30)$$

                                                                        •

At first sight it would seem that to apply (3.30) successfully would involve a vast amount of computation. If a general rule is to use at least 100 samples when bootstrapping, this would imply a total of $RM + R = 10\,100$ simulated samples and evaluations of t. But this is unnecessary, because of theoretical and computational techniques that can be used, as explained in Chapter 9. For the case of the bias B discussed here, the simulation variance of $B - C$ would be no greater than it was for B if we used $M = 1$ and increased R by a factor of about 5, so that a total of about 500 samples would seem reasonable; see Problem 3.19.

More complicated applications of the technique are discussed in Example 3.26 and in Chapters 4 and 5.

Theory

It may be intuitively clear that bootstrapping the bootstrap will reduce the order of bias in the original bootstrap calculation, at least in simple situations such as Example 3.18. However, in some situations the order of the reduction may not be clear. Here we outline a general calculation which provides the answer, so long as the quantity being estimated by the bootstrap can be expressed in terms of an estimating equation. For simplicity we focus on the single-sample case, but the calculations extend quite easily.

Suppose that the quantity $\beta = b(F)$ being estimated by the bootstrap is defined by the estimating equation

$$E\{h(\hat{F}, F; \beta) \mid F\} = 0, \tag{3.31}$$

where $h(G, F; \beta)$ is chosen to be of order one. The bootstrap solution is $\hat{\beta} = b(\hat{F})$, which therefore solves

$$E^*\{h(\hat{F}^*, \hat{F}; \hat{\beta}) \mid \hat{F}\} = 0.$$

In general $\hat{\beta}$ has a bias of order n^{-a}, say, where typically a is $\frac{1}{2}$, 1 or $\frac{3}{2}$. Therefore, for some $e(F)$ that is of order one, we can write

$$E\{h(\hat{F}, F; \hat{\beta}) \mid F\} \doteq e(F)n^{-a}. \tag{3.32}$$

To correct for this bias we introduce the ideal perturbation $\gamma = c_n(F)$ which modifies $b(\hat{F})$ to $b(\hat{F}, \gamma)$ in order to achieve

$$E[h\{\hat{F}, F; b(\hat{F}, \gamma)\} \mid F] = 0. \tag{3.33}$$

There is usually more than one way to define $b(\hat{F}, \gamma)$, but we shall assume that γ is defined to make $b(\hat{F}, 0) \equiv b(\hat{F})$. The bootstrap estimate for γ is $\hat{\gamma} = c_n(\hat{F})$, which is the solution to

$$E^*[h\{\hat{F}^*, \hat{F}; b(\hat{F}^*, \gamma)\} \mid \hat{F}] = 0,$$

and the adjusted value of $\hat{\beta}$ is then $\hat{\beta}_{adj} = b(\hat{F}, \hat{\gamma})$; it is $b(\hat{F}^*, \gamma)$ that requires the second level of resampling.

What we want to see is the effect of substituting $\hat{\beta}_{adj}$ for $\hat{\beta}$ in (3.32). First we approximate the solution to (3.33). Taylor expansion about $\gamma = 0$, together with (3.32), gives

$$E[h\{\hat{F}, F; b(\hat{F}, \gamma)\} \mid F] \doteq e(F)n^{-a} + d_n(F)\gamma, \qquad (3.34)$$

where

$$d_n(F) = \frac{\partial}{\partial \gamma} E[h\{\hat{F}, F; b(\hat{F}, \gamma)\} \mid F]\bigg|_{\gamma=0}.$$

Typically $d_n(F) \doteq d(F) \neq 0$, so that if we write $r(F) = e(F)/d(F)$ then (3.33) and (3.34) together imply that

$$\gamma = c_n(F) \doteq -r(F)n^{-a}.$$

This, together with the corresponding approximation for $\hat{\gamma} = c_n(\hat{F})$, gives

$$\hat{\gamma} - \gamma \doteq -n^{-a}\{r(\hat{F}) - r(F)\} = -n^{-a-1/2}X_n,$$

say. The quantity

$$X_n = n^{1/2}\{r(\hat{F}) - r(F)\}$$

is $O_p(1)$ because $\hat{F}$ and F differ by $O_p(n^{-1/2})$. It follows that, because $\gamma = O(n^{-a})$,

$$h\{\hat{F}, F; b(\hat{F}, \hat{\gamma})\} \doteq h\{\hat{F}, F; b(\hat{F}, \gamma)\} - n^{-a-1/2}X_n \frac{\partial}{\partial \gamma} h\{\hat{F}, F; b(\hat{F}, \gamma)\}\bigg|_{\gamma=0}. \qquad (3.35)$$

We can now assess the effect of the adjustment from $\hat{\beta}$ to $\hat{\beta}_{adj}$. Define the conditional quantity

$$k_n(X_n) = \frac{\partial}{\partial \gamma} E[h\{\hat{F}, F; b(\hat{F}, \gamma)\} \mid X_n, F]\bigg|_{\gamma=0},$$

which is $O_p(1)$. Then taking expectations in (3.35) we deduce that, because of (3.34),

$$E[h\{\hat{F}, F; b(\hat{F}, \hat{\gamma})\} \mid F] \doteq -n^{-a-1/2}E\{X_n k_n(X_n) \mid F\}. \qquad (3.36)$$

In most applications $E\{X_n k_n(X_n) \mid F\} = O(n^{-b})$ for $b = 0$ or $\frac{1}{2}$, so comparing (3.36) with (3.32) we see that the adjustment does reduce the order of bias by at least $\frac{1}{2}$.

Note that if the next term in expansion (3.34) were $O(n^{-a-c})$, then the right-hand side of (3.35) would strictly be $O(n^{-a-b-1/2}) + O(n^{-2a-1/2}) + O(n^{-a-c-1/2})$. In almost all cases this will lead to the same conclusion.

Example 3.19 (Adjusted bias estimate)   In the case of the bias $\beta = E(T \mid F) - \theta$, we take $h(\hat{F}, F; \beta) = t(\hat{F}) - t(F) - \beta$ and $b(F, \gamma) = b(F) - \gamma$. In regular problems the bias and its estimate are of order n^{-1}, and in (3.32) $a = 2$. It is easy to check that $d_n(F) = 1$, so that $X_n = n^{1/2}\{e(\hat{F}) - e(F)\}$ and

$$k_n(X_n) = \frac{d}{d\gamma} E\{t(\hat{F}) - t(F) - (\beta - \gamma) \mid e(\hat{F}), F\}\bigg|_{\gamma=0} = 1.$$

This implies that

$$\mathrm{E}\{X_n k_n(X_n) \mid F\} = n^{1/2}\mathrm{E}\{e(\hat{F}) - e(F) \mid F\} = O(n^{-1/2}).$$

Equation (3.36) then becomes $\mathrm{E}\{T - \theta - (\hat{\beta} - \hat{\gamma})\} = O(n^{-3})$. This generalizes the conclusion of Example 3.18, that the adjusted bootstrap bias estimate $\hat{\beta} - \hat{\gamma}$ is correct to second order. ∎

Further applications of the double bootstrap to significance tests and confidence limits are described in Sections 4.5 and 5.6 respectively.

3.9.2 Variation of properties of *T*

A somewhat different application of bootstrapping the bootstrap concerns assessment of how the distribution of *T* depends on the parameters of *F*. Suppose, for example, that we want to know how the variance of *T* depends upon θ and other unknown model parameters, but that this variance cannot be calculated theoretically. One possible application is to the search for a variance-stabilizing transformation.

The parametric case does not require nested bootstrap calculations. However, it is useful to outline the approach in a form that can be mimicked in the nonparametric case. The basic idea is to approximate $\mathrm{var}(T \mid \psi) = v(\psi)$ from simulated samples for an appropriately broad range of parameter values. Thus we would select a set of parameter values $\psi_1, \ldots, \psi_K$, for each of which we would simulate *R* samples from the corresponding parametric model, and compute the corresponding *R* values of *T*. This would give $t^*_{k1}, \ldots, t^*_{kR}$, say, for the model with parameter value ψ_k. Then the variance $v(\psi_k) = \mathrm{var}(T \mid \psi_k)$ would be approximated by

$$v(\psi_k) = R^{-1} \sum_{r=1}^{R} (t^*_{kr} - \bar{t}^*_k)^2, \tag{3.37}$$

where $\bar{t}^*_k = R^{-1} \sum_{r=1}^{R} t^*_{kr}$. Plots of $v(\psi_k)$ against components of ψ_k can then be used to see how $\mathrm{var}(T)$ depends on ψ. Example 2.13 shows an application of this. The same simulation results can also be used to approximate other properties, such as the bias or quantiles of *T*, or the variance of transformed *T*.

As described here the number of simulated datasets will be *RK*, but in fact this number can be reduced considerably, as we shall show in Section 9.4.4. The simulation can be bypassed completely if we estimate $v(\psi_k)$ by a delta-method variance approximation $v_L(\psi_k)$, based on the variance of the influence function under the parametric model. However, this will often be impossible.

In the nonparametric case there appears to be a major obstacle to performing calculations analogous to (3.37), namely the unavailability of models corresponding to a series of parameter values $\psi_1, \ldots, \psi_K$. But this obstacle can be overcome, at least partially. Suppose for simplicity that we have a single-sample problem, so that the EDF $\hat{F}$ is the fitted model, and imagine that we have drawn R independent bootstrap samples from this model. These bootstrap samples can be represented by their EDFs $\hat{F}_r^*$, which can be thought of as the analogues of parametric models defined by R different values of parameter ψ. Indeed the corresponding values of $\theta = t(F)$ are simply $t(\hat{F}_r^*) = t_r^*$, and other components of ψ can be defined similarly using the representation $\psi = p(F)$. This gives us the same framework as in the parametric case above. For example consider variance estimation. To approximate var(T) under parameter value $\psi_r^* = p(\hat{F}_r^*)$, we simulate M samples from the corresponding model $\hat{F}_r^*$; calculate the corresponding values of T, which we denote by $t_{rm}^{**}, m = 1, \ldots, M$; and then calculate the analogue of (3.37),

$$v_r^* = v(\psi_r^*) = M^{-1} \sum_{m=1}^{M} (t_{rm}^{**} - \bar{t}_r^{**})^2, \qquad (3.38)$$

with $\bar{t}_r^{**} = M^{-1} \sum_{m=1}^{M} t_{rm}^{**}$. The scatter plot of v_r^* against t_r^* will then be a proxy for the ideal plot of var($T \mid \psi$) against θ, and similarly for other plots.

Example 3.20 (City population data)   Figure 3.7 shows the results of the double bootstrap procedure outlined above, for the ratio estimator applied to the data in Table 2.1, with $n = 10$. The left panel shows the bias b_r^* estimated using $M = 50$ second-level bootstrap samples from each of $R = 999$ first-level bootstrap samples. The right panel shows the corresponding standard errors $v_r^{*1/2}$. The lines from applying a locally weighted robust smoother confirm the clear increase with the ratio in each panel.

The implication of Figure 3.7 is that the bias and variance of the ratio are not stable with $n = 10$. Confidence intervals for the true ratio θ based on normal approximations to the distribution of $T - \theta$ will therefore be poor, as will basic bootstrap confidence intervals, and those based on related quantities such as the studentized bootstrap are suspect. A reasonable interpretation of the right panel is that var(T) $\propto \theta^2$, so that log T should be more stable.   ∎

The particular application of variance estimation can be handled in a simpler way, at least approximately. If the nonparametric delta method variance approximation v_L (Sections 2.7.2 and 3.2.1) is fairly accurate, which is to say if the linear approximation (2.35) or (3.1) is accurate, then $v_r^* = v(\psi_r^*)$ can be estimated by $v_{Lr}^* = v_L(\hat{F}_r^*)$.

Example 3.21 (Transformed correlation)   An example where simple bootstrap methods tend to perform badly without the (explicit or implicit) use of transformation is the correlation coefficient. For a sample of size $n = 20$ from a bivariate normal distribution, with sample correlation $t = 0.74$, the left panel

Figure 3.7 Bias and standard error estimates for ratio applied to city population data, $n = 10$. For each of $R = 999$ bootstrap samples from the data, $M = 50$ second-level samples were drawn, and the resulting bias and standard error estimates b^* and $v^{*1/2}$ plotted against the bootstrapped ratio t^*. The lines are from a robust nonparametric curve fit to the simulations.

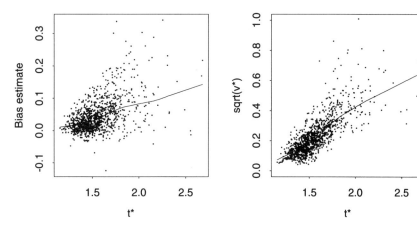

Figure 3.8 Scatter plot of v_L^* versus t^* for nonparametric simulation from a bivariate normal sample of size $n = 20$ with $R = 999$. The left panel is for t the sample correlation, with dotted line showing the theoretical relationship. The right panel is for transformed sample correlation.

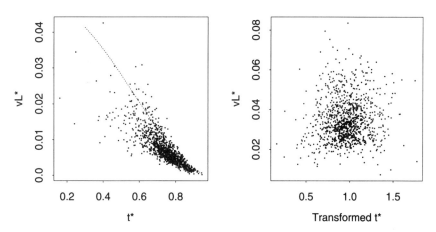

of Figure 3.8 contains a scatter plot of v_L^* versus t^* from $R = 999$ nonparametric simulations: the dotted line is the approximate normal-theory relationship $\mathrm{var}(T) \doteq n^{-1}(1 - \theta^2)^2$. The plot correctly shows strong instability of variance. The right panel shows the corresponding plot for bootstrapping the transformed estimate $\frac{1}{2}\log\{(1 + t)/(1 - t)\}$, whose variance is approximately n^{-1}: here v_L is computed as in Example 2.18. The plot correctly suggests quite stable variance. ∎

As presented here the selection of parameter values ψ_r^* is completely random, and R would need to be moderately large (at least 50) to get a reasonable spread of values of ψ_r^*. The total number of samples, $RM + R$, will then be very large. It is, however, possible to improve upon the algorithm; see Section 9.4.4. Another important problem is the roughness of variance estimates, apparent in both of the preceding examples. This is due not just to the size of M, but also to the noise in the EDFs $\hat{F}_r^*$ being used as models.

Frequency smoothing

One major difference between the parametric and nonparametric cases is that the parametric models vary smoothly with parameter values. A simple way to inject such smoothness into the nonparametric "models" $\hat{F}_r^*$ is to smooth them. For simplicity we consider the one-sample case.

Let $w(\cdot)$ be a symmetric density with mean zero and unit variance, and consider the smoothed frequencies

$$f_j^*(\theta, \varepsilon) \propto \frac{1}{R\varepsilon} \sum_{r=1}^{R} w\left(\frac{\theta - t_r^*}{\varepsilon}\right) f_{rj}^*, \quad j = 1, \dots, n. \tag{3.39}$$

Here $\varepsilon > 0$ is a smoothing parameter that determines the effective range of values of t^* over which the frequencies are smoothed. As is common with kernel smoothing, the value of ε is more important than the choice of $w(\cdot)$, which we take to be the standard normal density. Numerical experimentation suggests that close to $\theta = t$, values of ε in the range $0.2v^{1/2} - 1.0v^{1/2}$ are suitable, where v is an estimated variance for t. We choose the constant of proportionality in (3.39) to ensure that $\sum_j f_j^*(\theta, \varepsilon) = n$. For a given ε, the relative frequencies $n^{-1} f_j^*(\theta, \varepsilon)$ determine a distribution $\hat{F}_\theta^*$, for which the parameter value is $\theta^* = t(\hat{F}_\theta^*)$; in general θ^* is not equal to θ, although it is usually very close.

Example 3.22 (City population data) In continuation of Example 3.20, the top panels of Figure 3.9 show the frequencies f_j^* for four samples with values of t^* very close to 1.6. The variation in the f_j^* leads to the variability in both b^* and v^* that shows so clearly in Figure 3.7.

The lower panels show the smoothed frequencies (3.39) for distributions $\hat{F}_\theta^*$ with $\theta = 1.2, 1.52, 1.6, 1.9$ and $\varepsilon = 0.2v^{1/2}$. The corresponding values of the ratio are $\theta^* = 1.23, 1.51, 1.59$, and 1.89. The observations with the smallest empirical influence values are more heavily weighted when θ is less than the original value of the statistic, $t = 1.52$, and conversely. The third panel, for $\theta = 1.6$, results from averaging frequencies including those shown in the upper panels, and the distribution is much smoother than those. The results are not very sensitive to the value of ε, although the tilting of the frequencies is less marked for larger ε.

The smoothed frequencies can be used to assess how the bias and variance

Figure 3.9 Frequencies for city population data. The upper panels show frequencies f_j^* for four samples with values of t^* close to 1.6, plotted against empirical influence values l_j for the ratio. The lower panels show smoothed frequencies $f_j^*(\theta, \varepsilon)$ for distributions $\hat{F}_\theta^*$ with $\theta = 1.2, 1.52, 1.6, 1.9$ and $\varepsilon = 0.2v^{1/2}$.

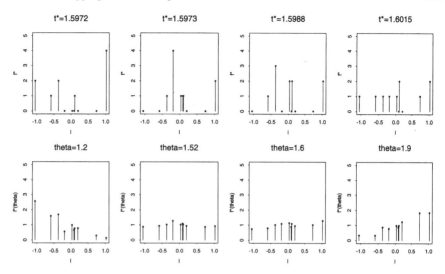

of T depend on θ. For each of a range of values of θ, we generate samples from the multinomial distribution $\hat{F}_\theta^*$ with expected frequencies (3.39), and calculate the corresponding values of t^*, $t_r^*(\theta)$, say. We then estimate the bias for sampling from $\hat{F}_\theta^*$ by $\bar{t}^*(\theta) - \theta^*$, where $\bar{t}^*(\theta)$ is the average of the $t_r^*(\theta)$. The variance is estimated similarly.

The top panel of Figure 3.10 shows values of $t_r^*(\theta)$ plotted against jittered values of θ for 100 samples generated from $\hat{F}_\theta^*$ at $\theta = 1.2, \ldots, 1.9$; we took $\varepsilon = 0.2$. The lower panels show that the corresponding biases and standard deviations, which are connected by the rougher solid lines, compare well with the double bootstrap results. The amount of computation is much less, however. The smoothed estimates are based on 1000 samples to estimate the $\hat{F}_\theta^*$, and then 100 samples at each of the eight chosen values of θ, whereas the double bootstrap required about 25 000 samples.   ■

Other applications of (3.39) are described in Chapters 9 and 10.

Variance stabilization

Experience suggests that bootstrap methods for confidence limits and significance tests based on estimators T are most effective when θ is essentially a location parameter, which is approximately induced by a variance-stabilizing transformation. Ideally such a transformation would be derived theoretically from (2.14) with variance function $v(\theta) = \text{var}(T \mid F)$.

In a nonparametric setting a suitable transformation may sometimes be suggested by analogy with a parametric problem, as in Example 3.21. If not, a transformation can be obtained empirically using the double bootstrap estimates of variance discussed earlier in the section. Suppose that we have bootstrap samples $\hat{F}_r^* \equiv (y_{r1}^*, \ldots, y_{rn}^*)$ and the corresponding statistics t_r^*, for

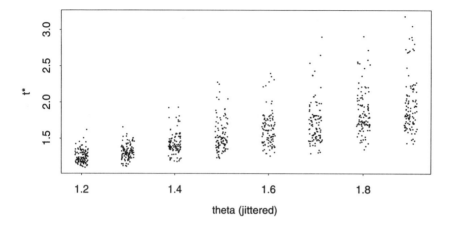

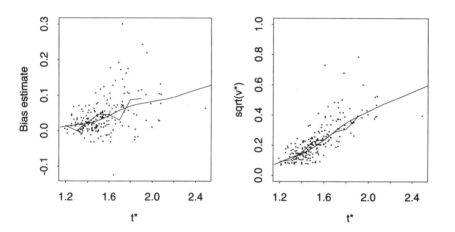

Figure 3.10 Use of smoothed nonparametric distributions to estimate bias and standard deviation functions for the ratio of the city population data. The top panel shows 100 bootstrapped ratios calculated from samples generated from $\hat{F}_{\theta}^{*}$, for each of $\theta = 1.2,\ldots,1.9$; for clarity the θ values are jittered. The lower panels show 200 of the points from Figure 3.7 and the estimated bias and standard deviation functions from that figure (smooth curves), with the biases and standard deviations estimated from the top panel (rougher curves).

$r = 1,\ldots,R$. Without loss of generality, suppose that $t_1^* \leq \cdots \leq t_R^*$. One way to implement empirical variance-stabilization is to choose R_1 of the t_r^* that are roughly evenly-spaced and that include t_1^* and t_R^*. For each of the corresponding $\hat{F}_r^*$ we then generate M bootstrap values t_{rm}^{**}, from which we estimate the variance of t_r^* to be v_r^* as defined in (3.38). We now smooth a plot of the v_r^* against the t_r^*, giving an estimate $\hat{v}(\theta)$ of the variance $\mathrm{var}(T \mid F)$ as a function of the parameter $\theta = t(F)$, and integrate numerically to obtain the estimated variance-stabilizing transformation

$$\hat{h}(t) = \int^{t} \frac{d\theta}{\{\hat{v}(\theta)\}^{1/2}}. \tag{3.40}$$

In general, but especially for small R_1, it will be better to fit a smooth curve to values of $\log v_r^*$, in part to avoid negative estimates $\hat{v}(\theta)$. Provided that a suitable smoothing method is used, inclusion of t_1^* and t_R^* in the set for which the v_r^* are estimated implies that all the transformed values $\hat{h}(t_r^*)$ can be calculated. The transformed estimator $\hat{h}(T)$ should have approximately unit variance.

Any of the common smoothers can be used to obtain $\hat{v}(\theta)$, and simple integration algorithms can be used for the integral (3.40). If the nested bootstrap is used only to obtain the variances of R_1 of the t_r^*, the total number of bootstrap samples required is $R + MR_1$. Values of R_1 and M in the ranges 50–100 and 25–50 will usually be adequate, so if $R = 1000$ the overall number of bootstrap samples required will be 2250–6000. If variance estimates for all the t_r^* are available, for example nonparametric delta method estimates, then the delta method shows that approximate standard errors for the $\hat{h}(t_r^*)$ will be $v_r^{*1/2}/\hat{v}(t_r^*)^{1/2}$; a plot of these against t_r^* will provide a check on the adequacy of the transformation.

The same procedure can be applied with second-level resampling done from smoothed frequencies, as in Example 3.22.

Example 3.23 (City population data) For the city population data of Example 2.8 the parameter of interest is the ratio θ, which is estimated by $t = \bar{x}/\bar{u}$. Figure 3.7 shows that the variance of T depends strongly on θ. We used the procedure outlined above to estimate a transformation based on $R = 999$ bootstrap samples, with $R_1 = 50$ and $M = 25$. The transformation is shown in the left panel of Figure 3.11: the right panel shows the standard errors $v_{Lr}^{*1/2}/\hat{v}(t_r^*)^{1/2}$ of the $\hat{h}(t_r^*)$. The transformation has been largely successful in stabilizing the variance.

In this case the variances v_{Lr}^* based on the linear approximation are readily calculated, and the transformation could have been estimated from them rather than from the nested bootstrap. ∎

3.10 Bootstrap Diagnostics

3.10.1 Jackknife-after-bootstrap

Sensitivity analysis is important in understanding the implications of a statistical calculation. A conclusion that depended heavily on just a few observations would usually be regarded as more tentative than one supported by all the data. When a parametric model is fitted, difficulties can be detected by a wide range of diagnostics, careful scrutiny of which is part of a parametric bootstrap analysis, as of any parametric modelling. But if a nonparametric bootstrap is used, the EDF $\hat{F}$ is in effect the model, and there is no baseline against which

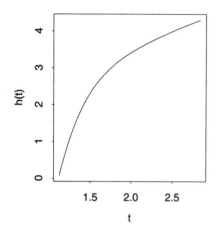
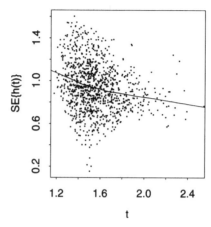

Figure 3.11
Variance-stabilization
for the city population
ratio. The left panel
shows the empirical
transformation $\hat{h}(\cdot)$, and
the right panel shows
the standard errors
$v_{Lr}^{*1/2}/\{\hat{v}(t_r^*)\}^{1/2}$ of the
$\hat{h}(t_r^*)$, with a smooth
curve.

to compare outliers, for example. In this situation we must focus on the effect
of individual observations on bootstrap calculations, to answer questions such
as "would the confidence interval differ greatly if this point were removed?",
or "what happens to the significance level when this observation is deleted?"

Nonparametric case

Once a nonparametric resampling calculation has been performed, a basic
question is how it would have been different if an observation, y_j, say, had
been absent from the original data. For example, it might be wise to check
whether or not a suspicious case has affected the quantiles used in a confidence
interval calculation. The obvious way to assess this is to do a further simulation
from the remaining observations, but this can be avoided. This is because a
resample in which y_j does not appear can be thought of as a random sample
from the data with y_j excluded. Expressed formally, if J^* is sampled uniformly
from $\{1,\ldots,n\}$, then the conditional distribution of J^* given that $J^* \neq j$
is the same as the distribution of I^*, where I^* is sampled uniformly from
$\{1,\ldots,j-1,j+1,\ldots,n\}$. The probability that y_j is not included in a bootstrap
sample is $(1 - n^{-1})^n \doteq e^{-1}$, so the number of simulations R_{-j} that do not
include y_j is roughly equal to $Re^{-1} \doteq 0.368R$.

So we can measure the effect of y_j on the calculations by comparing the full
simulation with the subset of $t_1^*,\ldots,t_R^*$ obtained from bootstrap samples where
y_j does not occur. In terms of the frequencies f_{rj}^* which count the number of
times y_j appears in the rth simulation, we simply restrict attention to replicates
with $f_{rj}^* = 0$. For example, the effect of y_j on the bias estimate B can be

	First son		Second son			First son		Second son	
	Len	Brea	Len	Brea		Len	Brea	Len	Brea
1	191	155	179	145	14	190	159	195	157
2	195	149	201	152	15	188	151	187	158
3	181	148	185	149	16	163	137	161	130
4	183	153	188	149	17	195	155	183	158
5	176	144	171	142	18	186	153	173	148
6	208	157	192	152	19	181	145	182	146
7	189	150	190	149	20	175	140	165	137
8	197	159	189	152	21	192	154	185	152
9	188	152	197	159	22	174	143	178	147
10	192	150	187	151	23	176	139	176	143
11	179	158	186	148	24	197	167	200	158
12	183	147	174	147	25	190	163	187	150
13	174	150	185	152					

measured by the scaled difference

$$n(B_{-j} - B) = n \left\{ \frac{1}{R_{-j}} \sum_{r:f_{rj}^* = 0} (t_r^* - t_{-j}) - \frac{1}{R} \sum_r (t_r^* - t) \right\}, \qquad (3.41)$$

where B_{-j} is the bias estimate from the resamples in which y_j does not appear, and t_{-j} is the value of t when y_j is excluded from the original data. Such calculations are applications of the jackknife method described in Section 2.7.3, so the technique applied to bootstrap results is called the *jackknife-after-bootstrap*. The scaling factor n in (3.41) is not essential.

A useful diagnostic is the plot of jackknife-after-bootstrap measures such as (3.41) against empirical influence values, possibly standardized. For this purpose any of the approximations to empirical influence values described in Section 2.7 can be used. The next example illustrates a related plot that shows how the distribution of $t^* - t$ changes when each observation is excluded.

Example 3.24 (Frets' heads)   Table 3.10 contains data on the head breadth and length of the first two adult sons in 25 families.

The correlations among the log measurements are given below the diagonal in Table 3.11. The values above the diagonal are the partial correlations. For example, the value 0.13 in the second row is the correlation between the log head breadth of the first son, b_1, and the log head length of the second son, l_2, after allowing for the other variables. In effect, this is the correlation between the residuals from separate regressions of b_1 and l_2 on the other two variables. The correlations are all large, but four of the partial correlations are small, which suggests the simple interpretation that each of the four pairs of measurements for first and second sons is independent conditionally on the values of the other two measurements.

116   3 · *Further Ideas*

| | | First son | | Second son | |
		Length	Breadth	Length	Breadth
First son	Length		0.43	0.21	0.17
	Breadth	0.75		0.13	0.22
Second son	Length	0.72	0.70		0.64
	Breadth	0.72	0.72	0.85	

Table 3.11 Correlations (below diagonal) and partial correlations (above diagonal) for log measurements on the head breadth and length of the first two adult sons in 25 families.

We focus on the partial correlation $t = 0.13$ between $\log b_1$ and $\log l_2$. The top panel of Figure 3.12 shows a jackknife-after-bootstrap plot for t, based on 999 bootstrap samples. The points at the left-hand end show the empirical 0.05, 0.1, 0.16, 0.5, 0.84, 0.9, and 0.95 quantiles of the values of $t_r^* - \bar{t}_{-2}^*$ for the 368 bootstrap samples in which case 2 was not selected; $\bar{t}_{-2}^*$ is the average of t_r^* for those samples. The dotted lines are the corresponding quantiles for all 999 values of $t^* - t$. The distribution is clearly much more peaked when case 2 is left out. The panel also contains the corresponding quantiles when other cases are excluded. The horizontal axis shows the empirical influence values for t: clearly putting more weight on case 2 sharply decreases the value of t.

The lower left panel of the figure shows that case 2 lies somewhat away from the rest, and the plot of residuals for the regressions of $\log b_1$ and $\log l_2$ on $(\log b_2, \log l_1)$ in the lower right panel accounts for the jackknife-after-bootstrap results. Case 2 seems outlying relative to the others: deleting it will clearly increase t substantially. The overall average and standard deviation of the t_r^* are 0.14 and 0.23, changing to 0.34 and 0.17 when case 2 is excluded. The evidence against zero partial correlation depends heavily on case 2. ■

Another version of the diagnostic plot uses case-deletion averages of the t_r^*, i.e. $\bar{t}_{-j}^* = R_{-j}^{-1} \sum_{r:f_{rj}^*=0} t_r^*$, instead of the empirical influence values. This more clearly reveals how the quantity of interest varies with parameter values.

Parametric case

In the parametric case different calculations are needed, because random samples from a case-deletion model are not simply an unweighted subset of the original bootstrap samples. Nevertheless, those original bootstrap samples can still be used if we make use of the following identity relating expectations under two different parameter values:

$$E\{h(Y) \mid \psi'\} = E\left\{h(Y)\frac{f(Y \mid \psi')}{f(Y \mid \psi)} \,\Big|\, \psi\right\}. \tag{3.42}$$

Suppose that the full-data estimate (e.g. maximum likelihood estimate) of the model parameter is $\hat{\psi}$, and that when case j is deleted the corresponding estimate is $\hat{\psi}_{-j}$. The idea is to use (3.42) with $\hat{\psi}$ and $\hat{\psi}_{-j}$ in place of ψ and ψ'

Figure 3.12 Jackknife-after-bootstrap analysis for the partial correlation between $\log b_1$ and $\log l_2$ for Frets' heads data. The top panel shows 0.05, 0.1, 0.16, 0.5, 0.84, 0.9 and 0.95 empirical quantiles of $t_r^* - \bar{t}_{-j}^*$ when each of the cases is dropped from the bootstrap calculation in turn. The lower panels show scatter plots of the raw values of $\log b_1$ and $\log l_2$, and of their residuals when regressed on the other two variables.

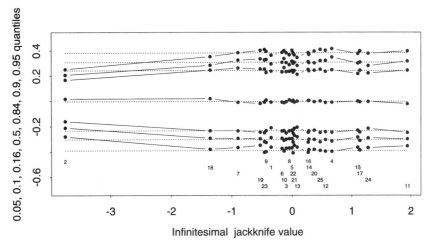

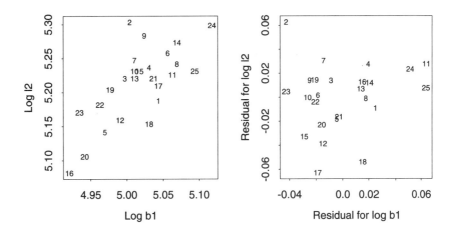

respectively. For example,

$$E^*(T^* \mid \hat{\psi}_{-j}) = E^* \left\{ T^* \frac{f(Y^* \mid \hat{\psi}_{-j})}{f(Y^* \mid \hat{\psi})} \,\Big|\, \hat{\psi} \right\}.$$

Therefore the parametric analogue of (3.41) is

$$n(B_{-j} - B) = n \left\{ \frac{1}{R} \sum_{r=1}^{R} (t_r^* - t_{-j}^*) \frac{f(y_r^* \mid \hat{\psi}_{-j})}{f(y_r^* \mid \hat{\psi})} - \frac{1}{R} \sum_{r=1}^{R} (t_r^* - t) \right\},$$

where the samples y_r^* are drawn from the full-data fitted model, that is with parameter value $\hat{\psi}$. Similar weighted calculations apply to other features of the distribution of $T^* - t$; see Problem 3.20. Other applications of the *importance reweighting* identity (3.42) will be discussed in Chapter 9.

3.10.2 Linearity

Statistical analysis is simplified when the statistic of interest T is close to linear. In this case the variance approximation v_L will be an accurate estimate of the bootstrap variance $\mathrm{var}(T \mid \hat{F})$, and saddlepoint methods (Section 9.5) can be applied to obtain accurate estimates of the distribution of t^*, without recourse to simulation. A linear statistic is not necessarily close to normally distributed, as Example 2.3 illustrates. Nor does linearity guarantee that T is directly related to a pivot and therefore useful in finding confidence intervals. On the other hand, experience from other areas in statistics suggests that these three properties will often occur together.

This suggests that we aim to find a transformation $h(\cdot)$ such that $h(T)$ is well described by the linear approximation that corresponds to (2.35) or (3.1). For simplicity we focus on the single-sample case here. The shape of $h(\cdot)$ would be revealed by a plot of $h(t)$ against t, but of course this is not available because $h(\cdot)$ is unknown. However, using Taylor approximation and (2.44) we do have

$$ h(t^*) \doteq h(t_L^*) \doteq h(t) + \dot{h}(t)\frac{1}{n}\sum_{j=1}^{n} f_j^* l_j = h(t) + \dot{h}(t)(t_L^* - t), \qquad \text{\small $\dot{h}(t)$ is $dh(t)/dt$.} $$

which shows that $t_L^* \doteq c + d h(t^*)$ with appropriate definitions of constants c and d. Therefore a plot of the values of $t_L^* = t + n^{-1}\sum f_j^* l_j$ against the t^* will look roughly like $h(\cdot)$, apart from a location and scale shift. We can now estimate $h(\cdot)$ from this plot, either by fitting a particular parametric form, or by nonparametric curve estimation.

Example 3.25 (City population data) The top left panel of Figure 3.13 shows t_L^* plotted against t^* for 499 bootstrap replicates of the ratio $t = \bar{x}/\bar{u}$ for the data in Table 2.1. The plot is highly nonlinear, and the logarithmic transformation, or one even more extreme, seems appropriate. Note that the plot has shape similar to that for the empirical variance-stabilizing transformation in Figure 3.11.

For a parametric transformation, we try a Box–Cox transformation, $h(t) = (t^\lambda - 1)/\lambda$, with the value of λ estimated by maximizing the log likelihood for the regression of the $h(t_r^*)$ on the t_{Lr}^*. This strongly suggests that we use $\lambda = -2$, for which the fitted curve is shown as the solid line on the plot. This is close to the result for a smoothing spline, shown as the dotted line. The top right panel shows the linear approximation for $h(t^*)$, i.e. $h(t) + \dot{h}(t)n^{-1}\sum_{j=1}^{n} f_j^* l_j$, plotted against $h(t^*)$. This plot is close to the line with unit gradient, and confirms the results of the analysis of transformations.

Figure 3.13 Linearity
transformation for the
ratio applied to the city
population data. The
top left panel shows
linear approximations t_L^*
plotted against
bootstrap replicates t^*,
with the estimated
parametric
transformation (solid)
and a transformation
estimated by a
smoothing spline (dots).
The top right panel
shows the same plot on
the transformed scale.
The lower left panel
shows the plot for the
studentized bootstrap
statistic. The lower right
panel shows a normal
Q-Q plot of the
studentized bootstrap
statistic for the
transformed values $h(t^*)$.

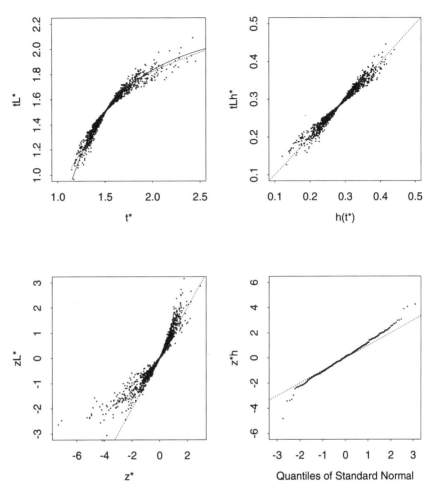

The lower panels show related plots for the studentized bootstrap statistics
on the original scale and on the new scale,

$$z^* = \frac{t^* - t}{v_L^{*1/2}}, \quad z_h^* = \frac{h(t^*) - h(t)}{\dot{h}(t)v_L^{*1/2}},$$

where $v_L^* = n^{-2}\sum f_j^* l_j^2$. The left panel shows that, like t^*, z^* is far from
linear. The lower right panel shows that the distribution of z_h^* is fairly close
to standard normal, though there are some outlying values. The distribution
of z^* is far from normal, as shown by the right panel of Figure 2.5. It
seems that, here, the transformation that gives approximate linearity of t^* also

makes the corresponding studentized bootstrap statistic roughly normal. The transformation based on the smoothing spline would give similar results. ∎

3.11 Choice of Estimator from the Data

In some applications we may want to choose an estimator or other procedure after looking at the data, especially if there is considerable prior uncertainty about the nature of random variation or of the form of relationship among variables. The simplest example with homogeneous data involves the choice of estimator for a population mean μ, when empirical evidence suggests that the underlying distribution F has long, non-normal tails.

Suppose that $T(1),\ldots,T(K)$ can all be considered potentially suitable estimators for μ, and for the moment assume that all are unbiased, which means that the underlying data distribution is symmetric. Then one natural criterion for choice among these estimators is variance or, since their exact variances will be unknown, estimated variance. So if the estimated variance of $T(i)$ is $V(i)$, a natural procedure is to select as estimate for a given dataset that $t(i)$ whose estimated variance is smallest. This defines the adaptive estimator T by

$$T = T(i) \quad \text{if} \quad V(i) = \min_{1 \le k \le K} V(k).$$

For most simple estimators we can use the nonparametric delta method variance estimates. But in general, and for more complicated problems, we use the bootstrap to implement this procedure. Thus we generate R bootstrap samples, compute the estimates $t_r^*(1),\ldots,t_r^*(K)$ for each sample, and then choose t to be that $t(i)$ for which the bootstrap estimate of variance

$$v(i) = (R-1)^{-1} \sum_{r=1}^{R} \{t_r^*(i) - \bar{t}^*(i)\}^2$$

is smallest; here $\bar{t}^*(i) = R^{-1} \sum_r t_r^*(i)$.

How we generate the bootstrap samples is important here. Having assumed symmetry of data distribution, the resampling distribution should be symmetric so that the $t^*(i)$ are unbiased for μ. Otherwise selection based on variance alone is questionable. Further discussion of this is postponed to Example 3.26.

So far the procedure is straightforward. But now suppose that we want to estimate the variance of T, or quantiles of $T - \mu$. For the variance, the minimum estimate $v(i)$ used to select $t = t(i)$ will tend to be too low: if I is the random index corresponding to the selected estimator, then $E\{V(I)\} < \text{var}\{T(I)\} = \text{var}(T)$. Similarly the resampling distribution of $T^* = T^*(I)$ will be artificially concentrated relative to that of T, so that empirical quantiles of the $t^*(i)$ values will tend to be too close to t. Whether or not this selection bias is serious depends on the context. However, the bias can be adjusted for by bootstrapping the whole procedure, as follows.

Let $y_1^*, \ldots, y_n^*$ be one of the R simulated samples. Suppose that we apply the procedure for choosing among $T(1), \ldots, T(K)$ to this bootstrap sample. That is, we generate M samples with equal probability from $y_1^*, \ldots, y_n^*$, and calculate the estimates $t_m^{**}(1), \ldots, t_m^{**}(K)$ for the mth such sample. Then choose the estimator with the smallest estimated variance

$$v^*(i) = (M-1)^{-1} \sum_{m=1}^{M} \{t_m^{**}(i) - \bar{t}^{**}(i)\}^2,$$

where $\bar{t}^{**}(i) = \sum_m t_m^{**}(i)$. That is,

$$t^* = t^*(i) \quad \text{if} \quad v^*(i) = \min_{1 \le k \le K} v^*(k).$$

Doing this for each of the R samples $y_1^*, \ldots, y_n^*$ gives $t_1^*, \ldots, t_R^*$, and the empirical distribution of the $t_r^* - t$ values approximates the distribution of $T - \mu$. For example, $v = (R-1)^{-1} \sum (t_r^* - t)^2$ estimates the variance of T, and by accounting for the selection bias should be more accurate than $v(i)$.

There are two byproducts of this double bootstrap procedure. One is information on how well-determined is the choice of estimator, if this is of interest, simply by examining the relative frequency with which each estimator is chosen. Secondly, the bias of $v(i)$ can be approximated: on the log scale bias is estimated by $R^{-1} \sum \log v_r^* - \log v$, where v_r^* is the smallest value of the $v^*(i)$s in the rth bootstrap sample.

Example 3.26 (Gravity data) Suppose that the data in Table 3.1 were only available as a combined sample of $n = 81$ measurements. The different dispersions of the ingredient series make the combined sample very non-normal, so that the simple average is a poor estimator of the underlying mean μ. One possible approach is to consider trimmed average estimates

$$t(k) = \frac{1}{n - 2k} \sum_{j=k+1}^{n-k} y_{(j)},$$

which are averages after dropping the k smallest and k largest order statistics $y_{(j)}$. The usual average and sample median correspond respectively to $k = 0$ and $\frac{1}{2}(n-1)$. The left panel of Figure 3.14 plots the trimmed averages against k. The mild downward trend in the plot suggests slight asymmetry of the data distribution. Our aim is to use the bootstrap to choose among the trimmed averages.

The trimmed averages will all be unbiased if the underlying data distribution is symmetric, and estimator variance will then be a sensible criterion on which to base choice. The bootstrap procedure must build in the assumed symmetry,

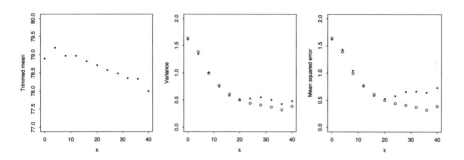

Figure 3.14 Trimmed averages and their estimated variances and mean squared errors for the pooled gravity data, based on $R = 1000$ bootstrap samples, using the ordinary bootstrap (•) and the symmetric bootstrap (∘).

and this can be done (cf. Example 3.4) by simulating samples $y_1^*, \ldots, y_n^*$ from a symmetrized version of $\hat{F}$ such as

$$\hat{F}_{sym}(y) = \tfrac{1}{2} \left\{ \hat{F}(y) + \hat{F}(2\hat{\mu} - y - 0) \right\},$$

which is simply the EDF of $y_1, \ldots, y_n, \hat{\mu} - (y_1 - \hat{\mu}), \ldots, \hat{\mu} - (y_n - \hat{\mu})$, with $\hat{\mu}$ an estimate of μ which for this purpose we take to be the sample median. The centre panel of Figure 3.14 shows bootstrap estimates of variance for eleven trimmed averages based on $R = 1000$ samples drawn from $\hat{F}_{sym}$. We conclude from this that $k = 36$ is best, but that there is little to choose among trimmed averages with $k = 24, \ldots, 40$. A similar conclusion emerges if we sample from $\hat{F}$, although the bootstrap variances are noticeably higher for $k \geq 24$.

If symmetry of the underlying distribution were in doubt, then we should take the biases of the estimators into account. One natural criterion then would be mean squared error. In this case our bootstrap samples would be drawn from $\hat{F}$, and we would select among the trimmed averages on the basis of bootstrap mean squared error

$$\text{mse}(i) = R^{-1} \sum_{r=1}^{R} \{t_r^*(i) - \bar{y}\}^2.$$

Note that mean squared error is measured relative to the mean $\bar{y}$ of the bootstrap population. The right panel of Figure 3.14 shows the bootstrap mean squared errors for our trimmed averages, and we see that the estimated biases do have an effect: now a value of k nearer 20 would appear to be best. Under the symmetric bootstrap, when the mean of $\hat{F}_{sym}$ is the sample median because we symmetrized about this point, bootstrap mean squared error equals bootstrap variance.

To focus the rest of the discussion, we shall assume symmetry and therefore choose t to be the trimmed average with $k = 36$. The value of t is 78.33, and the minimum bootstrap variance based on 1000 simulations is 0.321.

We now use the double bootstrap procedure to estimate the variance for t, and to determine appropriate quantiles for t. First we generate $R = 1000$

samples $y_1^*, \ldots, y_{81}^*$ from $\hat{F}_{sym}$. To each of these samples we then apply the original symmetric bootstrap procedure, generating $M = 100$ samples of size $n = 81$ from the symmetrized EDF of $y_1^*, \ldots, y_{81}^*$, choosing t^* to be that one of the 11 trimmed averages with smallest value of $v^*(i)$. The variance v of $t_1^*, \ldots, t_R^*$ equals 0.356, which is 10% larger than the original minimum variance. If we use this variance with a normal approximation to calculate a 95% confidence interval centred on t, the interval is [77.16, 79.50]. This is very similar to the intervals obtained in Example 3.2.

The frequencies with which the different trimming proportions are chosen are:

k	12	16	20	24	28	32	36	40
Frequency	1	25	54	96	109	131	498	86

Thus when symmetry of the underlying distribution is assumed, a fairly heavy degree of trimming seems desirable for these data, and the value $k = 36$ actually chosen seems reasonably well-determined. ∎

The general features of this discussion are as follows. We have a set of estimators $T(\alpha) = t(\alpha, \hat{F})$ for $\alpha \in A$, and for each estimator we have an estimated value $C(\alpha, \hat{F})$ for a criterion $C(\alpha, F) = \mathrm{E}\{c(T(\alpha), \theta) \mid F\}$ such as variance or mean squared error. The adaptive estimator is $T = t(\hat{\alpha}, \hat{F})$ where $\hat{\alpha} = \alpha(\hat{F})$ minimizes $C(\alpha, \hat{F})$ with respect to α. We want to know about the distribution of T, including for example its bias and variance. The distribution of $T - \theta = t(\hat{F}) - t(F)$ under sampling from F will be approximated by evaluating it under sampling from $\hat{F}$. That is, it will be approximated by the distribution of

$$T^* - t = t(\hat{F}^*) - t(\hat{F}) = t(\hat{\alpha}^*, \hat{F}^*) - t(\hat{\alpha}, \hat{F})$$

under sampling from $\hat{F}$. Here $\hat{F}^*$ is the analogue of $\hat{F}$ based on $y_1^*, \ldots, y_n^*$: if $\hat{F}$ is the EDF of the data, then $\hat{F}^*$ is the EDF of $y_1^*, \ldots, y_n^*$ sampled from $\hat{F}$.

Whether or not the allowance for selection bias is numerically important will depend upon the density of α values and the variability of $C(\alpha, \hat{F})$.

3.12 Bibliographic Notes

The extension of bootstrap methods to several unrelated samples has been used by several authors, including Hayes, Perl and Efron (1989) for a special contrast-estimation problem in particle physics; the application is discussed also in Efron (1992) and in Practical 3.4.

A general theoretical account of estimation in semiparametric models is given in the book by Bickel *et al.* (1993). The majority of applications of semiparametric models are in regression; see references for Chapters 6 and 7.

Efron (1979, 1982) suggested and studied empirically the use of smooth versions of the EDF, but the first systematic investigation of smoothed bootstraps was by Silverman and Young (1987). They studied the circumstances in which smoothing is beneficial for statistics for which there is a linear approximation. Hall, DiCiccio and Romano (1989) show that when the quantity of interest depends on a local property of the underlying CDF, as do quantiles, smoothing can give worthwhile theoretical reductions in the size of the mean squared error. Similar ideas apply to more complex situations such as L_1 regression (De Angelis, Hall and Young 1993); see however the discussion in Section 6.5. De Angelis and Young (1992) give a useful review of bootstrap smoothing, and discuss the empirical choice of how much smoothing to apply. See also Wang (1995). Romano (1988) describes a problem — estimation of the mode of a density — where the estimator is undefined unless the EDF is smoothed; see also Silverman (1981). In a spatial data problem, Kendall and Kendall (1980) used a form of bootstrap that jitters the observed data, in order to keep the rough configuration of points constant over the simulations; this amounts to sampling without replacement when applying the smoothed bootstrap. Young (1990) concludes that although this approach can outperform the unsmoothed bootstrap, it does not perform so well as the smoothed bootstrap described in Section 3.4.

General discussions of survival data can be found in the books by Cox and Oakes (1984) and Kalbfleisch and Prentice (1980), while Fleming and Harrington (1991) and Andersen et al. (1993) give more mathematical accounts. The product-limit estimator was derived by Kaplan and Meier (1958): it and variants are widely used in practice.

Efron (1981a) proposed the first bootstrap methods for survival data, and discussed the relation between traditional and bootstrap standard errors for the product-limit estimator. Akritas (1986) compared variance estimates for the median survival time from Efron's sampling scheme and a different approach of Reid (1981), and concluded that Efron's scheme is superior. The conditional method outlined in Section 3.5 was suggested by Hjort (1985), and subsequently studied by Kim (1990), who concluded that it estimates the conditional variance of the product-limit estimator somewhat better than does resampling cases. Doss and Gill (1992) and Burr and Doss (1993) give weak convergence results leading to confidence bands for quantiles of the survival time distribution. The asymptotic behaviour of parametric and non-parametric bootstrap schemes for censored data is described by Hjort (1992), while Andersen et al. (1993) discuss theoretical aspects of the weird bootstrap.

The general approach to missing-data problems via the EM algorithm is discussed by Dempster, Laird and Rubin (1977). Bayesian methods using multiple imputation and data augmentation are decribed by Tanner and Wong (1987) and Tanner (1996). A detailed treatment of multiple imputation techniques for missing-data problems, with special emphasis on survey data, is given by Rubin (1987). The principal reference for resampling in missing-data problems is Efron (1994), together with the useful, cautionary discussion by D. B. Rubin. The account in Section 3.6 puts more emphasis on careful choice of estimators.

Cochran (1977) is a standard reference on finite population sampling. Variance estimation by balanced subsampling methods was discussed in this context as early as McCarthy (1969), but the first attempt to apply the bootstrap directly was by Gross (1980), who describes what we have termed the "population bootstrap", but restricted to cases where N/n is an integer. This approach was subsequently developed by Bickel and Freedman (1984), while Chao and Lo (1994) also make a case for this approach. Booth, Butler and Hall (1994) describe the construction of studentized bootstrap confidence limits in this context. Presnell and Booth (1994) give a critical discussion of earlier literature and describe the superpopulation bootstrap. The use of modified sample sizes was proposed by McCarthy and Snowden (1985) and the mirror-match method by Sitter (1992). A different approach based on rescaling was introduced by Rao and Wu (1988). A comprehensive theoretical discussion of the jackknife and bootstrap in sample surveys is given in Chapter 6 of Shao and Tu (1995), with later developments described by Presnell and Booth (1994) and Booth, Butler and Hall (1994), on which the account in Section 3.7 is largely based.

Little has been written about resampling hierarchical data although two relevant references are given in the bibliographic notes for Chapter 7. Related methods for bootstrapping empirical Bayes estimates in hierarchical Bayes models are described by Laird and Louis (1987). Nonparametric estimation of the CDF for a random effect is discussed by Laird (1978).

Bootstrapping the bootstrap is described by Chapman and Hinkley (1986), and was applied to estimation of variance-stabilizing transformations by Tibshirani (1988). Theoretical aspects of adjustment of bootstrap calculations were developed by Hall and Martin (1988). See also the bibliographic notes for Chapters 4 and 5. Milan and Whittaker (1995) give a parametric bootstrap analysis of the data in Table 3.10, and discuss the difficulties that can arise when resampling in problems with a singular value decomposition.

Efron (1992) introduced the jackknife-after-bootstrap, and described a variety of ingenious uses for related calculations. Different graphical diagnostics for bootstrap reliability are developed in an asymptotic framework by Beran (1997). The linearity plot of Section 3.10.2 is due to Cook and Weisberg (1994).

Theoretical aspects of the empirical choice of estimator are discussed by Léger and Romano (1990a,b) and Léger, Politis and Romano (1992). Efron (1992) gives an example of choice of level of trimming of a robust estimator, without double bootstrapping. Some of the general issues, with examples, are discussed by Faraway (1992).

3.13 Problems

1   In a two-sample problem, with data $y_{ij}, j = 1, \ldots, n_i, i = 1, 2$, giving sample averages
    $\bar{y}_i$ and variances v_i, describe models for which it would be appropriate to resample
    the following quantities:
    (a) $e_{ij} = y_{ij} - \bar{y}_i$,
    (b) $e_{ij} = (y_{ij} - \bar{y}_i)/(1 + n_i^{-1})^{1/2}$,
    (c) $e_{ij} = (y_{ij} - \bar{y}_i)/\{v_i(1 + n_i^{-1})\}^{1/2}$,
    (d) $e_{ij} = \pm(y_{ij} - \bar{y}_i)/\{v_i(1 + n_i^{-1})\}^{1/2}$, where the signs are allocated with equal
    probabilities,
    (e) $e_{ij} = y_{ij}/\bar{y}_i$.
    In each case say how a simulated dataset would be constructed.
    What difficulties, if any, would arise from replacing $\bar{y}_i$ and v_i by more robust
    estimates of location and scale?
    (Sections 3.2, 3.3)

2   A slightly simplified version of the weighted mean of k samples, as used in
    Example 3.2, is defined by

$$t = \frac{\sum_{i=1}^{k} w_i \bar{y}_i}{\sum_{i=1}^{k} w_i},$$

where $w_i = n_i/\hat{\sigma}_i^2$, with $\bar{y}_i = n_i^{-1} \sum_j y_{ij}$ and $\hat{\sigma}_i^2 = n_i^{-1} \sum_j (y_{ij} - \bar{y}_i)^2$ estimates of
mean μ_i and variance σ_i^2 of the ith distribution. Show that the influence functions
for T are

$$L_{t,i}(y_i; F) = \frac{\omega_i}{\sum \omega_i} \left[y_i - \mu_i - (\mu_i - \theta) \left\{ (y_i - \mu_i)^2 - \sigma_i^2 \right\} / \sigma_i^2 \right],$$

where $\omega_i = n_i/\sigma_i^2$. Deduce that the first-order approximation under the constraint
$\mu_1 = \cdots = \mu_k$ for the variance of T is $v_L = 1/\sum \omega_i$, with empirical analogue $v_L =
1/\sum w_i$. Compare this to the corresponding formula based on the unconstrained
empirical influence values.
(Section 3.2.1)

3   Suppose that Y is bivariate with polar representation (X, ω), so that $Y^T =
(X \cos \omega, X \sin \omega)$. If it is known that ω has a uniform distribution on $[0, 2\pi)$,
independent of X, what would be an appropriate resampling algorithm based on
the random sample $y_1, \ldots, y_n$?
(Section 3.3)

4   Spherical data $y_1, \ldots, y_n$ are points on the sphere of unit radius. Suppose that it
    is assumed that these data come from a distribution that is symmetric about the
    unknown mean direction μ. In light of the symmetry assumption, what would be
    an appropriate resampling algorithm for simulating data $y_1^*, \ldots, y_n^*$?
    (Section 3.3; Ducharme *et al.*, 1985)

5   Two independent random samples $y_{11}, \ldots, y_{1n_1}$ and $y_{21}, \ldots, y_{2n_2}$ of positive data
    are obtained, and the ratio of sample means $t = \bar{y}_2/\bar{y}_1$ is used to estimate the
    corresponding population ratio $\theta = \mu_2/\mu_1$.
    (a) Show that the influence functions for t are

$$L_{t,1}(y_1; F) = -(y_1 - \mu_1)\theta/\mu_1, \quad L_{t,2}(y_2; F) = (y_2 - \mu_2)/\mu_1.$$

Hence obtain the formula

$$v_L = \left\{ n_1^{-2} t^2 \sum (y_{1j} - \bar{y}_1)^2 + n_2^{-2} \sum (y_{2j} - \bar{y}_2)^2 \right\} / \bar{y}_1^2$$

for the approximate variance of T.

(b) Describe an appropriate resampling algorithm. How could this be modified if one could assume a multiplicative model, i.e. $Y_{1j} = \mu_1 \varepsilon_{1j}$ and $Y_{2j} = \mu_2 \varepsilon_{2j}$ with all εs sampled from a common distribution of positive random variables?

(c) Show that under the multiplicative model the approximate variance formula can be changed to $v_L = t^2 \sum_{i,j}(e_{ij} - 1)^2/(n_1 n_2)$, where $e_{ij} = y_{ij}/\bar{y}_i$.
(Section 3.2.1)

6   The empirical influence values can be calculated more directly as follows. Consider only distributions supported on the data values, with probabilities $p_i = (p_{i1}, \ldots, p_{in_i})$ on the values in the ith sample for $i = 1, \ldots, k$. Then write $T = t(p_1, \ldots, p_k)$, so that $t = t(\hat{p}_1, \ldots, \hat{p}_k)$ with $\hat{p}_i = (\frac{1}{n_i}, \ldots, \frac{1}{n_i})$. Show that the empirical influence value l_{ij} corresponding to the jth case in sample i is given by

$$l_{ij} = \frac{d}{d\varepsilon} t \{\hat{p}_1, \ldots, (1-\varepsilon)\hat{p}_i + \varepsilon 1_j, \ldots, \hat{p}_k\} \Big|_{\varepsilon=0},$$

where 1_j is the vector with 1 in the jth position and zeroes elsewhere.
(Section 3.2.1)

7   Following on from the previous problem, re-express $t(p_1, \ldots, p_k)$ as a function $u(\pi)$ of a single probability vector $\pi = (\pi_{11}, \ldots, \pi_{1n_1}, \ldots, \pi_{kn_k})$. For example, for the ratio of means of two independent samples, $t = \bar{y}_2/\bar{y}_1$,

$$u(\pi) = \left(\sum y_{2j}\pi_{2j}/\sum \pi_{2j}\right)\Big/\left(\sum y_{1j}\pi_{1j}/\sum \pi_{1j}\right).$$

The observed value t is then equal to $u(\hat{\pi})$ where $\hat{\pi} = (\frac{1}{n}, \ldots, \frac{1}{n})$ with $n = \sum_{i=1}^{k} n_i$. Show that

$$\tilde{l}_{ij} = \frac{d}{d\varepsilon} u \{(1-\varepsilon)\hat{\pi} + \varepsilon 1_{ij}\} \Big|_{\varepsilon=0} = \frac{n}{n_i} l_{ij},$$

where 1_{ij} is the vector with 1 in the $(n_{i-1} + j)$th position, with $n_0 = 0$, and zeroes elsewhere. One consequence of this is that $v_L = n^{-2} \sum_{i=1}^{k} \sum_{j=1}^{n_i} \tilde{l}_{ij}^2$.

Apply these calculations to the ratio $t = \bar{y}_2/\bar{y}_1$.
(Section 3.2.1)

8   If $x_1, \ldots, x_n$ is a random sample from some distribution G with density g, suppose that this density is estimated by

$$\hat{g}_h(x) = \frac{1}{nh} \sum_{j=1}^{n} w\left(\frac{x - x_j}{h}\right) = \frac{1}{h} \int w\left(\frac{x - y}{h}\right) d\hat{G}(y),$$

where w is a symmetric PDF with mean zero and variance τ^2.

(a) Show that this density estimate has mean $\bar{x}$ and variance $n^{-1}\sum(x_j - \bar{x})^2 + h^2\tau^2$.

(b) Show that the random variable $\tilde{x} = x_J + h\varepsilon$ has PDF $\hat{g}_h$, where J is uniformly distributed on $(1, \ldots, n)$ and ε has PDF w. Hence describe an algorithm for bootstrap simulation from a smoothed version of the EDF.

(c) Show that the rescaled density

$$\frac{1}{nhb} \sum_{j=1}^{n} w\left(\frac{x - a - bx_j}{hb}\right)$$

will have the same first two moments as the EDF if $a = (1 - b)\bar{x}$ and $b = \{1 + nh^2\tau^2/\sum(x_j - \bar{x})^2\}^{-1/2}$. What algorithm simulates from this smoothed EDF?

(d) Discuss the special problems that arise from using $\hat{g}_h(x)$ when the range of x is $[0, \infty)$ rather than $(-\infty, \infty)$.

(e) Extend the algorithms in (b) and (c) to multivariate x.

(Section 3.4; Silverman and Young, 1987; Wand and Jones, 1995)

9   Consider resampling cases from censored data $(y_1, d_1), \ldots, (y_n, d_n)$, where $y_1 < \cdots < y_n$. Let f_j^* denote the number of times that (y_j, d_j) occurs in an ordinary bootstrap sample, and let $S_j^* = f_j^* + \cdots + f_n^*$.

(a) Show that when there is no censoring, the product-limit estimate puts mass n^{-1} on each observed failure $y_1 < \cdots < y_n$, so that $\hat{F}^0 \equiv \hat{F}$.

(b) Show that if $B(m, p)$ denotes binomial distribution with index m and probability p, then

$$f_j^* \mid S_j^* \sim B\left\{S_j^*, (n-j+1)^{-1}\right\}, \quad S_j^* \sim B\left(n, \tfrac{n-j+1}{n}\right).$$

(c) Show that the bootstrapped product-limit estimator $\hat{F}^{0*}$ satisfies

$$\log\left\{1 - \hat{F}^{0*}(y)\right\} = \sum_{j:y_j<y} d_j \log\left(1 - \frac{f_j^*}{S_j^*}\right),$$

and deduce that this has variance $\sum_{j:y_j<y} d_j \mathrm{var}\{\log(1 - f_j^*/S_j^*)\}$.

(d) Use the delta method to show that $\mathrm{var}[\log\{1-\hat{F}^{0*}(y)\}] \doteq \sum_{j:y_j<y} d_j/(n-j+1)^2$, and infer that

$$\mathrm{var}\left\{1 - \hat{F}^{0*}(y)\right\} \doteq \left\{1 - \hat{F}^0(y)\right\}^2 \sum_{j:y_j<y} \frac{d_j}{(n-j+1)^2}.$$

This equals the variance from Greenwood's formula, (3.10), apart from replacement of $(n-j+1)^2$ by $(n-j)(n-j+1)$.

(Section 3.5; Efron, 1981a; Cox and Oakes, 1984, Section 4.3)

10   Consider the weird bootstrap applied to a homogeneous sample of censored data, $(y_1, d_1), \ldots, (y_n, d_n)$, in which $y_1 < \cdots < y_n$. Let $d\hat{A}^{0*}(y_j) = N_j^*/(n-j+1)$, where the N_j^* are independent binomial variables with denominators $n-j+1$ and probabilities $d_j/(n-j+1)$.

(a) Show that the total number of failures under this resampling scheme is distributed as a sum of independent binomial observations.

(b) Show that

$$\mathrm{E}^*\left\{\int_0^y d\hat{A}^{0*}(u)\right\} = \hat{A}^0(y), \quad \mathrm{var}^*\left\{\int_0^y d\hat{A}^{0*}(u)\right\} = \sum_{j:y_j\leq y} \frac{d_j(n-j)}{(n-j+1)^3},$$

and that if $d_n = 1$ then $d\hat{A}^{0*}(y_n)$ always equals one.

(Section 3.5; Andersen *et al.*, 1993)

11   Suppose that $Y_j = (U_j, X_j), j = 1, \ldots, n$ are bivariate normal with mean vector μ and variance matrix Ω. When the Ys are observed, a random m cases have x missing. Obtain formulae for the maximum likelihood estimators of μ and Ω. Verify that these formulae agree with the multiple-imputation estimators constructed by the method of Section 3.6.

12   (a) Establish (3.15), and show that the sample variance c is an unbiased estimate of γ.

(b) Now suppose that $N = kn$ for some integer k. Show that under the population bootstrap,

$$E^*(\bar{Y}^*) = \bar{y}, \qquad \text{var}^*(\bar{Y}^*) = \frac{N(n-1)}{(N-1)n} \times (1-f)n^{-1}c.$$

(c) In the context of Example 3.16, suppose that the parameter of interest is a nonlinear function of θ, say $\eta = g(\theta)$, which is estimated by $g(T)$. Use the delta method to show that the bias of $g(T)$ is roughly $\frac{1}{2}g''(\theta)\text{var}(T)$, and that the bootstrap bias estimate is roughly $\frac{1}{2}g''(t)\text{var}^*(T^*)$. Under what conditions on n and N does the bootstrap bias estimate converge to the true bias?
(Section 3.7; Bickel and Freedman, 1984; Booth, Butler and Hall, 1994)

13 To model the superpopulation bootstrap, suppose that the original data are $y_1, \ldots, y_n$ and that $\mathcal{Y}^*$ contains $M_1, \ldots, M_n$ copies of $y_1, \ldots, y_n$; the joint distribution of the M_j is multinomial with probabilities n^{-1} and denominator N. If $Y_1^*, \ldots, Y_n^*$ are sampled without replacement from $\mathcal{Y}^*$ and if $\bar{Y}^* = n^{-1}\sum Y_j^*$, show that

$$E^*(\bar{Y}^*) = \bar{y}, \qquad E_M\left\{\text{var}^*(\bar{Y}^* \mid M)\right\} = \frac{n-1}{n} \times (1-f)n^{-1}c.$$

(Section 3.7; Presnell and Booth, 1994)

14 Suppose we wish to perform mirror-match resampling with k independent without-replacement samples of size m, but that $k = \{n(1-m/n)\}/\{\{m(1-f)\}$ is not an integer. Let K^* be the random variable such that

$$\Pr(K^* = k') = 1 - \Pr(K^* = k'+1) = k'(1+k'-k)/k,$$

where $k' = [k]$ is the integer part of k. Show that if the mirror-match algorithm is applied for an average $\bar{Y}^*$ with this distribution for K^*, $\text{var}^*(\bar{Y}^*) = (1-m/n)c/(mk)$. Show also that under mirror-match resampling with the simplifying assumption that randomization is not required because k is an integer,

$$E^*(C^*) = c\left\{1 - \frac{m(k-1)}{n(mk-1)}\right\},$$

where C^* is the sample variance of the Y_j^*.
What implications are there for variance estimation for more complex statistics?
(Section 3.7; Sitter, 1992)

15 Suppose that n is a large even integer and that $N = 5n/2$, and that instead of applying the population bootstrap we choose a population from which to resample according to

$$\mathcal{Y}^* = \begin{cases} y_1, \ldots, y_n, \quad y_1, \ldots, y_n, & \text{with probability } \frac{2}{5}, \\[2ex] y_1, \ldots, y_n, \quad y_1, \ldots, y_n, \quad y_1, \ldots, y_n, & \text{with probability } \frac{3}{5}. \end{cases}$$

Having selected $\mathcal{Y}^*$ we take a sample $Y_1^*, \ldots, Y_n^*$ from it without replacement and calculate $Z^* = (\bar{Y}^* - \bar{y})\{(1-f')n^{-1}c\}^{-1/2}$. Show that if $f' = n/N$ the approximate distribution of Z^* is the normal mixture $\frac{2}{5}N(0, \frac{5}{6}) + \frac{3}{5}N(0, \frac{10}{9})$, but that if $f' = n/\#\{\mathcal{Y}^*\}$ the approximate distribution of Z^* is $N(0,1)$. Check that in the first case, $E^*(Z^*) = 0$ and $\text{var}^*(Z^*) = 1$.
Comment on the implications for the use of randomization in finite population resampling.
(Section 3.7; Bickel and Freedman, 1984; Presnell and Booth, 1994)

$\#\{A\}$ is the number of elements in the set A.

16 Suppose that we have data $y_1,\ldots,y_n$, and that the bootstrap sample is taken to be

$$Y_j^* = \bar{y} + d(y_{I_j} - \bar{y}), \qquad j = 1,\ldots,n',$$

where $I_1,\ldots,I_{n'}$ are independently chosen at random from $1,\ldots,n$.
Show that when $d = \{n'(1-f)/(n-1)\}^{1/2}$, we have $\mathrm{E}^*(\bar{Y}^*) = \bar{y}$ and $\mathrm{var}^*(\bar{Y}^*) = (1-f)n^{-1}c$. How might the value of n' be chosen?
Discuss critically this resampling scheme.
(Section 3.7; Rao and Wu, 1988)

17 Suppose that $y_{ij} = x_i + z_{ij}, i = 1,\ldots,a$ and $j = 1,\ldots,b$, where the x_is are independent with mean μ and variance σ_x^2, and the z_{ij}s are independent with mean 0 and variance σ_z^2. Consider the resampling schemes

$$Y_{ij}^* = \bar{y}_{I_i} + (y_{K_iJ_j} - \bar{y}_{K_i}),$$

where $I_1,\ldots,I_a$ and $K_1,\ldots,K_a$ are randomly sampled with replacement from $\{1,\ldots,a\}$, and $J_1,\ldots,J_b$ are randomly sampled from $\{1,\ldots,b\}$ either with or without replacement. Show that the second-moment properties of the Y_{ij}^*s are given by (3.23) and (3.24).
(Section 3.8)

18 For the model of Problem 3.17, define estimates of the x_is and z_{ij}s by

$$\hat{x}_i = c\bar{y}_. + (1-c)\bar{y}_i, \quad \hat{z}_{ij} = d(y_{ij} - \bar{y}_i).$$

Show that the EDFs of $\hat{x}_i$ and $\hat{z}_{ij}$ have first two moments which are unbiased for the corresponding moments of the Xs and Zs if

$$(1-c)^2 = \frac{a}{a-1} - \frac{SS_W}{b(b-1)SS_B}, \quad d^2 = \frac{b}{b-1}.$$

(Section 3.8)

19 Consider the double bootstrap procedure for adjusting the estimated bias of T, as described in Section 3.9, when T is the average $\bar{Y}$. Show that the variance of simulation error for the adjusted bias estimate $B - C$ is

$$\mathrm{var}^*(B - C \mid \hat{F}) = \frac{(n-1)s^2}{Rn^2}\left(4 + \frac{n-1}{nM}\right),$$

with s^2 the sample variance.
Hence deduce that for fixed RM the best choice for M is 1. How would the results change for a statistic other than the average?
Derive the corresponding result for the bias correction of the bootstrap estimate of $\mathrm{var}(T)$.
(Sections 2.5.2, 3.9)

20 Extend the discussion following (3.42) to jackknife-after-bootstrap calculations for $v = (R-1)^{-1}\sum(t_r^* - \bar{t}^*)^2$.
Describe the calculation in detail when parametric simulation is performed from the exponential density.
(Section 3.10; Efron, 1992)

21 Let $t_p(F)$ denote the $p \times 100\%$ trimmed average of distribution F, i.e.

$$t_p(F) = \frac{1}{1-2p}\int_{F^{-1}(p)}^{F^{-1}(1-p)} y\,dF(y).$$

(a) If F_κ denotes the gamma distribution with index κ and unit mean, show that $t_p(F_\kappa) = \kappa(1-2p)^{-1}\{F_{\kappa+1}(y_{\kappa,1-p}) - F_{\kappa+1}(y_{\kappa,p})\}$, where $y_{\kappa,p}$ is the p quantile of F_κ. Hence evaluate $t_p(F_\kappa)$ for $\kappa = 1, 2, 5, 10$ and $p = 0, 0.1, 0.2, 0.3, 0.4, 0.5$.

(b) Suppose that the parameter of interest, $\theta = \sum_{i=1}^k c_i t_0(F_{i,\kappa_i})$, depends on several gamma distributions F_{i,κ_i}. Let $\hat{F}_i$ denote the EDF of a sample of size n_i from F_{i,κ_i}. Under what circumstances is $T = \sum_{i=1}^k c_i t_p(\hat{F}_i)$ (i) unbiased, (ii) nearly unbiased, as an estimate of θ? Test your conclusions by a small simulation experiment. (Section 3.11)

3.14 Practicals

1   To perform the analysis for the gravity data outlined in Example 3.2:

```
grav.fun <- function(data, i)
{ d <- data[i,]
  m <- tapply(d$g,d$series,mean)
  v <- tapply(d$g,d$series,var)
  n <- table(d$series)
  c(sum(m*n/v)/sum(n/v), 1/sum(n/v)) }
grav.boot <- boot(gravity, grav.fun, R=200, strata=gravity$series)
```

Plot the estimate and its variance. Is the simulation well-behaved? How normal are the bootstrapped estimates and studentized bootstrap statistics?

Now for a semiparametric analysis, as suggested in Section 3.3:

```
attach(gravity)
n <- table(series)
m <- rep(tapply(g, series, mean), n)
s <- rep(sqrt(tapply(g,series,var)),n)
res <- (g-m)/s
qqnorm(res); abline(0,1,lty=2)
grav <- data.frame(m, s, series, res)
grav.fun <- function(data, i)
{ e <- data$res[i]
  y <- data$m + data$s*e
  m <- tapply(y, data$series, mean)
  v <- tapply(y, data$series, var)
  n <- table(data$series)
  c(sum(m*n/v)/sum(n/v), 1/sum(n/v))
 }
grav1.boot <- boot(grav, grav.fun, R=200)
```

Do residuals `res` for the different series look similar? Compare the values of t^* and v^* for the two sampling schemes. Compare also 80% confidence intervals for g. (Section 3.2)

2   Dataframe `channing` contains data on the survival of 97 men and 365 women in a retirement home in California. The variables are sex, ages in months at which individuals entered and left the home, the time in months they spent there, and a censoring indicator (0/1 denoting censored due to leaving the home/died there). For details see Hyde (1980). We compare the variability of the survival probabilities at 75 and 85 years (900 and 1020 months), and of the estimated 0.75 and 0.5 quantiles of the survival distribution.

```
chan <- channing[1:97,]          # men only
chan$age <- chan$entry+chan$time
attach(chan)
chan.F <- survfit(Surv(age, cens))
chan.F
max(chan.F$surv[chan.F$time>900])
max(chan.F$surv[chan.F$time>1020])
chan.G <- survfit(Surv(age-0.01*cens,1-cens))
split.screen(c(2,1))
screen(1); plot(chan.F,xlim=c(760,1200),main="survival")
screen(2); plot(chan.G,xlim=c(760,1200),main="censoring")
chan.fun <- function(data)
{ s <- survfit(Surv(age,cens),data=data)
  c(max(s$surv[s$time>900]),  max(s$surv[s$time>1020]),
    min(s$time[(s$surv<=0.75)]), min(s$time[(s$surv<=0.5)])) }
chan.boot1 <- censboot(chan, chan.fun, R=99, sim = "ordinary")
chan.boot2 <- censboot(chan, chan.fun, R=99, F.surv=chan.F,
                       G.surv=chan.G, sim = "cond",index=c(6,5))
chan.boot3 <- censboot(chan, chan.fun, R=99, F.surv=chan.F,
                       sim = "weird",index=c(6,5))
```

Give normal-approximation confidence limits for each of the survival probabilities,
transformed if necessary, and compare them with those from chan.F. How do the
intervals for the different bootstraps compare?
(Section 3.5; Efron, 1981a)

3   To study the performance of censored data resampling schemes when the censoring
pattern is fixed, we perform a small simulation study. We apply a fixed censoring
pattern to samples of size 50 from the unit exponential distribution, and for each
sample we calculate $t = (t_1, t_2)$, where t_1 is the maximum likelihood estimate of the
distribution mean and t_2 is the number of censored observations. We apply each
bootstrap scheme to the sample, and record the mean and standard deviation of
t from the bootstrap simulation. (This is quite time-consuming: take nreps and R
as big as you dare.)

```
exp.fun <- function(d)
{ d.s <- survfit(Surv(y, cens),data=d)
  prob <- min(d.s$surv[d.s$time<1])
  med <- min(d.s$time[(1-d.s$surv)>=0.5])
  c(sum(d$y)/sum(d$cens), sum(1-d$cens)) }

results <- NULL; nreps <- 100; n <- 50; R <- 25
cens <- 3*runif(n)
for (i in 1:nreps)
{ y0 <- rexp(n)
  junk <- data.frame(y = pmin(y0,cens), cens = as.numeric(y0<cens))
  junk.F <- survfit(Surv(y,cens),data=junk)
  junk.G <- survfit(Surv(y,1-cens),data=junk)
  ord.boot <- censboot(junk, exp.fun, R=R)
  con.boot <- censboot(junk, exp.fun, R=R,
                       F.surv=junk.F, G.surv=junk.G, sim = "cond")
  wei.boot <- censboot(junk, exp.fun, R=R,
                       F.surv=junk.F, sim = "weird")
  res <- c(exp.fun(junk ),
           apply(ord.boot$t, 2, mean),
```

```
            apply(con.boot$t, 2, mean),
            apply(wei.boot$t, 2, mean),
            sqrt(apply(ord.boot$t, 2, var)),
            sqrt(apply(con.boot$t, 2, var)),
            sqrt(apply(wei.boot$t, 2, var)))
    results <- rbind(results, res) }
```

The estimated bias and standard deviation of t_1, and the bootstrap bias estimates are

```
mean(results[,1])-1
sqrt(var(results[,1]))
bias.o <- results[,3]-results[,1]
bias.c <- results[,5]-results[,1]
bias.w <- results[,7]-results[,1]
```

How do they compare? What about the estimated standard deviations? How do the numbers of censored observations vary under the schemes?
(Section 3.5; Efron, 1981a; Burr, 1994)

4 The tau particle is a heavy electron-like particle which decays into various collections of other charged particles shortly after its production. The decay usually involves one charged particle, in which case it can happen in a number of modes, the main four of which are labelled ρ, π, e, and μ. It takes a major research project to measure the rate of occurrence of single-particle decay, decay_1, or any of its component rates decay_ρ, decay_π, decay_e, and decay_μ, and just one of these can be measured in any one experiment. Thus dataframe `tau` on decay rates for 60 experiments represent several years of work. Here we use them to estimate and form a confidence interval for the parameter

$$\theta = \text{decay}_1 - \text{decay}_\rho - \text{decay}_\pi - \text{decay}_e - \text{decay}_\mu.$$

Suppose that we had thought of using the 0, 12.5, 25, 37.5 and 50% trimmed averages to estimate the difference. To calculate these and to obtain bootstrap confidence intervals for the estimates of θ:

```
tau.diff <- function(data)
{  y0  <- tapply(data[,1],data[,2],mean)
   y1 <- tapply(data[,1],data[,2],mean,trim=0.125)
   y2 <- tapply(data[,1],data[,2],mean,trim=0.25)
   y3 <- tapply(data[,1],data[,2],mean,trim=0.375)
   y4 <- tapply(data[,1],data[,2],median)
   y <- rbind(y0, y1, y2, y3, y4)
   y[,1]-apply(y[,-1],1,sum) }
tau.diff(tau)
tau.fun <- function(data, i)   tau.diff(data[i,])
tau.boot <- boot(tau,tau.fun,R=999,strata=tau$decay)
boot.ci(tau.boot, type=c("norm","basic"), index=1)
boot.ci(tau.boot, type=c("norm","basic"), index=2)
```

and so forth, with `index=3, 4, 5` for the remaining degrees of trim. Does the degree of trimming affect the interval much?
To see the jackknife-after-bootstrap plot when θ is estimated using the average:

```
jack.after.boot(tau.boot,index=1)
```

How does the degree of trim affect the bootstrap distributions of the different estimators of θ?

Now suppose that we want to choose the estimator from the data, by taking the trimmed average with smallest variance. For the original data this is the 25% trimmed average, so the estimate is 16.87. Its variance can be estimated by a double bootstrap, which we can implement as follows:

```
tau.nest <- function(data, i)
{ d <- data[i,]
    d.trim <- tau.diff(d)
    v.trim <- apply(boot(d, tau.fun, R=25, strata=d$decay)$t, 2, var)
    c(d.trim, v.trim)  }
tau.boot2 <- boot(tau, tau.nest, R=100, strata=tau$decay)
```

To see what degrees of trimming give the smallest variances, and to calculate the corresponding estimates and obtain their variance:

```
i <- matrix(1:5,5,tau.boot2$R)
i <- i[t(tau.boot2$t[,6:10]==apply(tau.boot2$t[,6:10],1,min))]
table(i)
t.best <- tau.boot2$t[cbind(1:tau.boot2$R,i)]
var(t.best)
```

Is the optimal degree of trimming well-determined?
How would you use the results of Problems 2.13 and 2.4 to avoid the second level of bootstrapping?
(Section 3.11; Efron, 1992)

5   We apply the jackknife-after-bootstrap to the correlation coefficient between plumage and behaviour in cross-bred ducks.

```
ducks.boot <- boot(ducks, corr, R=999, stype="w")
ducks.L <- empinf(data=ducks, statistic=corr)
split.screen(c(1,2))
screen(1)
split.screen(c(2,1))
screen(4)
attach(ducks)
plot(plumage,behaviour,type="n")
text(plumage,behaviour,round(ducks.L,2))
screen(3)
plot(plumage,behaviour,type="n")
text(plumage,behaviour,1:nrow(ducks))
screen(2)
jack.after.boot(boot.out=ducks.boot,useJ=F,stinf=F, L=ducks.L)
```

(a) The value of the correlation is $t = 0.83$. Will it increase or decrease if observation 7 is deleted from the sample? (Be careful.) What is the effect on t of deleting observation 6?
(b) What happens to the bootstrap distribution of $t^* - t$ when observation 8 is deleted from the sample? What about observation 6?
(c) Show that the probability that neither observation 5 nor observation 6 is in a bootstrap sample is $(1 - \frac{2}{11})^{11} \doteq 0.11$. Now suppose that observation 5 is deleted, and calculate the probability that observation 6 is not in a bootstrap sample. Does this explain what happens in (b)?

6   Suppose that we are interested in the largest eigenvalue of the covariance matrix between the baseline and one-year CD4 counts in cd4; see Practical 2.3. To

calculate this and its approximate variance using the nonparametric delta method (Problem 2.14), and to bootstrap it:

```
eigen.fun <- function(d, w = rep(1, nrow(d))/nrow(d))
{ w <- w/sum(w)
  n <- nrow(d)
  m <- crossprod(w, d)
  m2 <- sweep(d,2,m)
  v <- crossprod(diag(sqrt(w)) %*% m2)
  eig <- eigen(v,symmetric=T)
  stat <- eig$values[1]
  e <- eig$vectors[,1]
  i <- rep(1:n,round(n*w))
  ds <- sweep(d[i,],2,m)
  L <- (ds%*%e)^2 - stat
  c(stat, sum(L^2)/n^2)   }
cd4.boot <- boot(cd4,eigen.fun,R=999,stype="w")
```

Some diagnostic plots:

```
split.screen(c(1,2))
screen(1); split.screen(c(2,1))
screen(3)
plot(cd4.boot$t[,1],cd4.boot$t[,2],xlab="t*",ylab="vL*",pch=".")
screen(4)
plot(cd4[,1],cd4[,2],type="n",xlab="baseline",
     ylab="one year",xlim=c(1,7),ylim=c(1,7))
text(cd4[,1],cd4[,2],c(1:20),cex=0.7)
screen(2);  jack.after.boot(cd4.boot,useJ=F,stinf=F)
```

What is going on here?
(Section 3.10.1; Canty, Davison and Hinkley, 1996)

4

Tests

4.1 Introduction

Many statistical applications involve significance tests to assess the plausibility of scientific hypotheses. Resampling methods are not new to significance testing, since randomization tests and permutation tests have long been used to provide nonparametric tests. Also Monte Carlo tests, which use simulated datasets, are quite commonly used in certain areas of application. In this chapter we describe how resampling methods can be used to produce significance tests, in both parametric and nonparametric settings. The range of ideas is somewhat wider than the direct bootstrap approach introduced in the preceding two chapters. To begin with, we summarize some of the key ideas of significance testing.

The simplest situation involves a *simple null hypothesis* H_0 which completely specifies the probability distribution of the data. Thus, if we are dealing with a single sample $y_1, \ldots, y_n$ from a population with CDF F, then H_0 specifies that $F = F_0$, where F_0 contains no unknown parameters. An example would be "exponential with mean 1". The more usual situation in practice is that H_0 is a *composite null hypothesis*, which means that some aspects of F are not determined and remain unknown when H_0 is true. An example would be "normal with mean 1", the variance of the normal distribution being unspecified.

P-values

A statistical test is based on a *test statistic* T which measures the discrepancy between the data and the null hypothesis. In general discussion we shall follow the convention that large values of T are evidence against H_0. Suppose for the moment that this null hypothesis is simple. If the observed value of the test statistic is denoted by t then the level of evidence against H_0 is measured by the *significance probability*

$$p = \Pr(T \geq t \mid H_0),\tag{4.1}$$

often called the *P-value*. A corresponding notion is that of a critical value t_p for t, associated with testing at level p: if $t \geq t_p$ then H_0 is rejected at level p, or $100p\%$. Necessarily t_p is defined by $\Pr(T \geq t_p \mid H_0) = p$. The level p is also called the *error rate* or the *size* of the test, and $\{(y_1, \ldots, y_n) : t \geq t_p\}$ is called the *level p critical region* of the test. The distribution of T under H_0 is called the *null distribution* of T.

Under H_0 the P-value (4.1) has a uniform distribution on [0,1], if T is continuous, so that the corresponding random variable P has distribution

$$\Pr(P \leq p \mid H_0) = p.\tag{4.2}$$

This yields the error rate interpretation of the P-value, namely that if the observed test statistic were regarded as just decisive against H_0, then this is equivalent to following a procedure which rejects H_0 with error rate p. The same is not exactly true if T is discrete, and for this reason modifications to (4.1) are sometimes suggested for discrete data problems: we shall not worry about the distinction here.

It is important in applications to give a clear idea of the degree of discrepancy between data and null hypothesis, if not giving the P-value itself then at least indicating how it compares to several levels, say $p = 0.10, 0.05, 0.01$, rather than just testing at the 0.05 level.

Choice of test statistic

In the parametric setting, we have an explicit form for the sampling distribution of the data with a finite number of unknown parameters. Often the null hypothesis specifies numerical values for, or relationships between, some or all of these parameters. There is also an *alternative hypothesis H_A* which describes what alternatives to H_0 it is most important to detect, or what is thought likely to be true if H_0 is not. This alternative hypothesis guides the specific choice of T, usually through use of the likelihood function

$$L(\theta) = f_{Y_1,\ldots,Y_n}(y_1, \ldots, y_n \mid \theta),$$

i.e. the joint density of the observations. For example, when H_0 and H_A are both simple, say $H_0 : \theta = \theta_0$ and $H_A : \theta = \theta_A$, then the best test statistic is the likelihood ratio

$$T = L(\theta_A)/L(\theta_0).\tag{4.3}$$

A rather different situation is where we wish to test the goodness of fit of the parametric model. Sometimes this can be done by embedding the model into a larger model, with one or a few additional parameters corresponding to departure from the original model. We would then test those additional parameters. Otherwise general purpose goodness of fit tests will be used, for example chi-squared tests.

In the nonparametric setting, no particular forms are specified for the distributions. Then the appropriate choice of T is less clear, but it should be based on at least a qualitative notion of what is of concern should H_0 not be true. Usually T would be based on a statistical function $s(\hat{F})$ that reflects the characteristic of physical interest and for which the null hypothesis specifies a value. For example, suppose that we wish to test the null hypothesis H_0 that X and Y are independent, given the random sample $(X_1, Y_1), \ldots, (X_n, Y_n)$. The correlation $s(F) = \mathrm{corr}(X, Y) = \rho$ is a convenient measure of dependence, and $\rho = 0$ under H_0. If the alternative hypothesis is positive dependence, then a natural test statistic is $T = s(\hat{F})$, the raw sample correlation; if the alternative hypothesis is just "dependence", then the two-sided test statistic $T = s^2(\hat{F})$ could be used.

Conditional tests

In most parametric problems and all nonparametric problems, the null hypothesis H_0 is composite, that is it leaves some parameters unknown and therefore does not completely specify F. Therefore P-value (4.1) is not generally well-defined, because $\mathrm{Pr}(T \geq t \mid F)$ may depend upon which F satisfying H_0 is taken. There are two clean solutions to this difficulty. One is to choose T carefully so that its distribution is the same for all F satisfying H_0: examples include the Student-t test for a normal mean with unknown variance, and rank tests for nonparametric problems. The second and more widely applicable solution is to eliminate the parameters which remain unknown when H_0 is true by conditioning on the sufficient statistic under H_0. If this sufficient statistic is denoted by S, then we define the conditional P-value by

$$p = \mathrm{Pr}(T \geq t \mid S = s, H_0). \tag{4.4}$$

Familiar examples include the Fisher exact test for a 2×2 table and the Student-t test mentioned earlier. Other examples will be given in the next two sections.

A less satisfactory approach, which can nevertheless give good approximations, is to estimate F by a CDF $\hat{F}_0$ which satisfies H_0 and then calculate

$$p = \mathrm{Pr}(T \geq t \mid \hat{F}_0). \tag{4.5}$$

Typically this value will not satisfy (4.2) exactly, but will deviate by an amount which may be practically negligible.

Pivot tests

When the null hypothesis concerns a particular parameter value, the equivalence between significance tests and confidence sets can be used. This equivalence is that if the value θ_0 is outside a $1 - \alpha$ confidence set for θ, then θ differs from θ_0 with P-value less than α. The particular alternative hypothesis for which this applies is determined by the type of confidence set: for example, if the confidence set is all values to the right of a lower confidence limit, then the implied alternative is $H_A : \theta > \theta_0$. A specific form of test based on this equivalence is the *pivot test*. For example, suppose that T is an estimator for scalar θ, with estimated variance V. Suppose further that the studentized form $Z = (T - \theta)/V^{1/2}$ is a pivot, meaning that its distribution is the same for all relevant F, and in particular for all θ. The Student-t statistic is a familiar instance of this. For the one-sided test of $H_0 : \theta = \theta_0$ versus $H_A : \theta > \theta_0$, the P-value attached to the observed studentized test statistic $z_0 = (t - \theta_0)/v^{1/2}$ is

$$p = \Pr\{(T - \theta_0)/V^{1/2} \geq (t - \theta_0)/v^{1/2} \mid H_0\}.$$

But because Z is a pivot,

$$\Pr\{Z \geq (t - \theta_0)/v^{1/2} \mid H_0\} = \Pr\{Z \geq (t - \theta_0)/v^{1/2} \mid F\},$$

and therefore

$$p = \Pr\left(Z \geq z_0 \mid F\right). \tag{4.6}$$

The particular advantage of this, in the resampling context, is that we do not have to construct a special null hypothesis sampling distribution.

In parametric problems it is usually possible to express the model in terms of the parameter of interest ψ and other (nuisance) parameters λ, so that the null hypothesis concerns only ψ. In the above discussion of conditional tests, (4.4) would be independent of λ. One general approach to construction of a test statistic T is to generalize the simple likelihood ratio (4.3), and to define

$$LR = \frac{\max_{H_A} L(\psi, \lambda)}{\max_{H_0} L(\psi, \lambda)}.$$

For testing $H_0 : \psi = \psi_0$ versus $H_A : \psi \neq \psi_0$, this generalized likelihood ratio is equivalent to the more convenient expression

$$LR = \frac{L(\hat{\psi}, \hat{\lambda})}{L(\psi_0, \hat{\lambda}_0)} = \frac{\max_{\psi, \lambda} L(\psi, \lambda)}{\max_\lambda L(\psi_0, \lambda)}. \tag{4.7}$$

Of course this also applies when there is no nuisance parameter. For many models it is possible to show that $T = 2 \log LR$ has approximately the χ_d^2 distribution under H_0, where d is the dimension of ψ, so that

$$p \doteq \Pr(\chi_d^2 \geq t), \tag{4.8}$$

independently of λ. Thus the likelihood ratio LR is an approximate pivot.

There is a variety of related statistics, including the score statistic, and the signed likelihood ratio for one-parameter problems. With each likelihood-based statistic there is a simple approximation to the null distribution, and modifications to improve approximation in moderate-sized samples. The likelihood ratio method appears limited to parametric problems, but as we shall see in Chapter 10 it is possible to define analogues in the nonparametric case.

With all of the P-value calculations introduced thus far, simple approximations for p exist in many cases by appealing to limiting results as n increases. Part of the purpose of this chapter is to provide resampling alternatives to such approximations when they either fail to give appropriate accuracy or do not exist at all. Section 4.2 discusses ways in which resampling and simulation can help with parametric tests, starting with exact Monte Carlo tests. Section 4.3 briefly reviews permutation and randomization tests. This leads on to the wider topic of nonparametric bootstrap tests in Section 4.4. Section 4.5 describes a simple method for improving P-values when these are biased. Most of the examples in this chapter involve relatively simple applications. Chapters 6 and beyond contain more substantial applications.

4.2 Resampling for Parametric Tests

Broadly speaking, parametric resampling may be useful in any testing problem where either standard approximations do not apply or where the accuracy of such approximations is suspect. There is a wide range of such problems, including hypotheses with order constraints, hypotheses involving separate models, and graphical tests. In all of these problems, the basic method is to use a parametric resampling scheme as outlined in Section 2.2 except that here the simulation model must satisfy the relevant null hypothesis.

4.2.1 Monte Carlo tests

One special situation is when the null hypothesis distribution of T does not involve any nuisance parameters. Occasionally this happens directly, but more often it is induced, either by standardizing some initial statistic, or by conditioning on a sufficient statistic, as explained earlier. In the latter case the exact P-value is given by (4.4) rather than (4.1). In practice the exact P-value may be difficult or impossible to calculate, and Monte Carlo tests provide convenient approximations to the full tests. As we shall see, Monte Carlo tests are exact in their own right, and among bootstrap tests are special in this way.

The basic Monte Carlo test compares the observed statistic t to R independent values of T which are obtained from corresponding samples independently simulated under the null hypothesis model. If these simulated values are denoted by $t_1^*, \ldots, t_R^*$, then under H_0 all $R+1$ values $t, t_1^*, \ldots, t_R^*$ are equally likely values of T. That is, assuming T is continuous,

$$\Pr(T < T^*_{(r)} \mid H_0) = \frac{r}{R+1}, \tag{4.9}$$

where as usual $T^*_{(r)}$ denotes the rth ordered value. If exactly k of the simulated t^* values exceed t and none equal it, then

$$p = \Pr(T \geq t \mid H_0) \doteq p_{\mathrm{mc}} = \frac{k+1}{R+1}. \tag{4.10}$$

The right-hand side is referred to as the Monte Carlo P-value. If T is continuous, then it follows from (4.9) that under H_0 the distribution of the corresponding random variable P_{mc} is uniform on $(\frac{1}{R+1}, \ldots, \frac{R}{R+1}, 1)$. This result is the discrete analogue of (4.2), and guarantees that P_{mc} has the error rate interpretation. In this sense the Monte Carlo test is exact. It differs from the full test, which corresponds to $R = \infty$, by blurring the critical region of the full test for any attainable level.

If T is discrete, then repeat values of t^* can occur. If exactly l of the t^* values equal t, then it is sometimes advocated that one bounds the significance probability,

$$\frac{k+1}{R+1} \leq p_{\mathrm{mc}} \leq \frac{k+l+1}{R+1}.$$

Our strict interpretation of (4.1) would have us use the upper bound, and so we adopt the general definition

#(A) means the number of times the event A occurs.

$$p_{\mathrm{mc}} = \frac{1 + \#\{t^*_r \geq t\}}{R+1}. \tag{4.11}$$

Example 4.1 (Logistic regression) Suppose that $y_1, \ldots, y_n$ are independent binary outcomes, with corresponding scalar covariate values $x_1, \ldots, x_n$, and that we wish to test whether or not x influences y. If our chosen model is the logistic regression model

$$\log \frac{\Pr(Y_j = 1 \mid x_j)}{\Pr(Y_j = 0 \mid x_j)} = \lambda + \psi x_j, \quad j = 1, \ldots, n,$$

then the null hypothesis is $H_0 : \psi = 0$. Under H_0 the sufficient statistic for λ is $S = \sum Y_j$ and $T = \sum x_j Y_j$ is the natural test statistic; T is in fact optimal for the logistic model, but is also effective for monotone transformations of the odds ratio other than logarithm. The significance is to be calculated according to (4.4).

The null distribution of $Y_1, \ldots, Y_n$ given $S = s$ is uniform over all $\binom{n}{s}$ permutations of $y_1, \ldots, y_n$. Rather than generate all of these permutations to compute (4.4) exactly, we can generate R random permutations and apply (4.11). A simulated sample will then be $(x_1, y^*_1), \ldots, (x_n, y^*_n)$, where $y^*_1, \ldots, y^*_n$ is a random permutation of $y_1, \ldots, y_n$, and the associated test statistic will be $t^* = \sum x_j y^*_j$.

0	1	2	3	4	3	4	2	2	1
0	2	0	2	4	2	3	3	4	2
1	1	1	1	4	1	5	2	2	3
4	1	2	5	2	0	3	2	1	1
3	1	4	3	1	0	0	2	7	0

Table 4.1 $n = 50$ counts of balsam-fir seedlings in five feet square quadrats.

In some applications there will be repeats among the x values, or equivalently m_i binomial trials with a_i occurrences of $y = 1$ at the ith distinct value of x. If the data are expressed in the latter form, then the same random permutation procedure can be applied to the original expanded form of data with $n = \sum m_i$ individual ys.
■

Example 4.2 (Overdispersed counts)   The data in Table 4.1 are $n = 50$ counts of fir seedlings in small quadrats, part of a larger dataset. The actual spatial layout is preserved, although we are not concerned with this here. Rather we wish to test the null hypothesis that these data are a random sample from a Poisson distribution with unknown mean. The concern is that the data are overdispersed relative to the Poisson distribution, which strongly suggests that we take as test statistic the dispersion index $T = \sum(Y_j - \bar{Y})^2 / \bar{Y}$. Under the Poisson model $S = \sum Y_j$ is sufficient for the common mean, so we carry out a conditional test and apply (4.4). For the data, $t = 55.15$ and $s = 107$.

Now under the null hypothesis Poisson model, the conditional distribution of $Y_1, \ldots, Y_n$ given $\sum Y_j = s$ is multinomial with denominator s and n categories each having probability n^{-1}. It is easy to simulate from this distribution. In the first $R = 99$ simulated values t^*, 24 are larger than $t = 55.15$. So the Monte Carlo P-value (4.11) is equal to 0.25, and we conclude that the data dispersion is consistent with Poisson dispersion. Increasing R to 999 makes little difference, giving $p = 0.235$. The left panel of Figure 4.1 shows a histogram of all 999 values of $t^* - t$: the unshaded part of the histogram corresponds to values $t^* \geq t$ which count toward significance.

For this simple problem the null distribution of T given $S = s$ is approximately χ^2_{n-1}. That this approximation is accurate for our data is illustrated in the right panel of Figure 4.1, which plots the ordered values of t^* against quantiles of the χ^2_{49} distribution. The P-value obtained with this approximation is 0.253, close to the exact value. There are two points to make about this. First, the simulation results enable us to check on the accuracy of the theoretical approximation: if the approximation is good, then we can use it; but if it isn't, then we have the Monte Carlo P-value. Secondly, the Monte Carlo method does not require knowledge of a theoretical approximation, which may not even exist in more complicated problems, such as spatial analysis of these data. The Monte Carlo method applies very generally.
■

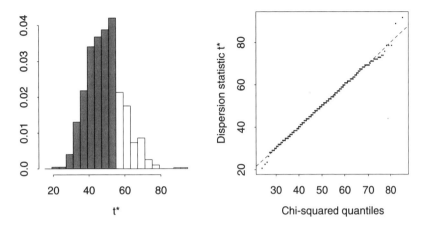

Figure 4.1 Simulation results for dispersion test. Left panel: histogram of $R = 999$ values of the dispersion statistic t^* obtained under multinomial sampling: the data value is $t = 55.15$ and $p_{mc} = 0.235$. Right panel: chi-squared plot of ordered values of t^*, dashed line corresponding to χ^2_{49} approximation to null conditional distribution.

It seems intuitively clear that the sensitivity of the Monte Carlo test increases with R. We shall discuss this issue later, but for now we note that it is advisable to take R to be at least 99.

There are two important aspects of the Monte Carlo test which make it widely useful. The first is that we only need to be able to simulate data under the null hypothesis, this being relatively simple even in some very complicated problems, such as those involving spatial processes (Chapter 8). Secondly, $t, t^*_1, \ldots, t^*_R$ do not need to be independent outcomes: the method remains valid so long as they are *exchangeable* outcomes, which is to say that the joint density of $T, T^*_1, \ldots, T^*_R$ under H_0 is invariant under permutation of its arguments. This allows us to apply Monte Carlo tests to quite complicated problems, as we see next.

4.2.2 Markov chain Monte Carlo tests

In some applications of the exact conditional test, with P-value given by (4.4), the conditional probability calculation is difficult or impossible to do directly. The Monte Carlo test is in principle appropriate here, since the null distribution (given s) does not depend upon unknown parameters. A practical obstacle is that in complicated problems it may be difficult to simulate independent samples directly from that conditional null distribution. However, as we observed before, the Monte Carlo test only requires exchangeable samples. This opens up a new possibility, the use of Markov chain Monte Carlo simulation, in which only the unconditional null distribution is needed.

The basic idea is to represent data $y = (y_1, \ldots, y_n)$ as the result of N steps of a Markov chain with some initial state $x = (x_1, \ldots, x_n)$, and to generate each y^* by an independent simulation of N steps with the same initial state x. If the Markov chain has equilibrium distribution equal to the null hypothesis distribution of $Y = (Y_1, \ldots, Y_n)$, then y and the R replicates of y^* are exchangeable outcomes under H_0 and (4.11) applies.

Suppose that under H_0 the data have joint density $f_0(y)$ for $y \in \mathcal{B}$, where both f_0 and $\mathcal{B}$ are conditioned on sufficient statistic s if we are dealing with a conditional test. For simplicity suppose that $\mathcal{B}$ has $|\mathcal{B}|$ elements, which we now regard as possible states labelled $(1, 2, \ldots, |\mathcal{B}|)$ of a Markov chain $\{Z_t, \ t = \ldots, -1, 0, 1, \ldots\}$ in discrete time. Consider the data y to be one realization of Z_N. We then have to fix an appropriate value or state for Z_0, and with this initial state simulate the R independent values of Z_N which are the R values of Y^*. The Markov chain is defined so that f_0 is the equilibrium distribution, which can be enforced by appropriate choice of the one-step forward transition probability matrix Q, say, with elements

$$q_{uv} = \Pr(Z_{t+1} = v \mid Z_t = u), \quad u, v \in \mathcal{B}.$$

For the moment suppose that Q is already known.

The first part of the simulation is to produce a value for Z_0. Starting from state y at time N, we simulate N backward steps of the Markov chain using the one-step backward transition probabilities

$$\Pr(Z_t = u \mid Z_{t+1} = v) = f_0(u)q_{uv}/f_0(v). \tag{4.12}$$

Let the final state, the realized value of Z_0, be x. Note that if H_0 is true, so that y was indeed sampled from f_0, then $\Pr(Z_0 = x) = f_0(x)$. In the second part of the simulation, which we repeat independently R times, we simulate N forward steps of the Markov chain, starting in state x and ending up in state $y^* = (y_1^*, \ldots, y_n^*)$. Since under H_0 the chain starts in equilibrium,

$$\Pr(Y^* = y^* \mid H_0) = \Pr(Z_N = y^*) = f_0(y^*).$$

That is, if H_0 is true, then the R replicates $y_1^*, \ldots, y_R^*$ and data y are all sampled from f_0, as we require. Moreover, the R replicates of y^* are jointly exchangeable with the data under H_0. To see this, we have first that

$$f(y, y_1^*, \ldots, y_R^* \mid H_0) = f_0(y) \sum_x \Pr(Z_0 = x \mid Z_N = y) \prod_{r=1}^{R} \Pr(Z_N = y_r^* \mid Z_0 = x),$$

using the independence of the replicate simulations from x. But by the definition of the first part of the simulation, where (4.12) applies,

$$f_0(y)\Pr(Z_0 = x \mid Z_N = y) = f_0(x)\Pr(Z_N = y \mid Z_0 = x),$$

and so

$$f(y, y_1^*, \ldots, y_R^* \mid H_0) = \sum_x f_0(x) \left\{ \Pr(Z_N = y \mid Z_0 = x) \prod_{r=1}^{R} \Pr(Z_N = y_r^* \mid Z_0 = x) \right\},$$

which is a symmetric function of $y, y_1^*, \ldots, y_R^*$ as required. Given that the data vector and simulated data vectors are exchangeable under H_0, the associated test statistic values $(t, t_1^*, \ldots, t_R^*)$ are also exchangeable outcomes under H_0. Therefore (4.11) applies for the P-value calculation.

To complete the description of the method, it remains to define the transition probability matrix Q so that the chain is irreducible with equilibrium distribution $f_0(y)$. There are several ways to do this, all of which use ratios $f_0(v)/f_0(u)$. For example, the Metropolis algorithm starts with a carrier Markov chain on state space $\mathcal{B}$ having any symmetric one-step forward transition probability matrix M, and defines one-step forward transition from state u in the desired Markov chain as follows:

- given we are in state u, select state v with probability m_{uv};
- accept the transition to v with probability $\min\{1, f_0(v)/f_0(u)\}$, otherwise reject it and stay in state u.

It is easy to check that the induced Markov chain has transition probabilities

$$q_{uv} = \min\{1, f_0(v)/f_0(u)\} m_{uv}, \quad u \neq v,$$

and

$$q_{uu} = m_{uu} + \sum_{v \neq u} \max\{0, 1 - f_0(v)/f_0(u)\} m_{uv},$$

and from this it follows that f_0 is indeed the equilibrium distribution of the Markov chain, as required. In applications it is not necessary to calculate the probabilities m_{uv} explicitly, although the symmetry and irreducibility of the carrier chain must be checked. If the matrix M is not symmetric, then the acceptance probability in the Metropolis algorithm must be modified to $\min\left[1, f_0(v) m_{vu}/\{f_0(u) m_{uv}\}\right]$.

The crucial feature of the Markov chain method is that f_0 itself is not needed, only ratios $f_0(v)/f_0(u)$ being involved. This means that for conditional tests, where f_0 is the conditional density for Y given $S = s$, only ratios of the unconditional null density for Y are needed:

$$\frac{f_0(v)}{f_0(u)} = \frac{\Pr(Y = v \mid S = s, H_0)}{\Pr(Y = u \mid S = s, H_0)} = \frac{\Pr(Y = v \mid H_0)}{\Pr(Y = u \mid H_0)}.$$

This greatly simplifies many applications.

The realizations of the Markov chain are symmetrically tied to the artificial starting value x, and this induces a symmetric correlation among $(t, t_1^*, \ldots, t_R^*)$.

This correlation depends upon the particular construction of Q, and reduces to zero at a rate which depends upon Q as m increases. While the correlation does not affect the validity of the P-value calculation, it does affect the power of the test: the higher the correlation, the lower the power.

Example 4.3 (Logistic regression)   We return to the problem of Example 4.1, which provides a very simple if artificial illustration. The data y are a binary sequence of length n with s ones, and calculations are to be conditional on $\sum Y_j = s$. Recall that direct Monte Carlo simulation is possible, since all $\binom{n}{s}$ possible data sequences are equally likely under the null hypothesis of constant probability of a unit response.

One simple Markov chain has one-step transitions which select a pair of subscripts i, j at random, and switch y_i and y_j. Clearly the chain is irreducible, since one can progress from any one binary sequence with s ones to any other. All ratios of null probabilities $f_0(v)/f_0(u)$ are equal to one, since all binary sequences with s ones are equally probable. Therefore if we run the Metropolis algorithm, all switches are accepted. But note that this Markov chain, while simple to implement, is inefficient and will require a large number of steps to induce approximate independence of the t_r^*s. The most effective Markov chain would have one-step transitions which are random permutations, and for this only one step would be required.   ■

Example 4.4 (AML data)   For data such as those in Example 3.9, consider testing the null hypothesis of proportional hazard functions. Denote the failure times by $z_1 < z_2 < \cdots < z_n$, assuming no ties for the moment, and define r_{ij} to be the number in group i who were at risk just prior to z_j. Further, let y_j be 0 or 1 according as the failure at z_j is in group 1 or 2, and denote the hazard function at time z for group i by $h_i(z)$. Then

$$\Pr(Y_j = 1) = \frac{r_{2j}h_2(z_j)}{r_{1j}h_1(z_j) + r_{2j}h_2(z_j)} = \frac{\theta_j}{a_j + \theta_j},$$

where $a_j = r_{1j}/r_{2j}$ and $\theta_j = h_2(z_j)/h_1(z_j)$ for $j = 1, \ldots, n$. The null hypothesis of proportional hazards implies the hypothesis $H_0 : \theta_1 = \cdots = \theta_n$.

For the data of Example 3.9, where $n = 18$, the values of y and a are given in Table 4.2; one tie has been randomly split. Note that censored data contribute only to the rs: the times are not used.

Of course the Y_js are not independent, because a_j depends upon the outcomes of $Y_1, \ldots, Y_{j-1}$. However, for the purposes of illustration here we shall pretend that the a_js are fixed, as well as the survival times and censoring times. That is, we shall treat the Y_js as independent Bernoulli variables with probabilities as given above. Under this pretence the conditional likelihood for

4.2 · Resampling for Parametric Tests

z	5	5	8	8	9	12	13	18	23	23	27	30	31	33	34	43	45	48
r_1	11	11	11	11	11	10	10	8	7	7	6	5	5	4	4	3	3	2
r_2	12	11	10	9	8	8	7	6	6	5	5	4	3	3	2	2	1	0
a	$\frac{11}{12}$	1	$\frac{11}{10}$	$\frac{11}{9}$	$\frac{11}{8}$	$\frac{10}{8}$	$\frac{10}{7}$	$\frac{8}{6}$	$\frac{7}{6}$	$\frac{7}{6}$	$\frac{6}{5}$	$\frac{5}{4}$	$\frac{5}{3}$	$\frac{4}{3}$	2	$\frac{3}{2}$	3	∞
y	1	1	1	1	0	1	0	0	1	0	1	1	0	1	0	1	1	0

Table 4.2 Ingredients of the conditional test for proportional hazards. Failure times as in Table 3.4; at time $z = 23$ the failure in group 2 is taken to occur first.

$\theta_1, \ldots, \theta_{18}$ is simply

$$\prod_{j=1}^{18} \left(\frac{\theta_j}{a_j + \theta_j} \right)^{y_j} \left(\frac{a_j}{a_j + \theta_j} \right)^{1-y_j}.$$

Note that because $a_{18} = \infty$, Y_{18} must be 0 whatever the value of θ_{18}, and so this final response is uninformative. We therefore drop y_{18} from the analysis. Having done this, we see that under H_0 the sufficient statistic for the common hazard ratio θ is $S = \sum_{j=1}^{17} Y_j$, whose observed value is $s = 11$.

Whatever the test statistic T, the exact conditional P-value (4.4) must be approximated. Direct simulation appears impossible, but a simple Markov chain simulation is possible. First, the state space of the chain is $\mathscr{B} = \{x = (x_1, \ldots, x_{17}) : \sum x_j = s\}$, that is all permutations of $y_1, \ldots, y_{17}$. For any two vectors x and $\tilde{x}$ in the state-space, the ratio of null conditional joint probabilities is

$$\frac{p(\tilde{x} \mid s, \theta_1 = \cdots = \theta_{17})}{p(x \mid s, \theta_1 = \cdots = \theta_{17})} = \prod_{j=1}^{17} a_j^{x_j - \tilde{x}_j}.$$

We take the carrier Markov chain to have one-step transitions which are random permutations: this guarantees fast movement over the state space. A step which moves from x to $\tilde{x}$ is then accepted with probability min $\left(1, \prod_{j=1}^{17} a_j^{x_j - \tilde{x}_j} \right)$. By symmetry the reverse chain is defined in exactly the same way.

The test statistic must be chosen to match the particular alternative hypothesis thought relevant. Here we suppose that the alternative is a monotone ratio of hazards, for which $T = \sum_{j=1}^{17} Y_j \log(Z_j)$ seems to be a reasonable choice. The Markov chain simulation is applied with $N = 100$ steps back to give the initial state x and 100 steps forward to state y^*, the latter repeated $R = 99$ times. Of the resulting t^* values, 48 are less than or equal to the observed value $t = 17.75$, so the P-value is $(1 + 48)/(1 + 99) = 0.49$. Thus there appears to be no evidence against the proportional hazards model.

Average acceptance probability in the Metropolis algorithm is approximately 0.7, and results for $N = 10$ and $N = 1000$ appear indistinguishable from those for $N = 100$. This indicates unusually fast convergence for applications of the Markov chain method. ∎

The use of R conditionally independent realizations of the Markov chain is sometimes referred to as the *parallel method*. In contrast is the *series method*, where only one realization is used. Since the successive states of the chain are dependent, a randomization device is needed to induce exchangeability. For details see Problem 4.2.

4.2.3 Parametric bootstrap tests

In many problems of course the distribution of T under H_0 will depend upon nuisance parameters which cannot be conditioned away, so that the Monte Carlo test method does not apply exactly. Then the natural approach is to fit the null model $\hat{F}_0$ and use (4.5) to compute the P-value, i.e. $p = \Pr(T \geq t \mid \hat{F}_0)$. For example, for the parametric model where we are testing $H_0 : \psi = \psi_0$ with λ a nuisance parameter, $\hat{F}_0$ would be the CDF of $f(y \mid \psi_0, \hat{\lambda}_0)$ with $\hat{\lambda}_0$ the maximum likelihood estimator (MLE) of the nuisance parameter when ψ is fixed equal to ψ_0. Calculation of the P-value by (4.5) is referred to as a bootstrap test.

If (4.5) cannot be computed exactly, or if there is no satisfactory approximation (normal or otherwise), then we proceed by simulation. That is, R independent replicate samples $y_1^*, \ldots, y_n^*$ are drawn from $\hat{F}_0$, and for the rth such sample the test statistic value t_r^* is calculated. Then the significance probability (4.5) will be approximated by

$$p_{\text{boot}} = \frac{1 + \#\{t_r^* \geq t\}}{R + 1}. \tag{4.13}$$

Ordinarily one would use a simple proportion here, but we have chosen to make the definition match that for the Monte Carlo test in (4.11).

Example 4.5 (Separate families test)   Suppose that we wish to choose between the alternative model forms $f_0(y \mid \eta)$ and $f_1(y \mid \zeta)$ for the PDF of the random sample $y_1, \ldots, y_n$. In some circumstances it may make sense to take one model, say f_0, as a null hypothesis, and to test this against the other model as alternative hypothesis. In the notation of Section 4.1, the nuisance parameter is $\lambda = (\eta, \zeta)$ and ψ is the binary indicator of model, with null value $\psi_0 = 0$ and alternative value $\psi_A = 1$. The likelihood ratio statistic (4.7) is equivalent to the more convenient form

$$T = n^{-1} \log \frac{L_1(\hat{\zeta})}{L_0(\hat{\eta})} = n^{-1} \sum_{j=1}^{n} \log \frac{f_1(y_j \mid \hat{\zeta})}{f_0(y_j \mid \hat{\eta})}, \tag{4.14}$$

where $\hat{\eta}$ and $\hat{\zeta}$ are the MLEs and L_0 and L_1 the likelihoods under f_0 and f_1 respectively. If the two families are strictly separate, then the chi-squared approximation (4.8) does not apply. There is a normal approximation for the null distribution of T, but this is often quite unreliable except for very large n. The parametric bootstrap provides a more reliable and simple option.

The parametric bootstrap works as follows. We generate R samples of size n by random sampling from the fitted null model $f_0(y \mid \hat{\eta})$. For each sample we calculate estimates $\hat{\eta}^*$ and $\hat{\zeta}^*$ by maximizing the simulated log likelihoods

$$\ell_1^*(\zeta) = \sum \log f_1(y_j^* \mid \zeta), \quad \ell_0^*(\eta) = \sum \log f_0(y_j^* \mid \eta),$$

and compute the simulated log likelihood ratio statistic

$$t^* = n^{-1}\{\ell_1^*(\hat{\zeta}^*) - \ell_0^*(\hat{\eta}^*)\}.$$

Then we calculate p using (4.13).

As a particular illustration, consider the failure-time data in Table 1.2. Two plausible models for this type of data are gamma and lognormal, that is

$$f_0(y \mid \eta) = \frac{\kappa(\kappa y)^{\kappa-1} \exp(-\kappa y/\mu)}{\mu^\kappa \Gamma(\kappa)}, \quad f_1(y \mid \zeta) = (\beta y)^{-1}\phi\left(\frac{\log y - \alpha}{\beta}\right), \quad y > 0.$$

For these data the MLEs of the gamma mean and index are $\hat{\mu} = \bar{y} = 108.083$ and $\hat{\kappa} = 0.707$, the latter being the solution to

$$\log(\kappa) - h(\kappa) = \log(\bar{y}) - \overline{\log y}$$

$\overline{\log y}$ and $s^2_{\log y}$ are the average and sample variance for the log y_j.

with $h(\kappa) = d\log\Gamma(\kappa)/d\kappa$, the digamma function. The MLEs of the mean and variance of the normal distribution for $\log Y$ are $\hat{\alpha} = \overline{\log y} = 3.829$ and $\hat{\beta}^2 = (n-1)s^2_{\log y}/n = 2.339$. The test statistic (4.14) is

$$t = -\hat{\kappa}\log(\hat{\kappa}/\bar{y}) - \hat{\kappa}\hat{\alpha} + \hat{\kappa} + \log\Gamma(\hat{\kappa}) - \tfrac{1}{2}\log(2\pi\hat{\beta}^2) - \tfrac{1}{2},$$

whose value for the data is $t = -0.465$. The left panel of Figure 4.2 shows a histogram of $R = 999$ values of t^* under sampling from the fitted gamma model: of these, 619 are greater than t and so $p = 0.62$.

Note that the histogram has a fairly non-normal shape in this case, suggesting that a normal approximation will not be very accurate. This is true also for the (rather complicated) studentized version Z of T: the right panel of Figure 4.2 shows the normal plot of bootstrap values z^*. The observed value of z is 0.4954, for which the bootstrap P-value is 0.34, somewhat smaller than that computed for t, but not changing the conclusion that there is no evidence to change from a gamma to a lognormal model for these data. There are good general reasons to studentize test statistics; see Section 4.4.1.

It should perhaps be mentioned that significance tests of this kind are not always helpful in distinguishing between models, in the sense that we could find evidence against either both or neither of them. This is especially true with small samples such as we have here. In this case the reverse test shows no evidence against the lognormal model. ∎

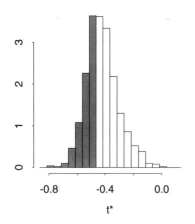
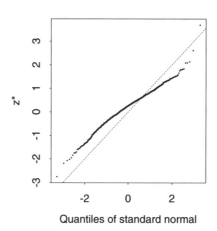

Figure 4.2 Null hypothesis resampling for failure data. Left panel shows histogram of t^* under gamma sampling. Right panel shows normal plot of z^*; $R = 999$ and gamma parameters $\hat{\mu} = 108.0833, \hat{\kappa} = 0.7065$; dotted line is theoretical $N(0, 1)$ approximation.

4.2.4 Graphical tests

Graphical methods are popular in model checking: examples include normal and half-normal plots of residuals in regression, plots of Cook distance in regression, plots of nonparametric hazard function estimates, and plots of intensity functions in spatial analysis (Section 8.3). In many cases the nominal shape of the plot is a straight line, which aids the detection of deviation from a null model. Whatever the situation, informed interpretation of the plot requires some notion of its probable variation under the model being checked, unless the sample size is so large that deviation is obvious (c.f. the plot of resampling results in Figure 4.2). The simplest and most common approach is to superimpose a "probable envelope", to which the original data plot is compared. This probable envelope is obtained by Monte Carlo or parametric resampling methods.

Graphical tests are not usually appropriate when a single specific alternative model is of interest. Rather they are used to suggest alternative models, depending upon the manner in which such a plot deviates from its null expected behaviour, or to find suspect data. (Indeed graphical tests are not tests in the usual sense, because there is usually no simple notion of "rejectable" behaviour: we comment more fully on this below.)

Suppose that the graph plots $T(a)$ versus a for $a \in \mathscr{A}$, a bounded set. The observed plot is $\{t(a) : a \in \mathscr{A}\}$. For example, in a normal plot $\mathscr{A}$ is a set of normal quantiles and the values of $t(a)$ are the ordered values of a sample, possibly studentized. The idea of the plot is to compare $t(a)$ with the probable behaviour of $T(a)$ for all $a \in \mathscr{A}$ when H_0 is true.

Example 4.6 (Normal plot) Consider the data in Table 3.1, and suppose in

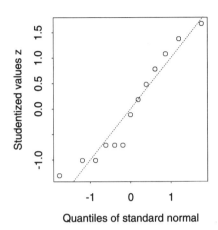

Figure 4.3 Normal plot of $n = 13$ studentized values for final sample in Table 3.1.

particular that we want to assess whether or not the last sample of $n = 13$ measurements can be assumed normal. A normal plot of the data is shown in Figure 4.3, which plots the ordered studentized values $z_{(i)} = (y_{(i)} - \bar{y})/s$ against the quantiles $a_i = \Phi^{-1}(\frac{i}{14})$ of the $N(0, 1)$ distribution. In the general notation $\mathscr{A}$ is the set of normal quantiles, and $t(a_i) = z_{(i)}$. The dotted line is the expected pattern, approximately, and the question is whether or not the points deviate sufficiently from this to suggest that the sample is non-normal.   ∎

Assume for the moment that the null hypothesis joint distribution of $\{T(a) : a \in \mathscr{A}\}$ involves no unknown nuisance parameters. This is true for a normal plot if we use studentized sample values z_i as in the previous example. Then for any fixed a we can subject $t(a)$ to a Monte Carlo test. For each of R independent sets of data $y_1^*, \ldots, y_n^*$, which are obtained by sampling from the null model, we compute the simulated plot

$$t^*(a), \quad a \in \mathscr{A}.$$

Under the null hypothesis, $T(a), T_1^*(a), \ldots, T_R^*(a)$ are independent and identically distributed for any fixed a, so that (4.9) applies with $T = T(a)$. That is,

$$\Pr\left(T(a) < T_{(j)}^*(a) \mid H_0\right) = \frac{j}{R+1}. \tag{4.15}$$

This leads to (4.11) as the one-sided P-value at the given value of a, if large values of $t(a)$ are evidence against the null model. There are obvious modifications if we want to test for small values of $t(a)$, or if we want a two-sided test.

The test as described applies for any single value of a. However, the graphical test does not look just at one fixed a, but rather at all $a \in \mathscr{A}$ simultaneously. In principle the Monte Carlo test could be applied at all values of $a \in \mathscr{A}$, but this would be time-consuming and difficult to interpret. To simplify matters, at each value of a we compute lower and upper critical values corresponding to fixed one-sided levels p, and plot these critical values against a to provide critical curves against which to compare the whole data plot $\{t(a), a \in \mathscr{A}\}$.

So the method is to choose integers R and k so that $\frac{k}{R+1} = p$, the desired one-sided test level, and then compute the critical values

$$t_{(k)}^*(a), t_{(R+1-k)}^*(a)$$

from the R simulated plots. If $t(a)$ exceeds the upper value, or falls below the lower value, then the corresponding one-sided P-value is at most p; the two-sided test which rejects H_0 if $t(a)$ falls outside the interval $[t_{(k)}^*(a), t_{(R+1-k)}^*(a)]$ has level equal to $2p$. The set of all upper and lower critical values defines the test envelope

$$\mathscr{E}^{1-2p} = \{[t_{(k)}^*(a), t_{(R+1-k)}^*(a)] : a \in \mathscr{A}\}. \tag{4.16}$$

Excursions of $t(a)$ outside $\mathscr{E}^{1-2p}$ are regarded as evidence against H_0, and this simultaneous comparison across all values of a is what is usually meant by the graphical test.

Example 4.7 (Normal plot, continued)   For the normal plot of the previous example, suppose we set $p = 0.05$. The smallest simulation size that works is $R = 19$, and then we take $k = 1$ in (4.16). The test envelope will therefore be the lines connecting the maxima and the minima. Because we are plotting studentized sample values, which eliminates mean and variance parameters, the simulation can be done with the $N(0, 1)$ distribution. Each simulated sample $y_1^*, \ldots, y_{13}^*$ is studentized to give $z_i^* = (y_i^* - \bar{y}^*)/s^*$, $i = 1, \ldots, 13$, whose ordered values are then plotted against the same normal quantiles $a_i = \Phi^{-1}(\frac{i}{14})$. The left panel of Figure 4.4 shows a set of $R = 19$ normal plots (plotted as connecting dashed lines) and their envelope (solid curves) for studentized values of simulated samples of $n = 13$ $N(0, 1)$ data. The right panel shows the envelope of these plots together with the original data plot. Note that one of the inner points falls just outside the envelope: this might be taken as mild evidence against normality of the data, but such an interpretation may be premature, in light of the discussion below.   ∎

The discussion so far assumes either that the null model involves no unknown parameters, or that it is possible to eliminate unknown parameters by standardization, as in the previous example. In the latter case simulated

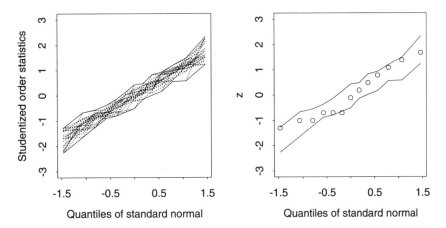

Figure 4.4 Graphical test of normality. Left panel: normal plots (dashed lines) of studentized values for $R = 19$ samples of $n = 13$ simulated from the $N(0, 1)$ distribution, together with their envelope (solid line). Right panel: envelope of the simulated plots superimposed on the original data plot.

samples can be generated from any null model F_0. When unknown model parameters cannot be eliminated, we would simulate from $\hat{F}_0$: then (4.15) will be approximately true provided n is not too small.

There are two aspects of the graphical test which need careful thought, namely the choice of R and the interpretation of the resulting plot. It seems clear from earlier discussion that for $p = 0.05$, say, $R = 19$ is too small: the test envelope is too random. $R = 99$ would seem to be a more sensible choice, provided this is not computationally difficult. But we should consider how formal is to be the interpretation of the graph. As it stands the notional one-sided significance levels p hold pointwise, and certainly the chance that the envelope captures an entire plot will be far less than $1 - 2p$. So it would not make sense to infer evidence against the null model if one arbitrarily placed point falls outside the envelope, as happened in Example 4.7. In fact in that example the chance is about 0.5 that some point will fall outside the simulation envelope, in contrast to the pointwise chance 0.1.

For some purposes it will be useful to know the overall error rate, i.e. the chance of a point falling outside the envelope, or even to control this rate. While this is difficult to do exactly, there is a simple empirical approach which works satisfactorily. Given the R simulated plots which were used to calculate the test envelope, we can simulate the graphical test by comparing $\{t_r^*(a), a \in \mathscr{A}\}$ to the envelope $\mathscr{E}_{-r}^{1-2p}$ that is obtained from the other $R - 1$ simulated plots. If we repeat this simulated test for $r = 1, \ldots, R$, then we obtain a resample estimate of the overall two-sided error rate

$$\frac{\#\{r : \{t_r^*(a), a \in \mathscr{A}\} \text{ exits } \mathscr{E}_{-r}^{1-2p}\}}{R}. \tag{4.17}$$

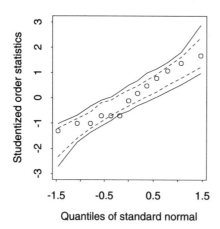

Figure 4.5 Normal plot of $n = 13$ studentized values for final sample in Table 3.1, together with simultaneous (solid lines) and pointwise (dashed lines) two-sided 0.10 test envelopes. $R = 199$

This is easy to calculate, since $\{t_r^*(a), a \in \mathscr{A}\}$ exits $\mathscr{E}_{-r}^{1-2p}$ if and only if

$$\text{rank}\{t_r^*(a)\} \leq k \quad \text{or} \quad \text{rank}\{t_r^*(a)\} \geq R + 1 - k$$

for at least one value of a, where as before $k = p(R + 1)$. Thus if the R plots are represented by a $R \times N$ array, we first compute columnwise ranks. Then we calculate the proportion of rows in which either the minimum rank is less than or equal to k, or the maximum rank is greater than or equal to $R + 1 - k$, or both. The corresponding one-sided error rates are estimated in the obvious way.

Example 4.8 (Normal plot, continued) For the normal plot of Example 4.6, an overall two-sided error rate of approximately 0.1 requires $R = 199$. Figure 4.5 shows a graphical test plot for $R = 199$ with outer envelope corresponding to overall two-sided error rate 0.1 and inner envelope corresponding to pointwise two-sided error rate 0.1; the empirical error rate (4.17) for the outer envelope is 0.10.   ■

In practice one might rather be looking for trends, manifested by sequences of points going outside the test envelope. Alternatively one might be focusing attention on particular regions of the plot, such as the tails of a probability plot. Because such plots may be used to detect several possible deviations from a hypothetical model, and hence be interpreted in several possible ways, it is not possible to make a single recommendation that will induce a controlled error rate. In the absence of a single criterion by which the plot is to be judged, it seems wise to plot envelopes corresponding to both pointwise one-sided error rate p and simultaneous one-sided error rate p, say with $p = 0.05$. This is relatively easy to do using (4.17). For a further illustration see Example 8.9.

4.2.5 Choice of R

In any simulation-based test, relatively few samples could be used if it quickly became clear that p was so large as to not be regarded as evidence against H_0. For example, if the event $t^* \geq t$ occurred 50 times in the first 100 samples, then it is reasonably certain that p will exceed 0.25, say, for much larger R, so there is little point in simulating further. On the other hand, if we observed $t^* \geq t$ only five times, then it would be worth sampling further to more accurately determine the level of significance.

One effect of not computing p exactly is to weaken the power of the test, essentially because the critical region of a fixed-level test has been randomly displaced. The effect can be quantified approximately as follows. Consider testing at level α, which is to say reject H_0 if $p \leq \alpha$. If the integer k is chosen equal to $(R+1)\alpha$, then the test rejects H_0 when $t^*_{(R+1-k)} < t$. For the alternative hypothesis H_A, the power of the test is

$$\pi_R(\alpha, H_A) = \Pr(\text{reject } H_0 \mid H_A) = \Pr(T^*_{(R+1-k)} < T \mid H_A).$$

To evaluate this probability, suppose for simplicity that T has a continuous distribution, with PDF $g_0(t)$ and CDF $G_0(t)$ under H_0, and density $g_A(t)$ under H_A. Then from the standard result for PDF of an order statistic we have

$$\pi_R(\alpha, H_A) = \int_{-\infty}^{\infty} \int_{-\infty}^{t} R\binom{R-1}{k-1} G_0(x)^{R-k} g_0(x) \{1 - G_0(x)\}^{k-1} g_A(t) dx dt.$$

After change of variable and some rearrangement of the integral, this becomes

$$\pi_R(\alpha, H_A) = \int_0^1 \pi_\infty(u, H_A) h_R(u; \alpha) du, \qquad (4.18)$$

where $\pi_\infty(u, H_A)$ is the power of the test using the exact P-value, and $h_R(u; \alpha)$ is the beta density on $[0, 1]$ with indices $(R+1)\alpha$ and $(R+1)(1-\alpha)$.

The next part of the calculation relies on $\pi_R(\alpha, H_A)$ being a concave function of α, as is usually the case. Then a lower bound for $\pi_\infty(u, H_A)$ is $\tilde{\pi}_\infty(u, H_A)$ which equals $u \pi_\infty(\alpha, H_A)/\alpha$ for $u \leq \alpha$ and $\pi_\infty(\alpha, H_A)$ for $u > \alpha$. It follows by applying (4.18) to $\tilde{\pi}_R(\alpha, H_A)$, and some manipulation, that

$$
\begin{aligned}
\pi_\infty(\alpha, H_A) - \pi_R(\alpha, H_A) &\leq \frac{\pi_\infty(\alpha, H_A)}{2\alpha} \int_0^1 |u - \alpha| h_R(u; \alpha) du \\
&= \frac{\pi_\infty(\alpha, H_A) \alpha^{(R+1)\alpha} (1-\alpha)^{(R+1)(1-\alpha)} \Gamma(R+1)}{(R+1)\alpha \Gamma((R+1)\alpha) \Gamma((R+1)(1-\alpha))}.
\end{aligned}
$$

We apply Stirling's approximation $\Gamma(x) \doteq (2\pi)^{1/2} x^{x-1/2} \exp(-x)$ for large x to the right-hand side and obtain the approximate bound

$$\frac{\pi_R(\alpha, H_A)}{\pi_\infty(\alpha, H_A)} \leq 1 - \left\{ \frac{1-\alpha}{2\pi(R+1)\alpha} \right\}^{1/2}. \qquad (4.19)$$

The following table gives some numerical values of this approximate bound.

simulation size R	19	39	99	199	499	999	9999
power ratio for $\alpha = 0.05$	0.61	0.73	0.83	0.88	0.92	0.95	0.98
power ratio for $\alpha = 0.01$	—	—	0.60	0.72	0.82	0.87	0.96

These values suggest that the loss of power with $R = 99$ is not serious for $\alpha \geq 0.05$, and that $R = 999$ should generally be safe. In fact the values can be quite conservative. For example, for testing a normal mean the power ratios for $\alpha = 0.05$ are usually above 0.85 and 0.97 for $R = 19$ and $R = 99$ respectively.

4.3 Nonparametric Permutation Tests

In many practical situations it is useful to have available statistical methods which do not depend upon specific parametric models, if only in order to provide backup to results of parametric methods. So, with significance testing, it is useful to have nonparametric tests such as the sign test and the signed-rank test for analysing paired data, either to confirm the results of applying the parametric paired t test, or to deal with evident non-normality of the paired differences.

Nonparametric tests in general compute significance without assuming forms for the data distributions. The choice of test statistic will usually be based firmly on the physical context of the problem, possibly reinforced by what we know would be a good choice if a plausible parametric model were applicable. So, in a comparison of two treatments where we believe that treatment effects are additive, it would be reasonable to choose as test statistic the difference of means, especially if we thought that the data distributions were not far from normal; for long-tailed data distributions the difference of medians would be more reasonable from a statistical point of view. If we are concerned about the nonrobustness of means, then we might first convert data values to relative ranks and then use an appropriate rank test.

There is a vast literature on various kinds of nonparametric tests, such as rank tests, U-statistic tests, and distance tests which compare EDFs in various ways. We shall not attempt to review these here. Rather our concern in this chapter is with resampling tests, and the simplest form of nonparametric resampling test is the permutation test.

Essentially a permutation test is a comparative test, where the test statistic involves some sort of comparison between EDFs. The special feature of the permutation test is that the null hypothesis implies a reduction of the nonparametric MLE of the data distributions to EDFs which play the role of sufficient statistic S in equation (4.4). The conditional probability distribution

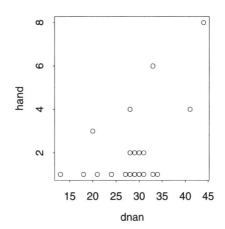

Figure 4.6 Scatter plot of $n = 37$ pairs of measurements in a study of handedness (provided by Dr Gordon Claridge, University of Oxford).

used in (4.4) is then a uniform distribution over a set of permutations of the data structure. The following example illustrates this.

Example 4.9 (Correlation test) Suppose that $Y = (U, X)$ is a random pair and that n such pairs are observed. The objective is to see if U and X are independent, this being the null hypothesis H_0. An illustrative dataset is plotted in Figure 4.6, where $u = $ dnan is a genetic measure and $x = $ hand is an integer measure of left-handedness. The alternative hypothesis is that x tends to be larger when u is larger. These data are clearly non-normal.

One simple test statistic is the sample correlation, $T = \rho(\hat{F})$ say. Note that here the EDF $\hat{F}$ puts probabilities n^{-1} on each of the n data pairs (u_i, x_i). The correlation is zero for any distribution that satisfies H_0. The correlation coefficient for the data in Figure 4.6 is 0.509.

When the form of F is unspecified, $\hat{F}$ is minimal sufficient for F. Under the null hypothesis, however, the minimal sufficient statistic is comprised of the ordered us and ordered xs, $s = (u_{(1)}, \dots, u_{(n)}, x_{(1)}, \dots, x_{(n)})$, equivalent to the two marginal EDFs. So here a conditional test can be applied, with (4.4) defining the P-value, which will therefore be independent of the underlying marginal distributions of U and X. Now when S is constrained to equal s, the random sample $(U_1, X_1), \dots, (U_n, X_n)$ is equivalent to $(u_{(1)}, X_1^*), \dots, (u_{(n)}, X_n^*)$ with $(X_1^*, \dots, X_n^*)$ a random permutation of $x_{(1)}, \dots, x_{(n)}$. Further, when H_0 is true all such permutations are equally likely, and there are $n!$ of them. Therefore the one-sided P-value is

$$p = \frac{\text{\# of permutations such that } T^* \geq t}{n!}. \tag{4.20}$$

In evaluating p, we can use the fact that all marginal sample moments

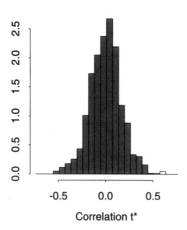

Figure 4.7 Histogram of correlation t^* values for $R = 999$ random permutations of data in Figure 4.6.

are constant across permutations. This implies that $T \geq t$ is equivalent to $\sum X_i U_i \geq \sum x_i u_i$. ∎

As a practical matter, it is rarely possible or necessary to compute the permutation P-value exactly. Typically a very large number of permutations is involved, for example more than 3 million in Example 4.9 when $n = 10$. In special cases involving linear statistics there will be theoretical approximations, such as normal approximations or improved versions of these: see Section 9.5. But for general use the most reliable approach is to make use of the Monte Carlo method of Section 4.2.1. That is, we take a large number R of random permutations, calculate the corresponding values $t_1^*, \ldots, t_R^*$ of T, and approximate p by

$$p \doteq p_{\mathrm{mc}} = \frac{1 + \#\{t_r^* \geq t\}}{R + 1}.$$

At least 99 and at most 999 random permutations should suffice.

Example 4.10 (Correlation test, ctd) For the dataset shown in Figure 4.6, the test of Example 4.9 was implemented by simulation, that is generating random permutations of the x-values, with $R = 999$. Figure 4.7 is a histogram of the correlation values. The unshaded part corresponds to the 4 t^* values which are greater than the observed correlation $t = 0.509$: the P-value is $p = (1 + 4)/(1 + 999) = 0.005$. ∎

One feature of permutation tests is that any test statistic is as easy to use as any other, at least in principle. So in the previous example it is just as easy to use the rank correlation (in which the us and xs are replaced by their relative ranks), a robust measure of correlation, or a complicated measure of distance between the bivariate EDF $\hat{F}$ and its null hypothesis version $\hat{F}_0$ which is the product of the EDFs of u and x. All that is required is that we be able to compute the test statistic for all permutations of the xs.

In the previous example the null hypothesis of independence led unambiguously to a sufficient statistic s and a permutation distribution. More generally the explicit null hypothesis may not be strong enough to do this, unless it can be taken to imply a stronger hypothesis. This depends upon the practical context, as we see in the following example.

Example 4.11 (Comparison of two means) Suppose that we want to compare the means of two populations, given random samples from each which are denoted by $(y_{11}, \ldots, y_{1n_1})$ and $(y_{21}, \ldots, y_{2n_2})$. The explicit null hypothesis is $H_0 : \mu_1 = \mu_2$, where μ_1 and μ_2 are the means for the respective populations. Now H_0 alone does not reduce the sufficient statistics from the two sets of ordered sample values. However, suppose we believe that the CDFs F_1 and F_2 have either of the special forms

$$F_1(y) = G(y - \mu_1), \quad F_2(y) = G(y - \mu_2)$$

or

$$F_1(y) = G(y/\mu_1), \quad F_2(y) = G(y/\mu_2),$$

for some unknown G. Then the null hypothesis implies a common CDF F for the two populations. In this case, the null hypothesis sufficient statistic s is the set of order statistics for the pooled sample

$$u_1 = y_{11}, \ldots, u_{n_1} = y_{1n_1}, u_{n_1+1} = y_{21}, \ldots, u_{n_1+n_2} = y_{2n_2},$$

that is $s = (u_{(1)}, \ldots, u_{(n_1+n_2)})$.

Situations where the special forms for F_1 and F_2 apply would include comparisons of two treatments which were both applied to a random selection of units from a common pool. The special forms would not necessarily apply to sets of physical measurements taken under different experimental conditions or using different apparatus, since then the samples could have unequal variablity even though H_0 were true.

Suppose that we test H_0 by comparing the sample means using test statistic $t = \bar{y}_2 - \bar{y}_1$, and suppose that the one-sided alternative $H_A : \mu_2 > \mu_1$ is appropriate. If we assume that H_0 implies a common distribution for the Y_{1i} and Y_{2j}, then the exact significance probability is given by (4.4), i.e.

$$p = \Pr(T \geq t \mid S = s, H_0).$$

Now when S is constrained to equal s, the concatenation of the two random samples $(Y_{11}, \ldots, Y_{1n_1}, Y_{21}, \ldots, Y_{2n_2})$ must form a permutation of s. The first

n_1 components of a permutation will give the first sample and the last n_2 components will give the second sample. Further, when H_0 is true all such permutations are equally likely, and there are $\binom{n_1+n_2}{n_1}$ of them. Therefore

$$p = \frac{\text{\# of permutations such that } T^* \geq t}{\binom{n_1+n_2}{n_1}}. \tag{4.21}$$

As in the previous example, this exact probability would usually be approximated by taking R random permutations of the type described, and applying (4.11). ∎

A somewhat more complicated two-sample test problem is provided by the following example.

Example 4.12 (AML data)   Figure 3.3 shows the product-limit estimates of the survivor function for times to remission of two groups of patients with acute myelogeneous leukaemia (AML), with one of the groups receiving maintenance chemotherapy. Does this treatment make a difference to survival?

A common test for comparison of estimated survivor functions is based on the log-rank statistic, which compares the actual number of failures in group 1 with its expected value at each time a failure is observed, under the null hypothesis that the survival distributions of the two groups are equal. To be more explicit, suppose that we pool the two groups and obtain ordered failure times $y_1 < \cdots < y_m$, with $m < n$ if there is censoring. Let f_{1j} and r_{1j} be the number of failures and the number at risk of failure in group 1 at time y_j, and similarly for group 2. Then the log-rank statistic is

$$T = \frac{\sum_{j=1}^m (f_{1j} - m_{1j})}{\left(\sum_{j=1}^m v_{1j}\right)^{1/2}},$$

where

$$m_{1j} = \frac{(f_{1j} + f_{2j})r_{1j}}{r_{1j} + r_{2j}}, \quad v_{1j} = \frac{(f_{1j} + f_{2j})r_{1j}r_{2j}(r_{1j} + r_{2j} - f_{1j} - f_{2j})}{(r_{1j} + r_{2j})^2(r_{1j} + r_{2j} - 1)}$$

are the conditional mean and variance of the number in group 1 to fail at time t_j, given the values of $f_{1j} + f_{2j}$, r_{1j} and r_{2j}. For the AML data $t = 1.84$. Is this evidence that chemotherapy lengthens survival times?

For a suitable null distribution we simply treat the observations in the rows of Table 3.4 as a single group and permute them, effectively randomly allocating group labels to the observations. For each of R permutations, we recalculate t, obtaining $t_1^*, \ldots, t_R^*$. Figure 4.8 shows the t_r^* plotted against order statistics from the $N(0,1)$ distribution, which is the asymptotic null distribution of T. The asymptotic P-value is 0.033, in reasonable agreement with the P-value $26/(999 + 1) = 0.026$ from the permutation test. ∎

Figure 4.8 Results of a
Monte Carlo
permutation test for
differences between the
survivor functions for
the two groups of AML
data, $R = 499$. The
dashed horizontal line
shows the observed
value of the statistic,
and values of t_r^* that
exceed it are hollow.
The dotted line is the
line $x = y$.

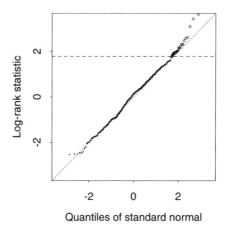

4.4 Nonparametric Bootstrap Tests

The permutation tests described in the previous section are special nonparametric resampling tests, in which resampling is done without replacement. In this section we discuss the direct application of nonparametric resampling methods, as introduced in Chapters 2 and 3. For tightly structured problems such as those in the previous section, this means resampling with replacement rather than without, which makes little difference. But bootstrap tests apply to a much wider class of testing problems.

The special nature of significance tests requires that probability calculations be done under a null hypothesis model. In this way the bootstrap calculations must differ from those in earlier chapters. For example, where in Chapter 2 we introduced the idea of resampling from the EDF $\hat{F}$, now we must resample from a distribution $\hat{F}_0$, say, which satisfies the relevant null hypothesis H_0. This has been illustrated already for parametric bootstrap tests in Section 4.2. Once the null resampling distribution $\hat{F}_0$ is decided, the basic bootstrap test will be to compute the P-value as

$$p_{\text{boot}} = \text{Pr}^*(T^* \geq t \mid \hat{F}_0),$$

or to approximate this by

$$p = \frac{1 + \#\{t_r^* \geq t\}}{R + 1},$$

using the results $t_1^*, \ldots, t_R^*$ from R bootstrap samples.

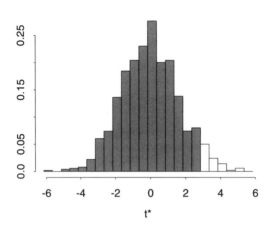

Figure 4.9 Histogram of test statistic values $t^* = \bar{y}_2^* - \bar{y}_1^*$ from $R = 999$ resamples of the two samples in Example 4.13. The data value of the test statistic is $t = 2.84$.

Example 4.13 (Comparison of two means, continued)   Consider the last two series of measurements in Example 3.1, which are reproduced here labelled samples 1 and 2:

sample 1	82	79	81	79	77	79	79	78	79	82	76	73	64
sample 2	84	86	85	82	77	76	77	80	83	81	78	78	78

Suppose that we want to compare the corresponding population means, μ_1 and μ_2, say with test statistic $t = \bar{y}_2 - \bar{y}_1$. If, as seems plausible, the shapes of the underlying distributions are identical, then under $H_0 : \mu_2 = \mu_1$ the two distributions are the same. It would then be sensible to choose for $\hat{F}_0$ the pooled EDF of the two samples. The resampling test will be the same as the permutation test of Example 4.11, except that random permutations will be replaced by random samples of size $n_1 + n_2 = 26$ drawn with replacement from the pooled data.

Figure 4.9 shows the results from applying this procedure to our two samples with $R = 999$. The unshaded area of the histogram corresponds to the 48 values of t^* larger than the observed value $t = 80.38 - 77.54 = 2.84$. The one-sided P-value for alternative $H_A : \mu_2 > \mu_1$ is $p = (48+1)/(999+1) = 0.049$. Application of the permutation test gave the same result.

It is worth stressing again that because the resampling method is wholly computational, any sensible test statistic is as easy to use as any other. So here, if outliers were present, it would be just as easy, and perhaps more sensible, to choose t to be the difference of trimmed means.

The question is: do we gain or lose anything by assuming that the two distributions have the same shape? ∎

The particular null fitted model used in the previous example was suggested in part by the permutation test, and is clearly not the only possibility. Indeed, a more reasonable null model in the context would be one which allowed different variances for the two populations sampled: an analogous model is used in Example 4.14 below. So in general there can be many candidates for null model in the nonparametric case, each corresponding to different restrictions imposed in addition to H_0. One must judge which is most appropriate on the basis of what makes sense in the practical context.

Semiparametric null models

If data are described by a semiparametric model, so that some features of underlying distributions are described by parameters, then it may be relatively easy to specify a null model. The following example illustrates this.

Example 4.14 (Comparison of several means) For the gravity data in Example 3.2, one point that we might check before proceeding with an aggregate estimation is that the underlying means for all eight series are in fact the same. One plausible model for the data, as mentioned in Section 3.2, is

$$y_{ij} = \mu_i + \sigma_i \varepsilon_{ij}, \quad j = 1, \ldots, n_i, i = 1, \ldots, 8,$$

where the ε_{ij} come from a single distribution G. The null hypothesis to be tested is $H_0 : \mu_1 = \cdots = \mu_8$, with general alternative. For this an appropriate test statistic is given by

$\bar{y}_i$ and s_i^2 are the average and sample variance for the ith series.

$$t = \sum_{i=1}^{8} w_i (\bar{y}_i - \hat{\mu}_0)^2, \quad w_i = n_i / s_i^2,$$

with $\hat{\mu}_0 = \sum w_i \bar{y}_i / \sum w_i$ the null estimate of the common mean. The null distribution of T would be approximately χ_7^2 were it not for the effect of small sample sizes. So a bootstrap approach is sensible.

The null model fit includes $\hat{\mu}_0$ and the estimated variances

$$\hat{\sigma}_{i0}^2 = (n_i - 1)s_i^2 / n_i + (\bar{y}_i - \hat{\mu}_0)^2.$$

The null model studentized residuals

$$e_{ij} = \frac{y_{ij} - \hat{\mu}_0}{\{\hat{\sigma}_{i0}^2 - (\sum w_i)^{-1}\}^{1/2}},$$

when plotted against normal quantiles, suggest mild non-normality. So, to be safe, we apply a nonparametric bootstrap. Datasets are simulated under the null model

$$y_{ij}^* = \hat{\mu}_0 + \hat{\sigma}_{i0} \varepsilon_{ij}^*,$$

i	$\bar{y}_i$	s_i^2	σ_{i0}^2	w_i
1	66.4	370.6	474.4	0.022
2	89.9	233.9	339.9	0.047
3	77.3	248.3	222.3	0.036
4	81.4	68.8	67.8	0.116
5	75.3	13.4	23.1	0.599
6	78.9	34.1	31.1	0.323
7	77.5	22.4	21.9	0.579
8	80.4	11.3	13.5	1.155

Table 4.3 Summary statistics for eight samples in gravity data, plus ingredients for significance test. The weighted mean is $\hat{\mu}_0 = 78.6$.

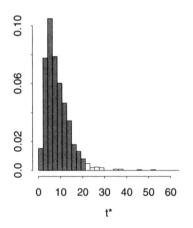 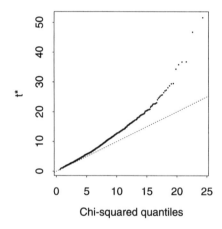

Figure 4.10 Resampling results for comparison of the means of the eight series of gravity data. Left panel: histogram of $R = 999$ values of t^* under nonparametric resampling from the null model with pooled studentized residuals; the unshaded area to right of observed value $t = 21.275$ gives $p = 0.029$. Right panel: ordered t^* values versus χ_7^2 quantiles; the dotted line is the theoretical approximation.

with ε_{ij}^*s randomly sampled from the pooled residuals $\{e_{ij}, i = 1,\ldots,8, j = 1,\ldots,n_i\}$. For each such simulated dataset we calculate sample averages and variances, then weights, the pooled mean, and finally t^*.

Table 4.3 contains a summary of the null model fit, from which we calculate $\hat{\mu}_0 = 78.6$ and $t = 21.275$.

A set of $R = 999$ bootstrap samples gave the histogram of t^* values in the left panel of Figure 4.10. Only 29 values exceed $t = 21.275$, so $p = 0.030$. The right panel of the figure plots ordered t^* values against quantiles of the χ_7^2 approximation, which is off by a factor of about 1.24 and gives the distorted P-value 0.0034. A normal-error parametric bootstrap gives results very similar to the nonparametric bootstrap.   ∎

Example 4.15 (Ratio test) Suppose that, as in Example 1.2, each observation y is a pair (u, x), and that we are interested in the ratio of means $\theta = E(X)/E(U)$. In particular suppose that we wish to test the null hypothesis $H_0 : \theta = \theta_0$. This problem could arise in a variety of contexts, and the context would help to determine the relevant null model. For example, we might have a paired-comparison experiment where the multiplicative effect θ is to be tested. Here θ_0 would be 1, and the marginal distributions of U and X should be the same under H_0. One natural null model $\hat{F}_0$ would then be the symmetrized EDF, i.e. the EDF of the expanded data $(u_1, x_1), \ldots, (u_n, x_n), (x_1, u_1), \ldots, (x_n, u_n)$. ∎

Fully nonparametric null models

In those few situations where the context of the problem does not help identify a suitable semiparametric null model, it is in principle possible to form a wholly nonparametric null model $\hat{F}_0$. Here we look at one general way to do this.

Suppose the test involves k distributions $F_1, \ldots, F_k$ for which the null hypothesis imposes a constraint, $H_0 : t(F_1, \ldots, F_k) = 0$. Then we can obtain a null model by nonparametric maximum likelihood, or a similar method, by adding the constraint to the usual derivation of the EDFs as MLEs. To be specific, suppose that we force the estimates of $F_1, \ldots, F_k$ to be supported on the corresponding sample values, as the EDFs are. Then the estimate for F_i will attach probabilities $p_i = (p_{i1}, \ldots, p_{in_i})$ to sample values $y_{i1}, \ldots, y_{in_i}$; the unconstrained EDF $\hat{F}_i$ corresponds to $\hat{p}_i = n_i^{-1}(1, \ldots, 1)$. Now measure the discrepancy between a possible F_i and the EDF $\hat{F}_i$ by $d(p_i, \hat{p}_i)$, say, such that the EDF probabilities $\hat{p}_i$ minimize this when no constraints other than $\sum_{j=1}^{n_i} p_{ij} = 1$ are imposed. Then a nonparametric null model is given by the probabilities which minimize the aggregate discrepancy subject to $t(F_1, \ldots, F_k) = 0$. That is, the null model minimizes the Lagrange expression

$$\sum_{i=1}^{k} d(p_i, \hat{p}_i) - \lambda t(p_1, \ldots, p_k) - \sum_{i=1}^{k} \alpha_i \left(\sum_{j=1}^{n_i} p_{ij} - 1 \right), \tag{4.22}$$

where $t(p_1, \ldots, p_k)$ is a re-expression of the original constraint function $t(F_1, \ldots, F_k)$. We denote the solutions of this constrained minimization problem by $\hat{p}_{i0}$, $i = 1, \ldots, k$.

The choice of discrepancy function $d(\cdot, \cdot)$ that corresponds to maximum likelihood estimation is the aggregate information distance

$$\sum_{i=1}^{k} \sum_{j=1}^{n_i} \hat{p}_{ij} \log(\hat{p}_{ij}/p_{ij}), \tag{4.23}$$

and a useful alternative is the reverse information distance

$$\sum_{i=1}^{k}\sum_{j=1}^{n_k} p_{ij} \log(p_{ij}/\hat{p}_{ij}). \tag{4.24}$$

Both are minimized by the set of EDFs when no constraints are imposed. The second measure has the advantage of automatically providing non-negative solutions. The following example illustrates the method and some of its implications.

Example 4.16 (Comparison of two means, continued) For the two-sample problem considered in Examples 4.11 and 4.13, we apply (4.22) with the discrepancy measure (4.24). The null hypothesis constraint is that the two means are equal, that is $\sum y_{1j} p_{1j} = \mu_1 = \mu_2 = \sum y_{2j} p_{2j}$, so that (4.22) becomes

$$\sum_{i=1}^{2}\sum_{j=1}^{n_i} p_{ij} \log(p_{ij}/\hat{p}_{ij}) - \lambda\left(\sum y_{1j} p_{1j} - \sum y_{2j} p_{2j}\right) - \sum_{i=1}^{2} \alpha_i \left(\sum_{j=1}^{n_i} p_{ij} - 1\right).$$

Setting derivatives with respect to p_{ij} equal to zero gives the equations

$$1 + \log p_{1j} - \alpha_1 - \lambda y_{1j} = 0, \quad 1 + \log p_{2j} - \alpha_2 + \lambda y_{2j} = 0,$$

which together with the initial constraints gives the solutions

$$\hat{p}_{1j,0} = \frac{\exp(\lambda y_{1j})}{\sum_{k=1}^{n_1} \exp(\lambda y_{1k})}, \quad \hat{p}_{2j,0} = \frac{\exp(-\lambda y_{2j})}{\sum_{k=1}^{n_2} \exp(-\lambda y_{2k})}. \tag{4.25}$$

The specific value of λ is uniquely determined by the null hypothesis constraint, which becomes

$$\frac{\sum y_{1j} \exp(\lambda y_{1j})}{\sum_k \exp(\lambda y_{1k})} = \frac{\sum y_{2j} \exp(-\lambda y_{2j})}{\sum_k \exp(-\lambda y_{2k})},$$

whose solution must be determined numerically. Distributions of the form (4.25) are usually called *exponential tilts* of the EDFs.

For our data $\lambda = 0.130$. The resulting null model probabilities are shown in the left panel of Figure 4.11. The right panel will be discussed later.

Having determined these null probabilities, the bootstrap test algorithm is as follows:

Algorithm 4.1 (Tilted bootstrap two-sample comparison) For $r = 1, \ldots, R$,

  1 Generate $(y_{11}^{*}, \ldots, y_{1n_1}^{*})$ by randomly sampling n_1 times from $(y_{11}, \ldots, y_{1n_1})$
     with weights $(\hat{p}_{11,0}, \ldots, \hat{p}_{1n_1,0})$.
  2 Generate $(y_{21}^{*}, \ldots, y_{2n_1}^{*})$ by randomly sampling n_2 times from $(y_{21}, \ldots, y_{2n_2})$
     with weights $(\hat{p}_{21,0}, \ldots, \hat{p}_{2n_2,0})$.
  3 Calculate the test statistic $t^{*} = \bar{y}_2^{*} - \bar{y}_1^{*}$.

Figure 4.11 Null
distributions for
comparison of two
means. Left panel: null
probability distributions
$\hat{p}_{10}$ (1) and $\hat{p}_{20}$ (2) with
equal means ($\lambda = 0.130$);
observations are marked
+. Right panel: smooth
densities corresponding
to null probability
distributions for
population 1 (dotted
curve) and population 2
(dashed curve), and
smooth density
corresponding to pooled
EDF (solid curve).

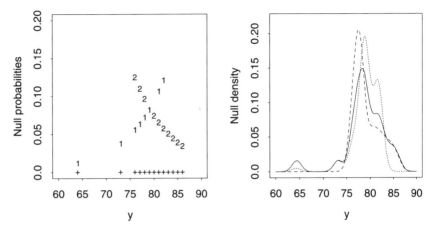

Table 4.4 Resampling
P-values for one-sided
comparison of two
means. The entries are
explained in
Examples 4.11, 4.13,
4.16, 4.19 and 4.20.

Null model	Statistic	P-value
pooled EDF	t and z	0.045
null variances	t	0.053
exponential tilt	t	0.006
	z	0.025
MLE	t	0.019
	z	0.017
(pivot)	z	0.015

Calculate

$$p = \frac{1 + \#\{t^* \geq t\}}{R + 1}.$$

Numerical results for $R = 999$ are given in Table 4.4 in the line labelled "exponential tilt, t". Results for other resampling tests are also given for comparison: z refers to a studentized version of t, "MLE" refers to use of constrained maximum likelihood (see Problem 4.8), "null variances" refers to the semiparametric method of Example 4.14. Clearly the choice of null model can have a strong effect on the P-value, as one might expect. The studentized test statistics z are discussed in Section 4.4.1. ∎

The method as illustrated here has strong similarity to use of empirical likelihood methods, as described in Chapter 10. In practice it seems wise to check the null model produced by the method, since resulting P-values are generally sensitive to model. Thus, in the previous example, we should look at Figure 4.11 to see if it makes practical sense. The smoothed versions of the null distributions in the right panel, which are obtained by kernel smoothing, are perhaps easier to interpret. One might well judge in this case that the two null distributions are more different than seems plausible. Despite this reservation about this example, the general method is a valuable tool to have in case of need.

There are, of course, situations where even this quite general approach will not work. Nevertheless the basic idea behind the approach can still be applied, as the following examples show.

Example 4.17 (Test for unimodality) One of the difficulties with nonparametric curve estimation is knowing whether particular features are "real". For example, suppose that we compute a density estimate $\hat{f}(y)$ and find that it has two modes. How do we tell if the minor mode is real? Bootstrap methods can be helpful in such problems. Suppose that a kernel density estimate is used, so that

$$\hat{f}(y;h) = \frac{1}{nh} \sum_{j=1}^{n} \phi\left(\frac{y-y_j}{h}\right),$$ (4.26)

where ϕ is the standard normal density. It is possible to show that the number of modes of $\hat{f}$ decreases as h increases. So one way to test unimodality is to see if an unusually large h is needed to make $\hat{f}$ unimodal. This suggests that we take as test statistic

$$t = \min_{h>0}\{h : \hat{f}(y;h) \text{ is unimodal}\}.$$

A natural candidate for the null sampling distribution is $\hat{f}(y;t)$, since this is the least smoothed version of the EDF which satisfies the null hypothesis of unimodality. By the convolution property of $\hat{f}$, random sample values from $\hat{f}(y;t)$ are given by

$$y_j^* = y_{I_j} + h\varepsilon_j, \quad j=1,\ldots,n,$$ (4.27)

where the ε_j are independent $N(0,1)$ variates and the I_j are random integers from $\{1,2,\ldots,n\}$. On general grounds it seems wise to modify $\hat{f}$ so as to have first two moments agree with the data (Problem 3.8), but this modification would have no effect here.

For any such sample $y_1^*,\ldots,y_n^*$ generated from the null distribution, we can check whether or not $t^* \geq t$ by checking whether or not the particular density estimate $\hat{f}^*(y;t)$ is unimodal. ∎

The next example applies a variation of this test.

Table 4.5 Perpendicular distances (miles) from an aerial line transect to schools of Southern Bluefin Tuna in the Great Australian Bight (Chen, 1996).

0.19	0.28	0.29	0.45	0.64	0.65	0.78	0.85
1.00	1.16	1.17	1.29	1.31	1.34	1.55	1.60
1.83	1.91	1.97	2.05	2.10	2.17	2.28	2.41
2.46	2.51	2.89	2.89	2.90	2.92	3.03	3.19
3.48	3.79	3.83	3.94	3.95	4.11	4.14	4.19
4.36	4.53	4.97	5.02	5.13	5.75	6.03	6.19
6.19	6.45	7.13	7.35	7.77	7.80	8.81	9.22
9.29	9.78	10.15	11.32	13.21	13.27	14.39	16.26

Example 4.18 (Tuna density estimate)   One method for estimating the abundance of a species in a region is to traverse a straight line of length L through the region, and to record the perpendicular distances from the line to positions where there are sightings. If there are n independent sightings and their (unsigned) distances $y_1, \ldots, y_n$ are presumed to have PDF $f(y)$, $y \geq 0$, the abundance density can be estimated by $n\hat{f}(0)/(2L)$, where $\hat{f}(0)$ is an estimate of the density at distance $y = 0$. The PDF $f(y)$ is proportional to a detection function that is assumed to decline monotonically with increasing distance, with non-monotonic decline suggesting that the assumptions that underlie line transect sampling must be questioned.

Table 4.5 gives data from an aerial survey of schools of Southern Bluefin Tuna in the Great Australian Bight. Figure 4.12 shows a histogram of the data. The figure also shows kernel density estimates

$$\hat{f}(y;h) = \frac{1}{nh} \sum_{j=1}^{n} \left\{ \phi\left(\frac{y - y_j}{h}\right) + \phi\left(\frac{y + y_j}{h}\right) \right\}, \quad y \geq 0, \quad (4.28)$$

with $h = 0.75, 1.5125$, and 3. This seemingly unusual density estimate is used because the probability of detection, and hence the distribution of signed distances, should be symmetric about the transect. The estimate is obtained by first calculating the EDF of the reflected distances $\pm y_1, \ldots, \pm y_n$, then applying the kernel smoother, and finally folding the result about the origin.

Although the estimated density falls monotonically for h greater than 1.5125, the estimate for smaller values suggests non-monotonic decline. Since we consider $\hat{f}(y;h)$ for positive values of y only, we are interested in whether the underlying density falls monotonically or not. We take the smallest h such that $\hat{f}(y;h)$ is unimodal to be the value of our test statistic t. This corresponds to monotonic decline of $\hat{f}(y;h)$ for $y \geq 0$, giving no modes for $y > 0$. The observed value of the test statistic is $t = 1.5125$, and we are interested in the significance probability

$$\Pr(T \geq t \mid \hat{F}_0),$$

for data arising from $\hat{F}_0$, an estimate of F that satisfies the null hypothesis of

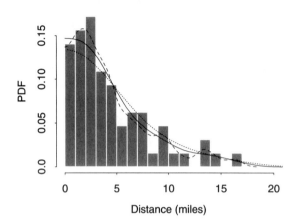

Figure 4.12 Histogram of the tuna data, and kernel density estimates (4.28) with bandwidths $h = 1.5125$ (solid), 0.75 (dashes), and 3 (dots).

monotone decline but is otherwise as close to the data as possible. That is, the null model is $\hat{f}(y;t)$.

To generate replicate datasets from the null model we use the convolution property of (4.28), which implies

$$y_j^* = |\pm y_{I_j} + t\varepsilon_j|, \quad j = 1, \ldots, n,$$

where the signs $\pm$ are assigned randomly, the I_j are random integers from $\{1, 2, \ldots, n\}$, and the ε_j are independent $N(0,1)$ variates; cf. (4.27). The kernel density estimate based on the y^* is $\hat{f}^*(y;h)$. We now calculate the test statistic as outlined in the previous example, and repeat the process $R = 999$ times to obtain an approximate significance probability. We restrict the hunt for modes to $0 < y < 10$, because it does not seem sensible to use so small a smoothing parameter in the density tails.

When the simulations were performed for these data, the frequencies of the number of modes of $\hat{f}^*(y;t)$ for $0 < y < 10$ were as follows.

Modes	0	1	2	3
Frequency	536	411	50	2

Like the fitted null distribution, a replicate where the full $\hat{f}^*(y;t)$ is unimodal will have no modes for $y > 0$. If we assume that the event $t^* = t$ is impossible, bootstrap datasets with no modes have $t^* < t$, so the significance probability is $(411 + 50 + 2 + 1)/(999 + 1) = 0.464$. There is no evidence against monotonic decline, giving no cause to doubt the assumptions underlying line transect methods. ∎

4.4.1 Studentized bootstrap method

For testing problems which involve parameter values, it is possible to obtain more stable significance tests by studentizing comparisons. One version of this is analogous to calculating a $1 - p$ confidence set by the studentized bootstrap method (Section 5.2.1), and concluding that the P-value is less than p if the null hypothesis parameter value is outside the confidence set. Section 4.1 outlined the application of this idea. Here we describe two possible resampling implementations.

For simplicity suppose first that θ is a scalar with estimator T, and that we want to test $H_0 : \theta = \theta_0$ versus $H_A : \theta > \theta_0$. The method suggested in Section 4.1 applies when

$$Z = \frac{T - \theta}{V^{1/2}}$$

is approximately a pivot, meaning that its distribution is approximately independent of unknown parameters. Then, with $z_0 = (t - \theta_0)/v^{1/2}$ denoting the observed studentized test statistic, the resampling analogue of (4.6) is

$$p = \mathrm{Pr}^*(Z^* \geq z_0 \mid \hat{F}), \tag{4.29}$$

which we can approximate by simulation without having to decide on a null model $\hat{F}_0$. The usual choice for v would be the nonparametric delta method estimate v_L of Section 2.7.2. The theoretical support for the use of Z is given in Section 5.4; in certain cases it will be advantageous to studentize a transformed estimate (Sections 5.2.2 and 5.7). In practice it would be appropriate to check on whether or not Z is approximately pivotal, using techniques described in Section 3.10.

Applications of this method are described in Section 6.2.5 and Section 6.3.2. The modifications for the other one-sided alternative and for the two-sided alternative are simply $p = \mathrm{Pr}^*(Z^* \leq z_0 \mid \hat{F})$ and $p = \mathrm{Pr}^*(Z^{*2} \geq z_0^2 \mid \hat{F})$.

Example 4.19 (Comparison of two means, continued) For the application considered in Examples 4.11, 4.13 and 4.16, where we compared two means using $t = \bar{y}_2 - \bar{y}_1$, it would be reasonable to suppose that the usual two-sample t statistic

$$Z = \frac{\bar{Y}_2 - \bar{Y}_1 - (\mu_2 - \mu_1)}{\left(S_2^2/n_2 + S_1^2/n_1\right)^{1/2}}$$

is approximately pivotal. Here $\hat{F}$ in (4.29) represents the EDFs of the two samples, given that no assumptions are made connecting the two distributions.

We calculate the observed value of the test statistic,

$$z_0 = \frac{\bar{y}_2 - \bar{y}_1}{\left(s_2^2/n_2 + s_1^2/n_1\right)^{1/2}},$$

whose value for these data is $2.846/1.610 = 1.768$. Then R values of

$$z^* = \frac{\bar{y}_2^* - \bar{y}_1^* - (\bar{y}_2 - \bar{y}_1)}{\left(s_2^{*2}/n_2 + s_1^{*2}/n_1\right)^{1/2}}$$

are generated, with each simulated dataset containing n_1 values sampled with replacement from sample 1 and n_2 values sampled with replacement from sample 2.

In $R = 999$ simulations we found 14 values in excess of 1.768, so the P-value is 0.015. This is entered in Table 4.4 in the row labelled "(pivot)". ∎

If θ is a vector with estimator T, and the null hypothesis is simple, $H_0 : \theta = \theta_0$, with general alternative $H_A : \theta \neq \theta_0$, then the analogous pivot is

$$Q = (T - \theta)^T V^{-1} (T - \theta),$$

with observed test statistic value

$$q_0 = (t - \theta_0)^T v^{-1} (t - \theta_0).$$

Again v_L is a standard choice for v, and again it may be beneficial first to transform T (Section 5.8). Test statistics for more complicated alternatives can be defined similarly; see Problem 4.10.

Studentized test statistics can also be used when Z or Q is not a pivot. The definitions will be slightly different,

$$Z = \frac{T - \theta_0}{V_0^{1/2}} \qquad (4.30)$$

for the scalar case and

$$Q = (T - \theta_0)^T V_0^{-1} (T - \theta_0)$$

for the vector case, where V_0 is an estimated variance under the null model. If Z_0 is used the bootstrap P-value will simply be

$$p = \text{Pr}^* (Z_0^* \geq z_0 \mid \hat{F}_0), \qquad (4.31)$$

with the obvious changes for a test based on Q_0. Even though the statistic is not pivotal, its use is likely to reduce the effects of nuisance parameters, and to give a P-value that is more nearly uniformly distributed under the null hypothesis than that calculated from T alone.

Example 4.20 (Comparison of two means, continued)   In Table 4.4 all the entries for z, except for the row labelled "(pivot)", were obtained using (4.30) with $t = \bar{y}_2 - \bar{y}_1$ and v_0 depending on the null model. For example, for the null models discussed in Example 4.16,

$$v_0 = \sum_{i=1}^{2} n_i^{-1} \sum_{j=1}^{n_i} (y_{ij} - \hat{\mu}_{i0})^2 \hat{p}_{ij,0},$$

where $\hat{\mu}_{i0} = \sum_{j=1}^{n_i} y_{ij} \hat{p}_{ij,0}$. For the two samples in question, under the exponential tilt null model both means equal 79.17 and $v_0 = 1.195$, the latter differing considerably from the variance estimate 2.59 used in the pivot method (Example 4.19).

The associated P-values computed from (4.31) are shown in Table 4.4 for all null models. These P-values are less dependent upon the particular model than those obtained with t unstudentized. ■

4.4.2 Conditional bootstrap tests

In parametric testing, conditioning plays an important role both in eliminating nuisance parameters and in fixing the information content of the data. In nonparametric testing the situation is less clear, because of the absence of a full model. Some aspects of conditioning are illustrated in Examples 5.16 and 5.17.

One simple example which does illustrate the possibility and effect of conditioning is the nonparametric bootstrap test for independence. In Example 4.9 we described an exact permutation test for this problem. The analogous bootstrap test would set the null model $\hat{F}_0$ to be the product of the marginal EDFs. Simulation under this model is equivalent to creating x_i^*s by random sampling with replacement from the xs, and independently creating z_i^*s by random sampling with replacement from the zs. However, we could view the marginal CDFs G and H as nuisance parameters and attempt to remove them from the analysis by conditioning on $\hat{G}^* = \hat{G}$ and $\hat{H}^* = \hat{H}$. This turns out to be exactly equivalent to using the permutation test, which does indeed completely eliminate G and H.

Adaptive tests

Conditioning occurs in a somewhat different way in the adaptive choice of test statistic. Suppose that we have possible test statistics $T_1, \ldots, T_k$ for which efficiency measures can be defined and estimated by $\hat{e}_1, \ldots, \hat{e}_k$: for example, if the T_i are alternative estimators for scalar parameter θ and H_0 concerns θ, then $\hat{e}_i$ might be the reciprocal of the estimated variance of T_i. The idea of the adaptive test is to use that T_i which is estimated to be most efficient for the observed data, and to condition on this fact.

We first partition the set $\mathcal{Y}$ of all possible null model resamples $y_1^*, \ldots, y_n^*$ into $\mathcal{Y}_1, \ldots, \mathcal{Y}_k$ such that

$$\mathcal{Y}_i = \{(y_1^*, \ldots, y_n^*) : \hat{e}_i^* = \max_{1 \le j \le k} \hat{e}_j^*\}.$$

Then if $y_1, \ldots, y_n$ is in $\mathcal{Y}_i$, so that t_i is preferred, the adaptive test computes the P-value as

$$p = \Pr{}^*(T_i^* \ge t_i \mid (y_1^*, \ldots, y_n^*) \in \mathcal{Y}_i).$$

For an example of this, see Problem 4.13. In the case of exact tests, such as permutation tests, the adaptive test is also exact.

4.4.3 Multiple testing

In some applications multiple tests of a hypothesis are based on a single set of data. This happens, for example, when pairwise comparisons of means are carried out for a several-sample analysis where the null hypothesis is equality of all means. In such situations the smallest of all test P-values is used, and it is clearly incorrect to interpret this smallest value in the usual way. Bootstrapping can be used to find the true significance level of the smallest P-value, as follows. Departing from our general notation, suppose that the test statistics are $S_1, \ldots, S_k$, with observed values $s_1, \ldots, s_k$, and that the null distribution of S_i is known to be $G_i(\cdot)$. Then the observed significance levels are $1 - G_i(s_i)$. The incorrect procedure would be treat the smallest P-value $\min\{1 - G_1(s_1), \ldots, 1 - G_k(s_k)\}$ as uniform on the interval $[0, 1]$. If the tests were exact and independent, the corresponding random variable would have distribution $1 - (1 - p)^k$ on $[0, 1]$, but in general we should take into account their (unknown) dependence. We can allow for the multiple testing by taking $t = \min\{1 - G_1(s_1), \ldots, 1 - G_k(s_k)\}$ to be the test statistic, and then the procedure is as follows. We generate data from the null hypothesis distribution, calculate the bootstrap statistics $s_1^*, \ldots, s_k^*$, and then take $t^* = \min\{1 - G_1(s_1^*), \ldots, 1 - G_k(s_k^*)\}$. We repeat this R times to get $t_1^*, \ldots, t_R^*$, and then obtain the P-value in the usual way. Notice that if all the $G_i(\cdot)$ equal $G(\cdot)$, say, the test is tantamount to bootstrapping $t = \max(s_1, \ldots, s_k)$, and then $G(\cdot)$ need not be known. If the $G_i(\cdot)$ are unequal, the procedure requires them to be known, in order to put the test statistics on a scale where they can be compared. If the $G_i(\cdot)$ are unknown, they can be estimated, but then a nested bootstrap (Section 3.9) is needed to obtain the P-value. The algorithm is the following.

Algorithm 4.2 (Multiple testing)   For $r = 1, \ldots, R$,

  1 Generate $y_1^*, \ldots, y_n^*$ independently from the fitted null distribution $\hat{F}_0$, and from them calculate $s_1^*, \ldots, s_k^*$.

  2 Fit the null distribution $\hat{F}_0^*$ to $y_1^*, \ldots, y_n^*$.

  3 For $m = 1, \ldots, M$, generate $y_1^{**}, \ldots, y_n^{**}$ independently from the fitted null distribution $\hat{F}_0^*$, and from them calculate $s_1^{**}, \ldots, s_k^{**}$.

  4 Calculate

$$t_r^* = \min \left\{ \frac{1 + \#\{s_1^{**} \ge s_1^*\}}{M + 1}, \ldots, \frac{1 + \#\{s_k^{**} \ge s_k^*\}}{M + 1} \right\}.$$

Calculate $p = (1 + \#\{t_r^* \ge t\})/(R + 1)$.   ●

The procedure is analogous to that used in Section 4.5, but in this case adjustment would require three levels of nested bootstrapping.

4.5 Adjusted P-values

So far we have described tests which compute P-values as $p = \Pr^*(T^* \geq t \mid \hat{F}_0)$ with $\hat{F}_0$ the working null sampling model. Ideally P should be uniformly distributed on [0,1] if the usual error rate interpretation is to be valid. This will be exactly or approximately correct for permutation and permutation-like bootstrap tests, but for other tests it can be far from correct. Preventive measures we can take are to transform t or studentize it, or both. However, these are not guaranteed to work. Here we describe a general method of adjustment, simple in principle but potentially very computer-intensive.

The idea behind adjusting P-values is simply to treat p as the observed test statistic: it is after all just a transformation of t. We estimate the distribution of the corresponding random variable P by resampling — under the null model, of course. Since small values of p are of interest, the adjusted P-value is defined by

$$p_{\text{adj}} = \Pr^*(P^* \leq p \mid \hat{F}_0), \tag{4.32}$$

where p is the observed P-value defined above. This requires bootstrapping the algorithm for computing P-values, another instance of increasing the accuracy of a bootstrap method by bootstrapping it, an idea introduced in Section 3.9.

The problem can be explained theoretically in either of two ways, perturbing the critical value of t for a fixed nominal error rate α, or adjusting for the bias in the P-value. We take the second approach, and since we are dealing with statistical error rather than simulation error (Section 2.5), we ignore the latter. The P-value computed for the data is written $p_0(\hat{F})$, where the function $p_0(\cdot)$ depends on the method used to obtain $\hat{F}_0$ from $\hat{F}$. When the null hypothesis is true, suppose that the particular null distribution F_0 obtains. Then the null distribution function for the P-value is

$$G(u, F_0) = \Pr\{p_0(\hat{F}) \leq u \mid F_0\}, \tag{4.33}$$

which with $u = \alpha$ is the true error rate corresponding to nominal error rate α. Now (4.33) implies that

$$\Pr\{G(p_0(\hat{F}), F_0) \leq \alpha \mid F_0\} = \alpha,$$

and so $G(p_0(\hat{F}), F_0)$ would be the ideal adjusted P-value, having actual error rate equal to the nominal error rate. Next notice that by substituting $\hat{F}_0$ for F_0 in (4.33) we can estimate $G(u, F_0)$ by

$$\Pr^*\{p_0(\hat{F}^*) \leq u \mid \hat{F}_0\}.$$

Finally, setting $u = p_0(\hat{F})$ we obtain

$$G(p_0(\hat{F}), F_0) \doteq \Pr^*\{p_0(\hat{F}^*) \le p_0(\hat{F}) \mid \hat{F}_0\}.$$

This we define to be the *adjusted P-value*, so when $p_0(\hat{F}) = p$,

$$p_{\text{adj}} = \Pr^*\{p_0(\hat{F}^*) \le p \mid \hat{F}_0\}, \qquad (4.34)$$

which is a more precise version of (4.32).

One must be careful to interpret $P^* = p_0(\hat{F}^*)$ properly in (4.34). Since the outer probability relates to sampling from $\hat{F}_0$, $\hat{F}^*$ in (4.34) denotes the EDF of a sample drawn from $\hat{F}_0$.

The adjusted P-value can be applied to advantage in both parametric and nonparametric testing, the key point being that it is more nearly uniformly distributed than the unadjusted P-value. Before discussing simulation implementation of the adjustment, we look at a simple example which illustrates the basic method.

Example 4.21 (Comparison of exponential means) Suppose that $x_1, \ldots, x_m$ and $y_1, \ldots, y_n$ are respectively random samples from exponential distributions with means μ_1 and μ_2, and that we wish to test $H_0 : \mu_1 = \mu_2$. For this problem there is an exact test based on $U = \bar{X}/\bar{Y}$, but we consider instead the test statistic $T = \bar{X} - \bar{Y}$, for which we show that the adjusted P-value automatically produces the P-value for the exact test.

For the parametric bootstrap test the null model sets the two sampling distributions equal to a common fitted exponential distribution with pooled mean

$$\hat{\mu} = \frac{m\bar{x} + n\bar{y}}{m + n}.$$

If $\bar{X}^*$ and $\bar{Y}^*$ denote averages of random samples of sizes m and n respectively from this exponential distribution, then the bootstrap P-value is $p = \Pr^*(\bar{X}^* - \bar{Y}^* \ge \bar{x} - \bar{y})$. This can be rewritten as

$$p = \Pr\left\{ m^{-1}G_m - n^{-1}G_n \ge \frac{(m+n)(u-1)}{mu+n} \right\}, \qquad (4.35)$$

where $u = \bar{x}/\bar{y}$, and G_m and G_n are independent gamma random variables with indices m and n respectively and unit scale parameters.

The bootstrap P-value (4.35) does not have a uniform distribution under the null hypothesis, so $P = p$ does not correspond to error rate p. This is fully corrected using the adjustment (4.34). To see this, write (4.35) as $p = h(u)$, so that $p_0(\hat{F}^*)$ equals

$$\Pr^{**}(T^{**} \ge T^* \mid \hat{F}_0^*) = h(U^*),$$

where $U^* = \bar{X}^*/\bar{Y}^*$. Since $h(\cdot)$ is decreasing, it follows that

$$p_{\text{adj}} = \Pr^*\{h(U^*) \le h(u) \mid \bar{x}, \bar{y}\} = \Pr^*(U^* \ge u \mid \bar{x}, \bar{y}) = \Pr(F_{2m,2n} \ge u),$$

which is the P-value of the exact test. Therefore p_{adj} is exactly uniform and the adjustment is perfectly successful. ■

In the previous example, the same result for p_{adj} would be achieved if the bootstrap distribution of T were replaced by a normal approximation. This might suggest that bootstrap calculation of p could be replaced by a rough theoretical approximation, thus removing one level of bootstrap sampling from calculation of p_{adj}. Unfortunately this is not always true, as is clear from the fact that if an approximate null distribution of T is used which does not depend upon $\hat{F}$ at all, then p_{adj} is just the ordinary bootstrap P-value.

In most applications it will be necessary to use simulation to approximate the adjusted P-value (4.34). Suppose that we have drawn R resamples from the null model $\hat{F}_0$, with corresponding test statistic values $t_1^*, \ldots, t_R^*$. The rth resample has EDF $\hat{F}_r^*$ (possibly a vector of EDFs), to which we fit the null model $\hat{F}_{r0}^*$. Resampling M times from $\hat{F}_{r0}^*$ gives samples from which we calculate t_{rm}^{**}, $m = 1, \ldots, M$. Then the Monte Carlo approximation for the adjusted P-value is

$$p_{\text{adj}} = \frac{1 + \#\{p_r^* \le p\}}{R + 1}, \qquad (4.36)$$

where for each r

$$p_r^* = \frac{1 + \#\{t_{rm}^{**} \ge t_r^*\}}{M + 1}. \qquad (4.37)$$

If p is calculated from the same R resamples, then a total of RM samples is generated. We can summarize the algorithm as follows:

Algorithm 4.3 (Double bootstrap test)   For $r = 1, \ldots, R$,

1   Generate $y_1^*, \ldots, y_n^*$ independently from the fitted null distribution $\hat{F}_0$ and calculate the test statistic t_r^* from them.
2   Fit the null distribution to $y_1^*, \ldots, y_n^*$, thereby obtaining $\hat{F}_{r0}^*$.
3   For $m = 1, \ldots, M$,

(a)   generate $y_1^{**}, \ldots, y_n^{**}$ independently from the fitted null distribution $\hat{F}_{r0}^*$; and
(b)   calculate from them the test statistic t_{rm}^{**}.

4   Calculate p_r^* as in (4.37).

Finally, calculate p_{adj} as in (4.36). ●

We discuss the choice of M after the following example.

Example 4.22 (Two-way table)   Table 4.6 contains a set of observed multinomial counts, for which we wish to test the null hypothesis of row–column independence, or additive loglinear model.

1	2	2	1	1	0	1
2	0	0	2	3	0	0
0	1	1	1	2	7	3
1	1	2	0	0	0	1
0	1	1	1	1	0	0

Table 4.6 Two-way table of counts (Newton and Geyer, 1994).

If the count in row i and column j is y_{ij}, then the null fitted values are $\hat{\mu}_{ij,0} = y_{i+}y_{+j}/y_{++}$, where $y_{i+} = \sum_j y_{ij}$ and so forth. The log likelihood ratio test statistic is

$$t = 2\sum_{i,j} y_{ij}\log(y_{ij}/\hat{\mu}_{ij,0}).$$

According to standard theory, T is approximately distributed as χ^2_d under the null hypothesis with $d = (7-1)\times(5-1) = 24$. Since $t = 38.52$, the approximate P-value is $\Pr(\chi^2_{24} \geq 38.52) = 0.031$. However, the chi-squared approximation is known to be quite poor for such a sparse table, so we apply the parametric bootstrap.

The model $\hat{F}_0$ is the fitted multinomial model, sample size $n = y_{++}$ and (i, j)th cell probability $\hat{\mu}_{ij,0}/n$. We generate R tables from this model and calculate the corresponding log likelihood ratio statistics $t^*_1, \ldots, t^*_R$. With $R = 999$ we obtain 47 statistics larger than the observed value $t = 38.52$, so the bootstrap P-value is $(1+47)/(1+999) = 0.048$. The inaccuracy of the chi-squared approximation is illustrated by Figure 4.13, which is a plot of ordered values of $\Pr(\chi^2_{24} \geq t^*)$ versus expected uniform order statistics: the straight line corresponds to the theoretical chi-squared approximation for T.

The bootstrap P-value turns out to be quite non-uniform. A double bootstrap calculation with $R = M = 999$ gives $p_{\text{adj}} = 0.076$.

Note that the test applied here conditions only on the total y_{++}, whereas in principle one would prefer to condition on all row and column sums, which are sufficient statistics under the null hypothesis: this would require more complex simulation methods, such as those of Section 4.2.1; see Problem 4.3. ∎

Choice of M

The general application of the double bootstrap algorithm involves simulation at two levels, with a total of RM samples. If we follow the suggestion to use as many as 1000 samples for calculation of probabilities, then here we would need as many as 10^6 samples, which seems impractical for other than simple problems. As in Section 3.9, we can determine approximately what a sensible choice for M would be. The calculation below of simulation mean squared error suggests that $M = 99$ would generally be satisfactory, and $M = 249$ would be safe. There are also ways of reducing considerably the total size of the simulation, as we shall show in Chapter 9.

Figure 4.13 Ordered
values of $\Pr(\chi^2_{24} \geq t^*)$
versus expected uniform
order statistics from
$R = 999$ bootstrap
simulations under the
null fitted model for
two-way table. Dotted
line is theoretical
approximation.

Figure 4.13 Ordered values of $\Pr(\chi^2_{24} \geq t^*)$ versus expected uniform order statistics from $R = 999$ bootstrap simulations under the null fitted model for two-way table. Dotted line is theoretical approximation.

To calculate the simulation mean squared error, we begin with equation (4.37), which we rewrite in the form

$I\{A\}$ is the indicator function of the event A.

$$p_r^* = \frac{1 + \sum_{m=1}^{M} I\{t_{rm}^{**} \geq t_r^*\}}{M + 1}.$$

In order to simplify the calculations, we suppose that, as $M \to \infty$, $p_r^* \to u_r$ such that the u_rs are a random sample from the uniform distribution on $[0,1]$. In this case there is no need to adjust the bootstrap P-value, so $p_{\text{adj}} = p$. Under this assumption $(M + 1)p_r^*$ is almost a $\text{Binom}(M, u_r)$ random variable, so that equation (4.36) can be approximated by

$$p_{\text{adj}} \doteq \frac{1 + \sum_{r=1}^{R} X_r}{R + 1},$$

where $X_r = I\{\text{Binom}(M, u_r) \leq (M+1)p\}$. We can now calculate the simulation mean and variance of p_{adj} by using the fact that

$$\mathrm{E}(X_r^k \mid u_r) = \Pr\{\text{Binom}(M, u_r) \leq (M+1)p\}$$

for $k = 1, 2$. First we have that for all r

$$\mathrm{E}(X_r^k) = \int_0^1 \sum_{j=0}^{[(M+1)p]} \binom{M}{j} u^j (1 - u)^{M-j} du = \frac{[(M+1)p]}{M+1},$$

where $[z]$ is the integer part of z. Since p_{adj} is proportional to the average of independent X_rs, it follows that

$$\mathrm{E}(p_{\text{adj}}) \doteq \frac{R[(M+1)p]}{(R+1)(M+1)},$$

which tends to the correct answer p as $R, M \to \infty$, and

$$\mathrm{var}(p_{\mathrm{adj}}) \doteq \frac{R[(M+1)p](M+1-[(M+1)p])}{(R+1)^2(M+1)^2}.$$

A simple aggregate measure of simulation error is the mean squared error relative to p,

$$MSE(p_{\mathrm{adj}}) \doteq \frac{[(M+1)p]\{M+1-[(M+1)p]\}}{R(M+1)^2} + \left\{p - \frac{[(M+1)p]}{M+1}\right\}^2. \quad (4.38)$$

Numerical evaluations of this result suggest that $M = 249$ would be a safe choice. If $0.01 \leq p < 0.10$ then $M = 99$ would be satisfactory, while $M = 49$ would be adequate for larger p. Note that two assumptions were made in the calculation, both of which are harmless. First, we assumed that p was independent of the t_r^*, whereas in fact it would likely be calculated from the same values. Secondly, our main interest is in cases where P-values are not exactly uniformly distributed. Problem 4.12 suggests a more flexible calculation, from which very similar conclusions emerge.

4.6 Estimating Properties of Tests

A statistical test involves two steps, collection of data and application of a particular test statistic to those data. Both steps involve choice, and resampling methods can have a role to play in such choices by providing estimates of test power.

Estimation of power

As regards collection of data, in simple problems of the kind under discussion in this chapter, the statistical contribution lies in recommendation of sample sizes via considerations of test *power*. If it is proposed to use test statistic T, and if the particular alternative H_A to the null hypothesis H_0 is of primary interest, then the power of the test is

$$\pi(p, H_A) = \Pr(T \geq t_p \mid H_A),$$

where t_p is defined by $\Pr(T \geq t_p \mid H_0) = p$. In the simplified language of testing theory, if we fix p and decide to reject H_0 when $t \geq t_p$, then $\pi(p, H_A)$ is the chance of rejection when H_A is true. An alternative specification is in terms of $E(P \mid H_A)$, the expected P-value. In many problems hypotheses are expressed in terms of parameters, and then power can be evaluated for arbitrary parameter values to give a power function. What is of interest to us here is the use of resampling to assess the power of a test, either as an aid to determination of appropriate sample sizes for a particular test, or as a way to choose from a set of possible tests.

Suppose, then, that a pilot set of data $y_1, \ldots, y_n$ is in hand, and that the model description is semiparametric (Section 3.3). The pilot data can be used to estimate the nonparametric component of the model, and to this can be added arbitrary values of the parametric component. This provides a family of alternative hypothesis models from which to simulate data and test statistic values. From these simulations we obtain approximations of test power, provided we have critical values t_p for the test statistic. This last condition will not always be met, but in many problems there will at least be a simple approximation, for example $N(0, 1)$ if we are using a studentized statistic. For many nonparametric tests, such as those based on ranks, critical values are distribution-free, and so are available. The following example illustrates this idea.

Example 4.23 (Maize height data) The EDFs plotted in the left panel of Figure 4.14 are for heights of maize plants growing in two adjacent rows, and differing only in a pollen sterility factor. The two samples can be modelled approximately by a semiparametric model with an unspecified baseline distribution F and one median-shift parameter θ. For analysis of such data it is proposed to test $H_0 : \theta = 0$ using the Wilcoxon test. Whether or not there are enough data can be assessed by estimating the power of this test, which does depend upon F.

Denote the observations in sample i by $y_{ij}, j = 1, \ldots, n_i$. The underlying distributions are assumed to have the forms $F(y)$ and $F(y - \theta)$, where θ is estimated by the difference in sample medians $\hat{\theta}$. To estimate F we subtract $\hat{\theta}$ from the second sample to give $\tilde{y}_{2j} = y_{2j} - \hat{\theta}$. Then $\hat{F}$ is the pooled EDF of the y_{1j}s and $\tilde{y}_{2j}$s. For these data $n_1 = n_2 = 12$ and $\hat{\theta} = -4.5$. The right panel of Figure 4.14 plots EDFs of the y_{1j}s and $\tilde{y}_{2j}$s.

The next step is to simulate data for selected values of θ and selected sample sizes N_1 and N_2 as follows. For group 1, sample data $y_{11}^*, \ldots, y_{1N_1}^*$ from $\hat{F}(y)$, i.e. randomly with replacement from

$$y_{11}, \ldots, y_{1n_1}, \tilde{y}_{21}, \ldots, \tilde{y}_{2n_2};$$

and for group 2, sample data $y_{21}^*, \ldots, y_{2N_2}^*$ from $\hat{F}(y - \theta)$, i.e. randomly with replacement from

$$y_{11} + \theta, \ldots, y_{1n_1} + \theta, \tilde{y}_{21} + \theta, \ldots, \tilde{y}_{2n_2} + \theta.$$

Then calculate test statistic t^*. With R repetitions of this, the power of the test at level p is the proportion of times that $t^* \geq t_p$, where t_p is the critical value of the Wilcoxon test for specified N_1 and N_2.

In this particular case, the simulations show that the Wilcoxon test at level $p = 0.01$ has power 0.26 for $\theta = \hat{\theta}$ and the observed sample sizes. Additional

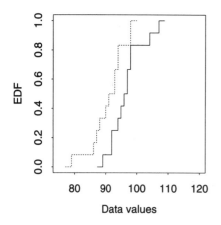
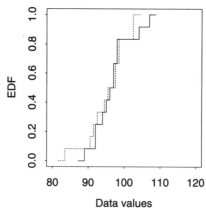

Figure 4.14 Power comparison for maize height data (Hand et al., 1994, p. 130). Left panel: EDFs of plant height for two groups. Right panel: EDFs for group 1 (unadjusted) and group 2 (adjusted by estimated median-shift $\hat{\theta} = -4.5$).

calculations show that both sample sizes need to be increased from 12 to at least 33 to have power 0.8 for $\theta = \hat{\theta}$.   ∎

If the proposed test uses the pivot method of Section 4.4.1, then calculations of sample size can be done more simply. For example, for a scalar θ consider a two-sided test of $H_0 : \theta = \theta_0$ with level 2α based on the pivot Z. The power function can be written

$$\pi(2\alpha, \theta) = 1 - \Pr\left\{z_{\alpha,N} + \frac{\theta_0 - \theta}{v_N^{1/2}} \leq Z_N \leq z_{1-\alpha,N} + \frac{\theta_0 - \theta}{v_N^{1/2}}\right\}, \qquad (4.39)$$

where the subscript N indicates sample size. A rough approximation to this power function can be obtained as follows. First simulate R samples of size N from $\hat{F}$, and use these to approximate the quantiles $z_{\alpha,N}$ and $z_{1-\alpha,N}$. Next set $v_N^{1/2} = n^{1/2} v_n^{1/2} / N^{1/2}$, where v_n is the variance estimate calculated from the pilot data. Finally, approximate the probability (4.39) using the same R bootstrap samples.

Sequential tests

Similar sorts of calculations can be done for sequential tests, where one important criterion is terminal sample size. In this context simulation can also be used to assess the likely eventual sample size, given data $y_1, \ldots, y_n$ at an interim stage of a test, with a specified protocol for termination. This can be done by simulating data continuation $y_{n+1}^*, y_{n+2}^*, \ldots$ up to termination, by sampling from fitted models or EDFs, as appropriate. From repetitions of this simulation one obtains an approximate distribution for terminal sample size N.

4.7 Bibliographic Notes

The standard theory of significance tests is described in Chapters 3–5 and 9 of Cox and Hinkley (1974). For detailed treatment of the mathematical theory see Lehmann (1986). In recent years much work has been done on obtaining improved distributional approximations for likelihood-based statistics, and most of this is covered by Barndorff-Nielsen and Cox (1994).

Randomization and permutation tests have long histories. R. A. Fisher (1935) introduced randomization tests as a device for explaining and justifying significance tests, both in simple cases and for complicated experimental designs: the randomization used in selecting a design can be used as the basis for inference, without appeal to specific error models. For a recent account see Manly (1991). A general discussion of how to apply randomization in complex problems is given by Welch (1990).

Permutation tests, which are superficially similar to randomization tests, are specifically nonparametric tests designed to condition out the unknown sampling distribution. The theory was developed by Pitman (1937a,b,c), and is summarized by Lehmann (1986). More recently Romano (1989, 1990) has examined properties of permutation tests and their relation to bootstrap tests for a variety of problems.

Monte Carlo tests were first suggested by Barnard (1963) and are particularly popular in spatial statistics, as described by Ripley (1977, 1981, 1987) and Besag and Diggle (1977). Graphical tests for regression diagnostics are described by Atkinson (1985), and Ripley (1981) applies them to model-checking in spatial statistics. Markov chain Monte Carlo methods for conditional tests were introduced by Besag and Clifford (1989); applications to contingency table analysis are given by Forster, McDonald and Smith (1996) and Smith, Forster and McDonald (1996), who give additional references. Gilks *et al.* (1996) is a good general reference on Markov chain Monte Carlo methods, including design of simulation.

The effect of simulation size R on power for Monte Carlo tests (with independent simulations) has been considered by Marriott (1979), Jöckel (1986) and by Hall and Titterington (1989); the discussion in Section 4.2.5 follows Jöckel. Sequential calculation of P-values is described by Besag and Clifford (1991) and Jennison (1992).

The use of tilted EDFs was introduced by Efron (1981b), and has subsequently had a strong impact on confidence interval methods; see Chapters 5 and 10.

Double bootstrap adjustment of P-values is discussed by Beran (1988), Loh (1987), Hinkley and Shi (1989), and Hall and Martin (1988). Applications are described by Newton and Geyer (1994). Geyer (1995) discusses tests for inequality-constrained hypotheses, which sheds light on possible inconsistency of bootstrap tests and suggests remedies. For references to discussions of improved simulation methods, see Chapter 9.

A variety of methods and applications for resampling in multiple testing are covered in the books by Noreen (1989) and Westfall and Young (1993).

Various aspects of resampling in the choice of test are covered in papers by Collings and Hamilton (1988), Hamilton and Collings (1991), and Samawi (1994). A general theoretical treatment of power estimation is given by Beran (1986). The brief discussion of adaptive tests in Section 4.4.2 is based on Donegani (1991), who refers to previous work on the topic.

4.8 Problems

1   For the dispersion test of Example 4.2, $y_1, \ldots, y_n$ are hypothetically sampled from a Poisson distribution. In the Monte Carlo test we simulate samples from the conditional distribution of $Y_1, \ldots, Y_n$ given $\sum Y_j = s$, with $s = \sum y_j$. If the exact multinomial simulation were not available, a Markov chain method could be used. Construct a Markov chain Monte Carlo algorithm based on one-step transitions from $(u_1, \ldots, u_n)$ to $(v_1, \ldots, v_n)$ which involve only adding and subtracting 1 from two randomly selected us. (Note that zero counts must not be reduced.)
Such an algorithm might be slow. Suggest a faster alternative.
(Section 4.2)

2   Suppose that $X_1, \ldots, X_n$ are continuous and have the same marginal CDF F, although they are not independent. Let I be a random integer between 1 and n. Show that $\text{rank}(X_I)$ has a uniform distribution on $\{1, 2, \ldots, n\}$.
Explain how to apply this result to obtain an exact Monte Carlo test using one realization of a suitable Markov chain.
(Section 4.2.2; Besag and Clifford, 1989)

3   Suppose that we have a $m \times m$ contingency table with entries y_{ij} which are counts.
(a) Consider the null hypothesis of row–column independence. Show that the sufficient statistic S_0 under this hypothesis is the set of row and column marginal totals. To assess the significance of the likelihood ratio test statistic conditional on these totals, a Markov chain Monte Carlo simulation is used. Develop a Metropolis-type algorithm using one-step transitions which modify the contents of a randomly selected tetrad $y_{ik}, y_{il}, y_{jk}, y_{jl}$, where $i \neq j, k \neq l$.
(b) Now consider the the null hypothesis of quasi-symmetry, which implies that in the loglinear model for mean cell counts, $\log E(Y_{ij}) = \mu + \alpha_i + \beta_j + \gamma_{ij}$, the interaction parameters satisfy $\gamma_{ij} = \gamma_{ji}$ for all i, j. Show that the sufficient statistic S_0 under this hypothesis is the set of totals $y_{ij} + y_{ji}, i \neq j$, together with the row and column totals and the diagonal entries. Again a conditional test is to be applied. Develop a Metropolis-type algorithm for Markov chain Monte Carlo simulation using one-step transitions which involve pairs of symmetrically placed tetrads.
(Section 4.2.2; Smith *et al.*, 1996)

4   Suppose that a one-sided bootstrap test at level α is to be applied with R simulated samples. Then the null hypothesis will be rejected if and only if the number of t^*s exceeding t is less than $k = (R+1)\alpha - 1$. If k_r is the number of t^*s exceeding t in the first r simulations, for what values of k_r would it be unnecessary to continue simulation?
(Section 4.2.5; Jennison, 1992)

5   (a) Consider the following rule for choosing the number of simulations in a Monte Carlo test. Choose k, and generate simulations $t_1^*, t_2^*, \ldots, t_l^*$ until the first l for which k of the t_r^* exceed the observed value t; then declare P-value $p = (k+1)/(l+1)$. Let the random variables corresponding to l and p be L and P. Show that

$$\Pr\{P \le (k+1)/(l+1)\} = \Pr(L > l-1) = k/l, \quad l = k, k+1, \ldots,$$

and deduce that L has infinite mean. Show that P has the distribution of a $U(0,1)$ random variable rounded to the nearest achievable significance level $1, k/(k+1), k/(k+2), \ldots$, and deduce that the test is exact.
(b) Consider instead stopping immediately if k of the t_r^* exceed t at any $l < R$, and anyway stopping when $l = R$, at which point m values exceed t. Show that this rule gives achievable significance levels

$$p = \begin{cases} (k+1)/(l+1), & m = k, \\ (m+1)/(R+1), & m < k. \end{cases}$$

Show that under this rule the null expected value of L is

$$E(L) = \sum_{l=1}^{R} \Pr(L \ge l) = k + k \sum_{l=k+1}^{R} l^{-1},$$

and evaluate this with $k = 49$ and 9 for $R = 999$.
(Section 4.2.5; Besag and Clifford, 1991)

6   Suppose that n subjects are allocated randomly to each of two treatments, A and B. In fact each subject falls in one of two relevant groups, such as gender, and the treatment allocation frequencies differ between groups. The response y_{ij} for the jth subject in the ith group is modelled as $y_{ij} = \gamma_i + \tau_{k(i,j)} + \varepsilon_{ij}$, where τ_A and τ_B are treatment effects and $k(i, j)$ is A or B according to which treatment was allocated to the subject. Our interest is in testing $H_0 : \tau_A = \tau_B$ with alternative that $\tau_A < \tau_B$, and the test statistic chosen is

$$T = \sum_{i,j:k(i,j)=B} r_{ij} - \sum_{i,j:k(i,j)=A} r_{ij},$$

where r_{ij} is the residual from regression of the ys on the group indicators.
(a) Describe how to calculate a permutation P-value for the observed value t using the method described above Example 4.12.
(b) A different calculation of the P-value is possible which conditions on the observed covariates, i.e. on the treatment allocation frequencies in the two groups. The idea is to first eliminate the group effects by reducing the data to differences $d_{ij} = y_{ij} - y_{i,j+1}$, and then to note that the joint probability of these differences under H_0 is constant under permutations of data within groups. That is, the minimal sufficient statistic S_0 under H_0 is the set of differences $Y_{i(j)} - Y_{i(j+1)}$, where $Y_{i(1)} \le Y_{i(2)} \le \cdots$ are the ordered values within the ith group. Show carefully how to calculate the P-value for t conditional on s_0.
(c) Apply the unconditional and conditional permutation tests to the following data:

	Group 1			Group 2	
A	3	5	4	4	1
B	0			2	1

(Sections 4.3, 6.3.2; Welch and Fahey, 1994)

7   A randomized matched-pair experiment to compare two treatments produces
    paired responses (y_{1j}, y_{2j}) from which the paired differences $d_j = y_{2j} - y_{1j}$ are
    calculated for $j = 1, \ldots, n$. The null hypothesis H_0 of no treatment difference
    implies that the d_js are sampled from a distribution that is symmetric with mean
    zero, whereas the alternative hypothesis implies a positive mean difference. For
    any test statistic t, such as $\bar{d}$, the exact randomization P-value $\Pr(T^* \geq t \mid H_0)$ is
    calculated under the null resampling model

    $$d_j^* = S_j d_j, \quad j = 1, \ldots n,$$

    where the S_j are independent and equally likely to be $+1$ and -1. What would
    be the corresponding nonparametric bootstrap sampling model $\hat{F}_0$? Would the
    resulting bootstrap P-value differ much from the randomization P-value?
    See Practical 4.4 to apply the randomization and bootstrap tests to the following
    data, which are differences of measurements in eighths of an inch on cross- and
    self-fertilized plants grown in the same pot (taken from R. A. Fisher's famous
    discussion of Darwin's experiment).

    49   –67   8   16   6   23   28   41   14   29   56   24   75   60   –48

    (Sections 4.3, 4.4; Fisher, 1935, Table 3)

8   For the two-sample problem of Example 4.16, consider fitting the null model by
    maximum likelihood. Show that the solution probabilities are given by

    $$\hat{p}_{1j,0} = \frac{1}{n_1(\alpha + \lambda y_{1j})}, \quad \hat{p}_{2j,0} = \frac{1}{n_2(\beta - \lambda y_{2j})},$$

    where α, β and λ are the solutions to the equations $\sum \hat{p}_{1j,0} = 1$, $\sum \hat{p}_{2j,0} = 1$, and
    $\sum y_{1j}\hat{p}_{1j,0} = \sum y_{2j}\hat{p}_{2j,0}$. Under what conditions does this solution not exist, or give
    negative probabilities? Compare this null model with the one used in Example 4.16.

9   For the ratio-testing problem of Example 4.15, obtain the nonparametric MLE of
    the joint distribution of (U, X). That is, if p_j is the probability attached to the data
    pair (u_j, x_j), maximize $\prod p_j$ subject to $\sum p_j(x_j - \theta_0 u_j) = 0$. Verify that the resulting
    distribution is the EDF of (U, X) when $\theta_0 = \bar{x}/\bar{u}$. Hence develop a numerical
    algorithm for calculating the p_js for general θ_0.
    Now choose probabilities $p_1, \ldots, p_n$ to minimize the distance

    $$d(p, q) = \sum p_j \log p_j - \sum p_j \log q_j,$$

    with $q = (\frac{1}{n}, \ldots, \frac{1}{n})$, subject to $\sum (x_j - \theta_0 u_j)p_j = 0$. Show that the solution is the
    exponential tilted EDF

    $$p_j \propto \exp\{\eta(x_j - \theta_0 u_j)\}.$$

    Verify that for small values of $\theta_0 - \bar{x}/\bar{u}$ these p_js are approximately the same as
    those obtained by the MLE method.
    (Section 4.4; Efron, 1981b)

10 Suppose that we wish to test the reduced-rank model $H_0 : g(\theta) = 0$, where $g(\cdot)$ is a
    p_1-dimensional reduction of p-dimensional θ. For the studentized pivot method we
    take $Q = \{g(T) - g(\theta)\}^T V_g^{-1}\{g(T) - g(\theta)\}$, with data test value $q_0 = g(t)^T v_g^{-1} g(t)$,
    where v_g estimates $\mathrm{var}\{g(T)\}$. Use the nonparametric delta method to show that
    $\mathrm{var}\{g(T)\} \doteq \dot{g}(t)V_L \dot{g}(t)^T$, where $\dot{g}(\theta) = \partial g(\theta)/\partial \theta^T$.
    Show how the method can be applied to test equality of p means given p indepen-
    dent samples, assuming equal population variances.
    (Section 4.4.1)

11 In a parametric situation, suppose that an exact test is available with test statistic U, that S is sufficient under the null hypothesis, but that a parametric bootstrap test is carried out using T rather than U. Will the adjusted P-value p_{adj} always produce the exact test?
(Section 4.5)

12 In calculating the mean squared error for the simulation approximation to the adjusted P-value, it might be more reasonable to assume that P-values u_r follow a Beta distribution with parameters a and b which are close to, but not equal to, one. Show that in this case

$$E(X_r^k) = \sum_{j=0}^{[(M+1)p]} \frac{\Gamma(M+1)\Gamma(a+j)\Gamma(b+M-j)\Gamma(a+b)}{\Gamma(j+1)\Gamma(M-j+1)\Gamma(a+b+M)\Gamma(a)\Gamma(b)},$$

where $X_r = I\{\mathrm{Binom}(M, u_r) \le (M+1)p\}$. Use this result to investigate numerically the choice of M.
(Section 4.5)

13 For the matched-pair experiment of Problem 4.7, suppose that we choose between the two test statistics $t_1 = \bar{d}$ and $t_2 = (n-2m)^{-1}\sum_{j=m+1}^{n-m} d_{(j)}$, for some m in the range $2, \ldots, [\tfrac{1}{2}n]$, on the basis of their estimated variances v_1 and v_2, where

$$v_1 = \frac{\sum(d_j - t_1)^2}{n^2},$$

$$v_2 = \frac{\sum_{j=m+1}^{n-m}(d_{(j)} - t_2)^2 + m(d_{(m+1)} - t_2)^2 + m(d_{(n-m)} - t_2)^2}{n(n-2m)}.$$

Give a detailed description of the adaptive test as outlined in Section 4.4.2. To apply it to the data of Problem 4.7 with $m = 2$, see Practical 4.4.
(Section 4.4.2; Donegani, 1991)

14 Suppose that we want critical values for a size α one-sided test of $H_0 : \theta = \theta_0$ versus $H_A : \theta > \theta_0$. The ideal value is the $1 - \alpha$ quantile $t_{0,1-\alpha}$ of the distribution of T under H_0, and this is estimated by the solution $\hat{t}_{0,1-\alpha}$ to $\Pr^*(T^* \ge t_0 \mid \hat{F}_0) = \alpha$. Typically $\hat{t}_{0,1-\alpha}$ is biased. Consider an adjusted critical value $\hat{t}_{0,1-\alpha-\gamma}$. Obtain the double bootstrap algorithm for choosing γ, and compare the resulting test to use of the adjusted P-value (4.34).
(Sections 4.5, 3.9.1; Beran, 1988)

4.9 Practicals

1   The data in dataframe dogs are from a pharmacological experiment. The two variables are cardiac oxygen consumption (MVO) and left ventricular pressure (LVP). Data for $n = 7$ dogs are

MVO	78	92	116	90	106	78	99
LVP	32	33	45	30	38	24	44

Apply a bootstrap test for the hypothesis of zero correlation between MVO and LVP. Use $R = 499$ simulations.
(Sections 4.3, 4.4)

2   For the permutation test outlined in Example 4.12,

```
aml.fun <- function(data, i)
{ d <- data[i, ]
    temp <- survdiff(Surv(d$time, d$cens) ~ data$group)
    s <- sign(temp$obs[2]-temp$exp[2])
    s*sqrt(temp$chisq) }
aml.perm <- boot(aml, aml.fun, R=499, sim="permutation")
(1+sum(aml.perm$t0<aml.perm$t))/(1+aml.perm$R)
o <- rank(aml.perm$t)
less <- (1:aml.perm$R)[aml.perm$t<aml.perm$t0]
o <- o/(1+aml.perm$R)
qqnorm(aml.perm$t,ylab="Log-rank statistic",type="n")
points(qnorm(o[less]),aml.perm$t[less])
points(qnorm(o[-less]),aml.perm$t[-less],pch=1)
abline(0,1,lty=2);
abline(h=aml.perm$t0,lty=3)
```

Compare this with the corresponding bootstrap test.
(Section 4.3)

3   For a graphical test of suitability of the exponential model for the data in Table 1.2,
    we generate data from the exponential distribution, and plot an envelope.

```
expqq.fun <- function(data, q) sort(data)/mean(data)
exp.gen <- function(data, mle) rexp(length(data), mle)
n <- nrow(aircondit)
qq <- qexp((1:n)/(n+1))
exp.boot <- boot(aircondit$hours,expqq.fun,R=999,sim="parametric",
            ran.gen=exp.gen,mle=1/mean(aircondit$hours),q=qq)
env <- envelope(exp.boot$t)
plot(qq,exp.boot$t0,xlab="Exponential quantiles",
     ylab="Scaled order statistics",xlim=c(0,max(qq)),
     ylim=c(0,max(c(exp.boot$t0,env$overall[2,]))),pch=1)
lines(qq,env$overall[1,]); lines(qq,env$overall[2,])
lines(qq,env$point[1,],lty=2); lines(qq,env$point[2,],lty=2)
```

Discuss the adequacy of the model. Check whether the gamma model is a better
fit.
(Section 4.2.4)

4   To apply the permutation test outlined in Problem 4.7,

```
darwin.gen <- function(data, mle)
{ sign <- sample(c(-1,1),mle,replace=T)
    data*sign }
darwin.rand <- boot(darwin$y, mean, R=999, sim="parametric",
                    ran.gen=darwin.gen, mle=nrow(darwin))
(1+sum(darwin.rand$t>darwin.rand$t0))/(1+darwin.rand$R)
```

Can you see how to modify darwin.gen to produce the bootstrap test?
To implement the adaptive test described in Problem 4.13, with $m = 2$:

```
darwin.f <- function(d)
{ n <- length(d); m <- 2
    t1 <- mean(d)
    v1 <- sum((d-t1)^2)/n^2
    d <- sort(d)[(m+1):(n-m)]
    t2 <- mean(d)
```

```
    v2 <- ((sum((d-t2)^2)+m*(min(d)-t2)^2+m*(max(d)-t2)^2))/(n*(n-2*m))
    c(t1, v1, t2, v2) }
darwin.ad <- boot(darwin$y, darwin.f, R=999, sim="parametric",
                  ran.gen=darwin.gen, mle=nrow(darwin))
darwin.ad$t0
i <- c(1:999)[darwin.ad$t[,2]>darwin.ad$t[,4]]
(1+sum(darwin.ad$t[i,3]>darwin.ad$t0[3]))/(1+length(i))
```

Is a different result obtained with the adaptive version of the bootstrap test?
(Sections 4.3, 4.4)

5 Dataframe `paulsen` contains data collected as part of an investigation into the quantal nature of neurotransmission in the brain, by Dr O. Paulsen of the Department of Pharmacology, University of Oxford, in collaboration with Professor P. Heggelund of the Department of Neurophysiology, University of Oslo. Two models have been proposed to explain such data. The first model suggests that the data are drawn from an underlying skewed unimodal distribution. The alternative model suggests that the data are drawn from a series of distributions with modes equal to integer multiples of a unit size. To distinguish between the two models, a bootstrap test of multimodality may be carried out, with the null hypothesis that the underlying distribution is unimodal.
To plot the data and a kernel density estimate with a Gaussian kernel and bandwidth $h = 1.5$, and to count its local maxima:

```
h <- 1.5
hist(paulsen$y,probability=T,breaks=c(0:30))
lines(density(paulsen$y,width=4*h,from=0,to=30))
peak.test <- function(y, h)
{dens <- density(y,width=4*h,n=100)
    sum(peaks(dens$y[(dens$x>=0)&(dens$x<=20)])) }
peak.test(paulsen$y, h)
```

Check that $h = 1.87$ is the smallest value giving just one peak.
For bootstrap analysis,

```
peak.gen <- function( d, mle)
{  n <- mle[1]; h <- mle[2]
    i <- sample(n,n,replace=T)
    d[i]+h*rnorm(n) }
paulsen.boot <- boot(paulsen$y, peak.test, R=999, sim="parametric",
                  ran.gen=peak.gen, mle=c(nrow(paulsen),1.87), h=1.87)
```

What is the significance level?
To repeat with a shrunk smoothed density estimate:

```
shrunk.gen <- function(d, mle)
{  n <- mle[1]; h <- mle[2]
    v <- var(d)
    (d[sample(n,n,replace=T)]+h*rnorm(n))/sqrt(1+h^2/v) }
paulsen.boot <- boot(paulsen$y, peak.test, R=999, sim="parametric",
                  ran.gen=shrunk.gen, mle=c(nrow(paulsen),1.87), h=1.87)
```

Bootstrap to obtain the P-value. Discuss your results.
(Section 4.4; Paulsen and Heggelund, 1994, Silverman, 1981).

6   For the cd4 data of Practicals 2.3 and 3.6, test the hypothesis that the distribution
     of CD4 counts after one year is the same as the baseline distribution. Test
     also whether the treatment affects the counts for each individual. Discuss your
     conclusions.

5

Confidence Intervals

5.1 Introduction

The assessment of uncertainty about parameter values is made using confidence intervals or regions. Section 2.4 gave a brief introduction to the ways in which resampling can be applied to the calculation of confidence limits. In this chapter we undertake a more thorough discussion of such methods, including more sophisticated ideas that are potentially more accurate than those mentioned previously.

Confidence region methods all focus on the same target properties. The first is that a confidence region with specified coverage probability γ should be a set $C_\gamma(y)$ of parameter values which depends only upon the data y and which satisfies

$$\Pr\{\theta \in C_\gamma(Y)\} = \gamma. \tag{5.1}$$

Implicit in this definition is that the probability does not depend upon any nuisance parameters that might be in the model. The confidence coefficient, or coverage probability, γ, is the relative frequency with which the confidence region would include, or cover, the true parameter value θ in repetitions of the process that produced the data y. In principle the coverage probability should be conditional on the information content of y as measured by ancillary statistics, but this may be difficult in practice without a parametric model; see Section 5.9.

The second important property of a confidence region is its shape. The general principle is that any value in C_γ should be more likely than all values outside C_γ, where "likely" is measured by a likelihood or similar function. This is difficult to apply in nonparametric problems, where strictly a likelihood function is not available; see, however, Chapter 10. In practice the difficulty is not serious for scalar θ, which is the major focus in this chapter, because in most applications the confidence region will be a single interval.

A confidence interval will be defined by limits $\hat{\theta}_{\alpha_1}$ and $\hat{\theta}_{1-\alpha_2}$, such that for any α

$$\Pr(\theta < \hat{\theta}_\alpha) = \alpha.$$

The coverage of the interval $[\hat{\theta}_{\alpha_1}, \hat{\theta}_{1-\alpha_2}]$ is $\gamma = 1 - (\alpha_1 + \alpha_2)$, and α_1 and α_2 are respectively the left- and right-tail error probabilities. For some applications only one limit is required, either a lower confidence limit $\hat{\theta}_\alpha$ or an upper confidence limit $\hat{\theta}_{1-\alpha}$, these both having coverage $1 - \alpha$. If a closed interval is required, then in principle we can choose α_1 and α_2, so long as they sum to the overall error probability 2α. The simplest way to do this, which we adopt for general discussion, is to set $\alpha_1 = \alpha_2 = \alpha$. Then the interval is equi-tailed with coverage probability $1 - 2\alpha$. In particular applications, however, one might well want to choose α_1 and α_2 to give approximately the shortest interval: this would be analogous to having the likelihood property mentioned earlier.

A single confidence region cannot give an adequate summary of the uncertainty about θ, so in practice one should give regions for three or four confidence levels between 0.50 and 0.99, say, together with the point estimate for θ. One benefit from this is that any asymmetry in the uncertainty about θ will be fairly clear.

So far we have assumed that a confidence region can be found to satisfy (5.1) exactly, but this is not possible except in a few special parametric models. The methods developed in this chapter are based on approximate probability calculations, and therefore involve a discrepancy between the nominal or target coverage, and the actual coverage probability.

In Section 5.2 we review briefly the standard approximate methods for parametric and nonparametric models, including the basic bootstrap methods already described in Section 2.4. More sophisticated methods, based on what is known as the percentile method, are the subject of Section 5.3. Section 5.4 compares the various methods from a theoretical viewpoint, using asymptotic expansions, and introduces the *ABC* method as an alternative to simulation methods. The use of significance tests to obtain confidence limits is outlined in Section 5.5. A nested bootstrap algorithm is introduced in Section 5.6. Empirical comparisons between methods are made in Section 5.7.

Confidence regions for vector parameters are described in Section 5.8. The possibility of conditional confidence regions is explored in Section 5.9 through discussion of two examples. Prediction intervals are discussed briefly in Section 5.10.

The discussion in this chapter is about how to use the results of bootstrap simulation algorithms to obtain confidence regions, irrespective of what the resampling algorithm is. The presentation supposes for the most part that we are in the simple situation of Chapter 2, where we have a single, complete homogeneous sample. Most of the methods described can be applied to more complex data structures, provided that appropriate resampling algorithms are used, but for most sorts of highly dependent data the theoretical properties of the methods are largely unknown.

5.2 Basic Confidence Limit Methods

5.2.1 Parametric models

One general approach to calculating a confidence interval is to make it surround a good point estimate of the parameter, which for parametric models will often be taken to be the maximum likelihood estimator. We begin by discussing various simple ways in which this approach can be applied.

Suppose that T estimates a scalar θ and that we want an interval with left- and right-tail errors both equal to α. For simplicity we assume that T is continuous. If the quantiles of $T - \theta$ are denoted by a_p, then

$$\Pr(T - \theta \leq a_\alpha) = \alpha = \Pr(T - \theta \geq a_{1-\alpha}). \tag{5.2}$$

Rewriting the events $T - \theta \leq a_\alpha$ and $T - \theta \geq a_{1-\alpha}$ as $\theta \geq T - a_\alpha$ and $\theta \leq T - a_{1-\alpha}$ respectively, we see that the $1 - 2\alpha$ equi-tailed interval has limits

$$\hat{\theta}_\alpha = t - a_{1-\alpha}, \quad \hat{\theta}_{1-\alpha} = t - a_\alpha. \tag{5.3}$$

This ideal solution rarely applies, because the distribution of $T - \theta$ is usually unknown. This leads us to consider various approximate methods, most of which are based on approximating the quantiles of $T - \theta$.

Normal approximation

The simplest approach is to apply a $N(0, v)$ approximation for $T - \theta$. This gives the approximate confidence limits

$$\hat{\theta}_\alpha, \hat{\theta}_{1-\alpha} = t \mp v^{1/2} z_{1-\alpha}, \tag{5.4}$$

where as usual $z_{1-\alpha} = \Phi^{-1}(1-\alpha)$. If T is a maximum likelihood estimator, then the approximate variance v can be computed directly from the log likelihood function $\ell(\theta)$. If there are no nuisance parameters, then we can use the reciprocal of either the observed Fisher information, $v = -1/\ddot{\ell}(\hat{\theta})$ or the estimated expected Fisher information $v = 1/i(\hat{\theta})$, where $i(\theta) = \mathrm{E}\{-\ddot{\ell}(\theta)\} = \mathrm{var}\{\dot{\ell}(\theta)\}$. The former is usually preferable. When there are nuisance parameters, we use the relevant element of the inverse of either $-\ddot{\ell}(\hat{\theta})$ or $i(\hat{\theta})$. More generally, if T is given by an estimating equation, then v can be calculated by the delta method; see Section 2.7.2. Equation (5.4) is the standard form for normal approximation confidence limits, although it is sometimes augmented by a bias correction which is based on the third derivative of the log likelihood function.

margin note: $\dot{\ell}(\theta) = \partial\ell(\theta)/\partial\theta$, and $\ddot{\ell}(\theta) = \partial^2\ell(\theta)/\partial\theta\partial\theta^T$.

In problems where the variance approximation v is hard to obtain theoretically, or is thought to be unreliable, the parametric bootstrap of Section 2.2 can be used. This requires simulation from the fitted model with parameter value $\hat{\theta}$. If the resampling estimates of bias and variance are denoted by b_R and v_R, then (5.4) is replaced by

$$\hat{\theta}_\alpha, \hat{\theta}_{1-\alpha} = t - b_R \mp v_R^{1/2} z_{1-\alpha}. \tag{5.5}$$

Whether or not a normal approximation method will work can be assessed by making a normal Q-Q plot of the simulated estimates $t_1^*, \ldots, t_R^*$, as illustrated in Section 2.2.2. If such a plot suggests that normal approximation is poor, then we can either try to improve the normal approximation in some way, or replace it completely. The basic resampling confidence interval methods of Section 2.4 do the latter, and we review them first.

Basic and studentized bootstrap methods

If we start again at the general confidence limit formula (5.3), we can estimate the quantiles a_α and $a_{1-\alpha}$ by the corresponding quantiles of $T^* - t$. Assuming that these are approximated by simulation, as in Section 2.2.2, the argument given in Section 2.4 leads to the confidence limits

$$\hat{\theta}_\alpha = 2t - t^*_{((R+1)(1-\alpha))}, \quad \hat{\theta}_{1-\alpha} = 2t - t^*_{((R+1)\alpha)}. \tag{5.6}$$

These we refer to as the *basic bootstrap confidence limits* for θ.

A modification of this is to use the form of the normal approximation confidence limit, but to replace the $N(0,1)$ approximation for $Z = (T-\theta)/V^{1/2}$ by a bootstrap approximation. Each simulated sample is used to calculate t^*, the variance estimate v^*, and hence the bootstrap version $z^* = (t^* - t)/v^{*1/2}$ of Z. The R simulated values of z^* are ordered and the p quantile of Z is estimated by the $(R + 1)p$th of these. Then the confidence limits (5.4) are replaced by

$$\hat{\theta}_\alpha = t - v^{1/2} z^*_{((R+1)(1-\alpha))}, \quad \hat{\theta}_{1-\alpha} = t - v^{1/2} z^*_{((R+1)\alpha)}. \tag{5.7}$$

These we refer to as *studentized bootstrap confidence limits*. They are also known as bootstrap-*t* limits, by analogy with the Student-*t* confidence limits for the mean of a normal distribution, to which they are equal under infinite simulation in that problem. In principle this method is superior to the previous basic method, for reasons outlined in Section 2.6.1 and discussed further in Section 5.4.

An empirical bias adjustment could be incorporated into the numerator of Z, but this is often difficult to calculate and is usually not worthwhile, because the effect is implicitly adjusted for in the bootstrap distribution.

For both (5.6) and (5.7) to apply exactly it is necessary that $(R + 1)\alpha$ be an integer. This can usually be arranged: with $R = 999$ we can handle most conventional values of α. But if for some reason $(R+1)\alpha$ is not an integer, then interpolation can be used. A simple method that works well for approximately normal estimators is linear interpolation on the normal quantile scale. For example, if we are trying to apply (5.6) and the integer part of $(R+1)\alpha$ is k, then we define

$$t^*_{((R+1)\alpha)} = t^*_{(k)} + \frac{\Phi^{-1}(\alpha) - \Phi^{-1}(\frac{k}{R+1})}{\Phi^{-1}(\frac{k+1}{R+1}) - \Phi^{-1}(\frac{k}{R+1})} (t^*_{(k+1)} - t^*_{(k)}), \quad k = [(R+1)\alpha]. \quad (5.8)$$

The same interpolation can be applied to the z^*s. Clearly such interpolations fail if $k = 0$, R or $R+1$.

Parameter transformation

The normal approximation method may fail to work well because it is being applied on the wrong scale, in which case it should help to apply the approximation on an appropriately transformed scale. Skewness in the distribution of T is often associated with var(T) varying with θ. For this reason the accuracy of normal approximation is often improved by transforming the parameter scale to stabilize the variance of the estimator, especially if the transformed scale is the whole real line. The accuracy of the basic bootstrap confidence limits (5.6) will also tend to be improved by use of such a transformation.

Suppose that we make a monotone increasing transformation of the parameter scale from θ to $\eta = h(\theta)$, and then transform t correspondingly to $u = h(t)$. Any confidence limit method can be applied for η, and untransforming the results will give confidence limits for θ. For example, consider applying the normal approximation limits (5.4) for η. By the delta method (Section 2.7.1) the variance approximation v for T transforms to

$\dot{h}(\theta)$ is $dh(\theta)/d\theta$.

$$\text{var}(U) = \text{var}\{h(T)\} \doteq \{\dot{h}(t)\}^2 v = v_U,$$

say. Then the confidence limits for η are $h(t) \mp v_U^{1/2} z_{1-\alpha}$, which transform back to the limits

$$\hat{\theta}_\alpha, \hat{\theta}_{1-\alpha} = h^{-1}\{h(t) \mp v_U^{1/2} z_{1-\alpha}\}. \quad (5.9)$$

Similarly the basic bootstrap confidence limits (5.6) become

$$\hat{\theta}_\alpha = h^{-1}\{2h(t) - h(t^*_{((R+1)(1-\alpha))})\}, \quad \hat{\theta}_{1-\alpha} = h^{-1}\{2h(t) - h(t^*_{((R+1)\alpha)})\}. \quad (5.10)$$

Whether or not the normal approximation is improved by transformation can be judged from a normal Q-Q plot of simulated $h(t^*)$ values.

How do we determine an appropriate transformation $h(\cdot)$? If var(T) is exactly or approximately equal to the known function $v(\theta)$, then the variance-stabilizing transformation is defined by (2.14); see Problem 5.2 for an example. If no theoretical approximation exists for var(T), then we can apply the empirical method outlined in Section 3.9.2. A simpler empirical approach which sometimes works is to make normal Q-Q plots of $h(t^*)$ for candidate transformations.

It is important to stress that the use of transformation can improve the basic bootstrap method considerably. Nevertheless it may still be beneficial to use the studentized method, after transformation. Indeed there is strong empirical evidence that the studentized method is improved by working on a scale with stable approximate variance. The studentized transformed estimator is

$$Z = \frac{h(T) - h(\theta)}{|\dot{h}(T)|V^{1/2}}.$$

Given R values of the bootstrap quantity $z^* = \{h(t^*) - h(t)\}/\{|\dot{h}(t^*)|v^{*1/2}\}$, the analogue of (5.10) is given by

$$\hat{\theta}_\alpha = h^{-1}\{h(t) - |\dot{h}(t)|v^{1/2}z^*_{((R+1)(1-\alpha))}\}, \quad \hat{\theta}_{1-\alpha} = h^{-1}\{h(t) - |\dot{h}(t)|v^{1/2}z^*_{((R+1)\alpha)}\}.$$
(5.11)

Note that if $h(\cdot)$ is given by (2.14) with no constant multiplier and $V = v(T)$, then the denominator of z^* and the multiplier $|\dot{h}(t)|v^{1/2}$ in (5.11) are both unity.

Likelihood ratio methods

When likelihood estimation is used, in principle the normal approximation confidence limits (5.4) are inferior to likelihood ratio limits. Suppose that the scalar θ is the only unknown parameter in the model, and define the log likelihood ratio statistic

$$w(\theta) = 2\{\ell(\hat{\theta}) - \ell(\theta)\}.$$

$\ell(\theta)$ is the log likelihood function

Quite generally the distribution of $W(\theta)$ is approximately chi-squared, with one degree of freedom since θ is a scalar. So a $1 - 2\alpha$ approximate confidence region is

$$C_{1-2\alpha} = \{\theta : w(\theta) \le c_{1,1-2\alpha}\},$$
(5.12)

where $c_{1,p}$ is the p quantile of the χ^2_1 distribution. This confidence region need not be a single interval, although usually it will be, and the left- and right-tail errors need not be even approximately equal. Separate lower and upper confidence limits can be defined using

$$z(\theta) = \text{sgn}(\hat{\theta} - \theta)\sqrt{w(\theta)},$$

$\text{sgn}(u) = u/|u|$ is the sign function.

which is approximately $N(0,1)$. The resulting confidence limits are defined implicitly by

$$z(\hat{\theta}_\alpha) = z_\alpha, \quad z(\hat{\theta}_{1-\alpha}) = z_{1-\alpha}.$$
(5.13)

When the model includes other unknown parameters λ, also estimated by maximum likelihood, $w(\theta)$ is calculated by replacing $\ell(\theta)$ with the profile log likelihood $\ell_{\text{prof}}(\theta) = \sup_\lambda \ell(\theta, \lambda)$.

These methods are invariant with respect to use of parameter transformation.

In most applications the accuracy will be very good, provided the model is correct, but it may nevertheless be sensible to consider replacing the theoretical quantiles by bootstrap approximations. Whether or not this is worthwhile can be judged from a chi-squared Q-Q plot of simulated values of

ℓ^* is the log likelihood for a set of data simulated using $\hat{\theta}$, for which the MLE is $\hat{\theta}^*$.

$$w^*(\hat{\theta}) = 2\{\ell^*(\hat{\theta}^*) - \ell^*(\hat{\theta})\},$$

or from a normal Q-Q plot of the corresponding values of $z^*(\hat{\theta})$.

Example 5.1 (Air-conditioning data) The data of Example 1.1 were used to illustrate various features of parametric resampling in Chapter 2. Here we look at confidence limit calculations for the underlying mean failure time μ under the exponential model for these data. The example is convenient in that there is an exact solution against which to compare the various approximations.

For the normal approximation method we use an estimate of the exact variance of the estimator $T = \bar{Y}$, $v = n^{-1}\bar{y}^2$. The observed value of $\bar{y}$ is 108.083 and $n = 12$, so $v = (31.20)^2$. Then the 95% confidence interval limits given by (5.4) with $\alpha = 0.025$ are

$$108.083 \pm 31.20 \times 1.96 = 46.9 \text{ and } 169.2.$$

These contrast sharply with the exact limits 65.9 and 209.2.

Transformation to the variance-stabilizing logarithmic scale does improve the normal approximation. Application of (2.14) with $v(\mu) = n^{-1}\mu^2$ gives $h(t) = \log(t)$, if we drop the multiplier $n^{1/2}$, and the approximate variance transforms to n^{-1}. The 95% confidence interval limits given by (5.9) are

$$\exp\{\log(108.083) \pm (12)^{-1/2} \times 1.96\} = 61.4 \text{ and } 190.3.$$

While a considerable improvement, the results are still not very close to the exact solution. A partial explanation for this is that there is a bias in $\log(T)$ and the variance approximation is no longer equal to the exact variance. Use of bootstrap estimates for the bias and variance of $\log(T)$, with $R = 999$, gives limits 58.1 and 228.8.

For the basic bootstrap confidence limits we use $R = 999$ simulations under the fitted exponential model, samples of size $n = 12$ being generated from the exponential distribution with mean 108.083; see Example 2.6. The relevant ordered values of $\bar{y}^*$ are the $(999 + 1)0.025$th and $(999 + 1)0.975$th, i.e. the 25th and 975th, which in our simulation were 53.3 and 176.4. The 95% confidence limits obtained from (5.6) are therefore

$$2 \times 108.083 - 176.4 = 39.8, \quad 2 \times 108.083 - 53.3 = 162.9.$$

These are no better than the normal approximation limits. However, application of the same method on the logarithmic scale gives much better results:

using the same ordered values of $\bar{y}^*$ in (5.10) we obtain the limits

$$\exp\{2\log(108.083)-\log(176.4)\} = 66.2, \ \exp\{2\log(108.083)-\log(53.4)\} = 218.8.$$

In fact these are simulation approximations to the exact limits, which are based on the exact gamma distribution of $\bar{Y}/\mu$. The same results are obtained using the studentized bootstrap limits (5.7) in this case, because $z = n^{1/2}(\bar{y}-\mu)/\bar{y}$ is a monotone function of $\log(\bar{y}) - \log(\mu) = \log(\bar{y}/\mu)$. Equation (5.11) also gives these results.

Note that if we had used $R = 99$, then the bootstrap confidence limits would have required interpolation, because $(99+1)0.025 = 2.5$ which is not an integer. The application of (5.8) would be

$$t^*_{(2.5)} = t^*_{(2)} + \frac{\Phi^{-1}(0.025) - \Phi^{-1}(0.020)}{\Phi^{-1}(0.030) - \Phi^{-1}(0.020)}(t^*_{(3)} - t^*_{(2)}).$$

This involves quite extreme ordered values and so is somewhat unstable.

The likelihood ratio method gives good results here, even using the chi-squared approximation.

Broadly similar comparisons among the methods apply under the more complicated gamma model for these data. As the comparisons made in Example 2.9 would predict, results for the gamma model are similar to those for nonparametric resampling, which are discussed in the next example. ∎

5.2.2 Nonparametric models

When no model is assumed for the data distribution, we are then in the situation of Section 2.3, if the data form a single homogeneous sample. Initially we assume that this is the case. Most of the methods just discussed for parametric models extend to this nonparametric situation with little difficulty. The major exception is the likelihood ratio method, which we postpone to Chapter 10.

Normal approximation

The simplest method is again to use a normal approximation, now with a nonparametric estimate of variance such as that provided by the nonparametric delta method described in Section 2.7.2. If l_j represents the empirical influence value for the jth case y_j, then the approximate variance is $v_L = n^{-2}\sum l_j^2$, so the nonparametric analogue of (5.4) for the limits of a $1 - 2\alpha$ confidence interval for θ is

$$t \mp v_L^{1/2} z_{1-\alpha}. \tag{5.14}$$

Section 2.7 outlines various ways of calculating or approximating the influence values.

If a small nonparametric bootstrap has been run to produce bias and variance estimates b_R and v_R, as described in Section 2.3, then the corresponding approximate $1 - 2\alpha$ confidence interval is

$$t - b_R \mp v_R^{1/2} z_{1-\alpha}. \tag{5.15}$$

In general we should expect this to be more accurate, provided R was large enough.

Basic and studentized bootstrap methods

For the basic bootstrap method, the only change from the parametric case is that the simulation model is the EDF $\hat{F}$. Otherwise equation (5.6) still applies. Whether or not the bootstrap method is likely to give improvement over the normal approximation method can again be judged from a normal Q-Q plot of the t^* values. Simulated resample values do give estimates of bias and variance which provide the more accurate normal approximation limits (5.15).

The studentized bootstrap method with confidence limits (5.7) likewise applies here. If the nonparametric delta method variance estimate v_L is used for v, then those confidence limits become

$$\hat{\theta}_\alpha = t - v_L^{1/2} z_{((R+1)(1-\alpha))}^*, \quad \hat{\theta}_{1-\alpha} = t - v_L^{1/2} z_{((R+1)\alpha)}^*, \tag{5.16}$$

where now $z^* = (t^* - t)/v_L^{*1/2}$. Note that the influence values must be recomputed for each bootstrap sample, because in expanded notation $l_j = l(y_j; \hat{F})$ depends upon the EDF of the sample. Therefore

$$v_L^* = n^{-2} \sum_{j=1}^n l^2(y_j^*; \hat{F}^*),$$

where $\hat{F}^*$ is the EDF of the bootstrap sample. A simple approximation to v_L^* can be made by substituting the approximation

$$l(y_j^*; \hat{F}^*) \doteq l(y_j^*; \hat{F}) - n^{-1} \sum_{k=1}^n l(y_k^*; \hat{F}),$$

but this is unreliable unless t is approximately linear; see Section 2.7.5 and Problem 2.20.

As in the parametric case, one might consider making a bias adjustment in the numerator of z, for example based on the empirical second derivatives of t. However, this rarely seems effective, and in any event an approximate adjustment is implicitly made in the bootstrap distribution of Z^*.

Example 5.2 (Air-conditioning data, continued) For the data of Example 1.1, confidence limits for the mean were calculated under an exponential model in Example 5.1. Here we apply nonparametric methods, simulated datasets being obtained by sampling with replacement from the data.

For the normal approximation, we use the nonparametric delta method estimate $v_L = n^{-2} \sum (y_j - \bar{y})^2$, whose data value is $1417.715 = (37.65)^2$. So the approximate 95% confidence interval is

$$108.083 \pm 37.65 \times 1.96 = 34.3 \text{ and } 181.9.$$

This, as with most of the numerical results here, is very similar to what is obtained under parametric analysis with the best-fitting gamma model; see Example 2.9.

For the basic bootstrap method with $R = 999$ simulated datasets, the 25th and 975th ordered values of $\bar{y}^*$ are 43.92 and 192.08, so the limits of the 95% confidence interval are

$$2(108.083) - 192.08 = 24.1 \text{ and } 2(108.083) - 43.92 = 172.3.$$

This is not obviously a poor result, unless compared with results for the gamma model (likelihood ratio limits 57 and 243), but the corresponding 99% interval has lower limit -27.3, which is clearly very bad! The studentized bootstrap fares better: the 25th and 975th ordered values of z^* are -5.21 and 1.66, so that application of (5.7) gives 95% interval limits

$$108.083 - 37.65 \times 1.66 = 45.7 \text{ and } 108.083 - 37.65 \times (-5.21) = 304.2.$$

But are these last results adequate, and how can we tell? The first part of this question we can answer both by comparison with the gamma model results, and by applying methods on the logarithmic scale, which we know is appropriate here. The basic bootstrap method gives 95% limits 66.2 and 218.8 when the log scale is used. So it would appear that the studentized bootstrap method limits are too wide here, but otherwise are adequate. If the studentized bootstrap method is applied in conjunction with the logarithmic transformation, the limits become 50.5 and 346.9.

How would we know in practice that the logarithmic transformation of T is appropriate, other than from experience with similar data? One way to answer this is to plot v_L^* versus t^*, as a surrogate for a "variance–parameter" plot, as suggested in Section 3.9.2. For this particular dataset, the equivalent plot of standard errors $v_L^{*1/2}$ is shown in the left panel of Figure 5.1 and strongly suggests that variance is approximately proportional to squared parameter, as it is under the parametric model. From this we would deduce, using (2.14), that the logarithmic transformation should approximately stabilize the variance. The right panel of the figure, which gives the corresponding plot for log-transformed estimates, shows that the transformation is quite successful. ∎

Parameter transformation

For suitably smooth statistics, the consistency of the studentized bootstrap method is essentially guaranteed by the consistency of the variance estimate V. In principle the method is more accurate than the basic bootstrap method,

Figure 5.1
Air-conditioning data:
nonparametric delta
method standard errors
for $t = \bar{y}$ (left panel) and
for $\log(t)$ (right panel) in
$R = 999$ nonparametric
bootstrap samples.

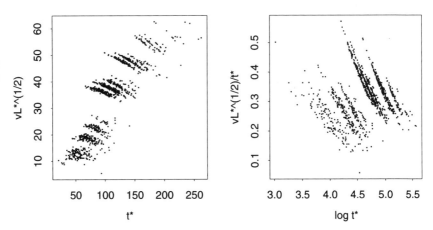

as we shall see in Section 5.4. However, variance approximations such as v_L can be somewhat unstable for small n, as in the previous example with $n = 12$. Experience suggests that the method is most effective when θ is essentially a location parameter, which is approximately induced by variance-stabilizing transformation (2.14). However, this requires knowing the variance function $v(\theta) = \mathrm{var}(T \mid F)$, which is never available in the nonparametric case.

A suitable transformation may sometimes be suggested by analogy with a parametric problem, as in the previous example. Then equations (5.10) and (5.11) will apply without change. Otherwise, a transformation can be obtained empirically using the technique described in Section 3.9.2, using either nested bootstrap estimates v^* or delta method estimates v_L^* with which to estimate values of the variance function $v(\theta)$. Equation (5.10) will then apply with estimated transformation $\hat{h}(\cdot)$ in place of $h(\cdot)$. For the studentized bootstrap interval (5.11), if the transformation is determined empirically by (3.40), then studentized values of the transformed estimates $\hat{h}(t_r^*)$ are

$$z_r^* = \hat{v}(t_r^*)^{1/2}\{\hat{h}(t_r^*) - \hat{h}(t)\}/v_{Lr}^{*1/2}.$$

On the original scale the $(1 - 2\alpha)$ studentized interval has endpoints

$$\hat{h}^{-1}\left\{\hat{h}(t) - v_L^{1/2}\hat{v}(t)^{-1/2}z_{((1-\alpha)(R+1))}^*\right\}, \quad \hat{h}^{-1}\left\{\hat{h}(t) - v_L^{1/2}\hat{v}(t)^{-1/2}z_{(\alpha(R+1))}^*\right\}. \tag{5.17}$$

In general it is wise to use the studentized interval even after transformation.

Example 5.3 (City population data) For the data of Example 2.8, with ratio θ estimated by $t = \bar{x}/\bar{u}$, we discussed empirical choice of transformation in Example 3.23. Application of the empirical transformation illustrated in

Figure 3.11 with the studentized bootstrap limits (5.17) leads to the 95% interval [1.23, 2.25]. This is similar to the 95% interval based on the $\hat{h}(t_r^*) - \hat{h}(t)$, [1.27, 2.21], while the studentized bootstrap interval on the original scale is [1.12, 1.88]. The effect of the transformation is to make the interval more like those from the percentile methods described in the following section.

To compare the studentized methods, we took 500 samples of size 10 without replacement from the full city population data in Table 1.3. Then for each sample we calculated 90% studentized bootstrap intervals on the original scale, and on the transformed scale with and without using the transformed standard error; this last interval is the basic bootstrap interval on the transformed scale. The coverages were respectively 90.4, 88.2, and 86.4%, to be compared to the ideal 90%. The first two are not significantly different, but the last is rather smaller, suggesting that it can be worthwhile to studentize on the transformed scale, when this is possible. The drawback is that studentized intervals that use the transformed scale tend to be longer than on the original scale, and their lengths are more variable.   ∎

5.2.3 Choice of R

What has been said about simulation size in earlier chapters, especially in Section 4.2.5, applies here. In particular, if confidence levels 0.95 and 0.99 are to be used, then it is advisable to have $R = 999$ or more, if practically feasible. Problem 5.5 outlines some relevant theoretical calculations.

5.3 Percentile Methods

We have seen in Section 5.2 that simple confidence limit methods can be made more accurate by working on a transformed scale. In many cases it is possible to use simulation results to get a reasonable idea of what a sensible transformation might be. A quite different approach is to find a method which implicitly uses the existence of a good transformation, but does not require that the transformation be found. This is what the percentile method and its modifications try to do.

5.3.1 Basic percentile method

Suppose that there is some unknown transformation of T, say $U = h(T)$, which has a symmetric distribution. Imagine that we knew h and calculated a $1 - 2\alpha$ confidence interval for $\phi = h(\theta)$ by applying the basic bootstrap method (5.6), except that we first use the symmetry to write $a_\alpha = -a_{1-\alpha}$ in the basic equation (5.3) as it applies to $U = h(T)$. This would mean that in applying (5.3) we would take $u - u^*_{((R+1)(1-\alpha))}$ instead of $u^*_{((R+1)\alpha)} - u$, and $u - u^*_{((R+1)\alpha)}$

instead of $u^*_{((R+1)(1-\alpha))} - u$, to estimate the α and $1 - \alpha$ quantiles of U. This swap would change the confidence interval limits (5.6) to

$$u^*_{((R+1)\alpha)}, \quad u^*_{((R+1)(1-\alpha))},$$

whose transformation back to the θ scale is

$$t^*_{((R+1)\alpha)}, \quad t^*_{((R+1)(1-\alpha))}. \tag{5.18}$$

Remarkably this $1 - 2\alpha$ interval for θ does not involve h at all, and so can be computed without knowing h. The interval (5.18) is known as the *bootstrap percentile interval*, and was initially recommended in place of (5.6).

As with most bootstrap methods, the percentile method applies for both parametric and nonparametric bootstrap sampling. Perhaps surprisingly, the method turns out not to work very well with the nonparametric bootstrap even when a suitable transformation h does exist. However, adjustments to the percentile method described below are successful for many statistics.

Example 5.4 (Air-conditioning data, continued) For the air-conditioning data discussed in Examples 5.1 and 5.2, the percentile method gives 95% intervals [70.8, 148.4] under the exponential model and [43.9, 192.1] under the nonparametric model. Neither is satisfactory, compared to accurate intervals such as the basic bootstrap interval using logarithmic transformation. ∎

5.3.2 Adjusted percentile method

For the percentile method to work well, it would be necessary that T be unbiased on the transformed scale, so that the swap of quantile estimates be correct. This does not usually happen. Also the method carries the defect of the basic bootstrap method, that the shape of the distribution of T changes as the sampling distribution changes from F to $\hat{F}$, even after transformation. In particular, the implied symmetrizing transformation often will not be quite the same as the variance-stabilizing transformation — this is the cause of the poor performance of the percentile method in Example 5.4. These difficulties need to be overcome if the percentile method is to be made accurate.

Parametric case with no nuisance parameters

We assume to begin with that the data are described by a parametric model with just the single unknown parameter θ, which is estimated by the maximum likelihood estimate $t = \hat{\theta}$. In order to develop the adjusted percentile method we make the simplifying assumption that for some unknown transformation $h(\cdot)$, unknown bias correction factor w and unknown skewness correction factor a, the transformed estimator $U = h(T)$ for $\phi = h(\theta)$ is normally distributed,

$$U \sim N\left(\phi - w\sigma(\phi), \sigma^2(\phi)\right) \quad \text{with } \sigma(\phi) = 1 + a\phi. \tag{5.19}$$

In fact this is an improved normal approximation, after applying the (unknown) normalizing transformation which eliminates the leading term in a skewness approximation. The usual factor n^{-1} has been taken out of the variance by scaling $h(\cdot)$ appropriately, so that both a and w will typically be of order $n^{-1/2}$. The use of a and w is analogous to the use of Bartlett correction factors in likelihood inference for parametric models.

The essence of the method is to calculate confidence limits for ϕ and then transform these back to the θ scale using the bootstrap distribution of T. To begin with, suppose that a and w are known, and write

$$U = \phi + (1 + a\phi)(Z - w),$$

where Z has the $N(0, 1)$ distribution with α quantile z_α. It follows that

$$\log(1 + aU) = \log(1 + a\phi) + \log\{1 + a(Z - w)\},$$

which is monotone increasing in ϕ. Therefore substitution of z_α for Z and u for U in this equation identifies the α confidence limit for ϕ, which is

$$\hat{\phi}_\alpha = u + \sigma(u)\frac{w + z_\alpha}{1 - a(w + z_\alpha)}.$$

Now the α confidence limit for θ is $\hat{\theta}_\alpha = h^{-1}(\hat{\phi}_\alpha)$, but $h(\cdot)$ is unknown. However, if we denote the distribution function of T^* by $\hat{G}$, then

$$\hat{G}(\hat{\theta}_\alpha) = \mathrm{Pr}^*(T^* < \hat{\theta}_\alpha \mid t) = \mathrm{Pr}^*(U^* < \hat{\phi}_\alpha \mid u) = \Phi\left(\frac{\hat{\phi}_\alpha - u}{\sigma(u)} + w\right)$$

$$= \Phi\left(w + \frac{w + z_\alpha}{1 - a(w + z_\alpha)}\right),$$

which is known. Therefore the α confidence limit for θ is

$$\hat{\theta}_\alpha = \hat{G}^{-1}\left\{\Phi\left(w + \frac{w + z_\alpha}{1 - a(w + z_\alpha)}\right)\right\}, \tag{5.20}$$

which expressed in terms of simulation values is

$$\hat{\theta}_\alpha = t^*_{((R+1)\tilde{\alpha})}, \quad \tilde{\alpha} = \Phi\left(w + \frac{w + z_\alpha}{1 - a(w + z_\alpha)}\right). \tag{5.21}$$

These limits are usually referred to as BC_a confidence limits. Note that they share the transformation invariance property of percentile confidence limits.

The use of $\hat{G}$ overcomes lack of knowledge of the transformation h. The values of a and w are unknown, of course, but they can be easily estimated. For w we can use the initial normal approximation (5.19) for U to write

$$\mathrm{Pr}^*(T^* < t \mid t) = \mathrm{Pr}^*(U^* < u \mid u) = \mathrm{Pr}(U < \phi \mid \phi) = \Phi(w),$$

so that

$$w = \Phi^{-1}\{\hat{G}(t)\}. \tag{5.22}$$

In terms of simulation values

# denotes the number
of times the event
occurs.

$$w = \Phi^{-1}\left(\frac{\#\{t_r^* \le t\}}{R+1}\right).$$

The value of a can be determined informally using (5.19). Thus if $\ell(\phi)$ denotes the log likelihood defined by (5.19), with derivative $\dot{\ell}(\phi)$, then it is easy to show that

$$\frac{E\{\dot{\ell}(\phi)^3\}}{\text{var}\{\dot{\ell}(\phi)\}^{3/2}} = 6a,$$

ignoring terms of order n^{-1}. But the ratio on the left of this equation is invariant under parameter transformation. So we transform back from ϕ to θ and deduce that, still ignoring terms of order n^{-1},

$$\frac{E\{\dot{\ell}(\theta)^3\}}{\text{var}\{\dot{\ell}(\theta)\}^{3/2}} = 6a.$$

To calculate a we approximate the moments of $\dot{\ell}(\theta)$ by those of $\dot{\ell}(\hat{\theta})$ under the fitted model with parameter value $\hat{\theta}$, so that the skewness correction factor is

$$a = \frac{1}{6}\frac{E^*\{\dot{\ell}^*(\hat{\theta})^3\}}{\text{var}^*\{\dot{\ell}^*(\hat{\theta})^{3/2}\}}, \qquad (5.23)$$

where ℓ^* is the log likelihood of a set of data simulated from the fitted model. More generally a is one-sixth the standardized skewness of the linear approximation to T.

One potential problem with the BC_a method is that if $\tilde{\alpha}$ in (5.21) is much closer to 0 or 1 than α, then $(R+1)\tilde{\alpha}$ could be less than 1 or greater than R, so that even with interpolation the relevant quantile cannot be calculated. If this happens, and if R cannot be increased, then it would be appropriate to quote the extreme value of t^* and the implied value of α. For example, if $(R+1)\tilde{\alpha} > R$, then the upper confidence limit $t_{(R)}^*$ would be given with implied right-tail error α_2 equal to one minus the solution to $\tilde{\alpha} = R/(R+1)$.

Example 5.5 (Air-conditioning data, continued)   Returning to the problem of Example 5.4 and the exponential bootstrap results for $R = 999$, we find that the number of $\bar{y}^*$ values below $\bar{y} = 108.083$ is 535, so by (5.22) $w = \Phi^{-1}(0.535) = 0.0878$. The log likelihood function is $\ell(\mu) = -n\log\mu - \mu^{-1}\sum y_j$, whose derivative is

$$\dot{\ell}(\mu) = \frac{\sum y_j}{\mu^2} - \frac{n}{\mu}.$$

The second and third moments of $\dot{\ell}(\mu)$ are $n\mu^{-2}$ and $2n\mu^{-3}$, so by (5.23)

$$a = \tfrac{1}{3}n^{-1/2} = 0.0962.$$

α	$\tilde{z}_\alpha = w + z_\alpha$	$\tilde{\alpha} = \Phi(w + \frac{\tilde{z}_\alpha}{1-a\tilde{z}_\alpha})$	$r = (R+1)\tilde{\alpha}$	$t^*_{(r)}$
0.025	−1.872	0.067	67.00	65.26
0.975	2.048	0.996	995.83	199.41
0.050	−1.557	0.103	102.71	71.19
0.950	1.733	0.985	984.89	182.42

Table 5.1 Calculation of adjusted percentile bootstrap confidence limits for μ with the data of Example 1.1, under the parametric exponential model with $R = 999$; $a = 0.0962, w = 0.0878$.

The calculation of the adjusted percentile limits (5.21) is illustrated in Table 5.1. The values of $r = (R+1)\tilde{\alpha}$ are not integers, so we have applied the interpolation formula (5.8).

Had we tried to calculate a 99% interval, we should have had to calculate the 999.88th ordered value of t^*, which does not exist. The implied right-tail error for $t^*_{(999)}$ is the value α_2 which solves

$$\frac{999}{1000} = \Phi\left(0.0878 + \frac{0.0878 + z_{1-\alpha_2}}{1 - 0.0962(0.0878 + z_{1-\alpha_2})}\right),$$

namely $\alpha_2 = 0.0125$. ∎

Parametric case with nuisance parameters

When θ is one of several unknown parameters, the previous development applies to a derived distribution called the *least-favourable family*. As usual we denote the nuisance parameters by λ and write $\psi = (\theta, \lambda)$. If the log likelihood function for ψ based on all the data is $\ell(\psi)$, then the expected Fisher information matrix is $i(\psi) = \mathrm{E}\{-\ddot{\ell}(\psi)\}$. Now define $\hat{\delta} = i^{-1}(\hat{\psi})(1, 0, \ldots, 0)^T$. $\ddot{\ell}(\psi)$ is $\partial^2\ell(\psi)/\partial\psi\partial\psi^T$. Then the least-favourable family of distributions is the one-parameter family obtained from the original model by restricting ψ to the curve $\hat{\psi} + \zeta\hat{\delta}$. With this restriction, the log likelihood is

$$\ell_{LF}(\zeta) = \ell(\hat{\psi} + \zeta\hat{\delta}),$$

akin to the profile log likelihood for θ. The MLE of ζ is $\hat{\zeta} = 0$.

The bias-corrected percentile method is now applied to the least-favourable family. Equations (5.21) and (5.22) still apply. The only change in the calculations is to the skewness correction factor a, which becomes

$$a = \frac{1}{6} \frac{\mathrm{E}^*\{\dot{\ell}^*_{LF}(0)^3\}}{\mathrm{var}^*\{\dot{\ell}^*_{LF}(0)\}^{3/2}}. \tag{5.24}$$

In this expression the parameter estimates $\hat{\psi}$ are regarded as fixed, and the moments are calculated under the fitted model.

A somewhat simpler expression for a can be obtained by noting that $\dot{\ell}_{LF}(0)$ is proportional to the influence function for t. The result in Problem 2.12 shows that

$$L_t(y_j; F_\psi) = ni^1(\psi)\dot{\ell}(\psi, y_j),$$

Table 5.2 Calculation
of adjusted percentile
bootstrap confidence
limits for μ with the
data of Example 1.1,
under the gamma
parametric model with
$\hat{\mu} = 108.0833$,
$\hat{\kappa} = 0.7065$ and
$R = 999$;
$a = 0.1145, w = 0.1372$.

α	$\tilde{z}_\alpha = w + z_\alpha$	$\tilde{\alpha} = \Phi(w + \frac{\tilde{z}_\alpha}{1-a\tilde{z}_\alpha})$	$r = (R+1)\tilde{\alpha}$	$t^*_{(r)}$
0.025	−1.823	0.085	85.20	62.97
0.975	2.097	0.998	998.11	226.00
0.050	−1.508	0.125	125.36	67.25
0.950	1.782	0.991	991.25	208.00

where $i^1(\psi)$ is the first row of the inverse of $i(\psi)$ and $\dot{\ell}(\psi, y_j)$ is the contribution to $\dot{\ell}(\psi)$ from the jth case. We can then rewrite (5.24) as

$$a = \frac{1}{6} \frac{\sum \mathrm{E}^*(L_j^{*3})}{\left\{ \sum \mathrm{var}^*(L_j^*) \right\}^{3/2}}, \tag{5.25}$$

where

$$L_j^* = ni^1(\hat{\psi})\dot{\ell}(\hat{\psi}, Y_j^*)$$

and Y_j^* follows the fitted distribution with parameter value $\hat{\psi}$. As before, to first order a is one-sixth the estimated standardized skewness of the linear approximation to t. In the form given, (5.25) will apply also to nonhomogeneous data.

The BC_a method can be extended to any smooth function of the original model parameters ψ; see Problem 5.7.

Example 5.6 (Air-conditioning data, continued) We now replace the exponential model used in the previous example, for the data of Example 2.3, with the two-parameter gamma model. The parameters are $\theta = \mu$ and $\lambda = \kappa$, the first still being the parameter of interest. The log likelihood function is

$$\ell(\mu, \kappa) = n\kappa \log(\kappa/\mu) + (\kappa - 1) \sum \log y_j - \kappa \sum y_j/\mu - n \log \Gamma(\kappa).$$

The information matrix is diagonal, so that the least-favourable family is the original gamma family with κ fixed at $\hat{\kappa} = 0.7065$. It follows quite easily that

$$\dot{\ell}^*_{LF}(0) \propto \bar{y}^* - \bar{y},$$

and so a is one-sixth of the skewness of the sample average under the fitted gamma model, that is $a = \frac{1}{3}(n\hat{\kappa})^{-1/2}$. The same result is obtained somewhat more easily via (5.25), since we know that the influence function for the mean is $L_t(y; F) = y - \mu$.

The numerical values of a and w for these data are 0.1145 and 0.1372 respectively, the latter from $R = 999$ simulated samples. Using these we compute the adjusted percentile bootstrap confidence limits as in Table 5.2. ∎

Just how flexible is the BC_a method? The following example presents a difficult challenge for all bootstrap methods, and illustrates how well the studentized bootstrap and BC_a methods can compensate for weaknesses in the more primitive methods.

Example 5.7 (Normal variance estimation)   Suppose that we have independent samples $(y_{i1}, \ldots, y_{im})$, $i = 1, \ldots, k$, from normal distributions with different means λ_i but common variance θ, the latter being the parameter of interest. The maximum likelihood estimator of the variance is $t = n^{-1} \sum_{i=1}^{k} \sum_{j=1}^{m} (y_{ij} - \bar{y}_i)^2$,   *$\bar{y}_i$ is the average of $y_{i1}, \ldots, y_{in_i}$.* where $n = mk$. In practice the more usual estimate would be the pooled mean square, with denominator $d = k(m - 1)$ rather than n, but here we leave the bias of T intact to see how well the bootstrap methods can cope.

The distribution of T is $n^{-1} \theta \chi_d^2$. This exact result allows us both to avoid the use of simulation, and to calculate exact coverages for all the confidence limit methods. Denote the α quantile of the χ_d^2 distribution by $c_{d,\alpha}$. Using the fact that $T^* = n^{-1} t \chi_d^2$ we see that the upper α confidence limits for θ under the basic bootstrap and percentile methods are respectively

$$2t - n^{-1} t c_{d,1-\alpha}, \quad n^{-1} t c_{d,\alpha}.$$

The coverages of these limits are calculated using the exact distribution of T. For example, for the basic bootstrap confidence limit

$$\Pr\left(\theta \leq 2T - n^{-1} T c_{d,1-\alpha}\right) = \Pr\left(\chi_d^2 \geq \frac{n}{2 - n^{-1} c_{d,1-\alpha}}\right).$$

For the BC_a method, (5.22) gives $w = \Phi^{-1}\{\Pr(\chi_d^2 \leq n)\}$ and (5.24) gives $a = \frac{1}{3} 2^{1/2} n^{-1/2}$. The upper α confidence limit, calculated by (5.20) with the exact distribution for T^*, is $n^{-1} t c_{d,\tilde{\alpha}}$. The exact coverage of this limit is $\Pr(\chi_d^2 \geq n^2 / c_{d,\tilde{\alpha}})$.

Finally, for the studentized bootstrap upper α confidence limit (5.7), we first calculate the variance approximation $v = 2n^{-1} t^2$ from the expected Fisher information matrix and then the confidence limit is $nt/c_{d,1-\alpha}$. The coverage of this limit is exactly α.

Table 5.3 shows numerical values of coverages for the four methods in the case $k = 10$ and $m = 2$, where $d = \frac{1}{2} n = 10$. The results show quite dramatically first how bad the basic and percentile methods can be if used without careful thought, and secondly how well studentized and adjusted percentile methods can do in a moderately difficult situation. Of course use of a logarithmic transformation would improve the basic bootstrap method, which would then give correct answers.   ∎

Table 5.3 Exact coverages (%) of confidence limits for normal variance based on maximum likelihood estimator for 10 samples each of size two.

Nominal	Basic	Studentized	Percentile	BC_a
1.0	0.8	1.0	0.0	1.0
2.5	2.5	2.5	0.0	2.5
5.0	4.8	5.0	0.0	5.0
95.0	35.0	95.0	1.6	91.5
97.5	36.7	97.5	4.4	100.0
99.0	38.3	99.0	6.9	100.0

Nonparametric case: single sample

The adjusted percentile method for the nonparametric case is developed by applying the method for the parametric case with no nuisance parameters to a specially constructed nonparametric exponential family with support on the data values, the least-favourable family derived from the multinomial distribution for frequencies of the data values under nonparametric resampling.

Specifically, if l_j denotes the empirical influence value for t at y_j, then the resampling model for an individual Y^* is the exponential tilted distribution

$$\Pr(Y^* = y_j) = p_j = \frac{\exp(\eta l_j)}{\sum_{k=1}^{n} \exp(\eta l_k)}. \tag{5.26}$$

The parameter of interest θ is a monotone function of η with inverse $\eta(\theta)$, say. The MLE of η is $\hat{\eta} = \eta(t) = 0$, which corresponds to the EDF $\hat{F}$ being the nonparametric MLE of the sampling distribution F.

The bias correction factor w is calculated as before from (5.22), but using nonparametric bootstrap simulation to obtain values of t^*. The skewness correction a is given by the empirical analogue of (5.23), where now

$\dot{\eta}(\theta)$ is the first derivative $d\eta(\theta)/d\theta$.

$$\dot{\ell}(\theta) = \dot{\eta}(\theta) \left\{ \sum l_j^* - n\mathrm{E}^*(L^*) \right\}.$$

When the moments needed in (5.23) are evaluated at $\hat{\theta}$, or equivalently at $\hat{\eta} = 0$, two simplifications occur. First we have $\mathrm{E}^*(L^*) = 0$, and secondly the multiplier $\dot{\eta}(t)$ cancels when (5.23) is applied. The result is that

$$a = \frac{1}{6} \frac{\sum l_j^3}{\left(\sum l_j^2 \right)^{3/2}}, \tag{5.27}$$

which is the direct analogue of (5.25).

Example 5.8 (Air-conditioning data, continued) The nonparametric version of the calculations in the preceding example involves the same formula (5.21), but now with $a = 0.0938$ and $w = 0.0728$. The former constant is calculated from (5.27) with $l_j = y_j - \bar{y}$. The confidence limit calculations are shown in Table 5.4 for 90% and 95% intervals. ∎

α	$\tilde{z}_\alpha = w + z_\alpha$	$\tilde{\alpha} = \Phi(w + \frac{z_\alpha}{1-a\tilde{z}_\alpha})$	$r = (R+1)\tilde{\alpha}$	$t^*_{(r)}$
0.025	−1.8872	0.0629	62.93	55.33
0.975	2.0327	0.9951	995.12	243.50
0.050	−1.5721	0.0973	97.26	61.50
0.950	1.7176	0.9830	983.01	202.08

Table 5.4 Calculation of adjusted percentile bootstrap confidence limits for μ in Example 1.1 using nonparametric bootstrap with $R = 999$; $a = 0.0938$, $w = 0.0728$.

If t is a function of sample moments, say $t = t(\bar{s})$ where $\bar{s}_i = n^{-1} \sum_{j=1}^{n} s_i(y_j)$ for $i = 1, \ldots, k$, then (5.26) is a one-dimensional reduction of a k-dimensional exponential family for $s_1(Y^*), \ldots, s_k(Y^*)$. By equation (2.38) the influence values l_j for t are given simply by $l_j = \dot{t}^T \{s(y_j) - \bar{s}\}$ with $\dot{t} = \partial t / \partial \bar{s}$.

The method as described will apply as given to any single-sample problem, and to most regression problems (Chapters 6 and 7), but not exactly to problems where statistics are based on several independent samples, including stratified samples.

Nonparametric case: several samples

In the parametric case the BC_a method as described applies quite generally through the unifying likelihood function. In the nonparametric case, however, there are predictable changes in the BC_a method. The background approximation methods are described in Section 3.2.1, which defines an estimator in terms of the EDFs of k samples, $t = t(\hat{F}_1, \ldots, \hat{F}_k)$. The empirical influence values l_{ij} for $j = 1, \ldots, n_i$ and $i = 1, \ldots, k$ and the variance approximation v_L are defined in (3.2) and (3.3).

If we return to the origin and development of the BC_a method, we see that the definition of bias correction w in (5.22) will remain the same. The skewness correction a will again be one-sixth the estimated standardized skewness of the linear approximation to t, which here is

$$a = \frac{1}{6} \frac{\sum_{i=1}^{k} n_i^{-3} \sum_{j=1}^{n_i} l_{ij}^3}{\left(\sum_{i=1}^{k} n_i^{-2} \sum_{j=1}^{n_i} l_{ij}^2 \right)^{3/2}}. \tag{5.28}$$

This can be verified as an application of the parametric method by constructing the least-favourable joint family of k distributions from the k multinomial distributions on the data values in the k samples.

Note that (5.28) can be expressed in the same form as (5.27) by defining $\tilde{l}_{ij} = n l_{ij} / n_i$, where $n = \sum n_i$, so that

$$v_L = n^{-2} \sum_{i,j} \tilde{l}_{ij}^2, \quad a = \frac{1}{6} \frac{\sum_{i,j} \tilde{l}_{ij}^3}{\left(\sum_{i,j} \tilde{l}_{ij}^2 \right)^{3/2}}; \tag{5.29}$$

see Problem 3.7. This can be helpful in writing an all-purpose algorithm for the BC_a method; see also the discussion of the ABC method in the next section.

An example is given at the end of the next section.

5.4 Theoretical Comparison of Methods

The studentized bootstrap and adjusted percentile methods for calculating confidence limits are inherently more accurate than the basic bootstrap and percentile methods. This is quite clear from empirical evidence. Here we look briefly at the theoretical side of the story for statistics which are approximately normal. Some aspects of the theory were discussed in Section 2.6.1. For simplicity we shall restrict most of the detailed discussion to the single-sample case, but the results generalize without much difficulty.

5.4.1 Second-order accuracy

To assess the accuracies of the various bootstrap confidence limits we calculate coverage probabilities up to the $n^{-1/2}$ terms in series approximations, these based on corresponding approximations for the CDFs of $U = (T - \theta)/v^{1/2}$ and $Z = (T - \theta)/V^{1/2}$. Here v is $\mathrm{var}(T)$ or any approximation which agrees to first order with v_L, the variance of the linear approximation to T. Similarly V is assumed to agree to first order with V_L. For example, in the scalar parametric case where T is the maximum likelihood estimator, v is the inverse of the expected Fisher information matrix. In all of the equations in this section equality is correct to order $n^{-1/2}$, i.e. ignoring errors of order n^{-1}.

The relevant approximations for CDFs are the one-term Cornish–Fisher approximations

$$\mathrm{Pr}(U \le u) = G(\theta + v^{1/2}u) = \Phi\left(u - n^{-1/2}(m_1 - \tfrac{1}{6}m_3 + \tfrac{1}{6}m_3u^2)\right), \quad (5.30)$$

where G is the CDF of T, and

$$K(z) = \mathrm{Pr}(Z \le z) = \Phi\left(u - n^{-1/2}\{m_1 - \tfrac{1}{6}m_3 - (\tfrac{1}{2}m_{11} - \tfrac{1}{6}m_3)u^2\}\right), \quad (5.31)$$

with the constants defined by

$$\mathrm{E}(U) = n^{-1/2}m_1, \ \mathrm{E}(U^3) = n^{-1/2}(m_3 - 3m_1), \ \mathrm{E}\{(V - v)(T - \theta)\} = n^{-1/2}m_{11};$$
$$(5.32)$$

note that the skewness of U is $n^{-1/2}m_3$. The corresponding approximations for quantiles of T (rather than U) and Z are

$$G^{-1}(\alpha) = \theta + v^{1/2}z_\alpha + n^{-1/2}v^{1/2}(m_1 - \tfrac{1}{6}m_3 + \tfrac{1}{6}m_3z_\alpha^2) \quad (5.33)$$

and

$$K^{-1}(\alpha) = z_\alpha + n^{-1/2}\left\{m_1 - \tfrac{1}{6}m_3 - (\tfrac{1}{2}m_{11} - \tfrac{1}{6}m_3)z_\alpha^2\right\}. \quad (5.34)$$

The analogous approximations apply to bootstrap distributions and quantiles, ignoring simulation error, by substituting appropriate estimates for the various constants. In fact, provided the estimates for m_1, m_3 and m_{11} have errors of order $n^{-1/2}$ or less, the $n^{-1/2}$ terms in the approximations will not change. This greatly simplifies the calculations that we are about to do.

Studentized bootstrap method

Consider the studentized bootstrap confidence limit $\hat{\theta}_\alpha = t - v^{1/2}\hat{K}^{-1}(1-\alpha)$. Since the right-hand side of (5.34) holds also for $\hat{K}^{-1}$ we see that to order n^{-1}

$$\hat{\theta}_\alpha = t - v^{1/2}z_{1-\alpha} - n^{-1/2}v^{1/2}\{m_1 - \tfrac{1}{6}m_3 - (\tfrac{1}{2}m_{11} - \tfrac{1}{6}m_3)z_{1-\alpha}^2\}. \qquad (5.35)$$

It then follows by applying (5.31) and expanding by Taylor series that

$$\Pr(\theta \le \hat{\theta}_\alpha) = \alpha + O(n^{-1}).$$

This property is referred to as *second-order accuracy*, as distinct from the first-order accuracy of the normal approximation confidence limit, whose coverage is $\alpha + O(n^{-1/2})$.

Adjusted percentile method

For the adjusted percentile limit (5.20) we use (5.33) with estimated constants as the approximation for $\hat{G}^{-1}(\cdot)$. For the normal integral inside (5.20) we can use the approximation $\Phi(z_\alpha + 2w + az_\alpha^2)$, because a and w are of order $n^{-1/2}$. Then the α confidence limit (5.20) is approximately

$$\hat{\theta}_\alpha = t + v^{1/2}z_\alpha + n^{-1/2}v^{1/2}\left\{2n^{1/2}w + m_1 - \tfrac{1}{6}m_3 + (n^{1/2}a + \tfrac{1}{6}m_3)z_\alpha^2\right\}. \qquad (5.36)$$

This will also be second-order accurate if it agrees with (5.35), which requires that to order $n^{-1/2}$,

$$a = n^{-1/2}(\tfrac{1}{2}m_{11} - \tfrac{1}{3}m_3), \quad w = -n^{-1/2}(m_1 - \tfrac{1}{6}m_3). \qquad (5.37)$$

To verify these approximations we use expressions for m_1, m_3 and m_{11} derived from the quadratic approximation for T described in Section 2.7.2.

In slightly simplified notation, the quadratic approximation (2.41) for T is

$$T = \theta + n^{-1}\sum_i L_t(Y_i) + \tfrac{1}{2}n^{-2}\sum_{i,j}Q_t(Y_j, Y_k). \qquad (5.38)$$

It will be helpful here and later to define the constants

$$a = \tfrac{1}{6}n^{-3}v^{-3/2}\sum_i E\{L_t^3(Y_i)\}, \qquad b = \tfrac{1}{2}n^{-2}\sum_i E\{Q_t(Y_i, Y_i)\},$$

$$\qquad \qquad (5.39)$$

$$c = \tfrac{1}{2}n^{-4}v^{-3/2}\sum_{j\neq k}E\{L_t(Y_j)L_t(Y_k)Q_t(Y_j, Y_k)\}.$$

Then calculations of the first and third moments of $T - \theta$ from the quadratic approximation show that

$$m_1 = n^{1/2} v^{-1/2} b, \quad m_3 = n^{1/2} (6a + 6c). \tag{5.40}$$

For m_{11}, it is enough to take V to be the delta method estimator, which in the full notation is $V_L = n^{-2} \sum L_t^2(Y_i; \hat{F})$. Then using the approximation

$$L_t(Y_i; \hat{F}) \doteq L_t(Y_i) - n^{-1} \sum_{j=1}^{n} L_t(Y_j) + n^{-1} \sum_{j=1}^{n} Q_t(Y_i, Y_j)$$

given in Problem 2.20, detailed calculation leads to

$$m_{11} = n^{1/2} (6a + 4c). \tag{5.41}$$

The results in (5.40) and (5.41) imply the identity for a in (5.37), after noting that the definitions of a in (5.23), (5.25) and (5.27) used in the adjusted percentile method are obtained by substituting estimates for moments of the influence function. The identity for w in (5.37) is confirmed by noting that the original definition $w = \Phi^{-1}\{\hat{G}(t)\}$ approximates $\Phi^{-1}\{G(\theta)\}$, which by applying (5.30) with $u = 0$ agrees with (5.37).

Basic and percentile methods

Similar calculations show that the basic bootstrap and percentile confidence limits are only first-order accurate. However, they are both superior to the normal approximation limits, in the sense that equi-tailed confidence intervals are second-order accurate. For example, consider the $1 - 2\alpha$ basic bootstrap confidence interval with limits

$$\hat{\theta}_\alpha, \hat{\theta}_{1-\alpha} = 2t - \hat{G}^{-1}(1 - \alpha), 2t - \hat{G}^{-1}(\alpha).$$

It follows from the estimated version of (5.33) that

$$2t - \hat{G}^{-1}(1 - \alpha) = t - v^{1/2} z_{1-\alpha} - n^{-1/2} v^{1/2} (m_1 - \tfrac{1}{6} m_3 + \tfrac{1}{6} m_3 z_{1-\alpha}^2),$$

and by (5.31) the error of this lower limit is

$$\Pr\{\theta \leq 2t - \hat{G}^{-1}(1 - \alpha)\} = 1 - \Phi(z_{1-\alpha} + n^{-1/2} m_{11} z_{1-\alpha}^2).$$

Correspondingly the error of the upper limit is

$$\Pr\{\theta \geq 2t - \hat{G}^{-1}(\alpha)\} = \Phi(z_\alpha + n^{-1/2} m_{11} z_\alpha^2).$$

Therefore the combined coverage error of the confidence interval is

$$1 - \Phi(z_{1-\alpha} + n^{-1/2} m_{11} z_{1-\alpha}^2) + \Phi(z_\alpha + n^{-1/2} m_{11} z_\alpha^2)$$

which, after expanding in Taylor series and dropping n^{-1} terms, and then noting that $z_\alpha^2 = z_{1-\alpha}^2$ and $\phi(z_\alpha) = \phi(z_{1-\alpha})$, turns out to equal

$$2\alpha + n^{-1/2} m_{11} \{ z_{1-\alpha}^2 \phi(z_{1-\alpha}) - z_\alpha^2 \phi(z_\alpha) \} = 2\alpha.$$

These results are suggestive of the behaviour that we observe in specific examples, that bootstrap methods in general are superior to normal approximation, but that only the adjusted percentile and studentized bootstrap methods correctly adjust for the effects of bias, nonconstant variance, and skewness. It would take an analysis including n^{-1} terms to distinguish between the preferred methods, and to see the effect of transformation prior to use of the studentized bootstrap method.

5.4.2 The ABC method

It is fairly clear that, to the order $n^{-1/2}$ considered above, there are many equivalent confidence limit methods. One of these, the ABC method, is of particular interest. The method rests on the approximation (5.35), which by using (5.40) and (5.41) can be re-expressed as

$$\hat{\theta}_\alpha = t + v^{1/2}\{z_\alpha + a + c - v^{-1/2}b + (2a+c)z_\alpha^2\}; \qquad (5.42)$$

here v has been approximated by v in the definition of m_1, and we have used $z_{1-\alpha} = -z_\alpha$.

The constants a, b and c in (5.42) are defined by (5.39), in which the expectations will be estimated. Special forms of the ABC method correspond to special-case estimates of these expectations. In all cases we take v to be v_L.

Parametric case

If the estimate t is a smooth function of sample moments, as is the case for an exponential family, then the constants in (5.39) are easy to estimate. With a temporary change of notation, suppose that $t = t(\bar{s})$ where $\bar{s} = n^{-1}\sum s(y_j)$ has p components, and define $\mu = E(\bar{S})$, so that $\theta = t(\mu)$. Then

$$L_t(Y_i) = \dot{t}(\mu)^T\{s(Y_j) - \mu\}, \quad Q_t(Y_j, Y_k) = \{s(Y_j) - \mu\}^T\ddot{t}(\mu)\{s(Y_k) - \mu\}. \quad (5.43)$$

> $\dot{t} = \partial t(s)/\partial s$, and $\ddot{t} = \partial^2 t(s)/\partial s \partial s^T$.

Estimates for a, b and c can therefore be calculated using estimates for the first three moments of $s(Y)$.

For the particular case where the distribution of $\bar{S}$ has the exponential family PDF

$$f_\eta(\bar{s}) = \exp\{\eta^T\bar{s} - \xi(\eta)\},$$

the calculations can be simplified. First, define $\Sigma(\mu) = \text{var}(\bar{S}) = \ddot{\xi}(\eta)$. Then

> $\ddot{\xi}(\eta) = \partial^2\xi(\eta)/\partial\eta\partial\eta^T$.

$$v_L = \dot{t}(\bar{s})^T\Sigma(\bar{s})\dot{t}(\bar{s}).$$

Substitution from (5.43) in (5.39), and estimation of the expectations, gives estimated constants which can be expressed simply as

$$a = \frac{1}{6v_L^{3/2}}\{\dot{t}(\bar{s})\}^T\frac{d^2\mu\{\hat{\eta} + \varepsilon\dot{t}(\bar{s})\}}{d\varepsilon^2}\bigg|_{\varepsilon=0}, \quad b = \frac{1}{2}\text{tr}\{\ddot{t}(\bar{s})\Sigma(\bar{s})\},$$

> tr(A) is the trace of the square matrix A.

$$c = \frac{1}{2v_L^{1/2}} \left. \frac{d^2 t(\bar{s} + k\varepsilon)}{d\varepsilon^2} \right|_{\varepsilon=0}, \tag{5.44}$$

where $k = \Sigma(\bar{s})\dot{t}(\bar{s})/v_L^{1/2}$.

The confidence limit (5.42) can also be approximated by an evaluation of the statistic t, analogous to the BC_a confidence limit (5.20). This follows by equating (5.42) with the right-hand side of the approximation $t(\bar{s} + v^{1/2}e) \doteq t(\bar{s}) + v^{1/2}e^T \dot{t}(\bar{s})$, with appropriate choice of e. The result is

$$\hat{\theta}_\alpha = t\left(\bar{s} + \frac{\tilde{z}_\alpha}{(1 - a\tilde{z}_\alpha)^2} k\right), \tag{5.45}$$

where

$$\tilde{z}_\alpha = w + z_\alpha = a + c - bv_L^{-1/2} + z_\alpha.$$

In this form the ABC confidence limit is an explicit approximation to the BC_a confidence limit.

If the several derivatives in (5.44) are calculated by numerical differencing, then only $4p + 4$ evaluations of t are necessary, plus one for every confidence limit calculated in the final step (5.45). Algorithms also exist for exact numerical calculation of derivatives.

Nonparametric case: single sample

If the estimate t is again a smooth function of sample moments, $t = t(\bar{s})$, then (5.43) still applies, and substitution of empirical moments leads to

$$a = \frac{1}{6} \frac{\sum l_j^3}{(\sum l_j^2)^{3/2}}, \quad b = \frac{1}{2} \text{tr}(\ddot{t}\hat{\Sigma}), \quad c = \frac{1}{2n} \frac{(\sum s_j l_j)^T \ddot{t}(\sum s_j l_j)}{(\sum l_j^2)^{3/2}}, \quad k = \frac{1}{n} \frac{\sum s_j l_j}{(\sum l_j^2)^{1/2}}. \tag{5.46}$$

An alternative, more general formulation is possible in which $\bar{s}$ is replaced by the multinomial proportions $n^{-1}(f_1, \ldots, f_n)$ attaching to the data values. Correspondingly μ is replaced by the probability vector p, and with distributions F restricted to the data values, we re-express $t(F)$ as $t(p)$; cf. Section 4.4. Now $\hat{F}$ is equivalent to $\hat{p} = (\frac{1}{n}, \ldots, \frac{1}{n})$ and $t = t(\hat{p})$. In this notation the empirical influence values and second derivatives are defined by

$$l_j = \left. \frac{d}{d\varepsilon} t\{(1 - \varepsilon)\hat{p} + \varepsilon 1_j\} \right|_{\varepsilon=0}, \tag{5.47}$$

and

$$q_{jj} = \left. \frac{d^2}{d\varepsilon^2} t\{(1 - \varepsilon)\hat{p} + \varepsilon 1_j\} \right|_{\varepsilon=0}, \tag{5.48}$$

where 1_j is the vector with 1 in the jth position and 0 elsewhere. Let us set $\dot{t}_j(p) = \partial t(p)/\partial p_j$, and $\ddot{t}_{jk}(p) = \partial^2 t(p)/\partial p_j \partial p_k$; see Section 2.7.2 and Problem 2.16. Then alternative forms for the vector l and the full matrix q are

$$l = (I - n^{-1}J)\dot{t}(\hat{p}), \quad q = (I - n^{-1}J)\ddot{t}(\hat{p})(I - n^{-1}J),$$

where $J = 11^T$. For each derivative the first form is convenient for approx-   1 is a vector of ones.
imation by numerical differencing, while the second form is often easier for
theoretical calculation.

Estimates for a and b can be calculated directly as empirical versions of
their definitions in (5.39), while for c it is simplest to use the analogue of the
representation in (5.44). The resulting estimates are

$$a = \frac{1}{6}\frac{\sum l_j^3}{(\sum l_j^2)^{3/2}}, \quad b = \frac{1}{2n^2}\sum q_{jj} = \frac{1}{2n^2}\text{tr}(q),$$

(5.49)

$$c = \frac{1}{2v_L^{1/2}}\frac{d^2t(\hat{p}+\varepsilon k)}{d\varepsilon^2}\bigg|_{\varepsilon=0} = \frac{1}{2n^4 v_L^{3/2}}\ddot{i}^T(I - n^{-1}J)\ddot{i}(I - n^{-1}J)\ddot{i}$$

where $k = n^{-2}v_L^{-1/2}1^T$ and $\dot{i},\ddot{i}$ are evaluated at $\hat{p}$.

The approximation (5.45) can also be used here, but now in the form

$$\hat{\theta}_\alpha = t\left(\hat{p} + \frac{\tilde{z}_\alpha}{(1-a\tilde{z}_\alpha)^2}k\right).$$

(5.50)

If the several derivatives are calculated by numerical differencing, then the
number of evaluations of $t(p)$ needed is only $2n+2$, plus one for each confidence
limit and the original value t. Note that the probability vector argument in
(5.50) is not constrained to be proper, or even positive, so that it is possible
for ABC confidence limits to be undefined.

Example 5.9 (Air-conditioning data, continued)   The adjusted percentile method
was applied to the air-conditioning data in Example 5.6 under the gamma
model and in Example 5.8 under the nonparametric model. Here we examine
how well the ABC method approximates the adjusted percentile confidence
limits. For the mean parameter, calculations are simple under all models. For
example, in the gamma case the exponential family is two-dimensional with
$s = (y, \log y)^T$,

$$\eta_1 = -n\kappa/\mu, \quad \eta_2 = n\kappa, \quad \psi(\eta) = -\eta_2\log(-\eta_1/n) + n\log\Gamma(\eta_2/n),$$

and $t(\bar{s}) = \bar{s}_1$. The last implies that $\dot{i} = (1,0)^T$ and $\ddot{i} = 0$. It then follows
straightforwardly that the constant a is given by $\frac{1}{3}(n\hat{\kappa})^{-1/2}$ as in Example 5.6,
that $b = c = 0$, and that $k = v_L^{1/2}(1,0)^T$. Similar calculations apply for the
nonparametric model, except that a is given by the corresponding value in
Example 5.8. So under both models

$$\hat{\theta}_{1-\alpha} = 108.083 + v_L^{1/2}\frac{a+z_{1-\alpha}}{\{1-a(a+z_{1-\alpha})\}^2}.$$

Numerical comparisons between the adjusted percentile confidence limits and

Table 5.5 Adjusted percentile (BC_a) and ABC confidence intervals for mean failure time μ for the air-conditioning data. $R = 999$ simulated samples for BC_a methods.

		Nominal confidence $1 - 2\alpha$		
		0.99	0.95	0.90
Gamma model	BC_a	51.5, 241.6	63.0, 226.0	67.2, 208.0
	ABC	52.5, 316.6	61.4, 240.5	66.9, 210.5
Nonparametric model	BC_a	44.6, 268.8	55.3, 243.5	61.5, 202.1
	ABC	46.6, 287.0	57.2, 226.7	63.6, 201.5

ABC limits are shown in Table 5.5. The ABC method appears to give reasonable approximations, except for the 99% interval under the gamma model.

∎

Nonparametric case: several samples

The estimated constants (5.49) for the single-sample case can be applied to several samples by using a single artificial probability vector π of length $n = \sum n_i$ as follows. The estimator will originally be defined by a function $t(p_1, \ldots, p_k)$, where $p_i = (p_{i1}, \ldots, p_{in_i})$ is the vector of probabilities on the ith sample values $y_{i1}, \ldots, y_{in_i}$. The artificial representation of the estimator in terms of the single probability vector

$$\pi = (\pi_{11}, \ldots, \pi_{1n_1}, \pi_{21}, \ldots, \pi_{kn_k})$$

of length n is $u(\pi) = t(p_1, \ldots, p_k)$ where p_i has elements

$$p_{ij} = \frac{\pi_{ij}}{\sum_{l=1}^{n_i} \pi_{il}}. \tag{5.51}$$

The set of EDFs is equivalent to $\hat{\pi} = (\frac{1}{n}, \ldots, \frac{1}{n})$ and the observed value of the estimate is $t = u(\hat{\pi})$. This artificial representation leads to expressions such as (5.29), in which the definition of $\tilde{l}_{ij}$ is obtained by applying (5.47) to $u(p)$. (Note that the real influence values l_{ij} and second derivatives $q_{i,jj}$ derived from $t(p_1, \ldots, p_k)$ should not be used.) That this method produces correct results is quite easy to verify using the several sample extension of the quadratic approximation (5.38); see Section 3.2.1 and Problem 3.7.

Example 5.10 (Air-conditioning data failure ratio) The data of Example 1.1 form one of several samples corresponding to different aircraft. The previous sample ($n_1 = 12$) and a second sample ($n_2 = 24$) are given in Table 5.6. Suppose that we want to estimate the ratio of failure rates for the two aircraft, and give confidence intervals for this ratio.

To set notation, let the mean failure times be μ_1 and μ_2 for the first and second aircraft, with $\theta = \mu_2/\mu_1$ the parameter of interest. The corresponding

First aircraft											
3	5	7	18	43	85	91	98	100	130	230	487

Second aircraft											
3	5	5	13	14	15	22	22	23	30	36	39
44	46	50	72	79	88	97	102	139	188	197	210

Table 5.6 Failure times for air-conditioning equipment in two aircraft (Proschan, 1963).

sample means are $\bar{y}_1 = 108.083$ and $\bar{y}_2 = 64.125$, so the estimate for θ is $t = \bar{y}_2/\bar{y}_1 = 0.593$.

The empirical influence values are (Problem 3.5)

$$l_{1j} = -t\frac{y_{1j} - \bar{y}_1}{\bar{y}_1}, \quad l_{2j} = \frac{y_{2j} - \bar{y}_2}{\bar{y}_1}.$$

We use (5.29) to calculate $v_L = 0.056\,14$ and $a = -0.0576$. In $R = 999$ nonparametric simulations there are 473 values of t^* below t, so by (5.22) $w = -0.0954$. With these values we can calculate BC_a confidence limit (5.21). For example, for $\alpha = 0.025$ and 0.975 the values of $\tilde{\alpha}$ are 0.0076 and 0.944 respectively, so that the limits of the 95% interval are $t^*_{(7.6)} = 0.227$ and $t^*_{(944)} = 1.306$; the first value is interpolated using (5.8).

The studentized bootstrap method gives 95% confidence interval $[0.131,1.255]$ using the original scale. The distribution of t^* values is highly skew here, and the logarithmic scale is strongly indicated by diagnostic plots. Figure 5.2 shows the normal Q-Q plot of the t^* values, the variance-parameter plots for original and logarithmic scales, and the normal Q-Q plot of z^* values after logarithmic transformation. Application of the studentized bootstrap method on the logarithmic scale leads to 95% confidence interval $[0.183,1.318]$ for θ, much closer to the BC_a limits.

For the ABC method, the original definition of the estimator is $t = t(p_1, p_2) = \sum y_{2j}p_{2j}/\sum y_{1j}p_{1j}$. The artificial definition in terms of a single probability vector π is

$$u(\pi) = \frac{\sum_{i=1}^{n_2} y_{2i}\pi_{2i}/\sum_{i=1}^{n_2} \pi_{2i}}{\sum_{j=1}^{n_1} y_{1j}\pi_{1j}/\sum_{j=1}^{n_1} \pi_{1j}}.$$

Application of (5.47) shows that the artificial empirical influence values are

$$\tilde{l}_{1j} = -t\left(\frac{n}{n_1}\right)\left(\frac{y_{1j} - \bar{y}_1}{\bar{y}_1}\right), \quad j = 1,\ldots,n_1,$$

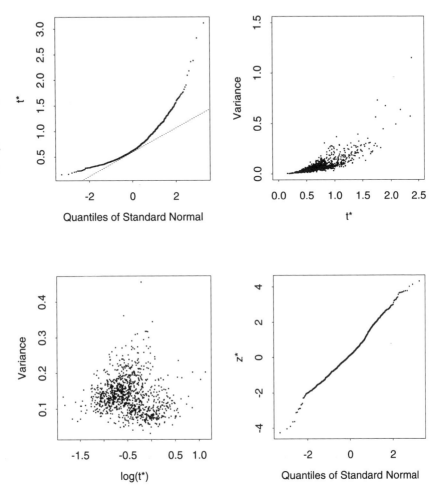

Figure 5.2 Diagnostic plots for air-conditioning data confidence intervals, based on $R = 999$ nonparametric simulations. Top left panel: normal Q-Q plot of t^*, dotted line is $N(t, v_L)$ approximation. Top right: variance-parameter plot, v_L^* versus t^*. Bottom left: variance-parameter plot after logarithmic transformation. Bottom right: normal Q-Q plot of z^* after logarithmic transformation.

and

$$\tilde{l}_{2j} = \left(\frac{n}{n_2}\right)\left(\frac{y_{2j} - \bar{y}_2}{\bar{y}_1}\right), \quad j = 1, \dots, n_2.$$

This leads to formulae in agreement with (5.29), which gives the values of a and v_L already calculated. It remains to calculate b and c.

For b, application of (5.48) gives

$$\tilde{q}_{1,jj} = \frac{2t}{\bar{y}_1}\left\{\frac{n^2(y_{1j} - \bar{y}_1)^2}{n_1^2 \bar{y}_1} + \frac{nn_2(y_{1j} - \bar{y}_1)}{n_1^2}\right\}$$

and

$$\tilde{q}_{2,jj} = -2\frac{nn_1(y_{2j} - \bar{y}_2)}{n_2^2\bar{y}_1},$$

so by (5.49) we have

$$b = n_1^{-2}\bar{y}_2\bar{y}_1^{-3}\sum(y_{1j} - \bar{y}_1)^2,$$

whose value is $b = 0.0720$. (The bootstrap estimates b and v are respectively 0.104 and 0.1125.) Finally, for c we apply the second form in (5.49) to $u(\pi)$, that is

$$c = \tfrac{1}{2}n^{-4}v_L^{-3/2}\tilde{l}^T\ddot{u}(\hat{\pi})\tilde{l},$$

and calculate $c = 0.3032$. The implied value of w is -0.0583, quite different from the bootstrap value -0.0954. The *ABC* formula (5.50) is now applied to $u(\pi)$ with $k = n^{-2}v_L^{-1/2}(\tilde{l}_{11},\ldots,\tilde{l}_{2,n_2})$. The resulting 95% confidence interval is [0.250,1.283], which is fairly close to the BC_a interval.

It seems possible that the approximation theory does not work well here, which would explain the larger-than-usual differences between BC_a, *ABC* and studentized bootstrap confidence limits; see Section 5.7.

One practical point is that the theoretical calculation of derivatives is quite time-consuming, compared to application of numerical differencing in (5.47)–(5.49).   ∎

5.5 Inversion of Significance Tests

There is a duality between significance tests for parameters and confidence sets for those parameters, in the sense that — for a prescribed level — a confidence region includes parameter values which are not rejected by an appropriate significance test. This can provide another option for calculating confidence limits.

Suppose that θ is an unknown scalar parameter, and that the model includes no other unknown parameters. If $R_\alpha(\theta_0)$ is a size α critical region for testing the null hypothesis $H_0 : \theta = \theta_0$, which means that

$$\Pr\{(Y_1,\ldots,Y_n) \in R_\alpha(\theta_0) \mid \theta_0\} = \alpha,$$

then the set

$$C_{1-\alpha}(Y_1,\ldots,Y_n) = \{\theta : (Y_1,\ldots,Y_n) \notin R_\alpha(\theta)\}$$

is a $1 - \alpha$ confidence region for θ. The shape of the region will be determined by the form of the test, including the alternative hypothesis for which the test is designed. In particular, an interval would usually be obtained if the alternative is two-sided, $H_A : \theta \neq \theta_0$; an upper limit if $H_A : \theta < \theta_0$; and a lower limit if $H_A : \theta > \theta_0$.

For definiteness, suppose that we want to calculate a lower $1 - \alpha$ confidence limit, which we denote by $\hat{\theta}_\alpha$. The associated test of $H_0 : \theta = \theta_0$ versus $H_A : \theta > \theta_0$ will be based on a test statistic $t(\theta_0)$ for which large values are evidence in favour of H_A: for example, $t(\theta_0)$ might be an estimate of θ minus θ_0. We will have an algorithm for approximating the P-value, which we can write as $p(\theta_0) = \Pr\{T(\theta_0) \geq t(\theta_0) \mid F_0\}$, where F_0 is the null hypothesis distribution with parameter value θ_0. The $1 - \alpha$ confidence set is all values of θ such that $p(\theta) \geq \alpha$, so the lower confidence limit $\hat{\theta}_\alpha$ is the smallest solution of $p(\theta) = \alpha$. A simple way to solve this is to evaluate $p(\theta)$ over a grid of, say, 20 values, and to interpolate via a simple curve fit. The grid can sometimes be determined from the normal approximation confidence limits (5.4). For the curve fit, a simple general method is to fit a logistic function to $p(\theta)$ using either a simple polynomial in θ or a spline. Once the curve is fitted, solutions to $p(\theta) = \alpha$ can be computed: usually there will be one solution, which is $\hat{\theta}_\alpha$.

For an upper $1 - \alpha$ confidence limit $\hat{\theta}_{1-\alpha}$, note that this is identical to a lower α confidence limit, so the same procedure as above with the same $t(\theta_0)$ can be used, except that we solve $p(\theta) = 1 - \alpha$. The combination of lower and upper $1 - \alpha$ confidence limits defines an equi-tailed $1 - 2\alpha$ confidence interval.

The following example illustrates this procedure.

Example 5.11 (Hazard ratio) For the AML data in Example 3.9, also analysed in Example 4.4, assume that the ratio of hazard functions $h_2(z)/h_1(z)$ for the two groups is a constant θ. As before, let r_{ij} be the number in group i who were at risk just prior to the jth failure time z_j, and let y_j be 0 or 1 according as the failure at z_j is in group 1 or 2. Then a suitable statistic for testing $H_0 : \theta = \theta_0$ is

$$t(\theta_0) = \sum_{j=1}^{n} \left(y_j - \frac{\theta_0 r_{2j}}{r_{1j} + \theta_0 r_{2j}} \right);$$

this is the score test statistic in the Cox proportional hazards model. Large values of $t(\theta_0)$ are evidence that $\theta > \theta_0$.

There are several possible resampling schemes that could be used here, including those described in Section 3.5 but modified to fix the constant hazard ratio θ_0. Here we use the simpler conditional model of Example 4.4, which holds fixed the survival and censoring times. Then for any fixed θ_0 the simulated values $y_1^*, \ldots, y_n^*$ are generated by

$$\Pr^*(Y_j^* = 1 \mid y_1^*, \ldots, y_{j-1}^*) = \frac{r_{2j}^* \theta_0}{r_{1j}^* + r_{2j}^* \theta_0},$$

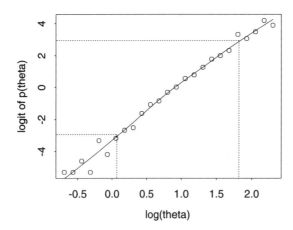

logit of p(theta)

log(theta)

Figure 5.3 Bootstrap
P-values $p(\theta_0)$ for testing
constant hazard ratio
θ_0, with $R = 199$ at each
point. Solid curve is
spline fit on logistic
scale. Dotted lines
interpolate solutions to
$p(\theta_0) = 0.05, 0.95$, which
are endpoints of 90%
confidence interval.

where the numbers at risk just prior to z_j are given by

$$r^*_{1j} = \max\left\{0, r_{11} - \sum_{k=1}^{j-1}(1 - y^*_k) - c_{1j}\right\}, \quad r^*_{2j} = \max\left\{0, r_{21} - \sum_{k=1}^{j-1} y^*_k - c_{2j}\right\},$$

with c_{ij} the number of censoring times in group i before z_j.

For the AML data we simulated $R = 199$ samples in this way, and calculated the corresponding values $t^*(\theta_0)$ for a grid of 21 values of θ_0 in the range $0.5 \le \theta_0 \le 10$. For each θ_0 we computed the one-sided P-value

$$p(\theta_0) = \frac{\#\{t^*(\theta_0) \ge t(\theta_0)\}}{200},$$

then on the logit scale we fitted a spline curve (in $\log\theta$), and interpolated the solutions to $p(\theta_0) = \alpha, 1-\alpha$ to determine the endpoints of the $(1-2\alpha)$ confidence interval for θ. Figure 5.3 illustrates this procedure for $\alpha = 0.05$, which gives the 90% confidence interval $[1.07, 6.16]$; the 95% interval is $[0.86, 7.71]$ and the point estimate is 2.52. Thus there is mild evidence that $\theta > 1$.

A more efficient approach would be to use $R = 99$ for the initial grid to determine rough values of the confidence limits, near which further simulation with $R = 999$ would provide accurate interpolation of the confidence limits. Yet more efficient algorithms are possible.   ■

In a more systematic development of the method, we must allow for a nuisance parameter λ, say, which also governs the data distribution but is not constrained by H_0. Then both $R_\alpha(\theta)$ and $C_{1-\alpha}(Y_1, \ldots, Y_n)$ must depend upon λ to make the inversion method work exactly. Under the bootstrap approach λ is replaced by an estimate.

Suppose, for example, that we want a lower $1 - \alpha$ confidence limit, which is obtained via the critical region for testing $H_0 : \theta = \theta_0$ versus the alternative hypothesis $H_A : \theta > \theta_0$. Define $\psi = (\theta, \lambda)$. If the test statistic is $T(\theta_0)$, then the size α critical region has the form

$$R_\alpha(\theta_0) = \{(y_1, \ldots, y_n) : \Pr\{T(\theta_0) \geq t(\theta_0) \mid \psi = (\theta_0, \lambda)\} \leq \alpha\},$$

and the exact lower confidence limit is the value $u_\alpha = u_\alpha(y, \lambda)$, such that

$$\Pr\{T(u_\alpha) \geq t(u_\alpha) \mid \psi = (u_\alpha, \lambda)\} = \alpha.$$

We replace λ by an estimate s, say, to obtain the lower $1 - \alpha$ bootstrap confidence limit $\hat{u}_{1-\alpha} = u_\alpha(y, s)$. The solution is found by applying for u the equation

$$\Pr^*\{T^*(u) \geq t(u) \mid \psi = (u, s)\} = \alpha,$$

where $T^*(u)$ follows the distribution under $\psi = (u, s)$. This requires application of an interpolation method such as the one illustrated in the previous example.

The simplest test statistic is the point estimate T of θ, and then $T(\theta_0) = T$. The method will tend to be more accurate if the test statistic is the studentized estimate. That is, if $\mathrm{var}(T) = \sigma^2(\theta, \lambda)$, then we take $Z = (T - \theta_0)/\sigma(\theta_0, S)$; for further details see Problem 5.11. The same remark would apply to score statistics, such as that in the previous example, where studentization would involve the observed or expected Fisher information.

Note that for the particular alternative hypothesis used to derive an upper limit, it would be standard practice to define the P-value as $\Pr\{T(\theta_0) \leq t(\theta_0) \mid F_0\}$, for example if $T(\theta_0)$ were an estimator for θ or its studentized form. Equivalently one can retain the general definition and solve $p(\theta_0) = 1 - \alpha$ for an upper limit.

In principle these methods can be applied to both parametric and semiparametric problems, but not to completely nonparametric problems.

5.6 Double Bootstrap Methods

Whether the basic or percentile bootstrap method is used to calculate confidence intervals, there is a possibly non-negligible difference between the nominal $1 - \alpha$ coverage and the actual probability coverage of the interval in repeated sampling, even if R is very large. The difference represents a bias in the method, and as indicated in Section 3.9 the bootstrap can be used to estimate and correct for such a bias. That is, by bootstrapping a bootstrap confidence interval method it can be made more accurate. This is analogous to the bootstrap adjustment for bootstrap P-values described in Section 4.5. One straightforward application of this idea is to the normal-approximation confidence interval (5.4), which produces the studentized bootstrap interval;

see Problem 5.12. A more ambitious application is bootstrap adjustment of the basic bootstrap confidence limit, which we develop here.

First we recall the full notations for the quantities involved in the basic bootstrap confidence interval method. The "ideal" upper $1 - \alpha$ confidence limit is $t(\hat{F}) - a_\alpha(F)$, where

$$\Pr\{T - \theta \leq a_\alpha(F) \mid F\} = \Pr\{t(\hat{F}) - t(F) \leq a_\alpha(F) \mid F\} = \alpha.$$

What is calculated, ignoring simulation error, is the confidence limit $t(\hat{F}) - a_\alpha(\hat{F})$. The bias in the method arises from the fact that $a_\alpha(\hat{F}) \neq a_\alpha(F)$ in general, so that

$$\Pr\{t(F) \leq t(\hat{F}) - a_\alpha(\hat{F}) \mid F\} \neq 1 - \alpha. \tag{5.52}$$

We could try to eliminate the bias by adding a correction to $a_\alpha(\hat{F})$, but a more successful approach is to adjust the subscript α. That is, we replace $a_\alpha(\hat{F})$ by $a_{q(\alpha)}(\hat{F})$ and estimate what the adjusted value $q(\alpha)$ should be. This is in the same spirit as the BC_a method.

Ideally we want $q(\alpha)$ to satisfy

$$\Pr\{t(F) \leq t(\hat{F}) - a_{q(\alpha)}(\hat{F}) \mid F\} = 1 - \alpha. \tag{5.53}$$

The solution $q(\alpha)$ will depend upon F, i.e. $q(\alpha) = q(\alpha, F)$. Because F is unknown, we estimate $q(\alpha)$ by $\hat{q}(\alpha) = q(\alpha, \hat{F})$. This means that we obtain $\hat{q}(\alpha)$ by solving the bootstrap version of (5.53), namely

$$\Pr^*\{t(\hat{F}) \leq t(\hat{F}^*) - a_{\hat{q}(\alpha)}(\hat{F}^*) \mid \hat{F}\} = 1 - \alpha. \tag{5.54}$$

This looks intimidating, but from the definition of $a_\alpha(F)$ we see that (5.54) can be rewritten as

$$\Pr^*\{\Pr^{**}(T^{**} \leq 2T^* - t \mid \hat{F}^*) \geq \hat{q}(\alpha) \mid \hat{F}\} = 1 - \alpha. \tag{5.55}$$

The same method of adjustment can be applied to any bootstrap confidence limit method, including the percentile method (Problem 5.13) and the studentized bootstrap method (Problem 5.14).

To verify that the nested bootstrap reduces the order of coverage error made by the original bootstrap confidence limit, we can apply the general discussion of Section 3.9.1. In general we find that coverage $1 - \alpha + O(n^{-a})$ is corrected to $1 - \alpha + O(n^{-a-1/2})$ for one-sided confidence limits, whether $a = \frac{1}{2}$ or 1. However, for equi-tailed confidence intervals coverage $1 - 2\alpha + O(n^{-1})$ is corrected to $1 - 2\alpha + O(n^{-2})$; see Problem 5.15.

Before discussing how to solve equation (5.55) using simulated samples, we look at a simple illustrative example where the solution can be found theoretically.

Example 5.12 (Exponential mean)   Consider the parametric problem of exponential data with unknown mean μ. The data estimate for μ is $t = \bar{y}$, $\hat{F}$ is the fitted exponential CDF with mean $\bar{y}$, and $\hat{F}^*$ is the fitted exponential CDF with mean $\bar{y}^*$ — the mean of a parametric bootstrap sample $y_1^*, \ldots, y_n^*$ drawn from $\hat{F}$. A result that we use repeatedly is that if $X_1, \ldots, X_n$ are independent exponential with mean γ, then $2n\bar{X}/\gamma$ has the χ^2_{2n} distribution.

The basic bootstrap upper $1 - \alpha$ confidence limit for μ is

$$2\bar{y} - \bar{y}c_{2n,\alpha}/(2n),$$

where $\Pr(\chi^2_{2n} \leq c_{2n,\alpha}) = \alpha$. To evaluate the left-hand side of (5.55), for the inner probability we have

$$\Pr^{**}(\bar{Y}^{**} \leq 2\bar{y}^* - \bar{y} \mid \hat{F}^*) = \Pr\{\chi^2_{2n} \leq 2n(2 - \bar{y}/\bar{y}^*)\},$$

which exceeds q if and only if $2n(2 - \bar{y}/\bar{y}^*) \geq c_{2n,q}$. Therefore the outer probability on the left-hand side of (5.55) is

$$\Pr^* \left\{ 2n(2 - \bar{y}/\bar{Y}^*) \geq c_{2n,q} \mid \hat{F} \right\} = \Pr \left\{ \chi^2_{2n} \geq \frac{2n}{2 - c_{2n,q}/(2n)} \right\}, \qquad (5.56)$$

with $q = \hat{q}(\alpha)$. Setting the probability on the right-hand side of (5.56) equal to $1 - \alpha$, we deduce that

$$\frac{2n}{2 - c_{2n,\hat{q}(\alpha)}/(2n)} = c_{2n,\alpha}.$$

Using $\hat{q}(\alpha)$ in place of α in the basic bootstrap confidence limit gives the adjusted upper $1 - \alpha$ confidence limit $2n\bar{y}/c_{2n,\alpha}$, which has exact coverage $1 - \alpha$. So in this case the double bootstrap adjustment is perfect.

Figure 5.4 shows the actual coverages of nominal $1 - \alpha$ bootstrap upper confidence limits when $n = 10$. There are quite large discrepancies for both basic and percentile methods, which are completely removed using the double bootstrap adjustment; see Problem 5.13. ∎

In general, and especially for nonparametric problems, the calculations in (5.55) cannot be done exactly and simulation or approximation methods must be used. A basic simulation algorithm is as follows. Suppose that we draw R samples from $\hat{F}$, and denote the model fitted to the rth sample by $\hat{F}^*_r$ — the EDF for one-sample nonparametric problems. Define

$$u_r^* = \Pr(T^{**} \leq 2t_r^* - t \mid \hat{F}^*_r).$$

This will be approximated by drawing M samples from $\hat{F}^*_r$, calculating the estimator values t_{rm}^{**} for $m = 1, \ldots, M$ and computing the estimate

$I\{A\}$ is the zero–one indicator function of the event A.

$$u_{M,r}^* = M^{-1} \sum_{m=1}^{M} I\{t_{rm}^{**} \leq 2t_r^* - t\}.$$

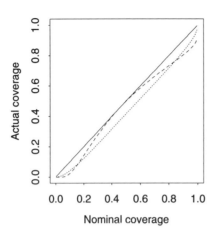

Figure 5.4 Actual coverages of percentile (dotted line) and basic bootstrap (dashed line) upper confidence limits for exponential mean when $n = 10$. Solid line is attained by nested bootstrap confidence limits.

Then the Monte Carlo version of (5.55) is

$$R^{-1} \sum_{r=1}^{R} I\{u_{M,r}^* \geq \hat{q}(\alpha)\} = 1 - \alpha,$$

which is to say that $\hat{q}(\alpha)$ is the α quantile of the $u_{M,r}^*$. The simplest way to obtain $\hat{q}(\alpha)$ is to order the values $u_{M,r}^*$ into $u_{M,(1)}^* \leq \cdots \leq u_{M,(R)}^*$, and then set $\hat{q}(\alpha) = u_{M,(\alpha(R+1))}^*$. What this amounts to is that the $(R+1)\alpha$th ordered value is read off from a Q-Q plot of the $u_{M,r}^*$ against quantiles of the $U(0,1)$ distribution, and that ordered value is then used to give the required quantile of the $t_r^* - t$. We illustrate this in the next example.

The total number of samples involved in this calculation is RM. Since we always think of simulating as many as 1000 samples to approximate probabilites, here this would suggest as many as 10^6 samples overall. The calculations of Section 4.5 would suggest something a bit smaller, say $M = 249$ to be safe, but this is still rather impractical. However, there are ways of greatly reducing the overall number of simulations, two of which are described in Chapter 9.

Example 5.13 (Kernel density estimate)   Bootstrap confidence intervals for the value of a density raise some awkward issues, which we now discuss, before outlining the use of the nested bootstrap in this context.

The standard kernel estimate of the PDF $f(y)$ given a random sample $y_1, \ldots, y_n$ is

$$\hat{f}(y; h) = \frac{1}{nh} \sum_{j=1}^{n} w\left(\frac{y - y_j}{h}\right),$$

where $w(\cdot)$ is a symmetric density with mean zero and unit variance, and h is the bandwidth. One source of difficulty is that if we consider the estimator to be $t(\hat{F})$, as we usually do, then $t(F) = h^{-1} \int w\{h^{-1}(y-x)\} f(x) dx$ is being estimated, not $f(y)$. The mean and variance of $\hat{f}(y;h)$ are approximately

$$f(y) + \tfrac{1}{2}h^2 f''(y), \quad (nh)^{-1} f(y) \int w^2(u)\, du, \tag{5.57}$$

for small h and large n. In general one assumes that as $n \to \infty$ so $h \to 0$ in such a way that $nh \to \infty$, and this makes both bias and variance tend to zero as n increases. The density estimate then has the form $t_n(\hat{F})$, such that $t_n(F) \to t(F) = f(y)$.

Because the variance in (5.57) is approximately proportional to the mean, it makes sense to work with the square root of the estimate. That is we take $T = \{\hat{f}(y;h)\}^{1/2}$ as estimator of $\theta = \{f(y)\}^{1/2}$. By the delta method of Section 2.7.1 we have from (5.57) that the approximate mean and variance of T are

$$\{f(y)\}^{1/2} + \tfrac{1}{4}\{f(y)\}^{-1/2}\left\{h^2 f''(y) - \tfrac{1}{2}(nh)^{-1}K\right\}, \quad \tfrac{1}{4}(nh)^{-1}K, \tag{5.58}$$

where $K = \int w^2(u)\, du$.

There remains the problem of choosing h. For point estimation of $f(y)$ it is usually suggested, on the grounds of minimizing mean squared error, that one take $h \propto n^{-1/5}$. This makes both bias and standard error of order $n^{-2/5}$. But there is no reason to do the same for setting confidence intervals, and in fact $h \propto n^{-1/5}$ turns out to be a poor choice, particularly for standard bootstrap methods, as we now show.

Suppose that we resample $y_1^*, \ldots, y_n^*$ from the EDF $\hat{F}$. Then the bootstrap version of the density estimate, that is

$$\hat{f}^*(y;h) = \frac{1}{nh} \sum_{j=1}^{n} w\left(\frac{y - y_j^*}{h}\right),$$

has mean exactly equal to $\hat{f}(y;h)$; the approximate variance is the same as in (5.57) except that $\hat{f}(y;h)$ replaces $f(y)$. It follows that $T^* = \{\hat{f}^*(y;h)\}^{1/2}$ has approximate mean and variance

$$\{\hat{f}(y;h)\}^{1/2} - \tfrac{1}{8}\{\hat{f}(y;h)\}^{-1/2}(nh)^{-1}K, \quad \tfrac{1}{4}(nh)^{-1}K. \tag{5.59}$$

Now consider the studentized estimates

$$Z = \frac{\{\hat{f}(y;h)\}^{1/2} - \{f(y)\}^{1/2}}{\tfrac{1}{2}(nh)^{-1/2}K^{1/2}}, \quad Z^* = \frac{\{\hat{f}^*(y;h)\}^{1/2} - \{\hat{f}(y;h)\}^{1/2}}{\tfrac{1}{2}(nh)^{-1/2}K^{1/2}}.$$

From (5.58) and (5.59) we see that if $h \propto n^{-1/5}$, then as n increases

$$Z \doteq \varepsilon + \{f(y)\}^{-1/2}K^{-1/2}\{f''(y) - \tfrac{1}{4}K\}, \quad Z^* \doteq \varepsilon^*,$$

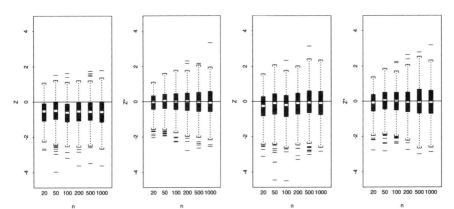

Figure 5.5 Studentized quantities for density estimation. The left panels show values of Z when $h = n^{-1/5}$ for 500 standard normal samples of sizes n and 500 bootstrap values for one sample at each n. The right panels show the corresponding values when $h = n^{-1/3}$.

where both ε and ε^* are $N(0,1)$. This means that quantiles of Z cannot be well approximated by quantiles of Z^*, no matter how large is n. The same thing happens for the untransformed density estimate.

There are several ways in which we can try to overcome this problem. One of the simplest is to change h to be of order $n^{-1/3}$, when calculations similar to those above show that $Z \doteq \varepsilon$ and $Z^* \doteq \varepsilon^*$. Figure 5.5 illustrates the effect. Here we estimate the density at $y = 0$ for samples from the $N(0,1)$ distribution, with $w(\cdot)$ the standard normal density. The first two panels show box plots of 500 values of z and z^* when $h = n^{-1/5}$, which is near-optimal for estimation in this case, for several values of n; the values of z^* are obtained by resampling from one dataset. The last two panels correspond to $h = n^{-1/3}$. The figure confirms the key points of the theory sketched above: that Z is biased away from zero when $h = n^{-1/5}$, but not when $h = n^{-1/3}$; and that the distributions of Z and Z^* are quite stable and similar when $h = n^{-1/3}$.

Under resampling from $\hat{F}$, the studentized bootstrap applied to $\{\hat{f}(y;h)\}^{1/2}$ should be consistent if $h \propto n^{-1/3}$. From a practical point of view this means considerable undersmoothing in the density estimate, relative to standard practice for estimation. A bias in Z of order $n^{-1/3}$ or worse will remain, and this suggests a possibly useful role for the double bootstrap.

For a numerical example of nested bootstrapping in this context we revisit Example 4.18, where we discussed the use of a kernel density estimate in estimating species abundance. The estimated PDF is

$$\hat{f}(y;h) = \frac{1}{nh} \sum_{j=1}^{n} \left\{ \phi\left(\frac{y - y_j}{h}\right) + \phi\left(\frac{y + y_j}{h}\right) \right\}, \quad y \geq 0,$$

where $\phi(\cdot)$ is the standard normal density, and the value of interest is $\hat{f}(0;h)$, which is used to estimate $f(0)$. In light of the previous discussion, we base

Figure 5.6 Adjusted bootstrap procedure for variance-stabilized density estimate $t = \{\hat{f}(0; 0.5)\}^{1/2}$ for the tuna data. The left panel shows the EDF of 1000 values of $t^* - t$. The right panel shows a plot of the ordered $u^*_{M,r}$ against quantiles $r/(R + 1)$ of the $U(0, 1)$ distribution. The dashed line shows how the quantiles of the u^* are used to obtain improved confidence limits, by using the right panel to read off the estimated coverage $\hat{q}(\alpha)$ corresponding to the required nominal coverage α, and then using the left panel to read off the $\hat{q}(\alpha)$ quantile of $t^* - t$.

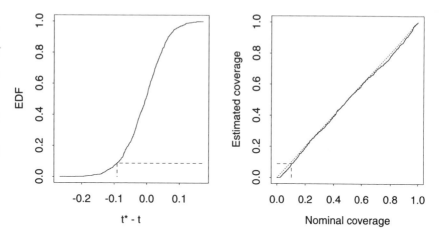

confidence intervals on the variance-stabilized estimate $t = \{\hat{f}(0; h)\}^{1/2}$. We also use a value of h considerably smaller than the value (roughly 1.5) used to estimate f in Example 4.18.

The right panel of Figure 5.6 shows the quantiles of the $u^*_{M,r}$ obtained when the double bootstrap bias adjustment is applied with $R = 1000$ and $M = 250$, for the estimate with bandwidth $h = 0.5$. If $T^* - t$ were an exact pivot, the distribution of the u^* would lie along the dotted line, and nominal and estimated coverage would be equal. The distribution is close to uniform, confirming our decision to use a variance-stabilized statistic.

The dashed line shows how the distribution of the u^*_r is used to remove the bias in coverage levels. For an upper confidence limit with nominal level $1 - \alpha = 0.9$, so that $\alpha = 0.1$, the estimated level is $\hat{q}(0.1) = 0.088$. The 0.088 quantile of the values of $t^*_r - t$ is $t^*_{(88)} - t = -0.091$, while the 0.10 quantile is $t^*_{(100)} - t = -0.085$. The corresponding upper 10% confidence limits for $f(0)^{1/2}$ are $t - (t^*_{(88)} - t) = 0.356 - (-0.091) = 0.447$ and $t - (t^*_{(100)} - t) = 0.356 - (-0.085) = 0.441$. For this value of α the adjustment has only a small effect.

Table 5.7 compares the 95% limits for $f(0)$ for different methods, using bandwidth $h = 0.5$, for which $\hat{f}(0; 0.5) = 0.127$. The longer upper tail for the double bootstrap interval is a result of adjusting the nominal $\alpha = 0.025$ to $\hat{q}(0.025) = 0.004$; at the upper tail we obtain $\hat{q}(0.975) = 0.980$. The lower tail of the interval agrees well with the other second-order correct methods.

For larger values of h the density estimates are higher and the confidence intervals narrower.

	Basic	Basic[†]	Student	Student[†]	Percentile	BC_a	Double
Upper	0.204	0.240	0.273	0.266	0.218	0.240	0.301
Lower	0.036	0.060	0.055	0.058	0.048	0.058	0.058

Table 5.7 Upper and lower endpoints of 95% confidence limits for $f(0)$ for the tuna data, with bandwidth $h = 0.5$; † indicates use of square-root transformation.

In Example 9.14 we describe how saddlepoint methods can greatly reduce the time taken to perform the double bootstrap in this problem. It might be possible to avoid the difficulties caused by the bias of the kernel estimate by using a clever resampling scheme, but it would be more complicated than the direct approach described above.   ∎

5.7 Empirical Comparison of Bootstrap Methods

The several bootstrap confidence limit methods can be compared theoretically on the basis of first- and second-order accuracy, as in Section 5.4, but this really gives only suggestions as to which methods we would expect to be good. The theory needs to be bolstered by numerical comparisons. One rather extreme comparison was described in Example 5.7. In this section we consider one moderately complicated application, estimation of a ratio of means, and assess through simulation the performances of the main bootstrap confidence limit methods. The conclusions appear to agree qualitatively with the results of other simulation studies involving applications of similar complexity: references to some of these are given in the bibliographic notes at the end of the chapter.

The application here is similar to that in Example 5.10, and concerns the ratio of means for data from two different gamma distributions. The first sample of size n_1 is drawn from a gamma distribution with mean $\mu_1 = 100$ and index 0.7, while the second independent sample of size n_2 is drawn from the gamma distribution with mean $\mu_2 = 50$ and index 1. The parameter $\theta = \mu_1/\mu_2$, whose value is 2, is estimated by the ratio of sample means $t = \bar{y}_1/\bar{y}_2$. For particular choices of sample sizes we simulated 10 000 datasets and to each applied several of the nonparametric bootstrap confidence limit methods discussed earlier, always with $R = 999$. We did not include the double bootstrap method. As a control we added the exact parametric method when the gamma indexes are known: this turns out not to be a strong control, but it does provide a check on simulation validity.

The results quoted here are for two cases, $n_1 = n_2 = 10$ and $n_1 = n_2 = 25$. In each case we assess the left- and right-tail error rates of confidence intervals, and their lengths.

Table 5.8 shows the empirical error rates for both cases, as percentages, for nominal rates between 1% and 10%: simulation standard errors are rates

Method	Nominal error rate							
	Lower limit				Upper limit			
	1	2.5	5	10	10	5	2.5	1
Exact	1.0	2.8	5.5	10.5	9.8	4.8	2.6	1.0
	1.0	2.3	4.8	9.9	10.2	4.9	2.5	1.1
Normal approximation	0.1	0.5	1.7	6.3	20.6	15.7	12.5	9.6
	0.1	0.5	2.1	6.4	16.3	11.5	8.2	5.5
Basic	0.0	0.0	0.2	1.8	24.4	21.0	18.6	16.4
	0.0	0.1	0.4	3.0	19.2	15.0	12.5	10.3
Basic, log scale	2.6	4.9	8.1	12.9	13.1	7.5	4.8	2.5
	1.6	3.2	6.0	11.4	11.5	6.3	3.3	1.7
Studentized	0.6	2.1	4.6	9.9	11.9	6.7	4.0	2.0
	0.8	2.3	4.6	9.9	10.9	5.9	3.0	1.4
Studentized, log scale	1.1	2.8	5.6	10.7	11.6	6.3	3.5	1.7
	1.1	2.5	5.0	10.1	10.8	5.7	2.9	1.3
Bootstrap percentile	1.8	3.6	6.5	11.6	14.6	8.9	5.9	3.3
	1.2	2.6	5.1	10.1	12.6	7.1	4.2	2.1
BC_a	1.9	4.0	6.9	12.3	14.0	8.3	5.3	3.0
	1.4	3.0	5.6	10.9	11.8	6.8	3.8	1.9
ABC	1.9	4.2	7.4	12.7	14.6	8.7	5.5	3.1
	1.3	3.0	5.7	11.0	12.1	6.8	3.7	1.9

Table 5.8 Empirical error rates (%) for nonparametric bootstrap confidence limits in ratio estimation: rates for sample sizes $n_1 = n_2 = 10$ are given above those for sample sizes $n_1 = n_2 = 25$. $R = 999$ for all bootstrap methods. 10 000 datasets generated from gamma distributions.

divided by 100. The normal approximation method uses the delta method variance approximation. The results suggest that the studentized method gives the best results, provided the log scale is used. Otherwise, the studentized method and the percentile, BC_a and ABC methods are comparable but only really satisfactory at the larger sample sizes.

Figure 5.7 shows box plots of the lengths of 1000 confidence intervals for both sample sizes. The most pronounced feature for $n_1 = n_2 = 10$ is the long — sometimes very long — lengths for the two studentized methods, which helps to account for their good error rates. This feature is far less prominent at the larger sample sizes. It is noticeable that the normal, percentile, BC_a and ABC intervals are short compared to the exact ones, and that taking logs improves the basic intervals. Similar comments apply when $n_1 = n_2 = 25$, but with less force.

5.8 Multiparameter Methods

When we want a confidence region for a vector parameter, the question of shape arises. Typically a rectangular region formed from intervals for each component parameter will not have high enough coverage probability, although a Bonferroni argument can be used to give a conservative confidence coefficient,

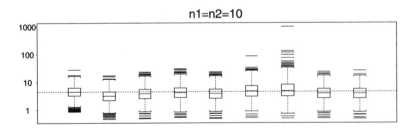

Figure 5.7 Box plots of
confidence interval
lengths for the first 1000
simulated samples in the
numerical experiment
with gamma data.

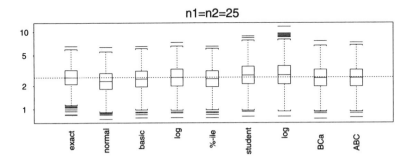

as follows. Suppose that θ has d components, and that the confidence region C_α is rectangular, with interval $C_{\alpha,i} = (\theta_{L,i}, \theta_{U,i})$ for the ith component θ_i. Then

$$\Pr(\theta \notin C_\alpha) = \Pr\left(\bigcup_i \{\theta_i \notin C_{\alpha,i}\}\right) \le \sum_i \Pr(\theta_i \notin C_{\alpha,i}) = \sum_i \alpha_i,$$

say. If we take $\alpha_i = \alpha/d$ then the region C_α has coverage at least equal to $1 - \alpha$. For certain applications this could be useful, in part because of its simplicity. But there are two potential disadvantages. First, the region could be very conservative — the true coverage could be considerably more than the nominal $1 - \alpha$. Secondly, the rectangular shape could be quite at odds with plausible likelihood contours. This is especially true if the estimates for parameter components are quite highly correlated, when also the Bonferroni method is more conservative.

One simple possibility for a joint bootstrap confidence region when T is approximately normal is to base it on the quadratic form

$$Q = (T - \theta)^T V^{-1}(T - \theta), \tag{5.60}$$

where V is the estimated variance matrix of T. Note that Q is the multivariate extension of the square of the studentized statistic of Section 5.2. If Q had exact p quantiles a_p, say, then a $1 - \alpha$ confidence set for θ would be

$$\{\theta : (T - \theta)^T V^{-1}(T - \theta) \le a_{1-\alpha}\}. \tag{5.61}$$

The elliptical shape of this set is correct if the distribution of T has elliptical contours, as the multivariate normal distribution does. So if T is approximately multivariate normal, then the shape will be approximately correct. Moreover, Q will be approximately distributed as a χ_d^2 variable. But as in the scalar case such distributional approximations will often be unreliable, so it makes sense to approximate the distribution of Q, and in particular the required quantiles $a_{1-\alpha}$, by resampling. The method then becomes completely analogous to the studentized bootstrap method for scalar parameters. The bootstrap analogue of Q will be

$$Q^* = (T^* - t)^T V^{*-1}(T^* - t),$$

which will be calculated for each of R simulated samples. If we denote the ordered bootstrap values by $q_1^* \leq \cdots \leq q_R^*$, then the $1 - \alpha$ bootstrap confidence region is the set

$$\{\theta : (t - \theta)^T v^{-1}(t - \theta) \leq q_{(R+1)(1-\alpha)}^*\}. \tag{5.62}$$

As in the scalar case, a common and useful choice for v is the delta method variance estimate v_L.

The same method can be applied on any scales which are monotone transformations of the original parameter scales. For example, if $h(\theta)$ has ith component $h_i(\theta_i)$, say, and if d is the diagonal matrix with elements $\partial h_i/\partial \theta_i$ evaluated at $\theta = t$, then we can apply (5.62) with the revised definition

$$q = \{h(t) - h(\theta)\}^T (d^T v d)^{-1}\{h(t) - h(\theta)\}.$$

If corresponding ordered bootstrap values are again denoted by q_r^*, then the bootstrap confidence region will be

$$\{\theta : \{h(t) - h(\theta)\}^T (d^T v d)^{-1}\{h(t) - h(\theta)\} \leq q_{(R+1)(1-\alpha)}^*\}. \tag{5.63}$$

A particular choice for $h(\cdot)$ would often be based on diagnostic plots of components of t^* and v^*, the objectives being to attain approximate normality and approximately stable variance for each component.

This method will be subject to the same potential defects as the studentized bootstrap method of Section 5.2. There is no vector analogue of the adjusted percentile methods, but the nested bootstrap method can be applied.

Example 5.14 (Air-conditioning data) For the air-conditioning data of Example 1.1, consider setting a confidence region for the two parameters $\theta = (\mu, \kappa)$ in a gamma model. The log likelihood function is

$$\ell(\mu, \kappa) = n\{\kappa \log(\kappa/\mu) - \log \Gamma(\kappa) + (\kappa - 1)\overline{\log y} - \kappa \bar{y}/\mu\},$$

$\bar{y}$ and $\overline{\log y}$ are the averages of the data and the log data.

from which we calculate the maximum likelihood estimators $T = (\hat{\mu}, \hat{\kappa})$. The numerical values are $\hat{\mu} = 108.083$ and $\hat{\kappa} = 0.7065$. A straightforward calculation shows that the delta method variance approximation, equal to the inverse of the expected information matrix as in Section 5.2, is

$$v_L = n^{-1}\text{diag}\left\{\hat{\kappa}^{-1}\hat{\mu}^2, \frac{d^2}{d\kappa^2}\log\Gamma(\hat{\kappa}) - \hat{\kappa}^{-1}\right\}. \qquad (5.64)$$

The standard likelihood ratio $1 - \alpha$ confidence region is the set of values of (μ, κ) for which

$$2\{\ell(\hat{\mu}, \hat{\kappa}) - \ell(\mu, \kappa)\} \le c_{2,1-\alpha},$$

where $c_{2,1-\alpha}$ is the $1 - \alpha$ quantile of the χ_2^2 distribution. The top left panel of Figure 5.8 shows the 0.50, 0.95 and 0.99 confidence regions obtained in this way. The top right panel is the same, except that $c_{2,1-\alpha}$ is replaced by a bootstrap estimate obtained from $R = 999$ samples simulated from the fitted gamma model. This second region is somewhat larger than, but of course has the same shape as, the first.

From the bootstrap simulation we have estimators $t^* = (\hat{\mu}^*, \hat{\kappa}^*)$ from each sample, from which we calculate the corresponding variance approximations using (5.64), and hence the quadratic forms $q^* = (t^* - t)^T v_L^{*-1}(t^* - t)$. We then apply (5.62) to obtain the studentized bootstrap confidence regions shown in the bottom left panel of Figure 5.8. This is clearly nothing like the likelihood-based confidence regions above, partly because it fails completely to take account of the mild skewness in the distribution of $\hat{\mu}$ and the heavy skewness in the distribution of $\hat{\kappa}$. These features are clear in the histogram plots of Figure 5.9.

Logarithmic transformation of both $\hat{\mu}$ and $\hat{\kappa}$ improves matters considerably: the bottom right panel of Figure 5.8 comes from applying the studentized bootstrap method after dual logarithmic transformation. Nevertheless, the solution is not completely satisfactory, in that the region is too wide on the κ axis and slightly narrow on the μ axis. This could be predicted to some extent by plotting v_L^* versus t^*, which shows that the log transformation of $\hat{\kappa}$ is not quite strong enough. Perhaps more important is that there is a substantial bias in $\hat{\kappa}$: the bootstrap bias estimate is 0.18.

One lesson from this example is that where a likelihood is available and usable, it should be used — with parametric simulation to check on, and if necessary replace, standard approximations for quantiles of the log likelihood ratio statistic.   ∎

Example 5.15 (Laterite data) The data in Table 5.9 are axial data consisting of 50 pole positions, in degrees of latitude and longitude, from a palaeo-magnetic study of New Caledonian laterites. The data take values only in the lower unit half-sphere, because an axis is determined by a single pole.

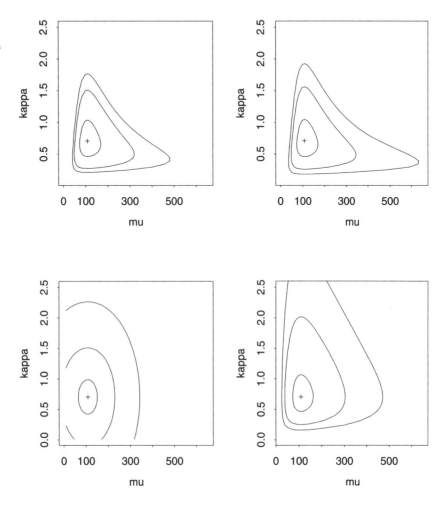

Figure 5.8 Bootstrap confidence regions for the parameters μ, κ of a gamma model for the air-conditioning data, with levels 0.50, 0.95 and 0.99. Top left: likelihood ratio region with χ_2^2 quantiles; top right: likelihood ratio region with bootstrap quantiles; bottom left: studentized bootstrap on original scales; bottom right: studentized bootstrap on logarithmic scales. $R = 999$ bootstrap samples from fitted gamma model with $\hat{\mu} = 108.083$ and $\hat{\kappa} = 0.7065$. + denotes MLE.

Let Y denote a unit vector on the lower half-sphere with cartesian coordinates $(\cos X \cos Z, \cos X \sin Z, \sin X)^T$, where X and Z are degrees of latitude and longitude. The population quantity of interest is the mean polar axis, $a(\theta, \phi) = (\cos \theta \cos \phi, \cos \theta \sin \phi, \sin \theta)^T$, defined as the axis given by the eigenvector corresponding to the largest eigenvalue of $E(Y Y^T)$. The sample value of this is given by the corresponding eigenvector of the matrix $n^{-1} \sum_j y_j y_j^T$, where y_j is the vector of cartesian coordinates of the jth pole position. The sample mean polar axis has latitude $\hat{\theta} = -76.3$ and longitude $\hat{\phi} = 83.8$. Figure 5.10 shows the original data in an equal-area projection onto a plane tangential to the South Pole, at $\theta = -90°$; the hollow circle represents the sample mean polar axis.

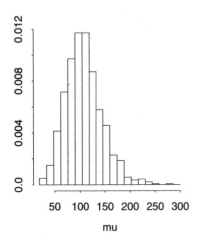
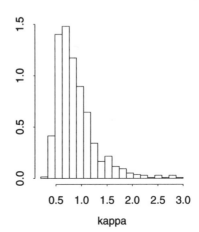

Figure 5.9 Histograms of $\hat{\mu}^*$ and $\hat{\kappa}^*$ from $R = 999$ bootstrap samples from gamma model with $\hat{\mu} = 108.083$ and $\hat{\kappa} = 0.7065$, fitted to air-conditioning data.

Lat	Long	Lat	Long	Lat	Long	Lat	Long
−26.4	324.0	−52.1	83.2	−80.5	108.4	−74.3	90.2
−32.2	163.7	−77.3	182.1	−77.7	266.0	−81.0	170.9
−73.1	51.9	−68.8	110.4	−6.9	19.1	−12.7	199.4
−80.2	140.5	−68.4	142.2	−59.4	281.7	−75.4	118.6
−71.1	267.2	−29.2	246.3	−5.6	107.4	−85.9	63.7
−58.7	32.0	−78.5	222.6	−62.6	105.3	−84.8	74.9
−40.8	28.1	−65.4	247.7	−74.7	120.2	−7.4	93.8
−14.9	266.3	−49.0	65.6	−65.3	286.6	−29.8	72.8
−66.1	144.3	−67.0	282.6	−71.6	106.4	−85.2	113.2
−1.8	256.2	−56.7	56.2	−23.3	96.5	−53.1	51.5
−38.3	146.8	−72.7	103.1	−60.2	33.2	−63.4	154.8
−17.2	89.9	−81.6	295.6	−40.4	41.0		
−56.2	35.6	−75.1	70.7	−53.6	59.1		

Table 5.9 Latitude (°) and longitude (°) of pole positions determined from the paleomagnetic study of New Caledonian laterites (Fisher *et al.*, 1987, p. 278).

In order to set a confidence region for the mean polar axis, or equivalently (θ, ϕ), we let

$$b(\theta, \phi) = (\sin\theta\cos\phi, \sin\theta\sin\phi, -\cos\theta)^T, \qquad c(\theta, \phi) = (-\sin\phi, -\cos\phi, 0)^T$$

denote the unit vectors orthogonal to $a(\theta, \phi)$. The sample values of these vectors are $\hat{a}$, $\hat{b}$ and $\hat{c}$, and the sample eigenvalues are $\hat{\lambda}_1 < \hat{\lambda}_2 < \hat{\lambda}_3$. Let A denote the 2×3 matrix $(\hat{b}, \hat{c})^T$ and B the 2×2 matrix with (j, k)th element

$$\frac{1}{(\hat{\lambda}_3 - \hat{\lambda}_1)(\hat{\lambda}_3 - \hat{\lambda}_2)} n^{-1} \sum_{j=1}^{n} (\hat{b}^T y_j)(\hat{c}^T y_j)(\hat{a}^T y_j)^2.$$

Figure 5.10 Equal-area projection of the laterite data onto the plane tangential to the South Pole (+). The sample mean polar axis is the hollow circle, and the square region is for comparison with Figures 5.11 and 10.3.

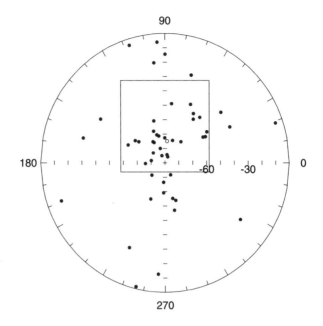

Then the analogue of (5.60) is

$$Q = na(\theta, \phi)^T A^T B^{-1} Aa(\theta, \phi), \tag{5.65}$$

which is approximately distributed as a χ_2^2 variable in large samples. In the bootstrap analogue of Q, a is replaced by $\hat{a}$, and A and B are replaced by the corresponding quantities calculated from the bootstrap sample.

Figure 5.11 shows results from setting confidence regions for the mean polar axis based on Q. The panels show the 0.5, 0.95 and 0.99 contours, using χ_2^2 quantiles and those based on $R = 999$ nonparametric bootstrap replicates q^*. The contours are elliptical in this projection. For this sample size it would not be misleading to use the asymptotic 0.5 and 0.95 quantiles, though the 0.99 quantiles differ by more. However, simulations with a random subset of size $n = 20$ gave dramatically different quantiles, and it seems to be essential to use the bootstrap quantiles for smaller sample sizes.

A different approach is to set $T = (\hat{\theta}, \hat{\phi})^T$, and then to base a confidence region for (θ, ϕ) on (5.60), with V taken to be nonparametric delta method estimate of the covariance matrix. This approach does not take into account the geometry of spherical data and works very poorly in this example, partly because the estimate t is close to the South Pole, which limits the range of $\hat{\theta}$.

∎

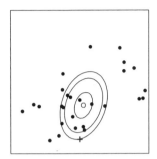 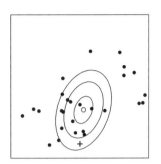

Figure 5.11 The 0.5, 0.95, and 0.99 confidence regions for the mean polar axis of the laterite data based on (5.65), using χ^2_2 quantiles (left) and bootstrap quantiles (right). The boundary of each panel is the square region in Figure 5.10; also shown are the South Pole (+) and the sample mean polar axis (○).

5.9 Conditional Confidence Regions

In parametric inference the probability calculations for confidence regions should in principle be made conditional on the ancillary statistics for the model, when these exist, the basic reason being to ensure that the inference accounts for the actual information content in the observed data. In parametric models what is ancillary is often specific to the mathematical form of F, and there is no nonparametric analogue. However, there are situations where there is a model-free ancillary indicator of the experiment, as with the design of a regression experiment (Chapter 6). In fact there is such an indicator in one of our earlier examples, and we now use this to illustrate some of the points which arise with conditional bootstrap confidence intervals.

Example 5.16 (City population data) For the ratio estimation problem of Example 1.2, the statistic $d = \bar{u}$ would often be regarded as ancillary. The reason rests in part on the notion of a model for linear regression of x on u with variation proportional to u. The left panel of Figure 5.12 shows the scatter plot of t^* versus d^* for the $R = 999$ nonparametric bootstrap samples used earlier. The observed value of d is 103.1. The middle and right panels of the figure show trends in the conditional mean and variance, $\mathrm{E}^*(T^* \mid d^*)$ and $\mathrm{var}^*(T^* \mid d^*)$, these being approximated by crude local averaging in the scatter plot on the left.

The calculation of confidence limits for the ratio $\theta = \mathrm{E}(X)/\mathrm{E}(U)$ is to be made conditional on $d^* = d$, the observed mean of u. Suppose, for example, that we want to apply the basic bootstrap method. Then we need to approximate the conditional quantiles $a_p(d)$ of $T - \theta$ given $D = d$ for $p = \alpha$ and $1 - \alpha$, and

Figure 5.12 City population data, $n = 49$. Scatter plot of bootstrap ratio estimates t^* versus d^*, and conditional means and variances of t^* given d^*. $R = 999$ nonparametric samples.

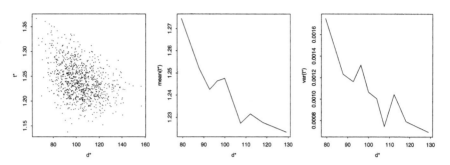

Table 5.10 City population data, $n = 49$. Comparison of unconditional and conditional cumulative probabilities for bootstrap ratio T^*. $R = 9999$ nonparametric samples, $R_d = 499$ used for conditional probabilities.

Unconditional	0.010	0.025	0.050	0.100	0.900	0.950	0.975	0.990
Conditional	0.006	0.020	0.044	0.078	0.940	0.974	0.988	1.000

use these in (5.3). The bootstrap estimate of $a_p(d)$ is the value $\hat{a}_p(d)$ defined by

$$\Pr\{T^* - t \le \hat{a}_p(d) \mid D^* = d\} = p,$$

and the simplest way to use our simulated samples to approximate this is to use only those samples for which d^* is "near" d. For example, we could take the $R_d = 99$ samples whose d^* values are closest to d and approximate $a_p(d)$ by the $100p$th ordered value of t^* in those samples.

Certainly stratification of the simulation results by intervals of d^* values shows quite strong conditional effects, as evidenced in Figure 5.12. The difficulty is that $R_d = 99$ samples is not enough to obtain good estimates of conditional quantiles, and certainly not to distinguish between unconditional quantiles and the conditional quantiles given $d^* \doteq d$, which is near the mean. Only with an increase of R to 9999, and using strata of $R_d = 499$ samples, does a clear picture emerge. Figure 5.13 shows plots of conditional quantile estimates from this larger simulation.

How different are the conditional and unconditional distributions? Table 5.10 shows bootstrap estimates of the cumulative conditional probabilities $\Pr(T \le a_p \mid D = d)$, where a_p is the unconditional p quantile, for several values of p. Each estimate is the proportion of times in $R_d = 499$ samples that t^* is less than or equal to the unconditional quantile estimate $t^*_{(10000p)}$. The comparison suggests that conditioning does not have a large effect in this case.

A more efficient use of bootstrap samples, which takes advantage of the smoothness of quantiles as a function of d, is to estimate quantiles for interval strata of R_d samples and then for each level p to fit a smooth curve. For example, if the kth such stratum gives quantile estimates $\hat{a}_{p,k}$ and average

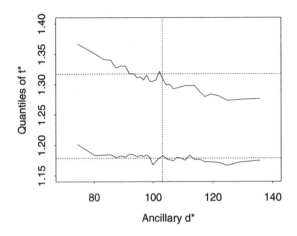

Figure 5.13 City population data, $n = 49$. Conditional 0.025 and 0.975 quantiles of bootstrap ratio t^* from $R = 9999$ samples, with strata of size $R_d = 499$. The horizonal dotted lines are unconditional quantiles, and the vertical dotted line is at $d^* = d$.

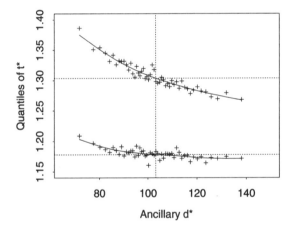

Figure 5.14 City population data, $n = 49$. Smooth spline fits to 0.025 and 0.975 conditional quantiles of bootstrap ratio t^* from $R = 9999$ samples, using overlapping strata of size $R_d = 199$.

value d_k for d^*, then we can fit a smoothing spline to the points $(d_k, \hat{a}_{p,k})$ for each p and interpolate the required value $\hat{a}_p(d)$ at the observed d. Figure 5.14 illustrates this for $R = 9999$ and non-overlapping strata of size $R_d = 199$, with $p = 0.025$ and 0.975. Note that interpolation is only needed at the centre of the curve. Use of non-overlapping intervals seems to give the best results. ∎

An alternative smoothing method is described in Problem 5.16. In Chapter 9 we shall see that in some cases, including the preceding example, it is possible to get accurate approximations to conditional quantiles using theoretical methods.

Figure 5.15 Annual
discharge of River Nile
at Aswan, 1871–1970
(Cobb, 1978).

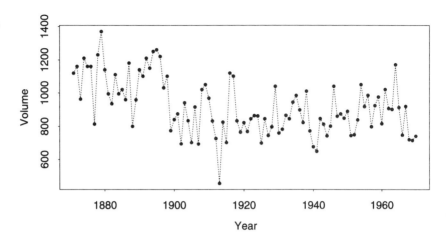

Just as with unconditional analysis, so with conditional analysis there is a
choice of bootstrap confidence interval methods. From our earlier discussion
the studentized bootstrap and adjusted percentile methods are likely to work
best for statistics that are approximately normal, as in the previous example.
The adjusted percentile method requires constants a, v_L and w, all of which
must now be conditional; see Problem 5.17. The studentized bootstrap method
can be applied as before with $Z = (T - \theta)/V^{1/2}$, except that now conditional
quantiles will be needed. Some simplification may occur if it is possible to
standardize with a conditional standard error.

The next example illustrates another way of overcoming the paucity of
bootstrap samples which satisfy the conditioning constraint.

Example 5.17 (Nile data)   The data plotted in Figure 5.15 are annual dis-
charges y of the River Nile at Aswan from 1871 to 1970. Interest lies in the
year $1870+\theta$ in which the mean discharge drops from $\mu_1 = 1100$ to $\mu_2 = 870$;
these mean values are estimated, but it is reasonable to ignore this fact and we
shall do so.

The least squares estimate of the integer θ maximizes

$$S(\theta) = \sum_{j=1}^{\theta} \{y_j - \tfrac{1}{2}(\mu_1 + \mu_2)\}.$$

Standard normal-theory likelihood analysis suggests that differences in $S(\theta)$
for θ near $\hat{\theta}$ are ancillary statistics. We shall reduce these differences to two
particular statistics which measure skewness and curvature of $S(\cdot)$ near $\hat{\theta}$,

c^*					b^*						
	...	−0.62	−0.37	−0.17	0	0.17	0.37	0.62	0.87	...	2.45
1.64	...	59	52	53	71	68	62	50	53	...	—
2.44	...	62	88	81	83	79	82	68	81	...	50
.	.	.	.	.	.	.	.	.	.	.	.
4.62	...	92	84	93	93	95	97	87	93	...	76
4.87	...	91	91	91	95	89	92	92	95	...	76
5.12	...	92	96	100	95	86	97	100	97	...	81
5.49	...	97	96	89	98	96	95	97	96	...	85
6.06	...	94	100	100	100	97	96	95	95	...	86
6.94	...	93	100	100	100	100	100	100	100	...	100

Table 5.11 Nile data. Part of the table of proportions (%) of bootstrap samples for which $|\hat{\theta}^* - \hat{\theta}| \leq 1$, for interval values of b^* and c^*. $R = 10\,000$ samples.

namely

$$B = S(\hat{\theta} + 5) - S(\hat{\theta} - 5), \quad C = S(\hat{\theta} + 5) - 2S(\hat{\theta}) + S(\hat{\theta} - 5);$$

for numerical convenience we rescale B and C by 0.0032. It is expected that B and C respectively influence the bias and variablity of $\hat{\theta}$. We are interested in the conditional confidence that should be attached to the set $\hat{\theta} \pm 1$, that is

$$\Pr(|\hat{\theta} - \theta| \leq 1 \mid b, c).$$

The data analysis gives $\hat{\theta} = 28$ (year 1898), $b = 0.75$ and $c = 5.5$.

With no assumption on the shape of the distribution of Y, except that it is constant, the obvious bootstrap sampling scheme is as follows. First calculate the residuals $e_j = x_j - \mu_1, j = 1, \ldots, 28$ and $e_j = x_j - \mu_2, j = 29, \ldots, 100$. Then simulate data series by $x_j^* = \mu_1 + \varepsilon_j^*, j = 1, \ldots, 28$ and $x_j^* = \mu_2 + \varepsilon_j^*, j = 29, \ldots, 100$, where ε_j^* is randomly sampled from $e_1, \ldots, e_{100}$. Each such sample series then gives $\hat{\theta}^*, b^*$ and c^*.

From $R = 10\,000$ bootstrap samples we find that the proportion of samples with $|\hat{\theta}^* - \hat{\theta}| \leq 1$ is 0.862, which is the unconditional bootstrap confidence. But when these samples are partitioned according to b^* and c^*, strong effects show up. Table 5.11 shows part of the table of proportions for outcome $|\hat{\theta}^* - \hat{\theta}| \leq 1$ for a 16×15 partition, 201 of these partitions being non-empty and most of them having at least 50 bootstrap samples. The proportions are consistently higher than 0.95 for (b^*, c^*) near (b, c), which strongly suggests that the conditional confidence $\Pr(|\hat{\theta} - \theta| \leq 1 \mid b = 0.75, c = 5.5)$ exceeds 0.95.

The conditional probability $\Pr(|\hat{\theta} - \theta| \leq 1 \mid b, c)$ will be smooth in b and c, so it makes sense to assume that the estimate

$$p(b^*, c^*) = \Pr^*(|\hat{\theta}^* - \hat{\theta}| \leq 1 \mid b^*, c^*)$$

is smooth in b^*, c^*. We fitted a logistic regression to the proportions in the 201 non-empty cells of the complete version of Table 5.11, the result being

$$\text{logit } \hat{p}(b^*, c^*) = -0.51 - 0.20b^{*2} + 0.68c^*.$$

The residual deviance is 223 on 198 degrees of freedom, which indicates an adequate fit for this simple model. The conditional bootstrap confidence is the fitted value of p at $b^* = b$, $c^* = c$, which is 0.972 with standard error 0.009. So the conditional confidence attached to $\theta = 28 \pm 1$ is much higher than the unconditional value.

The value of the standard error for the fitted value corresponds to a binomial standard error for a sample of size 3500, or 35% of the whole bootstrap simulation, which indicates high efficiency for this method of estimating conditional probability. ∎

5.10 Prediction

Closely related to confidence regions for parameters are confidence regions for future outcomes of the response Y, more usually called prediction regions. Applications are typically in more complicated contexts involving regression models (Chapters 6 and 7) and time series models (Chapter 8), so here we give only a brief discussion of the main ideas.

In the simplest situation we are concerned with prediction of one future response Y_{n+1} given observations $y_1, \ldots, y_n$ from a distribution F. The ideal upper γ prediction limit is the γ quantile of F, which we denote by $a_\gamma(F)$. The simplest approach to calculating a prediction limit is the plug-in approach, that is substituting the estimate $\hat{F}$ for F to give $\hat{a}_\gamma = a_\gamma(\hat{F})$. But this is clearly biased in the optimistic direction, because it does not allow for the uncertainty in $\hat{F}$. Resampling is used to correct for, or remove, this bias.

Parametric case

Suppose first that we have a fully parametric model, $F = F_\theta$, say. Then the prediction limit $a_\gamma(\hat{F})$ can be expressed more directly as $a_\gamma(\hat{\theta})$. The true coverage of this limit over repetitions of both data and predictand will not generally be γ, but rather

$$\Pr\{Y_{n+1} \le a_\gamma(\hat{\theta}) \mid \theta\} = h(\gamma), \tag{5.66}$$

say, where $h(\cdot)$ is unknown except that it must be increasing. (The coverage also depends on θ in general, but we suppress this from the notation for simplicity.) The idea is to estimate $h(\cdot)$ by resampling. So, for data $Y_1^*, \ldots, Y_n^*$ and predictand Y_{n+1}^* all sampled from $\hat{F} = F_{\hat{\theta}}$, we estimate (5.66) by

$$\hat{h}(\gamma) = \Pr^*\{Y_{n+1}^* \le a_\gamma(\hat{\theta}^*)\}, \tag{5.67}$$

where as usual $\hat{\theta}^*$ is the estimator calculated for data $Y_1^*,\ldots,Y_n^*$. In practice it would usually be necessary to use R simulated repetitions of the sampling and approximate (5.67) by

$$\hat{h}(\gamma) = \frac{\#\{y_{n+1,r}^* \le a_\gamma(\hat{\theta}_r^*)\}}{R+1}.\tag{5.68}$$

Once $\hat{h}(\gamma)$ has been calculated, the adjusted γ prediction limit is taken to be $\hat{a}_{\hat{g}(\gamma)} = a_{\hat{g}(\gamma)}(\hat{\theta})$, where

$$\hat{h}\{\hat{g}(\gamma)\} = \gamma.$$

Example 5.18 (Normal prediction limit)   Suppose that $Y_1,\ldots,Y_{n+1}$ are independently sampled from the $N(\mu,\sigma^2)$ distribution, where μ and σ are unknown, and that we wish to predict Y_{n+1} having observed $y_1,\ldots,y_n$. The plug-in method gives the basic γ prediction limit

$$\hat{a}_\gamma = \bar{y}_n + s_n\Phi^{-1}(\gamma),$$

where $\bar{y}_n = n^{-1}\sum y_j$ and $s_n^2 = n^{-1}\sum(y_j-\bar{y})^2$. If we write $Y_j = \mu+\sigma\varepsilon_j$, so that the ε_j are independent $N(0,1)$, then (5.66) becomes

$$h(\gamma) = \Pr\left\{\frac{\varepsilon_{n+1}-\bar{\varepsilon}_n}{s_n/\sigma} \le \Phi^{-1}(\gamma)\right\} = \Pr\left\{\left(\frac{n+1}{n-1}\right)^{1/2}Z_{n-1} \le \Phi^{-1}(\gamma)\right\},\tag{5.69}$$

where Z_{n-1} has the Student-t distribution with $n-1$ degrees of freedom. This leads directly to the Student-t prediction limit

$$\hat{a}_\gamma = \bar{y}_n + s_n\left(\frac{n+1}{n-1}\right)^{1/2}k_{n-1,\gamma},$$

where $k_{n-1,\gamma}$ is the γ quantile of the Student-t distribution with $n-1$ degrees of freedom.

In this particular case, then, $h(\cdot)$ does not need to be estimated. But if we had not recognized the occurrence of the Student-t distribution, then the first probability in (5.69) would have been estimated by applying (5.68) with samples generated from the $N(\bar{y}_n,s_n^2)$ distribution. Such an estimate (corresponding to infinite R) is plotted in Figure 5.16 for sample size $n=10$. The plot has logit scales to emphasize the discrepancy between $h(\gamma)$ and γ. Given values of the estimate $\hat{h}(\gamma)$, a smooth curve can be obtained by quadratic regression of their logits on logits of γ; this is illustrated in the figure, where the solid line is the regression fit. The required value $\hat{g}(\gamma)$ can be read off from the curve.   ∎

The preceding example suggests a more direct method for special cases involving means, which makes use of a point prediction $\hat{y}_{n+1}$ and the distribution of prediction error $\hat{Y}_{n+1} - Y_{n+1}$: resampling can be used to estimate this distribution directly. This method will be applied to linear regression models in Section 6.3.3.

Figure 5.16
Adjustment function
$h(\gamma)$ for prediction with
sample size $n = 10$ from
$N(\mu, \sigma^2)$, with quadratic
logistic fit (solid), and
line giving $h(\gamma) = \gamma$
(dots).

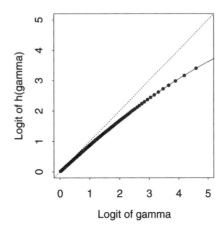

Nonparametric case

Now consider the nonparametric context, where $\hat{F}$ is the EDF of a single sample. The calculations outlined for the parametric case apply here also. First, if $r/n \leq \gamma < (r+1)/n$ then the plug-in prediction limit is $a_\gamma(\hat{F}) = y_{(r)}$; equivalently, $a_\gamma(\hat{F}) = y_{([n\gamma])}$, where $[\cdot]$ means integer part. Straightforward calculation shows that

$$\Pr(Y_{n+1} \leq Y_{(r)}) = r/(n+1),$$

which means that (5.66) becomes $h(\gamma) = [n\gamma]/(n+1)$. Therefore $[ng(\gamma)]/(n+1) = \gamma$, so that the adjusted prediction limit is $y_{([(n+1)\gamma])}$: this is exact if $(n+1)\gamma$ is an integer.

It seems intuitively clear that the efficiency of this nonparametric prediction limit relative to a parametric prediction limit would be considerably lower than would be the case for confidence limits on a parameter. For example, a comparison between the normal-theory and nonparametric methods for samples from a normal distribution shows the efficiency to be about $\frac{1}{2}$ for $\alpha = 0.05$.

For semiparametric problems similar calculations apply. One general approach which makes sense in certain applications, as mentioned earlier, bases prediction limits on point predictions, and uses resampling to estimate the distribution of prediction error. For further details see Sections 6.3.3 and 7.2.4.

5.11 Bibliographic Notes

Standard methods for obtaining confidence intervals are described in Chapters 7 and 9 of Cox and Hinkley (1974), while more recent developments in likelihood-based methods are outlined by Barndorff-Nielsen and Cox (1994). Corresponding methods based on resample likelihoods are described in Chapter 10.

Bootstrap confidence intervals were introduced in the original bootstrap paper by Efron (1979); bias adjustment and studentizing were discussed by Efron (1981b). The adjusted percentile method was developed by Efron (1987), who gives detailed discussion of the bias and skewness adjustment factors b and a. In part this development responded to issues raised by Schenker (1985). The ABC method and its theoretical justification were laid out by DiCiccio and Efron (1992). Hall (1988a, 1992a) contain rigorous developments of the second-order comparisons between competing methods, including the studentized bootstrap methods, and give references to earlier work dating back to Singh (1981). DiCiccio and Efron (1996) give an excellent review of the BC_a and ABC methods, together with their asymptotic properties and comparisons to likelihood-based methods. An earlier review, with discussion, was given by DiCiccio and Romano (1988).

Other empirical comparisons of the accuracy of bootstrap confidence interval methods are described in Section 4.4.4 of Shao and Tu (1995), while Lee and Young (1995) make comparisons with iterated bootstrap methods. Their conclusions and those of Canty, Davison and Hinkley (1996) broadly agree with those reached here.

Tibshirani (1988) discussed empirical choice of a variance-stabilizing transformation for use with the studentized bootstrap method.

Choice of simulation size R is investigated in detail by Hall (1986). See also the related references for Chapter 4 concerning choice of R to maintain high test power.

The significance test method has been studied by Kabaila (1993a) and discussed in detail by Carpenter (1996). Buckland and Garthwaite (1990) and Garthwaite and Buckland (1992) describe an efficient algorithm to find confidence limits in this context. The particular application discussed in Example 5.11 is a modified version of Jennison (1992). One intriguing application, to phylogenetic trees, is described by Efron, Halloran and Holmes (1996).

The double bootstrap method of adjustment in Section 5.6 is similar to that developed by Beran (1987) and Hinkley and Shi (1989); see also Loh (1987). The method is sometimes called bootstrap calibration. Hall and Martin (1988) give a detailed analysis of the reduction in coverage error. Lee and Young (1995) provide an efficient algorithm for approximating the method without simulation when the parameter is a smooth function of means. Booth and Hall

(1994) discuss the numbers of samples required when the nested bootstrap is used to calibrate a confidence interval.

Conditional methods have received little attention in the literature. Example 5.17 is taken from Hinkley and Schechtman (1987). Booth, Hall and Wood (1992) describe kernel methods for estimating the conditional distribution of a bootstrap statistic.

Confidence regions for vector parameters are almost untouched in the literature. There are no general analogues of adjusted percentile methods. Hall (1987) discusses likelihood-based shapes for confidence regions.

Geisser (1993) surveys several approaches to calculating prediction intervals, including resampling methods such as cross-validation.

References to confidence interval and prediction interval methods for regression models are given in the notes for Chapters 6 and 7; see also Chapter 8 for time series.

5.12 Problems

1   Suppose that we have a random sample $y_1, \ldots, y_n$ from a distribution F whose mean is unknown but whose variance is known and equal to σ^2. Discuss possible nonparametric resampling methods for obtaining confidence intervals for μ, including the following: (i) use $z = \sqrt{n}(\bar{y} - \mu)/\sigma$ and resample from the EDF; (ii) use $z = \sqrt{n}(\bar{y} - \mu)/s$ and resample from the EDF; (iii) as in (ii) but replace the EDF of the data by the EDF of values $\bar{y} + \sigma(y_i - \bar{y})/s$; (iv) as in (ii) but replace the EDF by a distribution on the data values whose mean and variance are $\bar{y}$ and σ^2.

> s^2 is the usual sample variance of $y_1, \ldots, y_n$.

2   Suppose that θ is the correlation coefficient for a bivariate distribution. If this distribution is bivariate normal, show that the MLE $\hat{\theta}$ is approximately $N(\theta, (1 - \theta^2)^2/n)$. Use the delta method to show that the transformed correlation parameter ζ for which $\hat{\eta}$ is approximately $N(0, n^{-1})$ is $\zeta = \frac{1}{2} \log\{(1 + \theta)/(1 - \theta)\}$.

Compare the use of normal approximations for $\hat{\theta}$ and $\hat{\zeta}$ with use of a parametric bootstrap analysis to obtain confidence intervals for θ: see Practical 5.1. (Section 5.2)

3   Independent measurements $y_1, \ldots, y_n$ come from a distribution with range $[0, \theta]$. Suppose that we resample by taking samples of size m from the data, and base confidence intervals on $Q = m(t - T^*)/t$, where $T^* = \max\{Y_1^*, \ldots, Y_m^*\}$. Show that this works provided that $m/n \to 0$ as $n \to \infty$, and use simulation to check its performance when $n = 100$ and Y has the $U(0, \theta)$ distribution. (Sections 2.6.1, 5.2)

4   The gamma model (1.1) with mean μ and index κ can be applied to the data of Example 1.1. For this model, show that the profile log likelihood for μ is

$$\ell_{\text{prof}}(\mu) = n\hat{\kappa}_\mu \log(\hat{\kappa}_\mu/\mu) + (\hat{\kappa}_\mu - 1)\sum \log y_j - \hat{\kappa}_\mu \sum y_j/\mu - n\log\Gamma(\hat{\kappa}_\mu),$$

where $\hat{\kappa}_\mu$ is the solution to the estimating equation

$$n\log(\kappa/\mu) + n + \sum \log y_j - \sum y_j/\mu - n\psi(\kappa) = 0,$$

with $\psi(\kappa)$ the derivative of $\log \Gamma(\kappa)$.

Describe an algorithm for simulating the distribution of the log likelihood ratio statistic $W(\mu) = 2\{\ell_{\mathrm{prof}}(\hat{\mu}) - \ell_{\mathrm{prof}}(\mu)\}$, where $\hat{\mu}$ is the overall maximum likelihood estimate.

(Section 5.2)

5   Consider simulation to estimate the distribution of $Z = (T - \theta)/V^{1/2}$, using R independent replicates with ordered values $z_1^* < \cdots < z_R^*$, where $z^* = (t^* - t)/v^{*1/2}$ is based on nonparametric bootstrapping of a sample $y_1, \ldots, y_n$. Let $\alpha = (r+1)/(R+1)$, so that a one-sided confidence interval for θ with nominal coverage α is $I_r = [t - v^{1/2}z_{r+1}^*, \infty)$.

(a) Show that

$$\mathrm{Pr}^*(\theta \in I_r \mid \hat{F}) = \mathrm{Pr}^*(z \le Z_{r+1}^*) = \sum_{s=0}^{r} \binom{R}{s} p^s (1-p)^{R-s},$$

where $p = p(\hat{F}) = \mathrm{Pr}^*(Z^* \le z \mid \hat{F})$. Let P be the random variable corresponding to $p(\hat{F})$, with CDF $G(\cdot)$. Hence show that the unconditional probability is

$$\mathrm{Pr}(\theta \in I_r) = \sum_{s=0}^{r} \binom{R}{s} \int_0^1 u^s (1-u)^{R-s} \, dG(u).$$

Note that $\mathrm{Pr}(P \le \alpha) = \mathrm{Pr}\{\theta \in [T - V^{1/2}Z_\alpha^*, \infty)\}$, where Z_α^* is the α quantile of the distribution of Z^*, conditional on $Y_1, \ldots, Y_n$.

(b) Suppose that it is reasonable to approximate the distribution of P by the beta distribution with density $u^{a-1}(1-u)^{b-1}/B(a,b)$, $0 < u < 1$; note that $a, b \to 1$ as $n \to \infty$. For some representative values of R, α, a and b, compare the coverage error of I_r with that of the interval $[T - V^{1/2}Z_\alpha^*, \infty)$.

(Section 5.2.3; Hall, 1986)

6   Capability or precision indices are used to indicate whether a process satisfies a specification of form (L, U), where L and U are the lower and upper specification limits. If the process is "in control", observations $y_1, \ldots, y_n$ on it are taken to have mean μ and standard deviation σ. Two basic capability indices are then $\theta = (U - L)/\sigma$ and $\eta = 2\min\{(U - \mu)/\sigma, (\mu - L)/\sigma\}$, with precision regarded as low if $\theta < 6$, medium if $6 \le \theta < 8$, and high if $\theta > 8$, and similarly for η, which is intended to be sensitive to the possibility that $\mu \ne \frac{1}{2}(L + U)$. Estimates of θ and η are obtained by replacing μ and σ with sample estimates, such as

(i) the usual estimates $\hat{\mu} = \bar{y} = n^{-1}\sum y_j$ and $\hat{\sigma} = \{(n-1)^{-1}\sum(y_j - \bar{y})^2\}^{1/2}$;

(ii) $\hat{\mu} = \bar{y}$ and $\hat{\sigma} = \bar{r}_k/d_k$, where $\bar{r}_k = b^{-1}\sum r_{k,i}$ and $r_{k,i}$ is the range $\max y_j - \min y_j$ of the ith block of k observations, namely $y_{k(i-1)+1}, \ldots, y_{ki}$, where $n = kb$. Here d_k is a scaling factor chosen so that r_k estimates σ.

(a) When estimates (i) are used, and the y_j are independent $N(\mu, \sigma^2)$ variables, show that an exact $(1 - 2\alpha)$ confidence interval for θ has endpoints

$$\hat{\theta}\left\{\frac{c_{n-1}(\alpha)}{n-1}\right\}^{1/2}, \quad \hat{\theta}\left\{\frac{c_{n-1}(1-\alpha)}{n-1}\right\}^{1/2},$$

where $c_v(\alpha)$ is the α quantile of the χ^2_v distribution.

(b) With the set-up in (a), suppose that parametric simulation from the fitted normal distribution is used to generate replicate values $\hat{\theta}_1^*, \ldots, \hat{\theta}_R^*$ of $\hat{\theta}$. Show that for $R = \infty$, the true coverage of the percentile confidence interval with nominal coverage $(1 - 2\alpha)$ is

$$\Pr\left\{\frac{(n-1)^2}{c_{n-1,1-\alpha}} \le \chi^2_{n-1} \le \frac{(n-1)^2}{c_{n-1,\alpha}}\right\},$$

where C has the χ^2_{n-1} distribution. Give also the coverages of the basic bootstrap confidence intervals based on $\hat{\theta}$ and $\log\hat{\theta}$.
Calculate these coverages for $n = 25, 50, 75$ and $\alpha = 0.05, 0.025$, and 0.005. Which of these intervals is preferable?
(c) See Practical 5.4, in which we take $d_5 = 2.236$.
(Section 5.3.1)

7 Suppose that we have a parametric model with parameter vector ψ, and that $\theta = h(\psi)$ is the parameter of interest. The adjusted percentile (BC_a) method is found by applying the scalar parameter method to the least-favourable family, for which the log likelihood $\ell(\psi)$ is replaced by $\ell_{LF}(\zeta) = \ell(\hat{\psi}+\zeta\hat{\delta})$, with $\hat{\delta} = i^{-1}(\hat{\psi})\dot{h}(\hat{\psi})$ and $\dot{h}(\cdot)$ is the vector of partial derivatives. Equations (5.21), (5.22) and (5.24) still apply.
Show in detail how to apply this extension of the BC_a method to the problem of calculating confidence intervals for the ratio $\theta = \mu_2/\mu_1$ of the means of two exponential distributions, given independent samples from those distributions. Use a numerical example (such as Example 5.10) to compare the BC_a method to the exact method, which is based on the fact that $\hat{\theta}/\theta$ has an F distribution.
(Sections 5.3.2, 5.4.2; Efron, 1987)

8 For the ratio of independent means in Example 5.10, show that the matrix of second derivatives $\ddot{u}(\hat{\pi})$ has elements

$$\ddot{u}_{1i,1j} = \frac{n^2 t}{n_1^2 \bar{y}_1}\left\{\frac{2(y_{1i} - \bar{y}_1)(y_{1j} - \bar{y}_1)}{\bar{y}_1} + (y_{1i} - \bar{y}_1) + (y_{1j} - \bar{y}_1)\right\},$$

$$\ddot{u}_{1i,2j} = -\frac{n^2}{n_1 n_2 \bar{y}_1^2}\{(y_{1i} - \bar{y}_1)(y_{2j} - \bar{y}_2)\},$$

and

$$\ddot{u}_{2i,2j} = -\frac{n^2}{n_2^2 \bar{y}_1}\{(y_{2i} - \bar{y}_2) + (y_{2j} - \bar{y}_2)\}.$$

Use these results to check the value of the constant c used in the ABC method in that example.

9 For the data of Example 1.2 we are interested in the ratio of means $\theta = E(X)/E(U)$. Define $\mu = (E(U), E(X))^T$ and write $\theta = t(\mu)$, which is estimated by $t = t(\bar{s})$ with $\bar{s} = (\bar{u}, \bar{x})^T$. Show that

$$\dot{t} = \begin{pmatrix} -\mu_2/\mu_1^2 \\ 1/\mu_1 \end{pmatrix}, \quad \ddot{t} = \begin{pmatrix} 2\mu_2/\mu_1^3 & -1/\mu_1^2 \\ -1/\mu_1^2 & 0 \end{pmatrix}.$$

From Problem 2.16 we have $l_j = e_j/\bar{u}$ with $e_j = x_j - tu_j$. Derive expressions for the constants a, b and c in the nonparametric ABC method, and note that $b = cv_L^{1/2}$.

Hence show that the *ABC* confidence limit is given by

$$\hat{\theta}_\alpha = \frac{\bar{x} + d_\alpha \sum x_j e_j / (n^2 v^{1/2} \bar{u})}{\bar{u} + d_\alpha \sum u_j e_j / (n^2 v^{1/2} \bar{u})},$$

where $d_\alpha = (a + z_\alpha) / \{1 - a(a + z_\alpha)\}^2$.
Apply this result to the full dataset with $n = 49$, for which $\bar{u} = 103.14$, $\bar{x} = 127.80$, $t = 1.239$, $v_L = 0.0119$, and $a = 0.0205$.
(Section 5.4.2)

10 Suppose that the parameter θ is estimated by solving the monotone estimating equation $S_Y(\theta) = 0$, with unique solution T. If the random variable $c(Y, \theta)$ has (approximately or exactly) the known, continuous distribution function G, and if $U \sim G$, then define t_U to be the solution to $c(y, t_U) = U$ for a fixed observation vector y. Show that for suitable A, $t - t_U \doteq -A^{-1} c(Y, \theta)$ has roughly the same distribution as $-A^{-1} U = -A^{-1} c(y, t_U) \doteq T - \theta$, and deduce that the distributions of $t - t_U$ and $T - \theta$ are roughly the same.
The distribution of $t - t_U$ can be approximated by simulation, and this provides a way to approximate the distribution of $T - \theta$. Comment critically on this resampling confidence limit method.
(Parzen, Wei and Ying, 1994)

11 Consider deriving an upper confidence limit for θ by test inversion. If T is an estimator for θ, and S is an estimator for nuisance parameter λ, and if $\mathrm{var}(T \mid \theta, \lambda) = \sigma^2(\theta, \lambda)$, then define $Z = (T - \theta_0)/\sigma(\theta_0, S)$. Show that an exact upper $1 - \alpha$ confidence limit is $u_{1-\alpha} = u_{1-\alpha}(t, s, \lambda)$ which satisfies

$$\Pr\left\{ \frac{T - u_{1-\alpha}}{\sigma(u_{1-\alpha}, S)} \le \frac{t - u_{1-\alpha}}{\sigma(u_{1-\alpha}, s)} \,\middle|\, \theta = (u_{1-\alpha}, \lambda) \right\} = \alpha.$$

The bootstrap confidence limit is $\hat{u}_{1-\alpha} = u_{1-\alpha}(t, s, s)$. Show that if S is a consistent estimator for λ then the method is consistent in the sense that $\Pr(\theta \le \hat{u}_{1-\alpha}) = 1 - \alpha + o(1)$. Further show that under certain conditions the coverage differs from $1 - \alpha$ by $O(n^{-1})$.
(Section 5.5; Kabaila, 1993a; Carpenter, 1996)

S is consistent for λ if $S = \lambda + o_p(1)$ as $n \to \infty$.

12 The normal approximation method for an upper $1 - \alpha$ confidence limit gives $\hat{\theta}_{1-\alpha} = \hat{\theta} + z_{1-\alpha} v^{1/2}$. Show that bootstrap adjustment of the nominal level $1 - \alpha$ in $z_{1-\alpha}$ leads to the studentized bootstrap method.
(Section 5.6; Beran, 1987)

13 The bootstrap method of adjustment can be applied to the percentile method. Show that the analogue of (5.55) is

$$\Pr^*\{\Pr^{**}(T^{**} \le t \mid \hat{F}^*) \le 1 - \hat{q}(\alpha) \mid \hat{F}\} = 1 - \alpha.$$

The adjusted $1 - \alpha$ upper confidence limit is then the $1 - \hat{q}(\alpha)$ quantile of T^*.
In the parametric bootstrap analysis for a single exponential mean, show that the percentile method gives upper $1 - \alpha$ limit $\bar{y} c_{2n, 1-\alpha}/(2n)$. Verify that the bootstrap adjustment of this limit gives the exact upper $1 - \alpha$ limit $2n\bar{y}/c_{2n, \alpha}$.
(Section 5.6; Beran, 1987; Hinkley and Shi, 1989)

$c_{v,\alpha}$ is the α quantile of the χ^2_v distribution.

14 Show how to make a bootstrap adjustment of the studentized bootstrap confidence limit method for a scalar parameter.
(Section 5.6)

15 For an equi-tailed $(1 - 2\alpha)$ confidence interval, the ideal endpoints are $t + \beta$ with values of β solving (3.31) with

$$h(\hat{F}, F; \beta) = I\{t(\hat{F}) - t(F) \le \beta\} - \alpha, \quad h(\hat{F}, F; \beta) = I\{t(\hat{F}) - t(F) \le \beta\} - (1 - \alpha).$$

Suppose that the bootstrap solutions are denoted by $\hat{\beta}_\alpha$ and $\hat{\beta}_{1-\alpha}$, and that in the language of Section 3.9.1 the adjustments $b(\hat{F}, \gamma)$ are $\hat{\beta}_{\alpha+\gamma_1}$ and $\hat{\beta}_{1-\alpha+\gamma_2}$. Show how to estimate γ_1 and γ_2, and verify that these adjustments modify coverage $1 - 2\alpha + O(n^{-1})$ to $1 - 2\alpha + O(n^{-2})$.
(Sections 3.9.1, 5.6; Hall and Martin, 1988)

16 Suppose that D is an approximate ancillary statistic and that we want to estimate the conditional probability $G(u \mid d) = \Pr(T - \theta \le u \mid D = d)$ using R simulated values (t_r^*, d_r^*). One smooth estimate is the kernel estimate

$$\hat{G}(u \mid d) = \frac{\sum_{r=1}^{R} w\left\{h^{-1}(d_r^* - d)\right\} I\left\{t_r^* - t \le u\right\}}{\sum_{r=1}^{R} w\left\{h^{-1}(d_r^* - d)\right\}},$$

where $w(\cdot)$ is a density symmetric about zero and h is an adjustable bandwidth. Investigate the bias and variance of this estimate in the case where (T, D) is approximately bivariate normal and $w(\cdot) = \phi(\cdot)$. Show that $h = R^{-1/2}$ is a reasonable choice.
(Section 5.9; Booth, Hall and Wood, 1992)

17 Suppose that (T, D) are approximately bivariate normal, with D an ancillary statistic upon whose observed value d we wish to condition when calculating confidence intervals. If the adjusted percentile method is to be used, then we need conditional evaluations of the constants a, v_L and w. One approach to this is based on selecting the subset of the R bootstrap samples for which $d^* \doteq d$. Then w can be calculated in the usual way, but restricted to this subset. For a and v_L we need empirical influence values, and these can be approximated by the regression method of Section 2.7.4, but using only the selected subset of samples.
Investigate whether or not this approach makes sense.
(Section 5.9)

18 Suppose that $y_1, \ldots, y_n$ are sampled from an unknown distribution, which is known to be symmetric about its median. Then to calculate a $1 - \alpha$ upper prediction limit for a further observation Y_{n+1}, the plug-in approach would use the $1 - \alpha$ quantile of the symmetrized EDF (Example 3.4). Develop a resampling algorithm for obtaining a bias-corrected prediction limit.
(Section 5.10)

19 For estimating the mean μ of a population with unknown variance, we want to find a $(1 - 2\alpha)$ confidence interval with specified length ℓ. Given data $y_1, \ldots, y_n$, consider the following approach. Create bootstrap samples of sizes $N = n, n+1, \ldots$ and calculate confidence intervals (e.g. by the studentized bootstrap method) for each N. Then choose as total sample size that N for which the interval length is ℓ or less. An additional $N - n$ data values are then obtained, and a bootstrap confidence interval applied. Discuss this approach, and investigate it numerically for the case where the data are sampled from a $N(\mu, \sigma^2)$ distribution.

5.13 Practicals

1 Suppose that we wish to calculate a 90% confidence interval for the correlation θ between the two counts in the columns of cd4; see Practical 2.3. To obtain

confidence intervals for θ under nonparametric resampling, using the empirical influence values to calculate v_L:

```
cd4.boot <- boot(cd4, corr.fun, stype="w", R=999)
boot.ci(cd4.boot,conf=0.9)
```

To obtain intervals on the variance-stabilized scale, i.e. based on

$$\hat{\zeta} = \tfrac{1}{2}\log\{(1+\hat{\theta})/(1-\hat{\theta})\} :$$

```
fisher <- function(r) 0.5*log((1+r)/(1-r))
fisher.dot <- function(r) 1/(1-r^2)
fisher.inv <- function(z) (exp(2*z)-1)/(exp(2*z)+1)
boot.ci(cd4.boot,h=fisher,hdot=fisher.dot,hinv=fisher.inv,conf=0.9)
```

How well do the intervals compare? Is the normal approximation reliable here? To compare intervals under parametric simulation from a fitted bivariate normal distribution:

```
cd4.rg <- function(data, mle)
{ d <- matrix(rnorm(2*nrow(data)), nrow(data), 2)
  d[,2] <- mle[5]*d[,1]+sqrt(1-mle[5]^2)*d[,2]
  d[,1] <- mle[1]+mle[3]*d[,1]
  d[,2] <- mle[2]+mle[4]*d[,2]
  d }
n <- nrow(cd4)
cd4.mle <- c(apply(cd4,2,mean),sqrt(apply(cd4,2,var)*(n-1)/n),
             corr(cd4))
cd4.para <- boot(cd4, corr.fun, R=999, sim="parametric",
                 ran.gen = cd4.rg, mle=cd4.mle)
boot.ci(cd4.para,type=c("norm","basic","stud","perc"),conf=0.9)
boot.ci(cd4.para,h=fisher,hdot=fisher.dot,hinv=fisher.inv,
        type=c("norm","basic","stud","perc"),conf=0.9)
```

To obtain the corresponding interval using the nonparametric ABC method:

```
abc.ci(cd4, corr, conf=0.9)
```

Do the differences among the various intervals reflect what you would expect? (Sections 5.2, 5.3, 5.4.2; DiCiccio and Efron, 1996).

2   Suppose that we wish to calculate a 90% confidence interval for the largest eigenvalue θ of the covariance matrix of the two counts in the columns of cd4; see Practicals 2.3 and 5.1. To obtain confidence intervals for θ under nonparametric resampling, using the empirical influence values to calculate v_L:

```
eigen.fun <- function(d, w = rep(1, nrow(d))/nrow(d))
{ w <- w/sum(w)
  n <- nrow(d)
  m <- crossprod(w, d)
  m2 <- sweep(d,2,m)
  v <- crossprod(diag(sqrt(w)) %*% m2)
  eig <- eigen(v,symmetric=T)
  stat <- eig$values[1]
  e <- eig$vectors[,1]
  i <- rep(1:n,round(n*w))
  ds <- sweep(d[i,],2,m)
```

```
L <- (ds%*%e)^2 - stat
c(stat, sum(L^2)/n^2) }
cd4.boot <- boot(cd4,eigen.fun,R=999,stype="w")
boot.ci(cd4.boot, conf=0.90)
abc.ci(cd4, eigen.fun, conf=0.9)
```

Discuss the differences among the various intervals.
(Sections 5.2, 5.3, 5.4.2; DiCiccio and Efron, 1996)

3   Dataframe amis contains data made available by G. Amis of Cambridgeshire
     County Council on the speeds in miles per hour of cars at pairs of sites on roads
     in Cambridgeshire. Speeds were measured at each site before and then again after
     the erection of a warning sign at one site of each pair. The quantity of interest is
     the mean relative change in the 0.85 quantile, η, of the speeds for each pair, i.e. the
     mean of the quantities $(\eta_{a1} - \eta_{b1}) - (\eta_{a0} - \eta_{b0})$; here η_{b1} and η_{a1} are the 0.85 quantiles
     of the speed distribution at the site where the sign was placed, before and after
     its erection. This quantity is chosen because the warning is particularly intended
     to slow faster drivers. About 100 speeds are available for each combination of
     14 pairs of sites and three periods, one before and two after the warnings were
     erected, but some of the pairs overlap. We work with a slightly smaller dataset, for
     which the ηs are:

```
amis1 <- amis[(amis$pair!=4)&(amis$pair!=6)&(amis$period!=3),]
tapply(amis1$speed, list(amis1$period,amis1$warning,amis1$pair),
       quantile, 0.85)
```

To attempt to set confidence intervals for θ, by stratified resampling from the
speeds at each combination of site and period:

```
amis.fun <- function(data, i)
{ d <- data[i, ]
  d <- tapply(d$speed,list(d$period,d$warning,d$pair),quantile,0.85)
  mean((d[2,1, ] - d[1,1, ]) - (d[2,2, ] - d[1,2, ]))  }
str <- 4*(amis1$pair-1)+2*(amis1$warning-1)+amis1$period
amis1.boot <- boot(amis1,amis.fun,R=99,strata=str)
amis1.boot$t0
qqnorm(amis1.boot$t)
abline(mean(amis1.boot$t),sqrt(var(amis1.boot$t)),lty=2)
boot.ci(amis1.boot,type=c("basic","perc","norm"),conf=0.9)
```

(There are 4800 cases in amis1 so this is demanding on memory: it may be
necessary to increase the object.size.) Do the resampled averages look normal?
Can you account for the differences among the intervals?
How big is the average effect of the warnings?
(Section 5.2)

4   Dataframe capability gives "data" from Bissell (1990) comprising 75 successive
     observations with specification limits $U = 5.79$ and $L = 5.49$; see Problem 5.6. To
     check that the process is "in control" and that the data are close to independent
     normal random variables:

```
par(mfrow=c(2,2))
tsplot(capability$y,ylim=c(5,6))
abline(h=5.79,lty=2); abline(h=5.49,lty=2)
qqnorm(capability$y)
acf(capability$y)
```

```
acf(capability$y,type="partial")
```

To find nonparametric confidence limits for η using the estimates given by (ii) in Problem 5.6:

```
capability.fun <- function(data, i, U=5.79, L=5.49, dk=2.236)
{ y <- data$y[i]
  m <- mean(y)
  r5 <- apply(matrix(y,15,5), 1, function(y) diff(range(y)))
  s <- mean(r5)/dk
  2*min((U-m)/s, (m-L)/s) }
capability.boot <- boot(capability, capability.fun, R=999)
boot.ci(capability.boot,type=c("norm","basic","perc"))
```

Do the values of t^* look normal? Why is there such a difference between the percentile and basic bootstrap limits? Which do you think are more reliable here? (Sections 5.2, 5.3)

5   Following on from Practical 2.3, we use a double bootstrap with $M = 249$ to adjust the studentized bootstrap interval for a correlation coefficient applied to the cd4 data.

```
nested.corr <- function(data, w, t0, M)
{ n <- nrow(data)
  i <- rep(1:n,round(n*w))
  t <- corr.fun(data, w )
  z <- (t[1]-t0)/sqrt(t[2])
  nested.boot <- boot(data[i,], corr.fun, R=M, stype="w")
  z.nested <- (nested.boot$t[,1]-t[1])/sqrt(nested.boot$t[,2])
  c(z, sum(z.nested<z)/(M+1)) }
cd4.boot <- boot(cd4, nested.corr, R=9, stype="w",
                          t0=corr(cd4), M=249)
```

To get some idea how long you will have to wait if you set $R = 999$ you can time the call to boot using unix.time or dos.time: beware of time and memory problems. It may be best to run a batch job, with contents

```
cd4.boot <- boot(cd4,nested.corr,R=99,stype="w",t0=corr(cd4),M=249)
junk <- boot(cd4,nested.corr,R=100,stype="w",t0=corr(cd4),M=249)
cd4.boot$t <- rbind(cd4.boot$t,junk$t)
cd4.boot$R <- cd4.boot$R+junk$R
```

but with the last three lines repeated eight further times.
cd4.nested contains a nested simulation we did earlier. To compare the actual and nominal coverage levels:

```
par(pty="s")
qqplot((1:cd4.nested$R)/(1+cd4.nested$R),cd4.nested$t[,2],
        xlab="nominal coverage",ylab="estimated coverage",pch=".")
lines(c(0,1),c(0,1))
```

How close to nominal is the estimated coverage? To read off the original and corrected 95% confidence intervals:

```
q <- c(0.975,0.025)
q.adj <- quantile(cd4.nested$t[,2],q)
t0 <- corr.fun(cd4)
z <- sort(cd4.nested$t[,1])
```

```
t0[1]-sqrt(t0[2])*z[floor((1+cd4.nested$R)*q)]
t0[1]-sqrt(t0[2])*z[floor((1+cd4.nested$R)*q.adj)]
```

Does the correction have much effect? Compare this interval with the corresponding *ABC* interval.
(Section 5.6)

6

Linear Regression

6.1 Introduction

One of the most important and frequent types of statistical analysis is regression analysis, in which we study the effects of explanatory variables or covariates on a response variable. In this chapter we are concerned with linear regression, in which the mean of the random response Y observed at value $x = (x_1, \ldots, x_p)^T$ of the explanatory variable vector is

$$\mathrm{E}(Y \mid x) = \mu(x) \equiv x^T \beta.$$

The model is completed by specifying the nature of random variation, which for independent responses amounts to specifying the form of the variance $\mathrm{var}(Y \mid x)$. For a full parametric analysis we would also have to specify the distribution of Y, be it normal, Poisson or whatever. Without this, the model is semiparametric.

For linear regression with normal random errors having constant variance, the least squares theory of regression estimation and inference provides clean, exact methods for analysis. But for generalizations to non-normal errors and non-constant variance, exact methods rarely exist, and we are faced with approximate methods based on linear approximations to estimators and central limit theorems. So, just as in the simpler context of Chapters 2–5, resampling methods have the potential to provide more accurate analysis.

We begin our discussion in Section 6.2 with simple least squares linear regression, where in ideal conditions resampling essentially reproduces the exact theoretical analysis, but also offers the potential to deal with non-ideal circumstances such as non-constant variance. Section 6.3 covers the extension to multiple explanatory variables. The related topics of aggregate prediction error and of variable selection based on predictive ability are discussed in Section 6.4. Robust methods of regression are examined briefly in Section 6.5.

Figure 6.1 Average body weight (kg) and brain weight (g) for 62 species of mammals, plotted on original scales and logarithmic scales (Weisberg, 1985, p. 144).

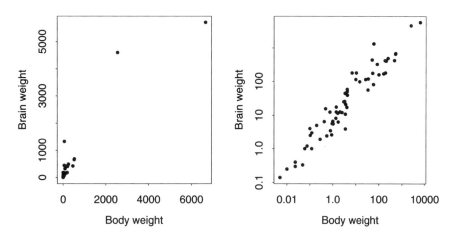

The further topics of generalized linear models, survival analysis, other non-linear regression, classification error, and nonparametric regression models are deferred to Chapter 7.

6.2 Least Squares Linear Regression

6.2.1 Regression fit and residuals

The left panel of Figure 6.1 shows the scatter plot of response "brain weight" versus explanatory variable "body weight" for $n = 62$ mammals. As the right panel of the figure shows, the data are well described by a simple linear regression after the two variables are transformed logarithmically, so that

$$y = \log(\text{brain weight}), \quad x = \log(\text{body weight}).$$

The simple linear regression model is

$$Y_j = \beta_0 + \beta_1 x_j + \varepsilon_j, \quad j = 1, \ldots, n, \tag{6.1}$$

where the ε_js are uncorrelated with zero means and equal variances σ^2. This constancy of variance, or homoscedasticity, seems roughly right for the example data. We refer to the data (x_j, y_j) as the jth case.

In general the values x_j might be controlled (by design), randomly sampled, or merely observed as in the example. But we analyse the data as if the x_is were fixed, because the amount of information about $\beta = (\beta_0, \beta_1)^T$ depends upon their observed values.

The simplest analysis of data under (6.1) is by the ordinary least squares method, on which we concentrate here. The least squares estimates for β are

$$\hat{\beta}_1 = \frac{\sum_{j=1}^{n}(x_j - \bar{x})y_j}{SS_x}, \quad \hat{\beta}_0 = \bar{y} - \hat{\beta}_1\bar{x}, \tag{6.2}$$

where $\bar{x} = n^{-1}\sum x_j$ and $SS_x = \sum_{j=1}^{n}(x_j - \bar{x})^2$. The conventional estimate of the error variance σ^2 is the residual mean square

$$s^2 = \frac{1}{n-2}\sum_{j=1}^{n}e_j^2,$$

where

$$e_j = y_j - \hat{\mu}_j \tag{6.3}$$

are raw residuals with

$$\hat{\mu}_j = \hat{\beta}_0 + \hat{\beta}_1 x_j \tag{6.4}$$

the fitted values, or estimated mean values, for the response at the observed x values.

The basic properties of the parameter estimates $\hat{\beta}_0$, $\hat{\beta}_1$, which are easily obtained under model (6.1), are

$$E(\hat{\beta}_0) = \beta_0, \quad \text{var}(\hat{\beta}_0) = \sigma^2\left(\frac{1}{n} + \frac{\bar{x}^2}{SS_x}\right), \tag{6.5}$$

and

$$E(\hat{\beta}_1) = \beta_1, \quad \text{var}(\hat{\beta}_1) = \frac{\sigma^2}{SS_x}. \tag{6.6}$$

The estimates are normally distributed and optimal if the errors ε_j are normally distributed, they are often approximately normal for other error distributions, but they are not robust to gross non-normality of errors or to outlying response values.

The raw residuals e_j are important for various aspects of model checking, and potentially for resampling methods since they estimate the random errors ε_j, so it is useful to summarize their properties also. Under (6.1),

$$e_j = \sum_{k=1}^{n}h_{jk}\varepsilon_k, \tag{6.7}$$

where

$$h_{jk} = n^{-1}\delta_{jk} + \frac{(x_j - \bar{x})(x_k - \bar{x})}{SS_x},$$

with δ_{jk} equal to 1 if $j = k$ and zero otherwise. The quantities h_{jj} are known as *leverages*, and for convenience we denote them by h_j. It follows from (6.7) that

$$E(e_j) = 0, \quad \text{var}(e_j) = \sigma^2(1 - h_j). \tag{6.8}$$

One consequence of this last result is that the estimator S^2 that corresponds to s^2 has expected value σ^2, because $\sum(1 - h_j) = n - 2$. Note that with the intercept β_0 in the model, $\sum e_j = 0$ automatically.

The raw residuals e_j can be modified in various ways to makes them suitable for diagnostic methods, but the most useful modification for our purposes is to change them to have constant variance, that is

$$r_j = \frac{y_j - \hat{\mu}_j}{(1 - h_j)^{1/2}}. \tag{6.9}$$

Standardized residuals are called studentized residuals by some authors.

We shall refer to these as *modified residuals*, to distinguish them from *standardized residuals* which are in addition divided by the sample standard deviation. A normal Q-Q plot of the r_j will reveal obvious outliers, or clear non-normality of the random errors, although the latter may be obscured somewhat because of the averaging property of (6.7).

A simpler modification of residuals is to use $1 - \bar{h} = 1 - 2n^{-1}$ instead of individual leverages $1 - h_j$, where $\bar{h}$ is the average leverage; this will have a very similar effect only if the leverages h_j are fairly homogeneous. This simpler modification implies multiplication of all raw residuals e_j by $(1 - 2n^{-1})^{-1/2}$: the average will equal zero automatically because $\sum e_j = 0$.

If (6.1) holds with homoscedastic random errors ε_j and if those random errors are normally distributed, or if the dataset is large, then standard distributional results will be adequate for drawing inferences with the least squares estimates. But if the errors are very non-normal or heteroscedastic, meaning that their variances are unequal, then those standard results may not be reliable and a resampling method may offer genuine improvement. In Sections 6.2.3 and 6.2.4 we describe two quite different resampling methods, the second of which is robust to failure of the model assumptions.

If strong non-normality or heteroscedasticity (which can be difficult to distinguish) appear to be present, then robust regression estimates may be considered in place of least squares estimates. These will be discussed in Section 6.5.

6.2.2 Alternative models

The linear regression model (6.1) can arise in two ways, and for our purposes it can be useful to distinguish them.

First formulation

The first possibility is that the pairs are randomly sampled from a bivariate distribution F for (X, Y). Then linear regression refers to linearity of the conditional mean of Y given $X = x$, that is

$$E(Y \mid X = x) = \mu_y + \gamma(x - \mu_x), \quad \gamma = \sigma_{xy}/\sigma_x^2, \tag{6.10}$$

with $\mu_x = E(X)$, $\mu_y = E(Y)$, $\sigma_x^2 = \text{var}(X)$ and $\sigma_{xy} = \text{cov}(X, Y)$. This conditional mean corresponds to the mean in (6.1), with

$$\beta_0 = \mu_y - \gamma\mu_x, \quad \beta_1 = \gamma. \tag{6.11}$$

The parameters $\beta = (\beta_0, \beta_1)^T$ are here seen to be statistical functions of the kind met in earlier chapters, in this case based on the first and second moments of F. The random errors ε_j in (6.1) will be homoscedastic with respect to x if F is bivariate normal, for example, but not in general.

The least squares estimators (6.2) correspond to the use of sample moments in (6.10). For future reference we note (Problem 6.1) that the influence function for the least squares estimators $t = (\hat{\beta}_0, \hat{\beta}_1)^T$ is the vector

$$L_t\{(x, y); F\} = \begin{pmatrix} 1 + \mu_x^2/\sigma_x^2 & -\mu_x/\sigma_x^2 \\ -\mu_x/\sigma_x^2 & 1/\sigma_x^2 \end{pmatrix} \begin{pmatrix} 1 \\ x \end{pmatrix} (y - \beta_0 - \beta_1 x). \tag{6.12}$$

The empirical influence values as defined in Section 2.7.2 are therefore

$$l_j = \begin{pmatrix} 1 - n\bar{x}(x_j - \bar{x})/SS_x \\ n(x_j - \bar{x})/SS_x \end{pmatrix} e_j. \tag{6.13}$$

The nonparametric delta method variance approximation (2.36) applied to $\hat{\beta}_1$ gives

$$v_L = \frac{\sum(x_j - \bar{x})^2 e_j^2}{SS_x^2}. \tag{6.14}$$

This makes no assumption of homoscedasticity. In practice we modify the variance approximation to account for leverage, replacing e_j by r_j as defined in (6.9).

Second formulation

The second possibility is that at any value of x, responses Y_x can be sampled from a distribution $F_x(y)$ whose mean and variance are $\mu(x)$ and $\sigma^2(x)$, such that $\mu(x) = \beta_0 + \beta_1 x$. Evidently $\beta_0 = \mu(0)$, and the slope parameter β_1 is a linear contrast of mean values $\mu(x_1), \mu(x_2), \ldots$, namely

$$\beta_1 = \frac{\sum(x_j - \bar{x})\mu(x_j)}{SS_x}.$$

In principle several responses could be obtained at each x_j. Simple linear regression with homoscedastic errors, with which we are initially concerned, corresponds to $\sigma(x) \equiv \sigma$ and

$$F_x(y) \equiv G\{y - \mu(x)\}. \tag{6.15}$$

So G is the distribution of random error, with mean zero and variance σ^2. Any particular application is characterized by the design $x_1, \ldots, x_n$ and the corresponding distributions F_x, the means of which are defined by linear regression.

The influence function for the least squares estimator is again given by (6.12), but with μ_x and σ_x^2 respectively replaced by $\bar{x}$ and $n^{-1}\sum(x_j - \bar{x})^2$. Empirical influence values are still given by (6.13). The analogue of linear approximations (2.35) and (3.1) is $\hat{\beta} = \beta + n^{-1}\sum_{j=1}^{n} L_t\{(x_j, y_j); F\}$, with variance $n^{-2}\sum_{j=1}^{n} \text{var}\left[L_t\{(x_j, Y_j); F\}\right]$. If the assumed homoscedasticity of errors is used to evaluate this, with the constant variance σ^2 estimated by $n^{-1}\sum e_j^2$, then the delta method variance approximation for $\hat{\beta}_1$, for example, is

$$\frac{\sum e_j^2}{nSS_x};$$

strictly speaking this is a semiparametric approximation. This differs by a factor of $(n-2)/n$ from the standard estimate, which is given by (6.6) with residual mean square s^2 in place of σ^2.

The standard analysis for linear regression as outlined in Section 6.2.1 is the same for both situations, provided the random errors ε_j have equal variances, as would usually be judged from plots of the residuals.

6.2.3 Resampling errors

To extend the resampling algorithms of Chapters 2–3 to regression, we have first to identify the underlying model F. Now if (6.1) is literally correct with homoscedastic errors, then those errors are effectively sampled from a single distribution. If the x_js are treated as fixed, then the second formulation of Section 6.2.2 applies, G being the common error distribution. The model F is the series of distributions F_x for $x = x_1, \ldots, x_n$, defined by (6.15). The resampling model is the corresponding series of estimated distributions $\hat{F}_x$ in which each $\mu(x_j)$ is replaced by the regression fit $\hat{\mu}(x_j)$ and G is estimated from all residuals.

For parametric resampling we would estimate G according to the assumed form of error distribution, for example the $N(0, s^2)$ distribution if normality were judged appropriate. (Of course resampling is not necessary for the normal linear model, because exact theoretical results are available.) For nonparametric resampling, on which we concentrate in this chapter, we need a generalization of the EDF used in Chapter 2. If the random errors ε_j were known, then their EDF would be appropriate. As it is we have the raw residuals e_j which estimate the ε_j, and their EDF will usually be consistent for G. But for practical use it is better to use the residuals r_j defined in (6.9), because their variances agree with those of the $\{\varepsilon_j\}$. Noting that G is assumed to have mean zero in the model, we then estimate G by the EDF of $r_j - \bar{r}$, where $\bar{r}$ is the average of the r_j. These centred residuals have mean zero, and we refer to their EDF as $\hat{G}$.

The full resampling model is taken to have the same "design" as the data, that is $x_j^* \equiv x_j$; it then specifies the conditional distribution of Y_j^* given x_j^*

through the estimated version of (6.1), which is

$$Y_j^* = \hat{\mu}_j + \varepsilon_j^*, \quad j = 1, \ldots, n, \tag{6.16}$$

with $\hat{\mu}_j = \hat{\beta}_0 + \hat{\beta}_1 x_j^*$ and ε_j^* randomly sampled from $\hat{G}$. So the algorithm to generate simulated datasets and corresponding parameter estimates is as follows.

Algorithm 6.1 (Model-based resampling in linear regression)
For $r = 1, \ldots, R$,

1 For $j = 1, \ldots, n$,

   (a) set $x_j^* = x_j$;
   (b) randomly sample ε_j^* from $r_1 - \bar{r}, \ldots, r_n - \bar{r}$; then
   (c) set $y_j^* = \hat{\beta}_0 + \hat{\beta}_1 x_j + \varepsilon_j^*$.

2 Fit least squares regression to $(x_1^*, y_1^*), \ldots, (x_n^*, y_n^*)$, giving estimates $\hat{\beta}_{0,r}^*, \hat{\beta}_{1,r}^*, s_r^{*2}$.

$\bullet$

The resampling means and variances of $\hat{\beta}_0^*$ and $\hat{\beta}_1^*$ will agree very closely with standard least squares theory. To see this, consider for example the slope estimate, whose bootstrap sample value can be written

$$\hat{\beta}_1^* = \frac{\sum(x_j - \bar{x})y_j^*}{\sum(x_j - \bar{x})^2} = \hat{\beta}_1 + \frac{\sum(x_j - \bar{x})\varepsilon_j^*}{SS_x}.$$

Because $E^*(\varepsilon_j^*) = n^{-1}\sum(r_j - \bar{r}) = 0$, it follows that $E^*(\hat{\beta}_1^*) = \hat{\beta}_1$. Also, because $\text{var}^*(\varepsilon_j^*) = n^{-1}\sum_{i=1}^n (r_i - \bar{r})^2$ for all j,

$$\text{var}^*(\hat{\beta}_1^*) = \frac{\sum(x_j - \bar{x})^2 \text{var}^*(\varepsilon_j^*)}{SS_x^2} = n^{-1}\sum(r_j - \bar{r})^2/SS_x.$$

The latter will be approximately equal to the usual estimate s^2/SS_x, because $n^{-1}\sum(r_j - \bar{r})^2 \doteq (n-2)^{-1}\sum e_j^2 = s^2$. In fact if the individual h_j are replaced by their average $\bar{h}$, then the means and variances of $\hat{\beta}_0^*$ and $\hat{\beta}_1^*$ are given exactly by (6.5) and (6.6) with the estimates $\hat{\beta}_0$, $\hat{\beta}_1$ and s^2 substituted for parameter values. The advantage of resampling is improved quantile estimation when normal-theory distributions of the estimators $\hat{\beta}_0$, $\hat{\beta}_1$, S^2 are not accurate.

Example 6.1 (Mammals) For the data plotted in the right panel of Figure 6.1, the simple linear regression model seems appropriate. Standard analysis suggests that errors are approximately normal, although there is a small suspicion of heteroscedasticity: see Figure 6.2. The parameter estimates are $\hat{\beta}_0 = 2.135$ and $\hat{\beta}_1 = 0.752$.

From $R = 499$ bootstrap simulations according to the algorithm above, the

Figure 6.2 Normal
Q-Q plot of modified
residuals r_j and their
plot against leverage
values h_j for linear
regression fit to
log-transformed
mammal data.

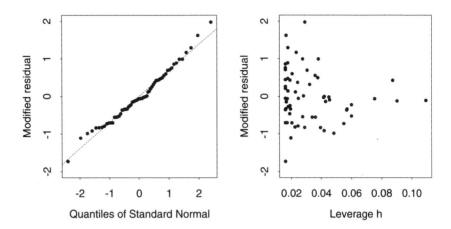

estimated standard errors of intercept and slope are respectively 0.0958 and
0.0273, compared to the theoretical values 0.0960 and 0.0285. The empirical
distributions of bootstrap estimates are almost perfectly normal, as they are
for the studentized estimates. The estimated 0.05 and 0.95 quantiles for the
studentized slope estimate

$$z = \frac{\hat{\beta}_1 - \beta_1}{SE(\hat{\beta}_1)},$$

where $SE(\hat{\beta}_1)$ is the standard error for $\hat{\beta}_1$ obtained from (6.6), are $z^*_{(25)} = -1.640$
and $z^*_{(475)} = 1.589$, compared to the standard normal quantiles ± 1.645. So, as
expected for a moderately large "clean" dataset, the resampling results agree
closely with those obtained from standard methods. ∎

Zero intercept

In some applications the intercept β_0 will not be included in (6.1). This affects
the estimation of β_1 and σ^2 in obvious ways, but the resampling algorithm will
also differ. First, the leverage values are different, namely

$$h_j = \frac{x_j^2}{\sum x_i^2},$$

so the modified residual will be different. Secondly, because now $\sum e_j \neq 0$, it is
essential to mean-correct the residuals before using them to simulate random
errors.

Repeated design points

If there are repeat observations at some or all values of x, this offers an
enhanced opportunity to detect heteroscedasticity: see Section 6.2.6. With

many such repeats it is in principle possible to estimate the CDFs F_x separately (Section 6.2.2), but there is rarely enough data for this to be useful in practice.

The main advantage of repeats is the opportunity it affords to test the adequacy of the linear regression formulation, by splitting the residual sum of squares into a "pure error" component and a "goodness-of-fit" component. To the extent that the comparison of these components through the usual F ratio is quite sensitive to non-normality and heteroscedasticity, resampling methods may be useful in interpreting that F ratio (Practical 6.3).

6.2.4 Resampling cases

A completely different approach would be to imagine the data as a sample from some bivariate distribution F of (X, Y). This will sometimes, but not often, mimic what actually happened. In this approach, as outlined in Section 6.2.2, the regression coefficients are viewed as statistical functions of F, and defined by (6.10). Model (6.1) still applies, but with no assumption on the random errors ε_j other than independence. When (6.10) is evaluated at $\hat{F}$ we obtain the least squares estimates (6.2).

With F now the bivariate distribution of (X, Y), it is appropriate to take $\hat{F}$ to be the EDF of the data pairs, and resampling will be from this EDF, just as in Chapter 2. The resampling simulation therefore involves sampling pairs with replacement from $(x_1, y_1), \ldots, (x_n, y_n)$. This is equivalent to taking $(x_i^*, y_i^*) = (x_I, y_I)$, where I is uniformly distributed on $\{1, 2, \ldots, n\}$. Simulated values $\hat{\beta}_0^*$, $\hat{\beta}_1^*$ of the coefficient estimates are computed from $(x_1^*, y_1^*), \ldots, (x_n^*, y_n^*)$ using the least squares algorithm which was applied to obtain the original estimates $\hat{\beta}_0$, $\hat{\beta}_1$. So the resampling algorithm is as follows.

The model $\mathrm{E}(Y \mid X = x) = \alpha + \beta_1(x - \bar{x})$, which some writers use in place of (6.1), is not useful here because $\alpha = \beta_0 + \beta_1 \bar{x}$ is a function not only of F but also of the data, through $\bar{x}$.

Algorithm 6.2 (Resampling cases in regression)

For $r = 1, \ldots, R$,

1 sample $i_1^*, \ldots, i_n^*$ randomly with replacement from $\{1, 2, \ldots, n\}$;

2 for $j = 1, \ldots, n$, set $x_j^* = x_{i_j^*}$, $y_j^* = y_{i_j^*}$; then

3 fit least squares regression to $(x_1^*, y_1^*), \ldots, (x_n^*, y_n^*)$, giving estimates $\hat{\beta}_{0,r}^*$, $\hat{\beta}_{1,r}^*$, s_r^{*2}.

There are two important differences between this second bootstrap method and the previous one using a parametric model and simulated errors. First, with the second method we make no assumption about variance homogeneity — indeed we do not even assume that the conditional mean of Y given $X = x$ is linear. This offers the advantage of potential robustness to heteroscedasticity, and the disadvantage of inefficiency if the constant-variance model is correct. Secondly, the simulated samples have different designs, because the values

Table 6.1 Mammals data. Comparison of bootstrap biases and standard errors of intercept and slope with theoretical results, standard and robust. Resampling cases with $R = 999$.

		Theoretical	Resampling cases	Robust theoretical
$\hat{\beta}_0^*$	bias	0	0.0006	—
	standard error	0.096	0.091	0.088
$\hat{\beta}_1^*$	bias	0	0.0002	—
	standard error	0.0285	0.0223	0.0223

$x_1^*, \ldots, x_n^*$ are randomly sampled. The design fixes the information content of a sample, and in principle our inference should be specific to the information in our data. The variation in $x_1^*, \ldots, x_n^*$ will cause some variation in information, but fortunately this is often unimportant in moderately large datasets; see, however, Examples 6.4 and 6.6.

Note that in general the resampling distribution of a coefficient estimate will not have mean equal to the data estimate, contrary to the unbiasedness property that the estimate in fact possesses. However, the difference is usually negligible.

Example 6.2 (Mammals) For the data of Example 6.1, a bootstrap simulation was run by resampling cases with $R = 999$. Table 6.1 shows the bias and standard error results for both intercept and slope. The estimated biases are very small. The striking feature of the results is that the standard error for the slope is considerably smaller than in the previous bootstrap simulation, which agreed with standard theory. The last column of the table gives robust versions of the standard errors, which are calculated by estimating the variance of ε_j to be r_j^2. For example, the robust estimate of the variance of $\hat{\beta}_1$ is

$$\frac{\sum (x_j - \bar{x})^2 r_j^2}{SS_x^2}. \tag{6.17}$$

This corresponds to the delta method variance approximation (6.14), except that r_j is used in preference to e_j. As we might have expected from previous discussion, the bootstrap gives an approximation to the robust standard error.

Figure 6.3 shows normal Q-Q plots of the bootstrap estimates $\hat{\beta}_0^*$ and $\hat{\beta}_1^*$. For the slope parameter the right panel shows lines corresponding to normal distributions with the usual and the robust standard errors. The distribution of $\hat{\beta}_1^*$ is close to normal, with variance much closer to the robust form (6.17) than to the usual form (6.6). ∎

One disadvantage of the robust standard error is its inefficiency relative to the usual standard error when the latter is correct. A fairly straightforward calculation (Problem 6.6) gives the efficiency, which is approximately 40% for the slope parameter in the previous example. Thus the effective degrees of freedom for the robust standard error is approximately 0.40 times 62, or 25.

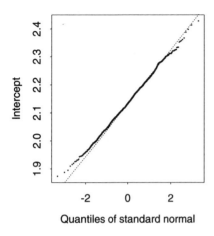
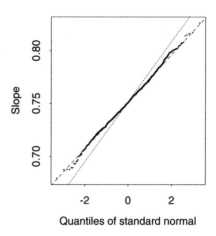

Figure 6.3 Normal plots for bootstrapped estimates of intercept (left) and slope (right) for linear regression fit to logarithms of mammal data, with $R = 999$ samples obtained by resampling cases. The dotted lines give approximate normal distributions based on the usual formulae (6.5) and (6.6), while the dashed line shows the normal distribution for the slope using the robust variance estimate (6.17).

The same loss of efficiency would apply approximately to bootstrap results for resampling cases.

6.2.5 Significance tests for slope

Suppose that we want to test whether or not the covariate x has an effect on the response y, assuming linear regression is appropriate. In terms of model parameters, the null hypothesis is $H_0 : \beta_1 = 0$. If we use the least squares estimate $\hat{\beta}_1$ as the basis for such a test, then this is equivalent to testing the Pearson correlation coefficient. This connection immediately suggests one nonparametric test, the permutation test of Example 4.9. However, this is not always valid, so we need also to consider other possible bootstrap tests.

Permutation test

The permutation test of correlation applies to the null hypothesis of independence between X and Y when these are both random. Equivalently it applies when the null hypothesis implies that the conditional distribution of Y given $X = x$ does not depend upon x. In the context of linear regression this means not only zero slope, but also constant error variance. The justification then rests simply on the exchangeability of the response values under the null hypothesis.

If we use $X_{(\cdot)}$ to denote the ordered values of $X_1, \ldots, X_n$, and so forth, then the exact level of significance for one-sided alternative $H_A : \beta_1 > 0$ and test statistic T is

$$
\begin{aligned}
p &= \Pr\left(T \geq t \mid X_{(\cdot)} = x_{(\cdot)}, Y_{(\cdot)} = y_{(\cdot)}, H_0\right) \\
&= \Pr\left[T \geq t \mid X = x, Y = \operatorname{perm}\{y_{(\cdot)}\}\right],
\end{aligned}
$$

where perm$\{\cdot\}$ denotes a permutation. Because all permutations are equally likely, we have

$$p = \frac{\#\text{of permutations such that } T \geq t}{n!},$$

as in (4.20). In the present context we can take $T = \hat{\beta}_1$, for which p is the same as if we used the sample Pearson correlation coefficient, but the same method applies for any appropriate slope estimator. In practice the test is performed by generating samples $(x_1^*, y_1^*), \ldots, (x_n^*, y_n^*)$ such that $x_j^* = x_j$ and $(y_1^*, \ldots, y_n^*)$ is a random permutation of $(y_1, \ldots, y_n)$, and fitting the least squares slope estimate $\hat{\beta}_1^*$. If this is done R times, then the one-sided P-value for alternative $H_A : \beta_1 > 0$ is

$$p = \frac{\#\{\hat{\beta}_1^* \geq \hat{\beta}_1\} + 1}{R + 1}.$$

It is easy to show that studentizing the slope estimate would not affect this test; see Problem 6.4. The test is exact in the sense that the P-value has a uniform distribution under H_0, as explained in Section 4.1; note that this uniform distribution holds conditional on the x values, which is the relevant property here.

First bootstrap test

A bootstrap test whose result will usually differ negligibly from that of the permutation test is obtained by taking the null model as the pair of marginal EDFs of x and y, so that the x_j^*s are randomly sampled with replacement from the x_js, and independently the y_j^*s are randomly sampled from the y_js. Again $\hat{\beta}_1^*$ is the slope fitted to the simulated data, and the formula for p is the same. As with the permutation test, the null hypothesis being tested is stronger than just zero slope.

The permutation method and its bootstrap look-alike apply equally well to any slope estimate, not just the least squares estimate.

Second bootstrap test

The next bootstrap test is based explicitly on the linear model structure with homoscedastic errors, and applies the general approach of Section 4.4. The null model is the null mean fit and the EDF of residuals from that fit. We calculate the P-value for the slope estimate under sampling from this fitted model. That is, data are simulated by

$$x_j^* = x_j, \quad y_j^* = \hat{\mu}_{j0} + \varepsilon_{j0}^*,$$

where $\hat{\mu}_{j0} = \bar{y}$ and the ε_{j0}^* are sampled with replacement from the null model residuals $e_{j0} = y_j - \bar{y}$, $j = 1, \ldots, n$. The least squares slope $\hat{\beta}_1^*$ is calculated from the simulated data. After R repetitions of the simulation, the P-value is calculated as before.

This second bootstrap test differs from the first bootstrap test only in that the values of explanatory variables x are fixed at the data values for every case. Note that if residuals were sampled without replacement, this test would duplicate the exact permutation test, which suggests that this bootstrap test will be nearly exact.

The test could be modified by standardizing the residuals before sampling from them, which here would mean adjusting for the constant null model leverage n^{-1}. This would affect the P-value slightly for the test as described, but not if the test statistic were changed to the studentized slope estimate. It therefore seems wise to studentize regression test statistics in general, if model-based simulation is used; see the discussion of bootstrap pivot tests below.

Testing non-zero slope values

All of the preceding tests can be easily modified to test a non-zero value of β_1. If the null value is $\beta_{1,0}$, say, then we apply the test to modified responses $y_j - \beta_{1,0}x_j$, as in Example 6.3 below.

Bootstrap pivot tests

Further bootstrap tests can be based on the studentized bootstrap approach outlined in Section 4.4.1. For simplicity suppose that we can assume homoscedastic errors. Then $Z = (\hat{\beta}_1 - \beta_1)/S_1$ is a pivot, where S_1 is the usual standard error for $\hat{\beta}_1$. As a pivot, Z has a distribution not depending upon parameter values, and this can be verified under the linear model (6.1). The null hypothesis is $H_0 : \beta_1 = 0$, and as before we consider the one-sided alternative $H_A : \beta_1 > 0$. Then the P-value is

$$p = \Pr\left(Z \geq \frac{\hat{\beta}_1}{s_1} \;\middle|\; \beta_1 = 0, \beta_0, \sigma\right) = \Pr\left(Z \geq \frac{\hat{\beta}_1}{s_1} \;\middle|\; \beta_1, \beta_0, \sigma\right),$$

because Z is a pivot. The probability on the right is approximated by the bootstrap probability

$$p = \Pr^*\left(Z^* \geq \frac{\hat{\beta}_1}{s_1}\right), \tag{6.18}$$

where $Z^* = (\hat{\beta}_1^* - \hat{\beta}_1)/S_1^*$ is computed from a sample simulated according to Algorithm 6.1, which uses the fit from the full model as in (6.16). So, applying the bootstrap as described in Section 6.2.3, we calculate the bootstrap P-value from the results of R simulated samples as

$$p = \frac{\#\{z^* \geq z_0\}}{R+1}, \tag{6.19}$$

where $z_0 = \hat{\beta}_1/s_1$.

The relation of this method to confidence limits is that if the lower $1 - \alpha$

$$z^* > z. \qquad \frac{\hat{\beta}_1^* - \hat{\beta}_1}{s_1^*} > \frac{\hat{\beta}_1}{s_1}$$

$$\hat{\beta}_1^* > \frac{s_1^*}{s_1}\hat{\beta}_1 + \hat{\beta}_1$$

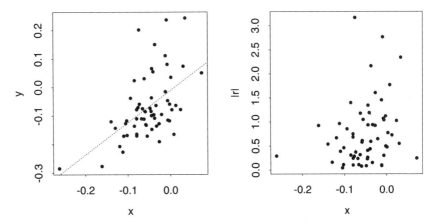

Figure 6.4 Linear regression model fitted to monthly excess returns over riskless rate y for one company versus excess market returns x. The left panel shows the data and fitted line. The right panel plots the absolute values of the standardized residuals against x (Simonoff and Tsai, 1994).

confidence limit for β_1 is above zero, then $p < \alpha$. Similar interpretations apply with upper confidence limits and confidence intervals.

The same method can be used with case resampling. If this were done as a precaution against error heteroscedasticity, then it would be appropriate to replace s_1 with the robust standard error defined as the square root of (6.17).

If we wish to test a non-zero value $\beta_{1,0}$ for the slope, then in (6.18) we simply replace $\hat{\beta}_1/s_1$ by $z_0 = (\hat{\beta}_1 - \beta_{1,0})/s_1$, or equivalently compare the lower confidence limit to $\beta_{1,0}$.

With all of these tests there are simple modifications if a different alternative hypothesis is appropriate. For example, if the alternative is $H_A : \beta_1 < 0$, then the inequalities "$\geq$" used in defining p are replaced by "$\leq$"; and the two-sided P-value is twice the smaller of the two one-sided P-values.

On balance there seems little to choose among the various tests described. The permutation test and its bootstrap look-alike are equally suited to statistics other than least squares estimates. The bootstrap pivot test with case resampling is the only one designed to test slope without assuming constant error variance under the null hypothesis. But one would usually expect similar results from all the tests.

The extensions to multiple linear regression are discussed in Section 6.3.2.

Example 6.3 (Returns data) The data plotted in Figure 6.4 are $n = 60$ consecutive cases of monthly excess returns y for a particular company and excess market returns x, where excess is relative to riskless rate. We shall ignore the possibility of serial correlation. A linear relationship appears to fit the data, and the hypothesis of interest is $H_0 : \beta_1 = 1$ with alternative $H_A : \beta_1 > 1$, the latter corresponding to the company outperforming the market.

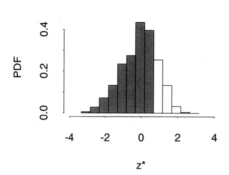

Figure 6.5 Returns data: histogram of $R = 999$ bootstrap values of studentized slope $z^* = (\hat{\beta}_1^* - \hat{\beta}_1)/s_{rob}^*$, obtained by resampling cases. Unshaded area corresponds to values in excess of data value $z_0 = (\hat{\beta}_1 - 1)/s_{rob} = 0.669$.

Figure 6.4 and plots of regression diagnostics suggest that error variation increases with x and is non-normal. It is therefore appropriate to apply the bootstrap pivot test with case resampling, using the robust standard error from (6.17), which we denote here by s_{rob}, to studentize the slope estimate.

Figure 6.5 shows a histogram of $R = 999$ values of z^*. The unshaded part corresponds to z^* greater than the data value

$$z_0 = (\hat{\beta}_1 - 1)/s_{rob} = (1.133 - 1)/0.198 = 0.669,$$

which happens 233 times. Therefore the bootstrap P-value is 0.234. In fact the use of the robust standard error makes little difference here: using the ordinary standard error gives P-value 0.252. Comparison of the ordinary t-statistic to the standard normal table gives P-value 0.28. ∎

6.2.6 Non-constant variance: weighted error resampling

In some applications the linear model (6.1) will apply, but with heteroscedastic random errors. If the heteroscedasticity can be modelled, then bootstrap simulation by resampling errors is still possible. We assume to begin with that ordinary, i.e. unweighted, least squares estimates are fitted, as before.

Known variance function

Suppose that in (6.1) the random error ε_j at $x = x_j$ has variance σ_j^2, where either $\sigma_j^2 = \kappa V(x_j)$ or $\sigma_j^2 = \kappa V(\mu_j)$, with $V(\cdot)$ a known function. It is possible to estimate κ, but we do not need to do this. We only require the modified residuals

$$r_j = \frac{y_j - \hat{\mu}_j}{\{V(x_j)(1 - h_j)\}^{1/2}} \quad \text{or} \quad \frac{y_j - \hat{\mu}_j}{\{V(\hat{\mu}_j)(1 - h_j)\}^{1/2}},$$

which will be approximately homoscedastic. The EDF of these modified residuals, after subtracting their mean, will estimate the distribution function G of the scaled, homoscedastic random errors δ_j in the model

$$Y_j = \beta_0 + \beta_1 x_j + V_j^{1/2}\delta_j, \tag{6.20}$$

where $V_j = V(x_j)$ or $V(\mu_j)$. Algorithm 6.1 for resampling errors is now modified as follows.

Algorithm 6.3 (Resampling errors with unequal variances)

For $r = 1, \ldots, R$,

1 For $j = 1, \ldots, n$,

       (*a*) set $x_j^* = x_j$;

       (*b*) randomly sample δ_j^* from $r_1 - \bar{r}, \ldots, r_n - \bar{r}$; then

       (*c*) set $y_j^* = \hat{\beta}_0 + \hat{\beta}_1 x_j + \hat{V}_j^{1/2}\delta_j^*$, where $\hat{V}_j$ is $V(x_j)$ or $V(\hat{\mu}_j)$ as appropriate.

2 Fit linear regression by ordinary least squares to data $(x_1^*, y_1^*), \ldots, (x_n^*, y_n^*)$, giving estimates $\hat{\beta}_{0r}^*, \hat{\beta}_{1r}^*, s_r^{*2}$.

                                                                               ●

Weighted least squares

Of course in this situation ordinary least squares is inferior to weighted least squares, in which ideally the jth case is given weight $w_j = V_j^{-1}$. If $V_j = V(x_j)$ then weighted least squares can be done in one pass through the data, whereas if $V_j = V(\mu_j)$ we first estimate μ_j by ordinary least squares fitted values $\hat{\mu}_j^0$, say, and then do a weighted least squares fit with the empirical weights $\hat{w}_j = 1/V(\hat{\mu}_j^0)$. In the latter case the standard theory assumes that the weights are fixed, which is adequate for first-order approximations to distributional properties. The practical effect of using empirical weights can be incorporated into the resampling, and so potentially more accurate distributional properties can be obtained; cf. Example 3.2.

For weighted least squares, the estimates of intercept and slope are

$$\hat{\beta}_1 = \frac{\sum w_j(x_j - \bar{x}_w)y_j}{\sum w_j(x_j - \bar{x}_w)^2}, \quad \hat{\beta}_0 = \bar{y}_w - \hat{\beta}_1\bar{x}_w,$$

where $\bar{x}_w = \sum w_j x_j / \sum w_j$ and $\bar{y}_w = \sum w_j y_j / \sum w_j$. Fitted values and raw residuals are defined as for ordinary least squares, but leverage values and modified residuals differ. The leverage values are now

$$h_j = \frac{w_j}{\sum w_i} + \frac{w_j(x_j - \bar{x}_w)^2}{\sum w_i(x_i - \bar{x}_w)^2},$$

and the modified residuals (standardized to equal variance) are

$$r_j = \frac{w_j^{1/2}(y_j - \hat{\mu}_j)}{(1 - h_j)^{1/2}}.$$

Standard theory gives the variance estimates

$$\operatorname{var}(\hat{\beta}_0) \doteq \hat{\kappa} \left\{ \frac{1}{\sum w_j} + \frac{\bar{x}_w^2}{\sum w_j(x_j - \bar{x}_w)^2} \right\}, \quad \operatorname{var}(\hat{\beta}_1) \doteq \frac{\hat{\kappa}}{\sum w_j(x_j - \bar{x}_w)^2},$$

where $\hat{\kappa} = s^2 = (n-2)^{-1} \sum w_j(y_j - \hat{\mu}_j)^2$ is the weighted residual mean square.

The algorithm for resampling errors is the same as for ordinary least squares, summarized in Algorithm 6.3, but with the full weighted least squares procedure implemented in the final step.

The situation where error variance depends on the mean is a special case of the generalized linear model, which is discussed more fully in Section 7.2.

Wild bootstrap

What if the variance function $V(\cdot)$ is unspecified? In some circumstances there may be enough data to model it from the pattern of residual variation, for example using a plot of modified residuals r_j (or their absolute values or squares) versus fitted values $\hat{\mu}_j$. This approach can work if there is a clear monotone relationship of variance with x or μ, or if there are clearly identifiable strata of constant variance (cf. Figure 7.14). But where the heteroscedasticity is unpatterned, either resampling of cases should be done with least squares estimates, or something akin to local estimation of variance will be required.

The most local approach possible is the *wild bootstrap*, which estimates variances from individual residuals. This uses the model-based resampling Algorithm 6.1, but with the jth resampled error ε_j^* taken from the two-point distribution

$$\Pr\left\{\varepsilon_j^* = e_j(1 - \sqrt{5})/2\right\} = \pi, \qquad \Pr\left\{\varepsilon_j^* = e_j(1 + \sqrt{5})/2\right\} = 1 - \pi, \quad (6.21)$$

where $\pi = (5 + \sqrt{5})/10$ and $e_j = y_j - \hat{\mu}_j$ is the raw residual. The first three moments of ε_j^* are zero, e_j^2 and e_j^3 (Problem 6.8). This algorithm generates at most 2^n different values of parameter estimates, and typically gives results that are underdispersed relative to model-based resampling or resampling cases. Note that if modified residuals r_j were used in place of raw residuals e_j, then the variance of $\hat{\beta}^*$ under the wild bootstrap would equal the robust variance estimate (6.17).

Example 6.4 (Returns data) As mentioned in Example 6.3, the data in Figure 6.4 show an increase in error variance with market return, x. Table 6.3 compares the bootstrap variances of the parameter estimates from ordinary least squares for case resampling and the wild bootstrap, with $R = 999$. The estimated variance of $\hat{\beta}_1$ from resampling cases is larger than for the wild

	All cases		Without case 22	
	$\hat{\beta}_0$	$\hat{\beta}_1$	$\hat{\beta}_0$	$\hat{\beta}_1$
Cases	0.32	44.3	0.42	73.2
Cases, subset	0.28	38.4	0.39	59.1
Wild, e_j	0.31	37.9	0.37	62.5
Wild, r_j	0.33	37.0	0.41	67.2
Robust theoretical	0.34	39.4	0.40	67.2

Table 6.2 Bootstrap variances ($\times 10^{-3}$) of ordinary least squares estimates for returns data, with $R = 999$.

bootstrap, and for the full data it makes little difference when the modified residuals are used.

Case 22 has high leverage, and its exclusion increases the variances of both estimates. The wild bootstrap is again less variable than bootstrapping cases, with the wild bootstrap of modified residuals intermediate between them.

We mentioned earlier that the design will vary when resampling cases. The left panel of Figure 6.6 shows the simulated slope estimates $\hat{\beta}_1^*$ plotted against the sums of squares $\sum(x_j^* - \bar{x}^*)^2$, for 200 bootstrap samples. The plotting character distinguishes the number of times case 22 occurs in the resamples: we return to this below. The variability of $\hat{\beta}_1^*$ decreases sharply as the sum of squares increases. Now usually we would treat the sum of squares as fixed in the analysis, and this suggests that we should calculate the variance of $\hat{\beta}_1^*$ from those bootstrap samples for which $\sum(x_j^* - \bar{x}^*)^2$ is close to the original value $\sum(x_j - \bar{x})^2$, shown by the dotted vertical line. If we take the subset between the dashed lines, the estimated variance is closer to that for the wild bootstrap, as shown the values in Table 6.2 and by the Q-Q plot in the right panel of Figure 6.6. This is also true when case 22 is excluded.

The main reason for the large variability of $\sum(x_j^* - \bar{x}^*)^2$ is that case 22 has high leverage, as its position at the bottom left of Figure 6.4 shows. Figure 6.6 shows that it has a substantial effect on the precision of the slope estimate: the most variable estimates are those where case 22 does not occur, and the least variable those where it occurs two or more times. ■

6.3 Multiple Linear Regression

The extension of the simple linear regression model (6.1) to several explanatory variables is

$$Y_j = \beta_0 x_{j0} + \beta_1 x_{j1} + \cdots + \beta_p x_{jp} + \varepsilon_j, \tag{6.22}$$

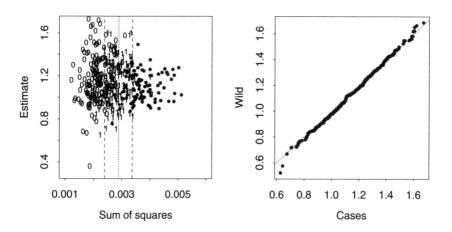

Figure 6.6 Comparison of wild bootstrap and bootstrapping cases for monthly returns data. The left panel shows 200 estimates of slope $\hat{\beta}_1^*$ plotted against sum of squares $\sum(x_j^* - \bar{x}^*)^2$ for case resampling. Resamples where case 22 occurred zero or one times are labelled accordingly. The right panel shows a Q-Q plot of the values of $\hat{\beta}_1^*$ for the wild bootstrap and the subset of the cases lying within the dashed lines in the left panel.

where for models with an intercept $x_{j0} \equiv 1$. In the more convenient vector form the model is

$$Y_j = x_j^T \beta + \varepsilon_j$$

with $x_j^T = (x_{j0}, x_{j1}, \ldots, x_{jp})$. The combined matrix representation for all responses $Y^T = (Y_1, \ldots, Y_n)$ is

$$Y = X\beta + \varepsilon \qquad (6.23)$$

with $X^T = (x_1, \ldots, x_n)$ and $\varepsilon^T = (\varepsilon_1, \ldots, \varepsilon_n)$. As before, the responses Y_j are supposed independent. This general linear model will encompass polynomial and interaction models, by judicious definition of x in terms of primitive variables; for example, we might have $x_{j1} = u_{j1}$ and $x_{j2} = u_{j1}^2$, or $x_{j3} = u_{j1}u_{j2}$, and so forth. When the x_{jk} are dummy variables representing levels of factors, we omit x_{j0} if the intercept is a redundant parameter.

In many respects the bootstrap analysis for multiple regression is an obvious extension of the analysis for simple linear regression in Section 6.2. We again concentrate on least squares model fitting. Particular issues which arise are: (i) testing for the effect of a subset of the explanatory variables, (ii) assessment of predictive accuracy of a fitted model, (iii) the effect of p large relative to n, and (iv) selection of the "best" model by suitable deletion of explanatory variables. In this section we focus on the first two of these, briefly discuss the third, and address variable selection methods in Section 6.4. We begin by outlining the extensions of Sections 6.2.1–6.2.4.

6.3.1 Bootstrapping the least squares fit

The ordinary least squares estimates of β for model (6.23) based on observed response vector y are

$$\hat{\beta} = (X^T X)^{-1} X^T y,$$

and corresponding fitted values are $\hat{\mu} = Hy$ where $H = X(X^T X)^{-1} X^T$ is the "hat" matrix, whose diagonal elements h_{jj} — again denoted by h_j for simplicity — are the leverage values. The raw residuals are $e = (I - H)y$.

Under homoscedasticity the standard formula for the estimated variance of $\hat{\beta}$ is

$$\operatorname{var}(\hat{\beta}) \doteq s^2 (X^T X)^{-1}, \tag{6.24}$$

with s^2 equal to the residual mean square $(n - p - 1)^{-1} e^T e$. The empirical influence values for ordinary least squares estimates are

$$l_j = n(X^T X)^{-1} x_j e_j, \tag{6.25}$$

which give rise to the robust estimate of $\operatorname{var}(\hat{\beta})$,

$$v_L = (X^T X)^{-1} \left(\sum_{j=1}^{n} x_j x_j^T e_j^2 \right) (X^T X)^{-1}; \tag{6.26}$$

see Problem 6.1. These generalize equations (6.13) and (6.14). The variance approximation is improved by using the modified residuals

$$r_j = \frac{e_j}{(1 - h_j)^{1/2}}$$

in place of the e_j, and then v_L generalizes (6.17).

Bootstrap algorithms generalize those in Sections 6.2.3–6.2.4. That is, model-based resampling generates data according to

$$Y_j^* = x_j^T \hat{\beta} + \varepsilon_j^*,$$

where the ε_j^* are randomly sampled from the modified residuals $r_1, \ldots, r_n$, or their centred counterparts $r_j - \bar{r}$. Case resampling operates by randomly resampling cases from the data. Pros and cons of the two methods are the same as before, provided p is small relative to n and the design is far from being singular. The situation where p is large requires special attention.

Large p

Difficulty can arise with both model-based resampling and case resampling if p is very large relative to n. The following theoretical example illustrates an extreme version of the problem.

Example 6.5 (One-way model)   Consider the regression model that corresponds to m independent samples each of size two. If the regression parameters $\beta_1, \ldots, \beta_m$ are the means of the populations sampled, then we omit the intercept term from the model, and the design matrix has $p = m$ columns and $n = 2m$ rows with dummy explanatory variables $x_{2i-1,i} = x_{2i,i} = 1$, $x_{j,i} = 0$ otherwise, $i = 1, \ldots, p$. That is,

$$X = \begin{pmatrix} 1 & 0 & 0 & \cdots & 0 & 0 \\ 1 & 0 & 0 & \cdots & 0 & 0 \\ 0 & 1 & 0 & \cdots & 0 & 0 \\ 0 & 1 & 0 & \cdots & 0 & 0 \\ \vdots & \vdots & \vdots & & \vdots & \vdots \\ 0 & 0 & 0 & \cdots & 0 & 1 \\ 0 & 0 & 0 & \cdots & 0 & 1 \end{pmatrix}.$$

For this model

$$\hat{\beta}_i = \tfrac{1}{2}(y_{2i} + y_{2i-1}), \quad i = 1, \ldots, p,$$

and

$$e_j = (-1)^j \tfrac{1}{2}(y_{2i} - y_{2i-1}), \quad h_j \equiv \tfrac{1}{2}, \quad j = 2i - 1, 2i, \quad i = 1, \ldots, p.$$

The EDF of the residuals, modified or not, could be very unlike the true error distribution: for example, the EDF will always be symmetric.

If the random errors are homoscedastic then the model-based bootstrap will give consistent estimates of bias and standard error for all regression coefficients. However, the bootstrap distributions must be symmetric, and so may be no better than normal approximations if true random errors are skewed. There appears to be no remedy for this. The problem is not so serious for contrasts among the $\hat{\beta}_i$. For example, if $\theta = \beta_1 - \beta_2$ then it is easy to see that $\hat{\theta}$ has a symmetric distribution, as does $\hat{\theta}^*$. The kurtosis is, however, different for $\hat{\theta}$ and $\hat{\theta}^*$; see Problem 6.10.

Case resampling will not work because in those samples where both y_{2i+1} and y_{2i+2} are absent β_i is inestimable: the resample design is singular. The chance of this is 0.48 for $m = 5$ increasing to 0.96 for $m = 20$. This can be fixed by omitting all bootstrap samples where $f_{2i-1}^* + f_{2i}^* = 0$ for any i. The resulting bootstrap variance for $\hat{\beta}_i^*$ consistently overestimates by a factor of about 1.3. Further details are given in Problem 6.9.   ∎

The implication for more general designs is that difficulties will arise with combinations $c^T \hat{\beta}$ where c is in the subspace spanned by those eigenvectors of $X^T X$ corresponding to small eigenvalues. First, model-based resampling will give adequate results for standard error calculations, but bootstrap distributions may not improve on normal approximations in calculating confidence limits for the β_is, or for prediction. Secondly, unconstrained case resampling

Table 6.3 Cement data (Woods, Steinour and Starke, 1932). The response y is the heat (calories per gram of cement) evolved while samples of cement set. The explanatory variables are percentages by weight of four constituents, tricalcium aluminate x_1, tricalcium silicate x_2, tetracalcium alumino ferrite x_3 and dicalcium silicate x_4.

	x_1	x_2	x_3	x_4	y
1	7	26	6	60	78.5
2	1	29	15	52	74.3
3	11	56	8	20	104.3
4	11	31	8	47	87.6
5	7	52	6	33	95.9
6	11	55	9	22	109.2
7	3	71	17	6	102.7
8	1	31	22	44	72.5
9	2	54	18	22	93.1
10	21	47	4	26	115.9
11	1	40	23	34	83.8
12	11	66	9	12	113.3
13	10	68	8	12	109.4

may induce near-collinearity in the design matrix X^*, or equivalently near-singularity in $X^{*T}X^*$, and hence produce grossly inflated bootstrap estimates of some standard errors. One solution would be to reject simulated samples where the smallest eigenvalue ℓ_1^* of $X^{*T}X^*$ is lower than a threshold just below the smallest eigenvalue ℓ_1 of X^TX. An alternative solution, more in line with the general thinking that analysis should be conditioned on X, is to use only those simulated samples corresponding to the middle half of the values of ℓ_1^*. This probably represents the best strategy for getting good confidence limits which are also robust to error heteroscedasticity. The difficulty may be avoided by an appropriate use of principal component regression.

Example 6.6 (Cement data) The data in Table 6.3 are classic in the regression literature as an example of near-collinearity. The four covariates are percentages of constituents which sum to nearly 100: the smallest eigenvalue of X^TX is $\ell_1 = 0.0012$, corresponding to eigenvector $(-1, 0.01, 0.01, 0.01, 0.01)$.

Theoretical and bootstrap standard errors for coefficients are given in Table 6.4. For error resampling the results agree closely with theory, as expected. The bootstrap distributions of $\hat\beta_i^*$ are very normal-looking: the hat matrix H is such that modified residuals r_j would look normal even for very skewed errors ε_j.

Case resampling gives much higher standard errors for coefficients, and the bootstrap distributions are visibly skewed with several outliers. Figure 6.7 shows scatter plots of two bootstrap coefficients versus smallest eigenvalue ℓ_1^* of $X^{*T}X^*$; plots for the other two coefficients are very similar. The variability of $\hat\beta_i^*$ increases substantially for small values of ℓ_1^*, whose reciprocal ranges from $\frac{1}{2}$ to 100 times the reciprocal of ℓ_1. Taking only those bootstrap samples which give the middle 500 values of ℓ_1^* (which are between 0.0005 and 0.0012)

	$\hat{\beta}_0$	$\hat{\beta}_1$	$\hat{\beta}_2$	$\hat{\beta}_3$	$\hat{\beta}_4$
Normal-theory	70.1	0.74	0.72	0.75	0.71
Error resampling, $R = 999$	66.3	0.70	0.69	0.72	0.67
Case resampling, all $R = 999$	108.5	1.13	1.12	1.18	1.11
Case resampling, middle 500	68.4	0.76	0.71	0.78	0.69
Case resampling, largest 800	67.3	0.77	0.69	0.78	0.68

Table 6.4 Standard errors of linear regression coefficients for cement data. Theoretical and error resampling assume homoscedasticity. Resampling results use $R = 999$ samples, but last two rows are based only on those samples with the middle 500 and the largest 800 values of ℓ_1^*.

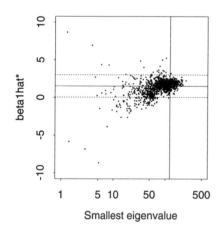
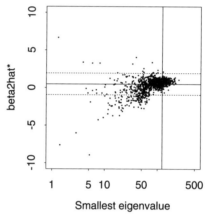

Figure 6.7 Bootstrap regression coefficients $\hat{\beta}_1^*$ and $\hat{\beta}_2^*$ versus smallest eigenvalue ℓ_1^* ($\times 10^{-5}$) of $X^{*T} X^*$ for $R = 999$ resamples of cases from the cement data. The vertical line is the smallest eigenvalue ℓ_1 of $X^T X$, and the horizontal lines show the original coefficients $\pm$ two standard errors.

gives more reasonable standard errors, as seen in the penultimate row of Table 6.4. The last row, corresponding to dropping the smallest 200 values of ℓ_1^*, gives very similar results.   ∎

Weighted least squares

The general discussion extends in a fairly obvious way to weighted least squares estimation, just as in Section 6.2.6 for the case $p = 1$. Suppose that $\text{var}(\varepsilon) = \kappa W^{-1}$ where W is the diagonal matrix of known case weights w_j. Then the weighted least squares estimates are

$$\hat{\beta} = (X^T W X)^{-1} X^T W y, \qquad (6.27)$$

the fitted values are $\hat{\mu} = X\hat{\beta}$, and the residual vector is $e = (I - H)y$, where now the hat matrix H is defined by

$$H = X(X^T W X)^{-1} X^T W, \qquad (6.28)$$

Note that H is not symmetric in general. Some authors prefer to work with the symmetric matrix $X'(X'^T X')^{-1} X'^T$, where $X' = W^{1/2} X$.

whose diagonal elements are the leverage values h_j. The residual vector e has variance $\text{var}(e) = \kappa(I - H)W^{-1}$, whose jth diagonal element is $\kappa(1 - h_j)w_j^{-1}$. So the modified residual is now

$$r_j = \frac{y_j - \hat{\mu}_j}{w_j^{-1/2}(1 - h_j)^{1/2}}. \tag{6.29}$$

Model-based resampling is defined by

$$Y_j^* = x_j^T \hat{\beta} + w_j^{-1/2} \varepsilon_j^*,$$

where ε_j^* is randomly sampled from the centred residuals $r_1 - \bar{r}, \ldots, r_n - \bar{r}$. It is not necessary to estimate κ to apply this algorithm, but if an estimate were required it would be $\hat{\kappa} = (n - p - 1)^{-1} y^T W(I - H)y$.

An important modification of case resampling is that each case must now include its weight w in addition to the response y and explanatory variables x.

6.3.2 Significance tests

Significance tests for the single covariate in simple linear regression were described in Section 6.2.5. Among those tests, which should all behave similarly, are the exact permutation test and a related bootstrap test. Here we look at the more usual practical problem, testing for the effect of one or a subset of several covariates. The tests are based on least squares estimates.

Suppose that the linear regression model is partitioned as

$$Y = X\beta + \varepsilon = X_0\alpha + X_1\gamma + \varepsilon,$$

where γ is a vector and we wish to test $H_0 : \gamma = 0$. Initially we assume homoscedastic errors. It would appear that the sufficiency argument which motivates the single-variable permutation test, and makes it exact, no longer applies. But there is a natural extension of that permutation test, and its motivation is clear from the development of bootstrap tests. The basic idea is to subtract out the linear effect of X_0 from both y and X_1, and then to apply the test described in Section 6.2.5 for simple linear regression.

The first step is to fit the null model, that is

$$\hat{\mu}_0 = X_0\hat{\alpha}_0, \quad \hat{\alpha}_0 = (X_0^T X_0)^{-1} X_0^T y.$$

We shall also need the residuals from this fit, which are $e_0 = (I - H_0)y$ with $H_0 = X_0(X_0^T X_0)^{-1} X_0^T$. The test statistic T will be based on the least squares estimate $\hat{\gamma}$ for γ in the full model, which can be expressed as

$$\hat{\gamma} = (X_{1\cdot0}^T X_{1\cdot0})^{-1} X_{1\cdot0}^T e_0$$

with $X_{1\cdot0} = (I - H_0)X_1$. The extension of the earlier permutation test is equivalent to applying the permutation test to "responses" e_0 and explanatory variables $X_{1 \cdot 0}$.

In the permutation-type test and its bootstrap analogue, we simulate data from the null model, assuming homoscedasticity; that is

$$y^* = \hat{\mu}_0 + \varepsilon_0^*,$$

where the components of the simulated error vector ε_0^* are sampled without (permutation) or with (bootstrap) replacement from the n residuals in e_0. Note that this makes use of the assumed homoscedasticity of errors. Each case keeps its original covariate values, which is to say that $X^* = X$. With the simulated data we regress y^* on X to calculate $\hat{\gamma}^*$ and hence the simulated test statistic t^*, as described below. When this is repeated R times, the bootstrap P-value is

$$\frac{\#\{t_r^* \geq t\} + 1}{R + 1}.$$

The permutation version of the test is not exact when nuisance covariates X_1 are present, but empirical evidence suggests that it is close to exact.

Scalar γ

What should t be? For testing a single component, so that γ is a scalar, suppose that the alternative hypothesis is one-sided, say $H_A : \gamma > 0$. Then we could take t to be $\hat{\gamma}$ itself, or possibly a studentized form such as $z_0 = \hat{\gamma}/v_0^{1/2}$, where v_0 is an appropriate estimate of the variance of $\hat{\gamma}$. If we compute the standard error using the null model residual sum of squares, then

$$v_0 = (n - q)^{-1} e_0^T e_0 (X_{1 \cdot 0}^T X_{1 \cdot 0})^{-1},$$

where q is the rank of X_0. The same formula is applied to every simulated sample to get v_0^* and hence $z^* = \hat{\gamma}^*/v_0^{*1/2}$.

When there are no nuisance covariates X_0, $v_0^* \equiv v_0$ in the permutation test, and studentizing has no effect: the same is true if the non-null standard error is used. Empirical evidence suggests that this is approximately true when X_0 is present; see the example below. Studentizing is necessary if modified residuals are used, with standardization based on the null model hat matrix.

An alternative bootstrap test can be developed in terms of a pivot, as described for single-variable regression in Section 6.2.5. Here the idea is to treat $Z = (\hat{\gamma} - \gamma)/V^{1/2}$ as a pivot, with $V^{1/2}$ an appropriate standard error. Bootstrap simulation under the full fitted model then produces the R replicates of z^* which we use to calculate the P-value. To elaborate, we first fit the full model $\hat{\mu} = X\hat{\beta}$ by least squares and calculate the residuals $e = y - \hat{\mu}$. Still assuming homoscedasticity, the standard error for $\hat{\gamma}$ is calculated using the residual mean square — a simple formula is

$$v = (n - p - 1)^{-1} e^T e (X_{1 \cdot 0}^T X_{1 \cdot 0})^{-1}.$$

Next, datasets are simulated using the model

$$y^* = X\hat{\beta} + \varepsilon^*, \quad X^* = X,$$

where the n errors in ε^* are sampled independently with replacement from the residuals e or modified versions of these. The full regression of y^* on X is then fitted, from which we obtain $\hat{\gamma}^*$ and its estimated variance v^*, these being used to calculate $z^* = (\hat{\gamma}^* - \hat{\gamma})/v^{*1/2}$. From R repeats of this simulation we then have the one-sided P-value

$$p = \frac{\#\{z_r^* \geq z_0\} + 1}{R + 1},$$

where $z_0 = \hat{\gamma}/v^{1/2}$. Although here we use p to denote a P-value as well as the number of covariates, no confusion should arise.

This test procedure is the same as calculating a $(1 - \alpha)$ lower confidence limit for γ by the studentized bootstrap method, and inferring $p < \alpha$ if the lower limit is above zero. The corresponding two-sided P-value is less than 2α if the equi-tailed $(1 - 2\alpha)$ studentized bootstrap confidence interval does not include zero.

One can guard against the effects of heteroscedastic errors by using case resampling to do the simulation, and by using a robust standard error for $\hat{\gamma}$ as described in Section 6.2.5. Also the same basic procedure can be applied to estimates other than least squares.

Example 6.7 (Rock data) The data in Table 6.5 are measurements on four cross-sections of each of 12 oil-bearing rocks, taken from two sites. The aim is to predict permeability from the other three measurements, which result from a complex image-analysis procedure. In all regression models we use logarithm of permeability as response y. The question we focus on here is whether the coefficient of shape is significant in a multiple linear regression on all three variables.

The problem is nonstandard in that there are four replicates of the explanatory variables for each response value. If we fit a linear regression to all 48 cases treating them as independent, strong correlation among the four residuals for each core sample is evident: see Figure 6.8, in which the residuals have unit variance.

Under a plausible model which accounts for this, which we discuss in Example 6.9, the appropriate linear regression for testing purposes uses core averages of the explanatory variables. Thus if we represent the data as responses y_j and replicate vectors of the explanatory variables x_{jk}, $k = 1, 2, 3, 4$, then the model for our analysis is

$$y_j = \bar{x}_{j.}^T \beta + \varepsilon_j,$$

where the ε_j are independent. A summary of the least squares regression

case	area	perimeter	shape	permeability
1	4990	2792	0.09	6.3
2	7002	3893	0.15	6.3
3	7558	3931	0.18	6.3
4	7352	3869	0.12	6.3
5	7943	3949	0.12	17.1
6	7979	4010	0.17	17.1
7	9333	4346	0.19	17.1
8	8209	4345	0.16	17.1
9	8393	3682	0.20	119.0
10	6425	3099	0.16	119.0
11	9364	4480	0.15	119.0
12	8624	3986	0.15	119.0
13	10651	4037	0.23	82.4
14	8868	3518	0.23	82.4
15	9417	3999	0.17	82.4
16	8874	3629	0.15	82.4
17	10962	4609	0.20	58.6
18	10743	4788	0.26	58.6
19	11878	4864	0.20	58.6
20	9867	4479	0.14	58.6
21	7838	3429	0.11	142.0
22	11876	4353	0.29	142.0
23	12212	4698	0.24	142.0
24	8233	3518	0.16	142.0
25	6360	1977	0.28	740.0
26	4193	1379	0.18	740.0
27	7416	1916	0.19	740.0
28	5246	1585	0.13	740.0
29	6509	1851	0.23	890.0
30	4895	1240	0.34	890.0
31	6775	1728	0.31	890.0
32	7894	1461	0.28	890.0
33	5980	1427	0.20	950.0
34	5318	991	0.33	950.0
35	7392	1351	0.15	950.0
36	7894	1461	0.28	950.0
37	3469	1377	0.18	100.0
38	1468	476	0.44	100.0
39	3524	1189	0.16	100.0
40	5267	1645	0.25	100.0
41	5048	942	0.33	1300.0
42	1016	309	0.23	1300.0
43	5605	1146	0.46	1300.0
44	8793	2280	0.42	1300.0
45	3475	1174	0.20	580.0
46	1651	598	0.26	580.0
47	5514	1456	0.18	580.0
48	9718	1486	0.20	580.0

Table 6.5 Rock data (Katz, 1995; Venables and Ripley, 1994, p. 251). These are measurements on four cross-sections of 12 core samples, with permeability (milli-Darcies), area (of pore space, in pixels out of 256×256), perimeter (pixels), and shape (perimeter/area)$^{1/2}$.

Figure 6.8 Rock data: standardized residuals from linear regression of all 48 cases, showing strong intra-core correlations.

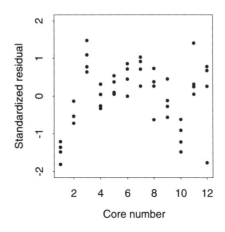

Table 6.6 Least squares results for multiple linear regression of rock data, all covariates included and core means used as response variable.

Variable	Coefficient	SE	t-value
intercept	3.465	1.391	2.49
area $(\times 10^{-3})$	0.864	0.211	4.09
peri $(\times 10^{-3})$	−1.990	0.400	−4.98
shape	3.518	4.838	0.73

is shown in Table 6.6. There is evidence of mild non-normality, but not heteroscedasticity of errors.

Figure 6.9 shows results from both the null model resampling method and the full model pivot resampling method, in both cases using resampling of errors. The observed value of z is $z_0 = 0.73$, for which the one-sided P-value is 0.234 under the first method, and 0.239 under the second method. Thus shape should not be included in the linear regression, assuming that its effect would be linear. Note that $R = 99$ simulations would have been sufficient here. ∎

Vector γ

For testing several components simultaneously, we take the test statistic to be the quadratic form

$$T = \hat{\gamma}^T (X_{1\cdot 0}^T X_{1\cdot 0}) \hat{\gamma},$$

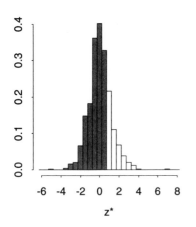 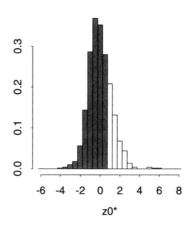

Figure 6.9 Resampling distributions of standardized test statistic for variable shape. Left: resampling z under null model, $R = 999$. Right: resampling pivot under full model, $R = 999$.

or equivalently the difference in residual sums of squares for the null and full model least squares fits. This can be standardized to

$$Z = \frac{n-q}{q} \times \frac{RSS_0 - RSS}{RSS_0},$$

where RSS_0 and RSS denote residual sums of squares under the null model and full model respectively.

We can apply the pivot method with full model simulation here also, using $Z = (\hat{\gamma} - \gamma)^T (X_{1\cdot 0}^T X_{1\cdot 0})(\hat{\gamma} - \gamma)/S^2$ with S^2 the residual mean square. The test statistic value is $z_0 = \hat{\gamma}^T(X_{1\cdot 0}^T X_{1\cdot 0})\hat{\gamma}/s^2$, for which the P-value is given by

$$\frac{\#\{z_r^* \geq z_0\} + 1}{R + 1}.$$

This would be equivalent to rejecting H_0 at level α if the $1 - \alpha$ confidence set for γ does not include the point $\gamma = 0$. Again, case resampling would provide protection against heteroscedasticity: z would then require a robust standard error.

6.3.3 Prediction

A fitted linear regression is often used for prediction of a new individual response Y_+ when the explanatory variable vector is equal to x_+. Then we shall want to supplement our predicted value by a prediction interval. Confidence limits for the mean response $x_+^T \beta$ can be found using the same resampling as is used to get confidence limits for individual coefficients, but limits for the response Y_+ itself — usually called prediction limits — require additional resampling to simulate the variation of Y_+ about $x_+^T \beta$.

The quantity to be predicted is $Y_+ = x_+^T \beta + \varepsilon_+$, say, and the point predictor is $\hat{Y}_+ = x_+^T \hat{\beta}$. The random error ε_+ is assumed to be independent of the random errors $\varepsilon_1, \ldots, \varepsilon_n$ in the observed responses, and for simplicity we assume that they all come from the same distribution: in particular the errors have equal variances.

To assess the accuracy of the point predictor, we can estimate the distribution of the prediction error

$$\delta = \hat{Y}_+ - Y_+ = x_+^T \hat{\beta} - (x_+^T \beta + \varepsilon_+)$$

by the distribution of

$$\delta^* = x_+^T \hat{\beta}^* - (x_+^T \hat{\beta} + \varepsilon_+^*), \qquad (6.30)$$

where ε_+^* is sampled from $\hat{G}$ and $\hat{\beta}^*$ is a simulated vector of estimates from the model-based resampling algorithm. This assumes homoscedasticity of random error. Unconditional properties of the prediction error correspond to averaging over the distributions of both ε_+ and the estimates $\hat{\beta}$, which we do in the simulation by repeating (6.30) for each set of values of $\hat{\beta}^*$. Having obtained the modified residuals r_j from the data fit, the algorithm to generate R sets each with M predictions is as follows.

Algorithm 6.4 (Prediction in linear regression)

For $r = 1, \ldots, R$,

    1 simulate responses y_r^* according to (6.16);

    2 obtain least squares estimates $\hat{\beta}_r^* = (X^T X)^{-1} X^T y_r^*$; then

    3 for $m = 1, \ldots, M$,

          (a) sample $\varepsilon_{+,m}^*$ from $r_1 - \bar{r}, \ldots, r_n - \bar{r}$, and

          (b) compute prediction error $\delta_{rm}^* = x_+^T \hat{\beta}_r^* - (x_+^T \hat{\beta} + \varepsilon_{+,m}^*)$.

                                                                       •

It is acceptable to use $M = 1$ here: the key point is that RM be large enough to estimate the required properties of δ^*. Note that if predictions at several values of x_+ are required, then only the third step of the algorithm needs to be repeated for each x_+.

The mean squared prediction error is estimated by the simulation mean squared error $(RM)^{-1} \sum_{r,m} (\delta_{rm}^* - \bar{\delta}^*)^2$. More useful would be a $(1 - 2\alpha)$ prediction interval for Y_+, for which we need the α and $(1 - \alpha)$ quantiles a_α and $a_{1-\alpha}$, say, of prediction error δ. Then the prediction interval would have limits

$$\hat{y}_+ - a_{1-\alpha}, \quad \hat{y}_+ - a_\alpha.$$

The exact, but unknown, quantiles are estimated by empirical quantiles of the pooled δ^*s, whose ordered values we denote by $\delta^*_{(1)} \leq \cdots \leq \delta^*_{(RM)}$. The bootstrap prediction limits are

$$\hat{y}_+ - \delta^*_{((RM+1)(1-\alpha))}, \quad \hat{y}_+ - \delta^*_{((RM+1)\alpha)}, \tag{6.31}$$

where $\hat{y}_+ = x_+^T \hat{\beta}$. This is analogous to the basic bootstrap method for confidence intervals (Section 5.2).

A somewhat better approach which mimics the standard normal-theory analysis is to work with studentized prediction error

$$Z = \frac{\hat{Y}_+ - Y_+}{S},$$

where S is the square root of residual mean square for the linear regression. The corresponding simulated values are $z^*_{rm} = \delta^*_{rm}/s^*_r$, with s^*_r calculated in step 2 of Algorithm 6.4. The α and $(1-\alpha)$ quantiles of Z are estimated by $z^*_{((RM+1)\alpha)}$ and $z^*_{((RM+1)(1-\alpha))}$ respectively, where $z^*_{(1)} \leq \cdots \leq z^*_{(RM)}$ are the ordered values of all RM z^*s. Then the studentized bootstrap prediction interval for Y_+ is

It is unnecessary to standardize also by the square root of $1 + x_+^T(X^TX)^{-1}x_+$, which would make the variance of Z close to 1, unless bootstrap results for different x_+ are pooled.

$$\hat{y}_+ - sz^*_{((RM+1)(1-\alpha))}, \quad \hat{y}_+ - sz^*_{((RM+1)\alpha)}. \tag{6.32}$$

Example 6.8 (Nuclear power stations)   Table 6.7 contains data on the cost of 32 light water reactors. The cost (in dollars $\times 10^{-6}$ adjusted to a 1976 base) is the response of interest, and the other quantities in the table are explanatory variables; they are described in detail in the data source.

We take log(cost) as the working response y, and fit a linear model with covariates PT, CT, NE, date, log(capacity) and log(N). The dummy variable PT indicates six plants for which there were partial turnkey guarantees, and it is possible that some subsidies may be hidden in their costs.

Suppose that we wish to obtain 95% prediction intervals for the cost of a station like case 32 above, except that its value for date is 73.00. The predicted value of log(cost) from the regression is $x_+^T\hat{\beta} = 6.72$, and the mean squared error from the regression is $s = 0.159$. With $\alpha = 0.025$ and a simulation with $R = 999$ and $M = 1$, $(RM+1)\alpha = 25$ and $(RM+1)(1-\alpha) = 975$. The values of $\delta^*_{(25)}$ and $\delta^*_{(975)}$ are −0.539 and 0.551, so the 95% limits (6.31) are 6.18 and 7.27, which are slightly wider than the normal-theory limits of 6.25 and 7.19. For the limits (6.32) we get $z^*_{(25)} = -3.680$ and $z^*_{(975)} = 3.512$, so the limits for log(cost) are 6.13 and 7.28. The corresponding prediction interval for cost is $[\exp(6.13), \exp(7.28)] = [459.4, 1451]$.

The usual caveats apply about extrapolating a trend outside the range of the data, and we should use these intervals with great caution. ∎

The next example involves an unusual data structure, where there is hierarchical variation in the covariates.

Table 6.7 Data on light water reactors constructed in the USA (Cox and Snell, 1981, p. 81).

	cost	date	T_1	T_2	capacity	PR	NE	CT	BW	N	PT
1	460.05	68.58	14	46	687	0	1	0	0	14	0
2	452.99	67.33	10	73	1065	0	0	1	0	1	0
3	443.22	67.33	10	85	1065	1	0	1	0	1	0
4	652.32	68.00	11	67	1065	0	1	1	0	12	0
5	642.23	68.00	11	78	1065	1	1	1	0	12	0
6	345.39	67.92	13	51	514	0	1	1	0	3	0
7	272.37	68.17	12	50	822	0	0	0	0	5	0
8	317.21	68.42	14	59	457	0	0	0	0	1	0
9	457.12	68.42	15	55	822	1	0	0	0	5	0
10	690.19	68.33	12	71	792	0	1	1	1	2	0
11	350.63	68.58	12	64	560	0	0	0	0	3	0
12	402.59	68.75	13	47	790	0	1	0	0	6	0
13	412.18	68.42	15	62	530	0	0	1	0	2	0
14	495.58	68.92	17	52	1050	0	0	0	0	7	0
15	394.36	68.92	13	65	850	0	0	0	1	16	0
16	423.32	68.42	11	67	778	0	0	0	0	3	0
17	712.27	69.50	18	60	845	0	1	0	0	17	0
18	289.66	68.42	15	76	530	1	0	1	0	2	0
19	881.24	69.17	15	67	1090	0	0	0	0	1	0
20	490.88	68.92	16	59	1050	1	0	0	0	8	0
21	567.79	68.75	11	70	913	0	0	1	1	15	0
22	665.99	70.92	22	57	828	1	1	0	0	20	0
23	621.45	69.67	16	59	786	0	0	1	0	18	0
24	608.80	70.08	19	58	821	1	0	0	0	3	0
25	473.64	70.42	19	44	538	0	0	1	0	19	0
26	697.14	71.08	20	57	1130	0	0	1	0	21	0
27	207.51	67.25	13	63	745	0	0	0	0	8	1
28	288.48	67.17	9	48	821	0	0	1	0	7	1
29	284.88	67.83	12	63	886	0	0	0	1	11	1
30	280.36	67.83	12	71	886	1	0	0	1	11	1
31	217.38	67.25	13	72	745	1	0	0	0	8	1
32	270.71	67.83	7	80	886	1	0	0	1	11	1

Example 6.9 (Rock data)   For the data discussed in Example 6.7, one objective is to see how well one can predict permeability from a single replicate of the three image-based measurements, as opposed to the four replicates obtained in the study. The previous analysis suggested that variable shape did not contribute usefully to a linear regression relationship for the logarithm of permeability, and this is confirmed by cross-validation analysis of prediction errors (Section 6.4.1). So here we concentrate on predicting permeability from the linear regression of $y = \log(\texttt{permeability})$ on area and peri.

In Example 6.7 we commented on the strong intra-core correlation among the explanatory variables, and that must be taken into account here if we are to correctly analyse prediction of core permeability from single measurements of area and peri. One way to do this is to think of the four replicate values of $u = (\texttt{area}, \texttt{peri})^T$ as unbiased estimates of an underlying core variable ξ, on which y has a linear regression. Then the data are modelled by

$$y_j = \alpha + \xi_j^T \gamma + \eta_j, \quad u_{jk} = \xi_j + \delta_{jk}, \tag{6.33}$$

	Method	Variable		
		Intercept	area ($\times 10^{-4}$)	peri ($\times 10^{-4}$)
$K = 1$	Direct regression on x_{jk}s	5.746	5.144	−16.16
	Normal-theory fit	5.694	5.300	−16.39
$K = 4$	Regression on $\bar{x}_j$·s	4.295	9.257	−21.78
	Normal-theory fit	4.295	9.257	−21.78

Table 6.8 Rock data: fits of linear regression models with K replicate values of explanatory variables area and peri. Normal-theory analysis is via model (6.33).

for $j = 1, \ldots, 12$ and $k = 1, \ldots, K$, where η_j and δ_{jk} are uncorrelated errors with zero means, and for our data $K = 4$.

Under normality assumptions on the errors and the ξ_j, the linear regression of y_j on $u_{j1}, \ldots, u_{jK}$ depends only on the core average $\bar{u}_j = K^{-1} \sum_{k=1}^K u_{jk}$. The regression coefficients depend strongly on K. For prediction from a single measurement u_+ we need the model with $K = 1$, and for resampling analysis we shall need the model with $K = 4$. These two versions of the observation regression model we write as

$$y_j = \bar{x}_j^T \beta^{(K)} + \varepsilon_j^{(K)} = \alpha^{(K)} + \bar{u}_j^T \gamma^{(K)} + \varepsilon_j^{(K)}, \tag{6.34}$$

for $K = 1$ and 4; the parameters α and γ in (6.33) correspond to $\alpha^{(K)}$ and $\gamma^{(K)}$ when $K = \infty$. Fortunately it turns out that both observation models can be fitted easily: for $K = 4$ we regress the y_js on the core averages $\bar{u}_j$; and for $K = 1$ we fit linear regression with all 48 individual cases as tabled, ignoring the intra-core correlation among the ε_{jk}s, i.e. pretending that y_j occurs four times independently. Table 6.8 shows the coefficients for both fits, and compares them to corresponding estimates based on exact normal-theory analysis.

Suppose, then, that we want to predict the new response y_+ given a single set of measurements u_+. If we define $x_+^T = (1, u_+^T)$, then the point prediction $\hat{Y}_+$ is $x_+^T \hat{\beta}^{(1)}$, where $\hat{\beta}^{(1)}$ are the coefficients in the fit of model (6.34) with $K = 1$, shown in the first row of Table 6.8. The EDF of the 48 modified residuals r_{jk} from this fit estimates the marginal distribution of the $\varepsilon_j^{(1)}$ in (6.34), and hence of the error ε_+ in

$$Y_+ = x_+^T \beta^{(1)} + \varepsilon_+.$$

Our concern is with the prediction error

$$\delta = \hat{Y}_+ - Y_+ = x_+^T (\hat{\beta}^{(1)} - \beta^{(1)}) - \varepsilon_+, \tag{6.35}$$

whose distribution is to be estimated by resampling.

The question is how to do the resampling, given the presence of intra-core correlation. A resampled dataset must consist of 12 subsets each with 4 replicates u_{jk}^* and a single response y_j^*, from which we shall fit $\hat{\beta}^{(1)*}$. The prediction error (6.35) will then be simulated by

$$\delta^* = \hat{y}_+^* - y_+^* = x_+^T(\hat{\beta}^{(1)*} - \hat{\beta}^{(1)}) - \varepsilon_+^*,$$

where ε_+^* is sampled from the EDF of the 48 modified residuals as mentioned above. It remains to decide how to simulate the data from which we calculate $\hat{\beta}^{(1)*}$.

Usually with error resampling we would fix the covariate values, so here we fix the 12 values of $\bar{u}_j$, which are surrogates for the ξ_js in model (6.33). Then we simulate responses from the fitted regression on these averages, and simulate the replicated measured covariates using an appropriate hierarchical-data algorithm. Specifically we take

$$u_{jk}^* = \bar{u}_j + d_{Jk},$$

where $d_{jk} = u_{jk} - \bar{u}_j$ and J is randomly sampled from $\{1,2,\ldots,12\}$. Our justification for this, in terms of retaining intra-core correlation, is given by the discussion in Section 3.8. It is potentially important to build the variation of u into the analysis. Since $\bar{u}_j^* \equiv \bar{u}_j$, the resampled responses are defined by

$$y_j^* = \bar{x}_j^T \hat{\beta}^{(4)} + \varepsilon_j^{(4)*},$$

where the $\varepsilon_j^{(4)*}$ are randomly sampled from the 12 mean-adjusted, modified residuals $r_j^{(4)} - \bar{r}^{(4)}$ from the regression of the y_js on the $\bar{u}_j$s. The estimates $\hat{\beta}^{(1)*}$ are now obtained by fitting the regression to the 48 simulated cases (u_{jk}^*, y_j^*), $k = 1,\ldots,4$ and $j = 1,\ldots,12$.

Figure 6.10 shows typical normal plots for prediction error $\hat{y}_+^* - y_+^*$, these for $x_+ = (1,4000,1000)$ and $x_+ = (1,10\,000,4000)$ which are near the edge of the observed space, from $R = 999$ resamples and $M = 1$. The skewness of prediction error is quite noticeable. The resampling standard deviations for prediction errors are 0.91 and 0.93, somewhat larger than the theoretical standard deviations 0.88 and 0.87 obtained by treating the 48 cases as independent.

To calculate 95% intervals we set $\alpha = 0.025$, so that $(RM + 1)\alpha = 25$ and $(RM + 1)(1 - \alpha) = 975$. The simulation values $\delta_{(25)}^*$ and $\delta_{(975)}^*$ are -1.63 and 1.93 at $x_+ = (1,4000,1000)$, and -1.57 and 2.19 at $x_+ = (1,10\,000,4000)$. The corresponding point predictions are 6.19 and 4.42, so 95% prediction intervals are $(4.26,7.82)$ at $x_+ = (1,4000,1000)$ and $(2.23,5.99)$ at $x_+ = (1,10\,000,4000)$. These intervals differ markedly from those based on normal theory treating all 48 cases as independent, those being $(4.44,7.94)$ and $(2.68,6.17)$. Much of the difference is due to the skewness of the resampling distribution of prediction error. ∎

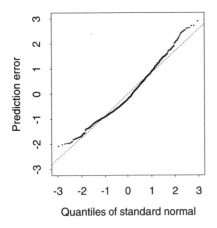
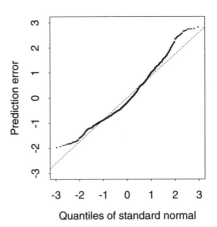

Figure 6.10 Rock data: normal plots of resampled prediction errors for $x_+ = (1, 4000, 1000)$ (left panel) and $x_+ = (1, 10\,000, 4000)$ (right panel), based on $R = 999$ and $M = 1$. Dotted lines correspond to theoretical means and standard deviations.

6.4 Aggregate Prediction Error and Variable Selection

In Section 6.3.3 our discussion of prediction focused on individual cases, and particularly on intervals of uncertainty around point predictions. For some applications, however, we are interested in an aggregate measure of prediction error — such as average squared error or misclassification error — which summarizes accuracy of prediction across a range of values of the covariates, using a given regression model. Such a measure may be of interest in its own right, or as the basis for comparing alternative regression models. In the first part of this section we outline the main resampling methods for estimating aggregate prediction error, and in the second part we discuss the closely related problem of variable selection for linear regression models.

6.4.1 Aggregate prediction error

The least squares fit of the linear regression model (6.22) provides the least squares *prediction rule* $\hat{y}_+ = x_+^T \hat{\beta}$ for predicting what a single response y_+ would be at value x_+ of the vector of covariates. What we want to know is how accurate this prediction rule will be for predicting data similar to those already observed. Suppose first that we measure accuracy of prediction by squared error $(y_+ - \hat{y}_+)^2$, and that our interest is in predictions for covariate values that exactly duplicate the data values $x_1, \ldots, x_n$. Then the *aggregate prediction error* is

$$D = n^{-1} \sum_{j=1}^{n} \mathrm{E}(Y_{+j} - x_j^T \hat{\beta})^2,$$

in which $\hat{\beta}$ is fixed and the expectation is over $Y_{+j} = x_j^T \beta + \varepsilon_{+j}$. We cannot calculate D exactly, because the model parameters are unknown, so we must settle for an estimate — which in reality is an estimate of $\Delta = \mathrm{E}(D)$, the average over all possible samples of size n. Our objective is to estimate D or Δ as accurately as possible.

As stated the problem is quite simple, at least under the ideal conditions where the linear model is correct and the error variance is constant, for then

X is the $n \times q$ matrix with rows $x_1^T, \ldots, x_n^T$, where $q = p + 1$ if there are p covariate terms and an intercept in the model.

$$
\begin{aligned}
D &= n^{-1} \sum \mathrm{var}(Y_{+j}) + n^{-1} \sum (x_j^T \beta - x_j^T \hat{\beta})^2 \\
&= \sigma^2 + n^{-1} (\hat{\beta} - \beta)^T X^T X (\hat{\beta} - \beta),
\end{aligned}
\tag{6.36}
$$

whose expectation is

$$
\Delta = \sigma^2 (1 + qn^{-1}),
\tag{6.37}
$$

where $q = p + 1$ is the number of regression coefficients. Since the residual mean square s^2 is an unbiased estimate for σ^2, we have the natural estimate

$$
\hat{\Delta} = s^2 (1 + qn^{-1}).
\tag{6.38}
$$

However, this estimate is very specialized, in two ways. First, it assumes that the linear model is correct and that error variance is constant, both unlikely to be exactly true in practice. Secondly, the estimate applies only to least squares prediction and the squared error measure of accuracy, whereas in practice we need to be able to deal with other measures of accuracy and other prediction rules — such as robust linear regression (Section 6.5) and linear classification, where y is binary (Section 7.2). There are no simple analogues of (6.38) to cover these situations, but resampling methods can be applied to all of them.

In order that our discussion apply as broadly as possible, we shall use general notation in which prediction error is measured by $c(y_+, \hat{y}_+)$, typically an increasing function of $|y_+ - \hat{y}_+|$, and the prediction rule is $\hat{y}_+ = \mu(x_+, \hat{F})$, where the EDF $\hat{F}$ represents the observed data. Usually $\mu(x_+, \hat{F})$ is an estimate of the mean response at x_+, a function of $x_+^T \hat{\beta}$ with $\hat{\beta}$ an estimate of β, and the form of this prediction rule is closely tied to the form of $c(y_+, \hat{y}_+)$. We suppose that the data $\hat{F}$ are sampled from distribution F, from which the cases to be predicted are also sampled. This implies that we are considering x_+ values similar to data values $x_1, \ldots, x_n$. Prediction accuracy is measured by the *aggregate prediction error*

$$
D \equiv D(F, \hat{F}) = \mathrm{E}_+ [c\{Y_+, \mu(X_+, \hat{F})\} \mid \hat{F}],
\tag{6.39}
$$

where E_+ emphasizes that we are averaging only over the distribution of (X_+, Y_+), with data fixed. Because F is unknown, D cannot be calculated, and so we look for accurate methods of estimating it, or rather its expectation

$$
\Delta \equiv \Delta(F) = \mathrm{E}\{D(F, \hat{F})\},
\tag{6.40}
$$

the average prediction accuracy over all possible datasets of size n sampled from F.

The most direct approach to estimation of Δ is to apply the bootstrap substitution principle, that is substituting the EDF $\hat{F}$ for F in (6.40). However, there are other widely used resampling methods which also merit consideration, in part because they are easy to use, and in fact the best approach involves a combination of methods.

Apparent error

The simplest way to estimate D or Δ is to take the average prediction error when the prediction rule is applied to the same data that was used to fit it. This gives the *apparent error*, sometimes called the *resubstitution error*,

$$\hat{\Delta}_{app} = D(\hat{F}, \hat{F}) = n^{-1} \sum_{j=1}^{n} c\{y_j, \mu(x_j, \hat{F})\}. \tag{6.41}$$

This is not the same as the bootstrap estimate $\Delta(\hat{F})$, which we discuss later.

It is intuitively clear that $\hat{\Delta}_{app}$ will tend to underestimate Δ, because the latter refers to prediction of new responses. The underestimation can be easily checked for least squares prediction with squared error, when $\hat{\Delta}_{app} = n^{-1}RSS$, the average squared residual. If the model is correct with homoscedastic random errors, then $\hat{\Delta}_{app}$ has expectation $\sigma^2(1 - qn^{-1})$, whereas from (6.37) we know that $\Delta = \sigma^2(1 + qn^{-1})$.

The difference between the true error and apparent error is the excess error, $D(F, \hat{F}) - D(\hat{F}, \hat{F})$, whose mean is the *expected excess error*,

$$e(F) = \mathrm{E}\{D(F, \hat{F}) - D(\hat{F}, \hat{F})\} = \Delta(F) - \mathrm{E}\{D(\hat{F}, \hat{F})\}, \tag{6.42}$$

where the expectation is taken over possible datasets $\hat{F}$. For squared error and least squares prediction the results in the previous paragraph show that $e(F) = 2qn^{-1}\sigma^2$. The quantity $e(F)$ is akin to a bias and can be estimated by resampling, so the apparent error can be modified to a reasonable estimate, as we see below.

Cross-validation

The apparent error is downwardly biased because it averages errors of predictions for cases at zero distance from the data used to fit the prediction rule. Cross-validation estimates of aggregate error avoid this bias by separating the data used to form the prediction rule and the data used to assess the rule. The general paradigm is to split the dataset into a *training set* $\{(x_j, y_j) : j \in S_t\}$ and a separate *assessment set* $\{(x_j, y_j) : j \in S_a\}$, represented by $\hat{F}_t$ and $\hat{F}_a$, say. The linear regression predictor is fitted to $\hat{F}_t$, used to predict responses y_j for

$j \in S_a$, and then Δ is estimated by

$$D(\hat{F}_a, \hat{F}_t) = n_a^{-1} \sum_{j \in S_a} c\{y_j, \mu(x_j, \hat{F}_t)\}, \tag{6.43}$$

with n_a the size of S_a. There are several variations on this estimate, depending on the size of the training set, the manner of splitting the dataset, and the number of such splits.

The version of cross-validation that seems to come closest to actual use of our predictor is *leave-one-out cross-validation*. Here training sets of size $n-1$ are taken, and all such sets are used, so we measure how well the prediction rule does when the value of each response is predicted from the rest of the data. If $\hat{F}_{-j}$ represents the $n-1$ observations $\{(x_k, y_k), k \neq j\}$, and if $\mu(x_j, \hat{F}_{-j})$ denotes the value predicted for y_j by the rule based on $\hat{F}_{-j}$, then the *cross-validation estimate of prediction error* is

$$\hat{\Delta}_{CV} = n^{-1} \sum_{j=1}^{n} c\{y_j, \mu(x_j, \hat{F}_{-j})\}, \tag{6.44}$$

which is the average error when each observation is predicted from the rest of the sample.

In general (6.44) requires n fits of the model, but for least squares linear regression only one fit is required if we use the case-deletion result (Problem 6.2)

$$\hat{\beta} - \hat{\beta}_{-j} = (X^T X)^{-1} x_j \frac{y_j - x_j^T \hat{\beta}}{1 - h_j},$$

where as usual h_j is the leverage for the jth case. For squared error in particular we then have

$$\hat{\Delta}_{CV} = n^{-1} \sum_{j=1}^{n} \frac{(y_j - x_j^T \hat{\beta})^2}{(1 - h_j)^2}. \tag{6.45}$$

From the nature of $\hat{\Delta}_{CV}$ one would guess that this estimate has only a small bias, and this is so: assuming an expansion of the form $\Delta(F) = a_0 + a_1 n^{-1} + a_2 n^{-2} + \cdots$, one can verify from (6.44) that $E(\hat{\Delta}_{CV}) = a_0 + a_1 (n-1)^{-1} + \cdots$, which differs from Δ by terms of order n^{-2} — unlike the expectation of the apparent error which differs by terms of order n^{-1}.

K-fold cross-validation

In general there is no reason that training sets should be of size $n-1$. For certain methods of estimation the number n of fits required for $\hat{\Delta}_{CV}$ could itself be a difficulty — although not for least squares, as we have seen in (6.45). There is also the possibility that the small perturbations in fitted model when single observations are left out makes $\hat{\Delta}_{CV}$ too variable, if fitted values $\mu(x, \hat{F})$ do not depend smoothly on $\hat{F}$ or if $c(y_+, \hat{y}_+)$ is not continuous. These potential problems can be avoided to a large extent by leaving out groups of observations, rather than single observations. There is more than one way to do this.

One obvious implementation of group cross-validation is to repeat (6.43) for a series of R different splits into training and assessment sets, keeping the size of the assessment set fixed at $n_a = m$, say. Then in a fairly obvious notation the estimate of aggregate prediction error would be

$$\hat{\Delta}_{CV} = R^{-1} \sum_{r=1}^{R} m^{-1} \sum_{j \in S_{a,r}} c\{y_j, \mu(x_j, \hat{F}_{t,r})\}. \qquad (6.46)$$

In principle there are $\binom{n}{m}$ possible splits, possibly an extremely large number, but it should be adequate to take R in the range 100 to 1000. It would be in the spirit of resampling to make the splits at random. However, consideration should be given to balancing the splits in some way — for example, it would seem desirable that each case should occur with equal frequency over the R assessment sets; see Section 9.2. Depending on the value of $n_t = n - m$ and the number p of explanatory variables, one might also need some form of balance to ensure that the model can always be fitted.

There is an efficient version of group cross-validation that does involve just one prediction of each response. We begin by splitting the data into K disjoint sets of nearly equal size, with the corresponding sets of case subscripts denoted by $C_1, \ldots, C_K$, say. These K sets define $R = K$ different splits into training and assessment sets, with $S_{a,k} = C_k$ the kth assessment set and the remainder of the data $S_{t,k} = \bigcup_{i \neq k} C_i$ the kth training set. For each such split we apply (6.43), and then average these estimates. The result is the K-fold cross-validation estimate of prediction error

$$\hat{\Delta}_{CV,K} = n^{-1} \sum_{j=1}^{n} c\{y_j, \mu(x_j, \hat{F}_{-k(j)})\}, \qquad (6.47)$$

where $\hat{F}_{-k(j)}$ represents the data from which the group containing the jth case has been deleted. Note that $\hat{\Delta}_{CV,K}$ is equal to the leave-one-out estimate (6.44) when $K = n$. Calculation of (6.47) requires just K model fits. Practical experience suggests that a good strategy is to take $K = \min\{n^{1/2}, 10\}$, on the grounds that taking $K > 10$ may be too computationally intensive when the prediction rule is complicated, while taking groups of size at least $n^{1/2}$ should perturb the data sufficiently to give small variance of the estimate.

The use of groups will have the desired effect of reducing variance, but at the cost of increasing bias. For example, it can be seen from the expansion used earlier for Δ that the bias of $\hat{\Delta}_{CV,K}$ is $a_1\{n(K-1)\}^{-1} + \cdots$, which could be substantial if K is small, unless n is very large. Fortunately the bias of $\hat{\Delta}_{CV,K}$ can be reduced by a simple adjustment. In a harmless abuse of notation, let

If $n/K = m$ is an integer, then all groups are of size m and $p_k \equiv 1/K$.

$\hat{F}_{-k}$ denote the data with the kth group omitted, for $k = 1, \ldots, K$, and let p_k denote the proportion of the data falling in the kth group. The *adjusted cross-validation estimate* of aggregate prediction error is

$$\hat{\Delta}_{ACV,K} = \hat{\Delta}_{CV,K} + D(\hat{F}, \hat{F}) - \sum_{k=1}^{K} p_k D(\hat{F}, \hat{F}_{-k}). \tag{6.48}$$

This has smaller bias than $\hat{\Delta}_{CV,K}$ and is almost as simple to calculate, because it requires no additional fits of the model. For a comparison between $\hat{\Delta}_{CV,K}$ and $\hat{\Delta}_{ACV,K}$ in a simple situation, see Problem 6.12.

The following algorithm summarizes the calculation of $\hat{\Delta}_{ACV,K}$ when the split into groups is made at random.

Algorithm 6.5 (K-fold adjusted cross-validation)

1 Fit the regression model to all cases, calculate predictions $\hat{y}_j$ from that model, and average the values of $c(y_j, \hat{y}_j)$ to get D.

2 Choose group sizes $m_1, \ldots, m_K$ such that $m_1 + \cdots + m_K = n$.

3 For $k = 1, \ldots, K$,

    (*a*) choose C_k by sampling m_k times without replacement from $\{1, 2, \ldots, n\}$ minus elements chosen for previous C_is;

    (*b*) fit the regression model to all data except cases $j \in C_k$;

    (*c*) calculate new predictions $\hat{y}_j = \mu(x_j, \hat{F}_{-k})$ for $j \in C_k$;

    (*d*) calculate predictions $\hat{y}_{kj} = \mu(x_j, \hat{F}_{-k})$ for all j; then

    (*e*) average the n values $c(y_j, \hat{y}_{kj})$ to give $D(\hat{F}, \hat{F}_{-k})$.

4 Average the n values of $c(y_j, \hat{y}_j)$ using $\hat{y}_j$ from step 3(c) to give $\hat{\Delta}_{CV,K}$.

5 Calculate $\hat{\Delta}_{ACV,K}$ as in (6.48) with $p_k = m_k/n$.

                                                                                                 •

Bootstrap estimates

A direct application of the bootstrap principle to $\Delta(F)$ gives the estimate

$$\hat{\Delta} = \Delta(\hat{F}) = E^* \{D(\hat{F}, \hat{F}^*)\},$$

where $\hat{F}^*$ denotes a simulated sample $(x_1^*, y_1^*), \ldots, (x_n^*, y_n^*)$ taken from the data by case resampling. Usually simulation is required to approximate this estimate, as follows. For $r = 1, \ldots, R$ we randomly resample cases from the data to obtain the sample $(x_{r1}^*, y_{r1}^*), \ldots, (x_{rn}^*, y_{rn}^*)$, which we represent by $\hat{F}_r^*$, and to this sample we fit the prediction rule and calculate its predictions $\mu(x_j, \hat{F}_r^*)$ of the data responses y_j for $j = 1, \ldots, n$. The aggregate prediction error estimate is then calculated as

$$R^{-1} \sum_{r=1}^{R} n^{-1} \sum_{j=1}^{n} c\{y_j, \mu(x_j, \hat{F}_r^*)\}. \tag{6.49}$$

Intuitively this bootstrap estimate is less satisfactory than cross-validation, because the simulated dataset $\hat{F}_r^*$ used to calculate the prediction rule is part of the data $\hat{F}$ used for assessment of prediction error. In this sense the estimate is a hybrid of the apparent error estimate and a cross-validation estimate, a point to which we return shortly.

As we have noted in previous chapters, care is often needed in choosing what to bootstrap. Here, an approach which works better is to use the bootstrap to estimate the expected excess error $e(F)$ defined in (6.42), which is the bias of the apparent error $\hat{\Delta}_{app}$, and to add this estimate to $\hat{\Delta}_{app}$. In theory the bootstrap estimate of $e(F)$ is

$$e(\hat{F}) = \mathrm{E}^*\{D(\hat{F}, \hat{F}^*) - D(\hat{F}^*, \hat{F}^*)\},$$

and its approximation from the simulations described in the previous paragraph defines the *bootstrap estimate of expected excess error*

$$\hat{e}_B = R^{-1} \sum_{r=1}^{R} \left[n^{-1} \sum_{j=1}^{n} c\{y_j, \mu(x_j, \hat{F}_r^*)\} - n^{-1} \sum_{j=1}^{n} c\{y_{rj}^*, \mu(x_{rj}^*, \hat{F}_r^*)\} \right]. \quad (6.50)$$

That is, for the rth bootstrap sample we construct the prediction rule $\mu(x, \hat{F}_r^*)$, then calculate the average difference between the prediction errors when this rule is applied first to the original data and secondly to the bootstrap sample itself, and finally average across bootstrap samples. We refer to the resulting estimate of aggregate prediction error, $\hat{\Delta}_B = \hat{e}_B + \hat{\Delta}_{app}$, as the *bootstrap estimate of prediction error*, given by

$$n^{-1} \sum_{j=1}^{n} R^{-1} \sum_{r=1}^{R} c\{y_j, \mu(x_j, \hat{F}_r^*)\} - R^{-1} \sum_{r=1}^{R} D(\hat{F}_r^*, \hat{F}_r^*) + D(\hat{F}, \hat{F}). \quad (6.51)$$

Note that the first term of (6.51), which is also the simple bootstrap estimate (6.49), is expressed as the average of the contributions $R^{-1} \sum_{r=1}^{R} c\{y_j, \mu(x_j, \hat{F}_r^*)\}$ that each original observation makes to the estimate of aggregate prediction error. These contributions are of interest in their own right, most importantly in assessing how the performance of the prediction rule changes with values of the explanatory variables. This is illustrated in Example 6.10 below.

Hybrid bootstrap estimates

It is useful to observe that the naive estimate (6.49), which is also the first term of (6.51), can be broken into two qualitatively different parts,

$$n^{-1} \sum_{j=1}^{n} \left(\frac{R_{-j}}{R} \right) \frac{1}{R_{-j}} \sum_{r:j \text{ out}} c\{y_j, \mu(x_j, \hat{F}_r^*)\} \quad (6.52)$$

and

$$n^{-1} \sum_{j=1}^{n} \left(\frac{R - R_{-j}}{R} \right) \frac{1}{R - R_{-j}} \sum_{r:j \text{ in}} c\{y_j, \mu(x_j, \hat{F}_r^*)\}, \tag{6.53}$$

where R_{-j} is the number of the R bootstrap samples $\hat{F}_r^*$ in which (x_j, y_j) does not appear. In (6.52) y_j is always predicted using data from which (x_j, y_j) is excluded, which is analogous to cross-validation, whereas (6.53) is similar to an apparent error calculation because y_j is always predicted using data that contain (x_j, y_j).

Now R_{-j}/R is approximately equal to the constant $e^{-1} \doteq 0.368$, so (6.52) is approximately proportional to

$$\hat{\Delta}_{BCV} = n^{-1} \sum_{j=1}^{n} \frac{1}{R_{-j}} \sum_{r:j \text{ out}} c\{y_j, \mu(x_j, \hat{F}_r^*)\}, \tag{6.54}$$

sometimes called the *leave-one-out bootstrap estimate of prediction error*. The notation refers to the fact that $\hat{\Delta}_{BCV}$ can be viewed as a bootstrap smoothing of the cross-validation estimate $\hat{\Delta}_{CV}$. To see this, consider replacing the term $c\{y_j, \mu(x_j, \hat{F}_{-j})\}$ in (6.44) by the expectation $\mathrm{E}_{-j}^*[c\{y_j, \mu(x_j, \hat{F}^*)\}]$, where E_{-j}^* refers to the expectation over bootstrap samples $\hat{F}^*$ of size n drawn from $\hat{F}_{-j}$. The estimate (6.54) is a simulation approximation of this expectation, because of the result noted in Section 3.10.1 that the R_{-j} bootstrap samples in which case j does not appear are equivalent to random samples drawn from $\hat{F}_{-j}$.

The smoothing in (6.54) may effect a considerable reduction in variance, compared to $\hat{\Delta}_{CV}$, especially if $c(y_+, \hat{y}_+)$ is not continuous. But there will also be a tendency toward positive bias. This is because the typical bootstrap sample from which predictions are made in (6.54) includes only about $(1 - e^{-1})n \doteq 0.632n$ distinct data values, and the bias of cross-validation estimates increases as the size of the training set decreases.

What we have so far is that the bootstrap estimate of aggregate prediction error essentially involves a weighted combination of $\hat{\Delta}_{BCV}$ and an apparent error estimate. Such a combination should have good variance properties, but may suffer from bias. However, if we change the weights in the combination it may be possible to reduce or remove this bias. This suggests that we consider the hybrid estimate

$$\hat{\Delta}_w = w\hat{\Delta}_{BCV} + (1 - w)\hat{\Delta}_{app}, \tag{6.55}$$

and then select w to make the bias as small as possible, ideally $\mathrm{E}(\hat{\Delta}_w) = \Delta + O(n^{-2})$.

Not unexpectedly it is difficult to calculate $\mathrm{E}(\hat{\Delta}_w)$ in general, but for quadratic error and least squares prediction it is relatively easy. We already know that the apparent error estimate has expectation $\sigma^2(1 - qn^{-1})$, and that the true

Apparent			K-fold (adjusted) cross-validation			
error	Bootstrap	0.632	32	16	10	6
2.0	3.2	3.5	3.6	3.7 (3.7)	3.8 (3.7)	4.4 (4.2)

Table 6.9 Estimates of aggregate prediction error ($\times 10^{-2}$) for data on nuclear power plants. Results for adjusted cross-validation are shown in parentheses.

aggregate error is $\Delta = \sigma^2(1 + qn^{-1})$. It remains only to calculate $E(\hat{\Delta}_{BCV})$, where here

$$\hat{\Delta}_{BCV} = n^{-1} \sum_{j=1}^{n} E^*_{-j}(y_j - x_j^T \hat{\beta}^*_{-j})^2,$$

with $\hat{\beta}^*_{-j}$ the least squares estimate of β from a bootstrap sample with the jth case excluded. A rather lengthy calculation (Problem 6.13) shows that

$$E(\hat{\Delta}_{BCV}) = \sigma^2(1 + 2qn^{-1}) + O(n^{-2}),$$

from which it follows that

$$E\{w\hat{\Delta}_{BCV} + (1 - w)\hat{\Delta}_{app}\} = \sigma^2(1 + 3wqn^{-1}) + O(n^{-2}),$$

which agrees with Δ to terms of order n^{-1} if $w = 2/3$.

It seems impossible to find an optimal choice of w for general measures of prediction error and general prediction rules, but detailed calculations do suggest that $w = 1 - e^{-1} = 0.632$ is a good choice. Heuristically this value for w is equivalent to an adjustment for the below-average distance between cases and bootstrap samples without them, compared to what we expect in the real prediction problem. That the value 0.632 is close to the value $2/3$ derived above is reassuring. The hybrid estimate (6.55) with $w = 0.632$ is known as the *0.632 estimator of prediction error* and is denoted here by $\hat{\Delta}_{0.632}$. There is substantial empirical evidence favouring this estimate, so long as the number of covariates p is not close to n.

Example 6.10 (Nuclear power stations)   Consider predicting the cost of a new power station based on the data of Example 6.8. We base our prediction on the linear regression model described there, so we have $\mu(x_j, \hat{F}) = x_j^T \hat{\beta}$, where $\hat{\beta}$ is the least squares estimate for a model with six covariates. The estimated error variance is $s^2 = 0.6337/25 = 0.0253$ with 25 degrees of freedom. The downwardly biased apparent error estimate is $\hat{\Delta}_{app} = 0.6337/32 = 0.020$, whereas the idealized estimate (6.38) is $0.025 \times (1 + \frac{7}{32}) = 0.031$. In this situation the prediction error for a particular station seems most useful, but before we turn to individual stations, we discuss the overall estimates, which are given in Table 6.9.

Those estimates show the pattern we would anticipate from the general

Figure 6.11
Components of
prediction error for
nuclear power data
based on 200 bootstrap
simulations. The top
panel shows the values
of $y_j - \mu(x_j, \hat{F}_r^*)$. The
lower left panel shows
the average error for
each case, plotted
against the residuals.
The lower right panel
shows the ratio of the
model-based to the
bootstrap prediction
standard errors.

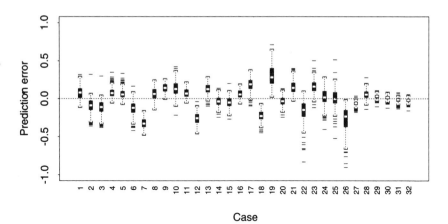

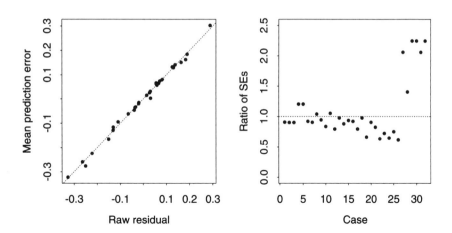

discussion. The apparent error is considerably smaller than other estimates.
The bootstrap estimate, with $R = 200$, is larger than the apparent error, but
smaller than the cross-validation estimates, and the 0.632 estimate agrees well
with the ordinary cross-validation estimate (6.44), for which $K = n = 32$.
Adjustment slightly decreases the cross-validation estimates. Note that the
idealized estimate appears to be quite accurate here, presumably because the
model fits well and errors are not far from homoscedastic — except for the
last six cases.

Now consider the individual predictions. Prediction error arises from two
components: the variability of the predictor $x_+^T \hat{\beta}$ and that of the associated
error ε_+. Figure 6.11 gives some insight into these. Its top panel shows the values

of $y_j - \mu(x_j, \hat{F}_r^*)$ for $r = 1, \ldots, R$, plotted against case number j. The variability of the average error corresponds to the variation of individual observations about their predicted values, while the variance within each group reflects parameter estimation uncertainty. A striking feature is the small prediction error for the last six power plants, whose variances and means are both small. The lower left panel shows the average values of $y_j - \mu(x_j, \hat{F}_r^*)$ over the 200 simulations, plotted against the raw residuals. They agree closely, as we should expect with a well-fitting model. The lower right panel shows the ratio of the model-based prediction standard error to the bootstrap prediction standard error. It confirms that the model-based calculation described in Example 6.8 overestimates the predictive standard error for the last six plants, which have the partial turnkey guarantee. The estimated bootstrap prediction error for these plants is 0.003, while it is 0.032 for the rest. The last six cases fall into three groups determined by the values of the explanatory variables: in effect they are replicated.

It might be preferable to plot $y_j - \mu(x_j, \hat{F}_r^*)$ only for those bootstrap samples which exclude the jth case, and then mean prediction error would better be compared to jackknifed residuals $y_j - x_j^T \hat{\beta}_{-j}$. For these data the plots are very similar to those we have shown.   ∎

Example 6.11 (Times on delivery suite)   For a more systematic comparison of prediction error estimates in linear regression, we use data provided by E. Burns on the times taken by 1187 women to give birth at the John Radcliffe Hospital in Oxford. An appropriate linear model has response the log time spent on delivery suite and dummy explanatory variables indicating the type of labour, the use of electronic fetal monitoring, the use of an intravenous drip, the reported length of labour before arriving at the hospital and whether or not the labour is the woman's first; seven parameters are estimated in all. We took 200 samples of size $n = 50$ at random from the full data. For each of these samples we fitted the model described above, and then calculated cross-validation estimates of prediction error $\hat{\Delta}_{CV,K}$ with $K = 50, 10, 5$ and 2 groups, the corresponding adjusted cross-validation estimates $\hat{\Delta}_{ACV,K}$, the bootstrap estimate $\hat{\Delta}_B$, and the hybrid estimate $\hat{\Delta}_{0.632}$. We took $R = 200$ for the bootstrap calculations.

The results of this experiment are summarized in terms of estimates of the expected excess error in Table 6.10. The average apparent error and excess error were 15.7×10^{-2} and 5.2×10^{-2}, the latter taken to be $e(F)$ as defined in (6.42). The table shows averages and standard deviations of the differences between estimates $\hat{\Delta}$ and $\hat{\Delta}_{app}$. The cross-validation estimate with $K = 50$, the bootstrap and the 0.632 estimate have similar properties, while other choices of K give estimates that are more variable; the half-sample estimate $\hat{\Delta}_{CV,2}$ is worst. Results for cross-validation with 10 and 5 groups are almost

Table 6.10 Summary results for estimates of prediction error for 200 samples of size $n = 50$ from a set of data on the times 1187 women spent on delivery suite at the John Radcliffe Hospital, Oxford. The table shows the average, standard deviation, and conditional mean squared error ($\times 10^{-2}$) for the 200 estimates of excess error. The 'target' average excess error is 5.2×10^{-2}.

			K-fold (adjusted) cross-validation			
	Bootstrap	0.632	50	10	5	2
Mean	4.6	5.3	5.3	6.0 (5.7)	6.2 (5.5)	9.2 (5.7)
SD	1.3	1.6	1.6	2.3 (2.2)	2.6 (2.3)	5.4 (3.3)
MSE	0.23	0.24	0.24	0.28 (0.26)	0.30 (0.27)	0.71 (0.33)

the same. Adjustment significantly improves cross-validation when group size is not small. The bootstrap estimate is least variable, but is downwardly biased.

The final row of the table gives the conditional mean squared error, defined as $(200)^{-1} \sum_{j=1}^{200} \{\hat{\Delta}_j - D_j(F, \hat{F})\}^2$ for each error estimate $\hat{\Delta}$. This measures the success of $\hat{\Delta}$ in estimating the true aggregate prediction error $D(F, \hat{F})$ for each of the 200 samples. Again the ordinary cross-validation, bootstrap, and 0.632 estimates perform best.

In this example there is little to choose between K-fold cross-validation with 10 and 5 groups, which both perform worse than the ordinary cross-validation, bootstrap, and 0.632 estimators of prediction error. K-fold cross-validation should be used with adjustment if ordinary cross-validation or the simulation-based estimates are not feasible. ∎

6.4.2 Variable selection

In many applications of multiple linear regression, one purpose of the analysis is to decide which covariate terms to include in the final model. The supposition is that the full model $y = x^T \beta + \varepsilon$ with p covariates in (6.22) is correct, but that it may include some redundant terms. Our aim is to eliminate those redundant terms, and so obtain the true model, which will form the basis for further inference. This is somewhat simplistic from a practical viewpoint, because it assumes that one subset of the proposed linear model is "true": it may be more sensible to assume that a few subsets may be equally good approximations to a complicated true relationship between mean response and covariates.

Given that there are p covariate terms in the model (6.22), there are 2^p candidates for true model because we can include or exclude each covariate. In practice the number of candidates will be reduced if prior information necessitates inclusion of particular covariates or combinations of them.

There are several approaches to variable selection, including various stepwise methods. But the approach we focus on here is the direct one of minimizing aggregate prediction error, when each candidate model is used to predict independent, future responses at the data covariate values. For simplicity we assume that models are fitted by least squares, and that aggregate prediction error is average squared error. It would be a simple matter to use other prediction rules and other measures of prediction accuracy.

First we define some notation. We denote an arbitrary candidate model by M, which is one of the 2^p possible linear models. Whenever M is used as a subscript, it refers to elements of that model. Thus the $n \times p_M$ design matrix X_M contains those p_M columns of the full design matrix X that correspond to covariates included in M; the jth row of X_M is x_{Mj}^T, the least squares estimates for regression coefficients in M are $\hat{\beta}_M$, and H_M is the hat matrix $X_M(X_M^T X_M)^{-1} X_M^T$ that defines fitted values $\hat{y}_M = H_M y$ under model M. The total number of regression coefficients in M is $q_M = p_M + 1$, assuming that an intercept term is always included.

Now consider prediction of single responses y_+ at each of the original design points $x_1, \ldots, x_n$. The average squared prediction error using model M is

$$n^{-1} \sum_{j=1}^{n} (y_{+j} - x_{Mj}^T \hat{\beta}_M)^2,$$

and its expectation under model (6.22), conditional on the data, is the aggregate prediction error

$$D(M) = \sigma^2 + n^{-1} \sum_{j=1}^{n} (\mu_j - x_{Mj}^T \hat{\beta}_M)^2,$$

where $\mu^T = (\mu_1, \ldots, \mu_n)$ is the vector of mean responses for the true multiple regression model. Taking expectation over the data distribution we obtain

$$\Delta(M) = \mathrm{E}\{D(M)\} = \left(1 + n^{-1} q_M\right) \sigma^2 + \mu^T (I - H_M) \mu, \qquad (6.56)$$

where $\mu^T (I - H_M) \mu$ is zero only if model M is correct. The quantities $D(M)$ and $\Delta(M)$ generalize D and Δ defined in (6.36) and (6.37).

In principle the best model would be the one that minimizes $D(M)$, but since the model parameters are unknown we must settle for minimizing a good estimate of $D(M)$ or $\Delta(M)$. Several resampling methods for estimating Δ were discussed in the previous subsection, so the natural approach would be to choose a good method and apply it to all possible models. However, accurate estimation of $\Delta(M)$ is not itself important: what is important is to accurately estimate the signs of differences among the $\Delta(M)$, so that we can identify which of the $\Delta(M)$s is smallest.

Of the methods considered earlier, the apparent error estimate $\hat{\Delta}_{app}(M) = n^{-1} RSS_M$ was poor. Its use here is immediately ruled out when we observe that it always decreases when covariates are added to a model, so minimization always leads to the full model.

Cross-validation

One good estimate, when used with squared error, is the leave-one-out cross-validation estimate. In the present notation this is

$$\hat{\Delta}_{CV}(M) = n^{-1} \sum_{j=1}^{n} \frac{(y_j - \hat{y}_{Mj})^2}{(1 - h_{Mj})^2},$$ (6.57)

where $\hat{y}_{Mj}$ is the fitted value for model M based on all the data and h_{Mj} is the leverage for case j in model M. The bias of $\hat{\Delta}_{CV}(M)$ is small, but that is not enough to make it a good basis for selecting M. To see why, note first that an expansion gives

$$n\hat{\Delta}_{CV}(M) \doteq \varepsilon^T (I - H_M)\varepsilon + 2p_M + \mu^T (I - H_M)\mu.$$ (6.58)

Then if model M is true, and M' is a larger model, it follows that for large n

$$\Pr\{\hat{\Delta}_{CV}(M) < \hat{\Delta}_{CV}(M')\} \doteq \Pr(\chi_d^2 < 2d),$$

where $d = p_{M'} - p_M$. This probability is substantially below 1 unless d is large. It is therefore quite likely that selecting M to minimize $\hat{\Delta}_{CV}(M)$ will lead to overfitting, even for large n. So although the term $\mu^T (I - H_M)\mu$ in (6.58) guarantees that, for large n, incorrect models will not be selected, minimization of $\hat{\Delta}_{CV}(M)$ does not provide consistent selection of the true model.

One explanation for this is that to estimate $\Delta(M)$ with sufficient accuracy we need both large amounts of data to fit model M and a large number of independent predictions. This can be accomplished using the more general cross-validation measure (6.43), under conditions given below. In principle we need to average (6.43) over all possible splits, but for practical purposes we follow (6.46). That is, using R different splits into training and assessment sets of sizes $n_t = n - m$ and $n_a = m$, we generalize (6.57) to

$$\hat{\Delta}_{CV}(M) = R^{-1} \sum_{r=1}^{R} m^{-1} \sum_{j \in S_{a,r}} \{y_j - \hat{y}_{Mj}(S_{t,r})\}^2,$$

where $\hat{y}_{Mj}(S_{t,r}) = x_{Mj}^T \hat{\beta}_M(S_{t,r})$ and $\hat{\beta}_M(S_{t,r})$ are the least squares estimates for coefficients in M fitted to the rth training set whose subscripts are in $S_{t,r}$. Note that the same R splits into training and assessment sets are used for all models. It can be shown that, provided m is chosen so that $n - m \rightarrow \infty$ and $m/n \rightarrow 1$ as $n \rightarrow \infty$, minimization of $\hat{\Delta}_{CV}(M)$ will give consistent selection of the true model as $n \rightarrow \infty$ and $R \rightarrow \infty$.

Bootstrap methods

Corresponding results can be obtained for bootstrap resampling methods. The bootstrap estimate of aggregate prediction error (6.51) becomes

$$\hat{\Delta}_B(M) = n^{-1}RSS_M + R^{-1}\sum_{r=1}^{R}n^{-1}\left\{\sum_{j=1}^{n}(y_j - x_{Mj,r}^{\bullet T}\hat{\beta}_{M,r}^{\bullet})^2 - RSS_{M,r}^{\bullet}\right\}, \quad (6.59)$$

where the second term on the right-hand side is an estimate of the expected excess error defined in (6.42). The resampling scheme can be either case resampling or error resampling, with $x_{Mj,r}^{\bullet} \equiv x_{Mj}$ for the latter.

It turns out that minimization of $\hat{\Delta}_B(M)$ behaves much like minimization of the leave-one-out cross-validation estimate, and does not lead to a consistent choice of true model as $n\to\infty$. However, there is a modification of $\hat{\Delta}_B(M)$, analogous to that made for the cross-validation procedure, which does produce a consistent model selection procedure. The modification is to make simulated datasets be of size $n - m$ rather than n, such that $m/n\to1$ and $n - m\to\infty$ as $n\to\infty$. Also, we replace the estimate (6.59) by the simpler bootstrap estimate

$$\hat{\Delta}_B(M) = R^{-1}\sum_{r=1}^{R}n^{-1}\sum_{j=1}^{n}(y_j - x_{Mj}^{T}\hat{\beta}_{M,r}^{\bullet})^2, \quad (6.60)$$

which is a generalization of (6.49). (The previous doubts about this simple estimate are less relevant for small $n - m$.) If case resampling is used, then $n - m$ cases are randomly selected from the full set of n. If model-based resampling is used, the model being M with assumed homoscedasticity of errors, then $X_M^{\bullet}$ is a random selection of $n - m$ rows from X_M and the $n - m$ errors $\varepsilon_j^{\bullet}$ are randomly sampled from the n mean-corrected modified residuals $r_{Mj} - \bar{r}_M$ for model M.

Bearing in mind the general advice that the number of simulated datasets should be at least $R = 100$ for estimating second moments, we should use at least that many here. The same R bootstrap resamples are used for each model M, as with the cross-validation procedure.

One major practical difficulty that is shared by the consistent cross-validation and bootstrap procedures is that fitting all candidate models to small subsets of data is not always possible. What empirical evidence there is concerning good choices for m/n suggests that this ratio should be about $\frac{2}{3}$. If so, then in many applications some of the R subsets will have singular designs $X_M^{\bullet}$ for big models, unless subsets are balanced by appropriate stratification on covariates in the resampling procedure.

Example 6.12 (Nuclear power stations)   In Examples 6.8 and 6.10 our analyses focused on a linear regression model that includes six of the $p = 10$ covariates available. Three of these covariates — date, log(cap) and NE — are highly

Figure 6.12 Aggregate prediction error estimates for sequence of models fitted to nuclear power stations data; see text. Leave-one-out cross-validation (solid line), bootstrap with $R = 100$ resamples of size 32 (dashed line) and 16 (dotted line).

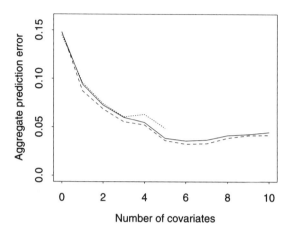

significant, all others having P-values of 0.1 or more. Here we consider the selection of variables to include in the model. The total number of possible models, $2^{10} = 1024$, is prohibitively large, and for the purposes of illustration we consider only the particular sequence of models in which variables enter in the order date, log(cap), NE, CT, log(N), PT, T1, T2, PR, BW: the first three are the highly significant variables.

Figure 6.12 plots the leave-one-out cross-validation estimates and the bootstrap estimates (6.60) with $R = 100$ of aggregate prediction error for the models with $0, 1, \ldots, 10$ covariates. The two estimates are very close, and both are minimized when six covariates are included (the six used in Examples 6.8 and 6.10). Selection of five or six covariates, rather than fewer, is quite clearcut. These results bear out the rough rule-of-thumb that variables are selected by cross-validation if they are significant at roughly the 0.1 level.

As the previous discussion would suggest, use of corresponding crossvalidation and bootstrap estimates from training sets of size 20 or less is precluded because for training sets of such sizes the models with more than five covariates are frequently unidentifiable. That is, the unbalanced nature of the covariates, coupled with the binary nature of some of them, frequently leads to singular resample designs. Figure 6.12 includes bootstrap estimates for models with up to five covariates and training set of size 16: these results were obtained by omitting many singular resamples. These rather fragmentary results confirm that the model should include at least five covariates.

A useful lesson from this is that there is a practical obstacle to what in theory is a preferred variable selection procedure. One way to try to overcome

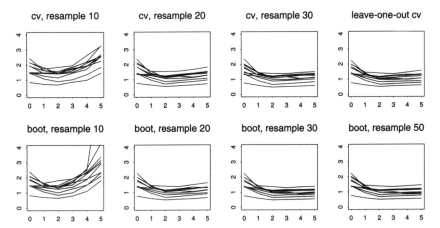

Figure 6.13
Cross-validation and bootstrap estimates of aggregate prediction error for sequence of six models fitted to ten datasets of size $n = 50$ with $p = 5$ covariates. The true model includes only two covariates.

this difficulty is to stratify on the binary covariates, but this is difficult to implement and does not work well here.   ∎

Example 6.13 (Simulation exercise)   In order to assess the variable selection procedures without the complication of singular resample designs, we consider a small simulation exercise in which procedures are applied to ten datasets simulated from a given model. There are $p = 5$ independent covariates, whose values are sampled from the uniform distribution on $[0, 1]$, and responses y are generated by adding $N(0, 1)$ variates to the means $\mu = x^T \beta$. The cases we examine have sample size $n = 50$, and $\beta_3 = \beta_4 = \beta_5 = 0$, so the true model includes an intercept and two covariate terms. To simplify calculations only six models are fitted, by successively adding $x_1, \ldots, x_5$ to an initial model with constant intercept. All resampling calculations are done with $R = 100$ samples. The number of datasets is admittedly small, but sufficient to make rough comparisons of performance.

The main results concern models with $\beta_1 = \beta_2 = 2$, which means that the two non-zero coefficients are about four standard errors away from zero. Each panel of Figure 6.13 shows, for the ten datasets, one variable selection criterion plotted against the number of covariates included in the model. Evidently the clearest indications of the true model occur when training set size is 10 or 20. Larger training sets give flat profiles for the criterion, and more frequent selection of overfitted models.

These indications match the evidence from more extensive simulations, which suggest that if training set size $n - m$ is about $n/3$ then the probability of correct model selection is 0.9 or higher, compared to 0.7 or less for leave-one-out cross-validation.

Further results were obtained with $\beta_1 = 2$ and $\beta_2 = 0.5$, the latter equal to one standard error away from zero. In this situation underfitting — failure to include x_2 in the selected model — occurred quite frequently even when using training sets of size 20. This degradation of variable selection procedures when coefficients are smaller than two standard errors is reputed to be typical. ∎

The theory used to justify the consistent cross-validation and bootstrap procedures may depend heavily on the assumptions that the dimension of the true model is small compared to the number of cases, and that the non-zero regression coefficients are all large relative to their standard errors. It is possible that leave-one-out cross-validation may work well in certain situations where model dimension is comparable to number of cases. This would be important, in light of the very clear difficulties of using small training sets with typical applications, such as Example 6.12. Evidently further work, both theoretical and empirical, is necessary to find broadly applicable variable selection methods.

6.5 Robust Regression

The use of least squares regression estimates is preferred when errors are near-normal in distribution and homoscedastic. However, the estimates are very sensitive to outliers, that is cases which deviate strongly from the general relationship. Also, if errors have a long-tailed distribution (possibly due to heteroscedasticity), then least squares estimation is not an efficient method. Any regression analysis should therefore include appropriate inspection of diagnostics based on residuals to detect outliers, and to determine if a normal assumption for errors is reasonable. If the occurrence of outliers does not cause a change in the regression model, then they will likely be omitted from the fitting of that model. Depending on the general pattern of residuals for remaining cases, we may feel confident in fitting by least squares, or we may choose to use a more robust method to be safe. Essentially the resampling methods that we have discussed previously in this chapter can be adapted quite easily for use with many robust regression methods. In this section we briefly review some of the main points.

Perhaps the most important point is that gross outliers should be removed before final regression analysis, including resampling, is undertaken. There are two reasons for this. The first is that methods of fitting that are resistant to outliers are usually not very efficient, and may behave badly under resampling. The second reason is that outliers can be disruptive to resampling analysis of methods such as least squares that are not resistant to outliers. For model-based resampling, the error distribution will be contaminated and in the resampling the outliers can then occur at any x values. For case resampling, outlying cases will occur with variable frequency and make the bootstrap estimates of coefficients too variable; see Example 6.4. The effects can be diagnosed from

Dose (rads)	117.5	235.0	470.0	705.0	940.0	1410
Survival %	44.000	16.000	4.000	0.500	0.110	0.700
	55.000	13.000	1.960	0.320	0.015	0.006
			6.120		0.019	

Table 6.11 Survival data (Efron, 1988).

the jackknife-after-bootstrap plots of Section 3.10.1 or similarly informative diagnostic plots, but such plots can fail to show the occurrence of multiple outliers.

For datasets with possibly multiple outliers, diagnosis is aided by initial use of a fitted method that is highly resistant to the effects of outliers. One preferred resistant method is least trimmed squares, which minimizes

$$\sum_{j=1}^{m} e_{(j)}^2(\beta), \tag{6.61}$$

the sum of the m smallest squares of deviations $e_j(\beta) = y_j - x_j^T \beta$. Usually m is taken to be $[\frac{1}{2}n] + 1$. Residuals from the least trimmed squares fit should clearly identify outliers. The fit itself is not very efficient, and should best be thought of as an initial step in a more efficient analysis. (It should be noted that in some implementations of least trimmed squares, local minima of (6.61) may be found far away from the global minimum.)

Here [·] denotes integer part.

Example 6.14 (Survival proportions)   The data in Table 6.11 and the left panel of Figure 6.14 are survival percentages for rats at a succession of doses of radiation, with two or three replicates at each dose. The theoretical relationship between survival rate and dose is exponential, so linear regression applies to

$$x = \text{dose}, \quad y = \log(\text{survival percentage}).$$

The right panel of Figure 6.14 plots these variables. There is a clear outlier, case 13, at $x = 1410$. The least squares estimate of slope is -59×10^{-4} using all the data, changing to -78×10^{-4} with standard error 5.4×10^{-4} when case 13 is omitted. The least trimmed squares estimate of slope is -69×10^{-4}.

From the scatter plot it appears that heteroscedasticity may be present, so we resample cases. The effect of the outlier on the resample least squares estimates is illustrated in Figure 6.15, which plots $R = 200$ bootstrap least squares slopes $\hat{\beta}_1^*$ against the corresponding values of $\sum(x_j^* - \bar{x}^*)^2$, differentiated by the frequency with which case 13 appears in the resample. There are three distinct groups of bootstrapped slopes, with the lowest corresponding to resamples in which case 13 does not occur and the highest to samples where it occurs twice or more. A jackknife-after-bootstrap plot would clearly reveal the effect of case 13. The resampling standard error of $\hat{\beta}_1^*$ is 15.3×10^{-4}, but only 7.6×10^{-4} for

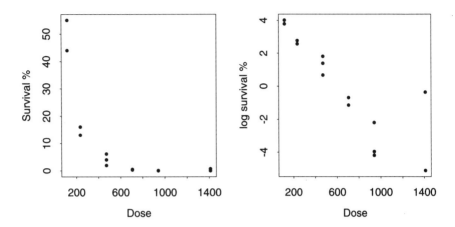

Figure 6.14 Scatter plots of survival data.

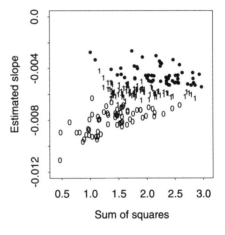

Figure 6.15 Bootstrap estimates of slope $\hat{\beta}_1^*$ and design sum-of-squares $\sum(x_j^* - \bar{x}^*)^2$ ($\times 10^5$), differentiated by frequency of case 13 (appears zero, one or more times), for case resampling with $R = 200$ from survival data.

samples without case 13. The corresponding resampling standard errors of the least trimmed squares slope are 20.5×10^{-4} and 18.0×10^{-4}, showing both the resistance and inefficiency of the least trimmed squares method.   ∎

Example 6.15 (Salinity data)   The data in Table 6.12 are $n = 28$ observations on the salinity of water in Pamlico Sound, North Carolina. The response in the second column is the bi-weekly average of salinity. The next three columns contain values of the covariates, respectively a lagged value of salinity, a trend

	Salinity sal	Lagged salinity lag	Trend indicator trend	River discharge dis
1	7.6	8.2	4	23.01
2	7.7	7.6	5	22.87
3	4.3	4.6	0	26.42
4	5.9	4.3	1	24.87
5	5.0	5.9	2	29.90
6	6.5	5.0	3	24.20
7	8.3	6.5	4	23.22
8	8.2	8.3	5	22.86
9	13.2	10.1	0	22.27
10	12.6	13.2	1	23.83
11	10.4	12.6	2	25.14
12	10.8	10.4	3	22.43
13	13.1	10.8	4	21.79
14	12.3	13.1	5	22.38
15	10.4	13.3	0	23.93
16	10.5	10.4	1	33.44
17	7.7	10.5	2	24.86
18	9.5	7.7	3	22.69
19	12.0	10.0	0	21.79
20	12.6	12.0	1	22.04
21	13.6	12.1	4	21.03
22	14.1	13.6	5	21.01
23	13.5	15.0	0	25.87
24	11.5	13.5	1	26.29
25	12.0	11.5	2	22.93
26	13.0	12.0	3	21.31
27	14.1	13.0	4	20.77
28	15.1	14.1	5	21.39

Table 6.12 Salinity data (Ruppert and Carroll, 1980).

indicator, and the river discharge. We consider a linear regression model with these three covariates.

The initial least squares analysis gives coefficients 0.78, −0.03 and −0.30, with intercept 9.70. The usual standard error for the trend coefficient is 0.16, so this coefficient would be judged not nearly significant. However, this fit is suspect, as can be seen not from the Q-Q plot of modified residuals but from the plot of cross-validation residuals versus leverages, where case 16 stands out as an outlier — due apparently to its unusual value of dis. The outlier is much more easily detected using the least trimmed squares fit, which has the quite different coefficient values 0.61, −0.15 and −0.86 with intercept 24.72: the residual of case 16 from this fit has standardized value 6.9. Figure 6.16 shows normal Q-Q plots of standardized residuals from least squares (left panel) and least trimmed squares fits (right panel); for the latter the scale factor is taken to be the median absolute residual divided by 0.6745, the value appropriate for estimating the standard deviation of normal errors.

Application of standard algorithms for least trimmed squares with default settings can give very different, incorrect solutions.

Figure 6.16 Salinity data: standardized residuals from least squares (left) and least trimmed squares (right) fits using all cases.

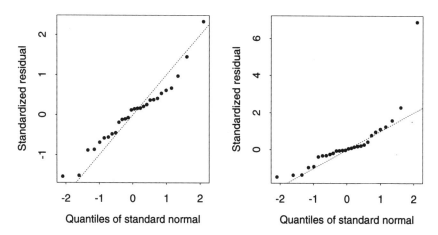

There is some question as to whether the outlier is really aberrant, or simply reflects the need for a quadratic term in dis. ∎

Robust methods

We suppose now that outliers have been isolated by diagnostic plots and set aside from further analysis. The problem now is whether or not that analysis should use least squares estimation: if there is evidence of a long-tailed error distribution, then we should downweight large deviations $y_j - x_j^T \beta$ by using a robust method. Two main options for this are now described.

One approach is to minimize not sums of squared deviations but sums of absolute values of deviations, $\sum |y_j - x_j^T \beta|$, so giving less weight to those cases with the largest errors. This is the L_1 method, which generalizes — and has efficiency comparable to — the sample median estimate of a population mean. There is no simple expression for approximate variance of L_1 estimators.

More efficient is M-estimation, which is analogous to maximum likelihood estimation. Here the coefficient estimates $\hat{\beta}$ for a multiple linear regression solve the estimating equation

$$\sum_{j=1}^{n} x_j \psi \left(\frac{y_j - x_j^T \hat{\beta}}{s} \right) = 0, \tag{6.62}$$

where $\psi(z)$ is a bounded replacement for z, and s is either the solution to a simultaneous estimating equation, or is fixed in advance. We choose the latter, taking s to be the median absolute deviation (divided by 0.6745) from the least trimmed squares regression fit. The solution to (6.62) is obtained by iterative weighted least squares, for which least trimmed squares estimates are good starting values.

With a careful choice of $\psi(\cdot)$, M-estimates should have smaller standard errors than least squares estimates for long-tailed distributions of random errors ε, yet have comparable standard errors should those errors be homoscedastic normal. One standard choice is $\psi(z) = z\min(1, c/|z|)$, Huber's winsorizing function, for which the coefficient estimates have approximate efficiency 95% relative to least squares estimates for homoscedastic normal errors when $c = 1.345$.

For large sample sizes M-estimates $\hat{\beta}$ are approximately normal in distribution, with approximate variance

$$\operatorname{var}(\hat{\beta}) \doteq \sigma^2 \frac{\mathrm{E}\{\psi^2(\varepsilon/\sigma)\}}{[\mathrm{E}\{\dot{\psi}(\varepsilon/\sigma)\}]^2}(X^TX)^{-1}, \tag{6.63}$$

$\dot{\psi}(u)$ is the derivative $d\psi(u)/du$.

under homoscedasticity. A more robust, empirical variance estimate is provided by the nonparametric delta method. First, the empirical influence values are, analogous to (6.25),

$$l_j = kn(X^TX)^{-1}x_j\psi\left(\frac{e_j}{s}\right),$$

where $k = sn^{-1}\sum_{j=1}^{n}\dot{\psi}(e_j/s)$ and $e_j = y_j - x_j^T\hat{\beta}$ is the raw residual; see Problem 6.7. The variance approximation is then

$$v_L = n^{-2}\sum_{j=1}^{n}l_jl_j^T = k^2(X^TX)^{-1}X^TDX(X^TX)^{-1}, \tag{6.64}$$

where $D = \operatorname{diag}\{\psi^2(e_1/s), \ldots, \psi^2(e_n/s)\}$; this generalizes (6.17).

Resampling

As with least squares estimation, so with robust estimates we have two simple choices for resampling: case resampling, or model-based resampling. Depending on which robust method is used, the resampling algorithm may need to be modified from the simple form that it takes for least squares estimation.

The L_1 estimates will behave like the sample median under either resampling scheme, so that the distribution of $\hat{\beta}^* - \hat{\beta}$ can be very discrete, and close to that of $\hat{\beta} - \beta$ only for very large samples. Use of the smooth bootstrap (Section 3.4) will improve accuracy. No simple studentization is possible for L_1 estimates.

For M-estimates case resampling should be satisfactory except for small datasets, especially those with unreplicated design points. The advantage of case resampling is simplicity. For model-based resampling, some modifications are required to the algorithm used to resample least squares estimation in Section 6.3. First, the leverage correction of raw residuals is given by

$$r_j = \frac{e_j}{(1 - dh_j)^{1/2}}, \qquad d = \frac{2\sum(e_j/s)\psi(e_j/s)}{\sum\dot{\psi}(e_j/s)} - \frac{\sum\psi^2(e_j/s)}{\{\sum\dot{\psi}(e_j/s)\}^2}.$$

Simulated errors are randomly sampled from the uncentred $r_1, \ldots, r_n$. Mean correction to the r_j is replaced by a slightly more complicated correction in the estimation equation itself. The resample version of (6.62) is

$$\sum_{j=1}^{n} x_j \left\{ \psi \left(\frac{y_j^* - x_j^T \hat{\beta}^*}{s^*} \right) - n^{-1} \sum_{k=1}^{n} \psi \left(\frac{r_j}{s^*} \right) \right\} = 0.$$

The scale estimate s^* is obtained by the same method as s, but from the resample data.

Studentization of $\hat{\beta}^* - \hat{\beta}$ is possible, using the resample analogue of the delta method variance (6.64) or more simply just using s^*.

Example 6.16 (Salinity data) In our previous look at the salinity data in Example 6.15, we identified case 16 as a clear outlier. We now set that case aside and re-analyse the linear regression with all three covariates. One objective is to determine whether or not the trend variable should be included in the model: the initial, incorrect least squares analysis suggested not.

A normal Q-Q plot of the modified residuals from the new least squares fit suggests somewhat long tails for the error disribution, so that robust methods may be worthwhile. We fit the model by four methods: least squares, Huber M-estimate (with $c = 1.345$), L_1 and least trimmed squares. Coefficient estimates are fairly similar under all methods, except for trend whose coefficients are -0.17, -0.22, -0.18 and -0.08.

For further analysis we apply case resampling with $R = 99$. Figure 6.17 illustrates the results for estimates of the coefficient of trend. The dotted lines on the top two panels correspond to the theoretical normal approximations: evidently the standard variance approximation — based on (6.63) — for the Huber estimate is too low. Note also the relatively large resampling variance for the least trimmed squares estimate, part of which may be due to unconverged estimates: two resampling outliers have been trimmed from this plot.

To assess the significance of trend we apply the studentized pivot method of Section 6.3.2 with both least squares and M-estimates, studentizing by the theoretical standard error in each case. The corresponding values of z are -1.25 and -1.80, with respectively 23 and 12 smaller values of z^* out of 99. So there appears to be little evidence of the need to include trend.

If we checked diagnostic plots for any of the four regression fits, a question might be raised about whether or not case 5 should be included in the analysis. An alternative view of this is provided by jackknife-after-bootstrap plots (Section 3.10.1) of the four fits: such plots correspond to case-deletion resampling. As an illustration, Figure 6.18 shows the jackknife-after-bootstrap plot for the coefficient of trend in the M-estimation fit. This shows clearly that case 5 has an appreciable effect on the resampling distribution, and that its omission would give tighter confidence limits on the coefficient. It also raises

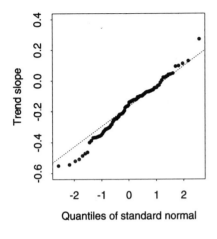

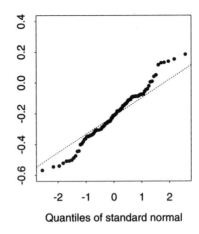

Figure 6.17 Salinity data: Normal Q-Q plots of resampled estimates of trend coefficient, based on case resampling ($R = 99$ for data excluding case 16. Clockwise from top left: least squares, Huber M-estimation, least trimmed squares, L_1. Dotted lines correspond to theoretical normal approximations.

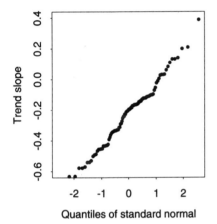

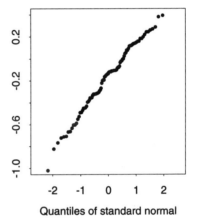

questions about two other cases. Clearly some further exploration is needed before firm conclusions can be reached. ■

The previous example illustrates the point that it is often worthwhile to incorporate robust methods into a regression analysis, both to help isolate outliers and to assess the reliability of conclusions based on the least squares fit to supposedly "clean" data. In some areas of applications, for example those involving relationships between financial series, long-tailed distributions may be quite common, and then robust methods will be especially important. To the extent that theoretical normal approximations are inaccurate for many robust estimates, resampling methods are a natural companion to robust analysis.

Figure 6.18 Jackknife-after-bootstrap plot for the coefficient of `trend` in the M-estimation fit to the salinity data, omitting case 16.

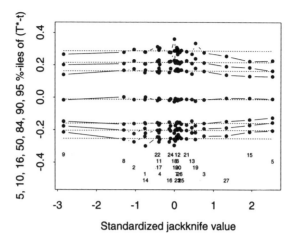

6.6 Bibliographic Notes

There are several comprehensive accounts of linear regression analysis, including the books by Draper and Smith (1981), Seber (1977), and Weisberg (1985). Diagnostic methods are described by Atkinson (1985) and by Cook and Weisberg (1982). A good general reference on robust regression is the book by Rousseeuw and Leroy (1987). Many linear regression methods and their properties are summarized, with illustrations using S-Plus, in Venables and Ripley (1994).

The use of bootstrap methods in regression was initiated by Efron (1979). Important early work on the theory of resampling for linear regression was by Freedman (1981) and Bickel and Freedman (1983). See also Efron (1988). Freedman (1984) and Freedman and Peters (1984a,b) assessed the methods in practical applications. Wu (1986) gives a quite comprehensive theoretical treatment, including comparisons between various resampling and jackknife methods; for further developments see Shao (1988) and Liu and Singh (1992b). Hall (1989b) shows that bootstrap methods can provide unusually accurate confidence intervals in regression problems.

Theoretical properties of bootstrap significance tests, including the use of both studentized pivots and F statistics, were established by Mammen (1993). Recent interest in resampling tests for econometric models is reviewed by Jeong and Maddala (1993).

Use of the bootstrap for calculating prediction intervals was discussed by Stine (1985). The asymptotic theory for the most elementary case was given by Bai and Olshen (1988). For further theoretical development see Beran (1992).

Olshen *et al.* (1989) described an interesting application to a complicated prediction problem.

The wild bootstrap is based on an idea suggested by Wu (1986), and has been explored in detail by Härdle (1989, 1990) and Mammen (1992). The effectiveness of the wild bootstrap, particularly for studentized coefficients, was demonstrated by Mammen (1993).

Cross-validation methods for the assessment of prediction error have a long history, but modern developments originated with Stone (1974) and Geisser (1975). What we refer to as K-fold cross-validation was proposed by Breiman *et al.* (1984), and further studied by Burman (1989). Important theoretical results were developed by Bunke and Droge (1984), Li (1987), and Shao (1993). The theoretical foundation of cross-validation and bootstrap estimates of prediction error, with particular emphasis on classification problems, was developed in Chapter 7 of Efron (1982) and by Efron (1983), the latter introducing the 0.632 estimate. Further developments, with applications and empirical studies, were given by Efron (1986) and Efron and Tibshirani (1997). The discussion of hybrid estimates in Section 6.4 is based on Hall (1995). In a simple case Davison and Hall (1992) attempt to explain the properties of the bootstrap and cross-validation error estimates.

There is a large literature on variable selection in regression, much of which overlaps with the cross-validation literature. Cross-validation is related to the the C_p method of linear model selection, proposed by Mallows (1973), and to the AIC method of Akaike (1973), as was shown by Stone (1977). For a summary discussion of various methods of model selection see Chapter 2 of Ripley (1996), for example. The consistent bootstrap methods outlined in Section 6.4 were developed by Shao (1996).

Asymptotic properties of resampled M-estimates were derived by Shorack (1982) who described the adjustment necessary for unbiasedness of the re-sampled coefficients. Mammen (1989) provided additional asymptotic support. Aspects of residuals from robust regression were discussed by Cook, Hawkins and Weisberg (1992) and McKean, Sheather and Hettsmansperger (1993), the latter showing how to standardize raw residuals in M-estimation. De Angelis, Hall and Young (1993) gave a detailed theoretical analysis of model-based resampling in L_1 estimation, which confirmed that a smooth bootstrap is advisable; further numerical results were provided by Stangenhaus (1987).

6.7 Problems

1 Show that for a multivariate distribution with mean vector μ and variance matrix Ω, the influence functions for the sample mean and variance are respectively

$$l_m(z) = z - \mu, \qquad l_s(z) = (z - \mu)(z - \mu)^T - \Omega.$$

Hence show that for the linear regression model derived as the conditional expectation $E(Y \mid X = x)$ of a multivariate CDF F, the empirical influence function values for linear regression parameters are

$$l_t(x_j, y_j) = n(X^T X)^{-1} x_j e_j,$$

where X is the matrix of explanatory variables.
(Sections 2.7.2, 6.2.2)

2   For homogeneous data as in Chapter 2, the empirical influence values for an estimator can be approximated using case-deletion values. Use the matrix identity

$$(X^T X - x_j x_j^T)^{-1} = (X^T X)^{-1} + \frac{(X^T X)^{-1} x_j x_j^T (X^T X)^{-1}}{1 - x_j^T (X^T X)^{-1} x_j}$$

to show that in the linear regression model with least squares fitting,

$$\hat{\beta} - \hat{\beta}_{-j} = (X^T X)^{-1} x_j \left(\frac{y_j - x_j^T \hat{\beta}}{1 - h_j} \right).$$

Compare this to the corresponding empirical influence value in Problem 6.1, and obtain the jackknife estimates of the bias and variance of $\hat{\beta}$.
(Sections 2.7.3, 6.2.2, 6.4)

3   For the linear regression model $y_j = x_j \beta + \varepsilon_j$, with no intercept, show that the least squares estimate of β is $\hat{\beta} = \sum x_j y_j / \sum x_j^2$. Define residuals by $e_j = y_j - x_j \hat{\beta}$. If the resampling model is $y_j^* = x_j \hat{\beta} + \varepsilon_j^*$, with ε_j^* randomly sampled from the e_js, show that the resample estimate $\hat{\beta}^*$ has mean and variance respectively

$\bar{e}$ and $\bar{x}$ are the averages of the e_j and x_j.

$$\hat{\beta} + \frac{n \bar{e} \bar{x}}{\sum x_j^2}, \qquad \frac{\sum (e_j - \bar{e})^2}{n \sum x_j^2}.$$

Thus in particular the resampling mean is incorrect. Examine the improvements made by leverage adjustment and mean correction of the residuals.
(Section 6.2.3)

4   The usual estimated variance of the least squares slope estimate $\hat{\beta}_1$ in simple linear regression can be written

$$v = \frac{\sum (y_j - \bar{y})^2 - \hat{\beta}_1^2 \sum (x_j - \bar{x})^2}{(n - 2) \sum (x_j - \bar{x})^2}.$$

If the x^*s and y^*s are random permutations of xs and ys, show that

$$v^* = \frac{\sum (y_j - \bar{y})^2 - \hat{\beta}_1^{*2} \sum (x_j - \bar{x})^2}{(n - 2) \sum (x_j - \bar{x})^2}.$$

Hence show that in the permutation test for zero slope, the R values of $\hat{\beta}_1^*$ are in the same order as those of $\hat{\beta}_1^* / v^{*1/2}$, and that $\hat{\beta}_1^* \geq \hat{\beta}_1$ is equivalent to $\hat{\beta}_1^* / v^{*1/2} \geq \hat{\beta}_1 / v^{1/2}$. This confirms that the P-value of the permutation test is unaffected by studentizing.
(Section 6.2.5)

5   For least squares regression, model-based resampling gives a bootstrap estimator $\hat{\beta}^*$ which satisfies

$$\hat{\beta}^* = \hat{\beta} + (X^T X)^{-1} \sum_{j=1}^{n} x_j \varepsilon_j^*,$$

where the ε_j^* are randomly sampled modified residuals. An alternative proposal is to bypass the resampling model for data and to define directly

$$\hat{\beta}^* = \hat{\beta} + (X^T X)^{-1} \sum_{j=1}^{n} u_j^*,$$

where the u_j^*s are randomly sampled from the vectors

$$u_j = x_j(y_j - x_j^T \hat{\beta}), \qquad j = 1, \ldots, n.$$

Show that under this proposal $\hat{\beta}^*$ has mean $\hat{\beta}$ and variance equal to the robust variance estimate (6.26). Examine, theoretically or through numerical examples, to what extent the skewness of $\hat{\beta}^*$ matches the skewness of $\hat{\beta}$.
(Section 6.3.1; Hu and Zidek, 1995)

6   For the linear regression model $y = X\beta + \varepsilon$, the improved version of the robust estimate of variance for the least squares estimates $\hat{\beta}$ is

$$v_{rob} = (X^T X)^{-1} X^T \mathrm{diag}(r_1^2, \ldots, r_n^2) X (X^T X)^{-1},$$

where r_j is the jth modified residual. If the errors have equal variances, then the usual variance estimate

$$v = s^2 (X^T X)^{-1}$$

would be appropriate and v_{rob} could be quite inefficient. To quantify this, examine the case where the random errors ε_j are independent $N(0, \sigma^2)$. Show first that

$$\mathrm{E}(r_j^2) = \sigma^2, \qquad \mathrm{cov}(r_j^2, r_k^2) = 2\sigma^4 \frac{(1 - h_{jk})^2}{(1 - h_{jj})(1 - h_{kk})}.$$

Hence show that the efficiency of the ith diagonal element of v_{rob} relative to the ith diagonal element of v, as measured by the ratio of their variances, is

h_{jk} is the (j,k)th element of hat matrix H and $h_{jj} = h_j$.

$$\frac{b_{ii}^2}{(n - p) g_i^T Q g_i},$$

where b_{ii} is the ith diagonal element of $(X^T X)^{-1}$, $g_i^T = (d_{i1}^2, \ldots, d_{in}^2)$ with $D = (X^T X)^{-1} X^T$, and Q has elements $(1 - h_{jk})^2 / \{(1 - h_j)(1 - h_k)\}$.
Calculate this relative efficiency for a numerical example.
(Sections 6.2.4, 6.2.6, 6.3.1; Hinkley and Wang, 1991)

7   The statistical function $\beta(F)$ for M-estimation is defined by the estimating equation

$$\int x \psi \left\{ \frac{y - x^T \beta(F)}{\sigma(F)} \right\} dF(x, y) = 0,$$

where $\sigma(F)$ is typically a robust scale parameter. Assume that the model contains an intercept, so that the covariate vector x includes the dummy variable 1. Use the technique of Problem 2.12 to show that the influence function for $\beta(F)$ is

$\dot{\psi}(u)$ is $d\psi(u)/du.$

$$L_\beta(x, y) = \left\{ \int xx^T \dot{\psi}(\varepsilon) dF(x, y) \right\}^{-1} \sigma x \psi(\varepsilon),$$

where $\varepsilon = (y - x^T\beta)/\sigma$; it is assumed that $\varepsilon\psi(\varepsilon)$ has mean zero.
If the distribution of the covariate vector is taken to be the EDF of $x_1, \ldots, x_n$, show that

$$L_\beta(x, y) = n\sigma k^{-1}(X^T X)^{-1} x\psi(\varepsilon),$$

where X is the usual covariate matrix and $k = \mathrm{E}\{\dot{\psi}(\varepsilon)\}$. Use the empirical version of this to verify the variance approximation

$$v_L = ns^2(X^T X)^{-1} \frac{\sum \psi^2(e_j/s)}{\{\sum \dot{\psi}(e_j/s)\}^2},$$

where $e_j = y_j - x_j^T \hat{\beta}$ and s is the estimated scale parameter.
(Section 6.5)

8 Given raw residuals $e_1, \ldots, e_n$, define independent random variables ε_j^* by (6.21).
Show that the first three moments of ε_j^* are 0, e_j^2, and e_j^3.
(a) Let $e_1, \ldots, e_n$ be raw residuals from the fit of a linear model $y = X\beta + \varepsilon$, and define bootstrap data by $y^* = X\hat{\beta} + \varepsilon^*$, where the elements of ε^* are generated according to the wild bootstrap. Show that the bootstrap least squares estimates $\hat{\beta}^*$ take at most 2^n values, and that

$$\mathrm{E}^*(\hat{\beta}^*) = \hat{\beta}, \qquad \mathrm{var}^*(\hat{\beta}^*) = v_{wild} = (X^T X)^{-1} X^T \hat{W} X (X^T X)^{-1},$$

where $\hat{W} = \mathrm{diag}(e_1^2, \ldots, e_n^2)$.
(b) Show that when all the errors have equal variances and the design is balanced, so that $h_j \equiv p/n$, v_{wild} is negatively biased as an estimate of $\mathrm{var}(\hat{\beta})$.
(c) Show that for the simple linear regression model (6.1) the expected value of $\mathrm{var}^*(\hat{\beta}^*)$ is

$$\frac{\sigma^2}{m_2} n^{-2}(n - 1 - m_4/m_2^2),$$

where $m_r = n^{-1}\sum(x_j - \bar{x})^r$. Hence show that if the x_j are uniformly spaced and the errors have equal variances, the wild bootstrap variance estimate is too small by a factor of about $1 - 14/(5n)$.
(d) Show that if the e_j are replaced by r_j, the difficulties in (b) and (c) do not arise.
(Sections 6.2.4, 6.2.6, 6.3.2)

9 Suppose that responses $y_1, \ldots, y_n$ with $n = 2m$ correspond to m independent samples of size two, where the ith sample comes from a population with mean μ_i and these means are of primary interest; the m population variances may differ. Use appropriate dummy variables x_i to express the responses in the linear model $y = X\beta + \varepsilon$, where $\beta_i = \mu_i$. With parameters estimated by least squares, consider estimating the standard error of $\hat{\beta}_i$ by case resampling.
(a) Show that the probability of getting a simulated sample in which all the parameters are estimable is

$$p = \sum_{j=0}^{m} (-1)^j \binom{m}{j} \left(1 - \frac{j}{m}\right)^{2m}.$$

(b) Consider constrained case resampling in which each of the m samples must be represented at least once. Show that the probability that there are r resample cases from the ith sample is

$$p^{-1}\binom{2m}{r}\left(\frac{1}{m}\right)^r\left(1-\frac{1}{m}\right)^{2m-r}\sum_{j=0}^{m-1}(-1)^j\binom{m-1}{j}\left(1-\frac{j}{m-1}\right)^{2m-r},$$

for $r = 1,\ldots,m+1$. Hence calculate the resampling mean of $\hat{\beta}_i$ and give an expression for its variance.
(Section 6.3; Feller, 1968, p. 102)

10 For the one-way model of Problem 6.9 with two observations per group, suppose that $\theta = \beta_2 - \beta_1$. Note that the least squares estimator of θ satisfies

$$\hat{\theta} = \theta + \tfrac{1}{2}(\varepsilon_3 + \varepsilon_4 - \varepsilon_1 - \varepsilon_2).$$

Suppose that we use model-based resampling with the assumption of error homoscedasticity. Show that the resample estimate can be expressed as

$$\hat{\theta}^* = \hat{\theta} + \tfrac{1}{2}\sum_{i=1}^4 \varepsilon_i^*,$$

where the ε_i^* are randomly sampled from the $2m$ modified residuals $\pm\frac{1}{\sqrt{2}}(\varepsilon_{2i}-\varepsilon_{2i-1})$, $i = 1,\ldots,m$. Use this representation to calculate the first four resampling moments of $\hat{\theta}^* - \hat{\theta}$. Compare the results with the first four moments of $\hat{\theta} - \theta$, and comment.
(Section 6.3)

11 Suppose that a 2^{-r} fraction of a 2^8 factorial experiment is run, where $1 \le r \le 4$. Under what circumstances would a bootstrap analysis based on case resampling be reliable?
(Section 6.3)

12 The several cross-validation estimates of prediction error can be calculated explicitly in the simple problem of least squares prediction for homogeneous data with no covariates. Suppose that data $y_1,\ldots,y_n$ and future responses y_+ are all sampled from a population with mean μ and variance σ^2, and consider the prediction rule $\mu(\hat{F}) = \bar{y}$ with accuracy measured by quadratic error.
(a) Verify that the overall prediction error is $\Delta = \sigma^2(1 + n^{-1})$, that the expectation of the apparent error estimate is $\sigma^2(1 - n^{-1})$, and that the cross-validation estimate $\hat{\Delta}_{CV}$ with training sets of size n_t has expectation $\sigma^2(1 + n_t^{-1})$.
(b) Now consider the K-fold cross-validation estimate $\hat{\Delta}_{CV,K}$ and suppose that $n = Km$ with m an integer. Re-label the data in the kth group as $y_{k1},\ldots,y_{km}$, and define $\bar{y}_k = m^{-1}\sum_{l=1}^m y_{kl}$. Verify that

$$\hat{\Delta}_{CV,K} = n^{-1}\sum_{k=1}^K\sum_{l=1}^m (y_{kl} - \bar{y}_k)^2 + K(K-1)^{-2}\sum_{k=1}^K (\bar{y}_k - \bar{y})^2,$$

and hence show that

$$E(\hat{\Delta}_{CV,K}) = \sigma^2\{1 + n^{-1} + n^{-1}(K - 1)^{-1}\}.$$

Thus the bias of $\hat{\Delta}_{CV,K}$ is $\sigma^2 n^{-1}(K - 1)^{-1}$.

(c) Extend the calculations in (b) to show that the adjusted estimate can be written

$$\hat{\Delta}_{ACV,K} = \hat{\Delta}_{CV,K} - K^{-1}(K-1)^{-2}\sum_{k=1}^{K}(\bar{y}_k - \bar{y})^2,$$

and use this to show that $E(\hat{\Delta}_{ACV,K}) = \Delta$.
(Section 6.4; Burman, 1989)

13   The leave-one-out bootstrap estimate of aggregate prediction error for linear prediction and squared error is equal to

$$\hat{\Delta}_{BCV} = n^{-1}\sum_{j=1}^{n} E_{-j}^*(y_j - x_j^T\hat{\beta}_{-j}^*)^2,$$

where $\hat{\beta}_{-j}^*$ is the least squares estimate of β from a bootstrap sample with the jth case excluded and E_{-j}^* denotes expectation over such samples. To calculate the mean of $\hat{\Delta}_{BCV}$, use the substitution

$$y_j - x_j^T\hat{\beta}_{-j}^* = y_j - x_j^T\hat{\beta}_{-j} + x_j^T(\hat{\beta}_{-j}^* - \hat{\beta}_{-j}),$$

and then show that

$$E(Y_j - X_j^T\hat{\beta}_{-j})^2 = \sigma^2\{1 + q(n-1)^{-1}\},$$
$$E\left[E_{-j}^*\{X_j^T(\hat{\beta}_{-j}^* - \hat{\beta}_{-j})(\hat{\beta}_{-j}^* - \hat{\beta}_{-j})^T X_j\}\right] = \sigma^2 q(n-1)^{-1} + O(n^{-2}),$$
$$E\{(Y_j - X_j^T\hat{\beta}_{-j})X_j^T E_{-j}^*(\hat{\beta}_{-j}^* - \hat{\beta}_{-j})\} = O(n^{-2}).$$

These results combine to show that $E(\hat{\Delta}_{BCV}) = \sigma^2(1 + 2qn^{-1}) + O(n^{-2})$, which leads to the choice $w = \frac{2}{3}$ for the estimate $\hat{\Delta}_w = w\hat{\Delta}_{BCV} + (1-w)\hat{\Delta}_{app}$.
(Section 6.4; Hall, 1995)

6.8 Practicals

1   Dataset catsM contains a set of data on the heart weights and body weights of 97 male cats. We investigate the dependence of heart weight (g) on body weight (kg). To see the data, fit a straight-line regression and do diagnostic plots:

```
catsM
plot(catsM$Bwt,catsM$Hwt,xlim=c(0,4),ylim=c(0,24))
cats.lm <- glm(Hwt~Bwt,data=catsM)
summary(cats.lm)
cats.diag <- glm.diag.plots(cats.lm,ret=T)
```

The summary suggests that the line passes through the origin, but we cannot rely on normal-theory results here, because the residuals seem skewed, and their variance possibly increases with the mean. Let us assess the stability of the fitted regression.
For case resampling:

```
cats.fit <- function(data) coef(glm(data$Hwt~data$Bwt))
cats.case <- function(data, i) cats.fit(data[i,])
cats.boot1 <- boot(catsM, cats.case, R=499)
cats.boot1
```

```
plot(cats.boot1,jack=T)
plot(cats.boot1,index=2,jack=T)
```

to see a summary and plots for the bootstrapped intercepts and slopes,. How
normal do they seem? Is the model-based standard error from the original fit
accurate? To what extent do the results depend on any single observation? We can
calculate the estimated standard error by the nonparametric delta method by

```
cats.L <- empinf(cats.boot1,type="reg")
sqrt(var.linear(cats.L))
```

Compare it with the quoted standard error from the regression output, and from
the empirical variance of the intercepts. Are the three standard errors in the order
you would expect?
For model-based resampling:

```
cats.res <- cats.diag$res*cats.diag$sd
cats.res <- cats.res - mean(cats.res)
cats.df <- data.frame(catsM,res=cats.res,fit=fitted(cats.lm))
cats.model <- function(data, i)
{ d <- data
  d$Hwt <- d$fit + d$res[i]
  cats.fit(d) }
cats.boot2 <- boot(cats.df, cats.model, R=499)
cats.boot2
plot(cats.boot2)
```

Compare the properties of these bootstrapped coefficients with those from case
resampling.
How would you use a resampling method to test the hypothesis that the line passes
through the origin?
(Section 6.2; Fisher, 1947)

2   The data of Example 6.14 are in dataframe survival. For a jackknife-after-
bootstrap plot for the regression slope $\hat{\beta}_1$:

```
survival.fun <- function(data, i)
{ d <- data[i,]
  d.reg <- glm(log(d$surv)~d$dose)
  c(coefficients(d.reg))}
survival.boot <- boot(survival, survival.fun, R=999)
jack.after.boot(survival.boot, index=2)
```

Compare this with Figure 6.15. What is happening?

3   poisons contains the survival times of animals in a 3×4 factorial experiment.
Each combination of three poisons and four treatments is used for four animals,
the allocation to the animals being completely randomized. The data are standard
in the literature as an example where transformation can be applied. Here we
apply resampling to the data on the original scale, and use it to test whether an
interaction between the two factors is needed. To calculate the test statistic, the
standard F statistic, and to see its significance using the usual F test:

```
poison.fun <- function(data)
{ assign("data.junk",data,frame=1)
  data.anova <- anova(glm(time~poison*treat,data=data.junk))
  dev <- as.numeric(unlist(data.anova[2]))
```

```
      df <- as.numeric(unlist(data.anova[1]))
      res.dev <- as.numeric(unlist(data.anova[4]))
      res.df <- as.numeric(unlist(data.anova[3]))
      (dev[4]/df[4])/(res.dev[4]/res.df[4]) }
poison.fun(poisons)
anova(glm(time~poison*treat,data=poisons),test="F")
```

To apply resampling analysis, using as the null model that with main effects:

```
poison.lm <- glm(time~poison+treat,data=poisons)
poison.diag <- glm.diag(poison.lm)
poison.mle <- list(fit=fitted(poison.lm),
                   res=residuals(poison.lm)/sqrt(1-poison.diag$h))
poison.gen <- function(data,mle)
{ i <- sample(48,replace=T)
  data$time <- mle$fit + mle$res[i]
  data }
poison.boot <- boot(poisons, poison.fun, R=199, sim="parametric",
                    ran.gen=poison.gen, mle=poison.mle)
sum(poison.boot$t>poison.boot$t0)
```

At what level does this give significance? Is this in line with the theoretical value? One assumption of the above analysis is homogeneity of variances, but the data cast some doubt on this. To test the hypothesis without this assumption:

```
poison.gen1 <- function(data,mle)
{ i <- matrix(1:48,4,12,byrow=T)
  i <- apply(i,1,sample,replace=T,size=4)
  data$time <- mle$fit + mle$res[i]
  data }
poison.boot <- boot(poisons, poison.fun, R=199, sim="parametric",
                    ran.gen=poison.gen1, mle=poison.mle)
sum(poison.boot$t>poison.boot$t0)
```

What do you conclude now?
(Section 6.3; Box and Cox, 1964)

4   For an example of prediction, we consider using the nuclear power station data to predict the cost of new stations like cases 27–32, except that their value for date is 73. We choose to make the prediction using the model with all covariates. To fit that model, and to make the 'new' station:

```
nuclear.glm <- glm(log(cost)~date+log(t1)+log(t2)+log(cap)+pr+ne
                   +ct+bw+log(cum.n)+pt,data=nuclear)
nuclear.diag <- glm.diag(nuclear.glm)
nuke <- data.frame(nuclear,fit=fitted(nuclear.glm),
                   res=nuclear.diag$res*nuclear.diag$sd)
nuke.p <- nuke[32,]
nuke.p$date <- 73
nuke.p$fit <- predict(nuclear.glm,nuke.p)
```

The bootstrap function and the call to boot are:

```
nuke.pred <- function(data,i,i.p,d.p)
{ d <- data
  d$cost <- exp(d$fit+d$res[i])
  d.glm <- glm(log(cost)~date+log(t1)+log(t2)+log(cap)+pr+ne
```

```
                +ct+bw+log(cum.n)+pt,data=d)
    predict(d.glm,d.p)-(d.p$fit+d$res[i.p]) }
nuclear.boot.pred <- boot(nuke,nuke.pred,R=199,m=1,d.p=nuke.p)
```

Finally the 95% prediction intervals are obtained by

```
as.vector(exp(nuke.p$fit-quantile(nuclear.boot.pred$t,
                            c(0.975,0.025)))))
```

How do these compare to those in Example 6.8?
Modify the above analysis to use a studentized pivot. What effect has this change
on your interval?
(Section 6.3.3; Cox and Snell, 1981, pp. 81–90)

5   Consider predicting the log brain weight of a mammal from its log body weight,
     using squared error cost. The data are in dataframe `mammals`. For an initial model,
     apparent error and ordinary cross-validation estimates of aggregate prediction
     error:

```
cost <- function(y, mu=0) mean((y-mu)^2)
mammals.glm <- glm(log(brain)~log(body),data=mammals)
muhat <- fitted(mammals.glm)
app.err <- cost(mammals.glm$y, muhat)
mammals.diag <- glm.diag(mammals.glm)
cv.err <- mean((mammals.glm$y-muhat)^2/(1-mammals.diag$h)^2)
```

For 6-fold unadjusted and adjusted estimates of aggregate prediction error:

```
cv.err.6 <- cv.glm(mammals, mammals.glm, cost, K=6)
```

Experiment with other values of K.
For bootstrap and 0.632 estimates, and plot of error components:

```
mammals.pred.fun <- function(data, i, formula)
{ d <- data[i,]
  d.glm <- glm(formula,data=d)
  D.F.hatF <- cost(log(data$brain), predict(d.glm,data))
  D.hatF.hatF <- cost(log(d$brain), fitted(d.glm))
  c(log(data$brain)-predict(d.glm,data), D.F.hatF - D.hatF.hatF)}
mam.boot <- boot(mammals, mammals.pred.fun, R=200,
                 formula=formula(mammals.glm))
n <- nrow(mammals)
err.boot <- app.err + mean(mam.boot$t[,n+1])
err.632 <- 0
mam.boot$f <- boot.array(mam.boot)
for (i in 1:n)
   err.632 <- err.632 + cost(mam.boot$t[mam.boot$f[,i]==0,i])/n
err.632 <- 0.368*app.err + 0.632*err.632
ord <- order(mammals.diag$res)
mam.pred <- mam.boot$t[,ord]
mam.fac <- factor(rep(1:n,rep(200,n)),labels=ord)
plot(mam.fac, mam.pred,ylab="Prediction errors",
     xlab="Case ordered by residual")
```

What are cases 34, 35, and 32?
(Section 6.4.1)

6   The data of Examples 6.15 and 6.16 are in dataframe `salinity`. For the linear regression model with all three covariates, consider the effect of discharge `dis` and the influence of case 16 on estimating this. Resample the least squares, L_1 and least trimmed squares estimates, and then look at the jackknife-after-bootstrap plots:

```
salinity.rob.fun <- function(data,i)
{ data.i <- data[i,]
  ls.fit <- lm(sal~lag+trend+dis, data=data.i)
  l1.fit <- l1fit(data.i[,-1],data.i[,1])
  lts.fit <- ltsreg(data.i[,-1],data.i[,1])
  c(ls.fit$coef,l1.fit$coef,lts.fit$coef) }
salinity.boot <- boot(salinity,salinity.rob.fun,R=1000)
jack.after.boot(salinity.boot,index=4)
jack.after.boot(salinity.boot,index=8)
jack.after.boot(salinity.boot,index=12)
```

What conclusions do you draw from these plots about (a) the shapes of the distributions of the estimates, (b) comparisons between the estimation methods, and (c) the effects of case 16?

One possible explanation for case 16 being an outlier with respect to the multiple linear regression model used previously is that a quadratic effect in `discharge` should be added to the model. We can test for this using the pivot method with least squares estimates and case resampling:

```
salinity.quad.fun <- function(data, i)
{ data.i <- data[i,]
  ls.fit <- lm(sal~lag+trend+poly(dis,2), data=data.i)
  ls.sum <- summary(ls.fit)
  ls.std <- sqrt(diag(ls.sum$cov))*ls.sum$sigma
  c(ls.fit$coef, ls.std) }
salinity.boot <- boot(salinity, salinity.quad.fun, R=99)
quad.z <- salinity.boot$t0[5]/salinity.boot$t0[10]
quad.z.star <- (salinity.boot$t[,5]-salinity.boot$t0[5])/
               salinity.boot$t[,10]
(1+sum(quad.z<quad.z.star))/(1+salinity.boot$R)
```

Out of curiosity, look at the normal Q-Q plots of raw and studentized coefficients:

```
qqnorm(salinity.boot$t[,5],ylab="discharge quadratic coefficient")
qqnorm(quad.z.star, ylab="discharge quadratic z statistic")
```

Is it reasonable to use least squares estimates here? See whether or not the same conclusion would be reached using other methods of estimation.

(Section 6.5; Ruppert and Carroll, 1980; Atkinson, 1985, p. 48)

7

Further Topics in Regression

7.1 Introduction

In Chapter 6 we showed how the basic bootstrap methods of earlier chapters extend to linear regression. The broad aim of this chapter is to extend the discussion further, to various forms of nonlinear regression models — especially generalized linear models and survival models — and to nonparametric regression, where the form of the mean response is not fully specified.

A particular feature of linear regression is the possibility of error-based resampling, when responses are expressible as means plus homoscedastic errors. This is particularly useful when our objective is prediction. For generalized linear models, especially for discrete data, responses cannot be described in terms of additive errors. Section 7.2 describes ways of generalizing error-based resampling for such models. The corresponding development for survival data is given in Section 7.3. Section 7.4 looks briefly at nonlinear regression with additive error, mainly to illustrate the useful contribution that resampling methods can make to analysis of such models. There is often a need to estimate the potential accuracy of predictions based on regression models, and Section 6.4 contained a general discussion of resampling methods for this. In Section 7.5 we focus on one type of application, the estimation of misclassification rates when a binary response y corresponds to a classification.

Not all relationships between a response y and covariates x can be readily modelled in terms of a parametric mean function of known form. At least for exploratory purposes it is useful to have flexible nonparametric curve-fitting methods, and there is now a wide variety of these. In Section 7.6 we examine briefly how resampling can be used in conjunction with some of these nonparametric regression methods.

326

7.2 Generalized Linear Models

7.2.1 Introduction

The generalized linear model extends the linear regression model of Section 6.3 in two ways. First, the distribution of the response Y has the property that the variance is an explicit function of the mean μ,

$$\text{var}(Y) = \phi V(\mu),$$

where $V(\cdot)$ is the known *variance function* and ϕ is the dispersion parameter, which may be unknown. This includes the important cases of binomial, Poisson, and gamma distributions in addition to the normal distribution. Secondly, the linear mean structure is generalized to

$$g(\mu) = \eta, \quad \eta = x^T \beta,$$

where $g(\cdot)$ is a specified monotone *link function* which "links" the mean to the linear predictor η. As before, x is a $(p+1) \times 1$ vector of explanatory variables associated with Y. The possible combinations of different variance functions and link functions include such things as logistic and probit regression, and log-linear models for contingency tables, without making ad-hoc transformations of responses.

The first extension was touched on briefly in Section 6.2.6 in connection with weighted least squares, which plays a key role in fitting generalized linear models. The second extension, to linear models for transformed means, represents a very special type of nonlinear model.

When independent responses y_j are obtained with explanatory variables x_j, the full model is usually taken to be

$$\text{E}(Y_j) = \mu_j, \quad g(\mu_j) = x_j^T \beta, \quad \text{var}(Y_j) = \kappa c_j V(\mu_j), \tag{7.1}$$

where κ may be unknown and the c_j are known weights. For example, for binomial data with probability $\pi(x_j)$ and denominator m_j, we take $c_j = 1/m_j$; see Example 7.3. The constant κ equals one for binomial, Poisson and exponential data. Notice that (7.1) strictly only specifies first and second moments of the responses, and in that sense is a semiparametric model. So, for example, we can model overdispersed count data by using the Poisson variance function $V(\mu) = \mu$ but allowing κ to be a free overdispersion parameter which is to be estimated.

One important point about generalized linear models is the non-unique definitions of residuals, and consequent non-uniqueness of nonparametric re-sampling algorithms.

After illustrating these ideas with an example we briefly review the main aspects of generalized linear models. We then go on to discuss resampling methods.

	Group 1			Group 2	
Case	x	y	Case	x	y
1	3.36	65	18	3.64	56
2	2.88	156	19	3.48	65
3	3.63	100	20	3.60	17
4	3.41	134	21	3.18	7
5	3.78	16	22	3.95	16
6	4.02	108	23	3.72	22
7	4.00	121	24	4.00	3
8	4.23	4	25	4.28	4
9	3.73	39	26	4.43	2
10	3.85	143	27	4.45	3
11	3.97	56	28	4.49	8
12	4.51	26	29	4.41	4
13	4.54	22	30	4.32	3
14	5.00	1	31	4.90	30
15	5.00	1	32	5.00	4
16	4.72	5	33	5.00	43
17	5.00	65			

Table 7.1 Survival times y (weeks) for two groups of acute leukaemia patients, together with $x = \log_{10}$ white blood cell count (Feigl and Zelen, 1965).

Example 7.1 (Leukaemia data) Table 7.1 contains data on the survival times in weeks of two groups of acute leukaemia victims, as a function of their white blood cell counts.

A simple model is that within each group survival time Y is exponential with mean $\mu = \exp(\beta_0 + \beta_1 x)$, where $x = \log_{10}$(white blood cell count). Thus the link function is logarithmic. The intercept is different for each group, but the slope is assumed common, so the full model for the jth response in group i is

$$\mathrm{E}(Y_{ij}) = \mu_{ij}, \quad \log(\mu_{ij}) = \beta_{0i} + \beta_1 x_{ij}, \quad \mathrm{var}(Y_{ij}) = V(\mu_{ij}) = \mu_{ij}^2.$$

The fitted means $\hat{\mu}$ and the data are shown in the left panel of Figure 7.1. The mean survival times for group 2 are shorter than those for group 1 at the same white blood cell count.

Under this model the ratios Y/μ are exponentially distributed with unit mean, and hence the Q-Q plot of $y_{ij}/\hat{\mu}_{ij}$ against exponential quantiles in the right panel of Figure 7.1 would ideally be a straight line. Systematic curvature might indicate that we should use a gamma density with index ν,

$$f(y \mid \mu, \nu) = \frac{y^{\nu-1}\nu^\nu}{\mu^\nu \Gamma(\nu)} \exp\left(-\frac{\nu y}{\mu}\right), \quad y > 0, \quad \mu, \nu > 0.$$

In this case $\mathrm{var}(Y) = \mu^2/\nu$, so the dispersion parameter is taken to be $\kappa = 1/\nu$ and $c_j \equiv 1$. In fact the exponential model seems to fit adequately. ∎

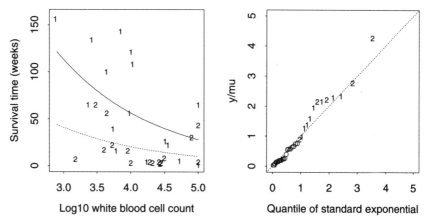

Figure 7.1 Summary plots for fits of an exponential model fitted to two groups of survival times for leukaemia patients. The left panel shows the times and fitted means as a function of their white blood cell count (group 1, fitted line solid; group 2, fitted line dots). The right panel shows an exponential Q-Q plot of the $y/\hat{\mu}$.

7.2.2 Model fitting and residuals

Estimation

Suppose that independent data $(x_1, y_1), \ldots, (x_n, y_n)$ are available, with response mean and variance described by (7.1). If the response distributions are assumed to be given by the corresponding exponential family model, then the maximum likelihood estimates of the regression parameters β solve the $(p+1) \times 1$ system of estimating equations

$$\sum_{j=1}^{n} \frac{y_j - \mu_j}{c_j V(\mu_j)} \times \frac{x_j}{\dot{g}(\mu_j)} = 0, \tag{7.2}$$

where $\dot{g}(\mu) = \partial\eta/\partial\mu$ is the derivative of the link function. Because the dispersion parameters are taken to have the form κc_j, the estimate $\hat{\beta}$ does not depend on κ. Note that although the estimates are derived as maximum likelihood estimates, their values depend only upon the regression relationship as expressed by the assumed variance function and the link function and choice of covariates.

The usual method for solving (7.2) is iterative weighted least squares, in which at each iteration the adjusted responses $z_j = \eta_j + (y_j - \mu_j)\dot{g}(\mu_j)$ are regressed on the x_j with weights w_j given by

$$w_j^{-1} = c_j V(\mu_j)\dot{g}^2(\mu_j); \tag{7.3}$$

all these quantities are evaluated at the current values of the estimates. The weighted least squares equation (6.27) applies at each iteration, with y replaced by the adjusted dependent variable z. The approximate variance matrix for $\hat{\beta}$

is given by the analogue of (6.24), namely

$$\text{var}(\hat{\beta}) \doteq \kappa (X^T W X)^{-1}, \tag{7.4}$$

with the diagonal weight matrix $W = \text{diag}(w_1, \ldots, w_n)$ evaluated at the final fitted values $\hat{\mu}_j$.

The corresponding 'hat' matrix is

$$H = X(X^T W X)^{-1} X^T W, \tag{7.5}$$

Some authors prefer to work with $X'(X'^T X')^{-1} X'^{1/2}$, where $X' = W^{1/2} X$.

as in (6.28). The relationship of H to fitted values is $\hat{\eta} = Hz$, where z is the vector of adjusted responses. Note that in general W, and hence H, depends upon the fitted values. The residual vector $e = y - \hat{\mu}$ has approximate variance matrix $(I - H)\text{var}(Y)$, this being exact only for linear regression with known W.

When the dispersion parameter κ is unknown, it is estimated by the analogue of residual mean square,

$$\hat{\kappa} = \frac{1}{n-p-1} \sum_{j=1}^{n} \frac{(y_j - \hat{\mu}_j)^2}{c_j V(\hat{\mu}_j)}. \tag{7.6}$$

For a linear model with $V(\mu) = 1$ and dispersion parameter $\kappa = \sigma^2$, this gives $\hat{\kappa} = s^2$, the residual mean square.

Let $\ell_j(\mu_j)$ denote the contribution that the jth observation makes to the overall log likelihood $\ell(\mu)$, parametrized in terms of the means μ_j. Then the fit of a generalized linear model is measured by the *deviance*

$$D = 2\kappa \{\ell(y) - \ell(\hat{\mu})\} = 2\kappa \sum_j \{\ell_j(y_j) - \ell_j(\hat{\mu}_j)\}, \tag{7.7}$$

which is the scaled difference between the maximized log likelihoods for the saturated model — which has a parameter for each observation — and the fitted model. The deviance corresponds to the residual sum of squares in the analysis of a linear regression model. For example, there are large reductions in the deviance when important explanatory variables are added to a model, and competing models may be compared via their deviances. When the fitted model is correct, the *scaled deviance* $\kappa^{-1}D$ will sometimes have an approximate chi-squared distribution on $n - p - 1$ degrees of freedom, analogous to the rescaled residual sum of squares in a normal linear model.

Significance tests

Individual coefficients β_j can be tested using studentized estimates, with standard errors estimated using (7.4), with κ replaced by the estimate $\hat{\kappa}$ if necessary. The null distributions of these studentized estimates will be approximately standard normal, but the accuracy of this approximation can be open to question. Allowance for estimation of κ can be made by using the t distribution with

$n-p-1$ degrees of freedom, as is justifiable for normal-theory linear regression, but in general the accuracy is questionable.

The analogue of analysis of variance is the analysis of deviance, wherein differences of deviances are used to measure effects. To test whether or not a particular subset of covariates has no effect on mean response, we use as test statistic the scaled difference of deviances, D for the full model with p covariates and D_0 for the reduced model with p_0 covariates. If κ is known, then the test statistic is $Q = (D_0 - D)/\kappa$. Approximate properties of log likelihood ratios imply that the null distribution of Q is approximately chi-squared, with degrees of freedom equal to $p - p_0$, the number of covariate terms being tested. If κ is estimated for the full model by $\hat{\kappa}$, as in (7.6), then the test statistic is

$$Q = (D_0 - D)/\hat{\kappa}. \tag{7.8}$$

In the special case of linear regression, $(p - p_0)^{-1}Q$ is the F statistic, and this motivates the use of the $F_{p-p_0,n-p-1}$ distribution as approximate null distribution for $(p-p_0)^{-1}Q$ here, although this has little theoretical justification.

Residuals

Residuals and other regression diagnostics for linear models may be extended to generalized linear models. The general form of residuals will be a suitably standardized version of $\delta(y, \hat{\mu})$ where $\delta(Y, \mu)$ matches some notion of random error.

The simplest way to define residuals is to mimic the earlier definitions for linear models, and to take the set of standardized differences, the *Pearson residuals*, $(y_j - \hat{\mu}_j)/\{c_j\hat{\kappa}V(\hat{\mu}_j)\}^{1/2}$. Leverage adjustment of these to compensate for estimation of β involves h_j, the jth diagonal element of the hat matrix H in (7.5), and yields *standardized Pearson residuals*

$$r_{Pj} = \frac{y_j - \hat{\mu}_j}{\{c_j\hat{\kappa}V(\hat{\mu}_j)(1 - h_j)\}^{1/2}}, \qquad j = 1, \ldots, n. \tag{7.9}$$

The standardized Pearson residuals are essentially scaled versions of the modified residuals defined in (6.29), except that the denominators of (7.9) may depend on the parameter estimates. In large samples one would expect the r_{Pj} to have mean and variance approximately zero and one, as they do for linear regression models.

In general the Pearson residuals inherit the skewness of the responses themselves, which can be considerable, and it may be better to standardize a transformed response. One way to do this is to define standardized residuals on the linear predictor scale,

$$r_{Lj} = \frac{g(y_j) - g(\hat{\mu}_j)}{\{c_j\hat{\kappa}\dot{g}^2(\hat{\mu}_j)V(\hat{\mu}_j)(1 - h_j)\}^{1/2}}, \qquad j = 1, \ldots, n. \tag{7.10}$$

For discrete data this definition must be altered if $g(y_j)$ is infinite, as for example when $g(y) = \log y$ and $y = 0$. For a non-identity link function one should not expect the mean and variance of r_{Lj} to be approximately zero and one, unless κ is unusually small; see Example 7.2.

An alternative approach to defining residuals is based on the fact that in a linear model the residual sum of squares equals the sum of squared residuals. This suggests that residuals for generalized linear models can be constructed from the contributions that individual observations make to the deviance. Suppose first that κ is known. Then the scaled deviance can be written as

$$\kappa^{-1}D = \sum d_j^2,$$

where $d_j = d(y_j, \hat{\mu}_j)$ is the signed square root of the scaled deviance contribution due to the jth case, the sign being that of $y_j - \hat{\mu}_j$. The *deviance residual* is d_j. Definition (7.7) implies that

$$d_j = \text{sign}(y_j - \hat{\mu}_j)[2\{\ell_j(y_j) - \ell_j(\hat{\mu}_j)\}]^{1/2}.$$

When ℓ is the normal log likelihood and $\kappa = \sigma^2$ is unknown, D is scaled by $\hat{\kappa} = s^2$ rather than κ before defining d_j. Similarly for the gamma log likelihood; see Example 7.2. In practice *standardized deviance residuals*

$$r_{Dj} = \frac{d_j}{(1 - h_j)^{1/2}}, \qquad j = 1, \ldots, n, \qquad (7.11)$$

are more commonly used than the unadjusted d_j.

For the linear regression model of Section 6.3, r_{Dj} is proportional to the modified residual (6.9). For other models the r_{Dj} can be seriously biased, but once bias-corrected they are typically closer to standard normal than are the r_{Pj} or r_{Lj}.

One general point to note about all of these residuals is that they are scaled, implicitly or explicitly, unlike the modified residuals of Chapter 6.

Quasilikelihood estimation

As we have noted before, only the link and variance functions must be specified in order to find estimates $\hat{\beta}$ and approximate standard errors. So although (7.2) and (7.6) arise from a parametric model, they are more generally applicable — just as least squares results are applicable beyond the normal-theory linear model. When no response distribution is assumed, the estimates $\hat{\beta}$ are referred to as *quasilikelihood* estimates, and there is an associated theory for such estimates, although this is not of concern here. The most common application is to data with a response in the form of counts or proportions, which are often found to be overdispersed relative to the Poisson or binomial distributions. One approach to modelling such data is to use the variance function appropriate to binomial or Poisson data, but to allow the dispersion parameter κ to be a free parameter, estimated by (7.6). This estimate is then used in calculating standard errors for $\hat{\beta}$ and residuals, as indicated above.

7.2.3 Sampling plans

Parametric simulation for a generalized linear model involves simulating new sets of data from the fitted parametric model. It has the usual disadvantage of the parametric bootstrap, that datasets generated from a poorly fitting model may not have the statistical properties of the original data. This applies particularly when count data are overdispersed relative to a Poisson or binomial model, unless the overdispersion has been modelled successfully.

Nonparametric simulation requires generating artificial data without assuming that the original data have some particular parametric distribution. A completely nonparametric approach is to resample cases, which applies exactly as described in Section 6.2.4. However, it is important to be clear what a case is in any particular application, because count and proportion data are often aggregated from larger datasets of independent variables.

Provided that the model (7.1) is correct, as would be checked by appropriate diagnostic methods, it makes sense to use the fitted model and generalize the semiparametric approach of resampling errors, as described in Section 6.2.3. We focus now on ways to do this.

Resampling errors

The simplest approach mimics the linear model sampling scheme but allows for the different response variances, just as in Section 6.2.6. So we define simulated responses by

$$y_j^* = \hat{\mu}_j + \{c_j \hat{\kappa} V(\hat{\mu}_j)\}^{1/2} \varepsilon_j^*, \qquad j = 1, \dots, n, \qquad (7.12)$$

where $\varepsilon_1^*, \dots, \varepsilon_n^*$ is a random sample from the mean-adjusted, standardized Pearson residuals $r_{Pj} - \bar{r}_P$ with r_{Pj} defined at (7.9). Note that for count data we are not assuming $\kappa = 1$. This resampling scheme duplicates the method of Section 6.2.6 for linear models, where the link function is the identity.

Because in general there is no explicit function connecting response y_j to random error ε_j, as there is for linear regression models, the resampling scheme (7.12) is not the only approach, and sometimes it is not suitable. One alternative is to use the same idea on the linear predictor scale. That is, we generate bootstrap data by setting

$$y_j^* = g^{-1} \left[x^T \hat{\beta} + \dot{g}(\hat{\mu}_j) \{c_j \hat{\kappa} V(\hat{\mu}_j)\}^{1/2} \varepsilon_j^* \right], \qquad j = 1, \dots, n, \qquad (7.13)$$

In these first two resampling schemes the scale factor $\hat{\kappa}^{-1/2}$ can be omitted provided it is omitted from both the residual definition and from the definition of y^*.

where $g^{-1}(\cdot)$ is the inverse link function and $\varepsilon_1^*, \dots, \varepsilon_n^*$ is a bootstrap sample from the residuals $r_{L1}, \dots, r_{Ln}$ defined at (7.10). Here the residuals should not be mean-adjusted unless $g(\cdot)$ is the identity link, in which case $r_{Lj} \equiv r_{Pj}$ and the two schemes (7.12) and (7.13) are the same.

A third approach is to use the deviance residuals as surrogate errors. If the deviance residual d_j is written as $d(y_j, \hat{\mu}_j)$, then imagine that corresponding random errors ε_j are defined by $\varepsilon_j = d(y_j, \mu_j)$. The distribution of these ε_j

is estimated by the EDF of the standardized deviance residuals (7.11). This suggests that we construct a bootstrap sample as follows. Randomly sample $\varepsilon_1^*, \ldots, \varepsilon_n^*$ from $r_{D1}, \ldots, r_{Dn}$ and let $y_1^*, \ldots, y_n^*$ be the solutions to

$$\varepsilon_j^* = d(y_j^*, \hat{\mu}_j), \qquad j = 1, \ldots, n. \tag{7.14}$$

This also gives the method of Section 6.2.3 for linear models, except for the mean adjustment of residuals.

None of these three methods is perfect. One obvious drawback is that they can all give negative or non-integer values of y^* when the original data are non-negative integer counts. A simple fix for discrete responses is to round the value of y_j^* from (7.12), (7.13), or (7.14) to the nearest appropriate value. For count data this is a non-negative integer, and if the response is a proportion with denominator m, it is a number in the set $0, 1/m, 2/m, \ldots, 1$. However, rounding can appreciably increase the proportion of extreme values of y^* for a case whose fitted value is near the end of its range.

A similar difficulty can occur when responses are positive with $V(\mu) = \kappa\mu^2$, as in Example 7.1. The Pearson residuals are $\hat{\kappa}^{-1/2}(y_j - \hat{\mu}_j)/\hat{\mu}_j$, all necessarily greater than $-\hat{\kappa}^{-1/2}$. But the standardized versions r_{Pj} are not so constrained, so that the result $y_j^* = \hat{\mu}_j(1 + \hat{\kappa}^{1/2}\varepsilon_j^*)$ from applying (7.12) can be negative. The obvious fix is to truncate y_j^* at zero, but this may distort the distribution of y^*, and so is not generally recommended.

Example 7.2 (Leukaemia data) For the data introduced in Example 7.1 the parametric model is gamma with log likelihood contributions

$$\ell_{ij}(\mu_{ij}) = -\kappa^{-1}\{\log(\mu_{ij}) + y_{ij}/\mu_{ij}\},$$

and the regression is additive on the logarithmic scale, $\log(\mu_{ij}) = \beta_{0i} + \beta_1 x_{ij}$. The deviance for the fitted model is $D = 40.32$ with 30 degrees of freedom, and equation (7.6) gives $\hat{\kappa} = 1.09$. The deviance residuals are calculated with κ set equal to $\hat{\kappa}$,

$$d_{ij} = \text{sign}(z_{ij} - 1)\{2\hat{\kappa}^{-1}(z_{ij} - 1 - \log z_{ij})\}^{1/2},$$

where $z_{ij} = y_{ij}/\hat{\mu}_{ij}$. The corresponding standardized values $r_{D,ij}$ have sample mean and variance respectively -0.37 and 1.15. The Pearson residuals are $\hat{\kappa}^{-1/2}(z_{ij} - 1)$.

The z_{ij} would be approximately a sample from the standard exponential distribution if in fact $\kappa = 1$, and the right-hand panel of Figure 7.1 suggests that this is a reasonable assumption.

Our basic parametric model for these data sets $\kappa = 1$ and puts $Y = \mu\varepsilon$, where ε has an exponential distribution with unit mean. Hence the parametric bootstrap involves simulating exponential data from the fitted model, that is setting $y^* = \hat{\mu}\varepsilon^*$, where ε^* is standard exponential. A slightly more cautious

Table 7.2 Lower and upper limits of 95% studentized bootstrap confidence intervals for β_{01} and β_1 for leukaemia data, based on 999 replicates of different simulation schemes.

	β_{01}		β_1	
	Lower	Upper	Lower	Upper
Exponential	5.16	11.12	−1.42	−0.04
Linear predictor, r_L	3.61	10.58	−1.53	0.17
Deviance, r_D	5.00	11.10	−1.46	0.02
Cases	0.31	8.78	−1.37	0.81

approach would be to generate gamma data with mean $\hat\mu$ and index $\hat\kappa^{-1}$, but we shall not do this here.

For nonparametric simulation, we consider all three schemes described earlier. First, with variance function $V(\mu) = \kappa\mu^2$, the Pearson residuals are $\hat\kappa^{-1/2}(y - \hat\mu)/\hat\mu$. Resampling Pearson residuals via (7.12) would be equivalent to setting $y^* = \hat\mu\varepsilon^*$, where ε^* is sampled at random from the zs (Problem 7.2). However, (7.12) cannot be used with the standardized Pearson residuals r_P, because negative values of y^* will occur, possibly as low as -4. Truncation at zero is not a sufficient remedy for this.

For the second resampling scheme (7.13), the logarithmic link gives $y^* = \hat\mu\exp(\hat\kappa^{1/2}\varepsilon^*)$, where ε^* is randomly sampled from the r_Ls which here are given by $r_L = \hat\kappa^{-1/2}(1-h)^{-1/2}\log(z)$. The sample mean and variance of r_L are -0.61 and 1.63, in very close agreement with those for the logarithm of a standard exponential variate. It is important that no mean correction be made to the r_L.

To implement the bootstrap for deviance residuals, the scheme (7.14) can be simplified as follows. We solve the equations $d(\tilde z_j, 1) = r_{Dj}$ for $j = 1,\ldots,n$ to obtain $\tilde z_1,\ldots,\tilde z_n$, and then set $y_j^* = \hat\mu_j\varepsilon_j^*$ for $j = 1,\ldots,n$, where $\varepsilon_1^*,\ldots,\varepsilon_n^*$ is a bootstrap sample from the $\tilde z$s (Problem 7.2).

Table 7.2 shows 95% studentized bootstrap confidence intervals for β_{01} (the intercept for Group 1) and β_1 using these schemes with $R = 999$. The variance estimates used are from (7.4) rather than the nonparametric delta method. The intervals for the three model-based schemes are very similar, while those for resampling cases are rather different, particularly for β_1, for which the bootstrap distribution of the studentized statistic is very non-normal.

Figure 7.2 compares simulated deviances with quantiles of the chi-squared distribution. Naive asymptotics would suggest that the scaled deviance $\hat\kappa D$ has approximately a chi-squared distribution on 30 degrees of freedom, but these asymptotics — which apply as $\kappa\to0$ — are clearly not useful here, even when data are in fact generated from the exponential distribution. The fitted deviance of 40.32 is not extreme, and the variation of the simulated estimates

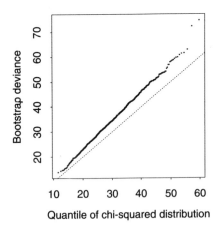
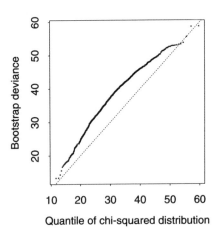

Figure 7.2 Leukaemia
data. Chi-squared Q-Q
plots of simulated
deviances for parametric
sampling from the fitted
exponential model (left)
and case resampling
(right).

$\hat{\kappa}^*$ is large enough that the observed value $\hat{\kappa} = 1.09$ could easily occur by
chance if the data were indeed exponential.   ∎

Comparison of resampling schemes

To compare the performances of the resampling schemes described above in
setting confidence intervals, we conducted a series of Monte Carlo experiments,
each based on 1000 sets of data of size $n = 15$, with linear predictor $\eta = \beta_0 + \beta_1 x$. In the first experiment, the values of x were generated from a
distribution uniform on the interval $(0, 1)$, we took $\beta_0 = \beta_1 = 4$, and responses
were generated from the exponential distribution with mean $\exp(\eta)$. Each
sample was then bootstrapped 199 times using case resampling and by model-
based resampling from the fitted model, with variance function $V(\mu) = \mu^2$,
by applying (7.13) and (7.14). For each of these resampling schemes, various
confidence intervals were obtained for parameters β_0, β_1, $\psi_1 = \beta_0\beta_1$ and
$\psi_2 = \beta_0/\beta_1$. The confidence intervals used were: the standard interval based
on the large-sample normal distribution of the estimate, using the usual rather
than a robust standard error; the interval based on a normal approximation
with bias and variance estimated from the resamples; the percentile and BC_a
intervals; and the basic bootstrap and studentized bootstrap intervals, the
latter using nonparametric delta method variance estimates. The first part of
Table 7.3 shows the empirical coverages of nominal 90% confidence intervals
for these combinations of resampling scheme, method of interval construction,
and parameter.

   The second experiment used the same design matrix, linear predictor, and
model-fitting and resampling schemes as the first, but the data were generated
from a lognormal model with mean $\exp(\eta)$ and unit variance on the log scale.

Table 7.3 Empirical coverages (%) for four parameters based on applying various resampling schemes with $R = 199$ to 1000 samples of size 15 generated from various models. Target coverage is 90%. The first two sets of results are for an exponential model fitted to exponential and lognormal data, and the second two are for a Poisson model fitted to Poisson and negative binomial data. See text for details.

	Cases				r_L or r_P				r_D			
	β_0	β_1	ψ_1	ψ_2	β_0	β_1	ψ_1	ψ_2	β_0	β_1	ψ_1	ψ_2
Standard	85	86	89	85	85	86	89	86	85	86	90	86
Normal	88	89	92	90	88	89	90	89	87	89	90	89
Percentile	85	87	83	89	86	89	86	89	86	88	86	89
BC_a	84	86	82	86	86	88	83	88	86	88	83	88
Basic	86	88	87	84	86	89	86	83	85	89	87	83
Student	89	89	86	81	92	92	89	84	92	92	89	84
Standard	79	79	82	81	79	78	82	82	79	78	82	82
Normal	81	81	84	85	81	80	84	84	82	80	84	84
Percentile	80	84	73	85	80	82	77	83	80	81	76	82
BC_a	78	83	72	81	80	80	74	79	79	81	74	80
Basic	78	78	82	78	81	80	83	80	80	81	84	80
Student	84	85	82	74	90	88	84	79	90	88	84	79
Standard	90	90	91	90	89	90	92	90	89	91	92	91
Normal	88	88	88	88	87	86	88	88	87	93	97	93
Percentile	87	87	85	86	89	88	88	88	90	94	97	91
BC_a	86	86	82	86	88	87	85	87	88	94	96	91
Basic	87	87	85	87	87	87	88	88	86	92	97	92
Student	95	90	80	92	90	89	89	89	90	93	92	91
Standard	69	64	59	70	69	63	59	69	67	64	60	71
Normal	87	84	86	90	88	84	84	89	87	89	92	94
Percentile	85	86	84	86	90	86	82	88	90	91	93	91
BC_a	85	85	80	85	88	83	77	86	87	89	88	89
Basic	86	84	83	85	88	84	83	87	87	89	91	91
Student	93	87	82	87	89	89	85	85	89	93	90	85

The third experiment used the same design matrix as the first two, but linear predictor $\eta = \beta_0 + \beta_1 x$, with $\beta_0 = \beta_1 = 2$ and Poisson responses with mean $\mu = \exp(\eta)$. The fourth experiment used the same means as the third, but had negative binomial responses with variance function $\mu + \mu^2/10$. The bootstrap schemes for these two experiments were case resampling and model-based resampling using (7.12) and (7.14).

Table 7.3 shows that while all the methods tend to undercover, the standard method can be disastrously bad when the random part of the fitted model is incorrect, as in the second and fourth experiments. The studentized method generally does better than the basic method, but the BC_a method does not improve on the percentile intervals. Thus here a more sophisticated method does not necessarily lead to better coverage, unlike in Section 5.7, and in particular there seems to be no reason to use the BC_a method. Use of the studentized interval on another scale might improve its performance for the ratio ψ_2, for which the simpler methods seem best. As far as the resampling schemes are concerned, there seems to be little to choose between the model-based schemes, which improve slightly on bootstrapping cases, even when the fitted variance function is incorrect.

We now consider an important caveat to these general comments.

Inhomogeneous residuals

For some types of data the standardized Pearson residuals may be very inhomogeneous. If y is Poisson with mean μ, for example, the distribution of $(y - \mu)/\mu^{1/2}$ is strongly positively skewed when $\mu < 1$, but it becomes increasingly symmetric as μ increases. Thus when a set of data contains both large and small counts, it is unwise to treat the r_P as exchangeable. One possibility for such data is to apply (7.12) but with fitted values stratified by the estimated skewness of their residuals.

Example 7.3 (Sugar cane) *Carvão da cana-de-açucar* — coal of sugar cane — is a disease of sugar cane that is common in some areas of Brazil, and its effects on production of the crop have led to a search for resistant varieties of cane. We use data kindly provided by Dr C. G. B. Demétrio of Escola Superior de Agricultura, Universidade de São Paulo, from a randomized block experiment in which the resistance to the disease of 45 varieties of cane was compared in four blocks of 45 plots. Fifty stems from a variety were put in a solution containing the disease agent, and then planted in a plot. After a fixed period, the total number of shoots appearing, m, and the number of diseased shoots, r, were recorded for each plot. Thus the data form a 4×45 layout of pairs (m, r). The purpose of analysis was to identify the most resistant varieties, for further investigation.

A simple model is that the number of diseased shoots r_{ij} for the ith block and jth variety is a binomial random variable with denominator m_{ij} and probability π_{ij}. For the generalized linear model formulation, the responses are taken to be $y_{ij} = r_{ij}/m_{ij}$ so that the mean response μ_{ij} is equal to the probability π_{ij} that a shoot is diseased. Because the variance of Y is $\pi(1 - \pi)/m$, the variance function is $V(\mu) = \mu(1 - \mu)$ and the dispersion parameters are $\phi = 1/m$, so that in the two-way version of (7.1), $c_{ij} = 1/m_{ij}$ and $\kappa = 1$. The probability of disease for the ith block and jth variety is related to the linear predictor $\eta_{ij} = \alpha_i + \beta_j$ through the logit link function $\eta = \log\{\pi/(1 - \pi)\}$. So the full model for all data is

$$\mathrm{E}(Y_{ij}) = \mu_{ij}, \quad \mu_{ij} = \exp(\alpha_i + \beta_j)/\{1 + \exp(\alpha_i + \beta_j)\},$$
$$\mathrm{var}(Y_{ij}) = m_{ij}^{-1} V(\mu_{ij}), \quad V(\mu_{ij}) = \mu_{ij}(1 - \mu_{ij}).$$

Interest focuses on the varieties with small values of β_j, which are likely to be the most resistant to the disease.

For an adequate fit, the deviance would roughly be distributed according to a χ^2_{132} distribution; in fact it is 1142.8. This indicates severe overdispersion relative to the model.

Figure 7.3 Model fit for the cane data. The left panel shows the estimated variety effects $\hat{\alpha}_1 + \hat{\beta}_j$ for block 1: varieties 1 and 3 are least resistant, and 31 is most resistant. The lines show the levels on the logit scale corresponding to $\pi = 0.5, 0.2, 0.05$ and 0.01. The right panel shows standardized Pearson residuals r_P plotted against $\hat{\alpha}_1 + \hat{\beta}_j$; the lines are at $0, \pm 3$.

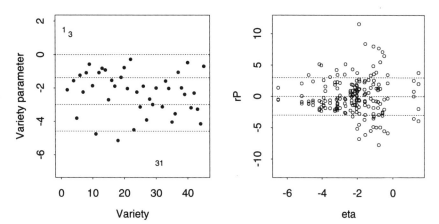

The left panel of Figure 7.3 shows estimated variety effects for block 1. Varieties 1 and 3 are least resistant to the disease, while variety 31 is most resistant. The right panel shows the residuals plotted against linear predictors. The skewness of the r_P drops as η increases.

Parametric simulation involves generating binomial observations from the fitted model. This greatly overstates the precision of conclusions, because this model clearly does not reflect the variability of the data. We could instead use the beta-binomial distribution. Suppose that, conditional on π, a response is binomial with denominator m and probability π, but instead of being fixed, π is taken to have a beta distribution. The resulting response has unconditional mean and variance

$$m\Pi, \quad m\Pi(1-\Pi)\{1+(m-1)\phi\}, \tag{7.15}$$

where $\Pi = E(\pi)$ and $\phi > 0$ controls the degree of overdispersion. Parametric simulation from this model is discussed in Problem 7.5.

Two variance functions for overdispersed binomial data are $V_1(\pi) = \phi\pi(1-\pi)$, with $\phi > 1$, and $V_2(\pi) = \pi(1-\pi)\{1+(m-1)\phi\}$, with $\phi > 0$. The first of these gives common overdispersion for all the observations, while the second allows proportionately greater spread when m is larger. We use the first, for which $\hat{\phi} = 8.3$, and perform nonparametric simulation using (7.12). The simulated responses are rounded to the nearest integer in $0, 1, \ldots, m$.

The left panel of Figure 7.4 shows box plots of the ratio of deviance to degrees of freedom for 200 simulations from the binomial model, the beta-binomial model, for nonparametric simulation by (7.12), and for (7.12) but with residuals stratified into groups for the fifteen varieties with the smallest values of $\hat{\beta}_j$, the middle fifteen values of $\hat{\beta}_j$, and the fifteen largest values of

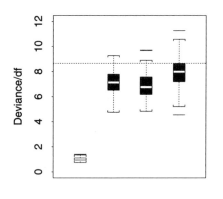

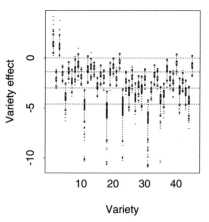

Figure 7.4 Resampling results for cane data. The left panel shows (left to right) simulated deviance/degrees of freedom ratios for fitted binomial and beta-binomial models, a nonparametric bootstrap, and a nonparametric bootstrap with residuals stratified by varieties; the dotted line is at the data ratio $8.66 = 1142.8/132$. The right panel shows the variety effects in 200 replicates of the stratified nonparametric resampling scheme.

$\hat{\beta}_j$. The dotted line shows the observed ratio. The binomial results are clearly quite inappropriate, those for the beta-binomial and unstratified simulation are better, and those for the stratified simulation are best.

To explain this, we return to the right panel of Figure 7.3. This shows that the residuals are not homogeneous: residuals for observations with small values of $\hat{\eta}$ are more positively skewed than those for larger values. This reflects the varying skewness of binomial data, which must be taken into account in the resampling scheme.

The right panel of Figure 7.4 shows the estimated variety effects for the 200 simulations from the stratified simulation. Varieties 1 and 3 are much less resistant than the others, but variety 31 is not much more resistant than 11, 18, and 23; other varieties are close behind. As might be expected, results for the binomial simulation are much less variable. The unstratified resampling scheme gives large negative estimated variety effects, due to inappropriately large negative residuals being used. To explain this, consider the right panel of Figure 7.3. In effect the unstratified scheme allows residuals from the right half of the panel to be sampled and placed at its left-hand end, leading to negative simulated responses that are rounded up to zero: the varieties for which this happens seem spuriously resistant.

Finer stratification of the residuals seems unnecessary for this application.

■

7.2.4 Prediction

In Section 6.3.3 we showed how to use resampling methods to obtain prediction intervals based on a linear regression fit. The same idea can be applied here.

Beyond having a suitable resampling algorithm to produce the appropriate variation in parameter estimates, we must also produce suitable response variation. In the linear model this is provided by the EDF of standardized residuals, which estimates the CDF of homoscedastic errors. Now we need to be able to produce the correct heteroscedasticity.

Suppose that we want to predict the response Y_+ at x_+, with a prediction interval. One possible point prediction is the regression estimate

$$\hat{\mu}_+ = g^{-1}(x_+^T \hat{\beta}),$$

although it would often be wise to make a bias correction. For the prediction interval, let us assume for the moment that some monotone function $\delta(Y, \mu)$ is homoscedastic, with pth quantile a_p, and that the mean value μ_+ of Y_+ is known. Then the $1 - 2\alpha$ prediction interval should be the values $y_{+,\alpha}$, $y_{+,1-\alpha}$ where $y_{+,p}$ satisfies $\delta(y, \mu_+) = a_p$. If μ is estimated by $\hat{\mu}$ independently of Y_+ and if $\delta(Y_+, \hat{\mu})$ has known quantiles, then the same method applies. So the appropriate bootstrap method is to estimate quantiles of $\delta(Y_+, \hat{\mu})$, and then set $\delta(y, \mu_+)$ equal to the estimated α and $1 - \alpha$ quantiles. The function $\delta(Y, \hat{\mu})$ will correspond to one of the definitions of residuals, and the bootstrap algorithm will use resampling from the corresponding standardized residuals, whose homoscedasticity is critical. The full resampling algorithm, which generalizes Algorithm 6.4, is as follows.

Algorithm 7.1 (Prediction in generalized linear models)

For $r = 1, \dots, R$,

1 create bootstrap sample response y_j^* at x_j by solving

$$\delta(y, \hat{\mu}_j) = \varepsilon_j^*, \quad j = 1, \dots, n,$$

   where the ε_j^* are randomly sampled from residuals $r_1, \dots, r_n$;

2 fit estimates $\hat{\beta}^*$ and $\hat{\kappa}^*$, and compute fitted value $\hat{\mu}_{+,r}^*$ corresponding to the new observation with $x = x_+$; then

3 for $m = 1, \dots, M$,

   (a) sample δ_{rm}^* from $r_1, \dots, r_n$,
   (b) set $y_{+,rm}^*$ equal to the solution of the equation $\delta(y, \hat{\mu}_+) = \delta_{rm}^*$,
   (c) compute simulated prediction 'errors' $d_{+,rm}^* = \delta(y_{+,rm}^*, \hat{\mu}_{+,r}^*)$.

Finally, order the RM values $d_{+,rm}^*$ to give $d_{+,(1)}^* \leq \cdots \leq d_{+,(RM)}^*$. Then calculate the prediction limits as the solutions to

$$\delta(y_+, \hat{\mu}_+) = d_{+,((RM+1)\alpha)}^*, \quad \delta(y_+, \hat{\mu}_+) = d_{+,((RM+1)(1-\alpha))}^*.$$

•

In principle any of the resampling methods in Section 7.2.3 could be used. In practice the homoscedasticity is important, and should be checked.

Example 7.4 (AIDS diagnoses)   Table 7.4 contains the number of AIDS reports in England and Wales to the end of 1992. They are cross-classified by diagnosis period and length of reporting delay, in three-month intervals. A blank in the table corresponds to an unknown entry, and $\geq$ indicates where an entry is a lower bound for the actual value. We shall treat these incomplete data as unknown in our analysis below. The problem was to predict the state of the epidemic at the time from the given data. This depends heavily on the values missing towards the foot of the table.

The data support the assumption that the reporting delay does not depend on the diagnosis period. In this case a simple model is that the number of reports in row j and column k of the table, y_{jk}, has a Poisson distribution with mean $\mu_{jk} = \exp(\alpha_j + \beta_k)$. If all the cells of the table are regarded as independent, the total diagnoses in period j have a Poisson distribution with mean $\sum_k \mu_{jk} = \exp(\alpha_j) \sum_k \exp(\beta_k)$. Hence the eventual total for an incomplete row can be predicted by adding the observed row total and the fitted values for the unobserved part of the row. How accurate is this prediction?

To assess this, we first simulate a complete table of bootstrap data, y_{jk}^*, using the fitted values $\hat{\mu}_{jk} = \exp(\hat{\alpha}_j + \hat{\beta}_k)$ from the original fit. We shall discuss below how to do this; for now simply note that this amounts to steps 1 and 3(b) of Algorithm 7.1. We then fit the two-way layout model to the simulated data, excluding the cells where the original table was incomplete, thereby obtaining parameter estimates $\hat{\alpha}_j^*$ and $\hat{\beta}_k^*$. We then calculate

$$y_{+,j}^* = \sum_{k \text{ unobs}} y_{jk}^*, \quad \hat{\mu}_{+,j}^* = \exp(\alpha_j^*) \sum_{k \text{ unobs}} \exp(\beta_k^*), \quad j = 1, \ldots, 38,$$

where the summation is over the cells of row j for which y_{jk} was unobserved; this is step 2. Note that $y_{+,j}^*$ is equivalent to the results of steps 3(a) and 3(b) with $M = 1$.

We take $\delta(y, \mu) = (y - \mu)/\mu^{1/2}$, corresponding to Pearson residuals for the Poisson distribution. This means that step 3(c) involves setting

$$d_{+,j}^* = \frac{y_{+,j}^* - \hat{\mu}_{+,j}^*}{\hat{\mu}_{+,j}^{*1/2}}.$$

We repeat this R times, to obtain values $d_{+,j,(1)}^* \leq \cdots \leq d_{+,j,(R)}^*$ for each j.

The final step is to obtain the bootstrap upper and lower limits $y_{+,j,\alpha}^*$, $y_{+,j,1-\alpha}^*$ for $y_{+,j}$, by solving the equations

$$\frac{y_{+,j} - \hat{\mu}_{+,j}}{\hat{\mu}_{+,j}^{1/2}} = d_{+,j,((R+1)\alpha)}^*, \quad \frac{y_{+,j} - \hat{\mu}_{+,j}}{\hat{\mu}_{+,j}^{1/2}} = d_{+,j,((R+1)(1-\alpha))}^*.$$

Table 7.4 Numbers of AIDS reports in England and Wales to the end of 1992 (De Angelis and Gilks, 1994). A ≥ sign in the body of the table indicates a count incomplete at the end of 1992, and † indicates a reporting-delay less than one month.

Year	Quarter	0†	1	2	3	4	5	6	7	8	9	10	11	12	13	≥14	Total reports to end 1992
1983	3	2	6	0	1	1	0	0	1	0	0	0	0	0	0	1	12
	4	2	7	1	1	1	0	0	0	0	0	0	0	0	0	0	12
1984	1	4	4	0	1	0	2	0	0	0	0	2	1	0	0	0	14
	2	0	10	0	1	1	0	0	0	1	1	1	0	0	0	0	15
	3	6	17	3	1	1	0	0	0	0	0	0	1	0	0	1	30
	4	5	22	1	5	2	1	0	2	1	0	0	0	0	0	0	39
1985	1	4	23	4	5	2	1	3	0	1	2	0	0	0	0	2	47
	2	11	11	6	1	1	5	0	1	1	1	1	0	0	0	1	40
	3	9	22	6	2	4	3	3	4	7	1	2	0	0	0	0	63
	4	2	28	8	8	5	2	2	4	3	0	1	1	0	0	1	65
1986	1	5	26	14	6	9	2	5	5	5	1	2	0	0	0	2	82
	2	7	49	17	11	4	7	5	7	3	1	2	2	0	1	4	120
	3	13	37	21	9	3	5	7	3	1	3	1	0	0	0	6	109
	4	12	53	16	21	2	7	0	7	0	0	0	0	0	1	1	120
1987	1	21	44	29	11	6	4	2	2	1	0	2	0	2	2	8	134
	2	17	74	13	13	3	5	3	1	2	2	0	0	0	3	5	141
	3	36	58	23	14	7	4	1	2	1	3	0	0	0	3	1	153
	4	28	74	23	11	8	3	3	6	2	5	4	1	1	1	3	173
1988	1	31	80	16	9	3	2	8	3	1	4	6	2	1	2	6	174
	2	26	99	27	9	8	11	3	4	6	3	5	5	1	1	3	211
	3	31	95	35	13	18	4	6	4	4	3	3	2	0	3	3	224
	4	36	77	20	26	11	3	8	4	8	7	1	0	0	2	2	205
1989	1	32	92	32	10	12	19	12	4	3	2	0	2	2	0	2	224
	2	15	92	14	27	22	21	12	5	3	0	3	3	0	1	1	219
	3	34	104	29	31	18	8	6	7	3	8	0	2	1	2		≥253
	4	38	101	34	18	9	15	6	1	2	2	2	3	2			≥233
1990	1	31	124	47	24	11	15	8	6	5	3	3	4				≥281
	2	32	132	36	10	9	7	6	4	4	5	0					≥245
	3	49	107	51	17	15	8	9	2	1	1						≥260
	4	44	153	41	16	11	6	5	7	2							≥285
1991	1	41	137	29	33	7	11	6	4	≥3							≥271
	2	56	124	39	14	12	7	10	≥1								≥263
	3	53	175	35	17	13	11	≥2									≥306
	4	63	135	24	23	12	≥1										≥258
1992	1	71	161	48	25	≥5											≥310
	2	95	178	39	≥6												≥318
	3	76	181	≥16													≥273
	4	67	≥66														≥133

This procedure takes into account two aspects of uncertainty that are important in prediction, namely the inaccuracy of parameter estimates, and the random fluctuations in the unobserved y_{jk}. The first enters through variation in $\hat{\alpha}_j^*$ and $\hat{\beta}_k^*$ from replicate to replicate, and the second enters through the sampling variability of the predictand $y_{+,j}^*$ over different replicates. The procedure does not allow for a third component of predictive error, due to uncertainty about the form of the model.

The model described above is a generalized linear model with Poisson errors and the log link function. It contains 52 parameters. The deviance of 716.5 on 413 degrees of freedom is strong evidence that the data are overdispersed relative to the Poisson distribution. The estimate of κ is $\hat{\kappa} = 1.78$, and in

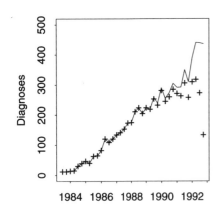
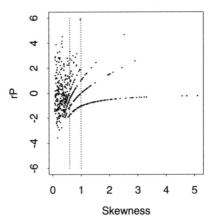

Figure 7.5 Results from the fit of a Poisson two-way layout to the AIDS data. The left panel shows predicted diagnoses (solid), together with the actual totals to the end of 1992 (+). The right panel shows standardized Pearson residuals plotted against estimated skewness, $\hat{\mu}^{-1/2}$; the vertical lines are at skewness 0.6 and 1.

fact a quasilikelihood model in which var$(Y) = \kappa\mu$ appears to fit the data; this corresponds to treating the counts in Table 7.4 as independent negative binomial random variables.

The predicted value $\exp(\hat{\alpha}_j)\sum_k \exp(\hat{\beta}_k)$ is shown as the solid line in the left panel of Figure 7.5, together with the observed total reports to the end of 1992. The right panel shows the standardized Pearson residuals plotted against the estimated skewness $\hat{\mu}^{-1/2}$. The banding of residuals at the right is characteristic of data containing small counts, with the lower band corresponding to zeroes in the original data, the next to ones, and so forth. The distributions of the r_P change markedly, and it would be inappropriate to treat them as a homogeneous group. The same conclusion holds for the standardized deviance residuals, although they are less skewed for larger fitted values. The dotted lines in the figure divide the observations into three strata, within each of which the residuals are more homogeneous. Finer stratification has little effect on the results described below.

One parametric bootstrap involves generating Poisson random variables Y_{jk}^* with means $\exp(\hat{\alpha}_j + \hat{\beta}_k)$. This fails to account for the overdispersion, which can be mimicked by parametric sampling from a fitted negative binomial distribution with the same means and estimated overdispersion.

Nonparametric resampling from standardized Pearson residuals will give overdispersion, but the right panel of Figure 7.5 suggests that the residuals should be stratified. Figure 7.6 shows the ratio of deviances to degrees of freedom for 999 samples taken under these four sampling schemes; the strata used in the lower right panel are shown in Figure 7.5. Parametric simulation from the Poisson model is plainly inappropriate because the data so generated

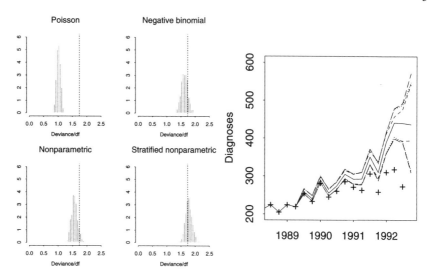

Figure 7.6 Resampling results for AIDS data. The left panels show deviances/degrees of freedom ratios for the four resampling schemes, with the observed ratio given as the vertical dotted line. The right panel shows predicted diagnoses (solid line), with pointwise 95% predictive intervals, based on 999 replicates of Poisson simulation (small dashes), of resampling residuals (dots), and of stratified resampling of residuals (large dashes).

Table 7.5 Bootstrap 95% prediction intervals for numbers of AIDS cases in England and Wales for the fourth quarters of 1990, 1991, and 1992.

	1990		1991		1992	
Poisson	296	315	294	327	356	537
Negative binomial	294	318	289	333	317	560
Nonparametric	294	318	289	333	314	547
Stratified nonparametric	292	319	288	335	310	571

are much less dispersed than the original data, for which the ratio is 716.5/413. The negative binomial simulation gives more appropriate results, which seem rather similar to those for nonparametric simulation without stratification. When stratification is used, the results mimic the overdispersion much better.

The pointwise 95% prediction intervals for the numbers of AIDS diagnoses are shown in the right panel of Figure 7.6. The intervals for simulation from the fitted Poisson model are considerably narrower than the intervals from resampling residuals, both of which are similar. The intervals for the last quarters of 1990, 1991, and 1992 are given in Table 7.5.

There is little change if intervals are based on the deviance residual formula for the Poisson distribution, $\delta(y, \mu) = \pm[2\{y \log(y/\mu) + \mu - y\}]^{1/2}$.

A serious drawback with this analysis is that predictions from the two-way layout model are very sensitive to the last few rows of the table, to the extent that the estimate $\hat{\alpha}_{38}$ for the last row is determined entirely by the bottom left cell. Some sort of temporal smoothing is preferable, and we reconsider these data in Example 7.12 ∎

7.3 Survival Data

Section 3.5 describes resampling methods for a single homogeneous sample of data subject to censoring. In this section we turn to problems where survival is affected by explanatory variables.

Suppose that the data (Y, D, x) on an individual consist of: a survival time Y; an indicator of censoring, D, that equals one if Y is observed and zero if Y is right-censored; and a covariate vector x. Under random censorship the observed value of Y is supposed to be $\min(Y^0, C)$, where C is a censoring variable with distribution G, and the true failure time Y^0 is a variable whose distribution $F(y; \beta, x)$ depends on the covariates x through a vector of parameters, β. More generally we might suppose that Y^0 and C are conditionally independent given x, and that C has distribution $G(c; \gamma, x)$. In either case, the value of C is supposed to be uninformative about the parameter β.

Parametric model

In a parametric model F is fully specified once β has been chosen. So if the data consist of measurements $(y_1, d_1, x_1), \ldots, (y_n, d_n, x_n)$ on independent individuals, we suppose that β is estimated, often by the maximum likelihood estimator $\hat{\beta}$. Parametric simulation is performed by generating values Y_j^{0*} from the fitted distributions $F(y; \hat{\beta}, x_j)$ and generating appropriate censoring times C_j^*, setting $Y_j^* = \min(Y_j^{0*}, C_j^*)$, and letting D_j^* indicate the event $Y_j^{0*} \leq C_j^*$. The censoring variables may be generating according to any one of the schemes outlined in Section 3.5, or otherwise if appropriate.

Example 7.5 (PET film data)   Table 7.6 contains data from an accelerated life test on PET film in gas insulated transformers; the film is used in electrical insulation. There are failure times y at each of four different voltages x. Three failure times are right-censored at voltage $x = 5$: according to the data source they were subject to censoring at a pre-determined time, but their values make it more likely that they were censored after a pre-determined number of failures, and we shall assume this in what follows.

The Weibull distribution is often used for such data. In this case plots suggest that both of its parameters depend on the voltage applied, and that there is an unknown threshold voltage x_0 below which failure cannot occur. Our model is that the distribution function for y at voltage x is given by

$$
\begin{aligned}
F(y \mid \beta, x) &= 1 - \exp\left\{-(y/\lambda)^\kappa\right\}, \qquad y > 0, \\
\lambda &= \exp\left\{\beta_0 - \beta_1 \log(x - 5 + e^{\beta_4})\right\}, \qquad (7.16) \\
\kappa &= \exp(\beta_2 - \beta_3 \log x).
\end{aligned}
$$

Voltage (kV)							
5	7131	8482	8559	8762	9026	9034	9104
	≥9104.25	≥9104.25	≥9104.25				
7	50.25	87.75	87.76	87.77	92.90	92.91	95.96
	108.30	108.30	117.90	123.90	124.30	129.70	135.60
	135.60						
10	15.17	19.87	20.18	21.50	21.88	22.23	23.02
	23.90	28.17	29.70				
15	2.40	2.42	3.17	3.75	4.65	4.95	6.23
	6.68	7.30					

Table 7.6 Failure times (hours) from an accelerated life test on PET film in SF_6 gas insulated transformers (Hirose, 1993). ≥ indicates right-censoring.

This parametrization is chosen so that the range of each parameter is unbounded; note that $x_0 = 5 - e^{\beta_4}$.

The upper panels of Figure 7.7 show the fit of this model when the parameters are estimated by maximizing the log likelihood ℓ. The left panel shows Q-Q plots for each of the voltages, and the right panel shows the fitted mean failure time and estimated threshold $\hat{x}_0$. The fit seems broadly adequate.

We simulate replicate datasets by generating observations from the Weibull model obtained by substituting the MLEs into (7.16). In order to apply our assumed censoring mechanism, we sort the observations simulated with $x = 5$ to get $y_{(1)}^* < \cdots < y_{(10)}^*$, say, and then set $y_{(8)}^*$, $y_{(9)}^*$, and $y_{(10)}^*$ equal to $y_{(7)}^* + 0.25$. We give these three observations censoring indicators $d^* = 0$, so that they are treated as censored, treat all the other observations as uncensored, and fit the Weibull model to the resulting data.

For sake of illustration, suppose that interest focuses on the mean failure time θ when $x = 4.9$. To facilitate this we reparametrize the model to have parameters θ and $\beta = (\beta_1, \ldots, \beta_4)$, where $\theta = 10^{-3}\lambda\Gamma(1 + 1/\kappa)$, with $x = 4.9$. The lower left panel of Figure 7.7 shows the profile log likelihood for θ, i.e.

$\Gamma(v)$ is the Gamma function $\int_0^\infty u^{v-1}e^{-u}\,du$.

$$\ell_{\text{prof}}(\theta) = \max_{\beta} \ell(\theta, \beta);$$

in the figure we renormalize the log likelihood to have maximum zero. Under the standard large-sample likelihood asymptotics outlined in Section 5.2.1, the approximate distribution of the likelihood ratio statistic

$$W(\theta) = 2\left\{\ell_{\text{prof}}(\hat{\theta}) - \ell_{\text{prof}}(\theta)\right\}$$

is χ_1^2, so a $1 - \alpha$ confidence set for the true θ is the set such that

$c_{v,p}$ is the p quantile of the χ_v^2 distribution.

$$\ell_{\text{prof}}(\theta) \geq \ell_{\text{prof}}(\hat{\theta}) - \tfrac{1}{2}c_{1,1-\alpha}.$$

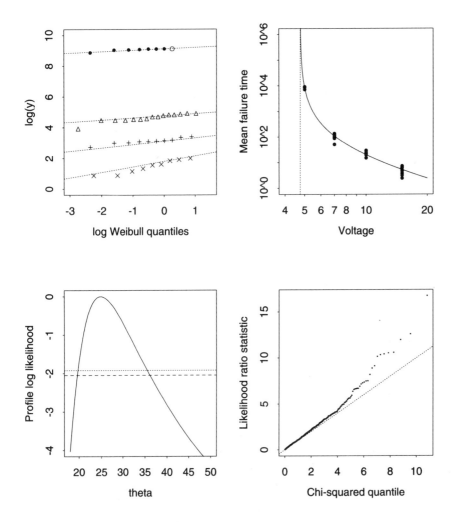

Figure 7.7 PET reliability data analysis. Top left panel: Q-Q plot of log failure times against quantiles of log Weibull distribution, with fitted model given by dotted lines, and censored data by ∘. Top right panel: Fitted mean failure time as a function of voltage x; the dotted line shows the estimated voltage $\hat{x}_0$ below which failure is impossible. Lower left panel: normalized profile log likelihood for mean failure time θ at $x = 4.9$; the dotted line shows the 95% confidence interval for θ using the asymptotic chi-squared distribution, and the dashed line shows the 95% confidence interval using bootstrap calibration of the likelihood ratio statistic. Lower right panel: chi-squared Q-Q plot for simulated likelihood ratio statistic, with dotted line showing its large-sample distribution.

where $\hat{\theta}$ is the overall MLE. For these data $\hat{\theta} = 24.85$ and the 95% confidence interval is $[19.75, 35.53]$; the confidence set contains values of θ for which $\ell_{\mathrm{prof}}(\theta)$ exceeds the dotted line in the bottom left panel of Figure 7.7.

The use of the chi-squared quantile to set the confidence interval presupposes that the sample is large enough for the likelihood asymptotics to apply, and this can be checked by the parametric simulation outlined above. The lower right panel of the figure is a Q-Q plot of likelihood ratio statistics $w^*(\hat{\theta}) = 2\{\ell^*_{\mathrm{prof}}(\hat{\theta}^*) - \ell^*_{\mathrm{prof}}(\hat{\theta})\}$ based on 999 sets of data simulated from the fitted model. The distribution of the $w^*(\hat{\theta})$ is close to chi-squared, but with

Table 7.7 Comparison of estimated biases and standard errors of maximum likelihood estimates for the PET reliability data, using standard first-order likelihood theory, parametric bootstrap simulation, and model-based nonparametric resampling.

Parameter	MLE	Likelihood		Parametric		Nonparametric	
		Bias	SE	Bias	SE	Bias	SE
β_0	6.346	0	0.117	0.007	0.117	0.001	0.112
β_1	1.958	0	0.082	0.007	0.082	0.006	0.080
β_2	4.383	0	0.850	0.127	0.874	0.109	0.871
β_3	1.235	0	0.388	0.022	0.393	0.022	0.393
x_0	4.758	0	0.029	-0.004	0.030	-0.002	0.028

mean 1.12, and their 0.95 quantile is $w^*_{(950)} = 4.09$, to be compared with $c_{1,0.95} = 3.84$. This gives bootstrap calibrated 95% confidence interval the set of θ such that $\ell_{\text{prof}}(\theta) \geq \ell_{\text{prof}}(\hat{\theta}) - \frac{1}{2} \times 4.09$, that is [19.62, 36.12], which is slightly wider than the standard interval.

Table 7.7 compares the bias estimates and standard errors for the model parameters using the parametric bootstrap described above and standard first-order likelihood theory, under which the estimated biases are zero, and the variance estimates are obtained as the diagonal elements of the inverse observed information matrix $(-\ddot{\ell})^{-1}$ evaluated at the MLEs. The estimated biases are small but significantly different from zero. The largest differences between the standard theory and the bootstrap results are for β_2 and β_3, for which the biases are of order 2–3%. The threshold parameter x_0 is well determined; the standard 95% confidence interval based on its asymptotic normal distribution is [4.701, 4.815], whereas the normal interval with estimated bias and variance is [4.703, 4.820].

A model-based nonparametric bootstrap may be performed by using residuals $e = (y/\hat{\lambda})^{\hat{\kappa}}$, three of which are censored, then resampling errors ε^* from their product-limit estimate, and then making uncensored bootstrap observations $\hat{\lambda}\varepsilon^{*1/\hat{\kappa}}$. The observations with $x = 5$ are then modified as outlined above, and the model refitted to the resulting data. The product-limit estimate for the residuals is very close to the survivor function of the standard exponential distribution, so we expect this to give results similar to the parametric simulation, and this is what we see in Table 7.7.

For censoring at a pre-determined time c, the simulation algorithms would work as described above, except that values of y^* greater than c would be replaced by c and the corresponding censoring indicators d^* set equal to zero. The number of censored observations in each simulated dataset would then be random; see Practical 7.3.

Plots show that the simulated MLEs are close to normally distributed: in this case standard likelihood theory works well enough to give good confidence intervals for the parameters. The benefit of parametric simulation is that the bootstrap estimates give empirical evidence that the standard theory can

$\ddot{\ell}$ is the matrix of second derivatives of ℓ with respect to θ and β.

be trusted, while providing alternative methods for calculating measures of uncertainty if the standard theory is unreliable. It is typical of first-order likelihood methods that the variability of likelihood quantities is underestimated, although here the effect is small enough to be unimportant.   ∎

Proportional hazards model

If it can be assumed that the explanatory variables act multiplicatively on the hazard function, an elegant and powerful approach to survival data analysis is possible. Under the usual form of *proportional hazards model* the hazard function for an individual with covariates x is $dA(y) = \exp(x^T\beta)dA^0(y)$, where $dA^0(y)$ is the 'baseline' hazard function that would apply to an individual with a fixed value of x, often $x = 0$. The corresponding cumulative hazard and survivor functions are

$$A(y) = \int_0^y \exp(x^T\beta)dA^0(u), \quad 1 - F(y;\beta,x) = \{1 - F^0(y)\}^{\exp(x^T\beta)},$$

where $1 - F^0(y)$ is the baseline survivor function for the hazard $dA^0(y)$.

The regression parameters β are usually estimated by maximizing the partial likelihood, which is the product over cases with $d_j = 1$ of terms

$$\frac{\exp(x^T\beta_j)}{\sum_{k=1}^n H(y_j - y_k)\exp(x^T\beta_k)}, \tag{7.17}$$

where $H(u)$ equals zero if $u < 0$ and equals one otherwise. Since (7.17) is unaltered by recentring the x_j, we shall assume below that $\sum x_j = 0$; the baseline hazard then corresponds to the average covariate value $x = 0$.

In terms of the estimated regression parameters the baseline cumulative hazard function is estimated by the *Breslow estimator*

$$\hat{A}^0(y) = \sum_{j:y_j \leq y} \frac{d_j}{\sum_{k=1}^n H(y_j - y_k)\exp(x^T\hat{\beta}_k)}, \tag{7.18}$$

a non-decreasing function that jumps at y_j by

$$d\hat{A}^0(y_j) = \frac{d_j}{\sum_{k=1}^n H(y_j - y_k)\exp(x^T\hat{\beta}_k)}.$$

One standard estimator of the baseline survivor function is

$$1 - \hat{F}^0(y) = \prod_{j:y_j \leq y} \left\{1 - d\hat{A}^0(y_j)\right\}, \tag{7.19}$$

which generalizes the product-limit estimate (3.9), although other estimators also exist. Whichever of them is used, the proportional hazards assumption implies that

$$\{1 - \hat{F}^0(y)\}^{\exp(x_j^T\hat{\beta})}$$

will be the estimated survivor function for an individual with covariate values x_j.

Under the random censorship model, the survivor function of the censoring distribution G is given by (3.11).

The bootstrap methods for censored data outlined in Section 3.5 extend straightforwardly to this setting. For example, if the censoring distribution is independent of the covariates, we generate a single sample under the conditional sampling plan according to the following algorithm.

Algorithm 7.2 (Conditional resampling for censored survival data)

For $j = 1, \ldots, n$,

  1 generate Y_j^{0*} from the estimated failure time survivor function $\{1 - \hat{F}^0(y)\}^{\exp(x_j^T \hat{\beta})}$;

  2 if $d_j = 0$, set $C_j^* = y_j$, and if $d_j = 1$, generate C_j^* from the conditional censoring distribution given that $C_j > y_j$, namely $\{\hat{G}(y) - \hat{G}(y_j)\}/\{1 - \hat{G}(y_j)\}$; then

  3 set $Y_j^* = \min(Y_j^{0*}, C_j^*)$, with $D_j^* = 1$ if $Y_j^* = Y_j^{0*}$ and zero otherwise.

       •

Under the more general model where the distribution G of C also depends upon the covariates and a proportional hazards assumption is appropriate for G, the estimated censoring survivor function when the covariate is x is

$$1 - \hat{G}(y; \hat{\gamma}, x) = \left\{1 - \hat{G}^0(y)\right\}^{\exp(x^T \hat{\gamma})},$$

where $\hat{G}^0(y)$ is the estimated baseline censoring distribution given by the analogues of (7.18) and (7.19), in which $1 - d_j$ and $\hat{\gamma}$ replace d_j and $\hat{\beta}$. Under model-based resampling, a bootstrap dataset is then obtained by

Algorithm 7.3 (Resampling for censored survival data)

For $j = 1, \ldots, n$,

  1 generate Y_j^{0*} from the estimated failure time survivor function $\{1 - \hat{F}^0(y)\}^{\exp(x_j^T \hat{\beta})}$, and independently generate C_j^* from the estimated censoring survivor function $\{1 - \hat{G}^0(y)\}^{\exp(x_j^T \hat{\gamma})}$; then

  2 set $Y_j^* = \min(Y_j^{0*}, C_j^*)$, with $D_j^* = 1$ if $Y_j^* = Y_j^{0*}$ and zero otherwise.

       •

The next example illustrates the use of these algorithms.

Example 7.6 (Melanoma data) To illustrate these ideas, we consider data on the survival of patients with malignant melanoma, whose tumours were removed by operation at the Department of Plastic Surgery, University Hospital of Odense, Denmark. Operations took place from 1962 to 1977, and patients were followed to the end of 1977. Each tumour was completely removed, together with about 2.5 cm of the skin around it. The following variables were available for 205 patients: time in days since the operation, possibly censored; status at the end of the study (alive, dead from melanoma, dead from other causes); sex; age; year of operation; tumour thickness in mm; and an indicator of whether or not the tumour was ulcerated. Ulceration and tumour thickness are important prognostic variables: to have a thick or ulcerated tumour substantially increases the chance of death from melanoma, and we shall investigate how they affect survival. We assume that censoring occurs at random.

We fit a proportional hazards model under the assumption that the baseline hazards are different for the ulcerated group of 90 individuals, and the non-ulcerated group, but that there is a common effect of tumour thickness. For a flexible assessment of how thickness affects the hazard function, we fit a natural spline with four degrees of freedom; its knots are placed at the empirical 0.25, 0.5 and 0.75 quantiles of the tumour thicknesses. Thus our model is that the survivor functions for the ulcerated and non-ulcerated groups are

$$1 - F_1(y; \beta, x) = \{1 - F_1^0(y)\}^{\exp(x^T\beta)}, \quad 1 - F_2(y; \beta, x) = \{1 - F_2^0(y)\}^{\exp(x^T\beta)},$$

where x has dimension four and corresponds to the spline, β is common to the groups, but the baseline survivor functions $1 - F_1^0(y)$ and $1 - F_2^0(y)$ may differ. For illustration we take the fitted censoring distribution to be the product-limit estimate obtained by setting censoring indicators $d' = 1 - d$, and fitting a model with no covariates, so $\hat{G}$ is just the product-limit estimate of the censoring time distribution. The left panel of Figure 7.8 shows the estimated survivor functions $1 - \hat{F}_1^0(y)$ and $1 - \hat{F}_2^0(y)$; there is a strong effect of ulceration. The right panel shows how the linear predictor $x^T\hat{\beta}$ depends on tumour thickness: from 0–3 mm the effect on the baseline hazard changes from about $\exp(-1) = 0.37$ to about $\exp(0.6) = 1.8$, followed by a slight dip and a gradual upward increase to a risk of about $\exp(1.2) = 3.3$ for a tumour 15 mm thick. Thus the hazard increases by a factor of about 10, but most of the increase takes place from 0–3 mm. However, there are too few individuals with tumours more than 10 mm thick for reliable inferences at the right of the panel.

The top left panel of Figure 7.9 shows the original fitted linear predictor, together with 19 replicates obtained by resampling cases, stratified by ulceration. The lighter solid lines in the panel below are pointwise 95% confidence limits, based on $R = 999$ replicates of this sampling scheme. In effect these are percentile method confidence limits for the linear predictor at each thickness.

Figure 7.8 Fit of a proportional hazards model for ulcer histology and survival of patients with malignant melanoma (Andersen *et al.*, 1993, pp. 709–714). Left panel: estimated baseline survivor functions for cases with ulcerated (dots) and non-ulcerated (solid) tumours. Right panel: fitted linear predictor $x^T\hat{\beta}$ for risk as a function of tumour thickness. The lower rug is for non-ulcerated patients, and the upper rug for ulcerated patients.

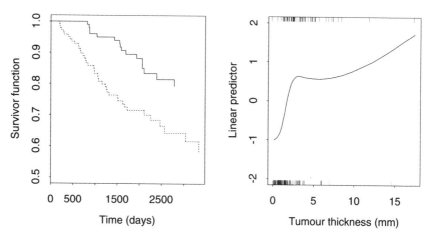

The sharp increase in risk for small thicknesses is clearly a genuine effect, while beyond 3mm the confidence interval for the linear predictor is roughly $[0, 1]$, with thickness having little or no effect.

Results from model-based resampling using the fitted model and applying Algorithm 7.3, and from conditional resampling using Algorithm 7.2 are also shown; they are very similar to the results from resampling cases. In view of the discussion in Section 3.5, we did not apply the weird bootstrap.

The right panels of Figure 7.9 show how the estimated 0.2 quantile of the survival distribution, $\hat{y}_{0.2} = \min\{y : \hat{F}_1(y; \hat{\beta}, x) \geq 0.2\}$ depends on tumour thickness. There is an initial sharp decrease from 3000 days to about 750 days as tumour thickness increases from 0–3 mm, but the estimate is roughly constant from then on. The individual estimates are highly variable, but the degree of uncertainty mirrors roughly that in the left panels. Once again results for the three resampling schemes are very similar.

Unlike the previous example, where resampling and standard likelihood methods led to similar conclusions, this example shows the usefulness of resampling when standard approaches would be difficult or impossible to apply. ∎

7.4 Other Nonlinear Models

A nonlinear regression model with independent additive errors is of form

$$y_j = \mu(x_j, \beta) + \varepsilon_j, \quad j = 1, \ldots, n, \tag{7.20}$$

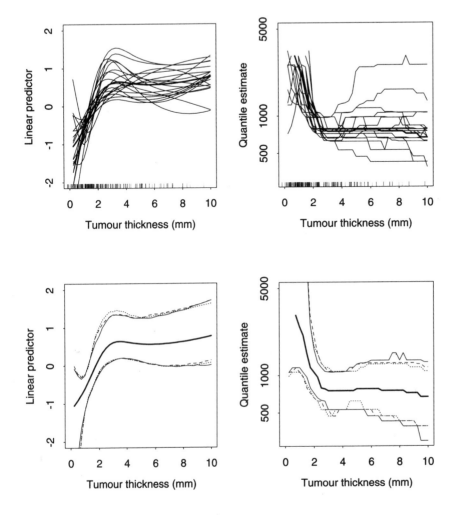

Figure 7.9 Bootstrap results for melanoma data analysis. Top left: fitted linear predictor (heavy solid) and 19 replicates from case resampling (solid); the rug shows observed thicknesses. Top right: estimated 0.2 quantile of survivor distribution as a function of tumour thickness, for an individual with an ulcerated tumour (heavy solid), and 19 replicates for case resampling (solid); the rug shows observed thicknesses. Bottom left: pointwise 95% percentile confidence limits for linear predictor, from case (solid), model-based (dots), and conditional (dashes) resampling. Bottom right: pointwise 95% percentile confidence limits for 0.20 quantile of survivor distribution, from case (solid), model-based (dots), and conditional (dashes) resampling, $R = 999$.

with $\mu(x, \beta)$ nonlinear in the parameter β, which may be vector or scalar. The linear algebra associated with least squares estimates for linear regression no longer applies exactly. However, least squares theory can be developed by linear approximation, and the least squares estimate $\hat{\beta}$ can often be computed accurately by iterative linear fitting.

The linear approximation to (7.20), obtained by Taylor series expansion, gives

$$y_j - \mu(x_j, \beta') \doteq u_j^T(\beta - \beta') + \varepsilon_j, \quad j = 1, \dots, n, \qquad (7.21)$$

where

$$u_j = \left. \frac{\partial \mu(x_j, \beta)}{\partial \beta} \right|_{\beta = \beta'}.$$

This defines an iteration that starts at β' using a linear regression least squares fit, and at the final iteration $\beta' = \hat{\beta}$. At that stage the left-hand side of (7.21) is simply the residual $e_j = y_j - \mu(x_j, \hat{\beta})$. Approximate leverage values and other diagnostics are obtained from the linear approximation, that is using the definitions in previous sections but with the u_js evaluated at $\beta' = \hat{\beta}$ as the values of explanatory variable vectors. This use of the linear approximation can give misleading results, depending upon the "intrinsic curvature" of the regression surface. In particular, the residuals will no longer have zero expectation in general, and standardized residuals r_j will no longer have constant variance under homoscedasticity of true errors.

The usual normal approximation for the distribution of $\hat{\beta}$ is also based on the linear approximation. For the approximate variance, (6.24) applies with X replaced by $U = (u_1, \ldots, u_n)^T$ evaluated at $\hat{\beta}$. So with s^2 equal to the residual mean square, we have

$$\hat{\beta} - \beta \;\; \dot{\sim} \;\; N\left(0, s^2(U^T U)^{-1}\right). \tag{7.22}$$

The accuracy of this approximation will depend upon two types of curvature effects, called parameter effects and intrinsic effects. The first of these is specific to the parametrization used in expressing $\mu(x, \cdot)$, and can be reduced by careful choice of parametrization. Of course resampling methods will be the more useful the larger are the curvature effects, and the worse the normal approximation.

Resampling methods apply here just as with linear regression, either simulating data from the fitted model with resampled modified residuals or by resampling cases. For the first of these it will generally be necessary to make a mean adjustment to whatever residuals are being used as the error population. It would also be generally advisable to correct the raw residuals for bias due to nonlinearity: we do not show how to do this here.

Example 7.7 (Calcium uptake data) The data plotted in Figure 7.10 show the calcium uptake of cells, y, as a function of time x after being suspended in a solution of radioactive calcium. Also shown is the fitted curve

$$\mu(x, \hat{\beta}) = \hat{\beta}_0 \left\{ 1 - \exp(-\hat{\beta}_1 x) \right\}.$$

The least squares estimates are $\hat{\beta}_0 = 4.31$ and $\hat{\beta}_1 = 0.209$, and the estimate of σ is 0.55 with 25 degrees of freedom. The standard errors for $\hat{\beta}_0$ and $\hat{\beta}_1$ based on (7.22) are 0.30 and 0.039.

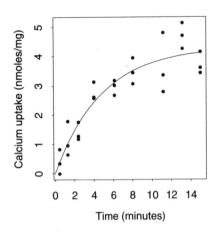
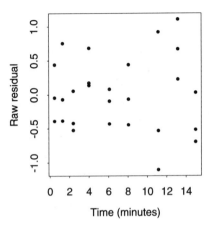

Figure 7.10 Calcium uptake data and fitted curve (left panel), with raw residuals (right panel) (Rawlings, 1988, p. 403).

	Estimate	Bootstrap bias	Theoretical SE	Bootstrap SE
$\hat{\beta}_0$	4.31	0.028	0.30	0.38
$\hat{\beta}_1$	0.209	0.004	0.039	0.040

Table 7.8 Results from $R = 999$ replicates of stratified case resampling for nonlinear regression model fitted to calcium data.

The right panel of Figure 7.10 shows that homogeneity of variance is slightly questionable here, so we resample cases by stratified sampling. Estimated biases and standard errors for $\hat{\beta}_0$ and $\hat{\beta}_1$ based on 999 bootstrap replicates are given in Table 7.8. The main point to notice is the appreciable difference between theoretical and bootstrap standard errors for $\hat{\beta}_0$.

Figure 7.11 illustrates the results. Note the non-elliptical pattern of variation and the non-normality: the z-statistics are also quite non-normal. In this case the bootstrap should give better results for confidence intervals than normal approximations, especially for β_0. The bottom right panel suggests that the parameter estimates are closer to normal on logarithmic scales.

Results for model-based resampling assuming homoscedastic errors are fairly similar, although the standard error for $\hat{\beta}_0$ is then 0.32. The effects of nonlinearity are negligible in this case: for example, the maximum absolute bias of residuals is about 0.012σ.

Suppose that we want confidence limits on some aspect of the curve, such as the "proportion of maximum" $\pi = 1 - \exp(-\beta_1 x)$. Ordinarily one might

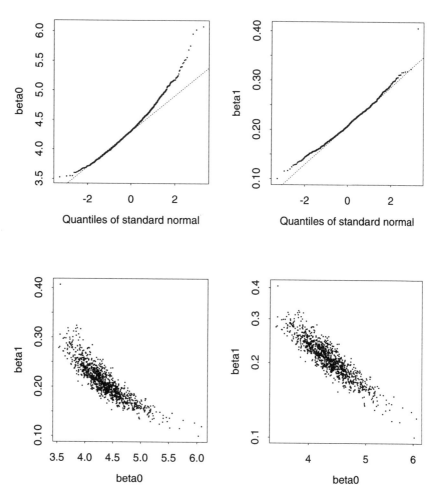

Figure 7.11 Parameter estimates for case resampling of calcium data, with $R = 999$. The upper panels show normal plots of $\hat{\beta}_0^*$ and $\hat{\beta}_1^*$, while the lower panels show their joint distributions on the original (left) and logarithmic scales (right).

approach this by applying the delta method together with the bivariate normal approximation for least squares estimates, but the bootstrap can deal with this using only the simulated parameter estimates. So consider the times $x = 1$, 5, 15, at which the estimates $\hat{\pi} = 1 - \exp(-\hat{\beta}_1 x)$ are 0.188, 0.647 and 0.956 respectively. The top panel of Figure 7.12 shows bootstrap distributions of $\hat{\pi}^* = 1 - \exp(-\hat{\beta}_1^* x)$: note the strong non-normality at $x = 15$.

The constraint that π must lie in the interval $(0, 1)$ means that it is unwise to construct basic or studentized confidence intervals for π itself. For example, the basic bootstrap 95% interval for π at $x = 15$ is [0.922, 1.025]. The solution is to do all the calculations on the logit scale, as shown in the lower panel of Figure 7.12, and untransform the limits obtained at the end. That is, we obtain

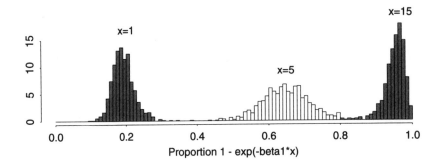

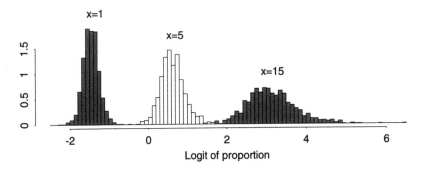

Figure 7.12 Calcium uptake data: bootstrap histograms for estimated proportion of maximum $\pi = 1 - \exp(-\beta_1 x)$ at $x = 1$, 5 and 15 based on $R = 999$ resamples of cases.

intervals $[\eta_1, \eta_2]$ for $\eta = \log\{\pi/(1 - \pi)\}$, and then take

$$\left[\frac{\exp(\eta_1)}{1 + \exp(\eta_1)}, \frac{\exp(\eta_2)}{1 + \exp(\eta_2)} \right]$$

as the corresponding intervals for π. The resulting 95% intervals are $[0.13, 0.26]$ at $x = 1$, $[0.48, 0.76]$ at $x = 5$, and $[0.83, 0.98]$ at $x = 15$. The standard linear theory gives slightly different values, e.g. $[0.10, 0.27]$ at $x = 1$ and $[0.83, 1.03]$ at $x = 15$.   ■

7.5 Misclassification Error

The discussion of aggregate prediction error in Section 6.4.1 was expressed in a general notation that would apply also to the regression models described in this chapter, with appropriate definitions of prediction rule $\hat{y}_+ = \mu(x_+, \hat{F})$ for a response y_+ at covariate values x_+, and measure of accuracy $c(y_+, \hat{y}_+)$. The general conclusions of Section 6.4.1 concerning bootstrap and cross-validation estimates of aggregate prediction error should apply here also. In particular the adjusted K-fold cross-validation estimate and the 0.632 bootstrap estimate should be preferred in most situations.

One type of problem that deserves special attention, in part because it differs most from the examples of Section 6.4.1, is the estimation of prediction error for binary responses, supposing these to be modelled by a generalized linear model of the sort discussed in Section 7.2. If the binary response corresponds to a classification indicator, then prediction of response y_+ for an individual with covariate vector x_+ is equivalent to classification of that individual, and incorrect prediction $(y_+ \neq \hat{y}_+)$ is a misclassification error.

Suppose, then, that the response y is 0 or 1, and that the prediction rule $\mu(x_+, \hat{F})$ is an estimate of $\Pr(Y_+ = 1 \mid x_+)$ for a new case (x_+, y_+). We imagine that this estimated probability is translated into a prediction of y_+, or equivalently a classification of the individual with covariate x_+. For simplicity we set $\hat{y}_+ = 1$ if $\mu(x_+, \hat{F}) \geq \frac{1}{2}$, and $\hat{y}_+ = 0$ otherwise; this would be modified if incidence rates for the two classes differed. If costs of both types of misclassification error are equal, as we shall assume, then it is enough to set

$$c(y_+, \hat{y}_+) = \begin{cases} 1, & y_+ \neq \hat{y}_+, \\ 0, & \text{otherwise.} \end{cases} \tag{7.23}$$

The aggregate prediction error D is simply the overall *misclassification rate,* equal to the proportion of cases where y_+ is wrongly predicted.

The special feature of this problem is that the prediction and the measure of error are not continuous functions of the data. According to the discussion in Section 6.4.1 we should then expect bootstrap methods for estimating D or its expected value Δ to be superior to cross-validation estimates, in terms of variability. Also leave-one-out cross-validation is no longer attractive on computational grounds, because we now have to refit the model for each resample.

Example 7.8 (Urine data)   For an example of the estimation of misclassification error, we take binary data on the presence of calcium oxalate crystals in 79 samples of urine. Explanatory variables are specific gravity, i.e. the density of urine relative to water, pH, osmolarity (mOsm), conductivity (mMho milliMho), urea concentration (millimoles per litre), and calcium concentration (millimoles per litre). After dropping two incomplete cases, 77 remain.

Consider how well the presence of crystals can be predicted from the explanatory variables. Analysis of deviance for binary logistic regression suggests the model which includes the $p = 4$ covariates specific gravity, conductivity, log calcium concentration, and log urine density, and we base our predictions on this model. The simplest estimate of the expected aggregate prediction error Δ is the average number of misclassifications, $\hat{\Delta}_{app} = n^{-1} \sum c(y_j, \hat{y}_j)$, with $c(\cdot, \cdot)$ given by (7.23); it would be equivalent to use instead

$$c(y, \hat{\mu}) = \begin{cases} 1, & |y - \hat{\mu}| > \frac{1}{2}, \\ 0, & \text{otherwise.} \end{cases}$$

			K-fold (adjusted) cross-validation				
Bootstrap	0.632	77	38	10	7	2
24.7	22.1	23.4	23.4 (23.7)	20.8 (21.0)	26.0 (25.4)	20.8 (20.8)

Table 7.9 Estimates of aggregate prediction error ($\times 10^{-2}$), or misclassification rate, for urine data (Andrews and Herzberg, 1985, pp. 249–251).

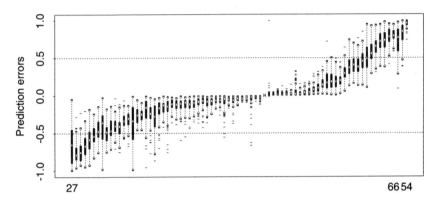

Case ordered by residual

Figure 7.13 Components of 0.632 estimate of prediction error, $y_j - \mu(x_j; \hat{F}_r^*)$, for urine data based on 200 bootstrap simulations. Values within the dotted lines make no contribution to prediction error. The components from cases 54 and 66 are the rightmost and the fourth from rightmost sets of errors shown; the components from case 27 are leftmost.

In this case $\hat{\Delta}_{app} = 20.8 \times 10^{-2}$. Other estimates of aggregate prediction error are given in Table 7.9. For the bootstrap and 0.632 estimates, we used $R = 200$ bootstrap resamples.

The discontinuous nature of prediction error gives more variable results than for the examples with squared error in Section 6.4.1. In particular the results for K-fold cross-validation now depend more critically on which observations fall into the groups. For example, the average and standard deviation of $\hat{\Delta}_{CV,7}$ for 40 repeats were 23.0×10^{-2} and 2.0×10^{-2}. However, the broad pattern is similar to that in Table 6.9.

Figure 7.13 shows box plots of the quantities $y_j - \mu(x_j; \hat{F}_r^*)$ that contribute to the 0.632 estimate of prediction error, plotted against case j ordered by the residual; only three values of j are labelled. There are about 74 contributions at each value of j. Only values outwith the horizontal dotted lines contribute to prediction error. The pattern is broadly what we would expect: observations with residuals close to zero are generally well predicted, and make little contribution to prediction error. More extreme residuals contribute most to prediction error. Note cases 66 and 54, which are always misclassified; their standardized Pearson residuals are 2.13 and 2.54. The figure suggests that case

Table 7.10 Summary results for estimates of prediction error for 200 samples of size $n = 50$ from data on low birth weights (Hosmer and Lemeshow, 1989, pp. 247–252; Venables and Ripley, 1994, p. 193). The table shows the average, standard deviation, and conditional mean squared error ($\times 10^{-2}$) for the 200 estimates of excess error. The "target" average excess error is 8.3×10^{-2}.

| | | | \multicolumn{5}{c}{K-fold (adjusted) cross-validation} | | | | |
	Bootstrap	0.632	50	25	10	5	2
Mean	9.1	8.8	11.5	11.7 (11.5)	12.2 (11.7)	12.4 (11.3)	15.3 (11.1)
SD	1.2	1.9	4.4	4.5 (4.2)	5.0 (4.6)	4.8 (3.9)	7.1 (4.6)
MSE	0.38	0.29	0.62	0.64 (0.63)	0.76 (0.73)	0.64 (0.54)	1.14 (0.59)

54 is outlying. At the other end is case 27, whose residual is -1.84; this was misclassified 42 times out of 65 in our simulation.   ∎

Example 7.9 (Low birth weights)   In order to compare the properties of estimates of misclassification error under repeated sampling, we took data on 189 births at a US hospital to be our population F. The binary response equals zero for babies with birth weight less than 2.5 kg, and equals one otherwise. We took 200 samples of size $n = 50$ from these data, and to each sample we fitted a binary logistic model with nine regression parameters expressing dependence on maternal characteristics — weight, smoking status, number of previous premature labours, hypertension, uterine irritability and the number of visits to the physician in the first trimester. For each of the samples we calculated various cross-validation and bootstrap estimates of misclassification rate, using $R = 200$ bootstrap resamples.

Table 7.10 shows the results of this experiment, expressed in terms of estimates of the excess error, which is the difference between true misclassification rate D and the apparent error rate $\hat{\Delta}_{app}$ found by applying the prediction rule to the data. The "target" value of the average excess error over the 200 samples was 8.3×10^{-2}; the average apparent error was 20.0×10^{-2}.

The bootstrap and 0.632 excess error estimates again perform best overall in terms of mean, variability, and conditional mean squared error. Note that the standard deviations for the bootstrap and 0.632 estimates suggest that $R = 50$ would have given results accurate enough for most purposes.

Ordinary cross-validation is significantly better than K-fold cross-validation, unless $K = 25$. However, the results for K-fold adjusted cross-validation are not significantly different from those for unadjusted cross-validation, even with $K = 2$. Thus if cross-validation is to be used, adjusted K-fold cross-validation offers considerable computational savings over ordinary cross-validation, and is about equally accurate.

For reasons outlined in Example 3.6, the EDF of the data may be a poor estimate of the original CDF when there are binary responses y_j. One way to overcome this is to switch the response value with small probability, i.e. to replace (x_j^*, y_j^*) with $(x_j^*, 1 - y_j^*)$ with probability (say) 0.1. This corresponds to a binomial simulation using probabilities shrunk somewhat towards 0.5

from the observed values of 0 and 1. It should produce results that are smoother than those obtained under case resampling from the original data. Our simulation experiment included this randomized bootstrap, but although typically it improves slightly on bootstrap results, the results here were very similar to those for the ordinary bootstrap.   ∎

In principle resampling estimates of misclassification rates could be used to select which covariates to include in the prediction rule, along the lines given for linear regression in Section 6.4.2. It seems likely, in the light of the preceding example, that the bootstrap approach would be preferable.

7.6 Nonparametric Regression

So far we have considered regression models in which the mean response is related to covariates x through a function of known form with a small number of unknown parameters. There are, however, occasions when it is useful to assess the effects of covariates x without completely specifying the form of the relationship between mean response μ and x. This is done using nonparametric regression methods, of which there are now a large number.

The simplest nonparametric regression relationship for scalar x is

$$Y = \mu(x) + \varepsilon,$$

where $\mu(x)$ has completely unknown form but would be assumed continuous in many applications, and ε is a random error with zero mean. A typical application is illustrated by the scatter plot in Figure 7.14. Here no simple parametric regression curve seems appropriate, so it makes sense to fit a smooth curve (which we do later in Example 7.10) with as few restrictions as possible.

Often nonparametric regression is used as an exploratory tool, either directly by producing a curve estimate for visual interpretation, or indirectly by providing a comparison with some tentative parametric model fit via a significance test. In some applications the rather different objective of prediction will be of interest. Whatever the application, the complicated nature of nonparametric regression methods makes it unlikely that probability distributions for statistics of interest can be evaluated theoretically, and so resampling methods will play a prominent role.

It is not possible here to describe all of the nonparametric regression methods that are now available, and in any event many of them do not yet have fully developed companion resampling methods. We shall limit ourselves to a brief discussion of some of the main methods, and to applications in generalized additive models, where nonparametric regression is used to extend the generalized linear models of Section 7.2.

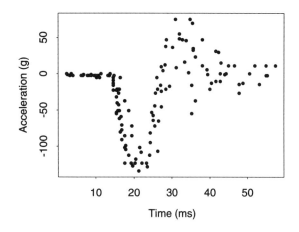

Figure 7.14 Motorcycle impact data. Acceleration y (g) at a time x milliseconds after impact (Silverman, 1985).

7.6.1 Nonparametric curves

Several nonparametric curve-fitting algorithms are variants on the idea of local averaging. One such method is *kernel smoothing*, which estimates mean response $E(Y \mid x) = \mu(x)$ by

$$\hat{\mu}(x) = \frac{\sum y_j w\{(x - x_j)/b\}}{\sum w\{(x - x_j)/b\}}, \tag{7.24}$$

with $w(\cdot)$ a symmetric density function and b an adjustable "bandwidth" constant that determines how widely the averaging is done. This estimate is similar in many ways to the kernel density estimate discussed in Example 5.13, and as there the choice of b depends upon a trade-off between bias and variability of the estimate: small b gives small bias and large variance, whereas large b has the opposite effects. Ideally b would vary with x, to reflect large changes in the derivative of $\mu(x)$ and heteroscedasticity, both evident in Figure 7.14.

Modifications to the estimate (7.24) are needed at the ends of the x range, to avoid the inherent bias when there is little or no data on one side of x. In many ways more satisfactory are the local regression methods, where a local linear or quadratic curve is fitted using weights $w\{(x - x_j)/b\}$ as above, and then $\hat{\mu}(x)$ is taken to be the fitted value at x. Implementations of this idea include the *lowess* method, which also incorporates trimming of outliers. Again the choice of b is critical.

A different approach is to define a curve in terms of basis functions, such as powers of x which define polynomials. The fitted model is then a linear combination of basis functions, with coefficients determined by least squares regression. Which basis to use depends on the application, but polynomials are

generally bad because fitted values become increasingly variable as x moves
toward the ends of its data range — polynomial extrapolation is notoriously
poor. One popular choice for basis functions is cubic splines, with which $\mu(x)$
is modelled by a series of cubic polynomials joined at "knot" values of x, such
that the curve has continuous second derivatives everywhere. The least squares
cubic spline fit minimizes the penalized least squares criterion for fitting $\mu(x)$,

$$\sum\{y_j - \mu(x_j)\}^2 + \lambda \int \{\ddot{\mu}(x)\}^2 dx;$$

weighted sums of squares can be used if necessary. In most software implementations the spline fit can be determined either by specifying the degrees of
freedom of the fitted curve, or by applying cross-validation (Section 6.4.1).

A spline fit will generally be biased, unless the underlying curve is in fact a
cubic. That such bias is nearly always present for nonparametric curve fits can
create difficulties. The other general feature that makes interpretation difficult
is the occurrence of spurious bumps and bends in the curve estimates, as we
shall see in Example 7.10.

Resampling methods

Two types of applications of nonparametric curves are use in checking a parametric curve, and use in setting confidence limits for $\mu(x)$ or prediction limits
for $Y = \mu(x) + \varepsilon$ at some values of x. The first type is quite straightforward, because data would be simulated from the fitted parametric model: Example 7.11
illustrates this. Here we look briefly at confidence limits and prediction limits,
where the nonparametric curve is the only "model".

The basic difficulty for resampling here is similar to that with density
estimation, illustrated in Example 5.13, namely bias. Suppose that we want
to calculate a confidence interval for $\mu(x)$ at one or more values of x. Case
resampling cannot be used with standard recommendations for nonparametric
regression, because the resampling bias of $\hat{\mu}^*(x)$ will be smaller than that
of $\hat{\mu}(x)$. This could probably be corrected, as with density estimation, by
using a larger bandwidth or equivalent tuning constant. But simpler, at least
in principle, is to apply the idea of model-based resampling discussed in
Chapter 6.

The naive extension of model-based resampling would generate responses
$y_j^* = \hat{\mu}(x_j) + \varepsilon_j^*$, where $\hat{\mu}(x_j)$ is the fitted value from some nonparametric
regression method, and ε_j^* is sampled from appropriately modified versions
of the residuals $y_j - \hat{\mu}(x_j)$. Unfortunately the inherent bias of most nonparametric regression methods distorts both the fitted values and the residuals,
and thence biases the resampling scheme. One recommended strategy is to
use as simulation model a curve that is oversmoothed relative to the usual
estimate. For definiteness, suppose that we are using a kernel method or a local
smoothing method with tuning constant b, and that we use cross-validation

to determine the best value of b. Then for the simulation model we use the corresponding curve with, say, $2b$ as the tuning constant. To try to eliminate bias from the simulation errors ε_j^*, we use residuals from an undersmoothed curve, say with tuning constant $b/2$. As with linear regression, it is appropriate to use modified residuals, where leverage is taken into account as in (6.9). This is possible for most nonparametric regression methods, since they are linear. Detailed asymptotic theory shows that something along these lines is necessary to make resampling work, but there is no clear guidance as to precise relative values for the tuning constants.

Example 7.10 (Motorcycle impact data)   The response y here is acceleration measured x milliseconds after impact in an accident simulation experiment. The full data were shown in Figure 7.14, but for computational reasons we eliminate replicates for the present analysis, which leaves $n = 94$ cases with distinct x values. The solid line in the top left panel of Figure 7.15 shows a cubic spline fit for the data of Figure 7.14, chosen by cross-validation and having approximately 12 degrees of freedom. The top right panel of the figure gives the plot of modified residuals against x for this fit. Note the heteroscedasticity, which broadly corresponds to the three strata separated by the vertical dotted lines. The estimated variances for these strata are approximately 4, 600 and 140. Reciprocals of these were used as weights for the spline fit in the left panel. Bias in these residuals is evident at times 10–15 ms, where the residuals are first mostly negative and then positive because the curve does not follow the data closely enough.

There is a rough correspondence between kernel smoothing and spline smoothing and this, together with the previous discussion, suggests that for model-based resampling we use $y_j^* = \tilde{\mu}(x_j) + \varepsilon_j^*$, where $\tilde{\mu}$ is the spline fit obtained by doubling the cross-validation choice of λ. This fit is the dotted line in the top left panel of Figure 7.15. The random errors ε_j^* are sampled from the modified residuals for another spline fit in which λ is half the cross-validation value. The lower right panel of the figure displays these residuals, which show less bias than those for the original fit, though perhaps a smaller bandwidth would be better still. The sampling is stratified, to reflect the very strong heteroscedasticity.

We simulated $R = 999$ datasets in this way, and to each fitted the spline curve $\hat{\mu}^*(x)$, with the bandwidth chosen by cross-validation each time. We then calculated 90% confidence intervals at six values of x, using the basic bootstrap method modified to equate the distributions of $\hat{\mu}^*(x) - \tilde{\mu}(x)$ and $\hat{\mu}(x) - \mu(x)$. For example, at $x = 20$ the estimates $\hat{\mu}$ and $\tilde{\mu}$ are respectively -110.8 and -106.2, and the 950th ordered value of $\hat{\mu}^*$ is -87.2, so that the upper confidence limit is $-110.8 - \{-87.2 - (-106.2)\} = -129.8$. The resulting confidence intervals are shown in the bottom left panel of Figure 7.15, together with the original

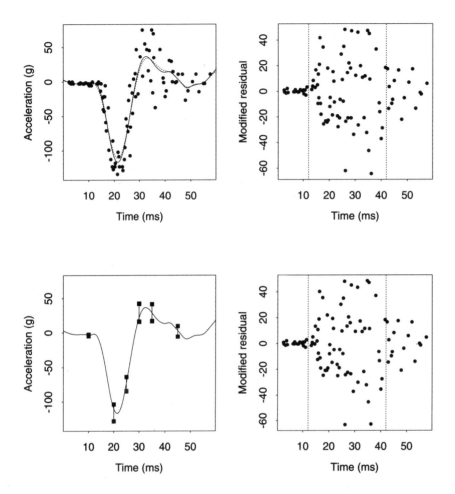

Figure 7.15 Bootstrap analysis of motorcycle data, without replicate responses. Top left: data, original cubic spline fit (solid) and oversmoothed fit (dots). Top right: residuals from original fit; note their bias at times 10–15 ms. Bottom right: residuals from undersmoothed fit. The lines in these plots show strata used in the resampling. Bottom left: original fit and 90% basic bootstrap confidence intervals at six values of x; they are not centred on the fitted curve.

fit. Note how the confidence limits are centred on the convex side of the fitted curve in order to account for its bias; this is most evident at $x = 20$. ∎

7.6.2 Generalized additive models

The structural part of a generalized linear model, as outlined in Section 7.2.1, is the linear predictor $\eta = x^T \beta$, which is additive in the components x_i of x. It may not always be the case that we know whether x_i or some transformation of it should be used in the linear predictor. Then it makes sense, at least for exploratory purposes, to include in η a nonparametric curve component $s_i(x_i)$ for each component x_i (except those corresponding to qualitative factors). This still assumes additivity of the effects of the x_is on the linear predictor scale.

The result is the *generalized additive model*

$$g\{\mu(x)\} = \eta(x) = \sum_{i=1}^{p} s_i(x_i), \qquad (7.25)$$

where $g(\cdot)$ is a known link function, as before. As for a generalized linear model, the model specification is completed by a variance function, $\mathrm{var}(Y) = \kappa V(\mu)$.

In practice we might force some terms $s_i(x_i)$ in (7.25) to be linear, depending upon what is known about the application. Each nonparametric term is typically fitted as a linear term plus a nonlinear term, the latter using smoothing splines or a local smoother. This means that the corresponding generalized linear model is a sub-model, so that the effects of nonlinearity can be assessed using differences of residual deviances, suitably scaled, as in (7.8). In standard computer implementations each nonparametric curve $s_i(x_i)$ has (approximately) three degrees of freedom for nonlinearity. Standard distributional approximations for the resulting test statistics are sometimes quite unreliable, so that resampling methods are particularly helpful in this context. For tests of this sort the null model for resampling is the generalized linear model, and the approach taken can be summarized by the following algorithm.

Algorithm 7.4 (Comparison of generalized linear and generalized additive models)

For $r = 1, \ldots, R$,

1 fix the covariate values at those observed;
2 generate bootstrap responses $y_1^*, \ldots, y_n^*$ by resampling from the fitted generalized linear null model;
3 fit the generalized linear model to the bootstrap data and calculate the residual deviance $d_{0,r}^*$;
4 fit the generalized additive model to the bootstrap data, calculate the residual deviance d_r^* and dispersion $\hat{\kappa}_r^*$; then
5 calculate $t_r^* = (d_{0,r}^* - d_r^*)/\hat{\kappa}_r^*$.

Finally, calculate the P-value as $\left[1 + \#\{t_r^* \geq t\} \right]/(R+1)$, where $t = (d_0 - d)/\hat{\kappa}$ is the scaled difference of deviances for the original data. •

The following example illustrates the use of nonparametric curve fits in model-checking.

Example 7.11 (Leukaemia data) For the data in Example 7.1, we originally fitted a generalized linear model with gamma variance function and linear predictor group $+ x$ with logarithmic link, where group is a factor with two levels. The fitted mean function for that model is shown as two solid curves in Figure 7.16, the upper curve corresponding to Group 1. Here we consider

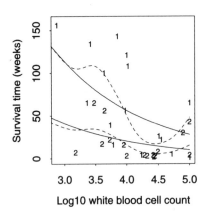

Figure 7.16
Generalized linear
model fits (solid) and
generalized additive
model fits (dashed) for
leukaemia data of
Example 7.1.

whether or not the effect of x is linear. To do this, we compare the original fit to that of the generalized additive model in which x is replaced by $s(x)$, which is a smoothing spline with three degrees of freedom. The link and variance functions are unchanged. The fitted mean function for this model is shown as dashed curves in the figure.

Is the smooth curve a significantly better fit? To answer this we use the test statistic Q defined in (7.8), where here D corresponds to the residual deviance for the generalized additive model, $\hat{\kappa}$ is the dispersion for that model, and D_0 is the residual deviance for the smaller generalized linear model. For these data $D = 40.32$ with 30 degrees of freedom, $\hat{\kappa} = 0.725$, and $D_0 = 30.75$ with 27 degrees of freedom, so that $q = (40.32 - 30.75)/0.725 = 13.2$. The standard approximation for the null distribution of Q is chi-squared with degrees of freedom equal to the difference in model dimensions, here $p - p_0 = 3$, so the approximate P-value is 0.004. Alternatively, to allow for estimation of the dispersion, $(p - p_0)^{-1}Q$ is compared to the F distribution with denominator degrees of freedom $n - p - 1$, here 27, and this gives approximate P-value 0.012. It looks as though there is strong evidence against the simpler, loglinear model. However, the accuracies of the approximations used here are somewhat questionable, so it makes sense to apply the resampling analysis.

To calculate a bootstrap P-value corresponding to $q = 13.2$, we simulate the distribution of Q under the fitted null model, that is the original generalized linear model fit, but with nonparametric resampling. The particular resampling scheme we choose here uses the linear predictor residuals r_{Lj} defined in (7.10), one advantage of which is that positive simulated responses are guaranteed. The residuals in this case are

$$r_{Lj} = \frac{\log(y_j) - \log(\hat{\mu}_{0j})}{\hat{\kappa}_0^{1/2}(1 - h_{0j})^{1/2}},$$

Figure 7.17
Chi-squared Q-Q plot of
standardized deviance
differences q^* for
comparing generalized
linear and generalized
additive model fits to
the leukaemia data. The
lines show the
theoretical χ_3^2
approximation (dashes)
and the F
approximation (dots).
Resampling uses
Pearson residuals on
linear predictor scale,
with $R = 999$.

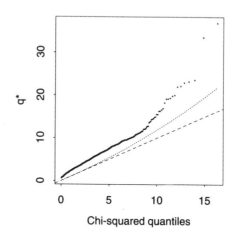

where h_{0j}, $\hat{\mu}_{0j}$ and $\hat{\kappa}_0$ are the leverage, fitted value and dispersion estimate for the null (generalized linear) model. These residuals appear quite homogeneous, so no stratification is used. Thus step 2 of Algorithm 7.4 consists of sampling $\varepsilon_1^*, \ldots, \varepsilon_n^*$ randomly with replacement from $r_{L1}, \ldots, r_{Ln}$ (without mean correction), and then generating responses $y_j^* = \hat{\mu}_{0j} \exp(\hat{\kappa}_0^{1/2} \varepsilon_j^*)$ for $j = 1, \ldots, n$.

Applying this algorithm with $R = 999$ for our data gives the P-value 0.035, larger than the theoretical approximations, but still suggesting that the linear term in x is not sufficient. The bootstrap null distribution of q^* deviates markedly from the standard χ_3^2 approximation, as the Q-Q plot in Figure 7.17 shows. The F approximation is also inaccurate.

A jackknife-after-bootstrap plot reveals that quantiles of q^* are moderately sensitive to case 2, but without this case the P-value is virtually unchanged.

Very similar results are obtained under parametric resampling with the exponential model, as might be expected from the original data analysis. ∎

Our next example illustrates the use of semiparametric regression in prediction.

Example 7.12 (AIDS diagnoses) In Example 7.4 we discussed prediction of AIDS diagnoses based on the data in Table 7.4. A smooth time trend seems preferable to fitting a separate parameter for each diagnosis period, and accordingly we consider a model where the mean number of diagnoses in period j reported with delay k, the mean for the (j,k) cell of the table, equals

$$\mu_{jk} = \exp\{\alpha(j) + \beta_k\}.$$

We take $\alpha(j)$ to be a locally quadratic lowess smooth with bandwidth 0.5.

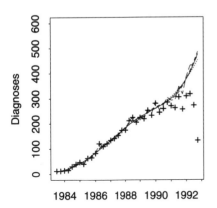
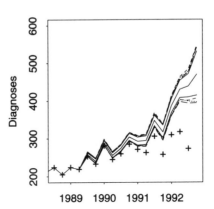

Figure 7.18
Generalized additive
model prediction of UK
AIDS diagnoses. The
left panel shows the
fitted curve with
bandwidth 0.5 (smooth
solid line), the predicted
diagnoses from this fit
(jagged dashed line),
and the fitted curves
with bandwidths 0.7
(dots) and 0.3 (dashes),
together with the
observed totals (+). The
right panel shows the
predicted quarterly
diagnoses for 1989–92
(central solid line), and
pointwise 95%
prediction limits from
the Poisson bootstrap
(solid), negative
binomial bootstrap
(dashes), and
nonparametric
bootstrap without (dots)
and with (dot-dash)
stratification.

The delay distribution is so sharply peaked here that although we could take a smooth function in the delay time, it is equally parsimonious to take 15 separate parameters β_k. We use the same variance function as in Example 7.4, which assumes that the observed counts y_{jk} are overdispersed Poisson with means μ_{jk}, and we fit the model as a generalized additive model. The residual deviance is 751.7 on 444.2 degrees of freedom, increased from 716.5 and 413 in the previous fit. The curve shown in the left panel of Figure 7.18 fits well, and is much more plausible as a model for underlying trend than the curve in Figure 7.5. The panel also shows the predicted values from this curve, which of course are heavily affected by the observed diagnoses in Table 7.4.

As mentioned above, in resampling from fitted curves it is important to take residuals from an undersmoothed curve, in order to avoid bias, and to add them to an oversmoothed curve. We take Pearson residuals $(y - \hat{\mu})/\hat{\mu}^{1/2}$ from a similar curve with bandwidth 0.3, and add them to a curve with bandwidth 0.7. These fits have deviances 745.3 on 439.2 degrees of freedom and 754.1 on 446.1 degrees of freedom. Both of these curves are shown in Figure 7.18. Leverage adjustment is awkward for generalized additive models, but the large number of degrees of freedom here makes such adjustments unnecessary. We modify resampling scheme (7.12), and repeat the calculations as for Algorithm 7.1 applied to Example 7.4, with $R = 999$.

Table 7.11 shows the resulting prediction intervals for the last quarters of 1990, 1991, and 1992. The intervals for 1992 are substantially shorter than those in Table 7.5, because of the different model. The generalized additive model is based on an underlying smooth trend in diagnoses, so predictions for the last few rows of the table depend less critically on the values observed

Table 7.11 Bootstrap
95% prediction intervals
for numbers of AIDS
cases in England and
Wales for the fourth
quarters of 1990, 1991,
and 1992, using
generalized additive
model.

	1990		1991		1992	
Poisson	295	314	302	336	415	532
Negative binomial	293	317	298	339	407	547
Nonparametric	294	316	296	337	397	545
Stratified nonparametric	293	315	295	338	394	542

in those rows. This contrasts with the Poisson two-way layout model, for which the predictions depend completely on single rows of the table and are much more variable. Compare the slight forecast drop in Figure 7.6 with the predicted increase in Figure 7.18.

The dotted lines in Figure 7.18 show pointwise 95% prediction bands for the AIDS diagnoses. The prediction intervals for the negative binomial and nonparametric schemes are similar, although the effect of stratification is smaller. Stratification has no effect on the deviances. The negative binomial deviances are typically about 90 larger than those generated under the nonparametric scheme.

The plausibility of the smooth underlying curve and its usefulness for prediction is of course central to the approach outlined here. ∎

7.6.3 Other methods

Often a nonparametric regression fit will be compared to a parametric fit, but not all applications are of this kind. For example, we may want to see whether or not a regression curve is monotone without specifying its form. The following application is of this kind.

Example 7.13 (Downs syndrome)   Table 7.12 contains a set of data on incidence of Downs syndrome babies for mothers in various age ranges. Mean age is approximate mean age of the m mothers whose babies included y babies with Downs syndrome. These data are plotted on the logistic scale in Figure 7.19, together with a generalized additive spline fit as an exploratory aid in modelling the incidence rate.

What we notice about the curve is that it *decreases* with age for young mothers, contrary to intuition and expert belief. A similar phenomenon occurs for other datasets. We want to see if this dip is real, as opposed to a statistical artefact. So a null model is required under which the rate of occurrence is increasing with age. Linear logistic regression is clearly inappropriate, and most other standard models give non-increasing rates. The approach taken is *isotonic regression*, in which the rates are fitted nonparametrically subject to their increasing with age. Further, in order to make the null model a special

x	17.0	18.5	19.5	20.5	21.5	22.5	23.5	24.5	25.5	26.5
m	13555	13675	18752	22005	23896	24667	24807	23986	22860	21450
y	16	15	16	22	16	12	17	22	15	14
x	27.5	28.5	29.5	30.5	31.5	32.5	33.5	34.5	35.5	36.5
m	19202	17450	15685	13954	11987	10983	9825	8483	7448	6628
y	27	14	9	12	12	18	13	11	23	13
x	37.5	38.5	39.5	40.5	41.5	42.4	43.5	44.5	45.5	47.0
m	5780	4834	3961	2952	2276	1589	1018	596	327	249
y	17	15	30	31	33	20	16	22	11	7

Table 7.12 Number y of Downs syndrome babies in m births for mothers with age groups centred on x years (Geyer, 1991).

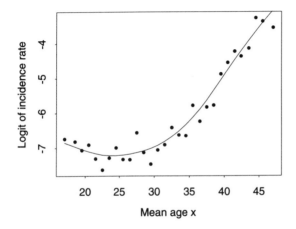

Figure 7.19 Logistic scale plot of Downs syndrome incidence rates. Solid curve is generalized additive spline fit with 3 degrees of freedom

case of the general model, the latter is taken to be an arbitrary convex curve for the logit of incidence rate.

If the incidence rate at age x_i is $\pi(x_i)$ with $\text{logit}\{\pi(x_i)\} = \eta(x_i) = \eta_i$, say, for $i = 1,\ldots,k$, then the binomial log likelihood is

$$\ell(\eta_1,\ldots,\eta_k) = \sum_{i=1}^{k}\{y_i\eta_i - m_i\log(1 + e^{\eta_i})\}.$$

A convex model is one in which

$$\eta_i \le \frac{x_{i+1} - x_i}{x_{i+1} - x_{i-1}}\eta_{i-1} + \frac{x_i - x_{i-1}}{x_{i+1} - x_{i-1}}\eta_{i+1}, \quad i = 2,\ldots,k-1.$$

The general model fit will maximize the binomial log likelihood subject to these constraints, giving estimates $\hat{\eta}_1,\ldots,\hat{\eta}_k$. The null model satisfies the constraints $\eta_i \le \eta_{i+1}$ for $i = 1,\ldots,k-1$, which are equivalent to the previous convexity

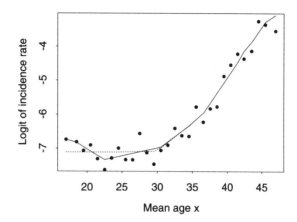

Figure 7.20 Logistic scale plot of incidence rates for Downs syndrome data, with convex fit (solid line) and isotonic fit (dotted line).

constraints plus the single constraint $\eta_1 \le \eta_2$. The null fit essentially pools adjacent age groups for which the general estimates $\hat{\eta}_i$ violate the monotonicity of the null model. If the null estimates are denoted by $\hat{\eta}_{0,i}$, then we take as our test statistic the deviance difference

$$T = 2\{\ell(\hat{\eta}_1, \ldots, \hat{\eta}_k) - \ell(\hat{\eta}_{0,1}, \ldots, \hat{\eta}_{0,k})\}.$$

The difficulty now is that the standard chi-squared approximation for deviance differences does not apply, essentially because there is not a fixed value for the degrees of freedom. There is a complicated large-sample approximation which may well not be reliable. So a parametric bootstrap is used to calculate the P-value. This requires simulation from the binomial model with sample sizes m_i, covariate values x_i and logits $\hat{\eta}_{0,i}$.

Figure 7.20 shows the convex and isotone regression fits, which clearly differ for age below 30. The deviance difference for these fits is $t = 5.873$. Simulation of $R = 999$ binomial datasets from the isotone model gave 33 values of t^* in excess of 5.873, so the P-value is 0.034 and we conclude that the dip in incidence rate may be real. (Further analysis with additional data does not support this conclusion.) Figure 7.21 is a histogram of the t^* values.

It is possible that the null distribution of T is unstable with respect to parameter values, in which case the nested bootstrap procedure of Section 4.5 should be used, possibly in conjunction with the recycling method of Section 9.4.4 to accelerate the computation. ∎

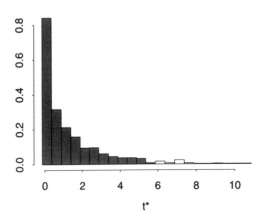

Figure 7.21 Histogram of 999 resampled deviance test statistics for the Downs syndrome data. The unshaded portion corresponds to values exceeding observed test statistic $t = 5.873$.

7.7 Bibliographic Notes

A full treatment of all aspects of generalized linear models is given by McCullagh and Nelder (1989). Dobson (1990) is a more elementary discussion, while Firth (1991) gives a useful shorter account. Davison and Snell (1991) describe methods of checking such models. Books by Chambers and Hastie (1992) and Venables and Ripley (1994) cover most of the basic methods discussed in this chapter, but restricted to implementations in S and S-Plus.

Published discussions of bootstrap methods for generalized linear models are usually limited to one-step iterations from the model fit, with resampling of Pearson residuals; see, for example, Moulton and Zeger (1991). There appears to be no systematic study of the various schemes described in Section 7.2.3. Nelder and Pregibon (1987) briefly discuss a more general application. Moulton and Zeger (1989) discuss bootstrap analysis of repeated measure data, while Booth (1996) describes methods for use when there is nested variation.

Books giving general accounts of survival data are mentioned in Section 3.12. Hjort (1985) describes model-based resampling methods for proportional hazards regression, and studies their theoretical properties such as confidence interval accuracy. Burr and Doss (1993) outline how the double bootstrap can be used to provide confidence bands for a median survival time, and compare its performance with simulated bands based on asymptotic results. Lo and Singh (1986) and Horváth and Yandell (1987) make theoretical contributions to bootstrapping survival data. Bootstrap and permutation tests for comparison of survivor functions are discussed by Heller and Venkatraman (1996).

Burr (1994) studies empirically various bootstrap confidence interval methods for the proportional hazards model. She finds no overall best combination, but concludes that normal-theory asymptotic confidence intervals and basic bootstrap intervals are generally good for regression parameters β, while percentile intervals are satisfactory for survival probabilities derived from the product-limit estimate. Results from the conditional bootstrap are more erratic than those for resampling cases or from model-based resampling, and the latter is generally preferred.

Altman and Andersen (1989), Chen and George (1985) and Sauerbrei and Schumacher (1992) apply case resampling to variable selection in survival data models, but there seems to be little theoretical justification of this. The use of bootstrap methods in general assessment of model uncertainty in regression is discussed by Faraway (1992).

Bootstrap methods for general nonlinear regression models are usually studied theoretically via linear approximation. See Huet, Jolivet and Messéan (1990) for some simulation results. There appears to be no literature on incorporating curvature effects into model-based resampling. The behaviour of residuals, leverages and diagnostics for nonlinear regression models are developed by Cook, Tsai and Wei (1986) and St. Laurent and Cook (1993).

The large literature on prediction error as related to discrimination is surveyed by McLachlan (1992). References for bootstrap estimation of prediction error are mentioned in Section 6.6. Those dealing particularly with misclassification error include Efron (1983) and Efron and Tibshirani (1997). Gong (1983) discusses a particular case where the prediction rule is based on a logistic regression model obtained by forward selection.

References to bootstrap methods for model selection are mentioned in Section 6.6. The treatment by Shao (1996) covers both generalized linear models and nonlinear models.

There are now numerous accounts of nonparametric regression, such as Hastie and Tibshirani (1990) on generalized additive models, and Green and Silverman (1994) on penalized likelihood methods. A useful treatment of local weighted regression by Hastie and Loader (1993) is followed by a discussion of the relative merits of various kernel-type estimators. Venables and Ripley (1994) discuss implementation in S-Plus with examples; see also Chambers and Hastie (1992). Considerable theoretical work has been done on bootstrap methods for setting confidence bands on nonparametric regression curves, mostly focusing on kernel estimators. Härdle and Bowman (1988) and Härdle and Marron (1991) both emphasize the need for different levels of smoothing in the components of model-based resampling schemes. Hall (1992b) gives a detailed theoretical assessment of the properties of such confidence band methods, and emphasizes the benefits of the studentized bootstrap. There appears to be no corresponding treatment for spline smoothing methods, nor for the many complex methods now used for fitting surfaces to model the effects of multiple covariates.

A summary of much of the theory for resampling in nonlinear and non-parametric regression is given in Chapter 8 of Shao and Tu (1995).

7.8 Problems

1   The estimator $\hat{\beta}$ in a generalized linear model may be defined as the solution to the theoretical counterpart of (7.2), namely

$$\int \frac{y-\mu}{cV(\mu)} \frac{x}{\partial\eta/\partial\mu} \, dF(x,y) = 0,$$

where μ is regarded as a function of β through the link function $g(\mu) = \eta = x^T\beta$. Use the result of Problem 2.12 to show that the empirical influence value for $\hat{\beta}$ based on data $(x_1, c_1, y_1), \ldots, (x_n, c_n, y_n)$ is

$$l_j = n(X^T W X)^{-1} x_j \frac{y_j - \hat{\mu}_j}{c_j V(\hat{\mu}_j)\partial\eta_j/\partial\mu_j},$$

evaluated at the fitted model, where W is the diagonal matrix with elements given by (7.3).
Hence show that the approximate variance matrix for $\hat{\beta}^*$ for case resampling in a generalized linear model is

$$\hat{\kappa}(X^T W X)^{-1} X^T W \mathscr{E} X (X^T W X)^{-1},$$

where $\mathscr{E} = \mathrm{diag}(r_{P1}^2, \ldots, r_{Pn}^2)$ with the r_{Pj} standardized Pearson residuals (7.9). Show that for the linear model this yields the modified version of the robust variance matrix (6.26).
(Section 7.2.2; Moulton and Zeger, 1991)

2   For the gamma model of Examples 7.1 and 7.2, verify that $\mathrm{var}(Y) = \kappa\mu^2$ and that the log likelihood contribution from a single observation is

$$\ell(y, \mu) = -\kappa^{-1}\{\log(\mu) + y/\mu\}.$$

Show that the unstandardized Pearson and deviance residuals are respectively $\hat{\kappa}^{-1/2}(z-1)$ and $\mathrm{sign}(z-1)[2\hat{\kappa}^{-1/2}\{z-1-\log(z)\}]^{1/2}$, where $z = y/\hat{\mu}$. If the regression is loglinear, meaning that the log link is used, verify that the unstandardized linear predictor residuals are simply $\hat{\kappa}^{-1/2}\log(z)$.
What are the possible ranges of the standardized residuals r_P, r_L and r_D? Calculate these for the model fitted in Example 7.2.
If the deviance residual is expressed as $d(y, \mu)$, check that $d(y, \mu) = d(z, 1)$. Hence show that the resampling scheme based on standardized deviance residuals can be expressed as $y_j^* = \hat{\mu}_j z_j^*$, where z_j^* is defined by $d(z_j^*, 1) = \varepsilon_j^*$ with ε_j^* randomly sampled from $r_{D1}, \ldots, r_{Dn}$. What further simplification can be made?
(Sections 7.2.2, 7.2.3)

3   The figure below shows the fit to data pairs $(x_1, y_1), \ldots, (x_n, y_n)$ of a binary logistic model

$$\Pr(Y = 1) = 1 - \Pr(Y = 0) = \frac{\exp(\beta_0 + \beta_1 x)}{1 + \exp(\beta_0 + \beta_1 x)}.$$

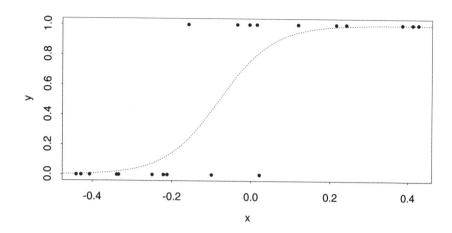

(a) Under case resampling, show that the maximum likelihood estimate $\hat{\beta}_1^*$ for a bootstrap sample is infinite with probability close to e^{-2}. What effect has this on the different types of bootstrap confidence intervals for β_1?

(b) Bias-corrected maximum likelihood estimates are obtained by modifying response values $(0,1)$ to $(h_j/2, 1+h_j)$, where h_j is the jth leverage for the model fit to the original data. Do infinite parameter estimates arise when bootstrapping cases from the modified data?

(Section 7.2.3; Firth, 1993; Moulton and Zeger, 1991)

4   Investigate whether resampling schemes given by (7.12), (7.13), and (7.14) yield Algorithm 6.1 for bootstrapping the linear model.

5   Suppose that conditional on $P = \pi$, Y has a binomial distribution with probability π and denominator m, and that P has a beta density

$$f(\pi \mid \alpha, \beta) = \frac{\Gamma(\alpha + \beta)}{\Gamma(\alpha)\Gamma(\beta)} \pi^{\alpha-1}(1 - \pi)^{\beta-1}, \quad 0 < \pi < 1, \quad \alpha, \beta > 0.$$

Show that Y has unconditional mean and variance (7.15) and express Π and ϕ in terms of α and β.

Express α and β in terms of Π and ϕ, and hence explain how to generate data with mean and variance (7.15) by generating π from a beta distribution, and then, conditional on the probabilities, generating binomial variables with probabilities π and denominators m.

How should your algorithm be amended to generate beta-binomial data with variance function $\phi\Pi(1 - \Pi)$?

(Example 7.3)

6   For generalized linear models the analogue of the case-deletion result in Problem 6.2 is

$$\hat{\beta}_{-j} \doteq \hat{\beta} - (X^T W X)^{-1} w_j \hat{\kappa}^{-1/2} x_j \frac{y_j - \hat{\mu}_j}{1 - h_j}.$$

(a) Use this to show that when the jth case is deleted the predicted value for y_j is

$$\mu(x_j; \hat{F}_{-j}) \doteq g^{-1}\left(\hat{\eta}_j - w_j^{-1/2}(1 - h_j)^{-1/2} h_j r_{Pj}\right).$$

(b) Use (a) to give an approximation for the leave-one-out cross-validation estimate of prediction error for a binary logistic regression with cost (7.23).
(Sections 6.4.1,7.2.2)

7.9 Practicals

1   Dataframe `remission` contains data from Freeman (1987) concerning a measure of cancer activity, the LI values, for 27 cancer patients, of whom 9 went into remission. Remission is indicated by the binary variable $r = 1$. Consider testing the hypothesis that the LI values do not affect the probability of remission. First, fit a binary logistic model to the data, plot them, and perform a permutation test:

```
attach(remission)
plot(LI+0.03*rnorm(27),r,pch=1,xlab="LI, jittered",xlim=c(0,2.5))
rem.glm <- glm(r~LI,binomial,data=remission)
summary(rem.glm)
x <- seq(0.4,2.0,0.02)
eta <- cbind(rep(1,81),x)%*%coefficients(rem.glm)
lines(x,inv.logit(eta),lty=2)
rem.perm <- function(data, i)
{ d <-data
  d$LI<- d$LI[i]
  d.glm <- glm(r~LI,binomial,data=d)
  coefficients(d.glm) }
rem.boot <- boot(remission, rem.perm, R=199, sim="permutation")
qqnorm(rem.boot$t[,2],ylab="Coefficient of LI",ylim=c(-3,3))
abline(h=rem.boot$t0[2],lty=2)
```

Compare this significance level with that from using a normal approximation for the coefficient of LI in the fitted model.
Construct bootstrap tests of the hypothesis by extending the methods outlined in Section 6.2.5.
(Freeman, 1987; Hall and Wilson, 1991)

2   Dataframe `breslow` contains data from Breslow (1985) on death rates from heart disease among British male doctors. A standard model is that the numbers of deaths y have a Poisson distribution with mean $n\lambda$, where n is the number of person-years and λ is the death rate. The focus of interest is how death rate depends on two explanatory variables, a factor representing the age group and an indicator of smoking status, x. Two competing models are

$$\lambda = \exp(\alpha_{age} + \beta x), \qquad \lambda = \alpha_{age} + \beta x;$$

these are respectively multiplicative and additive. To fit these models we proceed as follows:

```
breslow.mult <- glm(y~offset(log(n))+age+smoke,poisson(log),
                    data=breslow)
breslow.add <- glm(y~n:age+ns-1,poisson(identity),data=breslow)
```

Here `ns` is a variable for the effect of smoking, constructed to allow for the difficulty in applying an offset in fitting the additive model. The deviances of the fitted models are $D_{add} = 7.43$ and $D_{mult} = 12.13$. Although it appears that the additive model is the better fit, these models are not nested, so a chi-squared approximation cannot be applied to the difference of deviances. For bootstrap assessment of fit based on the difference of deviances, we simulate in turn from each fitted model. Because fits of the additive model fail if there are no deaths in the lowest age group, and this happens with appreciable probability, we constrain the simulation so that there are deaths at each age.

```
breslow.fun <- function(data)
{  mult <- glm(y~offset(log(n))+age+smoke,poisson(log),data=data)
   add <- glm(y~n:age+ns-1,poisson(identity),data=data)
   deviance(mult)-deviance(add) }
breslow.sim <- function(data, mle)
{ data$y <- rpois(nrow(data), mle)
  while(min(data$y)==0) data$y <- rpois(nrow(data), mle)
  data }
add.mle <- fitted(breslow.add)
add.boot <- boot(breslow, breslow.fun, R=99, sim="parametric",
                 ran.gen=breslow.sim, mle=add.mle)
mult.mle <- fitted(breslow.mult)
mult.boot <- boot(breslow, breslow.fun, R=99, sim="parametric",
                  ran.gen=breslow.sim, mle=mult.mle)
boxplot(mult.boot$t,add.boot$t,ylab="Deviance difference",
        names=c("multiplicative","additive"))
abline(h=mult.boot$t0,lty=2)
```

What does this tell you about the relative fit of the models?

A different strategy would be to use parametric simulation, simulating not from the fitted models, but from the model with separate Poisson distributions for each of the original data. Discuss critically this approach.

(Section 7.2; Example 4.5; Wahrendorf, Becher and Brown, 1987; Hall and Wilson, 1991)

3   Dataframe `hirose` contains the PET reliability data of Table 7.6. Initially we consider estimating the bias and variance of the MLEs of the parameters $\beta_0, \ldots, \beta_4$ and x_0 discussed in Example 7.5, using parametric simulation from the fitted Weibull model, but assuming that the data were subject to censoring at the fixed time 9104.25. Functions to calculate the minus log likelihood (in parametrization $\beta_0, \ldots, \beta_4$) and to find the MLEs are:

```
hirose.lik <- function(mle, data)
{ x0 <- 5-exp(mle[5])
  lambda <- exp(mle[1]+mle[2]*(-log(data$volt-x0)))
  beta <- exp(mle[3]+mle[4]*(-log(data$volt)))
  z <- (data$time/lambda)^beta
  sum(z - data$cens*log(beta*z/data$time)) }
hirose.fun <- function(data, start)
{ d <- nlminb(start, hirose.lik, data=data)
  conv <- (d$message=="RELATIVE FUNCTION CONVERGENCE")
  c(conv, d$objective, d$parameters) }
```

The MLEs for the original data can be obtained by setting `hirose.start <- c(6,2,4,1,1)` (obtained by introspection), and then iterating the following lines

```
hirose.start <- hirose.fun(hirose, start=hirose.start)[3:7]
hirose.start
```

a few times.

New data are generated by

```
hirose.gen <- function(data, mle)
{ x0 <- 5 - exp(mle[5])
  x1 <- -log(data$volt-x0)
  xb <- -log(data$volt)
  lambda <- exp(mle[1]+mle[2]*x1)
  beta <- exp(mle[3]+mle[4]*xb)
  y <- rweibull(nrow(data), shape=beta, scale=lambda)
  data$cens <- ifelse(y<=9104.25,1,0)
  data$time <- ifelse(data$cens==1,y,9104.25)
  data }
```

and the bootstrap results are obtained by

```
hirose.mle <- hirose.start
hirose.boot <- boot(hirose, hirose.fun, R=19, sim="parametric",
                    ran.gen=hirose.gen, mle=hirose.mle,
                    start=hirose.start)
hirose.boot$t[,7] <- 5-exp(hirose.boot$t[,7])
hirose.boot$t0[7] <- 5-exp(hirose.boot$t0[7])
hirose.boot
```

Try this with a larger value of R — but don't hold your breath.
For a full likelihood analysis for the parameter θ, the log likelihood must be
maximized over $\beta_1,\ldots,\beta_4$ for a given value of θ. A little thought shows that the
necessary code is

```
beta0 <- function(theta, mle)
{ x49 <- -log(4.9-(5-exp(mle[4])))
  x <- -log(4.9)
  log(theta*10^3) - mle[1]*x49-lgamma(1 + exp(-mle[2]-mle[3]*x)) }
hirose.lik2 <- function(mle, data, theta)
{ x0 <- 5-exp(mle[4])
  lambda <- exp(beta0(theta,mle)+mle[1]*(-log(data$volt-x0)))
  beta <- exp(mle[2]+mle[3]*(-log(data$volt)))
  z <- (data$time/lambda)^beta
  sum(z - data$cens*log(beta*z/data$time)) }
hirose.fun2 <- function(data, start, theta)
{ d <- nlminb(start, hirose.lik2, data=data, theta=theta)
  conv <- (d$message=="RELATIVE FUNCTION CONVERGENCE")
  c(conv, d$objective, d$parameters) }
hirose.f <- function(data, start, theta)
            c( hirose.fun(data,i,start),
               hirose.fun2(data,i,start[-1],theta))
```

so that `hirose.f` does likelihood fits when θ is fixed and when it is not.
The quantiles of the simulated likelihood ratio statistic are then obtained by

```
make.theta <- function(mle, x=hirose$volt)
{ x0 <- 5-exp(mle[5])
  lambda <- exp(mle[1]-mle[2]*log(x-x0))/10^3
  beta <- exp(mle[3]-mle[4]*log(x))
  lambda*gamma(1+1/beta) }
theta <- make.theta(hirose.mle,4.9)
hirose.boot <- boot(hirose, hirose.f, R=19, "parametric",
                    ran.gen=hirose.gen, mle=hirose.mle,
                    start=hirose.start, theta=theta)
```

```
R <- hirose.boot$R
i <- c(1:R)[(hirose.boot$t[,1]==1)&(hirose.boot$t[,8]==1)]
w <- 2*(hirose.boot$t[i,9]-hirose.boot$t[,2])
qqplot(qchisq(c(1:length(w))/(1+length(w)),1),w)
abline(0,1,lty=2)
```

Again, try this with a larger *R*.
Can you see how the code would be modified for nonparametric simulation?
(Section 7.3; Hirose, 1993)

4   Dataframe `nodal` contains data on 53 patients with prostate cancer. For each
    patient there are five explanatory variables, each with two levels. These are `aged`
    (<60, ≥60); `stage`, a measure of the seriousness of the tumour; `grade`, a measure
    of the pathology of the tumour; a measure of the seriousness of an `xray`; and
    `acid`, the level of serum acid phosphatase. The higher level of each of the last four
    variables indicates a more severe condition. The response *r* indicates whether the
    cancer has spread to the neighbouring lymph nodes. The data were collected to
    see whether nodal involvement can be predicted from the explanatory variables.
    Analysis of deviance for a binary logistic regression model suggests that the
    response depends only on `stage`, `xray` and `acid`, and we base our predictions on
    the model with these variables. Our measure of error is the average number of
    misclassifications $n^{-1} \sum c(y_j, \mu_j)$, where $c(y, \mu)$ is given by (7.23).
    For an initial model, apparent error, and ordinary and *K*-fold cross-validation
    estimates of prediction error:

```
attach(nodal)
cost <- function(r, pi=0) mean(abs(r-pi)>0.5)
nodal.glm <- glm(r~stage+xray+acid,binomial,data=nodal)
nodal.diag <- glm.diag(nodal.glm)
app.err <- cost(r, fitted(nodal.glm))
cv.err <- cv.glm(nodal, nodal.glm, cost, K=53)$delta
cv.11.err <- cv.glm(nodal, nodal.glm, cost, K=11)$delta
```

For resampling-based estimates and plot for 0.632 errors:

```
nodal.pred.fun <- function(data, i, model)
{ d <- data[i,]
  d.glm <- update(model,data=d)
  pred <- predict(d.glm,data,type="response")
  D.F.Fhat <- cost(data$r, pred)
  D.Fhat.Fhat <- cost(d$r, fitted(d.glm))
  c(data$r-pred, D.F.Fhat - D.Fhat.Fhat) }
nodal.boot <- boot(nodal, nodal.pred.fun, R=200, model=nodal.glm)
nodal.boot$f <- boot.array(nodal.boot)
n <- nrow(nodal)
err.boot <- mean(nodal.boot$t[,n+1]) + app.err
ord <- order(nodal.diag$res)
nodal.pred <- nodal.boot$t[,ord]
err.632 <- 0
n.632 <- NULL
pred.632 <- NULL
for (i in 1:n)  {
    inds <- nodal.boot$f[,i]==0
    err.632 <- err.632 + cost(nodal.pred[inds,i])/n
    n.632 <- c(n.632, sum(inds))
    pred.632 <- c(pred.632, nodal.pred[inds,i]) }
```

```
err.632 <- 0.368*app.err + 0.632*err.632
nodal.fac <- factor(rep(1:n,n.632),labels=ord)
plot(nodal.fac, pred.632,ylab="Prediction errors",
     xlab="Case ordered by residual")
abline(h=-0.5,lty=2); abline(h=0.5,lty=2)
```

Cases with errors entirely outside the dotted lines are always misclassified, and conversely.
Estimate the misclassification error using the model with all five explanatory variables.
(Section 7.5; Brown, 1980)

5   Dataframe cloth records the number of faults y in lengths x of cloth. Is it true that $E(y) \propto x$?

```
plot(cloth$x,cloth$y)
cloth.glm <- glm(y~offset(log(x)),poisson,data=cloth)
lines(cloth$x,fitted(cloth.glm))
summary(cloth.glm)
cloth.diag <- glm.diag(cloth.glm)
cloth.gam <- gam(y~s(log(x)),poisson,data=cloth)
lines(cloth$x,fitted(cloth.gam),lty=2)
summary(cloth.gam)
```

There is some overdispersion relative to the Poisson model with identity link, and strong evidence that the generalized additive model fit cloth.gam improves on the straight-line model in which y is Poisson with mean $\beta_0 + \beta_1 x$. We can try parametric simulation from the model with the linear fit (the null model) to assess the significance of the decrease; cf. Algorithm 7.4:

```
cloth.gen <- function(data, fits)
{ y <- rpois(n=nrow(data),fits)
  data.frame(x=data$x,y=y) }
cloth.fun <- function(data)
{ d.glm <- glm(y~offset(log(x)),poisson,data=data)
  d.gam <- gam(y~s(log(x)),poisson,data=data)
  c(deviance(d.glm),deviance(d.gam)) }
cloth.boot <- boot(cloth, cloth.fun, sim="parametric", R=99,
                    ran.gen=cloth.gen, mle=fitted(cloth.glm))
```

Are the simulated drops in deviance roughly χ_3^2, as they would be if standard asymptotics applied? How significant is the observed drop?
In addition to the hypothesis that we want to test — that $E(y)$ depends linearly on x — the parametric bootstrap imposes the constraint that the data are Poisson, which is not intended to be part of the null hypothesis. We avoid this by a nonparametric bootstrap, as follows:

```
cloth1 <- data.frame(cloth,fits=fitted(cloth.glm),
                      pearson=cloth.diag$rp)
cloth.fun1 <- function(data, i)
{ y <- data$fits+sqrt(data$fits)*data$pearson[i]
  y <- round(y)
  y[y<0] <- 0
  d.glm <- glm(y~offset(log(data$x)),poisson)
  d.gam <- gam(y~s(log(data$x)),poisson)
  c(deviance(d.glm),deviance(d.gam)) }
cloth.boot <- boot(cloth1, cloth.fun1, R=99)
```

Here we have used resampled standardized Pearson residuals for the null model, obtained by `cloth.diag$rp`.

How significant is the observed drop in deviance under this resampling scheme? (Section 7.6.2; Bissell, 1972; Firth, Glosup and Hinkley, 1991)

6 The data `nitrofen` are taken from a test of the toxicity of the herbicide nitrofen on the zooplankton *Ceriodaphnia dubia*, an important species that forms the basis of freshwater food chains for the higher invertebrates and for fish and birds. The standard test measures the survival and reproductive output of 10 juvenile *C. dubia* in each of four concentrations of the herbicide, together with a control in which the herbicide is not present. During the 7-day period of the test each of the original individuals produces three broods of offspring, but for illustration we analyse the total offspring.

A previous model for the data is that at concentration x the total offspring y for each individual is Poisson distributed with mean $\exp(\beta_1 + \beta_1 x + \beta_2 x^2)$. The fit of this model to the data suggests that low doses of nitrofen augment reproduction, but that higher doses inhibit it.

One thing required from analysis is an estimate of the concentration x_{50} of nitrofen at which the mean brood size is halved, together with a 95% confidence interval for x_{50}. A second issue is posed by the surprising finding from a previous analysis that brood sizes are slightly larger at low doses of herbicide than at high or zero doses: is this true?

A wide variety of nonparametric curves could be fitted to the data, though care is needed because there are only five distinct values of x. The data do not look Poisson, but we use models with Poisson errors and the log link function to ensure that fitted values and predictions are positive. To compare the fits of the generalized linear model described above and a robustified generalized additive model with Poisson errors:

```
nitro <- rbind(nitrofen,nitrofen,nitrofen,nitrofen,nitrofen)
nitro <- rbind(nitro,nitro,nitro,nitro,nitro)
nitro$conc <- seq(0,310,length=nrow(nitro))
attach(nitrofen)
plot(conc,jitter(total),ylab="total")
nitro.glm <- glm(total~conc+conc^2,poisson,data=nitrofen)
lines(nitro$conc,predict(nitro.glm,nitro,"response"),lty=3)
nitro.gam <- gam(total~s(conc,df=3),robust(poisson),data=nitrofen)
lines(nitro$conc,predict(nitro.gam,nitro,"response"))
```

To compare bootstrap confidence intervals for x_{50} based on these models:

```
nitro.fun <- function(data, i, nitro)
{ assign("d",data[i,],frame=1)
  d.fit <- gam(total~s(conc,df=3),robust(poisson),data=d)
  f <- predict(d.fit,nitro,"response")
  f.gam <- max(nitro$conc[f>0.5*f[1]])
  d.fit <- glm(total~conc+conc^2,poisson,data=d)
  f <- predict(d.fit,nitro,"response")
  f.glm <- max(nitro$conc[f>0.5*f[1]])
  c(f.gam, f.glm) }
nitro.boot <- boot(nitrofen, nitro.fun, R=499,
                 strata=rep(1:5,rep(10,5)), nitro=nitro)
boot.ci(nitro.boot,index=1,type=c("norm","basic","perc","bca"))
boot.ci(nitro.boot,index=2,type=c("norm","basic","perc","bca"))
```

Do the values of x_{50}^* look normal? What is the bias estimate for $\hat{x}_{50}$ using the two models?

To perform a bootstrap test of whether the peak is a genuine effect, we simulate from a model satisfying the null hypothesis of no peak to see if the observed value of a suitable test statistic t, say, is unusual. This involves fitting a model with no peak, and then simulating from it. We read fitted values $\hat{m}_0(x)$ from the robust generalized additive model fit, but with 2.2 df (chosen by eye as the smallest for which the curve is flat through the first two levels of concentration). We then generate bootstrap responses by setting $y^* = \hat{m}_0(x) + \varepsilon^*$, where the ε^* are chosen randomly from the modified residuals at that x. We take as test statistic the difference between the highest fitted value and the fitted value at $x = 0$.

```
nitro.test <- fitted(gam(total~s(conc,df=2.2),robust(poisson),
                         data=nitrofen))
f <- predict(nitro.glm,nitro,"response")
nitro.orig <- max(f) - f[1]
res <- (nitrofen$total-nitro.test)/sqrt(1-0.1)
nitro1 <- data.frame(nitrofen,res=res,fit=nitro.test)
nitro1.fun <- function(data, i, nitro)
{ assign("d",data[i,],frame=1)
  d$total <- round(d$fit+d$res[i])
  d.fit <- glm(total~conc+conc^2,poisson,data=d)
  f <- predict(d.fit,nitro,"response")
  max(f)-f[1] }
nitro1.boot <- boot(nitro1, nitro1.fun, R=99,
                    strata=rep(1:5,rep(10,5)), nitro=nitro)
(1+sum(nitro1.boot$t>nitro.orig))/(1+nitro1.boot$R)
```

Do your conclusions change if other smooth curves are fitted?
(Section 7.6.2; Bailer and Oris, 1994)

8

Complex Dependence

8.1 Introduction

In previous chapters our models have involved variables independent at some level, and we have been able to identify independent components that can be simulated. Where a model can be fitted and residuals of some sort identified, the same ideas can be applied in the more complex problems discussed in this chapter. Where that model is parametric, parametric simulation can in principle be used to obtain resamples, though Markov chain Monte Carlo techniques may be needed in practice. But in nonparametric situations the dependence may be so complex, or our knowledge of it so limited, that neither of these approaches is feasible. Of course some assumption of repeatedness within the data is essential, or it is impossible to proceed. But the repeatability may not be at the level of individual observations, but of groups of them, and there is typically dependence between as well as within groups. This leads to the idea of constructing bootstrap data by taking blocks of some sort from the original observations. The area is in rapid development, so we avoid a detailed mathematical exposition, and merely sketch key aspects of the main ideas. In Section 8.2 we describe some of the resampling schemes proposed for time series. Section 8.3 outlines some ideas useful in resampling point processes.

8.2 Time Series

8.2.1 Introduction

A time series is a sequence of observations arising in succession, usually at times spaced equally and taken to be integers. Most models for time series assume that the data are stationary, in which case the joint distribution of any subset of them depends only on their times of occurrence relative to each other and not on their absolute position in the series. A weaker assumption used in data analysis is that the joint second moments of observations depend only on their relative positions; such a series is said to be second-order or weakly stationary.

Time domain

There are two basic types of summary quantities for stationary time series. The first, in the time domain, rests on the joint moments of the observations. Let $\{Y_j\}$ be a second-order stationary time series, with zero mean and *autocovariance function* γ_j. That is, $\mathrm{E}(Y_j) = 0$ and $\mathrm{cov}(Y_k, Y_{k+j}) = \gamma_j$ for all k and j; the variance of Y_j is γ_0. Then the *autocorrelation function* of the series is $\rho_j = \gamma_j/\gamma_0$, for $j = 0, \pm 1, \ldots$, which measures the correlation between observations at lag j apart; of course $-1 \leq \rho_j \leq 1$, $\rho_0 = 1$, and $\rho_j = \rho_{-j}$. An uncorrelated series would have $\rho_j \equiv 0$, and if the data were normally distributed this would imply that the observations were independent.

For example, the stationary moving average process of order one, or MA(1) model, has

$$Y_j = \varepsilon_j + \beta \varepsilon_{j-1}, \qquad j = \ldots, -1, 0, 1, \ldots, \tag{8.1}$$

where $\{\varepsilon_j\}$ is a *white noise process* of innovations, that is, a stream of independent observations with mean zero and variance σ^2. The autocorrelation function for the $\{Y_j\}$ is $\rho_1 = \beta/(1 + \beta^2)$ and $\rho_j \equiv 0$ for $|j| > 1$; this sharp cut-off in the autocorrelations is characteristic of a moving average process. Only if $\beta = 0$ is the series Y_j independent. On the other hand the stationary autoregressive process of order one, or AR(1) model, has

$$Y_j = \alpha Y_{j-1} + \varepsilon_j, \qquad j = \ldots, -1, 0, 1, \ldots, \qquad |\alpha| < 1. \tag{8.2}$$

The autocorrelation function for this process is $\rho_j = \alpha^{|j|}$ for $j = \pm 1, \pm 2$ and so forth, so large α gives high correlation between successive observations. The autocorrelation function decreases rapidly for both models (8.1) and (8.2).

A close relative of the autocorrelation function is the *partial autocorrelation function*, defined as $\rho'_j = \gamma'_j/\gamma_0$, where γ'_j is the covariance between Y_k and Y_{k+j} after adjusting for the intervening observations. The partial autocorrelations for the MA(1) model are

$$\rho'_j = -(-\beta)^j (1 - \beta^2)\{1 - \beta^{2(j+1)}\}^{-1}, \qquad j = \pm 1, \pm 2, \ldots.$$

The AR(1) model has $\rho'_1 = \alpha$, and $\rho'_j \equiv 0$ for $|j| > 1$; a sharp cut-off in the partial autocorrelations is characteristic of autoregressive processes.

The sample estimates of ρ_j and ρ'_j are basic summaries of the structure of a time series. Plots of them against j are called the *correlogram* and *partial correlogram* of the series.

One widely used class of linear time series models is the autoregressive-moving average or ARMA process. The general ARMA(p, q) model is defined by

$$Y_j = \sum_{k=1}^{p} \alpha_k Y_{j-k} + \varepsilon_j + \sum_{k=1}^{q} \beta_k \varepsilon_{j-k}, \qquad (8.3)$$

where $\{\varepsilon_j\}$ is a white noise process. If all the α_k equal zero, $\{Y_j\}$ is the moving average process MA(q), whereas if all the β_k equal zero, it is AR(p). In order for (8.3) to represent a stationary series, conditions must be placed on the coefficients. Packaged routines enable models (8.3) to be fitted readily, while series from them are easily simulated using a given innovation series $\dots, \varepsilon_{-1}, \varepsilon_0, \varepsilon_1, \dots$.

Frequency domain

The second approach to time series is based on the frequency domain. The *spectrum* of a stationary series with autocovariances γ_j is

$$g(\omega) = \gamma_0 + 2 \sum_{j=1}^{\infty} \gamma_j \cos(\omega j), \qquad 0 \leq \omega \leq \pi. \qquad (8.4)$$

This summarizes the values of all the autocorrelations of $\{Y_j\}$. A white noise process has the flat spectrum $g(\omega) \equiv \gamma_0$, while a sharp peak in $g(\omega)$ corresponds to a strong periodic component in the series. For example, the spectrum for a stationary AR(1) model is $g(\omega) = \sigma^2 \{1 - 2\alpha \cos(\omega) + \alpha^2\}^{-1}$.

The empirical Fourier transform plays a key role in data analysis in the frequency domain. The treatment is simplified if we relabel the series as $y_0, \dots, y_{n-1}$ and suppose that $n = 2n_F + 1$ is odd. Let $\zeta = e^{2\pi i/n}$ be the nth complex root of unity, so $\zeta^n = 1$. Then the *empirical Fourier transform* of the data is the set of n complex-valued quantities

$$\tilde{y}_k = \sum_{j=0}^{n-1} \zeta^{jk} y_j, \qquad k = 0, \dots, n-1;$$

note that $\tilde{y}_0 = n\bar{y}$ and that the complex conjugate of $\tilde{y}_k$ is $\tilde{y}_{n-k}$, for $k = 1, \dots, n-1$. For different k the vectors $(1, \zeta^k, \dots, \zeta^{k(n-1)})^T$ are orthogonal. It is straightforward to see that

$$\frac{1}{n} \sum_{k=0}^{n-1} \zeta^{-jk} \tilde{y}_k = y_j, \qquad j = 0, \dots, n-1,$$

so this *inverse Fourier transform* retrieves the data. Now define the *Fourier frequencies* $\omega_k = 2\pi k/n$, for $k = 1, \dots, n_F$. The sample analogue of the spectrum at ω_k is the *periodogram*,

$$I(\omega_k) = n^{-1} |\tilde{y}_k|^2 = n^{-1} \left[\left\{ \sum_{j=0}^{n-1} y_j \cos(\omega_k j) \right\}^2 + \left\{ \sum_{j=0}^{n-1} y_j \sin(\omega_k j) \right\}^2 \right].$$

The orthogonality properties of the vectors involved in the Fourier transform imply that the overall sum of squares of the data may be expressed as

$$\sum_{j=0}^{n-1} y_j^2 = I(0) + 2\sum_{k=1}^{n_F} I(\omega_k). \tag{8.5}$$

The empirical Fourier transform and its inverse can be rapidly calculated by an algorithm known as the *fast Fourier transform*.

If the data arise from a stationary process $\{Y_j\}$ with spectrum $g(\omega)$, where $Y_j = \sum_{l=-\infty}^{\infty} a_{j-l}\varepsilon_l$, with $\{\varepsilon_l\}$ a normal white noise process, then as n increases and provided the terms $|a_l|$ decrease sufficiently fast as $l \to \pm\infty$, the real and imaginary parts of the complex-valued random variables $\tilde{y}_1, \ldots, \tilde{y}_{n_F}$ are asymptotically independent normal variables with means zero and variances $ng(\omega_1)/2, \ldots, ng(\omega_{n_F})/2$; furthermore the $\tilde{y}_k$ at different Fourier frequencies are asymptotically independent. This implies that as $n \to \infty$ for such a process, the periodogram values $I(\omega_k)$ at different Fourier frequencies will be independent, and that $I(\omega_k)$ will have an exponential distribution with mean $g(\omega_k)$. (If n is even $I(\pi)$ must be added to (8.5); $I(\pi)$ is approximately independent of the $I(\omega_k)$ and its asymptotic distribution is $g(\pi)\chi_1^2$.) Thus (8.5) decomposes the total sum of squares into asymptotically independent components, each associated with the amount of variation due to a particular Fourier frequency. Weaker versions of these results hold when the process is not linear, or when the process $\{\varepsilon_l\}$ is not normal, the key difference being that the joint limiting distribution of the periodogram values holds only for a finite number of fixed frequencies.

If the series is white noise, under mild conditions its periodogram ordinates $I(\omega_1), \ldots, I(\omega_{n_F})$ are roughly a random sample from an exponential distribution with mean γ_0. Tests of independence may be based on the *cumulative periodogram ordinates*,

$$\frac{\sum_{j=1}^k I(\omega_j)}{\sum_{j=1}^{n_F} I(\omega_j)}, \qquad k = 1, \ldots, n_F - 1.$$

When the data are white noise these ordinates have roughly the same joint distribution as the order statistics of $n_F - 1$ uniform random variables.

Example 8.1 (Rio Negro data)   The data for our first time series example are monthly averages of the daily stages — heights — of the Rio Negro, 18 km upstream at Manaus, from 1903 to 1992, made available to us by Professors H. O'Reilly Sternberg and D. R. Brillinger of the University of California at Berkeley. Because of the tiny slope of the water surface and the lower courses of its flatland affluents, these data may be regarded as a reasonable approximation of the water level in the Amazon River at the confluence of the

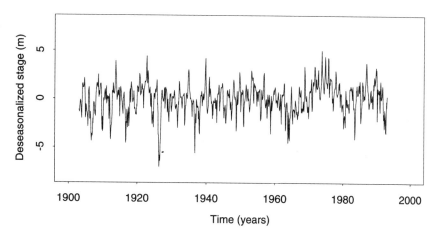

Figure 8.1
Deseasonalized monthly
average stage (metres)
of the Rio Negro at
Manaus, 1903–1992
(Sternberg, 1995).

two rivers. To remove the strong seasonal component, we subtract the average value for each month, giving the series of length $n = 1080$ shown in Figure 8.1.

For an initial example, we take the first ten years of observations. The top panels of Figure 8.2 show the correlogram and partial correlogram for this shorter series, with horizontal lines showing approximate 95% confidence limits for correlations from a white noise series. The shape of the correlogram and the cut-off in the partial correlogram suggest that a low-order autoregressive model will fit the data, which are quite highly correlated. The lower left panel of the figure shows the periodogram of the series, which displays the usual high variability associated with single periodogram ordinates. The lower right panel shows the cumulative periodogram, which lies well outside its overall 95% confidence band and clearly does not correspond to a white noise series.

An AR(2) model fitted to the shorter series gives $\hat{\alpha}_1 = 1.14$ and $\hat{\alpha}_2 = -0.31$, both with standard error 0.062, and estimated innovation variance 0.598. The left panel of Figure 8.3 shows a normal probability plot of the standardized residuals from this model, and the right panel shows the cumulative periodogram of the residual series. The residuals seem close to Gaussian white noise. ∎

8.2.2 Model-based resampling

There are two approaches to resampling in the time domain. The first and simplest is analogous to model-based resampling in regression. The idea is to fit a suitable model to the data, to construct residuals from the fitted model, and then to generate new series by incorporating random samples from the

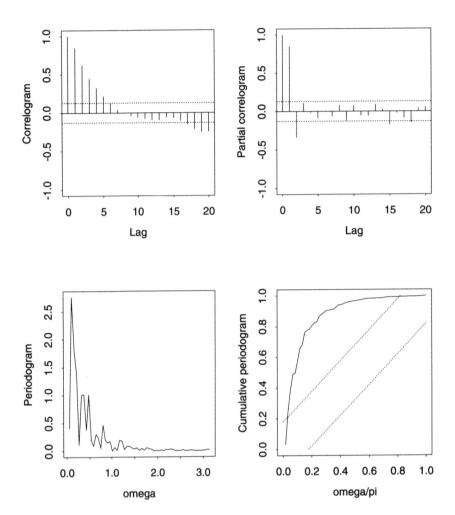

Figure 8.2 Summary plots for the Rio Negro data, 1903–1912. The top panels show the correlogram and partial correlogram for the series. The bottom panels show the periodogram and cumulative periodogram.

residuals into the fitted model. The residuals are typically recentred to have the same mean as the innovations of the model. About the simplest situation is when the AR(1) model (8.2) is fitted to an observed series $y_1, \ldots, y_n$, giving estimated autoregressive coefficient $\hat{\alpha}$ and estimated innovations

$$e_j = y_j - \hat{\alpha} y_{j-1}, \qquad j = 2, \ldots, n;$$

e_1 is unobtainable because y_0 is unknown. Model-based resampling might then proceed by equi-probable sampling with replacement from centred residuals $e_2 - \bar{e}, \ldots, e_n - \bar{e}$ to obtain simulated innovations $\varepsilon_0^*, \ldots, \varepsilon_n^*$, and then setting

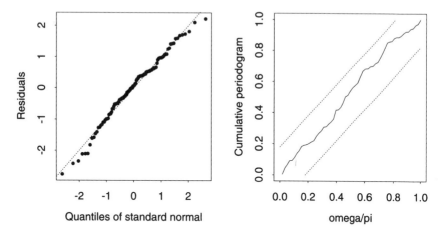

Figure 8.3 Plots for residuals from AR(2) model fitted to the Rio Negro data, 1903–1912: normal Q-Q plot of the standardized residuals (left), and cumulative periodogram of the residual series (right).

$y_0^* = \varepsilon_0^*$ and

$$y_j^* = \hat{\alpha} y_{j-1}^* + \varepsilon_j^*, \qquad j = 1, \dots, n; \tag{8.6}$$

of course we must have $|\hat{\alpha}| < 1$. In fact the series so generated is not stationary, and it is better to start the series in equilibrium, or to generate a longer series of innovations and start (8.6) at $j = -k$, where the 'burn-in' period $-k, \dots, 0$ is chosen large enough to ensure that the observations $y_1^*, \dots, y_n^*$ are essentially stationary; the values $y_{-k}^*, \dots, y_0^*$ are discarded.

Thus model-based resampling for time series is based on applying the defining equation(s) of the series to innovations resampled from residuals. This procedure is simple to apply, and leads to good theoretical behaviour for estimates based on such data when the model is correct. For example, studentized bootstrap confidence intervals for the autoregressive coefficients α_k in an AR(p) process enjoy the good asymptotic properties discussed in Section 5.4.1, provided that the model fitted is chosen correctly. Just as there, confidence intervals based on transformed statistics may be better in practice.

Example 8.2 (Wool prices) The Australian Wool Corporation monitors prices weekly when wool markets are held, and sets a minimum price just before each week's markets open. This reflects the overall price of wool for that week, but the prices actually paid can vary considerably relative to the minimum. The left panel of Figure 8.4 shows a plot of log(price paid/minimum price) for those weeks when markets were held from July 1976 to June 1984. The series does not seem stationary, having some of the characteristics of a random walk, as well as a possible overall trend.

If the log ratio in week j follows a random walk, we have $Y_j = Y_{j-1} + \varepsilon_j$,

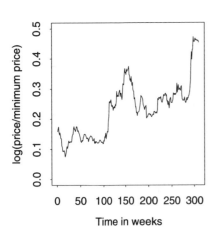
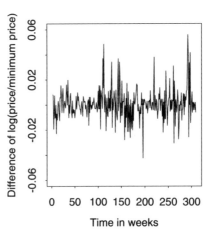

Figure 8.4 Weekly log ratio of price paid to minimum price for Australian wool from July 1976 to June 1984 (Diggle, 1990, pp. 229–237). Left panel: original data. Right panel: first differences of data.

where the ε_j are white noise; a non-zero mean for the innovations ε_j will lead to drift in y_j. The right panel of Figure 8.4 shows the differenced series, $e_j = y_j - y_{j-1}$, which appears stationary apart from a change in the innovation variance at about the 100th week. In our analysis we drop the first 100 observations, leaving a differenced series of length 208.

An alternative to the random walk model is the AR(1) model

$$(Y_j - \mu) = \alpha(Y_{j-1} - \mu) + \varepsilon_j; \tag{8.7}$$

this gives the random walk when $\alpha = 1$. If the innovations have mean zero and α is close to but less than one, (8.7) gives stationary data, though subject to the climbs and falls seen in the left panel of Figure 8.4. The implications for forecasting depend on the value of α, since the variance of a forecast is only asymptotically bounded when $|\alpha| < 1$. We test the unit root hypothesis that the data are a random walk, or equivalently that $\alpha = 1$, as follows.

Our test is based on the ordinary least squares estimate of α in the regression $Y_j = \gamma + \alpha Y_{j-1} + \varepsilon_j$ for $j = 2, \ldots, n$ using test statistic $T = (1 - \hat{\alpha})/S$, where S is the standard error for $\hat{\alpha}$ calculated using the usual formula for a straight-line regression model. Large values of T are evidence against the random walk hypothesis, with or without drift. The observed value of T is $t = 1.19$. The distribution of T is far from the usual standard normal, however, because of the regression of each observation on its predecessor.

Under the hypothesis that $\alpha = 1$ we simulate new time series $Y_1^*, \ldots, Y_n^*$ by generating a bootstrap sample $\varepsilon_2^*, \ldots, \varepsilon_n^*$ from the differences $e_2, \ldots, e_n$ and then setting $Y_1^* = Y_1, Y_2^* = Y_1^* + \varepsilon_2^*$, and $Y_j^* = Y_{j-1}^* + \varepsilon_j^*$ for subsequent j. This is (8.6) applied with the null hypothesis value $\hat{\alpha} = 1$. The value of T^* is then obtained from the regression of Y_j^* on Y_{j-1}^* for $j = 2, \ldots, n$. The left panel

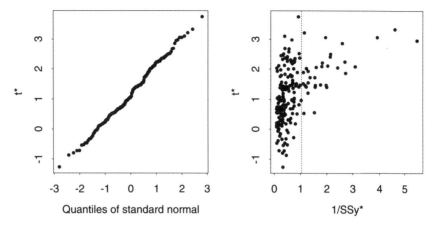

Figure 8.5 Results for 199 replicates of the random walk test statistic, T^*. The left panel is a normal plot of t^*. The right panel shows t^* plotted against the inverse sum of squares for the regressor, with the dotted line giving the observed value.

of Figure 8.5 shows the empirical distribution of T^* in 199 simulations. The distribution is close to normal with mean 1.17 and variance 0.88. The observed significance level for t is $(97 + 1)/(199 + 1) = 0.49$: there is no evidence against the random walk hypothesis.

The right panel of Figure 8.5 shows the values of t^* plotted against the inverse sum of squares for the regressor y^*_{j-1}. In a conventional regression, inference is usually conditional on this sum of squares, which determines the precision of the estimate. The dotted line shows the observed sum of squares. If the conditional distribution of t^* is thought to be appropriate here, the distribution of values of t^* close to the dotted line shows that the conditional significance level is even higher; there is no evidence against the random walk conditionally or unconditionally. ∎

Models are commonly fitted in order to predict future values of a time series, but as in other settings, it can be difficult to allow for the various sources of uncertainty that affect the predictions. The next example shows how bootstrap methods can give some idea of the relative contributions from innovations, estimation error, and model error.

Example 8.3 (Sunspot numbers) Figure 8.6 shows the much-analysed annual sunspot numbers $y'_1, \ldots, y'_{289}$ from 1700–1988. The data show a strong cycle with a period of about 11 years, and some hint of non-reversibility, which shows up as a lack of symmetry in the peaks. We use values from 1930–1979 to predict the numbers of sunspots over the next few years, based on fitting

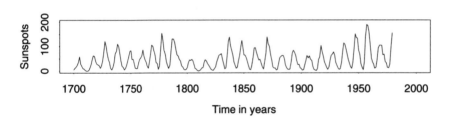

Figure 8.6 Annual sunspot numbers, 1700–1988 (Tong, 1990, p. 470).

	1980	81	82	83	84	85	86	87	1988
Actual	23.0	21.8	19.6	14.4	11.7	6.7	5.6	9.0	18.1
Predicted	21.6	18.9	14.9	12.2	9.1	7.5	6.8	8.8	13.6
					Standard error				
Nominal	2.0	2.9	3.2	3.2	3.2	3.2	3.3	3.4	3.4
Model, AR(9)	2.2	2.9	3.0	3.2	3.3	3.8	4.1	4.0	3.6
Model	2.3	3.3	3.6	3.5	3.5	3.6	3.8	3.9	3.8
Model, condit'l	2.5	3.6	4.1	3.9	3.8	3.8	3.9	4.0	4.1
Block, $l = 10$	7.8	7.0	6.9	6.9	6.7	6.6	6.7	6.8	6.5
Post-black'd, $l = 10$	2.1	3.3	3.9	4.0	3.6	3.6	3.9	4.3	4.3

Table 8.1 Predictions and their standard errors for $2\{(y_j' + 1)^{1/2} - 1\}$ for sunspot data, 1980–1988, based on data for 1930–1979. The standard errors are nominal, and also those obtained under model-based resampling assuming the simulated series y^* are AR(9), not assuming y^* is AR(9), and by a conditional scheme, and the block and post-blackened bootstraps with block length $l = 10$. See Examples 8.3 and 8.5 for details.

AR(p) models

$$Y_j - \mu = \sum_{k=1}^{p} \alpha_k(Y_{j-k} - \mu) + \varepsilon_j, \tag{8.8}$$

to the transformed observations $y_j = 2\{(y_j' + 1)^{1/2} - 1\}$; this transformation is chosen to stabilize the variance. The corresponding maximized log likelihoods are denoted $\hat{\ell}_p$. A standard approach to model selection is to select the model that minimizes $\text{AIC} = -2\hat{\ell}_p + 2p$, which trades off goodness of fit (measured by the maximized log likelihood) against model complexity (measured by p). Here the resulting "best" model is AR(9), whose predictions $\hat{y}_j$ for 1980–88 and their nominal standard errors are given at the top of Table 8.1. These standard errors allow for prediction error due to the new innovations, but not for parameter estimation or model selection, so how useful are they?

To assess this we consider model-based simulation from (8.8) using centred residuals and the estimated coefficients of the fitted AR(9) model to generate series $y_{r1}^*, \ldots, y_{r59}^*$, corresponding to the period 1930–1988, for $r = 1, \ldots, R$. We then fit autoregressive models up to order $p = 25$ to $y_{r1}^*, \ldots, y_{r50}^*$, select the model giving the smallest AIC, and use this model to produce predictions $\hat{y}_{rj}^*$ for $j = 51, \ldots, 59$. The prediction error is $y_{rj}^* - \hat{y}_{rj}^*$, and the estimated standard errors of this are given in Table 8.1, based on $R = 999$ bootstrap series. The orders of the fitted models were

Order	1	2	3	4	5	6	7	8	9	10	11	12
#	3	257	126	100	273	85	22	18	83	23	7	2

so the AR(9) model is chosen in only 8% of cases, and most of the models selected are less complicated. The fifth and sixth rows of Table 8.1 give the estimated standard errors of the $y_j^* - \hat{y}_j^*$ using the 83 simulated series for which the selected model was AR(9) and using all the series, based on the 999 replications. There is about a 10–15% increase in standard error due to parameter estimation, and the standard errors for the AR(9) models are mostly smaller.

Prediction errors should take account of the values of y_j immediately prior to the forecast period, since presumably these are relevant to the predictions actually made. Predictions that follow on from the observed data can be obtained by using innovations sampled at random except for the period $j = n - k + 1, \ldots, n$, where we use the residuals actually observed. Taking $k = n$ yields the original series, in which case the only variability in the y_{rj}^* is due to the innovations in the forecast period; the standard errors of the predictions will then be close to the nominal standard error. However, if k is small relative to n, the differences $y_{rj}^* - \hat{y}_{rj}^*$ will largely reflect the variability due to the use of estimated parameters, although the y_{rj}^* will follow on from y_n. The conditional standard errors in Table 8.1, based on $k = 9$, are about 10% larger than the unconditional ones, and substantially larger than the nominal standard errors.

The distributions of the $y_{rj}^* - \hat{y}_{rj}^*$ appear close to normal with zero means, and a summary of variation in terms of standard errors seems appropriate. There will clearly be difficulties with normal-based prediction intervals in 1985 and 1986, when the lower limits of 95% intervals for y are negative, and it might be better to give one-sided intervals for these years. It would be better to use a studentized version of $y_{rj}^* - \hat{y}_{rj}^*$ if an appropriate standard error were readily available.

When bootstrap series are generated from the AR(9) model fitted to the data from 1700–1979, the orders of the fitted models are

Order	5	9	10	11	12	13	14	15	16	17	18	19	20
#	1	765	88	57	28	21	11	11	5	1	4	2	5

so the AR(9) model is chosen in about 75% of cases. There is a tendency for AIC to lead to overfitting: just one of the models has order less than 9. For this longer series parameter estimation and model selection inflate the nominal standard error by at most 6%.

The above analysis gives the variability of predictions based on selecting the model that minimizes AIC on the basis that an AR(9) model is correct, and does not give a true reflection of the error otherwise. Is an autoregressive or more generally a linear model appropriate? A test for linearity of a time series can be based on the non-additivity statistic $T = w^2(n - 2m - 2)/(\text{RSS} - w^2)$, where RSS is the residual sum of squares for regression of $(y_{m+1}, \ldots, y_n)$ on the $(n - m) \times (m + 1)$ matrix X whose jth row is $(1, y_{m+j-1}, \ldots, y_j)$, with residuals q_j and fitted values g_j. Let q'_j denote the residuals from the regression of g_j^2 on X, and let w equal $\sum q_j q'_j / (\sum q_j'^2)^{1/2}$. Then the approximate distribution of T is $F_{1,n-2m-2}$, with large values of T indicating potential nonlinearity. The observed value of T when $m = 20$ is 5.46, giving significance level 0.02, in good agreement with bootstrap simulations from the fitted AR(9) model. The significance level varies little for values of m from 6 to 30. There is good evidence that the series is nonlinear. We return to these data in Example 8.5.

∎

The major drawback with model-based resampling is that in practice not only the parameters of a model, but also its structure, must be identified from the data. If the chosen structure is incorrect, the resampled series will be generated from a wrong model, and hence they will not have the same statistical properties as the original data. This suggests that some allowance be made for model selection, as in Section 3.11, but it is unclear how to do this without some assumptions about the dependence structure of the process, as in the previous example. Of course this difficulty is less critical when the model selected is strongly indicated by subject-matter considerations or is well-supported by extensive data.

8.2.3 Block resampling

The second approach to resampling in the time domain treats as exchangeable not innovations, but blocks of consecutive observations. The simplest version of this idea divides the data into b non-overlapping blocks of length l, where we suppose that $n = bl$. We set $z_1 = (y_1, \ldots, y_l)$, $z_2 = (y_{l+1}, \ldots, y_{2l})$, and so forth, giving blocks $z_1, \ldots, z_b$. The procedure is to take a bootstrap sample with equal probabilities b^{-1} from the z_j, and then to paste these end-to-end to form a new series. As a simple example, suppose that the original series is $y_1, \ldots, y_{12}$, and that we take $l = 4$ and $b = 3$. Then the blocks are $z_1 = (y_1, y_2, y_3, y_4)$, $z_2 = (y_5, y_6, y_7, y_8)$, and $z_3 = (y_9, y_{10}, y_{11}, y_{12})$. If the resampled blocks are $z_1^* = z_2$, $z_2^* = z_1$, and $z_3^* = z_2$, the new series of length 12 is

$$\{y_j^*\} \quad = \quad z_1^*, z_2^*, z_3^* \quad = \quad y_5, y_6, y_7, y_8, \quad y_1, y_2, y_3, y_4, \quad y_5, y_6, y_7, y_8.$$

In general, the resampled series are more like white noise than the original series, because of the joins between blocks where successive independently chosen z^* meet.

The idea that underlies this *block resampling* scheme is that if the blocks are long enough, enough of the original dependence will be preserved in the resampled series that statistics t^* calculated from $\{y_j^*\}$ will have approximately the same distribution as values t calculated from replicates of the original series. Clearly this approximation will be best if the dependence is weak and the blocks are as long as possible, thereby preserving the dependence more faithfully. On the other hand, the distinct values of t^* must be as numerous as possible to provide a good estimate of the distribution of T, and this points towards short blocks. Theoretical work outlined below suggests that a compromise in which the block length l is of order n^γ for some γ in the interval $(0, 1)$ balances these two conflicting needs. In this case both the block length l and the number of blocks $b = n/l$ tend to infinity as $n \to \infty$, though different values of γ are appropriate for different types of statistic t.

There are several variants on this resampling plan. One is to let the original blocks overlap, in our example giving the $n - l + 1 = 9$ blocks $z_1 = (y_1, \ldots, y_4)$, $z_2 = (y_2, \ldots, y_5)$, $z_3 = (y_3, \ldots, y_6)$, and so forth up to $z_9 = (y_9, \ldots, y_{12})$. This incurs end effects, as the first and last $l - 1$ of the original observations appear in fewer blocks than the rest. Such effects can be removed by wrapping the data around a circle, in our example adding the blocks $z_{10} = (y_{10}, y_{11}, y_{12}, y_1)$, $z_{11} = (y_{11}, y_{12}, y_1, y_2)$, and $z_{12} = (y_{12}, y_1, y_2, y_3)$. This ensures that each of the original observations has an equal chance of appearing in a simulated series. End correction by wrapping also removes the minor problem with the non-overlapping scheme that the last block is shorter than the rest if n/l is not an integer.

Post-blackening

The most important difficulty with resampling schemes based on blocks is that they generate series that are less dependent than the original data. In some circumstances this can lead to catastrophically bad resampling approximations, as we shall see in Example 8.4. It is clearly inappropriate to take blocks of length $l = 1$ when resampling dependent data, for the resampled series is then white noise, but the "whitening" can remain substantial for small and moderate values of l. This suggests a strategy intermediate between model-based and block resampling. The idea is to "pre-whiten" the series by fitting a model that is intended to remove much of the dependence between the original observations. A series of innovations is then generated by block resampling of residuals from the fitted model, and the innovation series is then "post-blackened" by applying the estimated model to the resampled innovations. Thus if an AR(1) model is used to pre-whiten the original data, new series are generated by applying (8.6) but with the innovation series $\{\varepsilon_j^*\}$ sampled not independently but in blocks taken from the centred residual series $e_2 - \bar{e}, \ldots, e_n - \bar{e}$.

Blocks of blocks

A different approach to removing the whitening effect of block resampling is to resample blocks of blocks. Suppose that the focus of interest is a statistic T which estimates θ and depends only on blocks of m successive observations. An example is the lag k autocovariance $(n-k)^{-1}\sum_{j=1}^{n-k}(y_j - \bar{y})(y_{j+k} - \bar{y})$, for which $m = k + 1$. Then unless $l \gg m$ the distribution of $T^* - t$ is typically a poor approximation to that of $T - \theta$, because a substantial proportion of the pairs (Y_j^*, Y_{j+k}^*) in a resampled series will lie across a join between blocks, and will therefore be independent. To implement resampling blocks of blocks we define a new m-variate process $\{Y_j'\}$ for which $Y_j' = (Y_j, \ldots, Y_{j+m-1})$, rewrite T so that it involves averages of the Y_j', and resample blocks of the new "data" $y_1', \ldots, y_{n-m+1}'$, each of the observations of which is a block of the original data. For the lag 1 autocovariance, for example, we set

$$(y_1', \ldots, y_{n-1}') \equiv \begin{pmatrix} y_{11}' & y_{12}' & \cdots & y_{1,n-1}' \\ y_{21}' & y_{22}' & \cdots & y_{2,n-1}' \end{pmatrix} = \begin{pmatrix} y_1 & y_2 & \cdots & y_{n-1} \\ y_2 & y_3 & \cdots & y_n \end{pmatrix}$$

and write $t = (n-1)^{-1}\sum(y_{1j}' - \bar{y}_{1.}')(y_{2j}' - \bar{y}_{2.}')$. The key point is that t should not compare observations adjacent in each row. With $n = 12$ and $l = 4$ a bootstrap replicate might be

$$\{y_j'^*\} \equiv \begin{pmatrix} y_5 & y_6 & y_7 & y_8 & y_1 & y_2 & y_3 & y_4 & y_7 & y_8 & y_9 & y_{10} \\ y_6 & y_7 & y_8 & y_9 & y_2 & y_3 & y_4 & y_5 & y_8 & y_9 & y_{10} & y_{11} \end{pmatrix}.$$

Since a bootstrap version of t based on this series will only contain products of (centred) adjacent observations of the original data, the whitening due to resampling blocks will be reduced, though not entirely removed.

This approach leads to a shorter series being resampled, but this is unimportant relative to the gain from avoiding whitening.

Stationary bootstrap

A further but less important difficulty with these block schemes is that the artificial series generated by them are not stationary, because the joint distribution of resampled observations close to a join between blocks differs from that in the centre of a block. This can be overcome by taking blocks of random length. The *stationary bootstrap* takes blocks whose lengths L are geometrically distributed, with density

$$\Pr(L = j) = (1 - p)^{j-1}p, \qquad j = 1, 2, \ldots.$$

This yields resampled series that are stationary with mean block length $l = p^{-1}$. Properties of this scheme are explored in Problems 8.1 and 8.2.

Example 8.4 (Rio Negro data) To illustrate these resampling schemes we consider the shorter series of river stages, of length 120, with its average subtracted. Figure 8.7 shows the original series, followed by three bootstrap

Figure 8.7 Resamples from the shorter Rio Negro data. The top panel shows the original series, followed by three series generated by model-based sampling from the fitted AR(2) model, then three series generated using the block bootstrap with $l = 24$ and no end correction, and three series made using the post-blackened method, with the same blocks as the block series and the fitted AR(2) model.

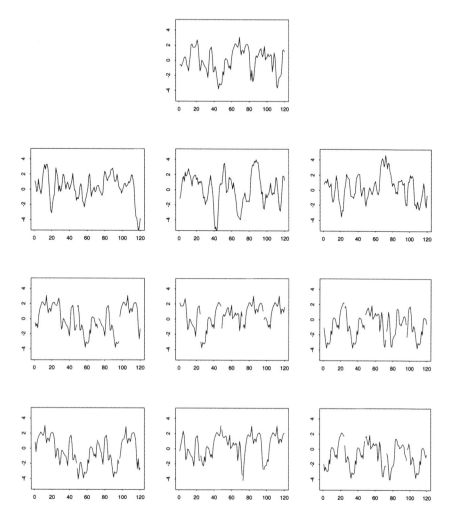

series generated by model-based sampling from the AR(2) model. The next three panels show series generated using the block bootstrap with length $l = 24$ and no wrapping. There are some sharp jumps at the ends of contiguous blocks in the resampled series. The bottom panels show series generated using the same blocks applied to the residuals, and then post-blackened using the AR(2) model. The jumps from using the block bootstrap are largely removed by post-blackening.

For a more systematic comparison of the methods, we generated 200 bootstrap replicates under different resampling plans. For each plan we calculated the standard error SE of the average $\bar{y}^*$ of the resampled series, and the average of the first three autocorrelation coefficients. The more dependent

			$\hat{\rho}_1$	$\hat{\rho}_2$	$\hat{\rho}_3$
Original values		—	0.85	0.62	0.45
Sampling SE		0.017	0.002	0.007	0.010
Resampling plan	Details	SE	$\bar{\rho}_1^{\bullet}$	$\bar{\rho}_2^{\bullet}$	$\bar{\rho}_3^{\bullet}$
Model-based	AR(2)	0.34	0.83	0.60	0.38
	AR(1)	0.49	0.82	0.67	0.54
	AR(3)	0.44	0.83	0.58	0.39
Blockwise	$l = 2$	0.20	0.41	−0.02	−0.01
	$l = 5$	0.26	0.67	0.35	0.14
	$l = 10$	0.33	0.75	0.47	0.27
	$l = 20$	0.33	0.79	0.54	0.35
Blocks of blocks	$l = 2$	0.20	0.85	0.63	0.45
	$l = 5$	0.26	0.85	0.63	0.45
	$l = 10$	0.33	0.85	0.64	0.47
	$l = 20$	0.33	0.85	0.64	0.48
Stationary	$l = 2$	0.25	0.40	0.13	0.03
	$l = 5$	0.28	0.66	0.37	0.20
	$l = 10$	0.31	0.74	0.47	0.28
	$l = 20$	0.28	0.79	0.54	0.36
Post-blackened	AR(2), $l = 2$	0.39	0.83	0.59	0.38
	AR(1), $l = 2$	0.58	0.85	0.69	0.56
	AR(3), $l = 2$	0.43	0.83	0.58	0.40

Table 8.2 Comparison of time-domain resampling plans applied to the average and first three autocorrelation coefficients for the Rio Negro data, 1903–1912.

the series, the larger we expect SE and the autocorrelation coefficients to be. Table 8.2 gives the results. The top two rows show the correlations in the data and approximate standard errors for the resampling results below.

The results for model-based simulation depend on the model used, although the overfitted AR(3) model gives results similar to the AR(2). The AR(1) model adds correlation not present in the original data.

The block method is applied with no end correction, but further simulations show that it makes little difference. Block length has a dramatic effect, and in particular, block length $l = 2$ essentially removes correlation at lags larger than one. Even blocks of length 20 give resampled data noticeably less dependent than the original series.

The whitening is overcome by resampling blocks of blocks. We took blocks of length $m = 4$, so that the m-variate series had length 117. The mean resampled autocorrelations are essentially unchanged even with $l = 2$, while SE$^{\bullet}$ does depend on block length.

The stationary bootstrap is used with end correction. The results are similar to those for the block bootstrap, except that the varying block length preserves slightly more of the original correlation structure; this is noticeable at $l = 2$.

Results for the post-blackened method with AR(2) and AR(3) models are similar to those for the corresponding model-based schemes. The results for the post-blackened AR(1) scheme are intermediate between AR(1) and AR(2) model-based resampling, reflecting the fact that the AR(1) model underfits the data, and hence structure remains in the residuals. Longer blocks have little effect for the AR(2) and AR(3) models, but they bring results for the AR(1) model more into line with those for the others. ∎

The previous example suggests that post-blackening generates resampled series with correlation structure similar to the original data. Correlation, however, is a measure of linear dependence. Is nonlinear dependence preserved by resampling blocks?

Example 8.5 (Sunspot numbers)   To assess the success of the block and post-blackened schemes in preserving nonlinearity, we applied them to the sunspot data, using $l = 10$. We saw in Example 8.3 that although the best autoregressive model for the transformed data is AR(9), the series is nonlinear. This nonlinearity must remain in the residuals, which are almost a linear transformation of the series. Figure 8.8 shows probability plots of the nonlinearity statistic T from Example 8.3, with $m = 20$, for the block and post-blackened bootstraps with $l = 10$. The results for model-based resampling of residuals are not shown but lie on the diagonal line, so it is clear that both schemes preserve some of the nonlinearity in the data, which must derive from lags up to 10. Curiously the post-blackened scheme seems to preserve more.

Table 8.1 gives the predictive standard errors for the years 1980–1988 when the simple block resampling scheme with $l = 10$ is applied to the data for 1930–1979. Once data for 1930–1988 have been generated, the procedure outlined in Example 8.3 is used to select, fit, and predict from an autoregressive model. Owing to the joins between blocks, the standard errors are much larger than for the other schemes, including the post-blackened one with $l = 10$, which gives results similar to but somewhat more variable than the model-based bootstraps. Unadorned block resampling seems inappropriate for assessing prediction error, as one would expect. ∎

Choice of block length

Suppose that we want to use the block bootstrap to estimate some feature κ based on a series of length n. An example would be the standard error of the series average, as in the third column of Table 8.2. Different block lengths l result in different bootstrap estimates $\hat{\kappa}(n, l)$. Which should we use?

A key result is that under suitable assumptions and for large n and l the

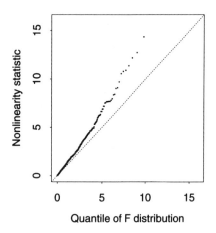
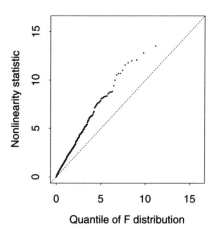

Figure 8.8
Distributions of
nonlinearity statistic for
block resampling
schemes applied to
sunspot data. The left
panel shows $R = 999$
replicates of a test
statistic for nonlinearity,
based on detecting
nonlinearity at up to 20
lags for the block
bootstrap with $l = 10$.
The right panel shows
the corresponding plot
for the post-blackened
bootstrap using the
AR(9) model.

mean squared error of $\hat{\kappa}(n, l)$ is proportional to

$$\frac{1}{n^d}\left(\frac{C_1}{l^2} + \frac{C_2 l^c}{n}\right),\tag{8.9}$$

where C_1 and C_2 depend only on κ and the dependence structure of the series. In (8.9) $d = 2$, $c = 1$ if κ is a bias or variance, $d = 1$, $c = 2$ if κ is a one-sided significance probability, and $d = 2$, $c = 3$ if κ is a two-sided significance probability. The justification for (8.9) when κ is a bias or a variance is discussed after the next example. The implication of (8.9) is that for large n, the mean squared error of of $\hat{\kappa}(n, l)$ is minimized by taking $l \propto n^{1/(c+2)}$, but we do not know the constant of proportionality. However, it can be estimated as follows.

We guess an initial value of l, and simulate to obtain $\hat{\kappa}(n, l)$. We then take $m < n$ and $k < l$ and calculate the values of $\hat{\kappa}_j(m, k)$ from the $n - m + 1$ series $y_j, \dots, y_{j+m-1}$ for $j = 1, \dots, n - m + 1$. The estimated mean squared error for $\hat{\kappa}(m, k)$ from a series of length m with block size k is then

$$\text{MSE}(m, k) = \frac{1}{n - m + 1}\sum_{j=1}^{n-m+1}\{\hat{\kappa}_j(m, k) - \hat{\kappa}(n, l)\}^2.$$

By repeating this procedure for different values of k but the same m, we obtain the value $\hat{k}$ for which $\text{MSE}(m, k)$ is minimized. We then choose

$$\hat{l} = \hat{k} \times (n/m)^{1/(c+2)}\tag{8.10}$$

as the optimum block length for a series of length n, and calculate $\hat{\kappa}(n, \hat{l})$. This procedure eliminates the constant of proportionality. We can check on the adequacy of $\hat{l}$ by repeating the procedure with initial value $l = \hat{l}$, iterating if necessary.

Figure 8.9 Ten-year
running average of
Manaus data (left),
together with
Abelson–Tukey
coefficients (right)
(Abelson and Tukey,
1963).

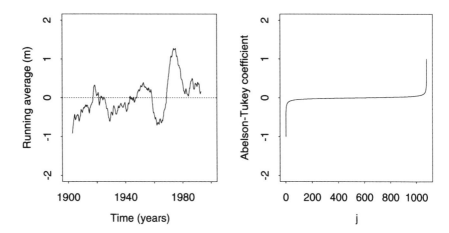

The minimum asymptotic mean squared error is $n^{-d-2/(c+2)}(C_1 + C_2)$, so if the block length selection procedure is applicable,

$$A(m) = \log \left\{ \min_k \mathrm{MSE}(m, k) \right\} + \{d + 2/(c + 2)\} \log m$$

should be approximately independent of m. This suggests that values of $A(m)$ for different m should be compared as a check on the asymptotics.

Example 8.6 (Rio Negro data)   There is concern that river heights at Manaus may be increasing due to deforestation, so we test for trend in the river series, a ten-year running average of which is shown in the left panel of Figure 8.9. There may be an upward trend, but it is hard to say whether the effect is real. To proceed, we suppose that the data consist of a stationary time series to which has been added a monotonic trend. Our test statistic is $T = \sum_{j=1}^{n} a_j Y_j$, where the coefficients

$$a_j = \left\{ (j - 1) \left(1 - \frac{j-1}{n+1} \right) \right\}^{1/2} - \left\{ j \left(1 - \frac{j}{n+1} \right) \right\}^{1/2}, \quad j = 1, \dots, n,$$

are optimal for detecting a monotonic trend in independent observations. The plot of the a_j in the right panel of Figure 8.9 shows that T strongly contrasts the ends of the series. We can think of T as almost being a difference of averages for the two ends of the series, and this falls into the class of statistics for which the method of choosing the block length described above is appropriate. Resampling blocks of blocks would not be appropriate here. The value of T for the full series is 7.908. Is this significantly large?

To simulate data under the null hypothesis of no trend, we use the stationary

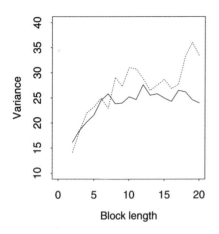 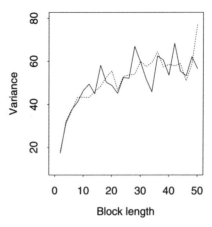

Figure 8.10 Estimated variances of T for Rio Negro data, for stationary (solid) and block (dots) bootstraps. The left panel is for 1903–1912 ($R = 999$), the right panel is for the whole series ($R = 199$).

bootstrap with wrapping to generate new series Y^*. We initially apply this to the shorter series of length 120, adjusted to have mean zero, for which T takes value 0.654. Under the null hypothesis the mean of $T = \sum a_j Y_j$ is zero and the distribution of T will be close to normal. We estimate its variance by taking the empirical variance of values T^* generated with the stationary bootstrap. The left panel of Figure 8.10 shows these variances $\hat{\kappa}(n, l)$ based on different mean block lengths l, for both stationary and block bootstraps. The stationary bootstrap smooths the variances for different fixed block lengths, resulting in a fairly stable variance for $l > 6$ or so. Variances of T^* based on the block bootstrap are more variable and increase to a higher eventual value. The variances for the full series are larger and more variable.

In order to choose the block length l, we took 50 randomly selected subseries of m consecutive observations from the series with $n = 120$, and for each value of $k = 2, \ldots, 20$ calculated values of $\hat{\kappa}(m, k)$ from $R = 50$ stationary bootstrap replicates. The left part of Table 8.3 shows the values $\hat{k}$ that minimize the mean squared error for different possible values of $\hat{\kappa}(n, l)$. Note that the values of $\hat{k}$ do not broadly increase with m, as the theory would predict. For smaller values of $\hat{\kappa}(n, l)$ the values of $\hat{k}$ vary considerably, and even for $\hat{\kappa}(n, l) = 30$ the corresponding values of $\hat{l}$ as given by (8.10) with $c = 1$ and $d = 2$ vary from 12 to 20. The left panel of Figure 8.10 shows that for l in this range, the variance $\hat{\kappa}(n, l)$ takes value roughly 25. For $\hat{\kappa}(n, l) = 25$, Table 8.3 gives $\hat{l}$ in the range 8–20, so overall we take $\hat{\kappa}(n, l) \doteq 25$ based on the stationary bootstrap.

The right part of Table 8.3 gives the values of $\hat{k}$ when the block bootstrap with wrapping is used. The series so generated are not exactly stationary, but are nearly so. Overall the values are more consistent than for the stationary

Table 8.3 Estimated values of $\hat{k}$ for Rio Negro data, 1903–1912, based on stationary bootstrap with mean length k applied to 50 subseries of length m (left figures) and block bootstrap with block length k applied to 50 subseries of length m (right figures).

$\hat{\kappa}(n,l)$	Stationary, m						Block, m					
	20	30	40	50	60	70	20	30	40	50	60	70
15	10	6	3	2	2	2	4	3	18	2	2	2
17.5	11	18	3	3	3	2	4	10	16	3	3	3
20	11	18	6	3	3	3	4	5	4	6	3	4
22.5	11	18	6	6	5	4	4	5	5	6	4	4
25	11	11	12	6	7	8	4	5	5	6	5	5
27.5	11	11	14	9	10	8	4	5	5	9	6	8
30	11	11	14	9	10	11	4	5	5	9	6	8

bootstrap, with broadly increasing values of $\hat{k}$ within each row, provided $\hat{\kappa}(n,l) > 20$. For these values of $\hat{\kappa}(n,l)$, the values of $\hat{k}$ suggest that $\hat{l}$ lies in the range 5–8, giving $\hat{\kappa}(n,l) \doteq 25$ or slightly less. Thus both the stationary and the block bootstrap suggest that the variance of T is roughly 25, and since $t = 0.654$, there is no evidence of trend in the first ten years of data.

For the stationary bootstrap, the values of $A(m)$ have smallest variance for $\hat{\kappa}(n,l) = 22.5$, when they are 13.29, 13.66, 14.18, 14.01, 13.99 and 13.59 for $m = 20,\ldots,70$. For the block bootstrap the variance is smallest when $\hat{\kappa}(n,l) = 27.5$, when the values are 13.86, 14.25, 14.63, 14.69, 14.73 and 14.44. However, the minimum mean squared error shows no obvious pattern for any value of $\hat{\kappa}(n,l)$, and it seems that the asymptotics apply adequately well here.

Overall Table 8.3 suggests that a range of values of m should be used, and that results for different m are more consistent for the block than for the stationary bootstrap. For given values of m and k, the variances $\hat{\kappa}_j(m,k)$ have approximate gamma distributions, but calculation of their mean squared error on the variance-stabilizing log scale does little to improve matters.

For the stationary bootstrap applied to the full series, we take l in the range $(8,20) \times (1080/120)^{1/3} = (17,42)$, which gives variances 46–68, with average variance roughly 55. The corresponding range of l for the block bootstrap is 10–17, which gives variances $\hat{\kappa}(n,l)$ in the range 43–53 or so, with average value 47. In either case the lowest reasonable variance estimate is about 45. Since the value of t for the full series is 7.9, an approximate significance level for the hypothesis of no trend based on a normal approximation to T^* is $1 - \Phi(7.9/45^{1/2}) \doteq 0.12$. The evidence for trend based on the monthly data is thus fairly weak. ∎

Some block theory

In order to gain some theoretical insight into block resampling and the fundamental approximation (8.9) which guides the choice of l, we examine the estimation of bias and variance for a special class of statistics.

Consider a stationary time series $\{Y_j\}$ with mean μ and covariances $\gamma_j = \mathrm{cov}(Y_0, Y_j)$, and suppose that the parameter of interest is $\theta = h(\mu)$. The obvious estimator of θ based on $Y_1, \ldots, Y_n$ is $T = h(\bar{Y})$, whose bias and variance are

$$
\beta = \mathrm{E}\left\{h(\bar{Y}) - h(\mu)\right\} \doteq \tfrac{1}{2} h''(\mu) \mathrm{var}(\bar{Y}),
$$

$$
(8.11)
$$

$$
v = \mathrm{var}\left\{h(\bar{Y})\right\} \doteq h'(\mu)^2 \mathrm{var}(\bar{Y}),
$$

$\bar{Y}$ is the average of $Y_1, \ldots, Y_n$.

by the delta method of Section 2.7.1. Note that

$$
\mathrm{var}(\bar{Y}) = n^{-2}\left\{n\gamma_0 + 2(n-1)\gamma_1 + \cdots + 2\gamma_{n-1}\right\} = n^{-2} c_0^{(n)},
$$

say, and that as $n \to \infty$,

$$
n^{-1} c_0^{(n)} = \gamma_0 + 2\sum_{j=1}^{n-1}(1 - j/n)\gamma_j \to \sum_{j=-\infty}^{\infty} \gamma_j = \zeta.
$$

Therefore $\beta \sim \tfrac{1}{2} h''(\mu) n^{-1}\zeta$, and $v \sim h'(\mu)^2 n^{-1}\zeta$ for large n. Now suppose that we estimate β and v by simple block resampling, with b non-overlapping blocks of length l, with $n = bl$, and use S_j to denote the average $l^{-1}\sum_{i=1}^{l} Y_{(j-1)l+i}$ of the jth block, for $j = 1, \ldots, b$. Thus $\bar{S} = \bar{Y}$, and $\bar{Y}^* = b^{-1}\sum_{j=1}^{b} S_j^*$, where the S_j^* are sampled independently from $S_1, \ldots, S_b$. The bootstrap estimates of the bias and variance of T are

$$
\hat{\beta} = \mathrm{E}^*\left\{h(\bar{Y}^*) - h(\bar{Y})\right\} \doteq h'(\bar{Y})\mathrm{E}^*(\bar{Y}^* - \bar{Y}) + \tfrac{1}{2}h''(\bar{Y})\mathrm{E}^*\left\{(\bar{Y}^* - \bar{Y})^2\right\},
$$

$$
(8.12)
$$

$$
\hat{v} = \mathrm{var}^*\left\{h(\bar{Y}^*)\right\} \doteq h'(\bar{Y})^2 \mathrm{var}^*(\bar{Y}^*).
$$

What we want to know is how the accuracies of $\hat{\beta}$ and $\hat{v}$ vary with l.

Since the blocks are non-overlapping,

$$
\mathrm{E}^*(\bar{Y}^*) = \bar{S}, \qquad \mathrm{var}^*(\bar{Y}^*) = b^{-2}\sum_{j=1}^{b}(S_j - \bar{S})^2.
$$

It follows by comparing (8.11) and (8.12) that the means of $\hat{\beta}$ and $\hat{v}$ will be asymptotically correct provided that when n is large, $\mathrm{E}\{b^{-1}\sum(S_j - \bar{S})^2\} \sim n^{-1}\zeta$. This will be so because $\sum(S_j - \bar{S})^2 = \sum(S_j - \mu)^2 - b(\bar{S} - \mu)^2$ has mean

$$
b\mathrm{var}(S_1) - b\mathrm{var}(\bar{S}) = b(l^{-2} c_0^{(l)} - n^{-2} c_0^{(n)}) \sim n^{-1}\zeta,
$$

if $l \to \infty$ and $l/n \to 0$ as $n \to \infty$. To calculate approximations for the mean squared errors of $\hat{\beta}$ and $\hat{v}$ requires more careful calculations and involves the variance of $\sum(S_j - \bar{S})^2$. This is messy in general, but the essential points remain under the simplifying assumptions that $\{Y_j\}$ is an m-dependent normal process. In this case $\gamma_{m+1} = \gamma_{m+2} = \cdots = 0$, and the third and higher cumulants of the process are zero. Suppose also that $m < l$. Then the variance of $\sum (S_j - \bar{S})^2$ is approximately

$$\text{var}\left\{\sum (S_j - \mu)^2\right\} = b\,\text{var}\left\{(S_1 - \mu)^2\right\} + 2(b-1)\text{cov}\left\{(S_1 - \mu)^2, (S_2 - \mu)^2\right\}.$$

For normal data,

$$\begin{aligned}
\text{var}\left\{(S_1 - \mu)^2\right\} &= 2\left\{\text{var}(S_1 - \mu)\right\}^2, \\
\text{cov}\left\{(S_1 - \mu)^2, (S_2 - \mu)^2\right\} &= 2\left\{\text{cov}(S_1 - \mu, S_2 - \mu)\right\}^2,
\end{aligned}$$

so

$$\text{var}\left\{\sum (S_j - \bar{S})^2\right\} \doteq 2b(l^{-2}c_0^{(l)})^2 + 4b(l^{-2}c_1^{(l)})^2,$$

where under suitable conditions on the process,

$$c_1^{(l)} = \gamma_1 + 2\gamma_2 + \cdots + l\gamma_l \to \sum_{j=1}^{\infty} j\gamma_j \sim \tfrac{1}{2}\tau,$$

say. After a delicate calculation we find that

$$\begin{aligned}
\text{E}(\hat{\beta}) - \beta &\sim -\tfrac{1}{2}h''(\mu) \times n^{-1}l^{-1}\tau, & \text{var}(\hat{\beta}) &\sim \left\{\tfrac{1}{2}h''(\mu)\right\}^2 \times 2ln^{-3}\zeta^2, & (8.13) \\
\text{E}(\hat{v}) - v &\sim -h'(\mu)^2 \times n^{-1}l^{-1}\tau, & \text{var}(\hat{v}) &\sim h'(\mu)^4 \times 2ln^{-3}\zeta^2, & (8.14)
\end{aligned}$$

thus establishing that the mean squared errors of $\hat{\beta}$ and $\hat{v}$ are of form (8.9).

This development can clearly be extended to multivariate time series, and thence to more complicated parameters of a single series. For example, for the first-order correlation coefficient of the univariate series $\{X_j\}$, we would apply the argument to the trivariate series $\{Y_j\} = \{(X_j, X_j^2, X_j X_{j-1})\}$ with mean $(\mu_1, \mu_{11}, \mu_{12})$, and set $\theta = h(\mu_1, \mu_{11}, \mu_{12}) = (\mu_{12} - \mu_1^2)/(\mu_{11} - \mu_1^2)$.

When overlapping blocks are resampled, the argument is similar but the details change. If the data are not wrapped around a circle, there are $n - l + 1$ blocks with averages $S_j = l^{-1}\sum_{i=1}^{l} Y_{i+j-1}$, and

$$\text{E}^*(\bar{Y}^* - \bar{Y}) = \frac{1}{l(n-l+1)}\left\{l(l-1)\bar{Y} - \sum_{j=1}^{l-1}(l-j)(Y_j + Y_{n-j+1})\right\}. \quad (8.15)$$

In this case the leading term of the expansion for $\hat{\beta}$ is the product of $h'(\bar{Y})$ and the right-hand side of (8.15), so the bootstrap bias estimate for $\bar{Y}$ as an estimator of $\theta = \mu$ is non-zero, which is clearly misleading since $\text{E}(\bar{Y}) = \mu$. With overlapping blocks, the properties of the bootstrap bias estimator depend on $\text{E}^*(\bar{Y}^*) - \bar{Y}$, and it turns out that its variance is an order of magnitude larger than for non-overlapping blocks. This difficulty can be removed by wrapping $Y_1, \ldots, Y_n$ around a circle and using n blocks, in which case $\text{E}^*(\bar{Y}^*) = \bar{Y}$, or by re-centring the bootstrap bias estimate to $\hat{\beta} = \text{E}^*\left\{h(\bar{Y}^*)\right\} - h\left\{\text{E}^*(\bar{Y}^*)\right\}$. In either case (8.13) and (8.14) apply. One asymptotic benefit of using overlapping blocks when the re-centred estimator is used is that $\text{var}(\hat\beta)$ and $\text{var}(\hat v)$ are reduced by a factor $\frac{2}{3}$, though in practice the reduction may not be visible for small n.

The corresponding argument for tail probabilities involves Edgeworth expansions and is considerably more intricate than that sketched above.

Apart from smoothness conditions on $h(\cdot)$, the key requirement for the above argument to work is that τ and ζ be finite, and that the autocovariances γ_j decrease sharply enough for the various terms neglected to be negligible. This is the case if $\gamma_j \sim \alpha^j$ for sufficiently large j and some α with $|\alpha| < 1$, as is the case for stationary finite ARMA processes. However, if for large j we find that $\gamma_j \sim j^{-\delta}$, where $\frac{1}{2} < \delta < 1$, ζ and τ are not finite and the argument will fail. In this case $g(\omega) \sim \omega^{-\delta}$ for small ω, so *long-range dependence* of this sort is characterized by a pole in the spectrum at the origin, where $\zeta = g(0)$ is the value of the spectrum. The data counterpart of this is a sharp increase in periodogram ordinates at small values of ω. Thus a careful examination of the periodogram near the origin and of the long-range correlation structure is essential before applying the block bootstrap to data.

8.2.4 Phase scrambling

Recall the basic stochastic properties of the empirical Fourier transform of a series $y_0,\ldots,y_{n-1}$ of length $n = 2n_F + 1$: for large n and under certain conditions on the process generating the data, the transformed values $\tilde y_k$ for $k = 1,\ldots,n_F$ are approximately independent, and their real and imaginary parts are approximately independent normal variables with means zero and variances $ng(\omega_k)/2$, where $\omega_k = 2\pi k/n$. The approximate independence of $\tilde y_1,\ldots,\tilde y_{n_F}$ suggests that, provided the conditions on the underlying process are met, the frequency domain is a better place to look for exchangeable components than the time domain. Expression (8.4) shows that the spectrum summarizes the covariance structure of the process $\{Y_j\}$, and correspondingly the periodogram values $I(\omega_k) = |\tilde y_k|^2/n$ summarize the second-order structure of the data, which as far as possible we should preserve when resampling. This suggests that we generate resamples by keeping fixed the moduli $|\tilde y_k|$, but randomizing their phases $u_k = \arg \tilde y_k$, which anyway are asymptotically uniformly distributed on the interval $[0, 2\pi)$, independent of the $|\tilde y_k|$. This *phase scrambling* can be done in a variety of ways, one of which is the following.

Algorithm 8.1 (Phase scrambling)

1 Compute from the data $y_0,\ldots,y_{n-1}$ the empirical Fourier transform

$$\tilde e_k = \sum_{j=0}^{n-1} \zeta^{jk}(y_j - \bar y), \quad k = 0,\ldots,n-1,$$

where $\zeta = \exp(2\pi i/n)$.

2 Set $\tilde{X}_k = \exp(iU_k^*)\tilde{e}_k$, $k = 0, \ldots, n-1$, where the U_k^* are independent variables uniform on $[0, 2\pi)$.

3 Set

$$\tilde{\varepsilon}_k^* = 2^{-1/2}\left(\tilde{X}_k + \tilde{X}_{n-k}^c\right), \quad k = 0, \ldots, n-1,$$

where superscript c denotes complex conjugate and we take $\tilde{X}_n \equiv \tilde{X}_0$.

4 Apply the inverse Fourier transform to $\tilde{e}_0^*, \ldots, \tilde{e}_{n-1}^*$ to obtain

$$Y_j^* = \bar{y} + n^{-1}\sum_{k=0}^{n-1} \zeta^{-jk}\tilde{e}_k^*, \quad j = 0, \ldots, n-1.$$

5 Calculate the bootstrap statistic T^* from $Y_0^*, \ldots, Y_{n-1}^*$.

•

Step 3 guarantees that $\tilde{Y}_k^*$ has complex conjugate $\tilde{Y}_{n-k}^*$, and therefore that the bootstrap series $Y_0^*, \ldots, Y_{n-1}^*$ is real. An alternative to step 2 is to resample the U_k^* from the observed phases $u_1, \ldots, u_{n-1}$.

The bootstrap series always has average $\bar{y}$, which implies that phase scrambling should be applied only to statistics that are invariant to location changes of the original series; in fact it is useful only for linear contrasts of the y_j, as we shall see below. It is straightforward to see that

$$Y_j^* = \bar{y} + \frac{2^{1/2}}{n}\sum_{l=0}^{n-1}(y_l - \bar{y})\sum_{k=0}^{n-1}\cos\left\{2\pi k(l-j)/n + U_k^*\right\}, \quad j = 0, \ldots, n-1,$$

$$(8.16)$$

from which it follows that the bootstrap data are stationary, with covariances equal to the circular covariances of the original series, and that all their odd joint cumulants equal zero (Problem 8.4). This representation also makes it clear that the resampled series will be essentially linear with normal margins.

The difference between phase scrambling and model-based resampling can be deduced from Algorithm 8.1. Under phase scrambling,

$$|\tilde{Y}_k^*|^2 = |\tilde{y}_k|^2\left\{1 + \cos(U_k^* + U_{n-k}^*)\right\}, \quad (8.17)$$

which gives

$$\mathrm{E}^*(|\tilde{Y}_k^*|^2) = |\tilde{y}_k|^2, \quad \mathrm{var}^*(|\tilde{Y}_k^*|^2) = \tfrac{1}{2}|\tilde{y}_k|^4.$$

Under model-based resampling the approximate distribution of $n^{-1}|\tilde{Y}_k^*|^2$ is $\hat{g}(\omega_k)X^*$, where $\hat{g}(\cdot)$ is the spectrum of the fitted model and X^* has a standard exponential distribution; this gives

$$\mathrm{E}^*(|\tilde{Y}_k^*|^2) \doteq \hat{g}(\omega_k), \quad \mathrm{var}^*(|\tilde{Y}_k^*|^2) \doteq \hat{g}^2(\omega_k).$$

Clearly these resampling schemes will give different results unless the quantities of interest depend only on the means of the $|\tilde{Y}_k^*|^2$, i.e. are essentially quadratic

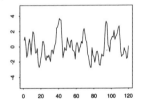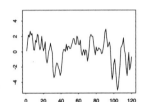

Figure 8.11 Three time
series generated by
phase scrambling the
shorter Rio Negro data.

in the data. Since the quantity of interest must also be location-invariant,
this restricts the domain of phase scrambling to such tasks as estimating the
variances of linear contrasts in the data.

Example 8.7 (Rio Negro data)   We assess empirical properties of phase scrambling using the first 120 months of the Rio Negro data, which we saw previously
were well-fitted by an AR(2) model with normal errors. Note that our statistic
of interest, $T = \sum a_j Y_j$, has the necessary structure for phase scrambling not
automatically to fail.

Figure 8.11 shows three phase scrambled datasets, which look similar to the
AR(2) series in the second row of Figure 8.7.

The top panels of Figure 8.12 show the empirical Fourier transform for the
original data and for one resample. Phase scrambling seems to have shrunk
the moduli of the series towards zero, giving a resampled series with lower
overall variability. The lower left panel shows smoothed periodograms for the
original data and for 9 phase scrambled resamples, while the right panel shows
corresponding results for simulation from the fitted AR(2) model. The results
are quite different, and show that data generated by phase scrambling are less
variable than those generated from the fitted model.

Resampling with 999 series generated from the fitted AR(2) model and by
phase scrambling, the distribution of T^* is close to normal under both schemes
but it is less variable under phase scrambling; the estimated variances are 27.4
and 20.2. These are similar to the estimates of about 27.5 and 22.5 obtained
using the block and stationary bootstraps.

Before applying phase scrambling to the full series, we must check that
it shows no sign of nonlinearity or of long-range dependence, and that it
is plausibly close to a linear series with normal errors. With $m = 20$ the
nonlinearity statistic described in Example 8.3 takes value 0.015, and no value
for $m \leq 30$ is greater than 0.84: this gives no evidence that the series is
nonlinear. Moreover the periodogram shows no signs of a pole as $\omega \to 0+$, so
long-range dependence seems to be absent. An AR(8) model fits the series
well, but the residuals have heavier tails than the normal distribution, with
kurtosis 1.2. The variance of T^* under phase scrambling is about 51, which

Figure 8.12 Phase scrambling for the shorter Rio Negro data. The upper left panel shows an Argand diagram containing the empirical Fourier transform $\tilde{y}_k$ of the data, with phase scrambled $\tilde{y}_k^*$ in the upper right panel. The lower panels show smoothed periodograms for the original data (heavy solid), 9 phase scrambled datasets (left) and 9 datasets generated from an AR(2) model (right); the theoretical AR(2) spectrum is the lighter solid line.

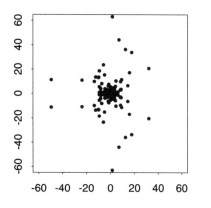
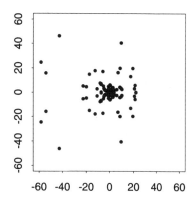
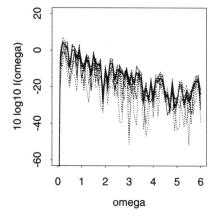
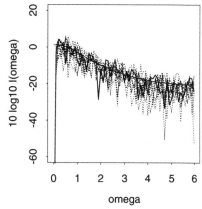

again is similar to the estimates from the block resampling schemes. Although this estimate may be untrustworthy, on the face of things it casts no doubt on the earlier conclusion that the evidence for trend is weak.   ■

The discussion above suggests that not only should phase scrambling be confined to statistics that are linear contrasts, but also that it should be used only after careful scrutiny of the data to detect nonlinearity and long-range dependence. With non-normal data there is the further difficulty that the Fourier transform and its inverse are averaging operations, which can produce resampled data quite unlike the original series; see Problem 8.4 and Practical 8.3. In particular, when phase scrambling is used in a test of the null hypothesis of linearity, it imposes on the distribution of the scrambled data the additional constraints of stationarity and a high degree of symmetry.

8.2.5 Periodogram resampling

Like time domain resampling methods, phase scrambling generates an entire new dataset. This is unnecessary for such problems as setting a confidence interval for the spectrum at a particular frequency or for assessing the variability of an estimate that is based on periodogram values. There are well-established limiting results for the distributions of periodogram values, which under certain conditions are asymptotically independent exponential random variables, and this suggests that we somehow resample periodogram values.

The obvious approach is to note that if $g^\dagger(\omega_k)$ is a suitable consistent estimate of $g(\omega_k)$ based on data $y_0, \ldots, y_{n-1}$, where $n = 2n_F + 1$, then for $k = 1, \ldots, n_F$ the residuals $e_k = I(\omega_k)/g^\dagger(\omega_k)$ are approximately standard exponential variables. This suggests that we generate bootstrap periodogram values by setting $I^*(\omega_k) = \tilde{g}(\omega_k)\varepsilon_k^*$, where $\tilde{g}(\omega_k)$ is also a consistent estimate of $g(\omega_k)$, and the ε_k^* are sampled randomly from the set $(e_1/\bar{e}, \ldots, e_{n_F}/\bar{e})$; this ensures that $E^*(\varepsilon_k^*) = 1$. The choice of $g^\dagger(\omega)$ and $\tilde{g}(\omega)$ is discussed below. Such a resampling scheme will only work in special circumstances. To see why, we consider estimation of $\theta = \int a(\omega)g(\omega)\,d\omega$ by a statistic that can be written in the form

$\bar{e}$ is the average of $e_1, \ldots, e_n$.

$$ T = \frac{\pi}{n_F} \sum_{k=1}^{n_F} a_k I_k, $$

where $I_k = I(\omega_k)$, $a_k = a(\omega_k)$, and ω_k is the kth Fourier frequency. For a linear process

$$ Y_j = \sum_{i=-\infty}^{\infty} b_i \xi_{j-i}, $$

where $\{\xi_i\}$ is a stream of independent and identically distributed random variables with standardized fourth cumulant κ_4, the means and covariances of the I_k are approximately

δ_{kl} is the Kronecker delta symbol, which equals one if $k = l$ and zero otherwise.

$$ E(I_k) \doteq g(\omega_k), \quad \text{cov}(I_k, I_l) \doteq g(\omega_k)g(\omega_l)(\delta_{kl} + n^{-1}\kappa_4). \tag{8.18} $$

From this it follows that under suitable conditions,

$$ E(T) \doteq \int a(\omega)g(\omega)\,d\omega, $$

$$ \text{var}(T) \doteq n^{-1}\left[2\pi \int a^2(\omega)g^2(\omega)\,d\omega + \kappa_4 \left\{ \int a(\omega)g(\omega)\,d\omega \right\}^2 \right]. $$

The bootstrap analogue of T is $T^* = \pi n_F^{-1} \sum_k a_k I_k^*$, and under the resampling scheme described above this has mean and variance

$$\mathrm{E}^*(T^*) \doteq \int a(\omega) \tilde{g}(\omega) \, d\omega, \quad \mathrm{var}^*(T^*) \doteq 2\pi n^{-1} \int a^2(\omega) \tilde{g}^2(\omega) \, d\omega.$$

For $\mathrm{var}^*(T^*)$ to converge to $\mathrm{var}(T)$ it is therefore necessary that $\kappa_4 = 0$ or that $\int a(\omega) g(\omega) \, d\omega$ be asymptotically negligible relative to the first variance term. A process with normal innovations will have $\kappa_4 = 0$, but since this cannot be ensured in general the structure of T must be examined carefully before this resampling scheme is applied; see Problem 8.6. One situation where it can be applied is kernel density estimation of $g(\cdot)$, as we now see.

Example 8.8 (Spectral density estimation) Suppose that our goal is inference for the spectral density $g(\eta)$ at some η in the interval $(0, \pi)$, and let our estimate of $g(\eta)$ be

$$T = \frac{\pi}{n_F h} \sum_{k=0}^{n_F} K\left(\frac{\omega_k - \eta}{h}\right) I_k,$$

where $K(\cdot)$ is a symmetric PDF with mean zero and unit variance and h is a positive smoothing parameter. Then

$$\mathrm{E}(T) \;\doteq\; h^{-1} \int K\left(\frac{\omega - \eta}{h}\right) g(\omega) \, d\omega \doteq g(\eta) + \tfrac{1}{2} h^2 g''(\eta),$$

$$\mathrm{var}(T) \;\doteq\; \frac{2\pi}{nh} \{g(\eta)\}^2 \int K^2(u) \, du + \frac{\kappa_4}{n} \left\{ h^{-1} \int K\left(\frac{\omega - \eta}{h}\right) g(\omega) \, d\omega \right\}^2.$$

Since we must have $h \to 0$ as $n \to \infty$ in order to remove the bias of T, the second term in the variance is asymptotically negligible relative to the first term, as is necessary for the resampling scheme outlined above to work with a time series for which $\kappa_4 \neq 0$. Comparison of the variance and bias terms implies that the asymptotic form of the relative mean squared error for estimation of $g(\eta)$ is minimized by taking $h \propto n^{-1/5}$. However, there are two difficulties in using resampling to make inference about $g(\eta)$ from T.

The first difficulty is analogous to that seen in Example 5.13, and appears on comparing T and its bootstrap analogue

$$T^* = \frac{\pi}{n_F h} \sum_{k=1}^{n_F} K\left(\frac{\omega_k - \eta}{h}\right) I_k^*.$$

We suppose that I_k^* is generated using a kernel estimate $\tilde{g}(\omega_k)$ with smoothing parameter $\tilde{h}$. The standardized versions of T and T^* are

$$Z = (nhc)^{1/2} \frac{T - g(\eta)}{g(\eta)}, \quad Z^* = (nhc)^{1/2} \frac{T^* - \tilde{g}(\eta)}{\tilde{g}(\eta)},$$

where $c = \{2\pi \int K^2(u)\,du\}^{-1}$. These have means

$$\mathrm{E}(Z) = (nhc)^{1/2}\frac{\mathrm{E}(T) - g(\eta)}{g(\eta)}, \quad \mathrm{E}^*(Z^*) = (nhc)^{1/2}\frac{\mathrm{E}^*(T^*) - \tilde{g}(\eta)}{\tilde{g}(\eta)}.$$

Considerations similar to those in Example 5.13 show that $\mathrm{E}^*(Z^*) \sim \mathrm{E}(Z)$ if $\tilde{h} \to 0$ such that $h/\tilde{h} \to 0$ as $n \to \infty$.

The second difficulty concerns the variances of Z and Z^*, which will both be approximately one if the rescaled residuals e_k have the same asymptotic distribution as the "errors" $I_k/g(\omega_k)$. For this to happen with $g^\dagger(\omega)$ a kernel estimate, it must have smoothing parameter $h^\dagger \propto n^{-1/4}$. That is, asymptotically $g^\dagger(\omega)$ must be undersmoothed compared to the estimate that minimizes the asymptotic relative mean squared error of T.

Thus the application of the bootstrap outlined above involves three kernel density estimates: the original, $\hat{g}(\omega)$, with $h \propto n^{-1/5}$; a surrogate $\tilde{g}(\omega)$ for $g(\omega)$ used when generating bootstrap spectra, with smoothing parameter $\tilde{h}$ asymptotically larger than h; and $g^\dagger(\omega)$, from which residuals are obtained, with smoothing parameter $h^\dagger \propto n^{-1/4}$ asymptotically smaller than h. This raises substantial difficulties for practical application, which could be avoided by explicit correction to reduce the bias of T or by taking h asymptotically narrower than $n^{-1/5}$, in which case the limiting means of Z and Z^* equal zero.

For a numerical assessment of this procedure, we consider estimating the spectrum $g(\omega) = \{1 - 2\alpha\cos(\omega) + \alpha^2\}^{-1}$ of an AR(1) process with $\alpha = 0.9$ at $\eta = \pi/2$. The kernel $K(\cdot)$ is the standard normal PDF. Table 8.4 compares the means and variances of Z with the average means and variances of Z^* for 1000 time series of various lengths, with normal and χ_1^2 innovations. The first set of results has bandwidths $h = an^{-1/5}$, $h^\dagger = an^{-1/4}$, and $\tilde{h} = an^{-1/6}$, with a chosen to minimize the asymptotic relative mean squared error of $\hat{g}(\eta)$.

Even for time series of length 1025, the means and variances of Z and Z^* can be quite different, with the variances more sensitive to the distribution of innovations. For the second block of numbers we took a non-optimal bandwidth $h = an^{-1/4}$, and $h^\dagger = \tilde{h} = h$. Although in this case the true and bootstrap moments agree better for normal innovations, the results for chi-squared innovations are almost as bad as previously, and it would be unwise to rely on the results even for fairly long series.

Mean and variance only summarize limited aspects of the distributions, and for a more detailed comparison we compare 1000 values of Z and of Z^* for a particular series of length 257. The left panel of Figure 8.13 shows that the Z^* are far from normally distributed, while the right panel compares the simulated Z^* and Z. Although Z^* captures the shape of the distribution of Z quite well, there is a clear difference in their means and variances, and confidence intervals for $g(\eta)$ based on Z^* can be expected to be poor. ∎

Table 8.4 Comparison of actual and bootstrap means and variances for a standardized kernel spectral density estimate Z. For the means the upper figure is the average of Z from 1000 AR(1) time series with $\alpha = 0.9$ and length n, and the lower figure is the average of $E^*(Z^*)$ for those series; for the variances the upper and lower figures are estimates of $\mathrm{var}(Z)$ and $E\{\mathrm{var}(Z^*)\}$. The upper 8 lines of results are for $h \propto n^{-1/5}$, $h^\dagger \propto n^{-1/4}$, and $\tilde{h} \propto n^{-1/6}$; for the lower 8 lines $h = h^\dagger = \tilde{h} \propto n^{-1/4}$.

Innovations			n					
			65	129	257	513	1025	∞
Normal	Mean		1.4	0.9	0.8	0.7	0.6	0.5
			2.0	1.7	1.3	1.0	0.8	
	Variance		2.5	1.5	1.3	1.1	1.1	1.0
			2.7	2.0	1.7	1.5	1.3	
Chi-squared	Mean		1.2	1.0	0.8	0.7	0.7	0.5
			2.1	1.7	1.3	1.0	0.8	
	Variance		6.9	4.9	3.8	3.1	2.7	1.0
			2.8	2.0	1.6	1.4	1.3	
Normal	Mean		0.9	0.5	0.5	0.3	0.2	0.0
			0.6	0.4	0.3	0.3	0.2	
	Variance		2.3	1.3	1.1	1.1	1.0	1.0
			1.5	1.4	1.4	1.3	1.3	
Chi-squared	Mean		1.0	0.6	0.5	0.4	0.3	0.0
			0.7	0.4	0.3	0.3	0.2	
	Variance		5.6	3.7	3.1	2.5	2.2	1.0
			1.4	1.4	1.4	1.3	1.2	

Figure 8.13 Comparison of distributions of Z and Z^* for time series of length 257. The left panel shows a normal plot of 1000 values of Z. The right panel compares the distributions of Z and Z^*.

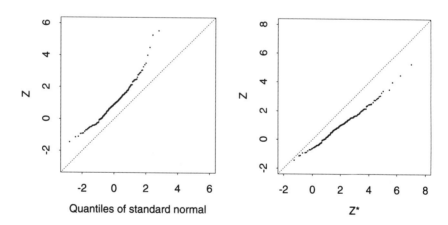

8.3 Point Processes

8.3.1 Basic ideas

A point process is a collection of events in a continuum. Examples are times of arrivals at an intensive care unit, positions of trees in a forest, and epicentres of earthquakes. Mathematical properties of such processes are determined by the joint distribution of the numbers of events in subsets of the continuum. Statistical analysis is based on some notion of repeatability, usually provided by assumptions of stationarity.

Let $N(A)$ denote the number of events in a set A. A point process is stationary if $\Pr\{N(A_1) = n_1, \ldots, N(A_k) = n_k\}$ is unaffected by applying the same translation to all the sets $A_1, \ldots, A_k$, for any finite k. Under second-order stationarity only the first and joint second moments of the $N(A_i)$ remain unchanged by translation.

For a stationary process $\mathrm{E}\{N(A)\} = \lambda|A|$, where λ is the intensity of the process and $|A|$ is the length, area, or volume of A. Second-order moment properties can be defined in various ways, with the most useful definition depending on the context.

The simplest stationary point process model is the homogeneous Poisson process, for which the random variables $N(A_1)$, $N(A_2)$ have independent Poisson distributions whenever A_1 and A_2 are disjoint. This completely random process is a natural standard with which to compare data, although it is rarely a plausible model. More realistic models of dependence can lead to estimation problems that seem analytically insuperable, and Monte Carlo methods are often used, particularly for spatial processes. In particular, simulation from fitted parametric models is often used as a baseline against which to judge data. This often involves graphical tests of the type outlined in Section 4.2.4.

In practice the process is observed only in a finite region. This can give rise to edge effects, which are increasingly severe in higher dimensions.

Example 8.9 (Caveolae)   The upper left panel of Figure 8.14 shows the positions of $n = 138$ caveolae in a 500 unit square region, originally a 2.65 μm square of muscle fibre. The upper right panel shows a realization of a binomial process, for which n points were placed at random in the same region; this is an homogeneous Poisson process conditioned to have 138 events. The data seem to have fewer almost-coincident points than the simulation, but it is hard to be sure.

Spatial dependence is often summarized by K-functions. Suppose that the process is orderly and isotropic, i.e. multiple coincident events are precluded and joint probabilities are invariant under rotation as well as translation. Then a useful summary of spatial dependence is Ripley's K-function,

$$K(t) = \lambda^{-1}\mathrm{E}\left(\#\{\text{events within distance } t \text{ of an arbitrary event}\}\right), \quad t \geq 0.$$

The mean- and variance-stabilized function $Z(t) = \{K(t)/\pi\}^{1/2} - t$ is sometimes used instead. For an homogeneous Poisson process, $K(t) = \pi t^2$. Empirical versions of $K(t)$ must allow for edge effects, as made explicit in Example 8.12.

The solid line in the lower left panel of Figure 8.14 is the empirical version

Figure 8.14 Muscle caveolae analysis. Top left: positions of 138 cavoelae in a 500 unit square of muscle fibre (Appleyard *et al.*, 1985). Top right: realization of an homogeneous binomial process with $n = 138$. Lower left: $\hat{Z}(t)$ (solid), together with pointwise 95% confidence bands (dashes) and overall 92% confidence bands (dots) based on $R = 999$ simulated binomial processes. Lower right: corresponding results for $R = 999$ realizations of a fitted Strauss process.

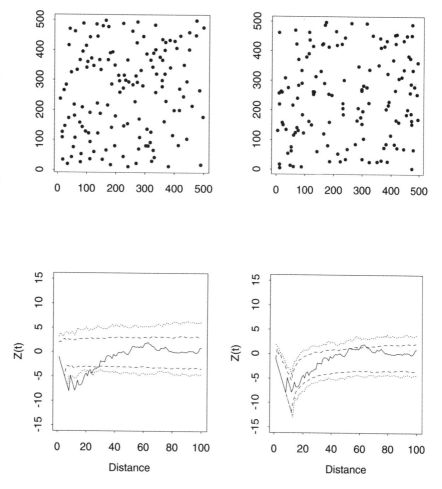

$\hat{Z}(t)$ of $Z(t)$. The dashed lines are pointwise 95% confidence bands from $R = 999$ realizations of the binomial process, and the dotted lines are overall bands with level about 92%, obtained by using the method outlined after (4.17) with $k = 2$. Relative to a Poisson process there is a significant deficiency of pairs of points lying close together, which confirms our previous impression.

The lower right panel of the figure shows the corresponding results for simulations from the Strauss process, a parametric model of interaction that can inhibit patterns in which pairs lie close together. This models the local behaviour of the data better than the stationary Poisson process. ∎

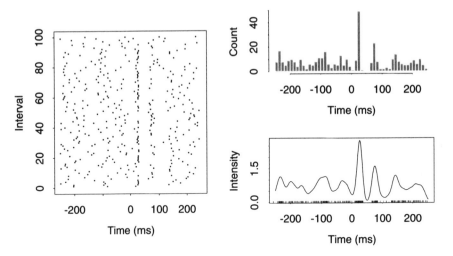

Figure 8.15
Neurophysiological
point process. The rows
of the left panel show
100 replicates of the
interval surrounding the
times at which a human
subject was given a
stimulus; each point
represents the time at
which the firing of a
neuron was observed.
The right panels shows
a histogram and kernel
intensity estimate
($\times 10^{-2}$ ms^{-1}) from
superposing the events
on the left, which are
shown by the rug in the
lower right panel.

8.3.2 Inhomogeneous Poisson processes

The sampling plans used in the previous example both assume stationarity of
the process underlying the data, and rely on simulation from fitted parametric
models. Sometimes independent cases can be identified, in which case it may
be possible to avoid the assumption of stationarity.

Example 8.10 (Neurophysiological point process)   The data in Figure 8.15
were recorded by Dr S. J. Boniface of the Clinical Neurophysiology Unit at
the Radcliffe Infirmary, Oxford, in a study of how a human subject responded
to a stimulus. Each row of the left panel of the figure shows the times at which
the firing of a motoneurone was observed, in an interval extending 250 ms
either side of 100 applications of the stimulus, which is taken to be at time
zero. Although little can be assumed about dependence within each interval,
the stimulus was given far enough apart for firings in different intervals to
be treated as independent. Firings occur at random about 100 ms apart prior
to the stimulus, but on about one-third of occasions a firing is observed
about 28 ms after it, and this partially synchronizes the firings immediately
following.

Theoretical results imply that under mild conditions the process obtained
by superposing all $N = 100$ intervals will be a Poisson process with time-
varying intensity, $N\lambda(y)$. Here it seems plausible that the conditions are met:
for example, 90 of the 100 intervals contain four or fewer events, so the overall
intensity is not dominated by any single interval. The superposed data have
$n = 389$ events whose times we denote by y_j.

The right panels of Figure 8.15 show a histogram of the superposed data and a rescaled kernel estimate of the intensity $\lambda(y)$ in units of 10^{-2} ms^{-1},

$$\hat{\lambda}(y;h) = 100 \times (Nh)^{-1} \sum_{j=1}^{n} w\left(\frac{y-y_j}{h}\right),$$

where $w(\cdot)$ is a symmetric density with mean zero and unit variance; we use the standard normal density with bandwidth $h = 7.5$ ms. Over the observation period this estimate integrates to $100n/N$. The estimated intensity is highly variable and it is unclear which of its features are spurious. We can try to construct a confidence region for $\lambda(y)$ at a set $\mathcal{Y}$ of y values of interest, but the same problems arise as in Examples 5.13 and 8.8.

Once again the key difficulty is bias: $\hat{\lambda}(y;h)$ estimates not $\lambda(y)$ but $\int w(u)\lambda(y - hu)\,du$. For large n and small h this means that

$$\mathrm{E}\{\hat{\lambda}(y;h)\} \doteq \lambda(y) + \tfrac{1}{2}h^2\lambda''(y), \quad \mathrm{var}\{\hat{\lambda}(y;h)\} \doteq c(Nh)^{-1}\lambda(y),$$

where $c = \int w^2(u)\,du$. As in Example 5.13, the delta method (Section 2.7.1) implies that $\hat{\lambda}(y;h)^{1/2}$ has approximately constant variance $\tfrac{1}{4}c(Nh)^{-1}$. We choose to work with the standardized quantities

$$Z(y;h) = \frac{\hat{\lambda}^{1/2}(y;h) - \lambda^{1/2}(y)}{\tfrac{1}{2}(Nh)^{-1/2}c^{1/2}}, \quad y \in \mathcal{Y}.$$

In principle an overall $1 - 2\alpha$ confidence band for $\lambda(y)$ over $\mathcal{Y}$ is determined by the quantiles $z_{L,\alpha}(h)$ and $z_{U,\alpha}(h)$ that satisfy

$$1 - \alpha = \mathrm{Pr}\{z_{L,\alpha}(h) \le Z(y;h), y \in \mathcal{Y}\} = \mathrm{Pr}\{Z(y;h) \le z_{U,\alpha}(h), y \in \mathcal{Y}\}. \quad (8.19)$$

The lower and upper limits of the band would then be

$$\begin{aligned} &\left\{\hat{\lambda}^{1/2}(y;h) - \tfrac{1}{2}(Nh)^{-1/2}c^{1/2}z_{U,\alpha}(h)\right\}^2, \\ &\left\{\hat{\lambda}^{1/2}(y;h) - \tfrac{1}{2}(Nh)^{-1/2}c^{1/2}z_{L,\alpha}(h)\right\}^2. \end{aligned} \quad (8.20)$$

In practice we must use resampling analogues $Z^*(y;h)$ of $Z(y;h)$ to estimate $z_{L,\alpha}(h)$ and $z_{U,\alpha}(h)$, and for this to be successful we must choose h and the resampling scheme to ensure that Z^* and Z have approximately the same distributions.

In this context there are a number of possible resampling schemes. The simplest is to take n events at random from the observed events. This relies on the independence assumptions for Poisson processes. A second scheme generates n^* events from the observed events, where n^* has a Poisson distribution with mean n. A more robust scheme is to superpose 100 resampled intervals, though this does not hold fixed the total number of events. These schemes would be inappropriate if the estimator of interest presupposed that events could not coincide, as did the K-function of Example 8.9.

For all of these resampling schemes the bootstrap estimators $\hat{\lambda}^*(y;h)$ are unbiased for $\hat{\lambda}(y;h)$. The natural resampling analogue of Z is

$$Z^*(y;h) = \frac{\left\{\hat{\lambda}^*(y;h)\right\}^{1/2} - \{\lambda^*(y)\}^{1/2}}{\frac{1}{2}(Nh)^{-1/2}c^{1/2}}, \qquad y \in \mathcal{Y},$$

but $E^*(Z^*) \doteq 0$ and $E(Z) \neq 0$. This situation is analogous to that of Example 5.13, and the conclusion is the same: to make the first two moments of Z and Z^* agree asymptotically, one must choose $h \propto N^{-\gamma}$ with $\gamma > \frac{1}{5}$. Further detailed calculations for the joint distributions over $\mathcal{Y}$ suggest also that $\gamma < \frac{1}{4}$. The essential idea is that h should be smaller than is commonly used for point estimation of the intensity.

A quite different approach is to generate realizations of an inhomogeneous Poisson process from a smooth estimate $\hat{\lambda}(y;\tilde{h})$ of the intensity. This can be achieved by using the smoothed bootstrap, as outlined in Section 3.4, and detailed in Problem 8.7. Under this scheme

$$E^*\left\{\hat{\lambda}^*(y;h)\right\} = \int \hat{\lambda}(y - hu;\tilde{h})w(u)\,du \doteq \hat{\lambda}(y;\tilde{h}) + \tfrac{1}{2}h^2\hat{\lambda}''(y;\tilde{h}),$$

and the resampling analogue of Z is

$$Z^*(y;h) = \frac{\{\hat{\lambda}^*(y;h)\}^{1/2} - \{\hat{\lambda}(y;\tilde{h})\}^{1/2}}{\frac{1}{2}(Nh)^{-1/2}c^{1/2}},$$

whose mean and variance closely match those of Z.

Whatever resampling scheme is employed, simulated values of Z^* will be used to estimate the quantiles $z_{L,\alpha}(h)$ and $z_{U,\alpha}(h)$ in (8.19). If R realizations are generated, then we take $\hat{z}_{L,\alpha}(h)$ and $\hat{z}_{U,\alpha}(h)$ to be respectively the $(R+1)\alpha$th ordered values of

$$\min_{\mathcal{Y}} z_r^*(y;h), \qquad \max_{\mathcal{Y}} z_r^*(y;h).$$

The upper panel of Figure 8.16 shows overall 95% confidence bands for $\lambda(y;5)$, using three of the sampling schemes described above. In each case $R = 999$, and $z_{L,0.025}(5)$ and $z_{U,0.025}(5)$ are estimated by the empirical 0.025 and 0.975 quantiles of the R replicates of $\min\{z^*(y;5), y = -250, -248, \ldots, 250\}$ and $\max\{z^*(y;5), y = -250, -248, \ldots, 250\}$. Results from resampling intervals and events are almost indistinguishable, while generating data from a fitted intensity gives slightly smoother results. In order to avoid problems at the boundaries, the set $\mathcal{Y}$ is taken to be $(-230, 230)$. The experimental setup implies that the intensity should be about 1×10^{-2} firings per second, the only significant departure from which is in the range 0–130 ms, where there is strong evidence that the stimulus affects the firing rate.

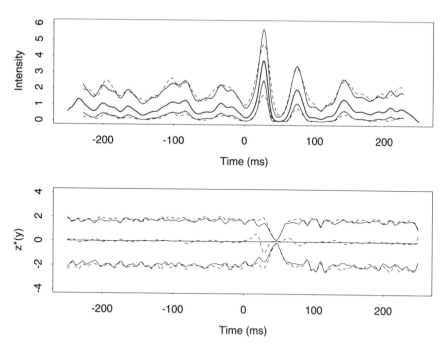

Figure 8.16 Confidence bands for the intensity of the neurophysiological point process data. The upper panel shows the estimated intensity $\hat{\lambda}(y; 5)$ $(10^{-2}$ ms$^{-1})$ (heavy solid), with overall 95% equi-tailed confidence bands based on resampling intervals (solid), resampling events (dots), and generating events from a fitted intensity (dashes). The outer lines in the lower panel show the 2.5% and 97.5% quantiles of the standardized quantile processes $z^*(y; h)$ for resampling intervals (solid) and generating from a fitted intensity (dashes), while the lines close to zero are the bootstrap bias estimates for $\hat{\lambda}$.

The lower panel of the figure shows $z^*_{0.025}(5)$, $z^*_{0.975}(5)$, and the bootstrap bias estimate for $\hat{\lambda}^*(y)$ for resampling intervals and for generating data from a fitted intensity function, with $\tilde{h} = 7.5$ ms. The quantile processes suggest that the variance-stabilizing transformation has worked well, but the double smoothing effect of the latter scheme shows in the bias. The behaviour of the quantile process when $y \doteq 50$ ms — where there are no firings — suggests that a variable bandwidth smoother might be better. ∎

Essentially the same ideas can be applied when the data are a single realization of an inhomogeneous Poisson process (Problem 8.8).

8.3.3 Tests of association

When a point process has events of different types, interest often centres on association between the different types of events or between events and associated covariates. Then permutation or bootstrap tests may be appropriate, although the simulation scheme will depend on the context.

Example 8.11 (Spatial epidemiology) Suppose that events of a point pattern correspond to locations y of cases of a rare disease $\mathcal{D}$ that is thought to be related to emissions from an industrial site at the origin, $y = 0$. A model for the incidence of $\mathcal{D}$ is that it occurs at rate $\lambda(y)$ per person-year at location y, where the suspicion is that $\lambda(y)$ decreases with distance from the origin. Since the disease is rare, the number of cases at y will be well approximated by a Poisson variable with mean $\lambda(y)\mu(y)$, where $\mu(y)$ is the population density of susceptible persons at y. The null hypothesis is that $\lambda(y) \equiv \lambda_0$, i.e. that y has no effect on the intensity of cases, other than through $\mu(y)$. A crucial difficulty is that $\mu(y)$ is unknown and will be hard to estimate from the data available.

One approach to testing for constancy of $\lambda(y)$ is to compare the point pattern for $\mathscr{D}$ to that of another disease $\mathscr{D}'$. This disease is chosen to have the same population of susceptible individuals as $\mathscr{D}$, but its incidence is assumed to be unrelated to emissions from the site and to incidence of $\mathscr{D}$, and so it arises with constant but unknown rate λ' per person-year. If $\mathscr{D}'$ is also rare, it will be reasonable to suppose that the number of cases of $\mathscr{D}'$ at y has a Poisson distribution with mean $\lambda'\mu(y)$. Hence the conditional probability of a case of $\mathscr{D}$ at y given that there is a case of $\mathscr{D}$ or $\mathscr{D}'$ at y is $\pi(y) = \lambda(y)/\{\lambda' + \lambda(y)\}$. If the disease locations are indicated by y_j, and d_j is zero or one according as the case at y_j has $\mathscr{D}'$ or $\mathscr{D}$, the likelihood is

$$\prod_j \pi(y_j)^{d_j}\{1 - \pi(y_j)\}^{1-d_j}.$$

If a suitable form for $\lambda(y)$ is assumed we can obtain the likelihood ratio or perhaps another statistic T to test the hypothesis that $\pi(y)$ is constant. This is a test of proportional hazards for $\mathscr{D}$ and $\mathscr{D}'$, but unlike in Example 4.4 the alternative is specified, at least weakly.

When $\lambda(y) \equiv \lambda_0$ an approximation to the null distribution of T can be obtained by permuting the labels on cases at different locations. That is, we perform R random reallocations of the labels $\mathscr{D}$ and $\mathscr{D}'$ to the y_j, recompute T for each such reallocation, and see whether the observed value of t is extreme relative to the simulated values $t_1^*,\ldots,t_R^*$.   ∎

Example 8.12 (Brambles) The upper left panel of Figure 8.17 shows the locations of 103 newly emergent and 97 one-year-old bramble canes in a 4.5 m square plot. It seems plausible that these two types of event are related, but how should this be tested? Events of both types are clustered, so a Poisson null hypothesis is not appropriate, nor is it reasonable to permute the labels attached to events, as in the previous example.

Let us denote the locations of the two types of event by $y_1,\ldots,y_n$ and $y_1',\ldots,y_{n'}'$. Suppose that a statistic $T = t(y_1,\ldots,y_n,y_1',\ldots,y_{n'}')$ is available that tests for association between the event types. If the extent of the observation region were infinite, we might construct a null distribution for T by applying random translations to events of one type. Thus we would generate values $T^* = t(y_1+U^*,\ldots,y_n+U^*,y_1',\ldots,y_{n'}')$, where U^* is a randomly chosen location in the plane. This sampling scheme has the desirable property of fixing the

Figure 8.17 Brambles
data. Top left: positions
of newly emergent (+)
and one-year bramble
canes (•) in a 4.5 m
square plot. Top right:
random toroidal shift of
the newly emergent
canes, with the original
edges shown by dotted
lines. Bottom left:
Original dependence
function Z_{12} (solid) and
20 replicates (dots)
under the null
hypothesis of no
association between
newly emergent and
one-year canes. Bottom
right: original
dependence function
and pointwise (dashes)
and overall (dots) 95%
null confidence sets. The
data used here are the
upper left quarter of
those displayed on
p. 113 of Diggle (1983).

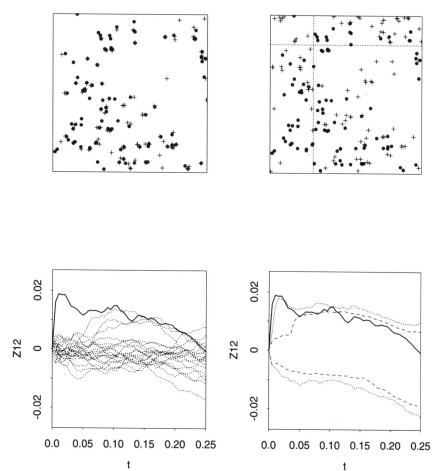

[·] denotes integer part.

relative locations of each type of event, but cannot be applied directly to the data in Figure 8.17 because the resampled patterns will not overlap by the same amount as the original.

We overcome this by random toroidal shifts, where we imagine that the pattern is wrapped on a torus, the random translation is applied, and the translated pattern is then unwrapped. Thus for points in the unit square we would generate $U^* = (U_1^*, U_2^*)$ at random in the unit square, and then map the event at $y_j = (y_{1j}, y_{2j})$ to $y_j^* = (y_{1j} + U_1^* - [y_{1j} + U_1^*], y_{2j} + U_2^* - [y_{2j} + U_2^*])$. The upper right panel of Figure 8.17 shows how such a shift uncouples the two types of events.

We can construct a test through an extension of the K-function to events of two types, that is the function

$$\lambda_2^{-1}\mathrm{E}\left(\#\{\text{type 2 events within distance } t \text{ of an arbitrary type 1 event}\}\right),$$

where λ_2 is the overall intensity of type 2 events. Suppose that there are n_1, n_2 events of types 1 and 2 in an observation region A of area $|A|$, that u_{ij} is the distance from the ith type 1 event to the jth type 2 event, that $w_i(u)$ is the proportion of the circumference of the circle that is centred at the ith type 1 event and has radius u that lies within A, and let $I(\cdot)$ denote the indicator of the event "$\cdot$". Then the sample version of this bivariate K-function is

$$\hat{K}_{12}(t) = (n_1 n_2)^{-1}|A| \sum_{i=1}^{n_1} \sum_{j=1}^{n_2} w_i^{-1}(u_{ij}) I(u_{ij} \leq t).$$

Although it is possible to base an overall statistic on $\hat{K}_{12}(t)$, for example taking $T = \int \hat{Z}_{12}(t)^2 \, dt$, where $\hat{Z}_{12}(t) = \{\hat{K}_{12}(t)/\pi\}^{1/2} - t$, a graphical test is usually more informative.

The lower left panel of Figure 8.17 shows results from 20 random toroidal shifts of the data. The original value of $Z_{12}(t)$ seems to show much stronger local association than do the simulations. This is confirmed by the lower right panel, which shows 95% pointwise and overall confidence bands for $Z_{12}(t)$ based on $R = 999$ shifts. There is clear evidence that the point patterns are not independent: as the original data suggest, new canes emerge close to those from the previous year.   ∎

8.3.4 Tiles

Little is known about resampling spatial processes when there is no parametric model. One nonparametric approach that has been investigated starts from a partition of the observation region $\mathscr{R}$ into disjoint tiles $\mathscr{A}_1,\ldots,\mathscr{A}_n$ of equal size and shape. If we abuse notation by identifying each tile with the pattern it contains, we can write the original value of the statistic as $T = t(\mathscr{A}_1,\ldots,\mathscr{A}_n)$. The idea is to create a resampled pattern by taking a random sample of tiles $\mathscr{A}_1^*,\ldots,\mathscr{A}_n^*$ from $\mathscr{A}_1,\ldots,\mathscr{A}_n$, with corresponding bootstrap statistic $T^* = t(\mathscr{A}_1^*,\ldots,\mathscr{A}_n^*)$. The hope is that if dependence is relatively short-range, taking large tiles will preserve enough dependence to make the properties of T^* close to those of T. If this is to work, the size of the tile must be chosen to trade off preserving dependence, which requires a few large tiles, and getting a good estimate of the distribution of T, which requires many tiles.

This idea is analogous to block resampling in time series, and is capable of similar variations. For example, rather than choosing the $\mathscr{A}_j^*$ independently from the fixed tiles $\mathscr{A}_1,\ldots,\mathscr{A}_n$, we may resample moving tiles by setting

Figure 8.18 Tile resampling for the caveolae data. The left panel shows the original data, with nine tiles sampled at random using toroidal wrapping. The right panel shows the resampled point pattern.

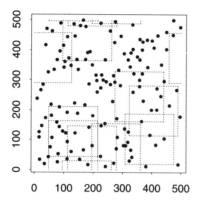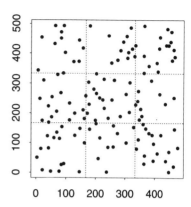

$\mathscr{A}_j^* = U_j^* + \mathscr{A}_j$, where U_j^* is a random vector chosen so that $\mathscr{A}_j^*$ lies wholly within $\mathscr{R}$; we can avoid bias due to undersampling near the boundaries of $\mathscr{R}$ by toroidal wrapping. As in all problems involving spatial data, edge effects are likely to play a critical role.

Example 8.13 (Caveolae)   Figure 8.18 illustrates tile resampling for the data of Example 8.9. The left panel shows the original caveolae data, with the dotted lines showing nine square tiles taken using the moving scheme with toroidal wrapping. The right panel shows the resampled pattern obtained when the tiles are laid side-by-side. For example, the centre top tile and middle right tiles were respectively taken from the top left and bottom right of the original data. Along the tile edges, events seem to lie closer together than in the left panel; this is analogous to the whitening that occurs in blockwise resampling of time series. No analogue of the post-blackened bootstrap springs to mind, however.

For a numerical evaluation of tile resampling, we experimented with estimating the variance θ of the number of events in an observation region $\mathscr{R}$ of side 200 units, using data generated from three random processes. In each case we generated 8800 events in a square of side 4000, then estimated θ from 2000 squares of side 200 taken at random. For each of 100 random squares of side 200 we calculated the empirical mean squared error for estimation of θ using bootstraps of size R, for both fixed and moving tiles. Data were generated from a spatial Poisson process ($\hat{\theta} = 23.4$), from the Strauss process that gave the results in the bottom right panel of Figure 8.14 ($\hat{\theta} = 17.5$), and from a sequential spatial inhibition process, which places points sequentially at random but not within 15 units of an existing event ($\hat{\theta} = 15.6$).

					n				
		4	16	36	64	100	144	196	256
Poisson	theory	224.2	77.9	47.3	36.3	31.2	28.4	26.7	25.6
	fixed	255.2	66.1	40.2	31.7	27.6	27.6	25.5	27.8
	moving	92.2	39.7	35.8	31.6	33.0	30.8	27.4	27.0
Strauss	fixed	129.1	49.1	27.9	19.2	16.4	19.3	20.8	21.9
	moving	53.2	26.4	19.0	17.4	15.9	18.9	18.7	17.9
SSI	fixed	123.8	37.7	14.8	13.5	17.9	25.1	34.6	42.4
	moving	36.5	12.9	11.2	15.6	18.3	21.2	28.6	35.4

Table 8.5 Mean squared errors for estimation of the variance of the number of events in a square of side 200, based on bootstrapping fixed and moving tiles. Data were generated from a Poisson process, a Strauss process with parameters chosen to match the data in Figure 8.14, and from a sequential spatial inhibition process with radius 15. In each case the mean number of events is 22. For $n \leq 64$, we took $R = 200$, for $n = 100, 144$, we took $R = 400$, and for $n \geq 196$ we took $R = 800$.

Table 8.5 shows the results. For the Poisson process the fixed tile results broadly agree with theoretical calculations (Problem 8.9), and the moving tile results accord with general theory, which predicts that mean squared errors for moving tiles should be lower than for fixed tiles. Here the mean squared error decreases to 22 as $n \to \infty$.

The fitted Strauss process inhibits pairs of points closer together than 12 units. The mean squared error is minimized when $n = 100$, corresponding to tiles of side 20; the average estimated variances from the 100 replicates are then 19.0 and 18.2. The mean squared errors for moving tiles are rather lower, but their pattern is similar.

The sequential spatial inhibition results are similar to those for the Strauss process, but with a sharper rise in mean squared error for larger n.

In this setting theory predicts that for a process with sufficiently short-range dependence, the optimal $n \propto |\mathcal{R}|^{1/2}$. If the caveolae data were generated by a Strauss process, results from Table 8.5 would suggest that we take $n \doteq 100 \times 500/200 \doteq 16^2$, so there would be 16 tiles along each side of $\mathcal{R}$. With $R = 200$ and fixed and moving tiles this gives variance estimates of 101.6 and 100.4, both considerably smaller than the variance for Poisson data, which would be 138.   ∎

8.4 Bibliographic Notes

There are many books on time series. Brockwell and Davis (1991) is a recent book aimed at a fairly mathematical readership, while Brockwell and Davis (1996) and Diggle (1990) are more suitable for the less theoretically inclined. Tong (1990) discusses nonlinear time series, while Beran (1994) covers long-memory processes. Bloomfield (1976), Brillinger (1981), Priestley (1981), and Percival and Walden (1993) are introductions to spectral analysis of time series.

Model-based resampling for time series was discussed by Freedman (1984), Freedman and Peters (1984a,b), Swanepoel and van Wyk (1986) and Efron and Tibshirani (1986), among others. Li and Maddala (1996) survey much of the related time domain literature, which has a somewhat theoretical emphasis; their account stresses econometric applications. For a more applied account of parametric bootstrapping in time series, see Tsay (1992). Bootstrap prediction in time series is discussed by Kabaila (1993b), while the bootstrapping of state-space models is described by Stoffer and Wall (1991). The use of model-based resampling for order selection in autoregressive processes is discussed by Chen *et al.* (1993).

Block resampling for time series was introduced by Carlstein (1986). In an important paper, Künsch (1989) discussed overlapping blocks in time series, although in spatial data the proposal of block resampling in Hall (1985) predates both. Liu and Singh (1992a) also discuss the properties of block resampling schemes. Politis and Romano (1994a) introduced the stationary bootstrap, and in a series of papers (Politis and Romano, 1993, 1994b) have discussed theoretical aspects of more general block resampling schemes. See also Bühlmann and Künsch (1995) and Lahiri (1995). The method for block length choice outlined in Section 8.2.3 is due to Hall, Horowitz and Jing (1995); see also Hall and Horowitz (1993). Bootstrap tests for unit roots in autoregressive models are discussed by Ferretti and Romo (1996). Hall and Jing (1996) describe a block resampling approach in which the construction of new series is replaced by Richardson extrapolation.

Bose (1988) showed that model-based resampling for autoregressive processes has good asymptotic higher-order properties for a wide class of statistics. Lahiri (1991) and Götze and Künsch (1996) show that the same is true for block resampling, but Davison and Hall (1993) point out that unfortunately — and unlike when the data are independent — this depends crucially on the variance estimate used.

Forms of phase scrambling have been suggested independently by several authors (Nordgaard, 1990; Theiler *et al.*, 1992), and Braun and Kulperger (1995, 1997) have studied its properties. Hartigan (1990) describes a method for variance estimation in Gaussian series that involves similar ideas but needs no randomization; see Problem 8.5.

Frequency domain resampling has been discussed by Franke and Härdle (1992), who make a strong analogy with bootstrap methods for nonparametric regression. It has been further studied by Janas (1993) and Dahlhaus and Janas (1996), on which our account is based.

Our discussion of the Rio Negro data is based on Brillinger (1988, 1989), which should be consulted for statistical details, while Sternberg (1987, 1995) gives accounts of the data and background to the problem.

Models based on point processes have a long history and varied provenance.

Daley and Vere-Jones (1988) and Karr (1991) provide careful accounts of their mathematical basis, while Cox and Isham (1980) give a more concise treatment. Cox and Lewis (1966) is a standard account of statistical methods for series of events, i.e. point processes in the line. Spatial point processes and their statistical analysis are described by Diggle (1983), Ripley (1981, 1988), and Cressie (1991). Spatial epidemiology has recently received attention from various points of view (Muirhead and Darby, 1989; Bithell and Stone, 1989; Diggle, 1993; Lawson, 1993). Example 8.11 is based on Diggle and Rowlingson (1994).

Owing to the impossibility of exact inference, a number of statistical procedures based on randomization or simulation originated in spatial data analysis. Examples include graphical tests, which were used extensively by Ripley (1977), and various approaches to parametric inference based on Markov chain Monte Carlo methods (Ripley, 1988, Chapters 4, 5). However, nonparametric bootstrap methods for spatial data have received little attention. One exception is Hall (1985), a pioneering work on the theory that underlies block resampling in coverage processes, a particular type of spatial data. Further discussion of resampling these processes is given by Hall (1988b) and Garcia-Soidan and Hall (1997). Possolo (1986) discusses subsampling methods for estimating the parameters of a random field. Other applications include Hall and Keenan (1989), who use the bootstrap to set confidence "gloves" for the outlines of hands, and Journel (1994), who uses parametric bootstrapping to account for estimation uncertainty in an application of kriging. Young (1986) describes bootstrap approaches to testing in some geometrical problems.

Cowling, Hall and Phillips (1996) describe the resampling methods for inhomogeneous Poisson processes that form the basis of Example 8.10, as well as outlining the related theory. Ventura, Davison and Boniface (1997) describe a different analysis of the neurophysiological data used in that example. Diggle, Lange and Beneš (1991) describe an application of the bootstrap to a point process problem in neuroanatomy.

8.5 Problems

1 Suppose that $y_1, \ldots, y_n$ is an observed time series, and let $z_{i,l}$ denote the block $y_i, \ldots, y_{i+l-1}$ of length l starting at y_i, where we set $y_i = y_{1+(i-1 \bmod n)}$ and $y_0 = y_n$. Also let $I_1, \ldots$ be a stream of random numbers uniform on the integers $1, \ldots, n$ and let $L_1, \ldots$ be a stream of random numbers having the geometric distribution $\Pr(L = l) = p(1 - p)^{l-1}$, $l = 1, \ldots$. The algorithm to generate a single stationary bootstrap replicate is

Algorithm 8.2 (Stationary bootstrap)

- Set $Y^* = z_{I_1, L_1}$ and set $i = 1$.
- While length$(Y^*) < n$, {increment i; replace Y^* with (Y^*, z_{I_i, L_i})}.

- Set $Y^* = Y_1^*, \ldots, Y_n^*$.

•

(a) Show that the algorithm above is equivalent to

Algorithm 8.3

- Set $Y_1^* = y_{I_1}$.
- For $i = 2, \ldots, n$, let $Y_i^* = y_{I_i}$ with probability p, and let $Y_i^* = y_{j+1}$ with probability $1 - p$, where $Y_{i-1}^* = y_j$.

•

(b) Define the empirical circular autocovariance

$$c_k = n^{-1} \sum_{j=1}^{n} (y_j - \bar{y})(y_{1+(j+k-1 \bmod n)} - \bar{y}), \quad k = 0, \ldots, n.$$

Show that conditional on $y_1, \ldots, y_n$,

$$E^*(Y_j^*) = \bar{y}, \quad \operatorname{cov}^*(Y_1^*, Y_{j+1}^*) = (1 - p)^j c_j$$

and deduce that y^* is second-order stationary.

(c) Show that if $y_1, \ldots, y_n$ are all distinct, Y^* is a first-order Markov chain. Under what circumstances is it a kth-order Markov chain?
(Section 8.2.3; Politis and Romano, 1994a)

2   Let $Y_1, \ldots, Y_n$ be a stationary time series with covariances $\gamma_j = \operatorname{cov}(Y_1, Y_{j+1})$. Show that

$$\operatorname{var}(\bar{Y}) = \gamma_0 + 2 \sum_{j=1}^{n} \left(1 - \frac{j}{n}\right) \gamma_j,$$

and that this approaches $\zeta = \gamma_0 + 2 \sum_1^\infty \gamma_j$ if $\sum_{j=1}^\infty j|\gamma_j|$ is finite.
Show that under the stationary bootstrap, conditional on the data,

$$\operatorname{var}^*(\bar{Y}^*) = c_0 + 2 \sum_{j=1}^{n-1} \left(1 - \frac{j}{n}\right) (1 - p)^j c_j,$$

where $c_0, c_1, \ldots$ are the empirical circular autocovariances defined in Problem 8.1.
(Section 8.2.3; Politis and Romano, 1994a)

3   (a) Using the setup described on pages 405–408, show that $\sum (S_j - \bar{S})^2$ has mean $v_{i,i} - b^{-1} v_{i,j}$ and variance

$$v_{i,i,j,j} + 2v_{i,j} v_{i,j} - 2b^{-1}(v_{i,i,j,k} + 2v_{i,j} v_{i,k}) + b^{-2}(v_{i,j,k,l} + 2v_{i,j} v_{k,l}),$$

where $v_{i,j} = \operatorname{cov}(S_i, S_j)$, $v_{i,j,k} = \operatorname{cum}(S_i, S_j, S_k)$ and so forth are the joint cumulants of the S_j, and summation is understood over each index.
(b) For an m-dependent normal process, show that provided $l > m$,

$$v_{i,j} = \begin{cases} l^{-1} c_0^{(l)}, & i = j, \\ l^{-2} c_1^{(l)}, & |i - j| = 1, \\ 0, & \text{otherwise}, \end{cases}$$

and show that $l^{-1} c_0^{(l)} \to \zeta$, $c_1^{(l)} \to \frac{1}{2}\tau$ as $l \to \infty$. Hence establish (8.13) and (8.14).
(Section 8.2.3; Appendix A; Hall, Horowitz and Jing, 1995)

4   Establish (8.16) and (8.17). Show that under phase scrambling,

$$n^{-1}\sum Y_j^* = \bar{y}, \quad \mathrm{cov}^*(Y_j^*, Y_{j+m}^*) = n^{-1}\sum(y_j - \bar{y})(y_{j+m} - \bar{y}),$$

where $j + m$ is interpreted mod n, and that all odd joint moments of the Y_j^* are zero.
This last result implies that the resampled series have a highly symmetric joint distribution. When the original data have an asymmetric marginal distribution, the following procedure has been proposed:

- let $x_j = \Phi^{-1}\{r_j/(n+1)\}$, where r_j is the rank of y_j among the original series $y_0,\ldots,y_{n-1}$;
- apply Algorithm 8.1 to $x_0,\ldots,x_{n-1}$, giving $X_0^*,\ldots,X_{n-1}^*$; then
- set $Y_j^* = y_{(r_j')}$, where r_j' is the rank of X_j^* among $X_0^*,\ldots,X_{n-1}^*$.

Discuss critically this idea (see also Practical 8.3).
(Section 8.2.4; Theiler *et al.*, 1992; Braun and Kulperger, 1995, 1997)

5   (a) Let $I_1,\ldots,I_m$ be independent exponential random variables with means μ_j, and consider the statistic $T = \sum_{j=1}^m a_j I_j$, where the a_j are unknown. Show that $V = \frac{1}{2}\sum_j a_j^2 I_j^2$ is an unbiased estimate of $\mathrm{var}(T) = \sum_j a_j^2 \mu_j^2$.
Now let $C = (c_0,\ldots,c_m)$ be an $(m+1)\times(m+1)$ orthogonal matrix with columns c_j, where c_0 is a vector of ones; the lth element of c_i is c_{li}. That is, for some constant b,

$$c_j^T c_i = 0, \quad i \neq j, \quad c_j^T c_j = b, \quad j = 1,\ldots,m.$$

Show that for a suitable choice of b, V is equal to

$$\frac{1}{2m(m+1)}\sum_{i=1}^{m+1}\sum_{l=1}^{m+1}(T_i - T_l)^2,$$

where for $i = 1,\ldots,m+1$, $T_i = \sum_{j=1}^m a_j(1 + c_{ij})I_j$.
(b) Now suppose that $Y_0,\ldots,Y_{n-1}$ is a time series of length $n = 2m+1$, with empirical Fourier transform $\tilde{Y}_0,\ldots,\tilde{Y}_{n-1}$ and periodogram ordinates $I_k = |\tilde{Y}_k|^2/n$, for $k = 0,\ldots,m$. For each $i = 1,\ldots,m+1$, let the perturbed periodogram ordinates be

$$\tilde{Y}_0^i = \tilde{Y}_0, \quad \tilde{Y}_k^i = (1 + c_{ik})^{1/2}\tilde{Y}_k, \quad \tilde{Y}_{n-k}^i = (1 + c_{ik})^{1/2}\tilde{Y}_{n-k}, \quad k = 1,\ldots,m,$$

from which the ith replacement time series is obtained by the inverse Fourier transform.
Let T be the value of a statistic calculated from the original series. Explain how the corresponding resample values, $T_1^*,\ldots,T_{m+1}^*$, may be used to obtain an approximately unbiased estimate of the variance of T, and say for what types of statistics you think this is likely to work.
(Section 8.2.4; Hartigan, 1990)

6   In the context of periodogram resampling, consider a *ratio statistic*

$$T = \frac{\sum_{k=1}^{n_F} a(\omega_k)I(\omega_k)}{\sum_{k=1}^{n_F} I(\omega_k)} = \frac{\int a(\omega)g(\omega)\,d\omega(1 + n_F^{-1/2}X_a)}{\int g(\omega)\,d\omega(1 + n_F^{-1/2}X_1)},$$

say. Use (8.18) to show that X_a and X_1 have means zero and that

$$\mathrm{var}(X_a) \doteq \pi I_{aagg}I_{ag}^{-2} + \tfrac{1}{2}\kappa_4, \quad \mathrm{var}(X_1) \doteq \pi I_{gg}I_g^{-2} + \tfrac{1}{2}\kappa_4,$$

$$\mathrm{cov}(X_1, X_a) \doteq \pi I_{agg}I_{ag}^{-1}I_g^{-1} + \tfrac{1}{2}\kappa_4,$$

where $I_{aagg} = \int a^2(\omega)g^2(\omega)\,d\omega$, and so forth. Hence show that to first order
the mean and variance of T do not involve κ_4, and deduce that periodogram
resampling may be applied to ratio statistics.
Use simulation to see how well periodogram resampling performs in estimating the
distribution of a suitable version of the sample estimate of the lag j autocorrelation,

$$\rho_j = \frac{\int_{-\pi}^{\pi} e^{-i\omega j} g(\omega)\,d\omega}{\int_{-\pi}^{\pi} g(\omega)\,d\omega}.$$

(Section 8.2.5; Janas, 1993; Dahlhaus and Janas, 1996)

7   Let $y_1,\ldots,y_n$ denote the times of events in an inhomogeneous Poisson process of
intensity $\lambda(y)$, observed for $0 \le y \le 1$, and let

$$\hat{\lambda}(y;h) = h^{-1}\sum_{j=1}^{n} w\left(\frac{y-y_j}{h}\right)$$

denote a kernel estimate of $\lambda(y)$, based on a kernel $w(\cdot)$ that is a PDF. Explain why
the following two algorithms for generating bootstrap data from the estimated
intensity are (almost) equivalent.

Algorithm 8.4 (Inhomogeneous Poisson process 1)

*   Let N have a Poisson distribution with mean $\hat{\Lambda} = \int_0^1 \hat{\lambda}(u;h)\,du$.
*   For $j = 1,\ldots,N$, independently take U_j^* from the $U(0,1)$ distribution, and
    then set $Y_j^* = \hat{F}^{-1}(U_j^*)$, where $\hat{F}(y) = \hat{\Lambda}^{-1}\int_0^y \hat{\lambda}(u;h)\,du$.

●

Algorithm 8.5 (Inhomogeneous Poisson process 2)

*   Let N have a Poisson distribution with mean $\hat{\Lambda} = \int_0^1 \hat{\lambda}(u;h)\,du$.
*   For $j = 1,\ldots,N$, independently generate I_j^* at random from the integers
    $\{1,\ldots,n\}$ and let ε_j^* be a random variable with PDF $w(\cdot)$. Set $Y_j^* = y_{I_j^*} + h\varepsilon_j^*$.

●

(Section 8.3.2)

8   Consider an inhomogeneous Poisson process of intensity $\lambda(y) = N\mu(y)$, where $\mu(y)$
is fixed and smooth, observed for $0 \le y \le 1$.
A kernel intensity estimate based on events at $y_1,\ldots,y_n$ is

$$\hat{\lambda}(y;h) = \frac{1}{h}\sum_{j=1}^{n} w\left(\frac{y-y_j}{h}\right),$$

where $w(\cdot)$ is the PDF of a symmetric random variable with mean zero and
variance one; let $K = \int w^2(u)\,du$.
(a) Show that as $N\to\infty$ and $h\to0$ in such a way that $Nh\to\infty$,

$$\mathrm{E}\left\{\hat{\lambda}(y;h)\right\} \doteq \lambda(y) + \tfrac{1}{2}h^2\lambda''(y), \quad \mathrm{var}\left\{\hat{\lambda}(y;h)\right\} \doteq Kh^{-1}\lambda(y);$$

you may need the facts that the number of events n has a Poisson distribution with
mean $\Lambda = \int_0^1 \lambda(u)\,du$, and that conditional on there being n observed events, their

times are independent random variables with PDF $\Lambda^{-1}\lambda(y)$. Hence show that the asymptotic mean squared error of $\hat{\lambda}(y;h)$ is minimized when $h \propto N^{-1/5}$. Use the delta method to show that the approximate mean and variance of $\hat{\lambda}^{1/2}(y;h)$ are

$$\lambda^{1/2}(y) + \tfrac{1}{4}\lambda^{-1/2}(y)\left\{h^2\lambda''(y) - \tfrac{1}{2}Kh^{-1}\right\}, \qquad \tfrac{1}{4}Kh^{-1}.$$

(b) Now suppose that resamples are formed by taking n observations at random from $y_1,\ldots,y_n$. Show that the bootstrapped intensity estimate

$$\hat{\lambda}^*(y;h) = \frac{1}{h}\sum_{j=1}^{n} w\left(\frac{y - y_j^*}{h}\right),$$

has mean $\mathrm{E}^*\{\hat{\lambda}^*(y;h)\} = \hat{\lambda}(y;h)$, and that the same is true when there are n^* resampled events, provided that $\mathrm{E}^*(n^*) = n$.

For a third resampling scheme, let n^* have a Poisson distribution with mean n, and generate n^* events independently from density $\hat{\lambda}(y;\tilde{h})/\int_0^1 \hat{\lambda}(u;\tilde{h})\,du$. Show that under this scheme

$$\mathrm{E}^*\{\hat{\lambda}^*(y;h)\} \doteq \int w(u)\hat{\lambda}(y - hu;\tilde{h})\,du.$$

(c) By comparing the asymptotic distributions of

$$Z(y;h) = \frac{\hat{\lambda}^{1/2}(y;h) - \lambda^{1/2}(y)}{\tfrac{1}{2}K^{1/2}h^{-1/2}}, \qquad Z^*(y;h) = \frac{\left\{\hat{\lambda}^*(y;h)\right\}^{1/2} - \hat{\lambda}^{1/2}(y;h)}{\tfrac{1}{2}K^{1/2}h^{-1/2}},$$

find conditions under which the quantiles of Z^* can estimate those of Z.
(Section 8.3.2; Example 5.13; Cowling, Hall and Phillips, 1996)

9 Consider resampling tiles when the observation region $\mathcal{R}$ is a square, the data are generated by a stationary planar Poisson process of intensity λ, and the quantity of interest is $\theta = \mathrm{var}(Y)$, where Y is the number of events in $\mathcal{R}$.

Suppose that $\mathcal{R}$ is split into n fixed tiles of equal size and shape, which are then resampled according to the usual bootstrap. Show that the bootstrap estimate of θ is $t = \sum(y_j - \bar{y})^2$, where y_j is the number of events in the jth tile. Use the fact that $\mathrm{var}(T) = (n-1)^2\{\kappa_4/n + 2\kappa_2^2/(n-1)\}$, where κ_r is the rth cumulant of Y_j, to show that the mean squared error of T is

$$\frac{\mu}{n^2}\left\{\mu + (n-1)(2\mu + n - 1)\right\},$$

where $\mu = \lambda|\mathcal{R}|$. Sketch this when $\mu > 1$, $\mu = 1$, and $\mu < 1$, and explain in qualitative terms its behaviour when $\mu > 1$.
Extend the discussion to moving tiles.
(Section 8.3)

8.6 Practicals

1 Dataframe `lynx` contains the Canadian lynx data, to the logarithm of which we fit the autoregressive model that minimizes AIC:

```
ts.plot(log(lynx))
lynx.ar <- ar(log(lynx))
lynx.ar$order
```

The best model is AR(11). How well determined is this, and what is the variance
of the series average? We bootstrap to see, using lynx.fun (given below), which
calculates the order of the fitted autoregressive model, the series average, and saves
the series itself.

Here are results for fixed-block bootstraps with block length $l = 20$:

```
lynx.fun <- function(tsb)
{ ar.fit <- ar(tsb, order.max=25)
  c(ar.fit$order, mean(tsb), tsb) }
lynx.1 <- tsboot(log(lynx), lynx.fun, R=99, l=20, sim="fixed")
tsplot(ts(lynx.1$t[1,3:116],start=c(1821,1)),
       main="Block simulation, l=20")
boot.array(lynx.1)[1,]
table(lynx.1$t[,1])
var(lynx.1$t[,2])
qqnorm(lynx.1$t[,2])
abline(mean(lynx.1$t[,2]),sqrt(var(lynx.1$t[,2])),lty=2)
```

To obtain similar results for the stationary bootstrap with mean block length
$l = 20$:

```
.Random.seed <- lynx.1$seed
lynx.2 <- tsboot(log(lynx), lynx.fun, R=99, l=20, sim="geom")
```

See if the results look different from those above. Do the simulated series using
blocks look like the original? Compare the estimated variances under the two
resampling schemes. Try different block lengths, and see how the variances of the
series average change.

For model-based resampling we need to store results from the original model:

```
lynx.model <- list(order=c(lynx.ar$order,0,0),ar=lynx.ar$ar)
lynx.res <- lynx.ar$resid[!is.na(lynx.ar$resid)]
lynx.res <- lynx.res - mean(lynx.res)
lynx.sim <- function(res,n.sim, ran.args)
{ rg1 <- function(n, res) sample(res, n, replace=T)
  ts.orig <- ran.args$ts
  ts.mod <- ran.args$model
  mean(ts.orig)+ts(arima.sim(model=ts.mod, n=n.sim,
                   rand.gen=rg1, res=as.vector(res))) }
.Random.seed <- lynx.1$seed
lynx.3 <- tsboot(lynx.res, lynx.fun, R=99, sim="model",
                 n.sim=114,ran.gen=lynx.sim,
                 ran.args=list(ts=log(lynx), model=lynx.model))
```

Check the orders of the fitted models for this scheme.

For post-blackening we need to define yet another function:

```
lynx.black <- function(res, n.sim, ran.args)
{ ts.orig <- ran.args$ts
  ts.mod <- ran.args$model
  mean(ts.orig) + ts(arima.sim(model=ts.mod,n=n.sim,innov=res)) }
.Random.seed <- lynx.1$seed
lynx.1b <- tsboot(lynx.res, lynx.fun, R=99, l=20, sim="fixed",
          n.sim=114,ran.gen=lynx.black,
          ran.args=list(ts=log(lynx), model=lynx.model))
```

Compare these results with those above, and try the post-blackened bootstrap with
`sim="geom"`.
(Sections 8.2.2, 8.2.3)

2   The data in `beaver` consist of a time series of $n = 100$ observations on the body
temperature $y_1,\ldots,y_n$ and an indicator $x_1,\ldots,x_n$ of activity of a female beaver,
Castor canadensis. We want to estimate and give an uncertainty measure for the
body temperature of the beaver. The simplest model that allows for the clear
autocorrelation of the series is

$$y_j = \beta_0 + \beta_1 x_j + \eta_j, \quad \eta_j = \alpha\eta_{j-1} + \varepsilon_j, \quad j = 1,\ldots,n, \tag{8.21}$$

a linear regression model in which the errors η_j form an AR(1) process, and the ε_j
are independent identically distributed errors with mean zero and variance σ^2.
Having fitted this model, estimated the parameters $\alpha, \beta_0, \beta_1, \sigma^2$ and calculated the
residuals $e_2,\ldots,e_n$ (e_1 cannot be calculated), we generate bootstrap series by the
following recipe:

$$y_j^* = \hat\beta_0 + \hat\beta_1 x_j + \eta_j^*, \quad \eta_j^* = \hat\alpha\eta_{j-1}^* + \varepsilon_j^*, \quad j = 1,\ldots,n, \tag{8.22}$$

where the error series $\{\eta_j^*\}$ is formed by taking a white noise series $\{\varepsilon_j^*\}$ at random
from the set $\{\hat\sigma(e_2 - \bar e),\ldots,\hat\sigma(e_n - \bar e)\}$ and then applying the second part of (8.22).
To fit the original model and to generate a new series:

```
fit <- function( data )
{ X <- cbind(rep(1,100),data$activ)
  para <- list( X=X,data=data)
  assign("para",para,frame=1)
  d <- arima.mle(x=para$data$temp,model=list(ar=c(0.8)),
                 xreg=para$X)
  res <- arima.diag(d,plot=F,std.resid=T)$std.resid
  res <- res[!is.na(res)]
  list(paras=c(d$model$ar,d$reg.coef,sqrt(d$sigma2)),
       res=res-mean(res),fit=X %*% d$reg.coef)  }
beaver.args <- fit(beaver)
white.noise <- function(n.sim, ts) sample(ts,size=n.sim,replace=T)
beaver.gen <- function(ts, n.sim, ran.args)
{ tsb <- ran.args$res
  fit <- ran.args$fit
  coeff <- ran.args$paras
  ts$temp <- fit + coeff[4]*arima.sim(model=list(ar=coeff[1]),
                            n=n.sim,rand.gen=white.noise,ts=tsb)
  ts }
new.beaver <- beaver.gen(beaver, 100, beaver.args)
```

Now we are able to generate data, we can bootstrap and see the results of
`beaver.boot` as follows:

```
beaver.fun <- function(ts) fit(ts)$paras
beaver.boot <- tsboot(beaver, beaver.fun, R=99,sim="model",
               n.sim=100,ran.gen=beaver.gen,ran.args=beaver.args)
names(beaver.boot)
beaver.boot$t0
beaver.boot$t[1:10,]
```

showing the original value of `beaver.fun` and its value for the first 10 replicate series. Are the estimated mean temperatures for the $R = 99$ simulations normal? Use `boot.ci` to obtain normal and basic bootstrap confidence intervals for the resting and active temperatures.

In this analysis we have assumed that the linear model with AR(1) errors is appropriate. How would you proceed if it were not?

(Section 8.2; Reynolds, 1994)

3 Consider scrambling the phases of the sunspot data. To see the original data, two replicates generated using ordinary phase scrambling, and two phase scrambled series whose marginal distribution is the same as that of the original data:

```
sunspot.fun <- function(ts) ts
sunspot.1 <- tsboot(sunspot,sunspot.fun,R=2,sim="scramble")
.Random.seed <- sunspot.1$seed
sunspot.2 <- tsboot(sunspot,sunspot.fun,R=2,sim="scramble",norm=F)
split.screen(c(3,2))
yl <- c(-50,200)
screen(1); ts.plot(sunspot,ylim=yl); abline(h=0,lty=2)
screen(3); tsplot(sunspot.1$t[1,],ylim=yl); abline(h=0,lty=2)
screen(4); tsplot(sunspot.1$t[2,],ylim=yl); abline(h=0,lty=2)
screen(5); tsplot(sunspot.2$t[1,],ylim=yl); abline(h=0,lty=2)
screen(6); tsplot(sunspot.2$t[2,],ylim=yl); abline(h=0,lty=2)
```

What features of the original data are preserved by the two algorithms? (You may find it helpful to experiment with different shapes for the figures.)

(Section 8.2.4; Problem 8.4; Theiler *et al.*, 1992)

4 coal contains data on times of explosions in coal mines from 15 March 1851 to 22 March 1962, often modelled as an inhomogeneous Poisson process. For a kernel intensity estimate (accidents per year):

```
coal.est <- function(y, h=5) length(y)*ksmooth(y,bandwidth=2.7*h,
          kernel="n",x.points=seq(1851,1963,2))$y
year <- seq(1851,1963,2)
plot(year,coal.est(coal$date),type="l",ylab="intensity",
     ylim=c(0,6))
rug(coal)
```

Try other choices of bandwidth h, noting that the estimate for the period $(1851 + 4h, 1962 - 4h)$ does not have edge effects. Do you think that the drop from about three accidents per year before 1900 to about one thereafter is spurious? What about the peaks at around 1910 and 1940?

For an equi-tailed 90% bootstrap confidence band for the intensity, we take $h = 5$ and $R = 199$ (a larger R will give more reliable results):

```
coal.fun <- function(data, i, h=5) coal.est(data[i], h)
coal.boot <- boot(coal$date, coal.fun, R=199)
A <- 0.5/sqrt(5*2*sqrt(pi))
Z <- sweep(sqrt(coal.boot$t),2,sqrt(coal.boot$t0))/A
Z.max <- sort(apply(Z,1,max))[190]
Z.min <- sort(apply(Z,1,min))[10]
top <- (sqrt(coal.boot$t0)-A*Z.min)^2
bot <- (sqrt(coal.boot$t0)-A*Z.max)^2
lines(year,top,lty=2); lines(year,bot,lty=2)
```

To see the quantile process:

```
Z <- apply(Z,2,sort)
Z.05 <- Z[10,]
Z.95 <- Z[190,]
plot(year,Z.05,type="l",ylab="Z",ylim=c(-3,3))
lines(year,Z.95)
```

Construct symmetric bootstrap confidence bands based on $z_\alpha(h)$ such that

$$\Pr\{|Z(y;h)| \le z_\alpha(h), y \in \mathscr{Y}\} = \alpha$$

(no more simulation is required). How different are they from the equi-tailed ones? For simulation with a random number of events, use

```
coal.gen <- function(data, n)
{ i <- sample(1:n,size=rpois(n=1,lambda=n),replace=T)
  data[i] }
coal.boot2 <- boot(coal$date, coal.est, R=199, sim="parametric",
                   ran.gen=coal.gen, mle=nrow(coal))
```

Does this make any difference?
(Section 8.3.2; Cowling, Hall and Phillips 1996; Hand *et al.*, 1994, p. 155)

9

Improved Calculation

9.1 Introduction

A few of the statistical questions in earlier chapters have been amenable to analytical calculation. However, most of our problems have been too complicated for exact solutions, and samples have been too small for theoretical large-sample approximations to be trustworthy. In such cases simulation has provided approximate answers through Monte Carlo estimates of bias, variance, quantiles, probabilities, and so forth. Throughout we have supposed that the simulation size is limited only by our impatience for reliable results.

Simulation of independent bootstrap samples and their use as described in previous chapters is usually easily programmed and implemented. If it takes up to a few hours to calculate enough values of the statistic of interest, T, *ordinary simulation* of this sort will be an efficient use of a researcher's time. But sometimes T is very costly to compute, or sampling is only a single component in a larger procedure — as in a double bootstrap — or the procedure will be repeated many times with different sets of data. Then it may pay to invest in methods of calculation that reduce the number of simulations needed to obtain a given precision, or equivalently increase the accuracy of an estimate based on a given simulation size. This chapter is devoted to such methods.

No lunch is free. The techniques that give the biggest potential variance reductions are usually the hardest to implement. Others yield less spectacular gains, but are more easily implemented. Thoughtless use of any of them may make matters worse, so it is essential to ensure that use of a variance reduction technique will save the investigator's time, which is much more valuable than computer time.

Most of our bootstrap estimates depend on averages. For example, in testing a null hypothesis (Chapter 4) we want to calculate the significance probability $p = \Pr^*(T^* \geq t \mid \hat{F}_0)$, where t is the observed value of test statistic T and the fitted model $\hat{F}_0$ is an estimate of F under the null hypothesis. The simple Monte Carlo estimate of p is $R^{-1}\sum_r I\{T_r^* \geq t\}$, where I is the indicator function and the T_r^* are based on R independent samples generated from $\hat{F}_0$. The variance of this estimate is cR^{-1}, where $c = p(1-p)$. Nothing can generally be done about the factor R^{-1}, but the constant c can be reduced if we use a more sophisticated Monte Carlo technique. Most of this chapter concerns such techniques. Section 9.2 describes methods for balancing the simulation in order to make it more like a full enumeration of all possible samples, and in Section 9.3 we describe methods based on the use of control variates. Section 9.4 describes methods based on importance sampling. In Section 9.5 we discuss one important method of theoretical approximation, the saddlepoint method, which eliminates the need for simulation.

9.2 Balanced Bootstraps

Suppose for simplicity that the data are a homogeneous random sample $y_1,\ldots,y_n$ with EDF $\hat{F}$, and that as usual we are concerned with the properties of a statistic T whose observed value is $t = t(y_1,\ldots,y_n)$. Our focus is $T^* = t(Y_1^*,\ldots,Y_n^*)$, where the Y_j^* are a random sample from $\hat{F}$. Consider the bias estimate for T, namely $B = E^*(T^* \mid \hat{F}) - t$. If g denotes the joint density of $Y_1^*,\ldots,Y_n^*$, then

$$B = \int t(y_1^*,\ldots,y_n^*)g(y_1^*,\ldots,y_n^*)dy_1^* \cdots dy_n^* - t.$$

This might be computable analytically if $t(\cdot)$ is simple enough, particularly for some parametric models. In the nonparametric case, if the calculation cannot be done analytically, we set g equal to n^{-n} for all possible samples $y_1^*, \ldots, y_n^*$ in the set $\mathscr{S} = \{y_1,\ldots,y_n\}^n$ and write

$$B = n^{-n}\sum_{\mathscr{S}} t(y_1^*,\ldots,y_n^*) - t. \tag{9.1}$$

This sum over all possible samples need involve only $\binom{2n-1}{n}$ calculations of t^*, since the symmetry of $t(\cdot)$ with respect to the sample can be used, but even so the *complete enumeration* of values t^* that (9.1) requires will usually be impracticable unless n is very small. So it is that, especially in nonparametric problems, we usually approximate the average in (9.1) by the average of R randomly chosen elements of $\mathscr{S}$ and so approximate B by $B_R = R^{-1}\sum T_r^* - t$.

This calculation with a random subset of $\mathscr{S}$ has a major defect: the values $y_1,\ldots,y_n$ typically do not occur with equal frequency in that subset. This is illustrated in Table 9.1, which reproduces Table 2.2 but adds (penultimate row) the aggregate frequencies for the data values; the final row is explained later. In the even simpler case of the sample average $t = \bar{y}$ we can see clearly

Table 9.1 $R = 9$ resamples for city population data, chosen by ordinary bootstrap sampling from $\hat{F}$.

		Data										
	j	1	2	3	4	5	6	7	8	9	10	
	u	138	93	61	179	48	37	29	23	30	2	
	x	143	104	69	260	75	63	50	48	111	50	

		Number of times j sampled										Statistic
Data		1	1	1	1	1	1	1	1	1	1	$t = 1.520$
Sample	1		3	2			1	2		1	1	$t_1^* = 1.466$
	2	1		1		2	2	1		2	1	$t_2^* = 1.761$
	3	1	1		1		1			4	2	$t_3^* = 1.951$
	4		1	2		1	1	2	2		1	$t_4^* = 1.542$
	5	3			1	3		1	1	1		$t_5^* = 1.371$
	6	1	1	2			1		1	1	3	$t_6^* = 1.686$
	7	1	1	2	2	2		1			1	$t_7^* = 1.378$
	8	2		1		3	1	1	1	1		$t_8^* = 1.420$
	9		1	1	1	2	1		2	1	1	$t_9^* = 1.660$
Aggregate		9	8	11	5	13	8	8	7	11	10	
$\bar{F}^*$		$\frac{9}{90}$	$\frac{8}{90}$	$\frac{11}{90}$	$\frac{5}{90}$	$\frac{13}{90}$	$\frac{8}{90}$	$\frac{8}{90}$	$\frac{7}{90}$	$\frac{11}{90}$	$\frac{10}{90}$	

that the unequal frequencies completely account for the fact that B_R differs from the correct value $B = 0$. The corresponding phenomenon for parametric bootstrapping is that the aggregated EDF of the R samples is not as close to the CDF of the fitted parametric model as it is to the same model with different parameter values.

There are two ways to deal with this difficulty. First, we can try to change the simulation to remove the defect; and secondly we can try to adjust the results of the existing simulation.

9.2.1 Balancing the simulation

The idea of *balanced resampling* is to generate tables of random frequencies, but to force them to be balanced in an appropriate way. A set of R bootstrap samples is said to have *first-order balance* if each of the original observations appears with equal frequency, i.e. exactly R times overall.

First-order balance is easy to achieve. A simple algorithm is as follows:

Algorithm 9.1 (Balanced bootstrap)

Concatenate R copies of $y_1, \ldots, y_n$ into a single set $\mathcal{Y}$ of size Rn.

Permute the elements of $\mathcal{Y}$ at random, giving $\mathcal{Y}^*$, say.

For $r = 1, \ldots, R$, take successive sets of n elements of $\mathcal{Y}^*$ to be the balanced resamples, y_r^*, and set $t_r^* = t(y_r^*)$.   •

Table 9.2 First-order balanced bootstrap with $R = 9$ for city population data.

		j: 1	2	3	4	5	6	7	8	9	10	Statistic
		Number of times j sampled										
Data		1	1	1	1	1	1	1	1	1	1	$t = 1.520$
Sample	1	1			1	3		2	1	1	1	$t_1^* = 1.632$
	2				2	1	1	2	1	1	2	$t_2^* = 1.823$
	3	2	2	2				1	1	1	1	$t_3^* = 1.334$
	4	2	2			2	1	1	1		1	$t_4^* = 1.317$
	5	1		3	1		2		1	2		$t_5^* = 1.531$
	6	2	1	1	1	1	1	1	1		1	$t_6^* = 1.344$
	7		2		1	1	1	1	1	2	1	$t_7^* = 1.730$
	8	1	2	2	1		1		1	1	1	$t_8^* = 1.424$
	9			1	2	1	2	1	1	1	1	$t_9^* = 1.678$
Aggregate		9	9	9	9	9	9	9	9	9	9	

Other algorithms (e.g. Problem 9.2) have been suggested that economize on the time and space needed to generate balanced samples, but the most time-consuming part of a bootstrap simulation is usually the calculation of the values of t^*, so the details of the simulation algorithm are rarely critical. Whatever the method used to generate the balanced samples, the result will be that individual observations have equal overall frequencies, just as for complete enumeration — a simple illustration is given below. Indeed, so far as the marginal frequencies of the data values are concerned, a complete enumeration has been performed.

Example 9.1 (City population data) Consider estimating the bias of the ratio estimate $t = \bar{x}/\bar{u}$ for the data in the second and third rows of Table 9.1. Table 9.2 shows the results for a balanced bootstrap with $R = 9$: each data value occurs exactly 9 times overall.

To see how well the balanced bootstrap works, we apply it with the more realistic number $R = 49$. The bias estimate is $B_R = \bar{T}^* - t = R^{-1}\sum_r T_r^* - t$, and its variance over 100 replicates of the ordinary resampling scheme is 7.25×10^{-4}. The corresponding figure for the balanced bootstrap is 9.31×10^{-5}, so the balanced scheme is about $72.5/9.31 = 7.8$ times more efficient for bias estimation. ■

Here and below we say that the efficiency of a bootstrap estimate such as B_R relative to the ordinary bootstrap is the variance ratio

$$\frac{\mathrm{var}^*_{ord}(B_R)}{\mathrm{var}^*_{bal}(B_R)},$$

where for this comparison the subscripts denote the sampling scheme under which B_R was calculated.

Table 9.3 Approximate
efficiency gains when
balancing schemes with
$R = 49$ are applied in
estimating biases for
estimates of nonlinear
regression model
applied to the calcium
uptake data, based on
100 repetitions of the
bootstrap.

	Cases		Stratified		Residuals	
	Balanced	Adjusted	Balanced	Adjusted	Balanced	Adjusted
$\hat{\beta}_0$	8.9	6.9	141	108	1.2	0.6
$\hat{\beta}_1$	13.1	8.9	63	49	1.4	0.6
$\hat{\sigma}$	11.1	9.1	18.7	18.0	15.3	13.5

So far we have focused on the application to bias estimation, for which the balance typically gives a big improvement. The same is not generally true for estimating higher moments or quantiles. For instance, in the previous example the balanced bootstrap has efficiency less than one for calculation of the variance estimate V_R.

The balanced bootstrap extends quite easily to more complicated sampling situations. If the data consist of several independent samples, as in Section 3.2, balanced simulation can be applied separately to each. Some other extensions are straightforward.

Example 9.2 (Calcium uptake data) To investigate the improvement in bias estimation for the parameters of the nonlinear regression model fitted to the data of Example 7.7, we calculated 100 replicates of the estimated biases based on 49 bootstrap samples. The resulting efficiencies are given in Table 9.3 for different resampling schemes; the results labelled "Adjusted" are discussed in Example 9.3. For stratified resampling the data are stratified by the covariate value, so there are nine strata each with three observations. The efficiency gains under stratified resampling are very large, and those under case resampling are worthwhile. The gains when resampling residuals are not worthwhile, except for $\hat{\sigma}^2$. ∎

First-order balance ensures that each observation occurs precisely R times in the R samples. In a scheme with *second-order balance*, each pair of observations occurs together precisely the same number of times, and so on for schemes with third- and higher-order balance. There is a close connection to certain experimental designs (Problem 9.7). Detailed investigation suggests, however, that there is usually no practical gain beyond first-order balance. An open question is whether or not there are useful "nearly balanced" designs.

9.2.2 Post-simulation balance

Consider again estimating the bias of T in a nonparametric context, based on an unbalanced array of frequencies such as Table 9.1. The usual bias estimate can be written in expanded notation as

$$B_R = R^{-1} \sum_{r=1}^{R} t(\hat{F}_r^*) - t(\hat{F}), \qquad (9.2)$$

where as usual $\hat{F}_r^*$ denotes the EDF corresponding to the rth row of the array. Let $\bar{F}^*$ denote the average of these EDFs, that is

$$\bar{F}^* = R^{-1}(\hat{F}_1^* + \cdots + \hat{F}_R^*).$$

For a frequency table such as Table 9.1, $\bar{F}^*$ is the CDF of the distribution corresponding to the aggregate frequencies of data values, as shown in the final row. The resulting *adjusted bias estimate* is

$$B_{R,adj} = R^{-1} \sum_{r=1}^{R} t(\hat{F}_r^*) - t(\bar{F}^*). \qquad (9.3)$$

This is sometimes called the re-centred bias estimate. In addition to the usual bootstrap values $t(\hat{F}_r^*)$, its calculation requires only $\bar{F}^*$ and $t(\bar{F}^*)$. Note that for adjustment to work, $t(\cdot)$ must be in a functional form, i.e. be defined independently of sample size n. For example, a variance must be calculated with divisor n rather than $n-1$.

The corresponding calculation for a parametric bootstrap is similar. In effect the adjustment compares the simulated estimates T_r^* to the parameter value $\hat{\theta}_R = t(\bar{F}^*)$ obtained by fitting the model to data with EDF $\bar{F}^*$ rather than $\hat{F}$.

Example 9.3 (Calcium uptake data)   Table 9.3 shows the efficiency gains from using $B_{R,adj}$ in the nonparametric resampling experiment described in Example 9.2. The gains are broadly similar to those for balanced resampling, but smaller.

For parametric sampling the quantities $\hat{F}_r^*$ in (9.3) represent sets of data generated by parametric simulation from the fitted model, and the average $\bar{F}^*$ is the dataset of size Rn obtained by concatenating the simulated samples. Here the simplest parametric simulation is to generate data $y_j^* = \hat{\mu}_j + \varepsilon_j^*$, where the $\hat{\mu}_j$ are the fitted values from Example 7.7 and the ε_j^* are independent $N(0, 0.55^2)$ variables. In 100 replicates of this bootstrap with $R = 49$, the efficiency gains for estimating the biases of $\hat{\beta}_0$, $\hat{\beta}_1$, and $\hat{\sigma}$ were 24.7, 42.5, and 20.7; the effect of the adjustment is much more marked for the parametric than for the nonparametric bootstraps.   ∎

The same adjustment does not apply to the variance approximation V_R, higher moments or quantiles. Rather the linear approximation is used as a conventional control variate, as described in Section 9.3.

9.2.3 Some theory

Some theoretical insight into both balanced simulation and post-simulation balancing can be gained by means of the nonparametric delta method (Section 2.7). As before, let $\hat{F}^*$ denote the EDF of a bootstrap sample $Y_1^*, \ldots, Y_n^*$. The expansion of $T^* = t(\hat{F}^*)$ about $\hat{F}$ is, to second-order terms,

$$t(\hat{F}^*) \doteq t_Q(\hat{F}^*) = t(\hat{F}) + n^{-1} \sum_{j=1}^{n} l_j^* + \tfrac{1}{2} n^{-2} \sum_{j=1}^{n} \sum_{k=1}^{n} q_{jk}^*, \qquad (9.4)$$

where $l_j^* \equiv l(Y_j^*; \hat{F})$ and $q_{jk}^* \equiv q(Y_j^*, Y_k^*; \hat{F})$ are values of the empirical first- and second-order derivatives of t at $\hat{F}$; equation (9.4) is the same as (2.41), but with $\hat{F}$ and F replaced by $\hat{F}^*$ and $\hat{F}$. We call the right-hand side of (9.4) the *quadratic approximation* to T^*. Omission of the final term leaves the linear approximation

$$t_L(\hat{F}^*) = t(\hat{F}) + n^{-1} \sum_{j=1}^{n} l_j^*, \qquad (9.5)$$

which is the basis of the variance approximation v_L; equation (9.5) is simply a recasting of (2.44).

In terms of the frequencies f_j^* with which the y_j appear in the bootstrap sample and the empirical influence values $l_j = l(y_j; \hat{F})$ and $q_{jk} = q(y_j, y_k; \hat{F})$, the quadratic approximation (9.4) is

$$T_Q^* = t + n^{-1} \sum_{j=1}^{n} f_j^* l_j + \tfrac{1}{2} n^{-2} \sum_{j=1}^{n} \sum_{k=1}^{n} f_j^* f_k^* q_{jk}, \qquad (9.6)$$

in abbreviated notation. Recall that $\sum_j l_j = 0$ and $\sum_j q_{jk} = \sum_k q_{jk} = 0$. We can now compare the resampling schemes through the properties of the frequencies f_j^*.

Consider bootstrap simulation to estimate the bias of T. Suppose that there are R simulated samples, and that y_j appears in the rth with frequency f_{rj}^*, while T takes value T_r^*. Then from (9.2) and (9.6) the bias approximation $B_R = R^{-1} \sum T_r^* - t$ can be approximated by

$$R^{-1} \sum_{r=1}^{R} \left(t + n^{-1} \sum_{j=1}^{n} f_{rj}^* l_j + \tfrac{1}{2} n^{-2} \sum_{j=1}^{n} \sum_{k=1}^{n} f_{rj}^* f_{rk}^* q_{jk} \right) - t. \qquad (9.7)$$

In the ordinary resampling scheme, the rows of frequencies $(f_{r1}^*, \ldots, f_{rn}^*)$ are independent samples from the multinomial distribution with denominator n and probability vector $(n^{-1}, \ldots, n^{-1})$. This is the case in Table 9.1. In this situation the first and second joint moments of the frequencies are

$$E^*(f_{rj}^*) = 1, \quad \text{cov}^*(f_{rj}^*, f_{sk}^*) = \delta_{rs}(\delta_{jk} - n^{-1}),$$

where $\delta_{jk} = 1$ if $j = k$ and zero otherwise, and so forth; the higher cumulants are given in Problem 2.19. Straightforward calculations show that approximation (9.7) has mean $\frac{1}{2}n^{-2}\sum_j q_{jj}$ and variance

$$\frac{1}{Rn^2}\left[\sum_{j=1}^n l_j^2 + \frac{1}{n}\sum_{j=1}^n l_j q_{jj}\right.$$

$$\left. + \frac{1}{4n^2}\left\{\sum_{j=1}^n q_{jj}^2 - \frac{1}{n}\left(\sum_{j=1}^n q_{jj}\right)^2 + \frac{2(n-1)}{n}\sum_{j=1}^n\sum_{k=1}^n q_{jk}^2\right\}\right]. \quad (9.8)$$

For the balanced bootstrap, the joint distribution of the $R \times n$ table of frequencies f_{rj}^* is hypergeometric with row sums n and column sums R. Because $\sum_j l_j = 0$ and $\sum_r f_{rj}^* = R$ for all j, approximation (9.7) becomes

$$\frac{1}{2Rn^2}\sum_{j=1}^n\sum_{k=1}^n q_{jk}\sum_{r=1}^R f_{rj}^* f_{rk}^*.$$

Under balanced resampling one can show (Problem 9.1) that

$$E^*(f_{rj}^*) = 1, \quad \text{cov}^*(f_{rj}^*, f_{sk}^*) = \frac{(n\delta_{jk}-1)(R\delta_{rs}-1)}{nR-1}, \quad (9.9)$$

so the bias approximation (9.7) has mean

$$\frac{1}{2}\frac{n(R-1)}{(nR-1)}n^{-2}\sum_{j=1}^n q_{jj};$$

more painful calculations show that its variance is approximately

$$\frac{1}{4Rn^4}\left\{-2R^{-1}\sum_{j=1}^n q_{jj}^2 + 2n^{-2}R^{-2}\left(\sum_{j=1}^n q_{jj}\right)^2 + 2(n-1)n^{-1}\sum_{j=1}^n\sum_{k=1}^n q_{jk}^2\right\}. \quad (9.10)$$

The mean is almost the same under both schemes, but the leading term of the variance in (9.10) is smaller than in (9.8) because the term in (9.7) involving the l_j is held equal to zero by the balance constraints $\sum_r f_{rj}^* = R$. First-order balance ensures that the linear term in the expansion for B_R is held equal to its value of zero for the complete enumeration.

Post-simulation balance is closely related to the balanced bootstrap. It is straightforward to see that the quadratic nonparametric delta method approximation of $B_{R,adj}$ in (9.3) equals

$$\frac{1}{2}n^{-2}\sum_{j=1}^n\sum_{k=1}^n\left\{R^{-1}\sum_{r=1}^R f_{rj}^* f_{rk}^* - \left(R^{-1}\sum_{r=1}^R f_{rj}^*\right)\left(R^{-1}\sum_{r=1}^R f_{rk}^*\right)\right\}q_{jk}. \quad (9.11)$$

Figure 9.1 Efficiency comparisons for estimating biases of normal eigenvalues. The left panel compares the efficiency gains over the ordinary bias estimate due to balancing and post-simulation adjustment. The right panel shows the gains for the balanced estimate, as a function of the correlation between the statistic and its linear approximation; the solid line shows the theoretical relation. See text for details.

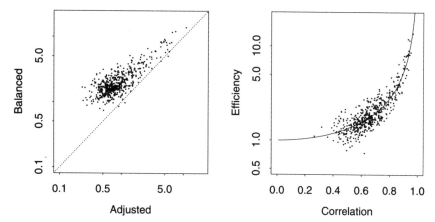

Like the balanced bootstrap estimate of bias, there are no linear terms in this expression. Re-centring has forced those terms to equal their population values of zero.

When the statistic T does not possess an expansion like (9.4), balancing may not help. In any case the correlation between the statistic and its linear approximation is important: if the correlation is low because the quadratic component of (9.4) is appreciable, then it may not be useful to reduce variation in the linear component. A rough approximation is that $\text{var}^*(B_R)$ is reduced by a factor equal to 1 minus the square of the correlation between T^* and T_L^* (Problem 9.5).

Example 9.4 (Normal eigenvalues)   For a numerical comparison of the efficiency gains in bias estimation from balanced resampling and post-simulation adjustment, we performed Monte Carlo experiments as follows. We generated n variates from the multivariate normal density with dimension 5 and identity covariance matrix, and took t to be the five eigenvalues of the sample covariance matrix. For each sample we used a large bootstrap to estimate the linear approximation t_L^* for each of the eigenvalues and then calculated the correlation c between t^* and t_L^*. We then estimated the gains in efficiency for balanced and adjusted estimates of bias calculated using the bootstrap with $R = 39$, using variances estimated from 100 independent bootstrap simulations.

Figure 9.1 shows the gains in efficiency for each of the 5 eigenvalues, for 50 sets of data with $n = 15$ and 50 sets with $n = 25$; there are 500 points in each panel. The left panel compares the efficiency gains for the balanced and adjusted schemes. Balanced sampling gives better gains than post-sample adjustment, but the difference is smaller at larger gains. The right panel shows the efficiency gains for the balanced scheme plotted against the correlation c. The solid line is the theoretical curve $(1 - c^2)^{-1}$. Knowledge of c would enable the efficiency gain to be predicted quite accurately, at least for $c > 0.8$. The potential improvement from balancing is not guaranteed to be worthwhile when $c < 0.7$. The corresponding plot for the adjusted estimates suggests that c must be at least 0.85 for a useful efficiency gain.   ■

This example suggests the following strategy when a good estimate of bias is required: perform a small standard unbalanced bootstrap, and use it to estimate the correlation between the statistic and its linear approximation. If that correlation exceeds about 0.7, it may be worthwhile to perform a balanced simulation, but otherwise it will not. If the correlation exceeds 0.85, post-simulation adjustment will usually be worthwhile, but otherwise it will not.

9.3 Control Methods

The basis of control methods is extra calculation during or after a series of simulations with the aim of reducing the overall variability of the estimator. This can be applied to nonparametric simulation in several ways. The post-simulation balancing described in the preceding section is a simple control method, in which we store the simulated random samples and make a single post-simulation calculation.

Most control methods involve extra calculations at the time of the simulation, and are applicable when there is a simple statistic that is highly correlated with T^*. Such a statistic is known as a *control variate*. The key idea is to write T^* in terms of the control variate and the difference between T^* and the control variate, and then to calculate the required properties for the control variate analytically, estimating only the differences by simulation.

Bias and variance

In many bootstrap contexts where T is an estimator, a natural choice for the control variate will be the linear approximation T_L^* defined in (2.44). The moments of T_L^* can be obtained theoretically using moments of the frequencies f_j^*. In ordinary random sampling the f_j^* are multinomial, so the mean and variance of T_L^* are

$$\mathrm{E}^*(T_L^*) = t, \quad \mathrm{var}^*(T_L^*) = n^{-2} \sum_{j=1}^{n} l_j^2 = v_L.$$

In order to use T_L^* as a control variate, we write $T^* = T_L^* + D^*$, so that D^* equals the difference $T^* - T_L^*$. The mean and variance of T^* can then be written

$$E^*(T^*) = E^*(T_L^*) + E^*(D^*), \quad \mathrm{var}^*(T^*) = \mathrm{var}^*(T_L^*) + 2\mathrm{cov}^*(T_L^*, D^*) + \mathrm{var}^*(D^*),$$

the leading terms of which are known. Only terms involving D^* need to be approximated by simulation. Given simulations $T_1^*, \ldots, T_R^*$ with corresponding linear approximations $T_{L,1}^*, \ldots, T_{L,R}^*$ and differences $D_r^* = T_r^* - T_{L,r}^*$, the mean and variance of T^* are estimated by

$$t + \bar{D}^*, \quad V_{R,con} = v_L + \frac{2}{R-1} \sum_{r=1}^{R} (T_{L,r}^* - \bar{T}_L^*)(D_r^* - \bar{D}^*) + \frac{1}{R-1} \sum_{r=1}^{R} (D_r^* - \bar{D}^*)^2,$$

$$(9.12)$$

where $\bar{T}_L^* = R^{-1} \sum_r T_{L,r}^*$ and $\bar{D}^* = R^{-1} \sum_r D_r^*$. Use of these and related approximations requires the calculation of the $T_{L,r}^*$ as well as the T_r^*.

The estimated bias of T^* based on (9.12) is $B_{R,con} = \bar{D}^*$. This is closely related to the estimate obtained under balanced simulation and to the re-centred bias estimate $B_{R,adj}$. Like them, it ensures that the linear component of the bias estimate equals its population value, zero. Detailed calculation shows that all three approaches achieve the same variance reduction for the bias estimate in large samples. However, the variance estimate in (9.12) based on linear approximation is less variable than the estimated variances obtained under the other approaches, because its leading term is not random.

Example 9.5 (City population data)   To see how effective control methods are in reducing the variability of a variance estimate, we consider the ratio statistic for the city population data in Table 2.1, with $n = 10$. For 100 bootstrap simulations with $R = 50$, we calculated the usual variance estimate $v_R = (R-1)^{-1} \sum (t_t^* - \bar{t}^*)^2$ and the estimate $v_{R,con}$ from (9.12). The estimated gain in efficiency calculated from the 100 simulations is 1.92, which though worthwhile is not large. The correlation between t^* and t_L^* is 0.94.

For the larger set of data in Table 1.3, with $n = 49$, we repeated the experiment with $R = 100$. Here the gain in efficiency is 7.5, and the correlation is 0.99.

Figure 9.2 shows scatter plots of the estimated variances in these experiments. For both sample sizes the values of $v_{R,con}$ are more concentrated than the values of v_R, though the main effect of control is to increase underestimates of the true variances.   ■

Example 9.6 (Frets heads)   The data of Example 3.24 are a sample of $n = 25$ cases, each consisting of 4 measurements. We consider the efficiency gains from using $v_{R,con}$ to estimate the bootstrap variances of the eigenvalues of their covariance matrix. The correlations between the eigenvalues and their linear approximations are 0.98, 0.89, 0.85 and 0.74, and the gains in efficiency estimated from 100 replicate bootstraps of size $R = 39$ are 2.3, 1.6, 0.95 and

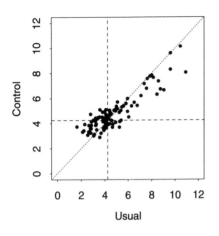 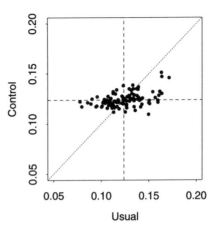

Figure 9.2 Comparison of estimated variances ($\times 10^{-2}$) for city population ratio, using usual and control methods, for $n = 10$ with $R = 50$ (left) and for $n = 49$ with $R = 100$ (right). The dotted line is the line $x = y$, and the dashed lines show the "true" variances, estimated from a much larger simulation.

1.3. The four left panels of Figure 9.3 show plots of the values of $v_{R,con}$ against the values of v_R. No strong pattern is discernible.

To get a more systematic idea of the effectiveness of control methods in this setting, we repeated the experiment outlined in Example 9.4 and compared the usual and control estimates of the variances of the five eigenvalues. The results for the five eigenvalues and $n = 15$ and 25 are shown in Figure 9.3. Gains in efficiency are not guaranteed unless the correlation between the statistic and its linear approximation is 0.80 or more, and they are not large unless the correlation is close to one. The line $y = (1 - x^4)^{-1}$ summarizes the efficiency gain well, though we have not attempted to justify this.   ∎

Quantiles

Control methods may also be applied to quantiles. Suppose that we have the simulated values $t_1^*, \ldots, t_R^*$ of a statistic, and that the corresponding control variates and differences are available. We now sort the differences by the values of the control variates. For example, if our control variate is a linear approximation, with $R = 4$ and $t_{L,2}^* < t_{L,1}^* < t_{L,4}^* < t_{L,3}^*$, we put the differences in order $d_2^*, d_1^*, d_4^*, d_3^*$. The procedure now is to replace the p quantile of the linear approximation by a theoretical approximation, t_p, for $p = 1/(R+1), \ldots, R/(R+1)$, thereby replacing $t_{(r)}^*$ with $t_{C,r}^* = t_p + d_{\pi(r)}^*$, where $\pi(r)$ is the rank of $t_{L,r}^*$. In our example we would obtain $t_{C,1}^* = t_{0.2} + d_2^*$, $t_{C,2}^* = t_{0.4} + d_1^*$, $t_{C,3}^* = t_{0.6} + d_4^*$, and $t_{C,4}^* = t_{0.8} + d_3^*$. We now estimate the pth quantile of the distribution of T by $t_{C,(r)}^*$, i.e. the rth quantile of $t_{C,1}^*, \ldots, t_{C,R}^*$. If the control variate is highly correlated with T^*, the bulk of the variability in the estimated quantiles will have been removed by using the theoretical approximation.

Figure 9.3 Efficiency comparisons for estimating variances of eigenvalues. The left panels compare the usual and control variance estimates for the data of Example 3.24, for which $n = 25$, when $R = 39$. The right panel shows the gains made by the control estimate in 50 samples of sizes 15 and 25 from the normal distribution, as a function of the correlation between the statistic and its linear approximation; the solid line shows the line $y = (1 - x^4)^{-1}$. See text for details.

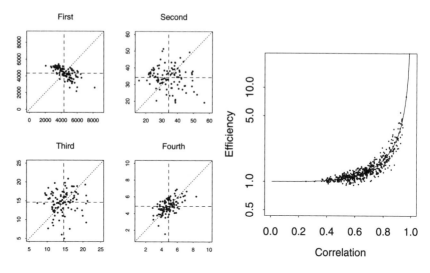

One desirable property of the control quantile estimates is that, unlike most other variance reduction methods, their accuracy improves with increasing n as well as R.

There are various ways to calculate the quantiles of the control variate. The preferred approach is to calculate the entire distribution of the control variate by saddlepoint approximation (Section 9.5), and to read off the required quantiles t_p. This is better than other methods, such as Cornish–Fisher expansion, because it guarantees that the quantiles of the control variate will increase with p.

Example 9.7 (Returns data)   To assess the usefulness of the control method just described, we consider setting studentized bootstrap confidence intervals for the rate of return in Example 6.3. We use case resampling to estimate quantiles of $T^* = (\hat{\beta}_1^* - \hat{\beta}_1)/S^*$, where $\hat{\beta}_1$ is the estimate of the regression slope, and S^2 is the robust estimated variance of $\hat{\beta}_1$ based on the linear approximation to $\hat{\beta}_1$.

For a single bootstrap simulation we calculated three estimates of the quantiles of T^*: the usual estimates, the order statistics $t^*_{(1)} < \cdots < t^*_{(R)}$; the control estimates $t^*_{C,(r)}$, taking the control variate to be the linear approximation to T^* based on exact empirical influence values; and the control estimates obtained using the linear approximation with empirical influence values estimated by regression on the frequency array for the same bootstrap. In each case the quantiles of the control variate were obtained by saddlepoint approximation, as outlined in Example 9.13 below. We used $R = 999$ and repeated the experiment 50 times in order to estimate the variance of the quantile estimates. We

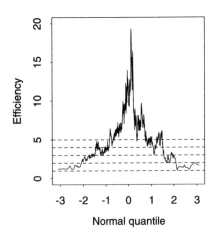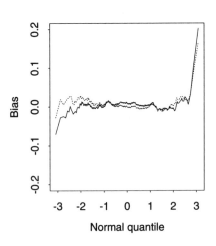

Figure 9.4 Efficiency and bias comparisons for estimating quantiles of a studentized bootstrap statistic for the returns data, based on a bootstrap of size $R = 999$. The left panel shows the variance of the usual quantile estimate divided by the variance of the control estimate based on an exact linear approximation, plotted against the corresponding normal quantile. The dashed lines show efficiencies of 1, 2, 3, 4 and 5. The right panel shows the estimated biases for the exact control (solid) and estimated control (dots) quantiles. See text for details.

estimated their bias by comparing them with quantiles of T^* obtained from 100 000 bootstrap resamples.

Figure 9.4 shows the efficiency gains of the exact control estimates relative to the usual estimates. The efficiency gain based on the linear approximation is not shown, but it is very similar. The right panel shows the biases of the two control estimates. The efficiency gains are largest for central quantiles, and are of order 1.5–3 for the quantiles of most interest, at about 0.025–0.05 and 0.95–0.975. There is some suggestion that the control estimates based on the linear approximation have the smaller bias, but both sets of biases are negligible at all but the most extreme quantiles.

The efficiency gains in this example are broadly in line with simulations reported in the literature; see also Example 9.10 below.   ∎

9.4 Importance Resampling

9.4.1 Basic estimators

Importance sampling

Most of our simulation calculations can be thought of as approximate integrations, with the aim of approximating

$$\mu = \int m(y^*)\, dG(y^*)$$

for some function $m(\cdot)$, where y^* is abbreviated notation for a simulated dataset. In expression (9.1), for example, $m(y^*) = t(y^*)$, and the distribution G for $Y^* = (Y_1^*, \ldots, Y_n^*)$ puts mass n^{-n} on each element of the set $\mathscr{S} = \{y_1, \ldots, y_n\}^n$.

When it is impossible to evaulate the integral directly, our usual approach is to generate R independent samples $Y_1^*, \ldots, Y_R^*$ from G, and to estimate μ by

$$\hat{\mu}_G = R^{-1} \sum_{r=1}^{R} m(Y_r^*).$$

This estimator has mean and variance

$$E_G^*(\hat{\mu}_G) = \int m(y^*) \, dG(y^*) = \mu, \quad \text{var}_G^*(\hat{\mu}_G) = R^{-1} \left\{ \int m(y^*)^2 \, dG(y^*) - \mu^2 \right\}, \tag{9.13}$$

and so is unbiased for μ. In the situation mentioned above, this is a re-expression of ordinary bootstrap simulation. We use notation such as $\hat{\mu}_G$ and E_G^* to indicate that estimates are calculated from random variables simulated from G, and that moment calculations are with respect to the distribution G.

One problem with $\hat{\mu}_G$ is that some values of y^* may contribute much more to μ than others. For example, suppose that the aim is to approximate the probability $\Pr^*(T^* \leq t_0 \mid \hat{F})$, for which we would take $m(y^*) = I\{t(y^*) \leq t_0\}$, where I is the indicator function. If the event $t(y^*) \leq t_0$ is rare, then most of the simulations will contribute zero to the integral. The aim of *importance sampling* is to sample more frequently from those "important" values of y^* whose contributions to the integral are greatest. This is achieved by sampling from a distribution that concentrates probability on these y^*, and then weighting the values of $m(y^*)$ so as to mimic the approximation we would have used if we had sampled from G. Importance sampling in the case of the nonparametric bootstrap amounts to re-weighting samples from the empirical distribution function $\hat{F}$, so in this context it is sometimes known as *importance resampling*.

The identity that motivates importance sampling is

$$\mu = \int m(y^*) \, dG(y^*) = \int m(y^*) \frac{dG(y^*)}{dH(y^*)} \, dH(y^*), \tag{9.14}$$

where necessarily the support of H includes the support of G. Importance sampling approximates the right-hand side of (9.14) using independent samples $Y_1^*, \ldots, Y_R^*$ from H. The new approximation for μ is the *raw importance sampling estimate*

$$\hat{\mu}_{H,raw} = R^{-1} \sum_{r=1}^{R} m(Y_r^*) w(Y_r^*), \tag{9.15}$$

where $w(y^*) = dG(y^*)/dH(y^*)$ is known as the *importance sampling weight*. The estimate $\hat{\mu}_{H,raw}$ has mean μ by virtue of (9.14), so is unbiased, and has variance

$$\text{var}_H^* \left(\hat{\mu}_{H,raw} \right) = R^{-1} \left\{ \int m(y^*)^2 w(y^*)^2 \, dH(y^*) - \mu^2 \right\} \tag{9.16}$$

$$= R^{-1} \left\{ \int m(y^*)^2 w(y^*) \, dG(y^*) - \mu^2 \right\}. \tag{9.17}$$

Our aim is now to choose H so that

$$\int m(y^*)^2 w(y^*) \, dG(y^*) < \int m(y^*)^2 \, dG(y^*).$$

Clearly the best choice is the one for which $m(y^*)w(y^*) = \mu$, because then $\hat\mu_{H,raw}$ has zero variance, but this is not usable because μ is unknown. In general it is hard to choose H, but sometimes the choice is straightforward, as we now outline.

Tilted distributions

A potentially important application is calculation of tail probabilities such as $\pi = \Pr^*(T^* \le t_0 \mid \hat F)$, and the corresponding quantiles of T^*. For probabilities $m(y^*)$ is taken to be the indicator function $I\{t(y^*) \le t_0\}$, and if $y_1, \ldots, y_n$ is a single random sample from the EDF $\hat F$ then $dG(y^*) = n^{-n}$. Any admissible nonparametric choice for H is a multinomial distribution with probability p_j on y_j, for $j = 1, \ldots, n$. Then

$$dH(y^*) = \prod_j p_j^{f_j^*},$$

where f_j^* counts how many components of Y^* equal y_j. We would like to choose the probabilities p_j to minimize $\mathrm{var}_H^*(\hat\mu_{H,raw})$, or at least to make this much smaller than $R^{-1}\pi(1-\pi)$. This appears to be impossible in general, but if T is close to normal we can get a good approximate solution.

Suppose that T^* has a linear approximation T_L^* which is accurate, and that the $N(t,v)$ approximation for T_L^* under ordinary resampling is accurate. Then the probability π we are trying to approximate is roughly $\Phi\left\{(t_0 - t)/v^{1/2}\right\}$. If we were using simulation to approximate such a normal probability directly, then provided that $t_0 \le t$ a good (near-optimal) importance sampling method would be to generate t^*s from the $N(t_0, v_L)$ distribution, where v_L is the nonparametric delta method variance. It turns out that we can arrange that this happen approximately for T^* by setting

$$p_j \propto \exp(\lambda l_j), \qquad j = 1, \ldots, n, \qquad (9.18)$$

where the l_j are the usual empirical influence values for t. The result of Problem 9.10 shows that under this distribution T^* is approximately $N(t + \lambda n v_L, v_L)$, so the appropriate choice for λ in (9.18) is approximately $\lambda = (t_0 - t)/(n v_L)$, again provided $t_0 \le t$; in some cases it is possible to choose λ to make T^* have mean exactly t_0. The choice of probabilities given by (9.18) is called an *exponential tilting* of the original values n^{-1}. This idea is also used in Sections 4.4, 5.3, and 10.2.2.

Table 9.4 shows approximate values of the efficiency $R^{-1}\pi(1-\pi)/\mathrm{var}^*(\hat\mu_{H,raw})$ of near-optimal importance resampling for various values of the tail probability π. The values were calculated using normal approximations for the distributions

Table 9.4 Approximate efficiencies for estimating tail probability π under importance sampling with optimal tilted EDF when T is approximately normal.

π	0.01	0.025	0.05	0.2	0.5	0.8	0.95	0.975	0.99
Efficiency	37	17	9.5	3.0	1.0	0.12	0.003	0.0005	0.00004

of T^* under G and H; see Problem 9.8. The entries in the table suggest that for $\pi \leq 0.05$ we could attain the same accuracy as with ordinary resampling with R reduced by a factor larger than about 10. Also shown in the table is the result of applying the exponential tilted importance resampling distribution when $t > t_0$, or $\pi > 0.5$: then importance resampling will be worse — possibly *much* worse — than ordinary resampling.

This last observation is a warning: straightforward importance sampling can be bad if misapplied. We can see how from (9.17). If $dH(y^*)$ becomes very small where $m(y^*)$ and $dG(y^*)$ are not small, then $w(y^*) = dG(y^*)/dH(y^*)$ will become very large and inflate the variance. For the tail probability calculation, if $t_0 > t$ then all samples y_r^* with $t(y_r^*) \leq t_0$ contribute $R^{-1}w(y_r^*)$ to $\hat{\mu}_{H,raw}$, and some of these contributions are enormous: although rare, they wreak havoc on $\hat{\mu}_{H,raw}$.

A little thought shows that for $t_0 > t$ one should apply importance sampling to estimate $1 - \pi = \mathrm{Pr}^*(T^* \geq t_0)$ and subtract the result from 1, rather than estimate π directly.

Quantiles

To see how quantiles are estimated, suppose that we want to estimate the α quantile of the distribution of T^*, and T^* is approximately $N(t, v_L)$ under $G = \hat{F}$. Then we take a tilted distribution for H such that T^* is approximately $N(t + z_\alpha v_L^{1/2}, v_L)$. For the situation we have been discussing, the exponential tilted distribution (9.18) will be near-optimal with $\lambda = z_\alpha/(nv_L^{1/2})$, and in large samples this will be superior to $G = \hat{F}$ for any $\alpha \neq \frac{1}{2}$. So suppose that we have used importance resampling from this tilted distribution to obtain values $t_1^* < \cdots < t_R^*$ with corresponding weights $w_1^*, \ldots, w_R^*$. Then for $\alpha < \frac{1}{2}$ the raw quantile estimate is t_M^*, where

$$\frac{1}{R+1}\sum_{r=1}^{M} w_r^* \leq \alpha < \frac{1}{R+1}\sum_{r=1}^{M+1} w_r^*, \tag{9.19}$$

while for $\alpha > \frac{1}{2}$ we define M by

$$\frac{1}{R+1}\sum_{r=M}^{R} w_r^* \leq 1 - \alpha < \frac{1}{R+1}\sum_{r=M+1}^{R} w_r^*;$$

see Problem 9.9. When there is no importance sampling we have $w_r^* \equiv 1$, and the estimate equals the usual $t_{((R+1)\alpha)}^*$.

The variation in $w(y^*)$ and its implications are illustrated in the following example. We discuss stabilizing modifications to raw importance resampling in the next subsection.

Example 9.8 (Gravity data)   For an example of importance resampling, we follow Example 4.19 and consider testing for a difference in means for the last two series of Table 3.1. Here we use the studentized pivot test, with observed test statistic

$$z_0 = \frac{\bar{y}_2 - \bar{y}_1}{\left(s_2^2/n_2 + s_1^2/n_1\right)^{1/2}}, \qquad (9.20)$$

where $\bar{y}_i$ and s_i^2 are the average and variance of the sample $y_{i1}, \ldots, y_{in_i}$, for $i = 1, 2$. The test compares z_0 to the general distribution of the studentized pivot

$$Z = \frac{\bar{Y}_2 - \bar{Y}_1 - (\mu_2 - \mu_1)}{\left(S_2^2/n_2 + S_1^2/n_1\right)^{1/2}};$$

z_0 is the value taken by Z under the null hypothesis $\mu_1 = \mu_2$. The observed value of z_0 is 1.84, with normal one-sided significance probability $\Pr(Z \geq z_0) = 0.033$.

We aim to estimate $\Pr(Z \geq z_0)$ by $\Pr^*(Z^* \geq z_0 \mid \hat{F})$, where $\hat{F}$ stands for the EDFs of the two samples. In this case $y^* = (y_{11}^*, \ldots, y_{1n_1}^*, y_{21}^*, \ldots, y_{2n_2}^*)$, and G is the joint density under the two EDFs, so the probability on each simulated dataset is $dG(y^*) = n_1^{-n_1} \times n_2^{-n_2}$.

Because $z_0 > 0$ and the P-value is clearly below $\frac{1}{2}$, raw importance sampling is appropriate and the estimated P-value is

$$\hat{\mu}_{H,raw} = R^{-1} \sum_{r=1}^R I\{z_r^* \geq z_0\} w_r^*, \qquad w_r^* = \frac{dG(y_r^*)}{dH(y_r^*)}.$$

The choice of H is made by analogy with the single-sample case discussed earlier. The two EDFs are tilted so as to make Z^* approximately $N(z_0, v_L)$, which should be near-optimal. This is done by working with the linear approximation

$$z_L^* = z + n_1^{-1} \sum_{j=1}^{n_1} f_{1j}^* l_{1j} + n_2^{-1} \sum_{j=1}^{n_2} f_{2j}^* l_{2j},$$

where f_{1j}^* and f_{2j}^* are the bootstrap sample frequencies of y_{1j} and y_{2j}, and the empirical influence values are

$$l_{1j} = -\frac{y_{1j} - \bar{y}_1}{\left(s_2^2/n_2 + s_1^2/n_1\right)^{1/2}}, \qquad l_{2j} = \frac{y_{2j} - \bar{y}_2}{\left(s_2^2/n_2 + s_1^2/n_1\right)^{1/2}}.$$

We take H to be the pair of exponential tilted distributions

$$p_{1j} = \Pr(Y_1^* = y_{1j}) \propto \exp(\lambda l_{1j}/n_1), \qquad p_{2j} = \Pr(Y_2^* = y_{2j}) \propto \exp(\lambda l_{2j}/n_2), \qquad (9.21)$$

Figure 9.5 Importance resampling to test for a location difference between series 7 and 8 of the gravity data. The solid points in the left panel are the weights w_r^* and bootstrap statistics z_r^* for $R = 99$ importance resamples; the hollow points are the pairs (z_r^*, w_r^*) for 99 ordinary resamples. The right panel compares the survivor function $\mathrm{Pr}^*(Z^* > z^*)$ estimated from 50 000 ordinary bootstrap resamples (heavy solid) with estimates of it based on the 99 ordinary bootstrap samples (dashes) and the 99 importance resamples (solid). The vertical dotted lines show z_0.

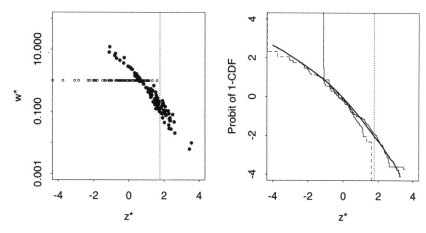

where λ is chosen so that Z_L^* has mean z_0: this should make Z^* approximately $N(z_0, v_L)$ under H. The explicit equation for λ is

$$\frac{\sum_{j=1}^{n_1} l_{1j} \exp(\lambda l_{1j}/n_1)}{\sum_{j=1}^{n_1} \exp(\lambda l_{1j}/n_1)} + \frac{\sum_{j=1}^{n_2} l_{2j} \exp(\lambda l_{2j}/n_2)}{\sum_{j=1}^{n_2} \exp(\lambda l_{2j}/n_2)} = z_0,$$

with approximate solution $\lambda = z_0$ since $v_L \doteq 1$. For our data the exact solution is $\lambda = 1.42$.

Figure 9.5 shows results for $R = 99$ simulations. The solid points in the left panel are the weights

$$w_r^* = \frac{dG(y_r^*)}{dH(y_r^*)} = \exp\left\{-\sum_{j=1}^{n_1} f_{1j}^* \log\left(n_1 p_{1j}\right) - \sum_{j=1}^{n_2} f_{2j}^* \log\left(n_2 p_{2j}\right)\right\}$$

plotted against the bootstrap values z_r^* for the importance resamples. These values of z_r^* are shifted to the right relative to the hollow points, which show the values of z_r^* and w_r^* (all equal to 1) for 99 ordinary resamples. The values of w_r^* for the importance re-weighting vary over several orders of magnitude, with the largest values when $z_r^* \ll z_0$. But only those for $z_r^* \geq z_0$ contribute to $\hat{\mu}_{H,raw}$.

How well does this single importance resampling distribution work for estimating all values of the survivor function $\mathrm{Pr}^*(Z^* \geq z)$? The heavy solid line in the right panel shows the "true" survivor function of Z^* estimated from 50 000 ordinary bootstrap simulations. The lighter solid line is the importance resampling estimate

$$R^{-1} \sum_{r=1}^{R} w_r^* I\{z_r^* \geq z\}$$

with $R = 99$, and the dotted line is the estimate based on 99 ordinary bootstrap samples from the null distribution. The importance resampling estimate follows the "true" survivor function accurately close to z_0 but does poorly for negative z^*. The usual estimate does best near $z^* = 0$ but poorly in the tail region of interest; the estimated significance probability is $\hat{\mu}_G = 0$. While the usual estimate decreases by R^{-1} at each z_r^*, the weighted estimate decreases by much smaller jumps close to z_0; the raw importance sampling tail probability estimate is $\hat{\mu}_{H,raw} = 0.015$, which is very close to the true value. The weighted survivor function estimate has large jumps in its left tail, where the estimate is unreliable.

In 50 repetitions of this experiment the ordinary and raw importance resampling tail probability estimates had variances 2.09×10^{-4} and 2.63×10^{-5}. For a tail probability of 0.015 this efficiency gain of about 8 is smaller than would be predicted from Table 9.4, the reason being that the distribution of z^* is rather skewed and the normal approximation to it is poor.　　　　■

In general there are several ways to obtain tilted distributions. We can use exponential tilting with exact empirical influence values, if these are readily available. Or we can estimate the influence values by regression using R_0 initial ordinary bootstrap resamples, as decribed in Section 2.7.4. Another way of using an initial set of bootstrap samples is to derive weighted smooth distributions as in (3.39): illustrations of this are given later in Examples 9.9 and 9.11.

9.4.2 Improved estimators

Ratio and regression estimators

One simple modification of the raw importance sampling estimate is based on the fact that the average weight $R^{-1} \sum_r w(Y_r^*)$ from any particular simulation will not equal its theoretical value of $E^*\{w(Y^*)\} = 1$. This suggests that the weights $w(Y_r^*)$ be normalized, so that (9.15) is replaced by the *importance resampling ratio estimate*

$$\hat{\mu}_{H,rat} = \frac{\sum_{r=1}^{R} m(Y_r^*)w(Y_r^*)}{\sum_{r=1}^{R} w(Y_r^*)}. \tag{9.22}$$

To some extent this controls the effect of very large fluctuations in the weights.

In practice it is better to treat the weight as a control variate or covariate. Since our aim in choosing H is to concentrate sampling where $m(\cdot)$ is largest, the values of $m(Y_r^*)w(Y_r^*)$ and $w(Y_r^*)$ should be correlated. If so, and if the average weight differs from its expected value of one under simulation from H, then the estimate $\hat{\mu}_{H,raw}$ probably differs from its expected value μ. This motivates the covariance adjustment made in the *importance resampling regression estimate*

$$\hat{\mu}_{H,reg} = \hat{\mu}_{H,raw} - b(\bar{w}^* - 1), \qquad (9.23)$$

where $\bar{w}^* = R^{-1} \sum_r w(Y_r^*)$, and b is the slope of the linear regression of the $m(Y_r^*)w(Y_r^*)$ on the $w(Y_r^*)$. The estimator $\hat{\mu}_{H,reg}$ is the predicted value for $m(Y^*)w(Y^*)$ at the point $w(Y^*) = 1$.

The adjustments made to $\hat{\mu}_{H,raw}$ in both $\hat{\mu}_{H,rat}$ and $\hat{\mu}_{H,reg}$ may induce bias, but such biases will be of order R^{-1} and will usually be negligible relative to simulation standard errors. Calculations outlined in Problem 9.12 indicate that for large R the regression estimator should outperform the raw and ratio estimators, but the improvement depends on the problem, and in practice the raw estimator of a tail probability or quantile is usually the best.

Defensive mixtures

A second improvement aims to prevent the weight $w(y^*)$ from varying wildly. Suppose that H is a mixture of distributions, $\pi H_1 + (1-\pi)H_2$, where $0 < \pi < 1$. The distributions H_1 and H_2 are chosen so that the corresponding probabilities are not both small simultaneously. Then the weights

$$dG(y^*)/\{\pi dH_1(y^*) + (1 - \pi)dH_2(y^*)\}$$

will vary less, because even if $dH_1(y^*)$ is very small, $dH_2(y^*)$ will keep the denominator away from zero and vice versa. This choice of H is known as a *defensive mixture distribution*, and it should do particularly well if many estimates, with different $m(y^*)$, are to be calculated. The mixture is applied by stratified sampling, that is by generating exactly πR observations from H_1 and the rest from H_2, and using $\hat{\mu}_{H,reg}$ as usual.

The components of the mixture H should be chosen to ensure that the relevant range of values of t^* is well covered, but beyond this the detailed choice is not critical. For example, if we are interested in quantiles of T^* for probabilities between α and $1 - \alpha$, then it would be sensible to target H_1 at the α quantile and H_2 at the $1 - \alpha$ quantile, most simply by the exponential tilting method described earlier. As a further precaution we might add a third component to the mixture, such as G, to ensure stable performance in the middle of the distribution. In general the mixture could have many components, but careful choice of two or three will usually be adequate. Always the application of the mixture should be by stratified sampling, to reduce variation.

Example 9.9 (Gravity data)   To illustrate the above ideas, we again consider the hypothesis testing problem of Example 9.8. The left panel of Figure 9.6

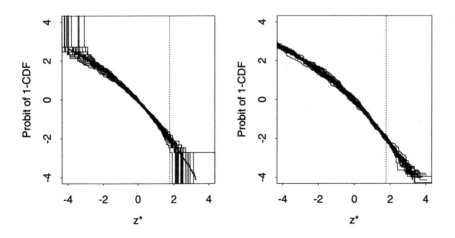

Figure 9.6 Importance resampling to test for a location difference between series 7 and 8 of the gravity data. In each panel the heavy solid line is the survivor function $\Pr^*(Z^* > z^*)$ estimated from 50 000 ordinary bootstrap resamples and the vertical dotted lines show z_0. The left panel shows the estimates for 20 ordinary bootstraps of size 299. The right panel shows 20 importance resampling estimates using 299 samples with a regression estimate following resampling from a defensive mixture distribution with three components. See text for details.

shows 20 replicate estimates of the null survivor function of z^*, using ordinary bootstrap resampling with $R = 299$. The right panel shows 20 estimates of the survivor function using the regression estimate $\hat{\mu}_{H,reg}$ after simulations with a defensive mixture distribution. This mixture has three components which are G (the two EDFs), and two pairs of exponential tilted distributions targeted at the 0.025 and 0.975 quantiles of Z^*. From our earlier discussion these distributions are given by (9.21) with $\lambda = \pm 2/v_L$: we shall denote the first pair of distributions by probabilities p_{1j} and p_{2j}, and the second by probabilities q_{1j} and q_{2j}. The first component G was used for $R_1 = 99$ samples, the second component (the ps) for $R_2 = 100$ and the third component (the qs) for $R_3 = 100$: the mixture proportions were therefore $\pi_j = R_j/(R_1 + R_2 + R_3)$ for $j = 1, 2, 3$. The importance resampling weights were

$$w(y^*) = \frac{n_1^{-n_1} n_2^{-n_2}}{\pi_1 \left(\frac{1}{n_1}\right)^{n_1} \left(\frac{1}{n_2}\right)^{n_2} + \pi_2 \prod p_{1j}^{f_{1j}^*} \prod p_{2j}^{f_{2j}^*} + \pi_3 \prod q_{1j}^{f_{1j}^*} \prod q_{2j}^{f_{2j}^*}},$$

where as before f_{1j}^* and f_{2j}^* respectively count how many times y_{1j} and y_{2j} appear in the resample.

For convenience we estimated the CDF of Z^* at the sample values z_s^*. The regression estimate at z_s^* is obtained by setting $m(y_r^*) = I\{z(y_r^*) \leq z(y_s^*)\}$ and calculating (9.23); this appears to involve 299 regressions for each CDF estimate, but Problem 9.13 shows how in fact just one matrix calculation is needed. The importance resampling estimate of the CDF is about as variable as the ordinary estimate over most of the distribution, but much less variable well into the tails.

For a more systematic comparison, we calculated the ratio of the mean

Table 9.5 Efficiency gains (ratios of mean squared errors) for estimating a tail probability, a bias, a variance and two quantiles for the gravity data, using importance resampling estimators together with defensive mixture distributions, compared to ordinary resampling. The mixtures have R_1 ordinary bootstrap samples mixed with R_2 samples exponentially tilted to the 0.025 quantile of z^*, and with R_3 samples exponentially tilted to the 0.975 quantile of z^*. See text for details.

Mixture			Estimate	Estimand				
R_1	R_2	R_3		$\mathrm{Pr}^*(Z^* \geq z_0)$	$\mathrm{E}^*(Z^*)$	$\mathrm{var}^*(Z^*)$	$z^*_{0.05}$	$z^*_{0.025}$
		299	Raw	11.2	0.04	0.03	0.07	—
			Ratio	3.5	0.06	0.05	0.06	0.05
			Regression	12.4	0.18	0.07	0.06	0.04
99	100	100	Raw	3.8	0.73	1.5	1.3	2.5
			Ratio	3.4	0.79	1.5	0.93	1.3
			Regression	4.0	0.93	1.6	0.87	1.2
19	140	140	Raw	3.9	0.34	1.2	0.96	2.6
			Ratio	2.3	0.43	0.82	0.48	1.1
			Regression	4.3	0.69	1.3	0.44	1.3

squared error from ordinary resampling to that when using defensive mixture distributions to estimate the tail probability $\mathrm{Pr}^*(Z^* \geq z_0)$ with $z_0 = 1.77$, two quantiles, and the bias $\mathrm{E}^*(Z^*)$ and the variance $\mathrm{var}^*(Z^*)$ for sampling from the two series. The mixture distributions have the same three components as before, but with different values for the numbers of samples R_1, R_2 and R_3 from each. Table 9.5 gives the results for three resampling mixtures with a total of $R = 299$ resamples in each case. The mean squared errors were estimated from 100 replicate bootstraps, with "true" values obtained from a single bootstrap of size 50 000. The main contribution to the mean squared error is from variance rather than bias.

The first resampling distribution is not a mixture, but simply the exponential tilt to the 0.975 quantile. This gives the best estimates of the tail probability, with efficiencies for raw and regression estimates in line with Example 9.8, but it gives very poor estimates of the other quantities. For the other two mixtures the regression estimates are best for estimating the mean and variance, while the raw estimates are best for the quantiles and not really worse for the tail probability. Both mixtures are about the same for tail quantiles, while the first mixture is better for the moments.

In this case the efficiency gains for tail probabilities and quantiles predicted by Table 9.4 are unrealistic, for two reasons. First, the table compares 299 ordinary simulations with just 100 tilted to each tail of the first mixture distribution, so we would expect the variance for a tail quantity based on the mixture to be larger by a factor of about three; this is just what we see when the first distribution is compared to the second. Secondly, the distribution of Z^* is quite skewed, which considerably reduces the efficiency out as far as the 0.95 quantile.

We conclude that the regression estimate is best for estimating central quantities, that the raw estimate is best for quantiles, that results for estimating quantiles are insensitive to the precise mixture used, and that theoretical gains may not be realized in practice unless a single tail quantity is to be estimated. This is in line with other studies.   ∎

9.4.3 Balanced importance resampling

Importance resampling works best for the extreme quantiles corresponding to small tail probabilities, but is less effective in the centre of a distribution. Balanced resampling, on the other hand, works best in the centre of a distribution. Balanced importance resampling aims to get the best of both worlds by combining the two, as follows.

Suppose that we wish to generate R balanced resamples in which y_j has overall probability p_j of occurring. To do this exactly in general is impossible for finite nR, but we can do so approximately by applying the following simple algorithm; a more efficient algorithm is described in Problem 9.14.

Algorithm 9.2 (Balanced importance resampling)

Choose $R_1 \doteq nRp_1, \ldots, R_n \doteq nRp_n$, such that $R_1 + \cdots + R_n = nR$.

Concatenate R_1 copies of y_1 with R_2 copies of y_2 with ... with R_n copies of y_n, to form $\mathcal{Y}$.

Permute the nR elements of $\mathcal{Y}$ at random to form $\mathcal{Y}^*$, and read off the R balanced importance resamples as sets of n successive elements of $\mathcal{Y}^*$.   •

A simple way to choose the R_j is to set $R'_j = 1 + [n(R-1)p_j]$, $j = 1, \ldots, n$, where $[\cdot]$ denotes integer part, and to set $R_j = R'_j + 1$ for the $d = nR - (R'_1 + \cdots + R'_n)$ values of j with the largest values of $nRp_j - R'_j$; we set $R_j = R'_j$ for the rest. This ensures that all the observations are represented in the bootstrap simulation.

Provided that R is large relative to n, individual samples will be approximately independent and hence the weight associated with a sample having frequencies $(f_1^*, \ldots, f_n^*)$ is approximately

$$\prod_{j=1}^{n} \left(\frac{R}{R_j} \right)^{f_j^*} \doteq \prod_{j=1}^{n} (np_j)^{-f_j^*};$$

this does not take account of the fact that sampling is without replacement.

Figure 9.7 shows the theoretical large-sample efficiencies of balanced resampling, importance resampling, and balanced importance resampling for estimating the quantiles of a normal statistic. Ordinary balance gives maximum efficiency of 2.76 at the centre of the distribution, while importance

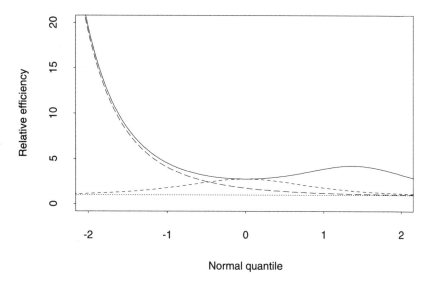

Figure 9.7 Asymptotic efficiencies of balanced importance resampling (solid), importance resampling (large dashes), and balanced resampling (small dashes) for estimating the quantiles of a normal statistic. The dotted horizontal line is at relative efficiency one.

resampling works well in the lower tail but badly in the centre and upper tail of the distribution. Balanced importance resampling dominates both.

Example 9.10 (Returns data) In order to assess how well these ideas might work in practice, we again consider setting studentized bootstrap confidence intervals for the slope in the returns example. We performed an experiment like that of Example 9.7, but with the $R = 999$ bootstrap samples generated by balanced resampling, importance resampling, and balanced importance resampling.

Table 9.6 shows the mean squared error for the ordinary bootstrap divided by the mean squared errors of the quantile estimates for these methods, using 50 replicate simulations from each scheme. This slightly different "efficiency" takes into account any bias from using the improved methods of simulation, though in fact the contribution to mean squared error from bias is small. The "true" quantiles are estimated from an ordinary bootstrap of size 100 000.

The first two lines of the table show the efficiency gains due to using the control method when the linear approximation is used as a control variate, with empirical influence values calculated exactly and estimated by regression from the same bootstrap simulation. The results differ little. The next two rows show the gains due to balanced sampling, both without and with the control

Method	Distribution	Quantile (%)								
		1	2.5	5	10	50	90	95	97.5	99
Control (exact)		1.7	2.7	2.8	4.0	11.2	5.5	2.4	2.6	1.4
Control (approx)		1.4	2.8	3.2	4.1	11.8	5.1	2.2	2.6	1.3
Balance		1.0	1.2	1.5	1.4	3.1	2.9	1.7	1.4	0.6
with control		1.4	1.8	3.0	2.8	4.4	4.7	2.5	2.2	1.5
Importance	H_1	7.8	3.7	3.6	1.8	0.4	3.5	2.3	3.1	5.5
	H_2	4.6	2.9	3.5	1.1	0.1	2.6	3.1	4.3	5.2
	H_3	3.6	3.7	2.0	1.7	0.5	2.4	2.2	2.6	3.6
	H_4	4.3	2.6	2.5	1.8	0.9	1.6	1.6	2.2	2.3
	H_5	2.6	2.1	0.7	0.3	0.4	0.5	0.6	1.6	2.1
Balanced	H_1	5.0	5.7	4.1	1.9	0.5	2.6	2.2	6.3	4.5
importance	H_2	4.2	3.4	2.4	1.8	0.2	2.0	3.6	4.2	3.9
	H_3	5.2	4.2	3.8	1.8	0.9	3.0	2.4	4.0	4.0
	H_4	4.3	3.3	3.4	2.2	2.1	2.7	3.7	3.3	4.3
	H_5	3.2	2.8	1.0	0.4	0.9	0.9	1.4	2.1	2.1

Table 9.6 Efficiencies for estimation of quantiles of studentized slope for returns data, relative to ordinary bootstrap resampling.

method, which gives a worthwhile improvement in performance, except in the tail.

The next five lines show the gains due to different versions of importance resampling, in each case using a defensive mixture distribution and the raw quantile estimate. In practice it is unusual to perform a bootstrap simulation with the aim of setting a single confidence interval, and the choice of importance sampling distribution H must balance various potentially conflicting requirements. Our choices were designed to reflect this. We first suppose that the empirical influence values l_j for t are known and can be used for exponential tilting of the linear approximation t_L^* to t^*. The first defensive mixture, H_1, uses 499 simulations from a distribution tilted to the α quantile of t_L^* and 500 simulations from a distribution tilted to the $1 - \alpha$ quantile of t_L^*, for $\alpha = 0.05$. The second mixture is like this but with $\alpha = 0.025$.

The third, fourth and fifth distributions are the sort that might be used in practice with a complicated statistic. We first performed an ordinary bootstrap of size R_0, which we used to estimate first the empirical influence values l_j by regression and then the tilt values η for the 0.05 and 0.95 quantiles. We then performed a further bootstrap of size $(R - R_0)/2$ using each set of tilted probabilities, giving a total of R simulations from three different distributions, one centred and two tilted in opposite directions. We took $R_0 = 199$ and $R_0 = 499$, giving H_3 and H_4. For H_5 we took $R_0 = 499$, but estimated the tilted distributions by frequency smoothing (Section 3.9.2) with bandwidth

$\varepsilon = 0.5v^{1/2}$ at the 0.05 and 0.95 quantiles of t^*, where $v^{1/2}$ is the standard error of t estimated from the ordinary bootstrap.

Balance generally improves importance resampling, which is not sensitive to the mixture distribution used. The effect of estimating the empirical influence values is not marked, while frequency smoothing does not perform so well as exponential tilting. Importance resampling estimates of the central quantiles are poor, even when the simulation is balanced. Overall, any of schemes H_1–H_4 leads to appreciably more accurate estimates of the quantiles usually of interest.   ∎

9.4.4 Bootstrap recycling

In Section 3.9 we introduced the idea of bootstrapping the bootstrap, both for making bias adjustments to bootstrap calculations and for studying the variation of properties of statistics. Further applications of the idea were described in Chapters 4 and 5. In both parametric and nonparametric applications we need to simulate samples from a series of distributions, themselves obtained from simulations in the nonparametric case. Recycling methods replace many sets of simulated samples by one set of samples and many sets of weights, and have the potential to reduce the computational effort greatly. This is particularly valuable when the statistic of interest is expensive to calculate, for example when it involves a difficult optimization, or when each bootstrap sample is costly to generate, as when using Markov chain Monte Carlo methods (Section 4.2.2).

The basic idea is repeated use of the importance sampling identity (9.14), as follows. Suppose that we are trying to calculate $\mu = \mathrm{E}\{m(Y)\}$ for a series of distributions $G_1, \ldots, G_K$. The naive Monte Carlo approach is to calculate each value $\mu_k = \mathrm{E}\{m(Y) \mid G_k\}$ independently, simulating R samples $y_1, \ldots, y_R$ from G_k and calculating $\hat{\mu}_k = R^{-1} \sum_{r=1}^{R} m(y_r)$. But for any distribution H whose support includes that of G_k we have

$$\mathrm{E}\{m(Y) \mid G_k\} = \int m(y) dG_k(y) = \int m(y) \frac{dG_k(y)}{dH(y)} dH(y) = \mathrm{E}\left\{ m(Y) \frac{dG_k(Y)}{dH(Y)} \middle| H \right\}.$$

We can therefore estimate all K values using one set of samples $y_1, \ldots, y_N$ simulated from H, with estimates

$$\hat{\mu}_k = N^{-1} \sum_{l=1}^{N} m(y_l) \frac{dG_k(y_l)}{dH(y_l)}, \quad k = 1, \ldots, K. \tag{9.24}$$

In some contexts we may choose N to be much larger than the value R we might use for a single simulation, but less than KR. It is important to choose H carefully, and to take account of the fact that the estimates are correlated.

Both N and the choice of H depend upon the use being made of the estimates and the form of $m(\cdot)$.

Example 9.11 (City population data) Consider again estimating the bias and variance functions for ratio $\theta = t(F)$ of the city population data with $n = 10$. In Example 3.22 we estimated $b(F) = E(T \mid F) - t(F)$ and $v(F) = \text{var}(T \mid F)$ for a range of values of $\theta = t(F)$ using a first-level bootstrap to calculate values of t^* for 999 bootstrap samples $\hat{F}^*$, and then doing a second-level bootstrap to estimate $b(\hat{F}^*)$ and $v(\hat{F}^*)$ for each of those samples. Here the second level of resampling is avoided by using importance re-weighting. At the same time, we retain the smoothing introduced in Example 3.22.

Rather than take each G_k to be one of the bootstrap EDFs $\hat{F}_r^*$, we obtain a smooth curve by using smooth distributions F_θ^* with probabilities $p_j^*(\theta)$ as defined by (3.39). Recall that the parameter value of F_θ^* is $t(F_\theta^*) = \theta^*$, say, which will differ slightly from θ. For H we take $\hat{F}$, the EDF of the original data, on the grounds that it has the correct support and covers the range of values for y^* well: it is not necessarily a good choice. Then we have weights

$$\frac{dG_k(y_r^*)}{dH(y_r^*)} = \frac{dF_\theta^*(y_r^*)}{dH(y_r^*)} = \prod_{j=1}^{n} \left\{ \frac{p_j^*(\theta)}{n^{-1}} \right\}^{f_{rj}^*} = w_r^*(\theta),$$

say, where as usual f_{rj}^* is the frequency with which y_j occurs in the rth bootstrap sample. We should emphasize that the samples y_r^* drawn from H here replace second-level bootstrap samples.

Consider the bias estimate. The weighted sum $R^{-1} \sum (t_r^* - \theta^*) w_r^*(\theta)$ is an unbiased estimate of the bias $E^{**}(T^{**} \mid F_\theta^*) - \theta^*$, and we can plot this estimate to see how the bias varies as a function of θ^* or θ. However, the weighted sum can behave badly if a few of the $w_r^*(\theta)$ are very large, and it is better to use the ratio and regression estimates (9.22) and (9.23).

The top left panel of Figure 9.8 shows raw, ratio, and regression estimates of the bias, based on a single set of $R = 999$ simulations, with the curve obtained from the double bootstrap calculation used in Figure 3.7. For example, the ratio estimate of bias for a particular value of θ is $\sum_r (t_r^* - \theta^*) w_r^*(\theta) / \sum_r w_r^*(\theta)$, and this is plotted as a function of θ^*. The raw and ratio estimates are rather poor, but the regression estimate agrees fairly well with the double bootstrap curve. The panel also shows the estimated bias from a defensive mixture with 499 ordinary samples mixed with 250 samples tilted to each of the 0.025 and 0.975 quantiles; this is the best estimate of those we consider. The panels below show 20 replicates of these estimated biases. These confirm the impression from the panel above: with ordinary resampling the regression estimator is best, but it is better to use the mixture distribution.

The top right panel shows the corresponding estimates for the standard

Figure 9.8 Estimated bias and standard error functions for the city population data ratio. In the top panels the heavy solid lines are the double bootstrap values shown in Figure 3.7, and the others are the raw estimate (large dashes), the ratio estimate (small dashes), the regression estimate (dots), and the regression estimate based on a defensive mixture distribution (light solid). The lower panels show 20 replicates of raw, ratio, and regression estimates from ordinary sampling, and the regression estimate from a defensive mixture (clockwise from upper left) for the panels above.

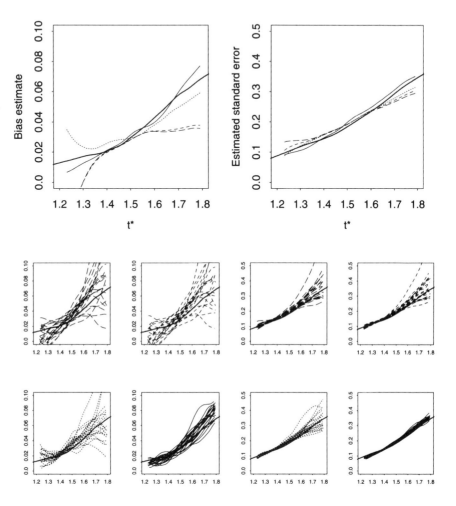

error of t. For each of a range of values of θ, we calculate this by estimating the bias and mean squared error

$$b(F_\theta^*) = \mathrm{E}^{**}(T^{**} - \theta^* \mid F_\theta^*), \qquad \mathrm{E}^{**}\{(T^{**} - \theta^*)^2 \mid F_\theta^*\}$$

by each of the raw, ratio, and regression methods, and plotting the resulting estimate

$$v^{1/2}(F_\theta^*) = [\mathrm{E}^{**}\{(T^{**} - \theta^*)^2 \mid F_\theta^*\} - \{\mathrm{E}^{**}(T^{**} - \theta^* \mid F_\theta^*)\}^2]^{1/2}.$$

The conclusions are the same as for the bias estimate.

As we saw in Example 3.22, here $T - \theta$ is not a stable quantity because its mean and variance depend heavily on θ.   ∎

The results for the raw estimate suggest that recycling can give very variable results, and it must be used with care, as the next example vividly illustrates.

Example 9.12 (Bias adjustment)   Consider the problem of adjusting the bootstrap estimate of bias of T, discussed in Section 3.9. The adjustment C in equation (3.30) is $(RM)^{-1} \sum_{r=1}^{R} \sum_{m=1}^{M} (t_{rm}^{**} - t_r^*) - B$, which uses M samples from each of the R models $\hat{F}_r^*$ fitted to samples from $\hat{F}$. The recycling method replaces each average $M^{-1} \sum_{m=1}^{M} (t_{rm}^{**} - t_r^*)$ by a weighted average of the form (9.24), so that C is estimated by

$$\frac{1}{RN} \sum_{r=1}^{R} \sum_{l=1}^{N} (t_l^{**} - t_r^*) \prod_{j=1}^{n} \frac{d\hat{F}_r^*(y_{lj}^{**})}{dH(y_{lj}^{**})} - B, \qquad (9.25)$$

where t_l^{**} is the value of T for the lth sample $y_{l1}^{**}, \ldots, y_{ln}^{**}$ drawn from the distribution H. If we applied recycling only to the first term of C, which estimates $E^{**}(T^{**})$, then a different — and as it turns out inferior — estimate would be obtained for C.

The support of H must include all R first-level bootstrap samples, so as in the previous example a natural choice is $H = \hat{F}$, the model fitted to (or the EDF of) the original sample. However, this can give highly unstable results, as one might predict from the leftmost panel in the second row of Figure 9.8. This can be illustrated by considering the case of the parametric model $Y \sim N(\theta, 1)$, with estimate $T = \bar{Y}$. Here the terms being summed in (9.25) have infinite variance; see Problem 9.15. The difficulty arises from the choice $H = \hat{F}$, and can be avoided by taking H to be a mixture as described in Section 9.4.2, with at least three components.   ∎

Instability due to the choice $H = \hat{F}$ does not occur with all applications of recycling. Indeed applications to bootstrap likelihood (Chapter 10) work well with this choice.

9.5 Saddlepoint Approximation

9.5.1 Basic approximations

Basic ideas

Let $W_1, \ldots, W_n$ be a random sample from a continuous distribution F with cumulant-generating function

$$K_W(\xi) = \log \int e^{\xi w} \, dF(w).$$

Suppose that we are interested in the linear combination $U = \sum a_j W_j$, and that this has exact PDF and CDF $g(u)$ and $G(u)$. Under suitable conditions, the *cumulant-generating function* of U, which is $K(\xi) = \sum K_W(\xi a_j)$, is the basis of highly accurate approximations to the PDF and CDF of U, known as *saddlepoint approximations*. The saddlepoint approximation to the density of U at u is

$$g_s(u) = \left\{ 2\pi K'' \left(\hat{\xi} \right) \right\}^{-1/2} \exp \left\{ K \left(\hat{\xi} \right) - \hat{\xi} u \right\}, \tag{9.26}$$

where the saddlepoint $\hat{\xi}$ satisfies the *saddlepoint equation*

$$K'(\hat{\xi}) = u, \tag{9.27}$$

and is therefore a function of u. Here K' and K'' are respectively the first and second derivatives of K with respect to ξ. A simple approximation to the CDF of U, $\Pr(U \le u)$, is

$$G_s(u) = \Phi \left\{ w + \frac{1}{w} \log \left(\frac{v}{w} \right) \right\}, \tag{9.28}$$

where $\Phi(\cdot)$ denotes the standard normal CDF, and

$$w = \text{sign}(\hat{\xi}) \left[2 \left\{ \hat{\xi} u - K \left(\hat{\xi} \right) \right\} \right]^{1/2}, \qquad v = \hat{\xi} \left\{ K'' \left(\hat{\xi} \right) \right\}^{1/2},$$

are both functions of u. An alternative to (9.28) is the *Lugannani–Rice formula*

$$\Phi(w) + \phi(w) \left(\frac{1}{w} - \frac{1}{v} \right), \tag{9.29}$$

but in practice the difference between them is small. When $\hat{\xi} = 0$ the CDF approximation is more complicated and we do not give it here. The approximations are constructed by numerical solution of the saddlepoint equation to obtain the value of $\hat{\xi}$ for each value of u of interest, from which the approximate PDF and CDF are readily calculated.

Formulae such as (9.26) and (9.28) can provide remarkably accurate approximations in many statistical problems. In fact,

$$g(u) = g_s(u) \left\{ 1 + O(n^{-1}) \right\}, \qquad G(u) = G_s(u) \left\{ 1 + O(n^{-3/2}) \right\},$$

for values of u such that $|w| < c$ for some positive c; the error in the CDF approximation rises to $O(n^{-1})$ when u is such that $|w| < cn^{1/2}$. A key feature is that the error is relative, so that the ratio of the true density of U to its saddlepoint approximation is bounded over the likely range of u. A consequence is that unlike other analytic approximations to densities and tail probabilities, (9.26), (9.28) and (9.29) are very accurate far into the tails of the density of U. If there is doubt about the accuracy of (9.28) and (9.29), G_s may be calculated by numerical integration of g_s.

The more complex formulae that are used for conditional and marginal density and distribution functions are given in Sections 9.5.2 and 9.5.3.

n		α (%)									
		0.1	0.5	1	2.5	5	95	97.5	99	99.5	99.9
10	Sim'n	7.8	10.9	12.8	15.4	18.1	78.5	85.1	96.0	102.1	116.4
	S'point	7.6	10.8	12.5	15.2	17.8	78.1	85.9	95.3	101.9	115.8
15	Sim'n	11.8	13.6	14.5	16.0	17.4	37.4	39.7	42.3	44.4	48.2
	S'point	11.7	13.5	14.4	15.9	17.4	37.4	39.7	42.4	44.3	48.2

Table 9.7 Comparison of saddlepoint approximation to bootstrap α quantiles ($\times 10^{-2}$) of a linear statistic for samples of sizes 10 and 15, with results from $R = 49\,999$ simulations.

Application to resampling

In the context of resampling, suppose that we are interested in the distribution of the average of a sample from $y_1, \ldots, y_n$, where y_j is sampled with probability p_j, $j = 1, \ldots, n$. Often, but not always, $p_j = n^{-1}$. We can write the average as $U^* = n^{-1} \sum f_j^* y_j$, where as usual $(f_1^*, \ldots, f_n^*)$ has a joint multinomial distribution with denominator n. Then U^* has cumulant-generating function

$$K(\xi) = n \log \left\{ \sum_j p_j \exp(\xi a_j) \right\}, \qquad (9.30)$$

where $a_j = y_j/n$. The function (9.30) can be used in (9.26) and (9.28) to give non-random approximations to the PDF and CDF of U^*. Unlike most of the methods described in this book, the error in saddlepoint approximations arises not from simulation variability, but from deterministic numerical error in using g_s and G_s rather than the exact density and distribution function.

In principle, of course, a nonparametric bootstrap statistic is discrete and so the density does not exist, but as we saw in Section 2.3.2, U^* typically has so many possible values that we can think of it as continuous away from the extreme tails of its distribution. Continuity corrections can sometimes be applied, but they make little difference in bootstrap applications.

When it is necessary to approximate the entire distribution of U^*, we calculate the values of $G_s(u)$ for m values of u equally spaced between $\min a_j$ and $\max a_j$ and use a spline smoother to interpolate between the corresponding values of $\Phi^{-1}\{G_s(u)\}$. Quantiles and cumulative probabilities for U^* can be read off the fitted curve. Experience suggests that $m = 50$ is usually ample.

Example 9.13 (Linear approximation)   A simple application of these ideas is to the linear approximation t_L^* for a bootstrap statistic t^*, as was used in Example 9.7. We write $T_L^* = t + n^{-1} \sum_j f_j^* l_j$, where as usual f_j^* is the frequency of the jth case in the bootstrap sample and l_j is the jth empirical influence value. The cumulant-generating function of $T_L^* - t$ is (9.30) with $a_j = l_j/n$ and

Figure 9.9 Comparison of the saddlepoint approximation (solid) to the PDF of a linear statistic with results from a bootstrap simulation with $R = 49\,999$, for samples of sizes 10 (left) and 15 (right).

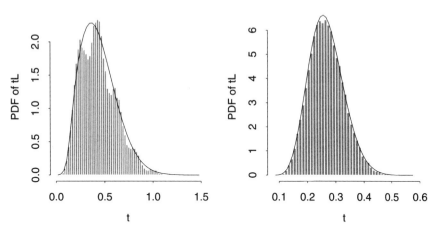

$p_j \equiv n^{-1}$, so the saddlepoint equation for approximation to the PDF and CDF of T_L^* at t_L^* is

$$\frac{\sum_{j=1}^n l_j \exp(\xi l_j/n)}{\sum_{j=1}^n \exp(\xi l_j/n)} = t_L^* - t,$$

whose solution is $\hat{\xi}$.

For a numerical example, we take the variance $t = n^{-1}\sum(y_j - \bar{y})^2$ for exponential samples of sizes 10 and 15; the empirical influence values are $l_j = (y_j - \bar{y})^2 - t$. Figure 9.9 compares the saddlepoint approximations to the PDFs of t_L^* with the histogram from bootstrap calculations with $R = 49\,999$. The saddlepoint approximation accurately reflects the skewed lower tail of the bootstrap distribution, whereas a normal approximation would not do so. However, the saddlepoint approximation does not pick up the multimodality of the density for $n = 10$, which arises for the same reason as in the right panels of Figure 2.9: the bulk of the variability of T_L^* is due to a few observations with large values of $|l_j|$, while those for which $|l_j|$ is small merely add noise. The figure suggests that with so small a sample the CDF approximation will be more useful. This is borne out by Table 9.7, which compares the simulation quantiles and quantiles obtained by fitting a spline to 50 saddlepoint CDF values.

In more complex applications the empirical influence values l_j would usually be estimated by numerical differentiation or by regression, as outlined in Sections 2.7.2, 2.7.4 and 3.2.1.   ∎

Example 9.14 (Tuna density estimate)   We return to the double bootstrap used in Example 5.13 to calibrate confidence intervals based on a kernel density estimate. This involved estimating the probabilities

$$\Pr^{**}(T^{**} \le 2t_r^* - t \mid \hat{F}_r^*),\tag{9.31}$$

where

$$t = \left[\frac{1}{nh} \sum_{j=1}^{n} \left\{ \phi\left(\frac{-y_j}{h}\right) + \phi\left(\frac{y_j}{h}\right) \right\} \right]^{1/2}$$

is the variance-stabilized estimate of the quantity of interest. The double bootstrap version of t can be written as $t^{**} = \left(\sum f_j^{**} a_j \right)^{1/2}$, where $a_j = (nh)^{-1}\{\phi(-y_j/h) + \phi(y_j/h)\}$ and f_j^{**} is the frequency with which y_j appears in a second-level bootstrap sample. Conditional on a first-level bootstrap sample $\hat{F}_r^*$ with frequencies $f_{r1}^*, \ldots, f_{rn}^*$, the f_j^{**} are independent multinomial variables with mean vector $(f_{r1}^*, \ldots, f_{rn}^*)$ and denominator n.

Now if $2t_r^* - t \le 0$, the probability (9.31) equals zero, because T is positive. If $2t_r^* - t > 0$, the event $T^{**} \le 2t_r^* - t$ is equivalent to $n^{-1} \sum f_j^{**} a_j \le (2t_r^* - t)^2$. Thus conditional on $\hat{F}_r^*$, if $2t_r^* - t > 0$, we can obtain a saddlepoint approximation to (9.31) by applying (9.28) and (9.30) with $u = (2t_r^* - t)^2$ and $p_j = n^{-1}f_{rj}^*$.

Including programming, it took about ten minutes to calculate 3000 values of (9.31) by saddlepoint approximation; direct simulation with 250 samples at the second level took about four hours on the same workstation. ∎

Estimating functions

One simple extension of the basic approximations is to statistics determined by monotonic estimating functions. Suppose that the value of a scalar bootstrap statistic T^* based on sampling from $y_1, \ldots, y_n$ is the solution to the estimating equation

$$U^*(t) = \sum_{j=1}^{n} a(t; y_j) f_j^* = 0,\tag{9.32}$$

where for each y the function $a(\theta; y)$ is decreasing in θ. Then $T^* \le t$ if and only if $U^*(t) \le 0$. Hence $\Pr^*(T^* \le t)$ may be estimated by $G_s(0)$ applied with cumulant-generating function (9.30) in which $a_j = a(t; y_j)$. A saddlepoint approximation to the density of T is

$$g_s(t) = \left| \frac{\dot{K}(\hat{\xi})}{\hat{\xi}} \right| \left\{ \frac{1}{2\pi K''(\hat{\xi})} \right\}^{1/2} \exp K(\hat{\xi}),\tag{9.33}$$

where $\dot{K}(\xi) = \partial K / \partial t$, and $\hat{\xi}$ solves the equation $K'(\xi) = 0$. The first term on the right in (9.33) corresponds to the Jacobian for transformation from the density of U^* to that of T^*.

Example 9.15 (Maize data) Problem 4.7 contains data from a paired comparison experiment performed by Darwin on the growth of maize plants. The data are reduced to 15 differences $y_1, \ldots, y_n$ between the heights (in eighths of an inch) of cross-fertilized and self-fertilized plants. When two large negative values are excluded, the differences have average $\bar{y} = 33$ and look close to normal, but when those values are included the average drops to 20.9.

When data may have been contaminated by outliers, robust M-estimates are useful. If we assume that $Y = \theta + \sigma\varepsilon$, where the distribution of ε is symmetric about zero but may have long tails, an estimate of location $\hat{\theta}$ can be found by solving the equation

$$\sum_{j=1}^{n} \psi\left(\frac{y_j - \theta}{\sigma}\right) = 0, \tag{9.34}$$

where $\psi(\varepsilon)$ is designed to downweight large values of ε. A common choice is the Huber estimate determined by

$$\psi(\varepsilon) = \begin{cases} -c, & \varepsilon \leq -c, \\ \varepsilon, & |\varepsilon| < c, \\ c, & c \leq \varepsilon. \end{cases} \tag{9.35}$$

With $c = \infty$ this gives $\psi(\varepsilon) = \varepsilon$ and leads to the normal-theory estimate $\hat{\theta} = \bar{y}$, but a smaller choice of c will give better behaviour when there are outliers.

With $c = 1.345$ and σ fixed at the median absolute deviation s of the data, we obtain $\hat{\theta} = 26.45$. How variable is this? We can get some idea by looking at replicates of $\hat{\theta}$ based on bootstrap samples $y_1^*, \ldots, y_n^*$. A bootstrap value $\hat{\theta}^*$ solves

$$\sum_{j=1}^{n} \psi\left(\frac{y_j^* - \hat{\theta}^*}{s}\right) = 0,$$

so the saddlepoint approximation to the PDF of bootstrap values is obtained starting from (9.32) with $a(t; y_j) = \psi\{(y_j - t)/s\}$. The left panel of Figure 9.10 compares the saddlepoint approximation with the empirical distribution of $\hat{\theta}^*$, and with the approximate PDF of the bootstrapped average. The saddlepoint approximation to $\hat{\theta}^*$ seems quite accurate, while the PDF of the average is wider and shifted to the left.

The assumption of symmetry underlies the use of the estimator $\hat{\theta}$, because the parameter θ must be the same for all possible choices of c. The discussion in Section 3.3 and Example 3.26 implies that our resampling scheme should take this into account by enlarging the resampling set to $y_1, \ldots, y_n$, $\tilde{\theta} - (y_1 - \tilde{\theta}), \ldots, \tilde{\theta} - (y_n - \tilde{\theta})$, for some very robust estimate of θ; we take $\tilde{\theta}$ to be the median. The cumulant-generating function required when taking samples

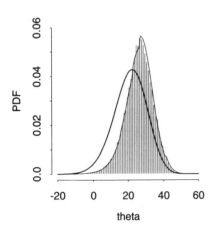 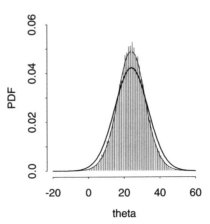

Figure 9.10
Comparison of the
saddlepoint
approximation to the
PDF of a robust
M-estimate applied to
the maize data (solid),
with results from a
bootstrap simulation
with $R = 50\,000$. The
heavy curve is the
saddlepoint
approximation to the
PDF of the average.
The left panel shows
results from resampling
the data, and the right
shows results from a
symmetrized bootstrap.

of size n from this set is

$$
n \log \left[(2n)^{-1} \sum_{j=1}^{n} \exp\{\xi a(t; y_j)\} + \exp\{\xi a(t; 2\tilde{\theta} - y_j)\} \right].
$$

The right panel of Figure 9.10 compares saddlepoint and Monte Carlo approximations to the PDF of $\hat{\theta}^*$ under this symmetrized resampling scheme; the PDF of the average is shown also. All are symmetric about $\tilde{\theta}$.

One difficulty here is that we might prefer to approximate the PDF of $\hat{\theta}^*$ when s is replaced by its bootstrap version s^*, and this cannot be done in the current framework. More fundamentally, the distribution of interest will often be for a quantity such as a studentized form of $\hat{\theta}^*$ derived from $\hat{\theta}^*$, s^*, and perhaps other statistics, necessitating the more sophisticated approximations outlined in Section 9.5.3. ∎

9.5.2 Conditional approximation

There are numerous ways to extend the discussion above. One of the most straightforward is to situations where U is a $q \times 1$ vector which is a linear function of independent variables $W_1, \ldots, W_n$ with cumulant-generating functions $K_j(\xi)$, $j = 1, \ldots, n$. That is, $U = A^T W$, where A is a $n \times q$ matrix with rows a_j^T.

The joint cumulant-generating function of U is

$$
K(\xi) = \log \mathrm{E} \exp(\xi^T A^T W) = \sum_{j=1}^{n} K_j(\xi^T a_j),
$$

and the saddlepoint approximation to the density of U at u is

$$g_s(u) = (2\pi)^{-q/2}|K''(\hat{\xi})|^{-1/2} \exp\left\{K(\hat{\xi}) - \hat{\xi}^T u\right\}, \qquad (9.36)$$

where $\hat{\xi}$ satisfies the $q \times 1$ system of equations $\partial K(\xi)/\partial\xi = u$, and $K''(\xi) = \partial^2 K(\xi)/\partial\xi\partial\xi^T$ is the $q \times q$ matrix of second derivatives of K; $|\cdot|$ denotes determinant.

Now suppose that U is partitioned into U_1 and U_2, that is, $U^T = (U_1^T, U_2^T)$, where U_1 and U_2 have dimension $q_1 \times 1$ and $(q - q_1) \times 1$ respectively. Note that $U_2 = A_2^T W$, where A_2 consists of the last $q - q_1$ columns of A. The cumulant-generating function of U_2 is simply $K(0, \xi_2)$, where $\xi^T = (\xi_1^T, \xi_2^T)$ has been partitioned conformably with U, so the saddlepoint approximation to the marginal density of U_2 is

$$g_s(u_2) = (2\pi)^{-(q-q_1)/2}|K_{22}''(0, \hat{\xi}_{20})|^{-1/2} \exp\left\{K(0, \hat{\xi}_{20}) - \hat{\xi}_{20}^T u_2\right\}, \qquad (9.37)$$

where $\hat{\xi}_{20}$ satisfies the $(q - q_1) \times 1$ system of equations $\partial K(0, \xi_2)/\partial\xi_2 = u_2$, and K_{22}'' is the $(q - q_1) \times (q - q_1)$ corner of K'' corresponding to U_2.

Division of (9.36) by (9.37) gives a *double saddlepoint* approximation to the conditional density of U_1 at u_1 given that $U_2 = u_2$. When U_1 is scalar, i.e. $q_1 = 1$, the approximate conditional CDF is again (9.28), but with

$$w = \operatorname{sign}(\hat{\xi}_1)\left(2\left[\left\{K(0, \hat{\xi}_{20}) - \hat{\xi}_{20}^T u_2\right\} - \left\{K(\hat{\xi}) - \hat{\xi}^T u\right\}\right]\right)^{1/2},$$

$$v = \hat{\xi}_1\left\{\frac{|K''(\hat{\xi})|}{|K_{22}''(0, \hat{\xi}_{20})|}\right\}^{1/2}.$$

Example 9.16 (City population data) A simple bootstrap application is to obtain the distribution of the ratio T^* in bootstrap sampling from the city population data pairs with $n = 10$. In order to avoid conflicts of notation we set $y_j = (z_j, x_j)$, so that T^* is the solution to the equation $\sum(x_j - tz_j)f_j^* = 0$.

For this we take the W_j to be independent Poisson random variables with equal means μ, so $K_j(\xi) = \mu(e^\xi - 1)$. We set

$$U^* = \begin{pmatrix} \sum(x_j - tz_j)W_j \\ \sum W_j \end{pmatrix}, \quad u = \begin{pmatrix} 0 \\ n \end{pmatrix}, \quad a_j = \begin{pmatrix} x_j - tz_j \\ 1 \end{pmatrix}.$$

Now $T^* \le t$ if and only if $\sum_j(x_j - tz_j)W_j \le 0$, where W_j is the number of times (z_j, x_j) is included in the sample. But the relation between the Poisson and multinomial distributions (Problem 9.19) implies that the joint conditional distribution of $(W_1, \ldots, W_n)$ given that $\sum W_j = n$ is the same as that of the multinomial frequency vector $(f_1^*, \ldots, f_n^*)$ in ordinary bootstrap sampling from a sample of size n. Thus the probability that $\sum_j(x_j - tz_j)W_j \le 0$ given that $\sum W_j = n$ is just the probability that $T^* \le t$ in ordinary bootstrap sampling from the data pairs.

α	Unconditional		Conditional		Without replacement	
	S'point	Sim'n	S'point	Sim'n	S'point	Sim'n
0.001	1.150	1.149	1.216	1.215	1.070	1.070
0.005	1.191	1.192	1.236	1.237	1.092	1.092
0.01	1.214	1.215	1.248	1.247	1.104	1.103
0.025	1.251	1.252	1.273	1.269	1.122	1.122
0.05	1.286	1.286	1.301	1.291	1.139	1.138
0.1	1.329	1.329	1.340	1.337	1.158	1.158
0.9	1.834	1.833	1.679	1.679	1.348	1.348
0.95	1.967	1.967	1.732	1.736	1.392	1.392
0.975	2.107	2.104	1.777	1.777	1.436	1.435
0.99	2.303	2.296	1.829	1.833	1.493	1.495
0.995	2.461	2.445	1.865	1.863	1.537	1.540
0.999	2.857	2.802	1.938	1.936	1.636	1.635

Table 9.8 Comparison of saddlepoint and simulation quantile approximations for the ratio when sampling from the city population data. The statistics are the ratio $\sum x_j / \sum z_j$ with $n = 10$, the ratio conditional on $\sum z_j = 640$ with $n = 10$, and the ratio in samples of size 10 taken without replacement from the full data. The simulation results are based on 100 000 bootstrap samples, with logistic regression used to estimate the simulated conditional probabilities, from which the quantiles were obtained by a spline fit.

In this situation it is of course more direct to use the estimating function method with $a(t; y_j) = x_j - tz_j$ and the simpler approximations (9.28) and (9.33). Then the Jacobian term in (9.33) is $|\sum z_j \exp\{\hat{\hat{\xi}}(x_j - tz_j)\} / \sum \exp\{\hat{\hat{\xi}}(x_j - tz_j)\}|$.

Another application is to conditional distributions for T^*. Suppose that the population pairs are related by $x_j = z_j\theta + z_j^{1/2}\varepsilon_j$, where the ε_j are a random sample from a distribution with mean zero. Then conditional on the z_j, the ratio $\sum x_j / \sum z_j$ has variance proportional to $(\sum z_j)^{-1}$. In some circumstances we might want to obtain an approximation to the conditional distribution of T^* given that $\sum Z_j^* = \sum z_j$. In this case we can use the approach outlined in the previous paragraph, but with two conditioning variables: we take the W_j to be independent Poisson variables with equal means, and set

$$U^* = \begin{pmatrix} \sum(x_j - tz_j)W_j \\ \sum z_j W_j \\ \sum W_j \end{pmatrix}, \quad u = \begin{pmatrix} 0 \\ \sum z_j \\ n \end{pmatrix}, \quad a_j = \begin{pmatrix} x_j - tz_j \\ z_j \\ 1 \end{pmatrix}.$$

A third application is to approximating the distribution of the ratio when a sample of size $m = 10$ is taken without replacement from the $n = 49$ data pairs. Again $T^* \le t$ is equivalent to the event $\sum_j (x_j - tz_j)W_j \le 0$, but now W_j indicates that (z_j, x_j) is included in the m cities chosen; we want to impose the condition $\sum W_j = m$. We take W_j to be binary variables with equal success probabilities $0 < \pi < 1$, giving $K_j(\xi) = \log(1 - \pi + \pi e^\xi)$, with π any value. We then apply the double saddlepoint approximation with

$$U^* = \begin{pmatrix} \sum(x_j - tz_j)W_j \\ \sum W_j \end{pmatrix}, \quad u = \begin{pmatrix} 0 \\ m \end{pmatrix}, \quad a_j = \begin{pmatrix} x_j - tz_j \\ 1 \end{pmatrix}.$$

Table 9.8 compares the quantiles of these saddlepoint distributions with

Monte Carlo approximations based on 100 000 samples. The general agreement is excellent in each case. ∎

A further application is to permutation distributions.

Example 9.17 (Correlation coefficient)   In Example 4.9 we applied a permutation test to the sample correlation t between variables x and z based on pairs $(x_1, z_1), \ldots, (x_n, z_n)$. For this statistic and test, the event $T \geq t$ is equivalent to $\sum_j x_j z_{\xi(j)} \geq \sum x_j z_j$, where $\xi(\cdot)$ is a permutation of the integers $1, \ldots, n$.

An alternative formulation is as follows. Let W_{ij}, $i, j = 1, \ldots, n$, denote independent binary variables with equal success probabilities $0 < \pi < 1$, for any π. Then consider the distribution of $U_1 = \sum_{i,j} x_i z_j W_{ij}$ conditional on $U_2 = (\sum_j W_{1j}, \ldots, \sum_j W_{nj}, \sum_i W_{i1}, \ldots, \sum_i W_{i,n-1})^T = u_2$, where u_2 is a vector of ones of length $2n - 1$. Notice that the condition $\sum_i W_{i,n} = 1$ is entailed by the other conditions and so is redundant. Each value of x_j and each value of z_j appears precisely once in the sum U_1, with equal probabilities, and hence the conditional distribution of U_1 given $U_2 = u_2$ is equivalent to the permutation distribution of T. Here $m = n^2$, $q = 2n$, and $q_1 = 1$.

Our limited numerical experience suggests that in this example the saddlepoint approximation can be inaccurate if the large number of constraints results in a conditional distribution on only a few values. ∎

9.5.3 Marginal approximation

The approximate distribution and density functions described so far are useful in contexts such as testing hypotheses, but they are harder to apply to such problems as setting studentized bootstrap confidence intervals. Although (9.26) and (9.28) can be extended to some types of complicated statistics, we merely outline the results.

Approximate cumulant-generating function

The simplest approach is direct approximation to the cumulant-generating function of the bootstrap statistic of interest, T^*. The key idea is to replace the cumulant-generating function $K(\xi)$ by the first four terms of its expansion in powers of ξ,

$$\xi \kappa_1 + \tfrac{1}{2} \xi^2 \kappa_2 + \tfrac{1}{6} \xi^3 \kappa_3 + \tfrac{1}{24} \xi^4 \kappa_4, \tag{9.38}$$

where κ_i is the ith cumulant of T^*. The exact cumulants are usually unavailable, so we replace them with the cumulants of the cubic approximation to T^* given by

$$T_C^* = t + n^{-1} \sum_{i=1}^n f_i^* l_i + \tfrac{1}{2} n^{-2} \sum_{i,j=1}^n f_i^* f_j^* q_{ij} + \tfrac{1}{6} n^{-3} \sum_{i,j,k=1}^n f_i^* f_j^* f_k^* c_{ijk},$$

where t is the original value of the statistic, and l_j, q_{ij} and c_{ijk} are the empirical linear, quadratic and cubic influence values; see also (9.6). To the order required the approximate cumulants are

$$
\begin{aligned}
\kappa_{C,1} &= t + \tfrac{1}{2} n^{-1} \left(n^{-1} \sum_i q_{ii} \right), \\
\kappa_{C,2} &= n^{-1} \left(n^{-1} \sum_i l_i^2 \right) + n^{-2} \left\{ \left(n^{-1} \sum_i l_i q_{ii} \right) \right. \\
&\qquad \left. + \tfrac{1}{2} \left(n^{-2} \sum_{ij} q_{ij}^2 \right) + \left(n^{-2} \sum_{ij} l_i c_{ijj} \right) \right\}, \\
\kappa_{C,3} &= n^{-2} \left\{ \left(n^{-1} \sum_i l_i^3 \right) + 3 \left(n^{-2} \sum_{ij} l_i l_j q_{ij} \right) \right\}, \\
\kappa_{C,4} &= n^{-3} \left\{ \left(n^{-1} \sum_i l_i^4 \right) - 3 \left(n^{-1} \sum_i l_i^2 \right)^2 + 12 \left(n^{-2} \sum_{ij} l_i^2 l_j q_{ij} \right) \right. \\
&\qquad \left. + 12 \left(n^{-3} \sum_{ijk} l_i l_j q_{ik} q_{jk} \right) + 4 \left(n^{-3} \sum_{ijk} l_i l_j l_k c_{ijk} \right) \right\},
\end{aligned}
$$

where the quantities in parentheses are of order one.

We get an approximate cumulant-generating function $K_C(\xi)$ by substituting the $\kappa_{C,i}$ into (9.38), and then use the standard approximations (9.26) and (9.28) with $K(\xi)$ replaced by $K_C(\xi)$. Detailed consideration establishes that this preserves the usual asymptotic accuracy of the saddlepoint approximations. From a practical point of view it may be better to sacrifice some theoretical accuracy but reduce the computational burden by dropping from $\kappa_{C,2}$ and $\kappa_{C,4}$ the terms involving the c_{ijk}; with this modification both PDF and CDF approximations have error of order n^{-1}.

In principle this approach is fairly simple, but in applications there is no guarantee that $K_C(\xi)$ is close to the true cumulant-generating function of T^* except for small ξ. It may be necessary to modify $K_C(\xi)$ to avoid multiple roots to the saddlepoint equation or if $\kappa_{C,4} < 0$, for then $K_C(\xi)$ cannot be convex. In these circumstances we can modify $K_C(\xi)$ to ensure that the cubic and quartic terms do not cause trouble, for example replacing it by

$$
K_{C,b}(\xi) = \xi \kappa_{C,1} + \tfrac{1}{2} \xi^2 \kappa_{C,2} + \left(\tfrac{1}{6} \xi^3 \kappa_{C,3} + \tfrac{1}{24} \xi^4 \kappa_{C,4} \right) \exp \left(-\tfrac{1}{2} n b^2 \xi^2 \kappa_{C,2} \right),
$$

where b is chosen to ensure that the second derivative of $K_{C,b}(\xi)$ with respect to ξ is positive; $K_{C,b}(\xi)$ is then convex. A suitable value is

$$
b = \max \left[\tfrac{1}{2}, \inf\{ a : K_{C,a}''(\xi) > 0, -\infty < \xi < \infty \} \right],
$$

and this can be found by numerical search.

Empirical Edgeworth expansion

The approximate cumulants can also be used in series expansions for the density and distribution of T^*. The Edgeworth expansion for the CDF of

$Z_C^* = (T^* - \kappa_{C,1})/\kappa_{C,2}^{1/2}$ is

$$\Pr{}^*(Z_C^* \le z) \doteq \Phi(z) + \{p_1(z) + p_2(z)\}\phi(z) + O_p(n^{-3/2}), \qquad (9.39)$$

where

$$
\begin{aligned}
p_1(z) &= -\tfrac{1}{6}\kappa_{C,3}\kappa_{C,2}^{-3/2}(z^2 - 1), \\
p_2(z) &= -z\left\{\tfrac{1}{24}\kappa_{C,4}\kappa_{C,2}^{-2}(z^2 - 3) + \tfrac{1}{72}\kappa_{C,3}^2\kappa_{C,2}^{-3}(z^4 - 10z^2 + 15)\right\}.
\end{aligned}
$$

Differentiation of (9.39) gives an approximate density for Z_C^* and hence for T^*. However, experience suggests that the saddlepoint approximations (9.28) and (9.29) are usually preferable if they can be obtained, primarily because (9.39) results in less accurate tail probability estimates: its error is absolute rather than relative. Further drawbacks are that (9.39) need not increase with z, and that the density approximation may become negative.

Derivation of the influence values that contribute to $\kappa_{C,1}, \ldots, \kappa_{C,4}$ can be tedious.

Example 9.18 (Studentized statistic) A statistic $T = t(\hat{F})$ studentized using the nonparametric delta method variance estimate obtained from its linear influence values $L_t(y; \hat{F})$ may be written as $Z = n^{1/2}W$, where

$$W = w(\hat{F}, F) = \frac{t(\hat{F}) - t(F)}{\left\{\int L_t(y; \hat{F})^2 \, d\hat{F}(y)\right\}^{1/2}},$$

with $\hat{F}$ the EDF of the data. The corresponding bootstrap statistic is $w(\hat{F}^*, \hat{F})$, where $\hat{F}^*$ is the EDF corresponding to a bootstrap sample. For economy of notation below we write

$$v = v(\hat{F}) = \int L_t(y; \hat{F})^2 \, d\hat{F}(y), \quad L_w(y_1) = L_w(y_1; \hat{F}), \quad Q_w(y_1, y_2) = Q_w(y_1, y_2; \hat{F}),$$

and so forth.

To obtain the linear, quadratic and cubic influence values for $w(G, F)$ at $G = F$, we replace $G(y)$ with

Here $H(x)$ is the Heaviside function, jumping from 0 to 1 at $x = 0$.

$$(1 - \varepsilon_1 - \varepsilon_2 - \varepsilon_3)F(y) + \varepsilon_1 H(y - y_1) + \varepsilon_2 H(y - y_2) + \varepsilon_3 H(y - y_3),$$

differentiate with respect to ε_1, ε_2, and ε_3, and set $\varepsilon_1 = \varepsilon_2 = \varepsilon_3 = 0$. The empirical influence values for W at $\hat{F}$ are then obtained by replacing F with $\hat{F}$. In terms of the influence values for t and v the result of this calculation is

$$
\begin{aligned}
L_w(y_1) &= v^{-1/2}L_t(y_1), \\
Q_w(y_1, y_2) &= v^{-1/2}Q_t(y_1, y_2) - \tfrac{1}{2}v^{-3/2}L_t(y_1)L_v(y_2)[2], \\
C_w(y_1, y_2, y_3) &= v^{-1/2}C_t(y_1, y_2, y_3) \\
&\quad - \tfrac{1}{2}v^{-3/2}\{Q_t(y_1, y_2)L_v(y_3) + Q_v(y_1, y_2)L_t(y_3)\}\,[3] \\
&\quad + \tfrac{3}{4}v^{-5/2}L_t(y_1)L_v(y_2)L_v(y_3)[3],
\end{aligned}
$$

where [k] after a term indicates that it should be summed over the permutations of its y_js that give the k distinct quantities in the sum. Thus for example

$$L_t(y_1)L_v(y_2)L_v(y_3)[3] = L_t(y_1)L_v(y_2)L_v(y_3) + L_t(y_3)L_v(y_1)L_v(y_2)$$
$$+L_t(y_2)L_v(y_3)L_v(y_1).$$

The influence values for z involve linear, quadratic, and cubic influence values for t, and linear and quadratic influence values for v, the latter given by

$$L_v(y_1) = L_t(y_1)^2 - \int L_t(x)^2 \, d\hat{F}(x) + 2 \int L_t(x)Q_t(x, y_1) \, d\hat{F}(x),$$

$$\tfrac{1}{2}Q_v(y_1, y_2) = L_t(y_1)Q_t(y_1, y_2)[2] - L_t(y_1)L_t(y_2)$$
$$- \int \{Q_t(x, y_1) + Q_t(x, y_2)\}L_t(x) \, d\hat{F}(x)$$
$$+ \int \{Q_t(x, y_2)Q_t(x, y_1) + L_t(x)C_t(x, y_1, y_2)\} \, d\hat{F}(x).$$

The simplest example is the average $t(\hat{F}) = \int x \, d\hat{F}(x) = \bar{y}$ of a sample of values $y_1, \ldots, y_n$ from F. Then $L_t(y_i) = y_i - \bar{y}$, $Q_t(y_i, y_j) \equiv C_t(y_i, y_j, y_k) \equiv 0$, the expressions above simplify greatly, and the required influence quantities are

$$l_i = L_w(y_i; \hat{F}) = v^{-1/2}(y_i - \bar{y}),$$
$$q_{ij} = Q_w(y_i, y_j; \hat{F}) = -\tfrac{1}{2}v^{-3/2}(y_i - \bar{y})\{(y_j - \bar{y})^2 - v\}[2],$$
$$c_{ijk} = C_w(y_i, y_j, y_k; \hat{F}) = 3v^{-3/2}(y_i - \bar{y})(y_j - \bar{y})(y_k - \bar{y})$$
$$+ \tfrac{3}{4}v^{-5/2}(y_i - \bar{y})\{(y_j - \bar{y})^2 - v\}\{(y_k - \bar{y})^2 - v\}[3],$$

where $v = n^{-1}\sum(y_i - \bar{y})^2$. The influence quantities for Z are obtained from those for W by multiplication by $n^{1/2}$. A numerical illustration of the use of the corresponding approximate cumulant-generating function $K_C(\xi)$ is given in Example 9.19. ∎

Integration approach

Another approach involves extending the estimating function approximation to the multivariate case, and then approximating the marginal distribution of the statistic of interest. To see how, suppose that the quantity T of interest is a scalar, and that T and $S = (S_1, \ldots, S_{q-1})^T$ are determined by a $q \times 1$ estimating function

$$U(t, s) = \sum_{j=1}^n a(t, s_1, \ldots, s_{q-1}; Y_j).$$

Then the bootstrap quantities T^* and S^* are the solutions of the equations

$$U^*(t, s) = \sum_{j=1}^n a_j(t, s)f_j^* = 0, \tag{9.40}$$

where $a_j(t,s) = a(t,s;y_j)$ and the frequencies $(f_1^*, \ldots, f_n^*)$ have a multinomial distribution with denominator n and mean vector $n(p_1, \ldots, p_n)$; typically $p_j \equiv n^{-1}$. We assume that there is a unique solution (t^*, s^*) to (9.40) for each possible set of f_j^*, and seek saddlepoint approximations to the marginal PDF and CDF of T^*.

For fixed t and s, the cumulant-generating function of U^* is

$$K(\xi; t, s) = n \log \left[\sum_{j=1}^n p_j \exp \left\{ \xi^T a_j(t,s) \right\} \right], \qquad (9.41)$$

and the joint density of the U^* at u is given by (9.36). The Jacobian needed to obtain the joint density of T^* and S^* from that of U^* is hard to obtain exactly, but can be approximated by

$$J(t,s;\xi) = \det \left\{ n \sum_{j=1}^n p_j'(t,s) \left(\frac{\partial a_j(t,s)}{\partial t}, \frac{\partial a_j(t,s)}{\partial s^T} \right) \right\},$$

where

$$p_j'(t,s) = \frac{p_j \exp \left\{ \xi^T a_j(t,s) \right\}}{\sum_{k=1}^n p_k \exp \left\{ \xi^T a_k(t,s) \right\}};$$

as usual for $r \times 1$ and $c \times 1$ vectors a and s with components a_i and s_d, we write $\partial a / \partial s^T$ for the $r \times c$ array whose (i,j) element is $\partial a_i / \partial s_j$. The Jacobian $J(t,s;\xi)$ reduces to the Jacobian term in (9.33) when s is not present. Thus the saddlepoint approximation to the density of (T^*, S^*) at (t,s) is

$$J(t,s;\hat{\xi})(2\pi)^{-q/2}|K''(\hat{\xi}; t, s)|^{-1/2} \exp K(\hat{\xi}; t, s), \qquad (9.42)$$

where $\hat{\xi} = \hat{\xi}(t,s)$ is the solution to the $q \times 1$ system of equations $\partial K / \partial \xi = 0$. Let us write $\Lambda(t,s) = -K\{\hat{\xi}(t,s); t, s\}$.

We require the marginal density and distribution functions of T^* at t. In principle they can be obtained by integration of (9.42) numerically with respect to s, but this is time-consuming when s is a vector. An alternative approach is analytical approximation using Laplace's method, which replaces the most important part of the integrand — the rightmost term in (9.42) — by a normal integral, suitably centred and scaled. Provided that the matrix $\partial^2 \Lambda(t,s)/\partial s \partial s^T$ is positive definite, the resulting approximate marginal density of T^* at t is

$$J(t,\tilde{s};\tilde{\xi})(2\pi)^{-1/2}|K''(\tilde{\xi}; t, \tilde{s})|^{-1/2} \left| \frac{\partial^2 \Lambda(t,\tilde{s})}{\partial s \partial s^T} \right|^{-1/2} \exp K(\tilde{\xi}; t, \tilde{s}), \qquad (9.43)$$

where $\tilde{\xi} = \tilde{\xi}(t)$ and $\tilde{s} = \tilde{s}(t)$ are functions of t that solve simultaneously the

$q \times 1$ and $(q - 1) \times 1$ systems of equations

$$\frac{\partial K(\xi;t,s)}{\partial \xi} = n \sum_{j=1}^{n} p'_j(t,s)a_j(t,s) = 0, \quad \frac{\partial K(\xi;t,s)}{\partial s} = n \sum_{j=1}^{n} p'_j(t,s)\frac{\partial a_j^T(t,s)}{\partial s}\xi = 0.$$

$$(9.44)$$

These can be solved using packaged routines, with starting values given by noting that when t equals its sample value t_0, say, s equals its sample value and $\xi = 0$.

The second derivatives of Λ needed to calculate (9.43) may be expressed as

$$\frac{\partial^2 \Lambda(t,s)}{\partial s \partial s^T} = \frac{\partial^2 K(\xi;t,s)}{\partial s \partial \xi^T} \left(\frac{\partial^2 K(\xi;t,s)}{\partial \xi \partial \xi^T} \right)^{-1} \frac{\partial^2 K(\xi;t,s)}{\partial \xi \partial s^T} - \frac{\partial^2 K(\xi;t,s)}{\partial s \partial s^T}, \quad (9.45)$$

where at the solutions to (9.44) the matrices in (9.45) are given by

$$\frac{\partial^2 K(\xi;t,s)}{\partial \xi \partial \xi^T} = n \sum_{j=1}^{n} p'_j(t,s)a_j(t,s)a_j(t,s)^T, \quad (9.46)$$

$$\frac{\partial^2 K(\xi;t,s)}{\partial \xi \partial s^T} = n \sum_{j=1}^{n} p'_j(t,s) \left\{ \frac{\partial a_j(t,s)}{\partial s^T} + a_j \xi^T \frac{\partial a_j(t,s)}{\partial s^T} \right\}, \quad (9.47)$$

$$\frac{\partial^2 K(\xi;t,s)}{\partial s_c \partial s_d} = n \sum_{j=1}^{n} p'_j(t,s) \left\{ \xi^T \frac{\partial^2 a_j(t,s)}{\partial s_c \partial s_d} + \xi^T \frac{\partial a_j(t,s)}{\partial s_c} \xi^T \frac{\partial a_j(t,s)}{\partial s_d} \right\}, \quad (9.48)$$

with s_c and s_d the cth and dth components of s.

The marginal CDF approximation for T^* at t is (9.28), with

$$w = \text{sign}(t - t_0) \{2K(\xi;t,s)\}^{1/2}, \quad (9.49)$$

$$v = -\frac{\partial K(\xi;t,s)}{\partial t} |K''(\xi;t,s)|^{1/2} \left| \frac{\partial^2 \Lambda(t,s)}{\partial s \partial s^T} \right|^{1/2} \{J(t,s;\xi)\}^{-1}, \quad (9.50)$$

evaluated at $s = \tilde{s}$, $\xi = \tilde{\xi}$; the only additional quantity needed here is

$$\frac{\partial K(\xi;t,s)}{\partial t} = n \sum_{j=1}^{n} p'_j(t,s)\xi^T \frac{\partial a_j(t,s)}{\partial t}. \quad (9.51)$$

Approximate quantiles of T^* can be obtained in the way described just before Example 9.13.

The expressions above look forbidding, but their implementation is relatively straightforward. The key point to note is that they depend only on the quantities $a_j(t,s)$, their first derivatives with respect to t, and their first two derivatives with respect to s. Once these have been programmed, they can be input to a generic routine to perform the saddlepoint approximations. Difficulties that sometimes arise with numerical overflow due to large exponents can usually be circumvented by rescaling data to zero mean and unit variance, which has no effect on location- and scale-invariant quantities such as studentized statistics. Remember, however, our initial comments in Section 9.1: the investment of time and effort needed to program these approximations is unlikely to be worthwhile unless they are to be used repeatedly.

Example 9.19 (Maize data) To illustrate these ideas we consider the bootstrap variance and studentized average for the maize data. Both these statistics are location-invariant, so without loss of generality we replace y_j with $y_j - \bar{y}$ and henceforth assume that $\bar{y} = 0$. With this simplification the statistics of interest are

$$V^* = n^{-1} \sum Y_j^{*2} - \bar{Y}^{*2}, \qquad Z^* = (n-1)^{1/2} \bar{Y}^* / V^{*1/2},$$

where $\bar{Y}^* = n^{-1} \sum Y_j^*$. A little algebra shows that

$$n^{-1} \sum Y_j^{*2} = V^* \left\{1 + Z^{*2}/(n-1)\right\}, \qquad n^{-1} \sum Y_j^* = Z^* V^{*1/2}(n-1)^{-1/2},$$

so to apply the integration approach we take $p_j \equiv n^{-1}$ and

$$a_j(z,v) = \begin{pmatrix} y_j - zv^{1/2}(n-1)^{-1/2} \\ y_j^2 - v\left\{1 + z^2/(n-1)\right\} \end{pmatrix},$$

from which the 2×1 matrices of derivatives

$$\frac{\partial a_j(z,v)}{\partial z}, \quad \frac{\partial a_j(z,v)}{\partial v}, \quad \frac{\partial^2 a_j(z,v)}{\partial z^2}, \quad \frac{\partial^2 a_j(z,v)}{\partial v^2},$$

needed to calculate (9.43)–(9.51) are readily obtained.

To find the marginal distribution of Z^*, we apply (9.43)–(9.51) with $t = z$ and $s = v$. For a given value of z, the three equations in (9.44) are easily solved numerically. The upper panels of Figure 9.11 compare the saddlepoint distribution and density approximations for Z^* with a large simulation. The analytical quantiles are very close to the simulated ones, and although the saddlepoint density seems to have integral greater than one it captures well the skewness of the distribution.

For V^* we take $t = v$ and $s = z$, but the lower left panel of Figure 9.11 shows that resulting PDF approximation fails to capture the bimodality of the density. This arises because V^* is deflated for resamples in which neither of the two smallest observations — which are somewhat separated from the rest — appear.

The contours of $-\Lambda(z,v)$ in the lower right panel reveal a potential problem with these methods. For $z = -3.5$, the Laplace approximation used to obtain (9.43) amounts to replacing the integral of $\exp\{-\Lambda(z,v)\}$ along the dashed vertical line by a normal approximation centred at A and with precision given by the second derivative of $\Lambda(z,v)$ at A along the line. But $\Lambda(-3.5,v)$ is bimodal for $v > 0$, and the Laplace approximation does not account for the second peak at B. As it turns out, this doesn't matter because the peak at B is so much

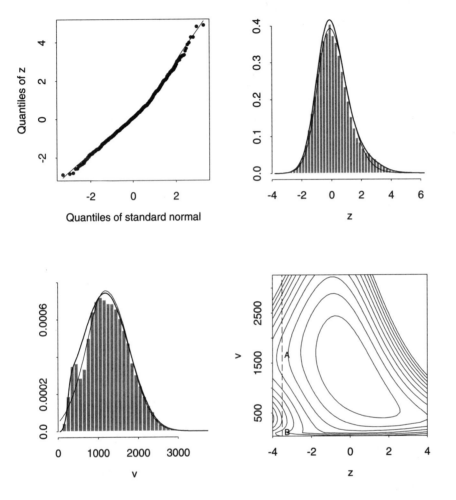

Figure 9.11
Saddlepoint
approximations for the
bootstrap variance V^*
and studentized average
Z^* for the maize data.
Top left:
approximations to
quantiles of Z^* by
integration saddlepoint
(solid) and simulation
using 50 000 bootstrap
samples (every 20th
order statistic is shown).
Top right: density
approximations for Z^*
by integration
saddlepoint (heavy
solid), approximate
cumulant-generating
function (solid), and
simulation using 50 000
bootstrap samples.
Bottom left:
corresponding
approximations for V^*.
Bottom right: contours
of $-\Lambda(z,v)$, with local
maxima along the
dashed line $z = -3.5$ at
A and at B.

lower than at A that it adds little to the integral, but clearly (9.43) would be catastrophically bad if the peaks at A and B were comparable. This behaviour occurs because there is no guarantee that $\Lambda(z,v)$ is a convex function of v and z. If the difficulty is thought to have arisen, numerical integration of (9.42) can be used to find the marginal density of Z^*, but the problem is not easily diagnosed except by checking that (9.45) is positive definite at any solution to (9.44) and by checking that different initial values of ξ and s lead to the the same solution for a given value of t. This may increase the computational burden to an extent that direct simulation is more efficient. Fortunately this difficulty is much rarer in larger samples.

The quantities needed for the approximate cumulant-generating function approach to obtaining the distribution of $n^{1/2}(n-1)^{-1/2}Z^*$ were given in Example 9.18. The approximate cumulants for Z^* are $\kappa_{C,1} = 0.13$, $\kappa_{C,2} = 1.08$, $\kappa_{C,3} = 0.51$ and $\kappa_{C,4} = 0.50$, with $\kappa_{C,2} = 0.89$ and $\kappa_{C,4} = -0.28$ when the terms involving the c_{ijk} are dropped. With or without these terms, the cumulants are some way from the values 0.17, 1.34, 1.05, and 1.55 estimated from 50 000 simulations. The upper right panel of Figure 9.11 shows the PDF approximation based on the modified cumulant-generating function; in this case $K_{C,0}(\xi)$ is convex. The modified PDF matches the centre of the distribution more closely than the integration PDF, but is poor in the upper tail.

For V^*, we have

$$l_i = (y_i - \bar{y})^2 - t, \quad q_{ij} = -2(y_i - \bar{y})(y_j - \bar{y}), \quad c_{ijk} = 0,$$

so the approximate cumulants are $\kappa_{C,1} = 1241$, $\kappa_{C,2}/\kappa_{C,1}^2 = 0.18$, $\kappa_{C,3}/\kappa_{C,1}^3 = 0.013$ and $\kappa_{C,4}/\kappa_{C,1}^4 = -0.0015$; the corresponding simulated values are 1243, 0.18, 0.018, 0.0010. Neither saddlepoint approximation captures the bimodality of the simulations, though the integration method is the better of the two. In this case $b = \frac{1}{2}$ for the approximate cumulant-generating function method, and the resulting density is clearly too close to normal.   ∎

Example 9.20 (Robust M-estimate)   For a second example of marginal approximation, we suppose that $\hat{\theta}$ and $\hat{\sigma}$ are M-estimates found from a random sample $y_1, \ldots, y_n$ by simultaneous solution of the equations

$$\sum_{j=1}^{n} \psi\left(\frac{y_j - \theta}{\sigma}\right) = 0, \quad \sum_{j=1}^{n} \chi\left(\frac{y_j - \theta}{\sigma}\right) = n\gamma.$$

The choice $\psi(\varepsilon) = \varepsilon$, $\chi(\varepsilon) = \varepsilon^2$, $\gamma = 1$ gives the non-robust estimates $\hat{\theta} = \bar{y}$ and $\hat{\sigma}^2 = n^{-1}\sum(y_j - \bar{y})^2$. Below we use the more robust Huber M-estimate specified by (9.35), with $\chi(\varepsilon) = \psi^2(\varepsilon)$ and with γ taken to equal $E\{\chi(\varepsilon)\}$, where ε is standard normal. For purposes of illustration we take $c = 1.345$.

Suppose we want to use $\hat{\theta}$ to get a confidence interval for θ. Since the nonparametric delta method estimate of $\text{var}(\hat{\theta})$ is $\hat{\sigma}^2 \sum \psi^2(e_j)/\{\sum \psi'(e_j)\}^2$ (Problem 6.7), where $e_j = (y_j - \hat{\theta})/\hat{\sigma}$, the studentized version of $\hat{\theta}$ is

$$Z = \frac{\hat{\theta} - \theta}{\hat{\sigma}} \times \frac{n^{-1}\sum_{j=1}^{n} \psi'(e_j)}{(\gamma/n)^{1/2}},$$

which is proportional to the usual Student-t statistic when $\psi(\varepsilon) \equiv \varepsilon$. In order to set studentized bootstrap confidence limits for θ, we need approximations to the bootstrap quantiles of Z. These may be obtained by applying the marginal saddlepoint approximation outlined above with $T = Z$, $S = (S_1, S_2)^T$, $p_j \equiv n^{-1}$,

					α (%)					
	0.1	1	2.5	5	10	90	95	97.5	99	99.9
Sim'n	−3.81	−2.68	−2.21	−1.86	−1.49	1.25	1.62	1.94	2.35	3.49
S'point	−3.68	−2.60	−2.11	−1.72	−1.31	1.24	1.62	1.97	2.42	3.57

Table 9.9 Comparison of results from 50 000 simulations with integration saddlepoint approximation to bootstrap α quantiles of a robust studentized statistic for the maize data.

and

$$a_j(t,s) = \begin{pmatrix} \psi\left(\hat{\sigma}e_j/s_1 - zd/s_2\right) \\ \psi^2\left(\hat{\sigma}e_j/s_1 - zd/s_2\right) - \gamma \\ \psi'\left(\hat{\sigma}e_j/s_1 - zd/s_2\right) - s_2 \end{pmatrix}, \tag{9.52}$$

where $d = (\gamma/n)^{1/2}$. For the Huber estimate, $s_2^* = n^{-1}\sum I\left(|\hat{\sigma}e_j^*/s_1^* - z^*d/s_2^*| \leq c\right)$ takes the discrete range of values j/n; here $I(A)$ is the indicator of the event A. In the extreme case with $c = \infty$, s_2^* always equals one, but even if c is finite it will be unwise to treat s_2^* as continuous unless n is very large. We therefore fix $s_2^* = s_2$, and modify a_j by dropping its third component, so that $q = 2$, and $S \equiv S_1$. With this change the quantities needed for the PDF and CDF approximations are

$$\frac{\partial a_j(t,s)}{\partial t} = \begin{pmatrix} -\psi'd/s_2 \\ -2\psi\psi'd/s_2 \end{pmatrix},$$

$$\frac{\partial a_j(t,s)}{\partial s} = \begin{pmatrix} -\hat{\sigma}e_j\psi'/s_1^2 \\ -2\hat{\sigma}e_j\psi\psi'/s_1^2 \end{pmatrix},$$

$$\frac{\partial^2 a_j(t,s)}{\partial s \partial s^T} = \begin{pmatrix} 2\hat{\sigma}e_j\psi'/s_1^3 \\ 4\hat{\sigma}e_j\psi\psi'/s_1^3 + 4\hat{\sigma}^2 e_j^2\psi'^2/s_1^4 \end{pmatrix},$$

where ψ and ψ' are evaluated at $\hat{\sigma}e_j/s_1 - zd/s_2$.

For the maize data the robust fit downweights the largest and two smallest observations, giving $\hat{\theta} = 26.68$ and $\hat{\sigma} = 25.20$. Table 9.9 compares saddlepoint and simulated quantiles of Z^*. The agreement is generally poorer than in the previous examples.

To investigate the properties of studentized bootstrap confidence intervals based on Z, we conducted a small simulation experiment. We generated 1000 samples of size n from the normal distribution, the t_5 distribution, the "slash" distribution — the distribution of an $N(0,1)$ variate divided by an independent $U(0,1)$ variate — and the χ_5^2 distribution. For each sample confidence intervals were obtained using the saddlepoint method described above. Table 9.10 shows the actual coverages of nominal 95% confidence intervals based on the integration saddlepoint approximation. For the symmetric distributions the results are remarkably good. The assumption of symmetric errors is false for the χ_5^2 distribution, and its results are poorer. In the symmetric cases the saddlepoint method failed to converge for about 2% of samples, for which

Table 9.10 Coverage (%) of nominal 90% and 95% confidence intervals based on the integration saddlepoint approximation to a studentized bootstrap statistic, based on 1 000 samples of size n from underlying normal, t_5, slash, and χ_5^2 distributions. Two-sided 90% and 95% coverages are given for all distributions, but for the asymmetric χ^2 distribution one-sided 5, 95, 2.5 and 97.5 % coverages are given also.

	Normal		t_5		Slash		Chi-squared					
	90	95	90	95	90	95	5	95	90	2.5	97.5	95
$n=20$	91	95	91	96	91	95	14	97	83	9	97	88
$n=40$	90	94	89	95	89	95	9	94	85	6	95	89

simulation would be needed to obtain confidence intervals; we simply left these samples out. Curiously there were no convergence problems for the χ_5^2 samples.

One complication arises from assuming that the error distribution is symmetric, in which case the discussion in Section 3.3 implies that our resampling scheme should be modified accordingly. We can do so by replacing (9.41) with

$$K(\xi;z,s_1) = n\log\left[\frac{1}{2}\sum_{j=1}^{n} p_j \exp\left\{\xi^T a_j(z,s_1)\right\} + \frac{1}{2}\sum_{j=1}^{n} p_j \exp\left\{\xi^T a_j'(z,s_1)\right\}\right],$$

where $a_j'(z,s_1)$ is obtained from (9.52) by replacing e_j with $-e_j$. However the odd cumulants of $\hat{\theta}^*$ are then zero, and a normal approximation to the distribution of Z will often be adequate.

Even without this modification, it seems that the method described above yields robust confidence intervals with coverages very close to the nominal level.

Relative timings for simulation and saddlepoint approximations to the bootstrap distribution of Z^* depend on how the methods are implemented. In our implementation for this example it takes about the same time to obtain 1000 values of Z^* by simulation as to calculate 50 saddlepoint approximations using the integration method, but this comparison is not realistic because the saddlepoint method gives accurate quantile estimates much further into the tails of the distribution of Z^*. If just two quantile estimates are needed, as would be the case for a 95% confidence interval, the saddlepoint method is about ten times faster. Other studies in the literature suggest that, once programmed, saddlepoint methods are 20–50 times faster than simulation, and that efficiency gains tend to be larger with larger samples. However, saddlepoint approximation fails on about 1–2% of samples, for which simulation is needed. ∎

9.6 Bibliographic Notes

Variance reduction methods for parametric simulation have a long history and a scattered literature. They are discussed in books on Monte Carlo methods, such as Hammersley and Handscomb (1964), Bratley, Fox and Schrage (1987), Ripley (1987), and Niederreiter (1992).

Balanced bootstrap simulation was introduced by Davison, Hinkley and Schechtman (1986). Ogbonmwan (1985) describes a slightly different method for achieving first-order balance. Graham et al. (1990) discuss second-order balance and the connections to classical experimental design. Algorithms for balanced simulation are described by Gleason (1988). Theoretical aspects of balanced resampling have been investigated by Do and Hall (1992b). Balanced sampling methods are related to number-theoretical methods for integration (Fang and Wang, 1994), and to Latin hypercube sampling (McKay, Conover and Beckman, 1979; Stein, 1987; Owen, 1992b). Diaconis and Holmes (1994) discuss the complete enumeration of bootstrap samples by methods based on Gray codes.

Linear approximations were used as control variates in bootstrap sampling by Davison, Hinkley and Schechtman (1986). A different approach was taken by Efron (1990), who suggested the re-centred bias estimate and the use of control variates in quantile estimation. Do and Hall (1992a) discuss the properties of this method, and provide comparisons with other approaches. Further discussion of control methods is contained in theses by Therneau (1983) and Hesterberg (1988).

Importance resampling was suggested by Johns (1988) and Davison (1988), and was exploited by Hinkley and Shi (1989) in the context of iterated bootstrap confidence intervals. Gigli (1994) outlines its use in parametric simulation for regression and certain time series problems. Hesterberg (1995b) suggests the application of ratio and regression estimators and of defensive mixture distributions in importance sampling, and describes their properties. The large-sample performance of importance resampling has been investigated by Do and Hall (1991). Booth, Hall and Wood (1993) describe algorithms for balanced importance resampling.

Bootstrap recycling was suggested by Davison, Hinkley and Worton (1992) and independently by Newton and Geyer (1994), following earlier ideas by J. W. Tukey; see Morgenthaler and Tukey (1991) for application of similar ideas to robust statistics. Properties of recycling in various applications are discussed by Ventura (1997).

Saddlepoint methods have a history in statistics stretching back to Daniels (1954), and they have been studied intensively in recent years. Reid (1988) reviews their use in statistical inference, while Jensen (1995) and Field and Ronchetti (1990) give longer accounts; see also Barndorff-Nielsen and Cox (1989). Jensen (1992) gives a direct account of the distribution function approximation we use. Saddlepoint approximation for permutation tests was proposed by Daniels (1955) and further discussed by Robinson (1982). Davison and Hinkley (1988), Daniels and Young (1991), and Wang (1993b) in-

vestigate their use in a number of resampling applications, and others have
investigated their use in confidence interval estimation (DiCiccio, Martin and
Young 1992a,b, 1994). The use of approximate cumulant-generating functions
is suggested by Easton and Ronchetti (1986), Gatto and Ronchetti (1996),
and Gatto (1994), while Wang (1992) shows how the approximation may be
modified to ensure the saddlepoint equation has a single root. Wang (1990)
discusses the accuracy of such methods in the bootstrap context. Booth and
Butler (1990) show how relationships among exponential family distributions
may be exploited to give saddlepoint approximations for a number of bootstrap and permutation inferences, while Wang (1993a) describes an alternative
approach for use in finite population problems. The marginal approximation
in Section 9.5.3 extends and corrects that of Davison, Hinkley and Worton
(1995); see also Spady (1991). The discussion in Example 9.18 follows Hinkley
and Wei (1984). Jing and Robinson (1994) give a careful discussion of the
accuracy of conditional and marginal saddlepoint approximations in bootstrap applications, while Chen and Do (1994) discuss the efficiency gains from
combining saddlepoint methods with importance resampling.

Other methods of variance reduction applied to bootstrap simulation include
antithetic sampling (Hall, 1989a) — see Problem 9.21 — and Richardson
extrapolation (Bickel and Yahav, 1988) — see Problem 9.22.

Appendix II of Hall (1992a) compares the theoretical properties of some of
the methods described in this chapter.

9.7 Problems

1 Under the balanced bootstrap the descending product factorial moments of the f^*_{rj}
are

$$E^* \left(\prod_{w=1}^m f^{\bullet(s_w)}_{t_w j_w} \right) = \prod_u n^{(p_u)} \prod_v R^{(q_v)} / (nR)^{(\sum s_w)},$$ (9.53)

where $f^{(a)} = f!/(f-a)!$, and

$$p_u = \sum_{w:t_w=u} s_w, \quad q_u = \sum_{w:j_w=v} s_w,$$

with u and v ranging over the distinct values of row and column subscripts on the
left-hand side of (9.53).
(a) Check the first- and second-order moments for the f^*_{rj} at (9.9), and verify that
the values in Problem 2.19 are recovered as $R \to \infty$.
(b) Use the results from (a) to obtain the mean of the bias estimate under balanced
resampling.
(c) Now suppose that T^* is a linear statistic, and let $V^* = (R-1)^{-1} \sum_r (T^*_r - \bar{T}^*)^2$
be the estimated variance of T based on the bootstrap samples. Show that the
mean of V^* under multinomial sampling is asymptotically equivalent to the mean
under hypergeometric sampling, as R increases.
(Section 9.2.1; Appendix A; Haldane, 1940; Davison, Hinkley and Schechtman,
1986)

2   Consider the following algorithm for generation of R balanced bootstrap samples from $y = (y_1, \ldots, y_n)$:

Algorithm 9.3 (Balanced bootstrap 2)
Concatenate y with itself R times to form a list $\mathcal{Y}$ of length nR.
For $l = nR, \ldots, 2$:
    (a) Generate a random integer i_l in the range $1, \ldots, l$.
    (b) Swap $\mathcal{Y}_l$ and $\mathcal{Y}_{i_l}$.

                                                  •

Show that this produces output equivalent to Algorithm 9.1.
Suggest a balanced bootstrap algorithm that uses storage $2n$, rather than the Rn used above.
(Section 9.2.1; Gleason, 1988; Booth, Hall and Wood, 1993)

3   Show that the re-centred estimate of bias, $B_{R,adj}$, can be approximated by (9.11), and obtain its mean and variance under ordinary bootstrap sampling. Compare the results with those obtained using the balanced bootstrap.
(Section 9.2.2; Appendix A; Efron, 1990)

4   Data $y_1, \ldots, y_n$ are sampled from a $N(\mu, \sigma^2)$ distribution and we estimate σ by the MLE $t = \{n^{-1} \sum (y_j - \bar{y})^2\}^{1/2}$. The bias of T can be estimated theoretically:

$$ B = \left\{ \frac{2^{1/2} \Gamma \left(\frac{n}{2} \right)}{n^{1/2} \Gamma \left(\frac{n-1}{2} \right)} - 1 \right\} t. $$

But suppose that we estimate the bias by parametric resampling; that is, we generate samples $y_1^*, \ldots, y_n^*$ from the $N(\bar{y}, t^2)$ distribution. Show that the raw and adjusted bootstrap estimates of B can be expressed as

$$ B_R = \left(n^{-1/2} R^{-1} \sum_{r=1}^{R} X_r^{1/2} - 1 \right) t $$

and

$$ B_{R,adj} = n^{-1/2} R^{-1} \left\{ \sum_{r=1}^{R} X_r^{1/2} - R^{1/2} \left(\sum_{r=1}^{R} X_r + X_{R+1} \right)^{1/2} \right\} t, $$

where $X_1, \ldots, X_R$ are independent χ_{n-1}^2 and X_{R+1} is independently χ_{R-1}^2.
Use simulation with these representations to show that the efficiencies of $B_{R,adj}$ are roughly 8 and 16 for $n = 10$ and 20, for any R.
(Section 9.2.2; Efron, 1990)

5   (a) Show that, for large n, the variance of the bias estimate under ordinary resampling, (9.8), can be written $(nA + 2B + C)/(Rn^2)$, while the variance of the bias estimate under balanced resampling, (9.11), is $C/(Rn^2)$; here A, B, and C are quantities of order one. Show also that the correlation ρ between a quadratic statistic T^* and its linear approximation T_L^* can be written as $(nA + B)/\{nA(nA + 2B + C)\}^{1/2}$, and hence verify that the variance of the bias estimate is reduced by a factor of $1 - \rho^2$ when balanced resampling is used.
(b) Give ρ in terms of sample moments when $t = n^{-1} \sum (y_j - \bar{y})^2$, and evaluate the resulting expression for samples of sizes $n = 10$ and 20 simulated from the normal and exponential distributions.
(Section 9.2.3)

6 Consider generating bootstrap samples $y_{r1}^*, \ldots, y_{rn}^*$, $r = 1, \ldots, R$, from $y_1, \ldots, y_n$. Write $y_{rj}^* = y_{\xi(r,j)}$, where the elements of the $R \times n$ matrix $\xi(r, j)$ take values in $1, \ldots, n$.

(a) Show that first-order balance can be arranged by ensuring that each column of ξ contains each of $1, \ldots, n$ with equal frequency, and deduce that when $R = n$ the matrix is a randomized block design with treatment labels $1, \ldots, n$ and with columns as blocks. Hence explain how to generate such a design when $R = kn$.

(b) Use the representation

$$f_{rj}^* = \sum_{i=1}^{n} \delta\{j - \xi(r, i)\},$$

where $\delta(u) = 1$ if $u = 0$ and equals zero otherwise, to show that the ξ-balanced design is balanced in terms of f_{rj}^*. Is the converse true?

(c) Suppose that we have a regression model $Y_j = \beta x_j + \varepsilon_j$, where the independent errors ε_j have mean zero and variance σ^2. We estimate β by $T = \sum Y_j x_j / \sum x_j^2$. Let $T^* = \sum (tx_j + \varepsilon_j^*) x_j / \sum x_j^2$ denote a resampled version of T, where ε_j^* is selected randomly from centred residuals $e_j - \bar{e}$, with $e_j = y_j - tx_j$ and $\bar{e} = n^{-1} \sum e_j$. Show that the average value of T^* equals t if R values of T^* are generated from a ξ-balanced design, but not necessarily if the design is balanced in terms of f_{rj}^*.
(Section 9.2.1; Graham et al., 1990)

7 (a) Following on from the previous question, a design is *second-order ξ-balanced* if all n^2 values of $(\xi(r, i), \xi(r, j))$ occur with equal frequency for any pair of columns i and j. With $R = n^2$, show that this is achieved by setting the first column of ξ to be $(1, \ldots, 1, 2, \ldots, 2, \ldots, n, \ldots, n)^T$, the second column to be $(1, 2, \ldots, n, \ldots, 1, 2, \ldots, n)^T$, and the remaining $n - 2$ columns to be the elements of $n - 2$ orthogonal Latin squares with treatment labels $1, \ldots, n$. Exhibit such a design for $n = 3$.

(b) Think of the design matrix as having rows as blocks, with treatment labels $1, \ldots, n$ to be allocated within blocks; take $R = kn$. Explain why a design is said to be *second-order f^*-balanced* if

$$\sum_{r=1}^{R} f_{rj}^{*2} = k(2n - 1), \quad \sum_{r=1}^{R} f_{rj}^* f_{rk}^* = k(n - 1), \quad j, k = 1, \ldots, n, \quad j \neq k.$$

Such a design is derived by replacing the treatment labels by $0, \ldots, n - 1$, choosing k initial blocks with these replacement labels, adding in turn $1, 2, \ldots, n - 1$, and reducing the values mod n. With $n = 5$ and $k = 3$, construct the design with initial blocks $(0, 1, 2, 3, 4)$, $(0, 0, 0, 1, 3)$, and $(0, 0, 0, 1, 2)$, and verify that it is first- and second-order balanced. Can the initial blocks be chosen at random?
(Section 9.2.1; Graham et al., 1990)

8 Suppose that you wish to estimate the normal tail probability $\int I\{z \leq a\} \phi(z) dz$, where $\phi(.)$ is the standard normal density function and $I\{A\}$ is the indicator of the event A, by importance sampling from a distribution $H(\cdot)$.

Let H be the normal distribution with mean μ and unit variance. Show that the maximum efficiency is

$$\frac{\Phi(a)\{1 - \Phi(a)\}}{\exp(\mu^2)\Phi(a + \mu) - \Phi(a)^2},$$

where μ is chosen to minimize $\exp(\mu^2)\Phi(a + \mu)$. Use the fact that $\Phi(z) \doteq -\phi(z)/z$ for $z \ll 0$ to give an approximate value for μ, and plot the corresponding approximate efficiency for $-3 < a < 0$. What happens when $a > 0$?
(Section 9.4.1)

9   Suppose that $T_1, \ldots, T_R$ is a random sample from PDF $h(\cdot)$ and CDF $H(\cdot)$, and let
     $g(\cdot)$ be a PDF with the same support as $h(\cdot)$ and with p quantile η_p, i.e.

$$p = \int_{-\infty}^{\eta_p} dG(t) = \int_{-\infty}^{\eta_p} \frac{g(t)}{h(t)} \, dH(t).$$

Let $T_{(1)} < \cdots < T_{(R)}$ denote the order statistics of the T_r, set

$$S_m = \frac{1}{R+1} \sum_{r=1}^{m} \frac{g(T_{(r)})}{h(T_{(r)})}, \qquad m = 1, \ldots, R,$$

and let M be the random index determined by $S_M \leq p < S_{M+1}$. Show that $T_{(M)} \to \eta_p$
as $R \to \infty$, and hence justify the estimate t_M^* given at (9.19).
(Section 9.4.1; Johns, 1988)

10   Suppose that T has a linear approximation T_L^*, and let p be the distribution on
     $y_1, \ldots, y_n$ with probabilities $p_j \propto \exp\{\lambda l_j / (n v_L^{1/2})\}$, where $v_L = n^{-2} \sum l_j^2$. Find the
     moment-generating function of T_L^* under sampling from p, and hence show that
     in this case T^* is approximately $N(t + \lambda v_L^{1/2}, v_L)$. You may assume that T_L^* is
     approximately $N(0, v_L)$ when $\lambda = 0$.
     (Section 9.4.1; Johns, 1988; Hinkley and Shi, 1989)

11   The linear approximation t_L^* for a single-sample resample statistic is typically
     accurate for t^* near t, but may not work well near quantiles of interest. For an
     approximation that is accurate near the α quantile of T^*, consider expanding
     $t^* = t(p^*)$ about $p_\alpha = (p_{1\alpha}, \ldots, p_{n\alpha})$ rather than about $(\frac{1}{n}, \ldots, \frac{1}{n})$.
     (a) Show that if $p_{j\alpha} \propto \exp(n^{-1} v_L^{-1/2} z_\alpha l_j)$, then $t(p_\alpha)$ will be close to the α quantile
     of T^* for large n.
     (b) Define

$$l_{j,\alpha} = \frac{d}{d\varepsilon} t\{(1-\varepsilon)p_\alpha + \varepsilon 1_j\} \bigg|_{\varepsilon=0}.$$

Show that

$$t^* \doteq t_{L,\alpha}^* = t(p_\alpha) + n^{-1} \sum_{j=1}^{n} f_j^* l_{j,\alpha}.$$

1_j is a vector with one
in the jth position and
zeroes elsewhere.

(c) For the ratio estimates in Example 2.22, compare numerically t_L^*, $t_{L,0.9}^*$ and the
quadratic approximation

$$t_Q^* = t + n^{-1} \sum_{j=1}^{n} f_j^* l_j + \tfrac{1}{2} n^{-2} \sum_{j=1}^{n} \sum_{k=1}^{n} f_j^* f_k^* q_{jk}$$

with t^*.
(Sections 2.7.4, 3.10.2, 9.4.1; Hesterberg, 1995a)

12   (a) The importance sampling ratio estimator of μ can be written as

$$\hat{\mu}_{H,rat} = \frac{\sum m(y_r)w(y_r)}{\sum w(y_r)} = \frac{\mu + R^{-1/2}\varepsilon_1}{1 + R^{-1/2}\varepsilon_0},$$

where $\varepsilon_1 = R^{-1/2} \sum \{m(y_r)w(y_r) - \mu\}$ and $\varepsilon_0 = R^{-1/2} \sum \{w(y_r) - 1\}$. Show that this
implies that

$$\text{var}(\hat{\mu}_{H,rat}) \doteq R^{-1} \text{var}\{m(Y)w(Y) - \mu w(Y)\}.$$

(b) The variance of the importance sampling regression estimator is approximately

$$\text{var}(\hat{\mu}_{H,reg}) \doteq R^{-1}\text{var}\{m(Y)w(Y) - aw(Y)\}, \tag{9.54}$$

where $a = \text{cov}\{m(Y)w(Y), w(Y)\}/\text{var}\{w(Y)\}$. Show that this choice of a achieves minimum variance among estimators for which the variance has form (9.54), and deduce that when R is large the regression estimator will always have variance no larger than the raw and ratio estimators.

(c) As an artificial illustration of (b), suppose that for $\theta > 0$ and some non-negative integer k we wish to estimate

$$\mu = \theta/(1+\theta)^{k+1} = \int m(y)g(y)\,dy = \int_0^\infty \frac{y^k e^{-y}}{k!} \times \theta e^{-\theta y}\,dy$$

by simulating from density $h(y) = \beta e^{-\beta y}$, $y > 0$, $\beta > 0$. Give $w(y)$ and show that $\text{E}\{m(Y)w(Y)\} = \mu$ for any β and θ, but that $\text{var}(\hat{\mu}_{H,rat})$ is only finite when $0 < \beta < 2\theta$. Calculate $\text{var}\{m(Y)w(Y)\}$, $\text{cov}\{m(Y)w(Y), w(Y)\}$, and $\text{var}\{w(Y)\}$. Plot the asymptotic efficiencies $\text{var}(\hat{\mu}_{H,raw})/\text{var}(\hat{\mu}_{H,rat})$ and $\text{var}(\hat{\mu}_{H,raw})/\text{var}(\hat{\mu}_{H,reg})$ as functions of β for $\theta = 2$ and $k = 0, 1, 2, 3$. Discuss your findings.

(Section 9.4.2; Hesterberg, 1995b)

13 Suppose that an application of importance resampling to a statistic T^* has resulted in estimates $t_1^* < \cdots < t_R^*$ and associated weights w_r^*, and that the importance re-weighting regression estimate of the CDF of T^* is required. Let A be the $R \times R$ matrix whose (r, s) element is $w_r^* I(t_s^* \le t_r^*)$ and B be the $R \times 2$ matrix whose rth row is $(1, w_r^*)$. Show that the regression estimate of the CDF at $t_1^*, \ldots, t_R^*$ equals $(1, 1)(B^T B)^{-1} B^T A$.

(Section 9.4.2)

14 (a) Let $I_k = (I_{k1}, \ldots, I_{kn})$, $k = 1, \ldots, nR$, denote independent identically distributed multinomial random variables with denominator 1 and probability vector $p = (p_1, \ldots, p_n)$. Show that $S_{nR} = \sum_{k=1}^{nR} I_k$ has a multinomial distribution with denominator nR and probability vector p, and that the conditional distribution of I_{nR} given that $S_{nR} = q$ is multinomial with denominator 1 and mean vector $(nR)^{-1}q$, where $q = (R_1, \ldots, R_n)$ is a fixed vector. Show also that

$$\Pr(I_1 = i_1, \ldots, I_{nR} = i_{nR} \mid S_{nR} = q)$$

equals

$$g(i_{nR} \mid S_{nR} = q) \prod_{j=1}^{nR-1} g\left(i_{nR-j} \mid S_{nR-j} = q - i_{nR-j+1} - \cdots - i_{nR}\right),$$

where $g(\cdot)$ is the probability mass function of its argument.

(b) Use (a) to justify the following algorithm:

Algorithm 9.4 (Balanced importance resampling)

Initialize by setting values of $R_1, \ldots, R_n$ such that $R_j \doteq nRp_j$ and $\sum R_j = nR$.
For $m = nR, \ldots, 1$:

    (a) Generate u from the $U(0, 1)$ distribution.
    (b) Find the j such that $\sum_{l=1}^{j-1} R_l \le um < \sum_{l=1}^{j} R_l$.
    (c) Set $I_m = j$ and decrease R_j to $R_j - 1$.

Return the sets $\{I_1, \ldots, I_n\}$, $\{I_{n+1}, \ldots, I_{2n}\}$, $\ldots$, $\{I_{n(R-1)+1}, \ldots, I_{nR}\}$ as the indices of the R bootstrap samples of size n.   ●

(Section 9.4.3; Booth, Hall and Wood, 1993)

15 For the bootstrap recycling estimate of bias described in Example 9.12, consider
    the case $T = \bar{Y}$ with the parametric model $Y \sim N(\theta, 1)$. Show that if H is taken to
    be the $N(\bar{y}, a)$ distribution, then the simulation variance of the recycling estimate
    of C is approximately

$$\frac{1}{n}\left[\frac{1}{R} + \left(\frac{a^2}{2a-1}\right)^{(n-1)/2}\left\{\frac{a(a-1)}{(2a-3)^{3/2}}\frac{1}{RN} + \frac{a^2}{8(a-1)^{3/2}}\frac{1}{N}\right\}\right],$$

provided $a > \frac{3}{2}$. Compare this to the simulation variance when ordinary double
bootstrap methods are used.

What are the implications for nonparametric double bootstrap calculations? Investigate the use of defensive mixtures for H in this problem.

(Section 9.4.4; Ventura, 1997)

16 Consider exponential tilting for a statistic whose linear approximation is

$$T_L^* = t + \sum_{s=1}^{S}\frac{1}{n_s}\sum_{j=1}^{n_s}f_{sj}^*l_{sj},$$

where the $(f_{s1}^*, \ldots, f_{sn_s}^*)$, $s = 1, \ldots, S$, are independent sets of multinomial frequencies.

(a) Show that the cumulant-generating function of T_L^* is

$$K(\xi) = \xi t + \sum_{s=1}^{S}n_s\log\left\{\frac{1}{n_s}\sum_{j=1}^{n_s}\exp(\xi l_{sj}/n_s)\right\}.$$

Hence show that choosing ξ to give $K'(\xi) = t_0$ is equivalent to exponential tilting
of T_L^* to have mean t_0, and verify the tilting calculations in Example 9.8.

(b) Explain how to modify (9.26) and (9.28) to give the approximate PDF and
CDF of T_L^*.

(c) How can stratification be accommodated in the conditional approximations of
Section 9.5.2?

(Section 9.5)

17 In a matched pair design, two treatments are allocated at random to each of n
pairs of experimental units, with differences d_j and average difference $\bar{d} = n^{-1}\sum d_j$.
If there is no real effect, all 2^n sequences $\pm d_1, \ldots, \pm d_n$ are equally likely, and so
are the values $\bar{D}^* = n^{-1}\sum S_j d_j$, where the S_j take values ± 1 with probability
$\frac{1}{2}$. The one-sided significance level for testing the null hypothesis of no effect is
$\Pr^*(\bar{D}^* \geq \bar{d})$.

(a) Show that the cumulant-generating function of $\bar{D}^*$ is

$$K(\xi) = \sum_{j=1}^{n}\log\cosh(\xi d_j/n),$$

and find the saddlepoint equation and the quantities needed for saddlepoint
approximation to the observed significance level. Explain how this may be fitted
into the framework of a conditional saddlepoint approximation.

(b) See Practical 9.5.

(Section 9.5.1; Daniels, 1958; Davison and Hinkley, 1988)

18 For the testing problem of Problem 4.9, use saddlepoint methods to develop an
approximation to the exact bootstrap P-value based on the exponential tilted EDF.
Apply this to the city population data with $n = 10$.

(Section 9.5.1)

19 (a) If $W_1, \ldots, W_n$ are independent Poisson variables with means $\mu_1, \ldots, \mu_n$, show that their joint distribution conditional on $\sum_j W_j = m$ is multinomial with probability vector $\pi = (\mu_1, \ldots, \mu_n)/\sum \mu_j$ and denominator m. Hence justify the first saddlepoint approximation in Example 9.16.

(b) Suppose that T^* is the solution to an estimating equation of form (9.32), but that $f_j^* = 0$ or 1 and $\sum f_j^* = m < n$; T^* is a delete-m jackknife value of the original statistic. Explain how to obtain a saddlepoint approximation to the PDF of T^*. How can this PDF be used to estimate $\text{var}^*(T^*)$? Do you think the estimate will be good when $m = n - 1$?

(Section 9.5.2; Booth and Butler, 1990)

20 (a) Show that the bootstrap correlation coefficient t^* based on data pairs (x_j, z_j), $j = 1, \ldots, n$, may be expressed as the solution to the estimating equation (9.40) with

$$
a_j(t, s) = \begin{pmatrix} x_j - s_1 \\ z_j - s_2 \\ (x_j - s_1)^2 - s_3 \\ (z_j - s_2)^2 - s_4 \\ (x_j - s_1)(z_j - s_2) - t(s_3 s_4)^{1/2} \end{pmatrix},
$$

where $s^T = (s_1, s_2, s_3, s_4)$, and show that the Jacobian $J(t, s; \xi) = n^5(s_3 s_4)^{1/2}$. Obtain the quantities needed for the marginal saddlepoint approximation (9.43) to the density of T^*.

(b) What further quantities would be needed for saddlepoint approximation to the marginal density of the studentized form of T^*?

(Section 9.5.3; Davison, Hinkley and Worton, 1995; DiCiccio, Martin and Young, 1994)

21 Let T_1^* be a statistic calculated from a bootstrap sample in which y_j appears with frequency f_j^* $(j = 1, \ldots, n)$, and suppose that the linear approximation to T_1^* is $T_L^* = t + n^{-1} \sum f_j^* l_j$, where $l_1 \leq l_2 \leq \cdots \leq l_n$. The statistic T_2^* antithetic to T_1^* is calculated from the bootstrap sample in which y_j appears with frequency f_{n+1-j}^*.

(a) Show that if T_1^* and T_2^* are antithetic,

$$
\text{var}\{\tfrac{1}{2}(T_1^* + T_2^*)\} \doteq \frac{1}{2n} \left(n^{-1} \sum_{j=1}^n l_j^2 + n^{-1} \sum_{j=1}^n l_j l_{n+1-j} \right),
$$

and that this is roughly $\tau^2/2n$ as $n \to \infty$, where

$$
\tau^2 = \tfrac{1}{2} \int_0^1 (\eta_p + \eta_{1-p})^2 \, dp
$$

and η_p is the pth quantile of the distribution of $L_t(Y; F)$.

(b) Show that if T_2^* is independent of T_1^* the corresponding variance is

$$
\text{var}\{\tfrac{1}{2}(T_1^* + T_2^*)\} = \frac{1}{2n^2} \sum_{j=1}^n l_j^2 \doteq \frac{1}{2n} \int_0^1 \eta_p^2 \, dp,
$$

and deduce that when T is the sample average and F is the exponential distribution the large-sample performance gain of antithetic resampling is $6/(12 - \pi^2) \doteq 2.8$.

(c) What happens if F is symmetric? Explain qualitatively why.

(Hall, 1989a)

22   Suppose that resampling from a sample of size n is used to estimate a quantity $z(n)$ with expansion

$$z(n) = z_0 + n^{-a}z_1 + n^{-2a}z_2 + \cdots, \tag{9.55}$$

where z_0, z_1, z_2 are unknown but a is known; often $a = \frac{1}{2}$. Suppose that we resample from the EDF $\hat{F}$, but with sample sizes n_0, n_1, where $1 < n_0 < n_1 < n$, instead of the usual n, giving simulation estimates $z^*(n_0)$, $z^*(n_1)$ of $z(n_0)$, $z(n_1)$.
(a) Show that $z^*(n)$ can be estimated by

$$\hat{z}^*(n) = z^*(n_0) + \frac{n^{-a} - n_0^{-a}}{n_0^{-a} - n_1^{-a}} \left\{ z^*(n_0) - z^*(n_1) \right\}.$$

(b) Now suppose that an estimate of $z^*(n_j)$ based on R_j simulations has variance approximately b/R_j and that the computational effort required to obtain it is cn_jR_j, for some constants b and c. Given n_0 and n_1, discuss the choice of R_0 and R_1 to minimize the variance of $\hat{z}^*(n)$ for a given total computational effort.
(c) Outline how knowledge of the limit z_0 in (9.55) can be used to improve $\hat{z}^*(n)$. How would you proceed if a were unknown? Do you think it wise to extrapolate from just two values n_0 and n_1?
(Bickel and Yahav, 1988)

9.8 Practicals

1   For ordinary bootstrap sampling, balanced resampling, and balanced resampling within strata:

```
y <- rnorm(10)
junk.fun <- function(y, i) var(y[i])
junk <- boot(y, junk.fun, R=9)
boot.array(junk)
apply(junk$t,2,sum)
junk <- boot(y, junk.fun, R=9, sim="balanced")
boot.array(junk)
apply(junk$t,2,sum)
junk <- boot(y, junk.fun, R=9, sim="balanced",
            strata=rep(1:2,c(5,5)))
boot.array(junk)
apply(junk$t,2,sum)
```

Now use balanced resampling in earnest to estimate the bias for the gravity data weighted average:

```
grav.fun <- function(data, i)
{   d <- data[i,]
    m <- tapply(d$g,d$series,mean)
    v <- tapply(d$g,d$series,var)
    n <- table(d$series)
    v <- (n-1)*v/n
    c(sum(m*n/v)/sum(n/v), sum(n/v)) }
grav.bal <- boot(gravity, grav.fun, R=49,
            strata=gravity$series, sim="balanced")
mean(grav.bal$t[,1])-grav.bal$t0[1]
```

For the adjusted estimate of bias:

```
grav.ord <- boot(gravity, grav.fun, R=49,
                 strata=gravity$series)
control(grav.ord,bias.adj=T)
```

Now a more systematic comparison, with 40 replicates each with $R = 19$:

```
R <- 19; nreps <- 40; bias <- matrix(,nreps,3)
for (i in 1:nreps) {
grav.ord <- boot(gravity, grav.fun, R=R, strata=gravity$series)
grav.bal <- boot(gravity, grav.fun, R=R,
                 strata=gravity$series, sim="balanced")
bias[i,] <- c(mean(grav.ord$t[,1])-grav.ord$t0[1],
              mean(grav.bal$t[,1])-grav.bal$t0[1],
              control(grav.ord,bias.adj=T)) }
bias
apply(bias,2,mean)
apply(bias,2,var)
split.screen(c(1,2))
screen(1)
qqplot(bias[,1],bias[,2],xlab="ordinary",ylab="balanced")
abline(0,1,lty=2)
screen(2)
qqplot(bias[,2],bias[,3],xlab="balanced",ylab="adjusted")
abline(0,1,lty=2)
```

What are the efficiency gains due to using balanced simulation and post-simulation adjustment for bias estimation here? Now a calculation to see the correlation between T^* and its linear approximation:

```
grav.ord <- boot(gravity, grav.fun, R=999, strata=gravity$series)
grav.L <- empinf(grav.ord,type="reg")
tL <- linear.approx(grav.ord,grav.L,index=1)
close.screen(all=T)
plot(tL,grav.ord$t[,1])
cor(tL,grav.ord$t[,1])
```

Finally, calculations for the estimates of bias, variance and quantiles using the linear approximation as control variate:

```
grav.cont <- control(grav.ord,L=grav.L,index=1)
grav.cont$bias
grav.cont$var
grav.cont$quantiles
```

2   To use importance resampling to estimate quantiles of the contrast of averages for the tau data of Practical 3.4, we first set up strata, a weighted version of the statistic *t*, a contrast of averages, and calculate the empirical influence values:

```
tau.w <- function(data, w)
{   d <- data$rate*w
    d <- tapply(d,data$decay,sum)/tapply(w,data$decay,sum)
    d[1]-sum(d[-1])    }
tau.L <- empinf(data=tau, statistic=tau.w, strata=tau$decay)
```

We could use exponential tilting to find distributions tilted to 14 and 18 (the original value of *t* is 16.16):

```
exp.tilt(tau.L,theta=c(14,18),t0=16.16)
```

Function `tilt.boot` does this automatically. Here we do 199 bootstraps without tilting, then 100 each tilted to the 0.05 and 0.95 quantiles of these 199 values of t^*. We then display the weights, without and with defensive mixture distributions:

```
tau.tilt <- tilt.boot(tau,tau.w,R=c(199,100,100),strata=tau$decay,
                  stype="w",L=tau.L,alpha=c(0.05,0.95))
split.screen(c(1,2))
screen(1); plot(tau.tilt$t,imp.weights(tau.tilt),log="y")
screen(2); plot(tau.tilt$t,imp.weights(tau.tilt,def=F),log="y")
```

The corresponding estimated quantiles are

```
imp.quantile(tau.tilt,alpha=c(0.05,0.95))
imp.quantile(tau.tilt,alpha=c(0.05,0.95),def=F)
```

The same can be done with frequency smoothing, but then the initial value of R must be larger:

```
tau.freq <- tilt.boot(tau, tau.w, R=c(499,250,250),
    strata=tau$decay, stype="w", tilt=F, alpha=c(0.05,0.95))
imp.quantile(tau.freq,alpha=c(0.05,0.95))
```

For balanced importance resampling we simply add `sim="balanced"` to the arguments of `tilt.boot`. For a small simulation study to see the potential efficiency gains over ordinary sampling, we compare the performance of ordinary sampling and importance resampling with and without balance, in estimating the 0.1 and 0.9 quantiles of the distribution of t^*.

```
tau.test <- NULL
for (irep in 1:10)
{ tau.boot <- boot(tau, tau.w, R=199, stype="w",
                  strata=tau$decay)
  q.ord <- sort(tau.boot$t)[c(20,180)]
  tau.tilt <- tilt.boot(tau, tau.w, R=c(99,50,50),
                        strata=tau$decay, stype="w", L=tau.L,
                        alpha=c(0.1,0.9))
  q.tilt <- imp.quantile(tau.tilt, alpha=c(0.1,0.9))$raw
  tau.bal <- tilt.boot(tau, tau.w, R=c(99,50,50),
                        strata=tau$decay, stype="w", L=tau.L,
                        alpha=c(0.1,0.9), sim="balanced")
  q.bal <- imp.quantile(tau.bal, alpha=c(0.1, 0.9))$raw
  tau.test <- rbind(tau.test, c(q.ord, q.tilt, q.bal)) }
sqrt(apply(tau.test, 2, var))
```

What are the efficiency gains of the two importance resampling methods?

3   Consider the bias and standard deviation functions for the correlation of the claridge data (Example 4.9). To estimate them, we perform a double bootstrap and plot the results, as follows.

```
clar.fun <- function(data, f)
{ r <- corr(data, f/sum(f))
  n <- nrow(data)
  d <- data[rep(1:n,f),]
  us <- (d[,1]-mean(d[,1]))/sqrt(var(d[,1]))
  xs <- (d[,2]-mean(d[,2]))/sqrt(var(d[,2]))
```

```
L <- us*xs - r*(us^2+xs^2)/2
v <- sum((L/n)^2)
clar.t <- boot(d, corr, R=25, stype="w")$t
i <- is.na(clar.t)
clar.t <- clar.t[!i]
c(r, v, mean(clar.t)-r, var(clar.t), sum(i)) }
clar.boot <- boot(claridge, clar.fun, R=999, stype="f")
split.screen(c(1,2))
screen(1)
plot(clar.boot$t[,1],clar.boot$t[,3],pch=".",
    xlab="theta*",ylab="bias")
lines(lowess(clar.boot$t[,1],clar.boot$t[,3],f=1/2),lwd=2)
screen(2)
plot(clar.boot$t[,1],sqrt(clar.boot$t[,4]),pch=".",
    xlab="theta*",ylab="SD")
l <- lowess(clar.boot$t[,1],clar.boot$t[,4],f=1/2)
lines(l$x,sqrt(l$y),lwd=2)
```

To obtain recycled estimates using only the results from a single bootstrap, and to compare them with those from the double bootstrap:

```
clar.rec <- boot(claridge, corr, R=999, stype="w")
IS.ests <- function(theta, boot.out, statistic, A=0.2)
{ f <- smooth.f(theta,boot.out,width=A)
  theta.f <- statistic(boot.out$data,f/sum(f))
  IS.w <- imp.weights(boot.out,q=f)
  moms <- imp.moments(boot.out,t=boot.out$t[,1]-theta.f,w=IS.w)
  c(theta, theta.f, moms$raw, moms$rat, moms$reg) }
IS.clar <- matrix(,41,8)
theta <- seq(0,0.8,length=41)
for (j in 1:41) IS.clar[j,] <- IS.ests(theta[j],clar.rec,corr)
screen(1,new=F)
lines(IS.clar[,2],IS.clar[,7])
lines(IS.clar[,2],IS.clar[,5],lty=3)
lines(IS.clar[,2],IS.clar[,3],lty=2)
screen(2, new=F)
lines(IS.clar[,2],sqrt(IS.clar[,8]))
lines(IS.clar[,2],sqrt(IS.clar[,6]),lty=3)
lines(IS.clar[,2],sqrt(IS.clar[,4]),lty=2)
```

Do you think these results are close enough to those from the double bootstrap? Compare the values of θ in IS.clar[,1] to the values of $\theta^* = t(\hat{F}_\theta^*)$ in IS.clar[,2].

4   Dataframe capability gives "data" from Bissell (1990) comprising 75 successive observations with specification limits $U = 5.79$ and $L = 5.49$; see Problem 5.6 and Practical 5.4. Suppose that we wish to use the range of blocks of 5 observations to estimate $\hat{\sigma}$, in which case $\hat{\theta} = k/\bar{r}_5$, where $k = (U - L)d_5$. Then $\hat{\theta}$ is the root of the estimating equation $\sum_j (k - r_{5,j}\theta) = 0$; this is just a ratio statistic. We estimate the PDF of $\hat{\theta}^*$ by saddlepoint methods as follows:

```
psi <- function(tt, r, k=2.236*(5.79-5.49)) k-r*tt
psi1 <-function(tt, r, k=2.236*(5.79-5.49)) r
det.psi <- function(tt, r, xi)
{ p <- exp(xi * psi(tt, r))
  length(r) * abs(sum(p * psi1(tt,r))/sum(p))  }
```

```
r5 <- apply(matrix(capability$y,15,5,byrow=T), 1,
            function(x) diff(range(x)))
m <- 300; top <- 10; bot <- 4
sad <- matrix(, m, 3)
th <- seq(bot,top,length=m)
for (i in 1:m)
{ sp <- saddle(A=psi(th[i], r5), u=0)
  sad[i,] <- c(th[i], sp$spa[1]*det.psi(th[i], r5, xi=sp$zeta.hat),
               sp$spa[2]) }
sad <- sad[!is.na(sad[,2])&!is.na(sad[,3]),]
plot(sad[,1],sad[,2],type="l",xlab="theta hat",ylab="PDF")
```

To obtain the quantiles of the distribution of $\hat{\theta}^*$, we use the following code; here capab.t0 contains $\hat{\theta}$ and its standard error.

```
theta.fun <- function(d, w, k=2.236*(5.79-5.49)) k*sum(w)/sum(d*w)
capab.v <- var.linear(empinf(data=r5, statistic=theta.fun))
capab.t0 <- c(2.236*(5.79-5.49)/mean(r5),sqrt(capab.v))
Afn <- function(t, data, k=2.236*(5.79-5.49)) k-t*data
ufn <- function(t, data, k=2.236*(5.79-5.49)) 0
capab.sp <- saddle.distn(A=Afn, u=ufn, t0=capab.t0, data=r5)
capab.sp
```

We can use the same ideas to apply the block bootstrap. Now we take $b = 15$ of the $n - l + 1$ blocks of successive observations of length $l = 5$. We concatenate them to form a new series, and then take the ranges of each block of successive observations. This is equivalent to selecting b ranges from among the $n - l + 1$ possible ranges, with replacement. The quantiles of the saddlepoint approximation to the distribution of $\hat{\theta}^*$ under this scheme are found as follows.

```
r5 <- NULL
for (j in 1:71) r5 <- c(r5, diff(range(capability$y[j:(j+4)])))
Afn <- function(t, data, k=2.236*(5.79-5.49)) cbind(k-t*data,1)
ufn <- function(t, data, k=2.236*(5.79-5.49)) c(0,15)
capab.sp1 <- saddle.distn(A=Afn,u=ufn,wdist="p",
                          type="cond",t0=capab.t0,data=r5)
capab.sp1$quantiles
```

Compare them with the quantiles above. How do they differ? Why?

5   To apply the saddlepoint approximation given in Problem 9.17 to the paired comparison data of Problem 4.7, and obtain a one-sided significance level $\Pr^*(\bar{D}^* \geq \bar{d})$:

```
K <- function(xi) sum(log(cosh(xi*darwin$y)))-xi*sum(darwin$y)
K2 <- function(xi) sum(darwin$y^2/cosh(xi*darwin$y)^2)
darwin.saddle <- saddle(K.adj=K,K2=K2)
darwin.saddle
1-darwin.saddle$spa[2]
```

10

Semiparametric Likelihood Inference

10.1 Likelihood

The likelihood function is central to inference in parametric statistical models. Suppose that data y are believed to have come from a distribution F_ψ, where ψ is an unknown $p \times 1$ vector parameter. Then the likelihood for ψ is the corresponding density evaluated at y, namely

$$L(\psi) = f_\psi(y),$$

regarded as a function of ψ. This measures the plausibility of the different values of ψ which might have given rise to y, and can be used in various ways.

If further information about ψ is available in the form of a prior probability density, $\pi(\psi)$, Bayes' theorem can be used to form a posterior density for ψ given the data y,

$$\pi(\psi \mid y) = \frac{\pi(\psi) f_\psi(y)}{\int \pi(\psi) f_\psi(y) \, d\psi}.$$

Inferences regarding ψ or other quantities of interest may then be based on this density, which in principle contains all the information concerning ψ.

If prior information about ψ is not available in a probabilistic form, the likelihood itself provides a basis for comparison of different values of ψ. The most plausible value is that which maximizes the likelihood, namely the *maximum likelihood estimate*, $\hat{\psi}$. The relative plausibility of other values is measured in terms of the log likelihood $\ell(\psi) = \log L(\psi)$ by the *likelihood ratio statistic*

$$W(\psi) = 2 \{\ell(\hat{\psi}) - \ell(\psi)\}.$$

A key result is that under repeated sampling of data from a regular model, $W(\psi)$ has approximately a chi-squared distribution with p degrees of freedom. This forms the basis for the primary method of calculating confidence regions in parametric models. One special feature is that the likelihood determines the shape of confidence regions when ψ is a vector.

Unlike many of the confidence interval methods described in Chapter 5, likelihood provides a natural basis for the combination of information from different experiments. If we have two independent sets of data, y and z, that bear on the same parameter, the overall likelihood is simply $L(\psi) = f(y \mid \psi)f(z \mid \psi)$, and tests and confidence intervals concerning ψ may be based on this. This type of combination is particularly useful in applications where several independent experiments are linked by common parameters; see Practical 10.1.

In applications we can often write $\psi = (\theta, \lambda)$, where the components of θ are of primary interest, while the so-called nuisance parameters λ are of secondary concern. In such situations inference for θ is based on the *profile likelihood,*

$$L_p(\theta) = \max_{\lambda} L(\theta, \lambda), \tag{10.1}$$

which is treated as if it were a likelihood. In some cases, particularly those where λ is high dimensional, the usual properties of likelihood statistics (consistency of maximum likelihood estimate, approximate chi-squared distribution of log likelihood ratio) do not apply without making an adjustment to the profile likelihood. The adjusted likelihood is

$$L_a(\theta) = L_p(\theta)|j_\lambda(\theta, \hat{\lambda}_\theta)|^{-1/2}, \tag{10.2}$$

where $\hat{\lambda}_\theta$ is the MLE of λ for fixed θ and $j_\lambda(\psi)$ is the observed information matrix for λ, i.e. $j_\lambda(\psi) = -\partial^2 \ell(\psi)/\partial\lambda\partial\lambda^T$.

Without a parametric model the definition of a parameter is more vexed. As in Chapter 2, we suppose that a parameter θ is determined by a statistical function $t(\cdot)$, so that $\theta = t(F)$ is a mean, median, or other quantity determined by, but not by itself determining, the unknown distribution F. Now the nuisance parameter λ is all aspects of F other than $t(F)$, so that in general λ is infinite dimensional. Not surprisingly, there is no unique way to construct a likelihood in this situation, and in this chapter we describe some of the different possibilities.

10.2 Multinomial-Based Likelihoods

10.2.1 Empirical likelihood

Scalar parameter

Suppose that observations $y_1, \ldots, y_n$ form a random sample from an unknown distribution F, and that we wish to construct a likelihood for a scalar parameter $\theta = t(F)$, where $t(\cdot)$ is a statistical function. One view of the EDF $\hat{F}$ is that it is the nonparametric maximum likelihood estimate of F, with corresponding nonparametric maximum likelihood estimate $t = t(\hat{F})$ for θ (Problem 10.1). The EDF is a multinomial distribution with denominator one and probability vector $(n^{-1}, \ldots, n^{-1})$ attached to the y_j. We can think of this distribution as embedded in a more general multinomial distribution with arbitrary probability vector $p = (p_1, \ldots, p_n)$ attached to the data values. If F is restricted to be such a multinomial distribution, then we can write $t(p)$ rather than $t(F)$ for the function which defines θ. The special multinomial probability vector $(n^{-1}, \ldots, n^{-1})$ corresponding to the EDF is $\hat{p}$, and $t = t(\hat{p})$ is the nonparametric maximum likelihood estimate of θ. This multinomial representation was used earlier in Sections 4.4 and 5.4.2.

Restricting the model to be multinomial on the data values with probability vector p, the parameter value is $\theta = t(p)$ and the likelihood for p is $L(p) = \prod_{j=1}^{n} p_j^{f_j}$, with f_j equal to the frequency of value y_j in the sample. But, assuming there are no tied observations, all f_j are equal to 1, so that $L(p) = p_1 \times \cdots \times p_n$: this is the analogue of $L(\psi)$ in the parametric case. We are interested only in $\theta = t(p)$, for which we can use the profile likelihood

$$L_{EL}(\theta) = \sup_{p\,:\,t(p)=\theta} \prod_{j=1}^{n} p_j, \qquad (10.3)$$

which is called the *empirical likelihood* for θ. Notice that the value of θ which maximizes $L_{EL}(\theta)$ corresponds to the value of p maximizing $L(p)$ with only the constraint $\sum p_j = 1$, that is $\hat{p}$. In other words, the empirical likelihood is maximized by the nonparametric maximum likelihood estimate t.

In (10.3) we maximize over the p_j subject to the constraints imposed by fixing $t(p) = \theta$ and $\sum p_j = 1$, which is effectively a maximization over $n - 2$ quantities when θ is scalar. Remarkably, although the number of parameters over which we maximize is comparable with the sample size, the approximate distributional results from the parametric situation carry over. Let θ_0 be the true value of θ, with T the maximum empirical likelihood estimator. Then under mild conditions on F and in large samples, the empirical likelihood ratio statistic

$$W_{EL}(\theta_0) = 2 \left\{ \log L_{EL}(T) - \log L_{EL}(\theta_0) \right\}$$

has an approximate chi-squared distribution with d degrees of freedom. Although the limiting distribution of $W_{EL}(\theta_0)$ is the same as that of $W_p(\theta_0)$ under a correct parametric model, such asymptotic results are typically less useful in the nonparametric setting. This suggests that the bootstrap be used to calibrate empirical likelihood, by using quantiles of bootstrap replicates of $W_{EL}(\theta_0)$, i.e. quantiles of $W_{EL}^*(\hat{\theta})$. This idea is outlined below.

Example 10.1 (Air-conditioning data)   We consider the empirical likelihood for the mean of the larger set of air-conditioning data in Table 5.6; $n = 24$

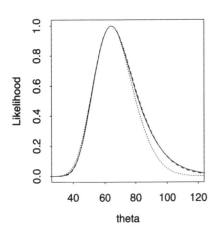
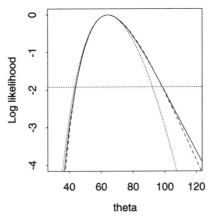

Figure 10.1 Likelihood
and log likelihoods for
the mean of the
air-conditioning data:
empirical (dots),
exponential (dashes),
and gamma profile
(solid). Values of θ
whose log likelihood lies
above the horizontal
dotted line in the right
panel are contained in
an asymptotic 95%
confidence set for the
true mean.

and $\bar{y} = 64.125$. The mean is $\theta = \int y\, dF(y)$, which equals $\sum_j p_j y_j$ for the
multinomial distribution that puts masses p_j on the y_j. For a specified value of
θ, finding (10.3) is equivalent to maximizing $\sum \log p_j$ with respect to $p_1, \ldots, p_n$,
subject to the constraints that $\sum p_j = 1$ and $\sum p_j y_j = \theta$. Use of Lagrange
multipliers gives $p_j \propto \{1 + \eta_\theta(y_j - \theta)\}^{-1}$, where the Lagrange multiplier η_θ is
determined by θ and satisfies the equation

$$\sum_{j=1}^{n} \frac{y_j - \theta}{1 + \eta_\theta(y_j - \theta)} = 0. \tag{10.4}$$

Thus the log empirical likelihood, normalized to have maximum zero, is

$$\ell_{EL}(\theta) = -\sum_{j=1}^{n} \log\{1 + \eta_\theta(y_j - \theta)\}. \tag{10.5}$$

This is maximized at the sample average $\theta = \bar{y}$, where $\eta_\theta = 0$ and $p_j = n^{-1}$. It
is undefined outside $(\min y_j, \max y_j)$, because no multinomial distribution on
the y_j can have mean outside this interval.

Figure 10.1 shows $L_{EL}(\theta)$, which is calculated by successive solution of (10.4)
to yield η_θ at values of θ small steps apart. The exponential likelihood and
gamma profile likelihood for the mean are also shown. As we should expect,
the gamma profile likelihood is always higher than the exponential likelihood,
which corresponds to the gamma likelihood but with shape parameter $\kappa = 1$.
Both parametric likelihoods are wider than the empirical likelihood. Direct
comparison between parametric and empirical likelihoods is misleading, however, since they are based on different models, and here and in later figures

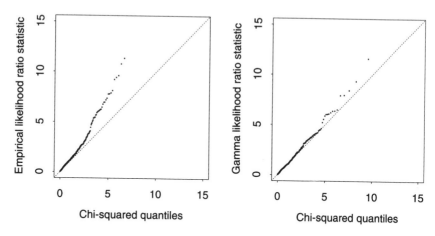

Figure 10.2 Simulated empirical likelihood ratio statistics (left panel) and gamma profile likelihood ratio statistics (right panel) for exponential samples of size 24. The dotted line corresponds to the theoretical χ_1^2 approximation.

we give the gamma likelihood purely as a visual reference. The circumstances in which empirical and parametric likelihoods are close are discussed in Problem 10.3.

The endpoints of an approximate 95% confidence interval for θ are obtained by reading off where $\ell_{EL}(\theta) = \frac{1}{2}c_{1,0.95}$, where $c_{d,\alpha}$ is the α quantile of the chi-squared distribution with d degrees of freedom. The interval is $(43.3, 92.3)$, which compares well with the nonparametric BC_a interval of $(42.4, 93.2)$. The likelihood ratio intervals for the exponential and gamma models are $(44.1, 98.4)$ and $(44.0, 98.6)$.

Figure 10.2 shows the empirical likelihood and gamma profile likelihood ratio statistics for 500 exponential samples of size 24. Though good for the parametric statistic, the chi-squared approximation is poor for W_{EL}, whose estimated 95% quantile is 5.92 compared to the χ_1^2 quantile of 3.84. This suggests strongly that the empirical likelihood-based confidence interval given above is too narrow. However, the simulations are only relevant when the data are exponential, in which case we would not be concerned with empirical likelihood.

We can use the bootstrap to estimate quantiles for $W_{EL}(\theta_0)$, by setting $\theta_0 = \bar{y}$ and then calculating $W^*(\theta_0)$ for bootstrap samples from the original data. The resulting Q-Q plot is less extreme than the left panel of Figure 10.2, with a 95% quantile estimate of 4.08 based on 999 bootstrap samples; the corresponding empirical likelihood ratio interval is $(42.8, 93.3)$. With a sample of size 12, 41 of the 999 simulations gave infinite values of $W_{EL}(\theta_0)$ because $\bar{y}$ did not lie within the limits $(\min y_j^*, \max y_j^*)$ of the bootstrap sample. With a sample of size 24, this problem did not arise. ∎

Vector parameter

In principle, empirical likelihood is straightforward to construct when θ has dimension $d < n - 1$. Suppose that $\theta = (\theta_1, \ldots, \theta_d)^T$ is determined implicitly as the root of the simultaneous equations

$$\int u(\theta; y) \, dF(y) = 0, \quad i = 1, \ldots, d,$$

where $u(\theta; y)$ is a $d \times 1$ vector whose ith element is $u_i(\theta; y)$. Then the estimate $\hat{\theta}$ is the solution to the d estimating equations

$$\sum_{j=1}^{n} u(\hat{\theta}; y_j) = 0. \tag{10.6}$$

An extension of the argument in Example 10.1, involving the vector of Lagrange multipliers $\eta_\theta = (\eta_{\theta 1}, \ldots, \eta_{\theta d})^T$, shows that the log empirical likelihood is

$$\ell_{EL}(\theta) = -\sum_{j=1}^{n} \log \left\{ 1 + \eta_\theta^T u_j(\theta) \right\}, \tag{10.7}$$

where $u_j(\theta) \equiv u(\theta; y_j)$. The value of η_θ is determined by θ through the simultaneous equations

$$\sum_{j=1}^{n} \frac{u_j(\theta)}{1 + \eta_\theta^T u_j(\theta)} = 0. \tag{10.8}$$

The simplest approximate confidence region for the true θ is the set of values such that $W_{EL}(\theta) \leq c_{d,1-\alpha}$, but in small samples it will again be preferable to replace the χ_d^2 quantile by its bootstrap estimate.

10.2.2 Empirical exponential family likelihoods

Another data-based multinomial likelihood can be based on an empirical exponential family construction. Suppose that $\hat{\theta}_1, \ldots, \hat{\theta}_d$ are defined as the solutions to the equations (10.6). Then rather than putting probability $n^{-1}\{1 + \eta_\theta^T u_j(\theta)\}^{-1}$ on y_j, corresponding to (10.7), we can take probabilities proportional to $\exp\{\xi_\theta^T u_j(\theta)\}$; this is the exponential tilting construction described in Example 4.16 and in Sections 5.3 and 9.4. Here $\xi_\theta = (\xi_{\theta 1}, \ldots, \xi_{\theta d})^T$ is determined by θ through

$$\sum_{j=1}^{n} u_j(\theta) \exp \left\{ \xi_\theta^T u_j(\theta) \right\} = 0. \tag{10.9}$$

This is analogous to (10.8), but it may be solved using a program that fits regression models for Poisson responses (Problem 10.4), which is often more convenient to deal with than the optimization problems posed by empirical likelihood. The log likelihood obtained by integrating (10.9) is $\ell_{EEF}(\theta) = \sum \exp\{\xi_\theta^T u_j(\theta)\}$. This can be close to $\ell_{EL}(\theta)$, which suggests that both the corresponding log likelihood ratio statistics share the same rather slow approach to their large-sample distributions.

In addition to likelihood ratio statistics from empirical exponential families and empirical likelihood, many other related statistics can be defined. For example, we can regard ξ_θ as the parameter in a Poisson regression model and construct a quadratic form

$$Q_{EEF}(\theta) = \left\{\sum_{j=1}^{n} u_j(\theta)\right\}^T \left\{\sum_{j=1}^{n} u_j(\theta)u_j(\theta)^T\right\}^{-1} \left\{\sum_{j=1}^{n} u_j(\theta)\right\} \qquad (10.10)$$

based on the score statistic that tests the hypothesis $\xi_\theta = 0$. There is a close parallel between $Q_{EEF}(\theta)$ and the quadratic forms used to set confidence regions in Section 5.8, but the nonlinear relationship between θ and $Q_{EEF}(\theta)$ means that the contours of (10.10) need not be elliptical. As discussed there, for example, theory suggests that when the true value of θ is θ_0, $Q_{EEF}(\theta_0)$ has a large-sample χ_d^2 distribution. Thus an approximate $1 - \alpha$ confidence region for θ is the set of values of θ for which $Q_{EEF}(\theta)$ does not exceed $c_{d,1-\alpha}$. And as there, it is generally better to use bootstrap estimates of the quantiles of $Q_{EEF}(\theta)$.

Example 10.2 (Laterite data) We consider again setting a confidence region based on the data in Example 5.15. Recall that the quantity of interest is the mean polar axis,

$$a(\theta, \phi) = (\cos\theta \cos\phi, \cos\theta \sin\phi, \sin\theta)^T,$$

which is the axis given by the eigenvector corresponding to the largest eigenvalue of $\mathrm{E}(YY^T)$. The data consist of positions on the lower half-sphere, or equivalently the sample values of $a(\theta, \phi)$, which we denote by y_j, $j = 1, \ldots, n$.

In order to set an empirical likelihood confidence region for the mean polar axis, or equivalently for the spherical polar coordinates (θ, ϕ), we let

$$b(\theta, \phi) = (\sin\theta \cos\phi, \sin\theta \sin\phi, -\cos\theta)^T, \qquad c(\theta, \phi) = (-\sin\phi, -\cos\phi, 0)^T$$

denote the unit vectors orthogonal to $a(\theta, \phi)$. Then since the eigenvectors of $\mathrm{E}(YY^T)$ may be taken to be orthogonal, the population values of (θ, ϕ) satisfy simultaneously the equations

$$b(\theta, \phi)^T \mathrm{E}(YY^T)a(\theta, \phi) = 0, \qquad c(\theta, \phi)^T \mathrm{E}(YY^T)a(\theta, \phi) = 0,$$

with sample equivalents

$$b(\theta, \phi)^T \left(n^{-1}\sum_{j=1}^{n} y_j y_j^T\right) a(\theta, \phi) = 0, \qquad c(\theta, \phi)^T \left(n^{-1}\sum_{j=1}^{n} y_j y_j^T\right) a(\theta, \phi) = 0.$$

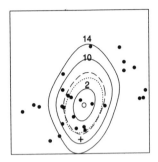 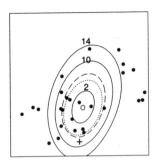

Figure 10.3 Contours of W_{EL} (left) and Q_{EEF} (right) for the mean polar axis, in the square region shown in Figure 5.10. The dashed lines show the 95% confidence regions using bootstrap quantiles. The dotted ellipse is the 95% confidence region based on a studentized statistic (Fisher, Lewis and Embleton, 1987, equation 6.9).

In terms of the previous general discussion, we have $d = 2$ and

$$u_j(\theta) \equiv u(\theta, \phi; y_j) = \begin{pmatrix} b(\theta, \phi)^T y_j y_j^T a(\theta, \phi) \\ c(\theta, \phi)^T y_j y_j^T a(\theta, \phi) \end{pmatrix}.$$

The left panel of Figure 10.3 shows the empirical likelihood contours based on (10.7) and (10.8), in the square region shown in Figure 5.10. The corresponding contours for $Q_{EEF}(\theta)$ are shown on the right. The dashed lines show the boundaries of the 95% confidence regions for (θ, ϕ) using bootstrap calibration; these differ little from those based on the asymptotic χ_2^2 distribution. In each panel the dotted ellipse is a 95% confidence region based on a studentized form of the sample mean polar axis, for which the contours are ellipses. The elliptical contours are appreciably tighter than those for the likelihood-based statistics.

Table 10.1 compares theoretical and bootstrap quantiles for several likelihood-based statistics and the studentized bootstrap statistic, Q, for the full data and for a random subset of size 20. For the full data, the quantiles for Q_{EEF} and W_{EL} are close to those for the large-sample χ_2^2 distribution. For the subset, Q_{EEF} is close to its nominal distribution, but the other statistics seem considerably more variable. Except for Q_{EEF}, it would be misleading to rely on the asymptotic results for the subsample.   ∎

Theoretical work suggests that W_{EL} should have better properties than statistics such as W_{EEF} or Q_{EEF}, but since simulations do not always confirm this, bootstrap quantiles should generally be used to set the limits of confidence regions from multinomial-based likelihoods.

Table 10.1 Bootstrap p quantiles of likelihood-based statistics for mean polar axis data.

p	χ_2^2	Full data, $n = 50$				Subset, $n = 20$			
		Q	W_{EL}	W_{EEF}	Q_{EEF}	Q	W_{EL}	W_{EEF}	Q_{EEF}
0.80	3.22	3.23	3.40	3.37	3.15	3.67	3.70	3.61	3.15
0.90	4.61	4.77	4.81	5.05	4.69	5.39	5.66	5.36	4.45
0.95	5.99	6.08	6.18	6.94	6.43	7.17	7.99	10.82	7.03

10.3 Bootstrap Likelihood

Basic idea

Suppose for simplicity that our data $y_1, \ldots, y_n$ form a homogeneous random sample for which statistic T takes value t. If the data were governed by a parametric model under which T had the density $f_T(\cdot; \theta)$, then a partial likelihood for θ based on T would be $f_T(t; \theta)$ regarded as a function of θ. In the absence of a parametric model, we may estimate the density of T at t, for different values of θ, by means of a nonparametric double bootstrap.

To be specific, suppose that we generate a first-level bootstrap sample $y_1^*, \ldots, y_n^*$ from $y_1, \ldots, y_n$, with corresponding estimator value t^*. This bootstrap sample is now considered as a population whose parameter value is t^*; the empirical distribution of $y_1^*, \ldots, y_n^*$ is the nonparametric analogue of a parametric model with $\theta = t^*$. We then generate M second-level bootstrap samples by sampling from our first-level sample, and calculate the corresponding values of T, namely $t_1^{**}, \ldots, t_M^{**}$. Kernel density estimation based on these second-level values provides an approximate density for T^{**}, and by analogy with parametric partial likelihood we take this density at $t^{**} = t$ to be the value of a nonparametric partial likelihood at $\theta = t^*$. If the density estimate uses kernel $w(\cdot)$ with bandwidth h, then this leads to the *bootstrap likelihood* value at $\theta = t^*$ given by

$$L(t^*) = f_{T^{**}}(t \mid t^*) = \frac{1}{Mh} \sum_{m=1}^{M} w\left(\frac{t_m^{**} - t}{h}\right). \tag{10.11}$$

On repeating this procedure for R different first-level bootstrap samples, we obtain R approximate likelihood values $L(t_r^*)$, $r = 1, \ldots, R$, from which a smooth likelihood curve $L_B(\theta)$ can be produced by nonparametric smoothing.

Computational improvements

There are various ways to reduce the large amount of computation needed to obtain a smooth curve. One, which was used earlier in Section 3.9.2, is to generate second-level samples from smoothed versions of the first-level samples. As before, probability distributions on the values $y_1, \ldots, y_n$ are denoted by vectors $p = (p_1,\ldots,p_n)$, and parameter values are expressed as $t(p)$; recall that $\hat{p} = (\frac{1}{n},\ldots,\frac{1}{n})$ and $t = t(\hat{p})$. The rth first-level bootstrap sample gives statistic value t_r^*, and the data value y_j occurs with frequency $f_{rj}^* = np_{rj}^*$, say. In the bootstrap likelihood calculation this bootstrap sample is considered as a population with probability distribution $p_r^* = (p_{r1}^*,\ldots,p_{rn}^*)$ on the data values, and $t_r^* = t(p_r^*)$ is considered as the θ-value for this population.

In order to obtain populations which vary smoothly with θ, we apply kernel smoothing to the p_r^*, as in Section 3.9.2. Thus for target parameter value θ^0 we define the vector $p^*(\theta^0)$ of probabilities

$$p_j^*(\theta^0) \propto \frac{1}{R\varepsilon}\sum_{r=1}^{R} w\left(\frac{\theta^0 - t_r^*}{\varepsilon}\right)p_{rj}^*, \quad j = 1,\ldots,n, \tag{10.12}$$

where typically $w(\cdot)$ is the standard normal density and $\varepsilon = v_L^{1/2}$; as usual v_L is the nonparametric delta method variance estimate for t. The distribution $p^*(\theta^0)$ will have parameter value not θ^0 but $\theta = t\left(p^*(\theta^0)\right)$. With the understanding that θ is defined in this way, we shall for simplicity write $p^*(\theta)$ rather than $p^*(\theta^0)$. For a fixed collection of R first-level samples and bandwidth $\varepsilon > 0$, the probability vectors $p^*(\theta)$ change gradually as θ varies over its range of interest.

Second-level bootstrap sampling now uses vectors $p^*(\theta)$ as sampling distributions on the data values, in place of the p_r^*s. The second-level sample values t^{**} are then used in (10.11) to obtain $L_B(\theta)$. Repeating this calculation for, say, 100 values of θ in the range $t \pm 4v_L^{1/2}$, followed by smooth interpolation, should give a good result.

Experience suggests that the value $\varepsilon = v_L^{1/2}$ is safe to use in (10.12) if the t_r^* are roughly equally spaced, which can be arranged by weighted first-level sampling, as outlined in Problem 10.6.

A way to reduce further the amount of calculation is to use recycling, as described in Section 9.4.4. Rather than generate second-level samples from each $p^*(\theta)$ of interest, one set of M samples can be generated using distribution p on the data values, and the associated values $t_1^{**},\ldots,t_M^{**}$ calculated. Then, following the general re-weighting method (9.24), the likelihood values are calculated as

$$L_B(\theta) = \frac{1}{Mh}\sum_{m=1}^{M} w\left(\frac{t_m^{**} - t}{h}\right)\prod_{j=1}^{n}\left\{\frac{p_j^*(\theta)}{p_j}\right\}^{f_{jm}^{**}}, \tag{10.13}$$

where f_{jm}^{**} is the frequency of the jth case in the mth second-level bootstrap sample. One simple choice for p is the EDF $\hat{p}$. In special cases it will be possible to replace the second level of sampling by use of the saddlepoint approximation method of Section 9.5. This would give an accurate and smooth approximation to the density of T^{**} for sampling from each $p^*(\theta)$.

Example 10.3 (Air-conditioning data)   We apply the ideas outlined above to

Figure 10.4 Bootstrap likelihood for mean of air-conditioning data. Left panel: bootstrap likelihood values obtained by saddlepoint approximation for 200 random samples, with smooth curve fitted to values obtained by smoothing frequencies from 1000 bootstrap samples. Right panel: gamma profile log likelihood (solid) and bootstrap log likelihood (dots).

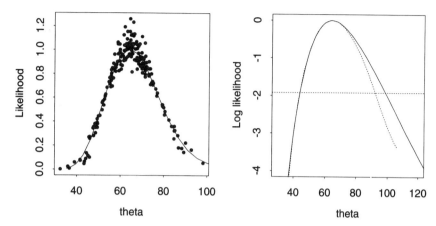

the data from Example 10.1. The solid points in the left panel of Figure 10.4 are bootstrap likelihood values for the mean θ for 200 resamples, obtained by saddlepoint approximation. This replaces the kernel density estimate (10.11) and avoids the second level of resampling, but does not remove the variation in estimated likelihood values for different bootstrap samples with similar values of t_r^*. A locally quadratic nonparametric smoother (on the log likelihood scale) could be used to produce a smooth likelihood curve from the values of $L(t_r^*)$, but another approach is better, as we now describe.

The solid line in the left panel of Figure 10.4 interpolates values obtained by applying the saddlepoint approximation using probabilities (10.12) at a few values of θ^0. Here the values of t_r^* are generated at random, and we have taken $\varepsilon = 0.5 v_L^{1/2}$; the results depend little on the value of ε.

The log bootstrap likelihood is very close to log empirical likelihood, with 95% confidence interval $(43.8, 92.1)$. ∎

Bootstrap likelihood is based purely on resampling and smoothing, which is a potential advantage over empirical likelihood. However, in its simplest form it is more computer-intensive. This precludes bootstrapping to estimate quantiles of bootstrap likelihood ratio statistics, which would involve three levels of nested resampling.

10.4 Likelihood Based on Confidence Sets

In certain circumstances it is possible to view confidence intervals as being approximately posterior probability sets, in the Bayesian sense. This encourages the idea of defining a confidence distribution for θ from the set of confidence limits, and then taking the PDF of this distribution as a likelihood function. That is, if we define the confidence distribution function C by $C(\hat{\theta}_\alpha) = \alpha$, then the associated likelihood would be the "density" $dC(\theta)/d\theta$. Leaving the philosophical arguments aside, we look briefly at where this idea leads in the context of nonparametric bootstrap methods.

10.4.1 Likelihood from pivots

Suppose that $Z(\theta) = z(\theta, \hat{F})$ is a pivot, with CDF $K(z)$ not depending on the true distribution F, and that $z(\theta)$ is a monotone function of θ. Then the confidence distribution based on confidence limits derived from z leads to the likelihood

$$L^\dagger(\theta) = |\dot{z}(\theta)| k\{z(\theta)\}, \qquad (10.14)$$

$\dot{z}(\theta)$ equals $\partial z(\theta)/\partial \theta$.

where $k(z) = dK(z)/dz$. Since k will be unknown in practice, it must be estimated.

In fact this definition of likelihood has a hidden defect. If the identification of confidence distribution with posterior distribution is accurate, as it is to a good approximation in many cases, then the effect of some prior distribution has been ignored in (10.14). But this effect can be removed by a simple device. Consider an imaginary experiment in which a random sample of size $2n$ is obtained, with outcome exactly two copies of the data y that we have. Then the likelihood would be the square of the likelihood $L_Z(\theta \mid y)$ we are trying to calculate. The ratio of the corresponding posterior densities would be simply $L_Z(\theta \mid y)$. This argument suggests that we apply the confidence density (10.14) twice, first with data y to give $L_n^\dagger(\theta)$, say, and second with data (y, y) to give $L_{2n}^\dagger(\theta)$. The ratio $L_{2n}^\dagger(\theta)/L_n^\dagger(\theta)$ will then be a likelihood with the unknown prior effect removed. In an explicit notation, this definition can be written

$$L_Z(\theta) = \frac{L_{2n}^\dagger(\theta)}{L_n^\dagger} = \frac{|\dot{z}_{2n}(\theta)| k_{2n}\{z_{2n}(\theta)\}}{|\dot{z}_n(\theta)| k_n\{z_n(\theta)\}}, \qquad (10.15)$$

where the subscripts indicate sample size. Note that $\hat{F}$ and t are the same for both sample sizes, but quantities such as variance estimates will depend upon sample size. Note also that the implied prior is estimated by $L_n^{\dagger 2}(\theta)/L_{2n}^\dagger(\theta)$.

Example 10.4 (Exponential mean)   If data $y_1, \ldots, y_n$ are sampled from an exponential distribution with mean θ, then a suitable choice for $z(\theta, \hat{F})$ is $\bar{y}/\theta$. The gamma distribution for $\bar{Y}$ can be used to check that the original definition (10.14) gives $L^\dagger(\theta) = \theta^{-n-1} \exp(-n\bar{y}/\theta)$, whereas the true likelihood is $\theta^{-n} \exp(-n\bar{y}/\theta)$. The true result is obtained exactly using (10.15). The implied prior is $\pi(\theta) \propto \theta^{-1}$, for $\theta > 0$.   ∎

In practice the distribution of Z must be estimated, in general by bootstrap sampling, so the densities k_n and k_{2n} in (10.15) must be estimated. To be specific, consider the particular case of the studentized quantity $z(\theta) = (t-\theta)/v_L^{1/2}$. Apart from a constant multiplier, the definition (10.15) gives

$$L^\dagger(\theta) = k_{2n}\left(\frac{t-\theta}{v_{2n,L}^{1/2}}\right) \Big/ k_n\left(\frac{t-\theta}{v_{n,L}^{1/2}}\right), \tag{10.16}$$

where $v_{n,L} = v_L$ and $v_{2n,L} = \frac{1}{2}v_L$, and we have used the fact that t is the estimate for both sample sizes. The densities k_n and k_{2n} are approximated using bootstrap sample values as follows. First R nonparametric samples of size n are drawn from $\hat{F}$ and corresponding values of $z_n^* = (t_n^* - t)/v_{n,L}^{*1/2}$ calculated. Then R samples of size $2n$ are drawn from $\hat{F}$ and values of $z_{2n}^* = (t_{2n}^* - t)/(v_{2n,L}^*)^{1/2}$ calculated. Next kernel estimates for k_n and k_{2n}, with bandwidths h_n and h_{2n} respectively, are obtained and substituted in (10.16). For example,

$$\hat{k}_n\left(\frac{t-\theta}{v_{n,L}^{1/2}}\right) = \frac{1}{h_n R}\sum_{r=1}^{R} w\left(\frac{t-\theta-v_{n,L}^{1/2}z_{n,r}^*}{h_n v_{n,L}^{1/2}}\right). \tag{10.17}$$

In practice these values can be computed via spline smoothing from a dense set of values of the kernel density estimates $\hat{k}_n(z)$.

There are difficulties with this method. First, just as with bootstrap likelihood, it is necessary to use a large number of simulations R. A second difficulty is that of ascertaining whether or not the chosen Z is a pivot, or else what prior transformation of T could be used to make Z pivotal; see Section 5.2.2. This is especially true if we extend (10.16) to vector θ, which is theoretically possible. Note that if the studentized bootstrap is applied to a transformation of t rather than t itself, then the factor $|\dot{z}(\theta)|$ in (10.14) can be ignored when applying (10.16).

10.4.2 Implied likelihood

In principle any bootstrap confidence limit method can be turned into a likelihood method via the confidence distribution, but it makes sense to restrict attention to the more accurate methods such as the studentized bootstrap used above. Section 5.4 discusses the underlying theory and introduces one other method, the *ABC* method, which is particularly easy to use as basis for a likelihood because no simulation is required.

First, a confidence density is obtained via the quadratic approximation (5.42), with a, b and c as defined for the nonparametric *ABC* method in (5.49). Then, using the argument that led to (10.15), it is possible to show that the induced likelihood function is

$$L_{ABC}(\theta) = \exp\{-\tfrac{1}{2}u^2(\theta)\}, \tag{10.18}$$

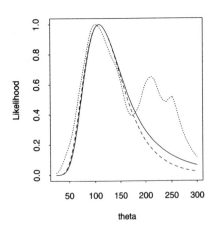 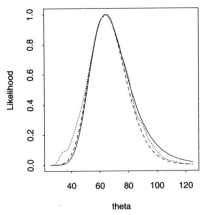

Figure 10.5 Gamma profile likelihood (solid), implied likelihood L_{ABC} (dashes) and pivot-based likelihood (dots) for air-conditioning dataset of size 12 (left panel) and size 24 (right panel). The pivot-based likelihood uses $R = 9999$ simulations and bandwidths 1.0.

where

$$u(\theta) = \frac{2r(\theta)}{1 + 2ar(\theta) + \{1 + 4ar(\theta)\}^{1/2}}, \quad r(\theta) = -\frac{2z(\theta)}{1 + \{1 - 4cz(\theta)\}^{1/2}},$$

with $z(\theta) = (t - \theta)/v_L^{1/2}$ as before. This is called the *implied likelihood*. Based on the discussion in Section 5.4, one would expect results similar to those from applying (10.16).

A further modification is to multiply $L_{ABC}(\theta)$ by $\exp\{(cv_L^{1/2} - b)\theta/v_L\}$, with b the bias estimate defined in (5.49). The effect of this modification is to make the likelihood even more compatible with the Bayesian interpretation, somewhat akin to the adjusted profile likelihood (10.2).

Example 10.5 (Air-conditioning data)   Figure 10.5 shows confidence likelihoods for the two sets of air-conditioning data in Table 5.6, samples of size 12 and 24 respectively. The implied likelihoods $L_{ABC}(\theta)$ are similar to the empirical likelihoods for these data. The pivotal likelihood $L_Z(\theta)$, calculated from $R = 9999$ samples with bandwidths equal to 1.0 in (10.17), is clearly quite unstable for the smaller sample size. This also occurred with bootstrap likelihood for these data and seems to be due to the discreteness of the simulations with so small a sample.   ∎

10.5 Bayesian Bootstraps

All the inferences we have described thus far have been frequentist: we have summarized uncertainty in terms of confidence regions for the unknown parameter θ of interest, based on repeated sampling from a distribution F. A

quite different approach is possible if prior information is available regarding
F. Suppose that the only possible values of Y are known to be $u_1, \ldots, u_N$, and
that these arise with unknown probabilities $p_1, \ldots, p_N$, so that

$$\Pr(Y = u_j \mid p_1, \ldots, p_N) = p_j, \qquad \sum p_j = 1.$$

If our data consist of the random sample $y_1, \ldots, y_n$, and f_j counts how many
y_i equal u_j, the probability of the observed data given the values of the
p_j is proportional to $\prod_{j=1}^{N} p_j^{f_j}$. If the prior information regarding the p_j is
summarized in the prior density $\pi(p_1, \ldots, p_N)$, the joint posterior density of the
p_j given the data is proportional to

$$\pi(p_1, \ldots, p_N) \prod_{j=1}^{N} p_j^{f_j},$$

and this induces a posterior density for θ. Its calculation is particularly straightforward when π is the Dirichlet density, in which case the prior and posterior
densities are respectively proportional to

$$\prod_{j=1}^{N} p_j^{a_j}, \qquad \prod_{j=1}^{N} p_j^{a_j + f_j};$$

the posterior density is Dirichlet also. *Bayesian bootstrap* samples and the
corresponding values of θ are generated from the joint posterior density for
the p_j, as follows.

Algorithm 10.1 (Bayesian bootstrap)
For $r = 1, \ldots, R$,

    1 Let $G_1, \ldots, G_N$ be independent gamma variables with shape parameters
       $a_j + f_j + 1$, and unit scale parameters, and for $j = 1, \ldots, N$ set $P_j^\dagger = G_j/(G_1 + \cdots + G_N)$.
    2 Let $\theta_r^\dagger = t(F_r^\dagger)$, where $F_r^\dagger \equiv (P_1^\dagger, \ldots, P_N^\dagger)$.
Estimate the posterior density for θ by kernel smoothing of $\theta_1^\dagger, \ldots, \theta_R^\dagger$.   •

    In practice with continuous data we have $f_j \equiv 1$. The simplest version of
the simulation puts $a_j = -1$, corresponding to an improper prior distribution
with support on $y_1, \ldots, y_n$; the G_j are then exponential. Some properties of this
procedure are outlined in Problem 10.10.

Example 10.6 (City population data) In the city population data of Example 2.8, for which $n = 10$, the parameter $\theta = t(F)$ and the rth simulated
posterior value $\theta_r^\dagger$ are

$$t(F) = \frac{\int x \, dF(u, x)}{\int u \, dF(u, x)}, \qquad t(F_r^\dagger) = \frac{\sum x_j P_{jr}^\dagger}{\sum u_j P_{jr}^\dagger}.$$

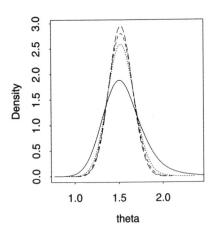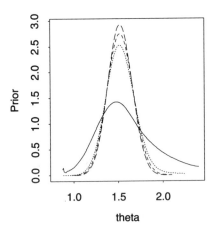

Figure 10.6 Bayesian bootstrap applied to city population data, with $n = 10$. The left panel shows posterior densities for ratio θ estimated from 999 Bayesian bootstrap simulations, with $a = -1, 2, 5, 10$; the densities are more peaked as a increases. The right panel shows the corresponding prior densities for θ.

The left panel of Figure 10.6 shows kernel density estimates of the posterior density of θ based on $R = 999$ simulations with all the a_j equal to $a = -1, 2, 5,$ and 10. The increasingly strong prior information results in posterior densities that are more and more sharply peaked.

The right panel shows the implied priors on θ, obtained using the data doubling device from Section 10.4. The priors seem highly informative, even when $a = -1$.   ∎

The primary use of the Bayesian bootstrap is likely to be for imputation when data are missing, rather than in inference for θ *per se*. There are theoretical advantages to such *weighted bootstraps*, in which the probabilities $P^\dagger$ vary smoothly, but as yet they have been little used in applications.

10.6 Bibliographic Notes

Likelihood inference is the core of parametric statistics. Many elementary textbooks contain some discussion of large-sample likelihood asymptotics, while adjusted likelihoods and higher-order approximations are described by Barndorff-Nielsen and Cox (1994).

Empirical likelihood was defined for single samples by Owen (1988) and extended to wider classes of models in a series of papers (Owen, 1990, 1991). Qin and Lawless (1994) make theoretical connections to estimating equations, while Hall and La Scala (1990) discuss some practical issues in using empirical likelihoods. More general models to which empirical likelihood has been applied include density estimation (Hall and Owen, 1993; Chen 1996), length-biased data (Qin, 1993), truncated data (Li, 1995), and time series (Monti,

1997). Applications to directional data are discussed by Fisher *et al.* (1996). Owen (1992a) reports simulations that compare the behaviour of the empirical likelihood ratio statistic with bootstrap methods for samples of size up to 20, with overall conclusions in line with those of Section 5.7: the studentized bootstrap performs best, in particular giving more accurate confidence intervals for the mean than the empirical likelihood ratio statistic, for a variety of underlying populations.

Related theoretical developments are due to DiCiccio, Hall and Romano (1991), DiCiccio and Romano (1989), and Chen and Hall (1993). From a theoretical viewpoint it is noteworthy that the empirical likelihood ratio statistic can be Bartlett-adjusted, though Corcoran, Davison and Spady (1996) question the practical relevance of this. Hall (1990) makes theoretical comparisons between empirical likelihood and likelihood based on studentized pivots.

Empirical likelihood has roots in certain problems in survival analysis, notably using the product-limit estimator to set confidence intervals for a survival probability. Related methods are discussed by Murphy (1995). See also Mykland (1995), who introduces the idea of dual likelihood, which treats the Lagrange multiplier in (10.7) as a parameter. Except in large samples, it seems likely that our caveats about asymptotic results apply here also.

Empirical exponential families have been discussed in Section 10.10 of Efron (1982) and DiCiccio and Romano (1990), among others; see also Corcoran, Davison and Spady (1996), who make comparisons with empirical likelihood statistics. Jing and Wood (1996) show that empirical exponential family likelihood is not Bartlett adjustable. A univariate version of the statistic Q_{EEF} in Section 10.2.2 is discussed by Lloyd (1994) in the context of M-estimation.

Bootstrap likelihood was introduced by Davison, Hinkley and Worton (1992), who discuss its relationship to empirical likelihood, while a later paper (Davison, Hinkley and Worton, 1995) describes computational improvements.

Early work on the use of confidence distributions to define nonparametric likelihoods was done by Hall (1987), Boos and Monahan (1986), and Ogbonmwan and Wynn (1986). The use of confidence distributions in Section 10.4 rests in part on the similarity of confidence distributions to Bayesian posterior distributions. For related theory see Welch and Peers (1963), Stein (1985) and Berger and Bernardo (1992). Efron (1993) discusses the likelihood derived from *ABC* confidence limits, shows a strong connection with profile likelihood and related likelihoods, and gives several applications; see also Chapter 24 of Efron and Tibshirani (1993).

The Bayesian bootstrap was introduced by Rubin (1981), and subsequently used by Rubin and Schenker (1986) and Rubin (1987) for multiple imputation in missing data problems. Banks (1988) has described some variants of the Bayesian bootstrap, while Newton and Raftery (1994) describe a variant which they name the weighted likelihood bootstrap. A comprehensive theoretical discussion of weighted bootstraps is given in Barbe and Bertail (1995).

10.7 Problems

1   Consider empirical likelihood for a parameter $\theta = t(F)$ defined by an estimating equation $\int u(t; y) \, dF(y) = 0$, based on a random sample $y_1, \ldots, y_n$.
(a) Use Lagrange multipliers to maximize $\sum \log p_j$ subject to the conditions $\sum p_j = 1$ and $\sum p_j u(t; y_j) = 0$, and hence show that the log empirical likelihood is given by (10.7) with $d = 1$. Verify that the empirical likelihood is maximized at the sample EDF, when $\theta = t(\hat{F})$.
(b) Suppose that $u(t; y) = y - t$ and $n = 2$, with $y_1 < y_2$. Show that η_θ can be written as $(\theta - \bar{y})/\{(\theta - y_1)(y_2 - \theta)\}$, and sketch it as a function of θ.
(Section 10.2.1)

2   Suppose that $x_1, \ldots, x_n$ and $y_1, \ldots, y_m$ are independent random samples from distributions with means μ and $\mu + \delta$. Obtain the empirical likelihood ratio statistic for δ.
(Section 10.2.1)

3   (a) In (10.5), suppose that $\theta = \bar{y} + n^{-1/2} \sigma \varepsilon$, where $\sigma^2 = \text{var}(y_j)$ and ε has an asymptotic standard normal distribution. Show that $\eta_\theta \doteq -n^{-1/2} \varepsilon / \sigma^2$, and deduce that near $\bar{y}$, $\ell_{EL}(\theta) \doteq -\frac{n}{2} (\bar{y} - \theta)^2 / \sigma^2$.
(b) Now suppose that a single observation from F has log density $\ell(\theta) = \log f(y; \theta)$ and corresponding Fisher information $i(\theta) = \text{E}\{-\ddot{\ell}(\theta)\}$. Use the fact that the MLE $\hat{\theta}$ satisfies the equation $\dot{\ell}(\hat{\theta}) = 0$ to show that near $\hat{\theta}$ the parametric log likelihood is roughly $\ell(\theta) \doteq -\frac{n}{2} i(\theta)(\hat{\theta} - \theta)^2$
(c) By considering the double exponential density $\frac{1}{2} \exp(-|y - \theta|)$, $-\infty < y < \infty$, and an exponential family density with mean θ, $a(y) \exp\{yb(\theta) - c(\theta)\}$, show that it may or may not be true that $\ell_{EL}(\theta) \doteq \ell(\theta)$.
(Section 10.2.1; DiCiccio, Hall and Romano, 1989)

4   Let θ be a scalar parameter defined by an estimating equation $\int u(\theta; y) \, dF(y) = 0$. Suppose that we wish to make likelihood inference for θ based on a random sample $y_1, \ldots, y_n$, using the empirical exponential family

$$\pi_j(\theta) = \Pr(Y = y_j) = \frac{e^{\xi_\theta u(\theta; y_j)}}{\sum_{k=1}^n e^{\xi_\theta u(\theta; y_k)}}, \quad j = 1, \ldots, n,$$

where ξ_θ is determined by

$$\sum_{j=1}^n \pi_j(\theta) u(\theta; y_j) = 0. \tag{10.19}$$

(a) Let $Z_1, \ldots, Z_n$ be independent Poisson variables with means $\exp(\xi u_j)$, where $u_j \equiv u(\theta; y_j)$; we treat θ as fixed. Write down the likelihood equation for ξ, and show that when the observed values of the Z_j all equal zero, it is equivalent to (10.19). Hence outline how software that fits generalized linear models may be used to find ξ_θ.
(b) Show that the formulation in terms of Poisson variables suggests that the empirical exponential family likelihood ratio statistic is the Poisson deviance $W_{EEF}(\theta_0)$,

while the multinomial form gives $W'_{EEF}(\theta_0)$, where

$$W_{EEF}(\theta_0) = 2\sum\{1 - \exp(\xi_\theta u_j)\},$$

$$W'_{EEF}(\theta_0) = 2\left[n\log\left\{n^{-1}\sum e^{\xi_\theta u_j}\right\} - \xi_\theta \sum u_j\right].$$

(c) Plot the log likelihood functions corresponding to W_{EEF} and W'_{EEF} for the data in Example 10.1; take $u_j = y_j - \theta$. Perform a small simulation study to compare the behaviour of W_{EEF} and W'_{EEF} when the underlying data are samples of size 24 from the exponential distribution.
(Section 10.2.2)

5 Suppose that $a = (\sin\theta, \cos\theta)^T$ is the mean direction of a distribution on the unit circle, and consider setting a nonparametric confidence set for a based on a random sample of angles $\theta_1, \ldots, \theta_n$; set $y_j = (\sin\theta_j, \cos\theta_j)^T$.
(a) Show that $\hat{a}$ is determined by the equation $\sum y_j^T b = 0$, where $b = (\cos\theta, -\sin\theta)^T$. Hence explain how to construct confidence sets based on statistics from empirical likelihood and from empirical exponential families.
(b) Extend the argument to data taking values on the unit sphere, with mean direction $a = (\cos\theta\cos\phi, \cos\theta\sin\phi, \sin\theta)^T$.
(c) See Practical 10.2.
(Section 10.2.2; Fisher et al., 1996)

6 Suppose that t has empirical influence values l_j, and set

$$p_j^\bullet(\theta^0) = \frac{e^{\xi l_j}}{\sum_{i=1}^n e^{\xi l_i}}, \tag{10.20}$$

where $\xi = v^{1/2}(\theta^0 - t)$ and $v = n^{-2}\sum l_j^2$.
(a) Show that $t(\hat{F}_\xi) \doteq \theta_0$, where $\hat{F}_\xi$ denotes the CDF corresponding to (10.20). Hence describe how to space out the values $t_r^\bullet$ in the first-level resampling for a bootstrap likelihood.
(b) Rather than use the tilted probabilities (10.12) to construct a bootstrap likelihood by simulation, suppose that we use those in (10.20). For a linear statistic, show that the cumulant-generating function of $T^{\bullet\bullet}$ in sampling from (10.20) is $\lambda t + n\{K(\xi + n^{-1}\lambda) - K(\xi)\}$, where $K(\xi) = \log(\sum e^{\xi l_j})$. Deduce that the saddlepoint approximation to $f_{T^{\bullet\bullet}|T^\bullet}(t \mid \theta^0)$ is proportional to $\exp\{-nK(\xi)\}$, where $\theta^0 = K'(\xi)$. Hence show that for the sample average, the log likelihood at $\theta^0 = \sum y_j e^{\xi y_j}/\sum e^{\xi y_j}$ is $n\{\xi t - \log(\sum e^{\xi y_j})\}$.
(c) Extend (b) to the situation where t is defined as the solution to a monotonic estimating equation.
(Section 10.3; Davison, Hinkley and Worton, 1992)

7 Consider the choice of h for the raw bootstrap likelihood values (10.11), when $w(\cdot)$ is the standard normal density. As is often roughly true, suppose that $T^\bullet \sim N(t, v)$, and that conditional on $T^\bullet = t^\bullet$, $T^{\bullet\bullet} \sim N(t^\bullet, v)$.
(a) Show that the mean and variance of the product of $v^{1/2}$ with (10.11) are I_1 and $M^{-1}(I_2 - I_1^2)$, where

$$I_k = (2\pi)^{-k/2}\gamma^{-(k-1)}(\gamma^2 + k)^{-1/2}\exp\left\{-\frac{k\delta^2}{2(\gamma^2 + k)}\right\},$$

where $\gamma = hv^{-1/2}$ and $\delta = v^{-1/2}(t^\bullet - t)$. Hence verify some of the values in the following table:

	$\delta = 0$			$\delta = 1$			$\delta = 2$		
γ	0	1	2	0	1	2	0	1	2
Density $\times 10^{-2}$	39.9	39.9	39.9	24.2	24.2	24.2	5.4	5.4	5.4
Bias $\times 10^{-2}$	-0.8	-2.9	-5.7	0	-0.1	-0.5	0.3	1.2	2.5
$M \times$ variance $\times 10^{-2}$	40.4	13.4	5.6	28.3	11.2	5.7	7.5	3.8	2.6

(b) If γ is small, show that the variance of (10.11) is roughly proportional to the square of its mean, and deduce that the variance is approximately constant on the log scale.

(c) Extend the calculations in (a) to (10.13).

(Section 10.3; Davison, Hinkley and Worton, 1992)

8   Let y represent data from a parametric model $f(y;\theta)$, and suppose that θ is estimated by $t(y)$. Assuming that simulation error may be ignored, under what circumstances would the bootstrap likelihood generated by parametric simulation from f equal the parametric likelihood? Illustrate your answer with the $N(\theta, 1)$ distribution, taking t to be (i) the sample average, (ii) the sample median.

(Section 10.3)

9   Suppose that we wish to construct an implied likelihood for a correlation coefficient θ based on its sample value T by treating $Z = \frac{1}{2}\log\{(1+T)/(1-T)\}$ as normal with mean $g(\theta) = \frac{1}{2}\log\{(1+\theta)/(1-\theta)\}$ and variance n^{-1}. Show that the implied likelihood and implied prior are proportional to

$$\exp\left[-\tfrac{n}{2}\{g(t) - g(\theta)\}^2\right], \qquad (1-\theta)^{-2}, \quad |\theta| < 1.$$

Is the prior here proper?

(Section 10.4)

10   The Dirichlet density with parameters $(\xi_1, \ldots, \xi_n)$ is

$$\frac{\Gamma(\xi_1 + \cdots + \xi_n)}{\Gamma(\xi_1) \cdots \Gamma(\xi_n)} p_1^{\xi_1 - 1} \cdots p_n^{\xi_n - 1}, \qquad p_j > 0, \quad \sum p_j = 1, \quad \xi_j > 0.$$

Show that the P_j have joint moments

$$\mathrm{E}(P_j) = \frac{\xi_j}{s}, \quad \mathrm{cov}(P_j, P_k) = \frac{\xi_j(\delta_{jk}s - \xi_k)}{s^2(t+1)},$$

where $\delta_{jk} = 1$ if $j = k$ and zero otherwise, and $s = \xi_1 + \cdots + \xi_n$.

(a) Let $y_1, \ldots, y_n$ be a random sample, and consider bootstrapping its average. Show that under the Bayesian bootstrap with $a_j \equiv a$,

$$\mathrm{E}^\dagger(P_j^\dagger) = n^{-1}, \quad \mathrm{cov}^\dagger(P_j^\dagger, P_k^\dagger) = \frac{\delta_{jk} - 1/n}{n(2n + an + 1)}. \tag{10.21}$$

Hence show that the posterior mean and variance of $\theta^\dagger = \sum y_j P_j^\dagger$ are $\bar{y}$ and $(2n + an + 1)^{-1} m_2$, where $m_2 = n^{-1}\sum(y_j - \bar{y})^2$.

(b) Now consider the average $\bar{Y}^\dagger$ of bootstrap samples generated as follows. We generate a distribution $F^\dagger \equiv (P_1^\dagger, \ldots, P_n^\dagger)$ on $y_1, \ldots, y_n$ under the Bayesian bootstrap, and then make $Y_1^\dagger, \ldots, Y_n^\dagger$ by independent multinomial sampling from $F^\dagger$. Show that

$$\mathrm{E}^\dagger(\bar{Y}^\dagger) = \bar{y}, \quad \mathrm{var}(\bar{Y}^\dagger) = \frac{n(a+3)}{(2n+an+1)}\frac{m_2}{n}.$$

Are the properties of this as $n \to \infty$ and $a \to \infty$ what you would expect? How does this compare with samples generated by the usual nonparametric bootstrap? (Section 10.5)

10.8 Practicals

1   We compare the empirical likelihoods and 95% confidence intervals for the mean of the data in Table 3.1, (a) pooling the eight series:

```
attach(gravity)
grav.EL <- EL.profile(g,tmin=70,tmax=85,n.t=51)
plot(grav.EL[,1],exp(grav.EL[,2]),type="l",xlab="mu",
    ylab="empirical likelihood")
lik.CI(grav.EL,lim=-0.5*qchisq(0.95,1))
```

and (b) treating the series as arising from separate distributions with the same mean and plotting eight individual likelihoods:

```
gravs.EL <- EL.profile(g[series==1],n.t=21)
plot(gravs.EL[,1],exp(gravs.EL[,2]),type="n",xlab="mu",
    ylab="empirical likelihood",xlim=range(g))
lines(gravs.EL[,1],exp(gravs.EL[,2]),lty=2)
for (s in 2:8)
{ gravs.EL <- EL.profile(g[series==s],n.t=21)
  lines(gravs.EL[,1],exp(gravs.EL[,2]),lty=2) }
```

Now we combine the individual likelihoods into a single likelihood by multiplying them together; we renormalize so that the product has maximum one.

```
lims <- matrix(NA,8,2)
for (s in 1:8) { x <- g[series==s]; lims[s,] <- range(x) }
mu.min <- max(lims[,1]);  mu.max <- min(lims[,2])
gravs.EL <- EL.profile(g[series==1],
                       tmin=mu.min,tmax=mu.max,n.t=21)
gravs.EL.L  <- gravs.EL[,2]
gravs.EL.mu <- gravs.EL[,1]
for (s in 2:8)
gravs.EL.L <- gravs.EL.L + EL.profile(g[series==s],
                       tmin=mu.min,tmax=mu.max,n.t=21)[,2]
gravs.EL.L <- gravs.EL.L - max(gravs.EL.L)
lines(gravs.EL.mu,exp(gravs.EL.L),lwd=2)
lik.CI(cbind(gravs.EL.mu,gravs.EL.L),lim=-0.5*qchisq(0.95,1))
```

Compare the intervals with those in Example 3.2. Does the result for (b) suggest a limitation of multinomial likelihoods in general?
Compare the empirical likelihoods with the profile likelihood (10.1) and the adjusted profile likelihood (10.2), obtained when the series are treated as independent normal samples with different variances but the same mean. (Section 10.2.1)

2   Dataframe `islay` contains 18 measurements (in degrees east of north) of palaeo-current azimuths from the Jura Quartzite on the Scottish island of Islay. We aim to use multinomial-based likelihoods to set 95% confidence intervals for the mean direction $a(\theta) = (\sin\theta, \cos\theta)^T$ of the distribution underlying the data; the vector $b(\theta) = (\cos\theta, -\sin\theta)^T$ is orthogonal to a. Let $y_j = (\sin\theta_j, \cos\theta_j)^T$ denote the vectors corresponding to the observed angles $\theta_1, \ldots, \theta_n$. Then the mean direction $\hat{\theta}$ is the angle subtended at the origin by $\sum y_j / \|\sum y_j\|$.
For the original estimate, plots of the data, log likelihoods and confidence intervals:

```
attach(islay)
th <- ifelse(theta>180,theta-360,theta)
a.t <- function(th) c(sin(th*pi/180), cos(th*pi/180))
b.t <- function(th) c(cos(th*pi/180), -sin(th*pi/180))
y <- t(apply(matrix(theta, 18,1), 1, a.t))
thetahat <- function(y)
{ m <- apply(y,2,sum)
  m <- m/sqrt(m[1]^2+m[2]^2)
  180*atan(m[1]/m[2])/pi }
thetahat(y)
u.t <- function(y, th) crossprod(b.t(th), t(y))
islay.EL <- EL.profile(y, tmin=-100, tmax=120, n.t=40, u=u.t)
plot(islay.EL[,1],islay.EL[,2],type="l",xlab="theta",
     ylab="log empirical likelihood",ylim=c(-25,0))
points(th,rep(-25,18)); abline(h=-3.84/2,lty=2)
lik.CI(islay.EL,lim=-0.5*qchisq(0.95,1))
islay.EEF <- EEF.profile(y, tmin=-100, tmax=120, n.t=40, u=u.t)
lines(islay.EEF[,1],islay.EEF[,2],lty=3)
lik.CI(islay.EEF,lim=-0.5*qchisq(0.95,1))
```

Discuss the shapes of the log likelihoods.
To obtain 0.95 quantiles of the bootstrap distributions of W_{EL} and W_{EEF}:

```
islay.fun <- function(y, i, angle)
{   u <- as.vector(u.t(y[i,], angle))
    z <- rep(0,length(u))
    EEF.fit <- glm(z~u-1,poisson)
    W.EEF <- 2*sum(1-fitted(EEF.fit))
    EL.loglik <- function(lambda) - sum(log(1 + lambda * u))
    EL.score <- function(lambda) - sum(u/(1 + lambda * u))
    assign("u",u,frame=1)
    EL.out <- nlmin(EL.loglik,0.001)
    W.EL <- -2*EL.loglik(EL.out$x)
    c(thetahat(y[i,]), W.EL, W.EEF, EL.out$converged) }
islay.boot <- boot(y,islay.fun,R=999,angle=thetahat(y))
islay.boot$R <- sum(islay.boot$t[,4])
islay.boot$t <- islay.boot$t[islay.boot$t[,4]==1,]
apply(islay.boot$t[,2:3],2,quantile,0.95)
```

How do the bootstrap-calibrated confidence intervals compare with those based on the χ_1^2 distribution, and with the basic bootstrap intervals using the $\hat{\theta}^*$?
(Sections 10.2.1, 10.2.2; Hand *et al.*, 1994, p. 198)

3   We compare posterior densities for the mean of the air-conditioning data using (a) the Bayesian bootstrap with $a_j \equiv -1$:

```
air1 <- data.frame(hours=aircondit$hours,G=1)
air.bayes.gen <- function(d, a)
{ out <- d
  out$G <- rgamma(nrow(d),shape=a+2)
  out }
air.bayes.fun <- function(d) sum(d$hours*d$G)/sum(d$G)
air.bayesian <- boot(air1, air.bayes.fun, R=999, sim="parametric",
                     ran.gen=air.bayes.gen,mle=-1)
plot(density(air.bayesian$t,n=100,width=25),type="l",
     xlab="theta",ylab="density",ylim=c(0,0.02))
```

and (b) an exponential model with mean θ for the data, with prior according to which θ^{-1} has a gamma distribution with index κ and scale λ^{-1}:

```
kappa <- 0; lambda <- 0
kappa.post <- kappa + length(air1$hours)
lambda.post <- lambda + sum(air1$hours)
theta <- 30:300
lines(theta,
      lambda.post/theta^2*dgamma(lambda.post/theta,kappa.post),
      lty=2)
```

Repeat this with different values of a in the Bayesian bootstrap and κ, λ in the parametric case, and discuss your results.
(Section 10.5)

11

Computer Implementation

11.1 Introduction

The key requirements for computer implementation of resampling methods are a flexible programming langauge with a suite of reliable quasi-random number generators, a wide range of built-in statistical procedures to bootstrap, and a reasonably fast processor. In this chapter we outline how to use one implementation, using the current (May 1997) commercial version Splus 3.3 of the statistical language S, although the methods could be realized in a number of other statistical computing environments.

The remainder of this section outlines the installation of the library, and gives a quick summary of features of Splus essential to our purpose. Each subsequent section describes aspects of the library needed for the material in the corresponding chapter: Section 11.2 corresponds to Chapter 2, Section 11.3 to Chapter 3, and so forth. These sections take the form of a tutorial on the use of the library functions. The outline given here is not intended to replace the help files distributed with the library, which can be viewed by typing help(boot,library="boot") within Splus. At various points below, you will need to consult these files for more details on functions.

The main functions in the library are summarized in Table 11.1.

The best way to learn to use software is to use it, and from Section 11.1.2 onwards, we assume that you, dear reader, know the basics of S, including how to write simple functions, that you are seated comfortably at your favourite computer with Splus launched and a graphics window open, and that you are working through this chapter. We do not show the Splus prompt >, nor the continuation prompt +.

522

Table 11.1 Functions in the Splus bootstrap library.

Function	Purpose
abc.ci	Nonparametric ABC confidence intervals
boot	Parametric and nonparametric bootstrap simulation
boot.array	Array of indices or frequencies from bootstrap simulation
boot.ci	Bootstrap confidence intervals
censboot	Bootstrap for censored and survival data
control	Control methods for estimation of quantiles, bias, variance, etc.
cv.glm	Cross-validation prediction error estimate for generalized linear model
empinf	Calculate empirical influence values
envelope	Calculate simulation envelope
exp.tilt	Exponential tilting to calculate probability distributions
glm.diag	Generalized linear model diagnostics
glm.diag.plot	Plot generalized linear model diagnostics
imp.moments	Importance resampling moment estimates
imp.prob	Importance resampling tail probability estimates
imp.quantile	Importance resampling quantile estimates
imp.weights	Calculate importance resampling weights
jack.after.boot	Jackknife-after-bootstrap plot
linear.approx	Calculate linear approximation to a statistic
saddle	Saddlepoint approximation
saddle.distn	Saddlepoint approximation for a distribution
simplex	Simplex method of linear programming
smooth.f	Frequency smoothing
tilt.boot	Automatic importance re-weighting bootstrap simulation
tsboot	Bootstrap for time series data

11.1.1 Installation

UNIX

The bootstrap library can be obtained from the home page for this book,

```
http://dmawww.epfl.ch/davison.mosaic/BMA/
```

in the form of a compressed shar file bootlib.sh.Z. This file should be uncompressed and moved to an appropriate directory. The file can then be unpacked by

```
sh bootlib.sh
rm bootlib.sh
```

You should then follow the instructions in the README file to complete the installation of the library.

It is best to set up an Splus library boot containing the library files; you may need to ask your system manager to do this. Once this is done, and once inside Splus in your usual working directory, the functions and data are accessed by typing

```
library(boot,first=T)
```

This will avoid cluttering your working directory with library files, and reduce the chance that you accidentally overwrite them.

Windows

The disk at the back of this book contains the library functions and documentation for use with Splus for Windows. For instructions on the installation, see the file README.TXT on the disk. The contents of the disk can also be retrieved in the form of a zip file from the home page for the book given above.

11.1.2 Some key Splus ideas

Quasi-random numbers

To put 20 quasi-random $N(0, 1)$ data into y and to see its contents, type

```
y <- rnorm(20)
y
```

Here <- is the assignment symbol. To see the contents of any S object, simply type its name, as above. This is often done below, and we do not show the output.

In general quasi-random numbers from a distribution are generated by the functions rexp, rgamma, rchisq, rt,..., with arguments to give parameters where needed. For example,

```
y <- rgamma(n=10,shape=2)
```

generates 10 gamma observations with shape parameter 2, and

```
y <- rgamma(n=10,shape=c(1:10))
```

generates a vector of ten gamma variables with shape parameters $1, 2, \ldots, 10$.

The function sample is used to sample from a set with or without replacement. For example, to get a random permutation of the numbers $1, \ldots, 10$, a random sample with replacement from them, a random permutation of 11, 22, 33, 44, 55, a sample of size 10 from them, and a sample of size 10 taken with unequal probabilities:

```
sample(10)
sample(10,replace=T)
set <- c(11,22,33,44,55)
sample(set)
sample(set,size=10,replace=T)
sample(set,size=10,replace=T,prob=c(0.1,0.1,0.1,0.1,0.6))
```

Subscripts

The city population data with $n = 10$ are

```
city
city$u
city$x
```

where the second two commands show the individual variables of `city`. This Splus object is a dataframe — an array of data in which rows correspond to cases, and the named columns to variables. Elements of an object are accessed by subscripts, so

```
city$x[1]
city$x[c(1:4)]
city$x[c(1,5,10)]
city[c(1,5,10),2]
city$x[-1]
city[c(1:3),]
```

give various subsets of the elements of `city`. To make a nonparametric bootstrap sample of the rows of `city`, you could type:

```
i <- sample(10,replace=T)
city[i,]
```

The row labels result from the algorithm used to give unique labels to rows, and can be ignored for our purposes.

11.2 Basic Bootstraps

11.2.1 Nonparametric bootstrap

The main bootstrap function, `boot`, works on a vector, a matrix, or a dataframe. A simple use of `boot` to bootstrap the ratio $t = \bar{x}/\bar{u}$ for the city population data of Example 2.8 is

```
city.fun <- function(data, i)
{ d <- data[i,]
  mean(d$x)/mean(d$u) }
city.boot <- boot(data=city, statistic=city.fun, R=50)
```

The function `city.fun` takes as input the dataframe `data` and the vector of indices `i`. Its first command sets up the bootstrapped dataframe, and its second makes and returns the bootstrapped ratio. The last command instructs the function `boot` to bootstrap the data in `city` $R = 50$ times, apply the statistic `city.fun` to each bootstrap dataset and put the results in `city.boot`.

Bootstrap objects

The result of a call to boot is a bootstrap object. This is implemented as a list
of quantities which is given the class "boot" and for which various methods
are defined. For example, typing

```
city.boot
```

prints the original statistic, its estimated bias and its standard error, while

```
plot(city.boot)
```

gives suitable summary plots.

To see the names of the elements of the bootstrap object city.boot, type

```
names(city.boot)
```

You see various names, of which city.boot$t0, city.boot$t, city.boot$R,
city.boot$seed contain the original value of the statistic, the bootstrap
values, the value of R, and the value of the Splus random number generation
seed when boot was invoked. To see their contents, type their names.

Timing

To repeat the simulation, checking how long it takes, type

```
unix.time(city.boot <- boot(city,city.fun,R=50))
```

on a UNIX system or

```
dos.time(city.boot <- boot(city,city.fun,R=50))
```

on a DOS system. The first number returned is the time the simulation took,
and is useful for estimating how long a larger simulation would take.

Although code is generally clearer when dataframes are used, the computation can be speeded up by avoiding them, as here:

```
mat <- as.matrix(city)
mat.fun <- function(data, i)
{ d <- data[i,]
  mean(d[,2])/mean(d[,1]) }
unix.time(mat.boot <- boot(mat,mat.fun,R=50))
```

Compare this with the time taken using the dataframe city.

Frequency array

To obtain the $R \times n$ array of bootstrap frequencies for city.boot and to
display its first 20 lines, type

```
f <- boot.array(city.boot)
f[1:20,]
```

The rows of f are the vectors of frequencies for individual bootstrap samples. The array is useful for many *post hoc* calculations, and is invoked by post-processing functions such as jack.after.boot and imp.weight, which are discussed below. It is calculated from city.boot$seed. The array of indices for the bootstrap samples can be obtained by boot.array(city.boot,index=T).

Types of statistic

For a nonparametric bootstrap, the function statistic can be of one of three types. We have already seen examples of the first, index type, where the arguments are the dataframe data and the vector of indices, i; this is specified by stype="i" (the default).

For the second, weighted type, the arguments are data and a vector of weights w. For example,

```
city.w <- function(data, w=rep(1,nrow(data))/nrow(data))
{ w <- w/sum(w)
  sum(w*data$x)/sum(w*data$u)}
city.boot <- boot(city, city.w, R=20, stype="w")
```

writes

$$\frac{\bar{x}^*}{\bar{u}^*} = \frac{\sum w_j^* x_j / \sum w_j^*}{\sum w_j^* u_j / \sum w_j^*},$$

where w_j^* is the weight put on the jth case of the dataframe in the bootstrap sample; the first line of city.w ensures that $\sum w_j^* = 1$. Setting w in the initial line of the function gives the default value for w, which is a vector of n^{-1}s; this enables the original value of t to be obtained by city.w(city). A more complicated example is given by the library correlation function corr. Not all statistics can be written in this form, but when they can, numerical differentiation can be used to obtain empirical influence values and *ABC* confidence intervals.

For the third, frequency type, the arguments are data and a vector of frequencies f. For example,

```
city.f <- function(data, f) mean(f*data$x)/mean(f*data$u)
city.boot <- boot(city, city.f, R=20, stype="f")
```

uses

$$\frac{\bar{x}^*}{\bar{u}^*} = \frac{n^{-1} \sum f_j^* x_j}{n^{-1} \sum f_j^* u_j},$$

where f_j^* is the frequency with which the jth row of the dataframe occurs in the bootstrap sample. Not all statistics can be written in this form. It differs from the preceding type in that whereas weights can in principle take any positive

values, frequencies must be integers. Of course in this example it would be
easiest to use the function city.fun given earlier.

Function statistic

The contents of statistic can be more-or-less arbitrarily complicated, provided that its output is a scalar or fixed-length vector. For example,

```
air.fun <- function(data, i)
{ d <- data[i,]
  c(mean(d), var(d)/nrow(data)) }
air.boot <- boot(data=aircondit, statistic=air.fun, R=200)
```

performs a nonparametric bootstrap for the average of the air-conditioning
data, and returns the bootstrapped averages and their estimated variances. We
give more complex examples below. Beware of memory and storage problems
if you make the output too long.

By default the first element of statistic (and so the first column of
boot.out$t) is treated as the main statistic for certain calculations, such as
calculation of empirical influence values, the jackknife-after-bootstrap plot, and
confidence interval calculations, which are described below. This is changed
by use of the index argument, usually a single number giving the column of
statistic to which the calculation is to be applied.

Further arguments can be passed to statistic using the ... argument to
boot. For example,

```
city.subset <- function(data, i, n=10)
{  d <- data[i[1:n],]
   mean(d[,2])/mean(d[,1]) }
city.boot <- boot(data=city, statistic=city.subset, R=200, n=5)
```

gives resampled ratios for bootstrap samples of size 5. Note that the frequency
array for city.boot would not be useful in this case. The indices can be
obtained by

```
boot.array(city.boot,indices=T)[,1:5]
```

11.2.2 Parametric bootstrap

For a parametric bootstrap, the first argument to statistic remains a vector,
matrix, or dataframe, but statistic need take no second argument. Instead
three further arguments to boot must be supplied. The first, ran.gen, tells boot
how to simulate bootstrap data, and is a function that takes two arguments,
the original data, and an object containing any other parameters, mle. The
output of ran.gen should have the same form and attributes as the original
dataset. The second new argument to boot is a value for mle itself. The third

new argument to boot, sim="parametric", tells boot to perform a parametric simulation: by default the simulation is nonparametric and sim="ordinary". Other possible values for sim are described below.

For example, for parametric simulation from the exponential model fitted to the air-conditioning data in Table 1.2, we set

```
aircondit.fun <- function(data) mean(data$hours)
aircondit.sim <- function(data, mle)
{ d <- data
  d$hours <- rexp(n=nrow(data), rate=mle)
  d }
aircondit.mle <- 1/mean(aircondit$hours)
aircondit.para <- boot(data=aircondit, statistic=aircondit.fun,
               R=20, sim="parametric", ran.gen=aircondit.sim,
               mle=aircondit.mle)
```

Air-conditioning data for a different aircraft are given in aircondit7. Obtain their sample average, and perform a parametric bootstrap of the average using the fitted exponential model. Give the bias and variance estimates for the average. Do the bootstrapped averages look normal for this sample size?

A more complicated example is parametric simulation based on a log bivariate normal distribution fitted to the city population data:

```
l.city <- log(city)
city.mle <- c(apply(l.city,2,mean),sqrt(apply(l.city,2,var)),
             corr(l.city))
city.sim <- function(data, mle)
{ n <- nrow(data)
  d <- matrix(rnorm(2*n),n,2)
  d[,2] <- mle[2] + mle[4]*(mle[5]*d[,2]+sqrt(1-mle[5]^2)*d[,1])
  d[,1] <- mle[1] + mle[3]*d[,1]
  data$x <- exp(d[,2])
  data$u <- exp(d[,1])
  data }
city.f <- function(data) mean(data[,2])/mean(data[,1])
city.para <- boot(city, city.f, R=200, sim="parametric",
               ran.gen=city.sim, mle=city.mle)
```

With this definition of city.f, a nonparametric bootstrap can be performed by

```
city.boot <- boot(data=city,
    statistic=function(data, i) city.f(data[i,]), R=200)
```

This is useful when comparing parametric and nonparametric bootstraps for the same problem. Compare them for the `city` data.

11.2.3 Empirical influence values

For a statistic `boot.fun` in weighted form, function `empinf` returns the empirical influence values l_j, obtained by numerical differentiation. For the ratio function `city.w` given above, for example, these and the exact values (Problem 2.9) are

```
L.diff <- empinf(data=city, statistic=city.w, stype="w")
cbind(L.diff,(city$x-city.w(city)*city$u)/mean(city$u))
```

Empirical influence values can also be obtained from the output of boot by regression of the values of t^* on the frequency array. For example,

```
city.boot   <- boot(city, city.fun, R=999)
L.reg <- empinf(city.boot)
L.reg
```

uses regression with the 999 samples in `city.boot` to estimate the l_j.

Jackknife values can be obtained by

```
J <- empinf(data=city,statistic=city.fun,stype="i",type="jack")
```

The argument `type` controls how the influence values are to be calculated, but this also depends on the quantities input to `empinf`: for details see the help file.

Variance approximations

`var.linear` uses empirical influence values to calculate the nonparametric delta method variance approximation for a statistic:

```
var.linear(L.diff)
var.linear(L.reg)
```

Linear approximation

`linear.approx` uses output from a nonparametric bootstrap simulation to calculate the linear approximations to the bootstrapped quantities. The empirical influence values can be supplied, but if not, they are estimated by a call to `empinf`. For the city population ratio,

```
city.tL.reg <- linear.approx(city.boot)
city.tL.diff <- linear.approx(city.boot, L=L.diff)
split.screen(c(1,2))
screen(1); plot(city.tL.reg,city.boot$t); abline(0,1,lty=2)
screen(2); plot(city.tL.diff,city.boot$t); abline(0,1,lty=2)
```

calculates the linear approximation for the two sets of empirical influence values and plots the actual t^* against them.

11.3 Further Ideas

11.3.1 Stratified sampling

Stratified sampling is performed by including argument `strata` in the call to boot. Suppose that we wish to bootstrap the difference in the trimmed averages for the last two groups of gravity data (Example 3.2):

```
gravity
grav <- gravity[as.numeric(gravity$series)>=7,]
grav
grav.fun <- function(data, i, trim=0.125)
{ d <- data[i,]
  m <- tapply(d$g, d$series, mean, trim=trim)
  m[7]-m[8] }
grav.boot <- boot(grav, grav.fun, R=200, strata=grav$series)
```

Check that the expected properties of `boot.array(grav.boot)` hold.

Empirical influence values, linear approximations, and nonparametric delta method variance approximations are calculated by

```
grav.L <- empinf(grav.boot)
grav.tL <- linear.approx(grav.boot)
var.linear(grav.L, strata=grav$series)
```

`grav.boot$strata` contains the strata used in the resampling, which are taken into account automatically if `grav.boot` is used, but otherwise must be supplied, as in the final line of the code above.

11.3.2 Smoothing

The neatest way to perform smooth bootstrapping is to use `sim="parametric"`. For example, to estimate the variance of the median of the data in y, using smoothing parameter $h = 0.5$:

```
y <- rnorm(99)
h <- 0.5
y.gen <- function(data, mle)
{ n <- length(data)
  i <- sample(n, n, replace=T)
  data[i] + mle*rnorm(n) }
```

```
y.boot <- boot(y, median, R=200, sim="parametric",
               ran.gen=y.gen, mle=h)
var(y.boot$t)
```

This guarantees that y.boot$t0 contains the original median. For shrunk smoothing, see Practical 4.5.

11.3.3 Censored data

censboot is used to bootstrap censored data. Suppose that we wish to assess the variability of the median survival time and the probability of survival beyond 20 weeks for the first group of AML data (Example 3.9).

```
aml1 <- aml[aml$group==1,]
aml1.fun <- function(data)
{  surv <- survfit(Surv(data$time,data$cens))
   p1 <- min(surv$surv[surv$time<20])
   m1 <- min(surv$time[surv$surv<0.5])
   c(p1, m1) }
aml1.ord <- censboot(data=aml1, statistic=aml1.fun, R=50)
aml1.ord
```

This involves ordinary bootstrap resampling, and hence could be performed with boot, although aml1.fun would then have to be rewritten to have another argument. For conditional simulation, two additional arguments must be supplied containing the estimated survivor functions for the times to failure and the censoring distribution:

```
aml1.fail <- survfit(Surv(time,cens),data=aml1)
aml1.cens <- survfit(Surv(time-0.01*cens,1-cens),data=aml1)
aml1.con <- censboot(data=aml1, statistic=aml1.fun, R=50,
               F.surv=aml1.fail, G.surv=aml1.cens, sim="cond")
```

11.3.4 Bootstrap diagnostics

Jackknife-after-bootstrap

Function jack.after.boot produces a jackknife-after-bootstrap plot of the first column of boot.out$t based on a nonparametric simulation. For example, for the city data ratio:

```
city.fun <- function(data, i)
 { d <- data[i,]
    rat <- mean(d$x)/mean(d$u)
    L <- (d$x-rat*d$u)/mean(d$u)
    c(rat, sum(L^2)/nrow(d)^2, L) }
```

```
city.boot <- boot(city, city.fun, R=999)
city.L <- city.boot$t0[3:12]
split.screen(c(1,2)); screen(1); split.screen(c(2,1)); screen(4)
attach(city)
plot(u,x,type="n",xlim=c(0,300),ylim=c(0,300))
text(u,x,round(city.L,2))
screen(3)
plot(u,x,type="n",xlim=c(0,300),ylim=c(0,300))
text(u,x,c(1:10)); abline(0,city.boot$t0[1],lty=2)
screen(2)
jack.after.boot(boot.out=city.boot, useJ=F, stinf=F, L=city.L)
close.screen(all=T)
```

The two left panels show the data with case numbers and empirical influence values as plotting symbols. The jackknife-after-bootstrap plot on the right shows the effect of deleting cases in turn: values of t^* are more variable when case 4 is deleted and less variable when cases 9 and 10 are deleted. We see from the empirical influence values that the distribution of t^* shifts downwards when cases with positive empirical influence values are deleted, and conversely.

This plot is also produced by setting true the jack argument to plot when applied to a bootstrap object, as in plot(city.boot,jack=T).

Other arguments for jack.after.boot control whether the influence values are standardized (by default they are, stinf=T), whether the empirical influence values are used (by default jackknife values are used, based on the simulation, so the default values are useJ=T and L=NULL).

Most post-processing functions allow the user to specify either an index for the component of interest, or a vector of length boot.out$R to be treated as the main statistic. Thus a jackknife-after-bootstrap plot using the second component of city.boot$t — the estimated variances for t^* — would be obtained by either of

```
jack.after.boot(city.boot,useJ=F,stinf=F,index=2)
jack.after.boot(city.boot,useJ=F,stinf=F,t=city.boot$t[,2])
```

Frequency smoothing

smooth.f smooths the frequencies of a nonparametric bootstrap object to give a "typical" distribution with expected value roughly at θ. In order to find the smoothed frequencies for $\theta = 1.4$ for the city ratio, and to obtain the corresponding value of t, we set

```
city.freq <- smooth.f(theta=1.4, boot.out=city.boot)
city.w(city, city.freq)
```

The smoothing bandwidth is controlled by the `width` argument to `smooth.f` and is width$\times v^{1/2}$, where v is the estimated variance of t — width=0.5 by default.

11.4 Tests

11.4.1 Parametric tests

Simple parametric tests can be conducted using parametric simulation. For example, to perform the conditional simulation for the data in `fir` (Example 4.2):

```
fir.mle <- c(sum(fir$count), nrow(fir))
fir.gen <- function(data, mle)
{ d <- data
  y <- sample(x=mle[2],size=mle[1],replace=T)
  d$count <- tabulate(y,mle[2])
  d }
fir.fun <- function(data)
 (nrow(data)-1)*var(data$count)/mean(data$count)
fir.boot <- boot(fir, fir.fun, R=999, sim="parametric",
                 ran.gen=fir.gen, mle=fir.mle)
qqplot(qchisq(c(1:fir.boot$R)/(fir.boot$R+1),df=49),fir.boot$t)
abline(0,1,lty=2); abline(h=fir.boot$t0)
```

The last two lines here display the results (almost) as in the right panel of Figure 4.1.

11.4.2 Permutation tests

Approximate permutation tests are performed by setting sim="permutation" when invoking boot. For example, suppose that we wish to perform a permutation test for zero correlation between the two columns of dataframe `ducks`:

```
perm.fun <- function(data, i)  cor(data[,1],data[i,2])
ducks.perm <- boot(ducks, perm.fun, R=499, sim="permutation")
(sum(ducks.perm$t>ducks.perm$t0)+1)/(ducks.perm$R+1)
qqnorm(ducks.perm$t,ylim=c(-1,1))
abline(h=ducks.perm$t0,lty=2)
```

If `strata` is included in the call to boot, permutation is performed independently within each stratum.

11.4.3 Bootstrap tests

For a bootstrap test of the hypothesis of zero correlation in the ducks data, we make a new dataframe and function:

```
duck <- c(ducks[,1],ducks[,2])
n <- nrow(ducks)
duck.fun <- function(data, i, n)
{ x <- data[i]
  cor(x[1:n],x[(n+1):(2*n)]) }
.Random.seed <- ducks.perm$seed
ducks.boot <- boot(duck, duck.fun, R=499,
                 strata=rep(c(1,2),c(n,n)), n=n)
(sum(ducks.boot$t>ducks.boot$t0)+1)/(ducks.boot$R+1)
```

This uses the same seed as for the permutation test, for a more precise comparison. Is the significance level similar to that for the permutation test?

Why cannot boot be directly applied to ducks to perform a bootstrap test?

Exponential tilting

The test of equality of means for two sets of data in Example 4.16 involves exponential tilting. The null distribution puts probabilities given by (4.25) on the two sets of data, and the tilt parameter λ solves the equation

$$\sum_{i=1}^{2} \frac{\sum_j z_{ij} \exp(\lambda z_{ij})}{\sum_j \exp(\lambda z_{ij})} = \theta,$$

where $z_{1j} = y_{1j}$, $z_{2j} = -y_{2j}$, and $\theta = 0$. The fitted null distribution is obtained using exp.tilt, as follows:

```
z <- grav$g
z[grav$series==8] <- -z[grav$series==8]
z.tilt <- exp.tilt(L=z, theta=0, strata=grav$series)
z.tilt
```

where z.tilt contains the fitted probabilities (which sum to one for each stratum) and the values of λ and θ. Other arguments can be input to exp.tilt: see its help file.

The significance probability is then obtained by using the weights argument to boot. This argument is a vector containing the probabilities with which to select the rows of data, when bootstrap sampling is to be performed with unequal probabilities. In this case the unequal probabilities are given by the tilted distribution, under which the expected value of the test statistic is zero. The code needed to perform the simulation and get the estimated significance level is:

```
grav.test <- function(data, i)
{ d <- data[i,]
  diff(tapply(d$g,d$series,mean))[7] }
grav.boot <- boot(data=grav, statistic=grav.test, R=999,
                  weights=z.tilt$p, strata=grav$series)
(sum(grav.boot$t>grav.boot$t0)+1)/(grav.boot$R+1)
```

11.5 Confidence Intervals

The main function for setting bootstrap confidence intervals is boot.ci, which takes as input a bootstrap object. For example, to get a 95% confidence interval for the ratio in the city data, using the city.boot object created in Section 11.3.4:

```
boot.ci(boot.out=city.boot)
```

By default the confidence level is 0.95, but other values can be obtained using the conf argument. Here invoking boot.ci shows the normal, basic, studentized bootstrap, percentile, and BC_a intervals. Subsets of these intervals are obtained using the type argument. For example, if city.boot$t only contained the ratio and not its estimated variance, it would be impossible to obtain the studentized bootstrap interval, and an appropriate use of boot.ci would be

```
boot.ci(boot.out=city.boot,type=c("norm","perc","basic","bca"),
        conf=c(0.8,0.9))
```

By default boot.ci assumes that the first and second columns of boot.out$t contain the statistic itself and its estimated variance; otherwise the index argument can be used, as outlined in the help file.

To calculate intervals for the parameter $h(\theta)$, and then back-transform them to the original scale, we use the h, hinv, and hdot arguments. For example, to calculate intervals for the city ratio, using $h(\cdot) = \log(\cdot)$, we set

```
boot.ci(city.boot, h=log, hinv=exp, hdot=function(u) 1/u)
```

where hinv and hdot are the inverse and first derivative of $h(\cdot)$. Note how transformation improves the basic bootstrap interval.

Nonparametric ABC intervals are calculated using abc.ci. For example

```
abc.ci(data=city, statistic=city.w)
```

calculates the 95% ABC interval for the city ratio; statistic must be in weighted form for this. As usual, strata are incorporated using the strata argument.

11.6 Linear Regression

11.6.1 Basic approaches

Resampling for linear regression models is performed using boot. It is simplest when bootstrapping cases. For example, to compare the biases and variances for parameter estimates from bootstrapping least squares and L_1 estimates for the mammals data:

```
fit.model <- function(data)
{  fit <- glm(log(brain)~log(body),data=data)
   l1 <- l1fit(log(data$body),log(data$brain))
   c(coef(fit), coef(l1)) }
mammals.fun <- function(data, i) fit.model(data[i,])
mammals.boot <- boot(mammals, mammals.fun, R=99)
mammals.boot
```

For model-based resampling it is simplest to set up an augmented dataframe containing the residuals and fitted values. Although the model is a straightforward linear model, we fit it using glm rather than lm so that we can calculate residuals using the library function glm.diag, which calculates various types of residuals, approximate Cook statistics, and measures of leverage for a glm object. (The diagnostics are exact for a linear model.) A related function is glm.diag.plots, which produces standard diagnostic plots for a generalized linear model fit:

```
mam.lm <- glm(log(brain)~log(body),data=mammals)
mam.diag <- glm.diag(mam.lm)
glm.diag.plots(mam.lm)
res <- (mam.diag$res-mean(mam.diag$res))*mam.diag$sd
mam <- data.frame(mammals,res=res,fit=fitted(mam.lm))
mam.fun <- function(data, i)
{ d <- data
  d$brain <- exp(d$fit+d$res[i])
  fit.model(d) }
mam.boot <- boot(mam, mam.fun, R=99)
mam.boot
```

Empirical influence values and the nonparametric delta method standard error for the slope of the linear model could be obtained by putting the slope estimate in weighted form:

```
mam.w <- function(data, w)
   coef(glm(log(data$brain)~log(data$body), weights=w))[2]
mam.L <- empinf(data=mammals, statistic=mam.w)
sqrt(var.linear(mam.L))
```

For more complicated regressions, for example with unequal response variances, more information must be added to the new dataframe.

Wild bootstrap

The wild bootstrap can be implemented using `sim="parametric"`, as follows:

```
mam.mle <- c(nrow(mam), (5+sqrt(5))/10)
mam.wild <- function(data, mle)
{ d <- data
  i <- 2*rbinom(mle[1], size=1, prob=1-mle[2])-1
  d$brain <- exp(d$fit+d$res*(1-i*sqrt(5))/2)
  d }
mam.boot.wild <- boot(mam, fit.model, R=20, sim="parametric",
                      ran.gen=mam.wild, mle=mam.mle)
```

11.6.2 Prediction

Now consider prediction of the log brain weight of new mammals with body weights equal to those for the chimpanzee and baboon. For this we introduce yet another argument to boot — m, which gives the number of ε^*_{rm} to be simulated with each bootstrap sample (see Algorithm 6.4). In this case we want to predict at $m = 2$ "new" mammals, with covariates contained in d.pred. The `statistic` function supplied to boot must now take at least one more argument, namely the additional indices for constructing the bootstrap versions of the two "new" mammals. We implement this as follows:

```
d.pred <- mam[c(46,47),]
pred <- function(data, d.pred)
  predict(glm(log(brain)~log(body),data=data), d.pred)
mam.pred <- function(data, i, i.pred, d.pred)
{ d <- data
  d$brain <- exp(d$fit+d$res[i])
  pred(d, d.pred) - (d.pred$fit + d$res[i.pred]) }
mam.boot.pred <- boot(mam, mam.pred, R=199, m=2, d.pred=d.pred)
orig <- matrix(pred(mam, d.pred),mam.boot.pred$R,2,byrow=T)
exp(apply(orig+mam.boot.pred$t,2,quantile,c(0.025,0.5,0.975)))
```

giving the 0.025, 0.5, and 0.975 prediction limits for the brain sizes of the "new" mammals. The actual brain sizes lie close to or above the upper limits of these intervals: primates tend to have larger brains than other mammals.

11.6.3 Aggregate prediction error and variable selection

Practical 6.5 shows how to obtain the various estimates of aggregate prediction error based on a given model.

For consistent bootstrap variable selection, a subset of size $n - m$ is used to fit each of the possible models. Consider Example 6.13, where a fake set of data is made by

```
x1 <- runif(50); x2 <- runif(50); x3 <- runif(50)
x4 <- runif(50); x5 <- runif(50); y <- rnorm(50)+2*x1+2*x2
fake <- data.frame(y,x1,x2,x3,x4,x5)
```

As in that example, we consider the six possible models with no covariates, with just x_1, with x_1, x_2, and so forth, finishing with $x_1, \ldots, x_5$. The function subset.boot fits these to a subset of n-size observations, and calculates the prediction mean squared error for all the data. It is then applied using boot:

```
subset.boot <- function(data, i, size=0)
{ n <- nrow(data)
  i.t <- i[1:(n-size)]
  data.t <- data[i.t, ]
  res0 <- data$y - mean(data.t$y)
  lm.d <- lm(y ~ x1, data=data.t)
  res1 <- data$y - predict.lm(lm.d, data)
  lm.d <- update(lm.d, .~.+x2)
  res2 <- data$y - predict.lm(lm.d, data)
  lm.d <- update(lm.d, .~.+x3)
  res3 <- data$y - predict.lm(lm.d, data)
  lm.d <- update(lm.d, .~.+x4)
  res4 <- data$y - predict.lm(lm.d, data)
  lm.d <- update(lm.d, .~.+x5)
  res5 <- data$y - predict.lm(lm.d, data)
  meansq <- function(y) mean(y^2)
  apply(cbind(res0,res1,res2,res3,res4,res5),2,meansq)/n }
fake.boot.40 <- boot(fake, subset.boot, R=100, size=40)
delta.hat.40 <- apply(fake.boot.40$t,2,mean)
plot(c(0:5),delta.hat.40,xlab="Number of covariates",
     ylab="Delta hat (M)",type="l",ylim=c(0,0.1))
```

For results with a different value of size, but re-using fake.boot.40$seed in order to reduce simulation variability:

```
.Random.seed <- fake.boot.40$seed
fake.boot.30 <- boot(fake, subset.boot, R=100, size=30)
delta.hat.30 <- apply(fake.boot.30$t,2,mean)
lines(c(0:5),delta.hat.30,lty=2)
```

Try this with various values of size.

Modify the code above to do variable selection using cross-validation, and compare it with the bootstrap results.

11.7 Further Topics in Regression

11.7.1 Nonlinear and generalized linear models

Nonlinear and generalized linear models are bootstrapped using the ideas in the preceding section. For example, to apply case resampling to the calcium data of Example 7.7:

```
calcium.fun <- function(data, i)
{ d <- data[i,]
  d.nls <- nls(cal~beta0*(1-exp(-time*beta1)),data=d,
            start=list(beta0=5,beta1=0.2))
  c(coefficients(d.nls),sum(d.nls$residuals^2)/(nrow(d)-2)) }
cal.boot <- boot(calcium,calcium.fun,R=19,strata=calcium$time)
```

Likewise, to apply model-based simulation to the leukaemia data of Example 7.1, resampling standardized deviance residuals according to (7.14),

```
leuk.glm <- glm(time~log10(wbc)+ag-1,Gamma(log),data=leuk)
leuk.diag <- glm.diag(leuk.glm)
muhat <- fitted(leuk.glm)
rL <- log(leuk$time/muhat)/sqrt(1-leuk.diag$h)
eps <- 10^(-4)
u <- -log(seq(from=eps,to=1-eps,by=eps))
d <- sign(u-1)*sqrt(2*(u-1-log(u)))/leuk.diag$sd
r.dev <- smooth.spline(d, u)
z <- predict(r.dev, leuk.diag$rd)$y
leuk.mle <- data.frame(muhat,rL,z)
fit.model <- function(data)
{ data.glm <- glm(time~log10(wbc)+ag-1,Gamma(log),data=data)
  c(coefficients(data.glm),deviance(data.glm)) }
leuk.gen <- function(data,mle)
{ i <- sample(nrow(data),replace=T)
  data$time <- mle$muhat*mle$z[i]
  data }
leuk.boot <- boot(leuk, fit.model, R=19, sim="parametric",
            ran.gen=leuk.gen, mle=leuk.mle)
```

The other procedures for model-based resampling of generalized linear models are applied similarly. Try to modify this code to resample the linear predictor residuals according to (7.13) (they are already calculated above).

11.7.2 Survival data

Further arguments to censboot are needed to bootstrap survival data. For illustration, we consider the melanoma data of Example 7.6, and fit a model in which survival depends on log tumour thickness. The initial fits are given by

```
mel.cox <- coxph(Surv(time,status==1)~log(thickness)
                 +strata(ulcer),data=melanoma)
mel.surv <- survfit(mel.cox)
mel.cens <- survfit(Surv(time-0.01*(status!=1),status!=1)~1,
             data=melanoma)
```

The bootstrap function mel.fun given below need only take one argument, a dataframe containing the data themselves. Note how the function uses a smoothing spline to interpolate fitted values for the full range of thickness; this avoids difficulties due to the variability of the covariate when resampling cases. The output of mel.fun is the vector of fitted linear predictors predicted by the spline.

```
mel.fun <- function(d)
{ attach(d)
  cox <- coxph(Surv(time,status==1)~log(thickness)+strata(ulcer))
  eta <- unique(cox$linear.predictors)
  u <- unique(thickness)
  sp <- smooth.spline(u,eta,df=20)
  th <- seq(from=0.25,to=10,by=0.25)
  eta <- predict(sp,th)$y
  detach("d")
  eta }
```

The next three commands give the syntax for case resampling, for model-based resampling and for conditional resampling. For either of these last two schemes, the baseline survivor functions for the survival times and censoring times, and the fitted proportional hazards (Cox) model for the survival distribution must be supplied via the F.surv, G.surv, and cox arguments.

```
attach(melanoma)
mel.boot <- censboot(melanoma, mel.fun, R=99, strata=ulcer)
mel.boot.mod <- censboot(melanoma, mel.fun, R=99,
        F.surv=mel.surv, G.surv=mel.cens, strata=ulcer,
        cox=mel.cox, sim="model")
mel.boot.con <- censboot(melanoma, mel.fun, R=99,
        F.surv=mel.surv, G.surv=mel.cens, strata=ulcer,
        cox=mel.cox, sim="cond")
```

The bootstrap results are best displayed graphically. Here is the code for the
analogue of the left panels of Figure 7.9:

```
th <- seq(from=0.25,to=10,by=0.25)
split.screen(c(2,1))
screen(1)
plot(th,mel.boot$t0,type="n",xlab="Tumour thickness (mm)",
     xlim=c(0,10),ylim=c(-2,2),ylab="Linear predictor")
lines(th,mel.boot$t0,lwd=3)
rug(jitter(thickness))
for (i in 1:19) lines(th,mel.boot$t[i,],lwd=0.5)
screen(2)
plot(th,mel.boot$t0,type="n",xlab="Tumour thickness (mm)",
     xlim=c(0,10),ylim=c(-2,2),ylab="Linear predictor")
lines(th,mel.boot$t0,lwd=3)
mel.env <- envelope(mel.boot$t,level=0.95)
lines(th,mel.env$point[1,],lty=1)
lines(th,mel.env$point[2,],lty=1)
mel.env <- envelope(mel.boot.mod$t,level=0.95)
lines(th,mel.env$point[1,],lty=2)
lines(th,mel.env$point[2,],lty=2)
mel.env <- envelope(mel.boot.con$t,level=0.95)
lines(th,mel.env$point[1,],lty=3)
lines(th,mel.env$point[2,],lty=3)
detach("melanoma")
```

Note how tight the confidence envelope is relative to that for the more highly
parametrized model used in the example. Try again with larger values of R, if
you have the patience.

11.7.3 Nonparametric regression

Nonparametric regression is bootstrapped in the same way as other regressions. Consider for example bootstrapping the smoothing spline fit to the
motorcycle data of Example 7.10. The data without repeats are in motor, with
components accel, times, strata, and v, the last two of which give the strata
for resampling and an estimated variance within each stratum. The three fits
are obtained by

```
attach(motor)
motor.smooth <- smooth.spline(times,accel,w=1/v)
motor.small <- smooth.spline(times,accel,w=1/v,
                            spar=motor.smooth$spar/2)
motor.big <- smooth.spline(times,accel,w=1/v,
                          spar=motor.smooth$spar*2)
```

Commands to set up and perform the resampling are as follows:

```
res <- (motor$accel-motor.small$y)/sqrt(1-motor.small$lev)
motor.mle <- data.frame(bigfit=motor.big$y,res=res)
xpoints <- c(10,20,25,30,35,45)
motor.fun <- function(data, x)
{ y.smooth <- smooth.spline(data$times,data$accel,w=1/data$v)
  predict(y.smooth,x)$y }
motor.gen <- function(data, mle)
{ d <- data
  i <- c(1:nrow(data))
  i1 <- sample(i[data$strata==1],replace=T)
  i2 <- sample(i[data$strata==2],replace=T)
  i3 <- sample(i[data$strata==3],replace=T)
  d$accel <- mle$bigfit + mle$res[c(i1,i2,i3)]
  d }
motor.boot <- boot(motor, motor.fun, R=999, sim="parametric",
                   ran.gen=motor.gen, mle=motor.mle, x=xpoints)
```

Finally, the 90% basic bootstrap confidence limits are obtained by

```
mu.big <- predict(motor.big,xpoints)$y
mu <- predict(motor.smooth,xpoints)$y
ylims <- apply(motor.boot$t,2,quantile,c(0.05,0.95))
ytop <- mu - (ylims[1,]-mu.big)
ybot <- mu - (ylims[2,]-mu.big)
```

What is the effect of using a smaller smoothing parameter when calculating the residuals?

Try altering this code to apply the wild bootstrap, and see what effect it has on the results.

11.8 Time Series

Model-based resampling for time series is analogous to regression. We consider the sunspot data of Example 8.3, to which we fit the autoregressive model that minimizes AIC:

```
sun <- 2*(sqrt(sunspot+1)-1)
ts.plot(sun)
sun.ar <- ar(sun)
sun.ar$order
```

The best model is AR(9). How well determined is this, and what is the variance of the series average? We bootstrap to see, using

```
sun.fun <- function(tsb)
{ ar.fit <- ar(tsb, order.max=25)
  c(ar.fit$order, mean(tsb), tsb) }
```

which calculates the order of the fitted autoregressive model, the series average, and saves the series itself.

Our function for bootstrapping time series is tsboot. Here are results for fixed-block bootstraps with block length $l = 20$:

```
sun.1 <- tsboot(sun, sun.fun, R=99, l=20, sim="fixed")
tsplot(sun.1$t[1,3:291],main="Block simulation, l=20")
table(sun.1$t[,1])
var(sun.1$t[,2])
qqnorm(sun.1$t[,2])
```

The statistic for tsboot takes only one argument, the time series. The first plot here shows the results for a single replicate using block simulation: note the occasional big jumps in the resampled series. Note also the large variation in the orders of the fitted autoregressive models.

To obtain similar results for the stationary bootstrap with mean block length $l = 20$:

```
sun.2 <- tsboot(sun, sun.fun, R=99, l=20, sim="geom")
```

Are the results similar to having blocks of fixed length?

For model-based resampling we need to store results from the original model, and to make residuals from that fit:

```
sun.model <- list(order=c(sun.ar$order,0,0),ar=sun.ar$ar)
sun.res <- sun.ar$resid[!is.na(sun.ar$resid)]
sun.res <- sun.res - mean(sun.res)
sun.sim <- function(res,n.sim, ran.args)
{ rg1 <- function(n, res) sample(res, n, replace=T)
  ts.orig <- ran.args$ts
  ts.mod <- ran.args$model
  mean(ts.orig)+rts(arima.sim(model=ts.mod, n=n.sim,
    rand.gen=rg1, res=as.vector(res))) }
sun.3 <- tsboot(sun.res, sun.fun, R=99, sim="model", n.sim=114,
    ran.gen=sun.sim,ran.args=list(ts=sun, model=sun.model))
```

Check the orders of the fitted models for this scheme. Are they similar to those obtained using the block schemes above?

For "post-blackening" we need to define yet another function:

```
sun.black <- function(res, n.sim, ran.args)
{ ts.orig <- ran.args$ts
```

```
  ts.mod <- ran.args$model
  mean(ts.orig)+rts(arima.sim(model=ts.mod,n=n.sim,innov=res)) }
sun.1b <- tsboot(sun.res, sun.fun, R=99, l=20, sim="fixed",
  ran.gen=sun.black, ran.args=list(ts=sun, model=sun.model),
  n.sim=length(sun))
```

Compare these results with those above, and try it with `sim="geom"`.

11.9 Improved Simulation

11.9.1 Balanced resampling

The balanced bootstrap is invoked via the `sim` argument to boot:

```
city.bal <- boot(city, city.fun, R=20, sim="balanced")
```

If `strata` is supplied, balancing takes place separately within each stratum.

11.9.2 Control methods

`control` applies the control methods, including post-simulation balance, to the output from an existing bootstrap simulation. For example,

```
control(city.boot, bias.adj=T)
```

produces the adjusted bias estimate, while

```
city.con <- control(city.boot)
```

gives a list consisting of the regression estimates of the empirical influence values, linear approximations to the bootstrap statistics, the control estimates of bias, variance, and the third cumulant of the t^*, control estimates of selected quantiles of the distribution of t^*, and a spline object that summarizes the approximate quantiles used to obtain the control quantile estimates. Saddlepoint approximation is used to obtain these approximate quantiles. Typing

```
city.con$L
city.con$bias
city.con$var
city.con$quantiles
```

gives some of the above-mentioned quantities. Arguments to `control` allow the user to specify the empirical influence values, the spline object, and other quantities to be used by control, if they are already available; see the help file for details.

11.9.3 Importance resampling

We have already met a use of nonparametric simulation with unequal probabilities in Section 11.4, using the `weights` argument to `boot`. The simplest form for `weights`, used there, is a vector containing the probabilities with which to select the rows of `data`, when bootstrap sampling is to be performed with unequal probabilities. If we wish to perform importance resampling using several distributions, we can set them up and then perform the sampling as follows:

```
city.top <- exp.tilt(L=city.L, theta=2, t0=city.w(city))
city.bot <- exp.tilt(L=city.L, theta=1.2, t0=city.w(city))
city.tilt <- boot(city, city.fun, R=c(100,99),
                  weights=rbind(city.top$p,city.bot$p))
```

which performs 100 simulations from the probabilities in `city.top$p` and 99 from the probabilities in `city.bot$p`. In the first two lines `exp.tilt` is used to solve the equation

$$ t_0 + \frac{\sum_j l_j \exp(\lambda l_j)}{\sum_j \exp(\lambda l_j)} = \theta, $$

corresponding to exponential tilting of the linear approximation to t to be centred at $\theta = 2$ and 1.2. In the call to `boot`, R is a vector, and `weights` a matrix with `length(R)` rows and `nrow(data)` columns, corresponding to the `length(R)` distributions from which resampling takes place.

The importance sampling weights, moments, and selected quantiles of the resamples in `city.tilt$[,1]` are calculated by

```
imp.weights(city.tilt)
imp.moments(city.tilt)
imp.quantile(city.tilt)
```

Each of these returns raw, ratio and regression estimates of the corresponding quantities. Some other uses of important resampling are exemplified by

```
imp.prob(city.tilt, t0=1.2, def=F)
z <- (city.tilt$t[,1]-city.tilt$t0[1])/sqrt(city.tilt$t[,2])
imp.quantile(boot.out=city.tilt, t=z)
```

The call to `imp.prob` calculates the importance sampling estimate of the probability that $t^* \leq 1.2$, without using defensive mixture distributions (by default `def=T`, i.e. defensive mixture distributions are used to obtain the weights and estimates). The last two lines show how importance sampling is used to estimate quantiles of the studentized bootstrap statistic.

For more details and further arguments to the functions, see their help files.

Function `tilt.boot`

The description above relies on exponential tilting to obtain the resampling probabilities, and requires knowing where to tilt to. If this is difficult, `tilt.boot` can be used to avoid this, by performing an initial bootstrap with equal resampling probabilities, then using frequency smoothing to estimate appropriate tilted probabilities. For example,

```
city.tilt <- tilt.boot(city, city.fun, R=c(500,250,249))
```

performs 500 ordinary bootstraps, uses the results to estimate probability distributions tilted to the 0.025 and 0.975 points of the simulations, and then performs 250 bootstraps tilted to the 0.025 quantile, and 249 tilted to the 0.975 quantile, before assigning the result to a bootstrap object. More complex uses of `tilt.boot` are possible; see its help file.

Importance re-weighting

These functions allow for importance re-weighting as well as importance sampling. For example, suppose that we require to re-weight the simulated values so that they appear to have been simulated from a distribution with expected ratio close to 1.4. We then use the q= option to the importance sampling functions as follows:

```
q <- smooth.f(theta=1.4, boot.out=city.tilt)
city.w(city, q)
imp.moments(city.tilt, q=q)
imp.quantile(city.tilt, q=q)
```

where the first line calculates the smoothed distribution, the second obtains the corresponding ratio, and the third and fourth obtain the moment and quantile estimates corresponding to simulation from the distribution q.

11.9.4 Saddlepoint methods

The function used for single saddlepoint approximation is `saddle`. Its simplest use is to obtain the PDF and CDF approximations for a linear statistic, such as the linear approximation $t + n^{-1} \sum f_j^* l_j$ to a general bootstrap statistic t^*. The same results are obtained by using the approximation $n^{-1} \sum f_j^* l_j$ to $t^* - t$, and this is what `saddle` does. To obtain the approximations at $t^* = 2$ for the city data, we set

```
saddle(A=city.L/nrow(city), u=2-city.w(city))
```

which returns the PDF and CDF approximations, and the value of $\hat{\zeta}$.

The function `saddle.distn` returns the saddlepoint estimate of an entire distribution, using the terms $n^{-1} l_j$ in the random sum and an initial idea of the centre and scale for the distribution of $T^* - t$:

```
city.t0 <- c(0, sqrt(var.linear(city.L)))
city.sad <- saddle.distn(A=city.L/nrow(city), t0=city.t0)
city.sad
```

The Lugannani–Rice formula can be applied by setting LR=T in the calls to saddle and saddle.dist; by default LR=F.

For more sophisticated applications, the arguments A and u to saddle.distn can be replaced by functions. For example, the bootstrapped ratio can be defined through the estimating equation

$$\sum_j f_j^*(x_j - t u_j) = 0, \qquad (11.1)$$

where the f_j^* have a joint multinomial distribution with equal probabilities and denominator $n = 10$, the number of rows of city, as outlined in Example 9.16. Accordingly we set

```
city.t0 <- c(city.w(city), sqrt(var.linear(city.L)))
Afn <- function(t, data) data$x-t*data$u
ufn <- function(t, data) 0
saddle(A=Afn(2, city), u=0)
city.sad <- saddle.distn(A=Afn, u=ufn, t0=city.t0, data=city)
```

The penultimate line here gives the exact version of the call to saddle that started this section, while the last line calculates the saddlepoint approximation to the exact distribution of T^*. For saddle.distn the quantiles of the distribution of T^* are estimated by obtaining the CDF approximation at a number of values of t, and then interpolating the CDF using a spline smoother. The range of values of t used is determined by the contents of t0, whose first value contains the original value of the statistic, and whose second value contains a measure of the spread of the distribution of T^*, such as its standard error.

Another use of saddle and saddle.distn is to give them directly the adjusted cumulant generating function $K(\xi) - t\xi$, and the second derivative $K''(\xi)$. For example, the city data above can be tackled as follows:

```
K.adj <- function(xi)
{ L <- city$x-city.t*city$u
  nrow(city)*log(sum(exp(xi*L))/nrow(city))-city.t*xi }
K2 <- function(xi)
{ L <- city$x-city.t*city$u
  p <- exp(L*xi)
  nrow(city)*(sum(L^2*p)/sum(p) - (sum(L*p)/sum(p))^2) }
city.t <- 2
saddle(K.adj=K.adj, K2=K2)
```

This is most useful when $K(\cdot)$ is not of the standard form that follows from a multinomial distribution.

Conditional approximations

Conditional saddlepoint approximation is applied by giving `Afn` and `ufn` more columns, and setting the `wdist` and `type` arguments to `saddle` appropriately. For example, suppose that we want to find the distribution of T^*, defined as the root of (11.1), but resampling 25 rather than 49 cases of `bigcity`. Then we set

```
bigcity.L <- (bigcity$x-city.w(bigcity)*bigcity$u)/
             mean(bigcity$u)
bigcity.t0 <- c(city.w(bigcity), sqrt(var.linear(bigcity.L)))
Afn <- function(t, data) cbind(data$x-t*data$u, 1)
ufn <- function(t, data) c(0,25)
saddle(A=Afn(1.4, bigcity), u=ufn(1.4, bigcity), wdist="p",
       type="cond")
city.sad <- saddle.distn(A=Afn, u=ufn, wdist="p", type="cond",
           data=bigcity, t0=bigcity.t0)
```

Here the `wdist` argument gives the distribution of the random variables W_j, which is Poisson in this case, and the `type` argument specifies that a conditional approximation is required. For resampling without replacement, see the help file. A further argument `mu` allows these variables to have differing means, in which case the conditional saddlepoint will correspond to sampling from multinomial or hypergeometric distributions with unequal probabilities.

11.10 Semiparametric Likelihoods

Basic functions only are provided for semiparametric likelihood inference.

To calculate and plot the log profile likelihood for the mean of a gamma model for the larger air conditioning data (Example 10.1):

```
gam.L <- function(y, tmin=min(y)+0.1, tmax=max(y)-0.1, n.t)
{ gam.loglik <- function(l.nu, mu, y)
  { nu <- exp(l.nu)
    -sum(log(dgamma(nu*y/mu, nu)*nu/mu)) }
  out <- matrix(NA, n.t+1, 3)
  for (it in 0:n.t)
  { t <- tmin + (tmax-tmin)*it/n.t
    fit <- nlminb(0, gam.loglik, mu=t, y=y)
    out[1+it,] <- c(t, exp(fit$parameters), -fit$objective) }
  out }
```

```
air.gam <- gam.L(aircondit7$hours, 40, 120, 100)
air.gam[,3] <- air.gam[,3] - max(air.gam[,3])
plot(air.gam[,1],air.gam[,3],type="l",xlab="theta",
     ylab="Log likelihood",xlim=c(40,120))
abline(h=-0.5*qchisq(0.95,1),lty=2)
```

Empirical and empirical exponential family likelihoods are obtained using the functions EL.profile and EEF.profile. They are included in the library for demonstration purposes only, and are not intended for serious use, nor are they currently supported as part of the library. These functions give log likelihoods for the mean of their first argument, calculated at n.t values of θ from tmin and tmax. The output of EL.profile is a n.t$\times$3 matrix whose first column is the values of θ, whose next column is the log profile likelihood, and whose final column is the values of the Lagrange multiplier. The output of EEF.profile is a n.t$\times$4 matrix whose first column is the values of θ, whose next two columns are versions of the log profile likelihood (see Example 10.4), and whose final column is the values of the Lagrange multiplier. For example:

```
air.EL <- EL.profile(aircondit7$hours,tmin=40,tmax=120,n.t=100)
lines(air.EL[,1],air.EL[,2],lty=2)
air.EEF <- EEF.profile(aircondit7$hours,tmin=40,tmax=120,
                       n.t=100)
lines(air.EEF[,1],air.EEF[,3],lty=3)
```

Note how close the two semiparametric log likelihoods are, compared to the parametric one. The practicals at the end of Chapter 10 give more examples of their use (and abuse).

More general (and more robust!) code to calculate empirical likelihoods is provided by Professor A. B. Owen at Stanford University; see World Wide Web reference http://playfair.stanford.edu/reports/owen/el.S.

APPENDIX A

Cumulant Calculations

In this book several chapters and some of the problems involve moment calculations, which are often simplified by using cumulants.

The cumulant-generating function of a random variable Y is

$$K(t) = \log \mathrm{E}\left(e^{tY}\right) = \sum_{s=1}^{\infty} \frac{1}{s!} t^s \kappa_s,$$

where κ_s is the sth cumulant, while the moment-generating function of Y is

$$M(t) = \mathrm{E}\left(e^{tY}\right) = \sum_{s=0}^{\infty} \frac{1}{s!} t^s \mu_s',$$

where $\mu_s' = \mathrm{E}(Y^s)$ is the sth moment. A simple example is a $N(\mu, \sigma^2)$ random variable, for which $K(t) = t\mu + \frac{1}{2}t^2\sigma^2$; note the appealing fact that its cumulants of order higher than two are zero. By equating powers of t in the expansions of $K(t)$ and $\log M(t)$ we find that $\kappa_1 = \mu_1'$ and that

$$\begin{aligned}
\kappa_2 &= \mu_2' - (\mu_1')^2, \\
\kappa_3 &= \mu_3' - 3\mu_2'\mu_1' + 2(\mu_1')^3, \\
\kappa_4 &= \mu_4' - 4\mu_3'\mu_1' - 3(\mu_2')^2 + 12\mu_2'(\mu_1')^2 - 6(\mu_1')^4,
\end{aligned}$$

with inverse formulae

$$\begin{aligned}
\mu_2' &= \kappa_2 + (\kappa_1)^2, \\
\mu_3' &= \kappa_3 + 3\kappa_2\kappa_1 + (\kappa_1)^3, \\
\mu_4' &= \kappa_4 + 4\kappa_3\kappa_1 + 3(\kappa_2)^2 + 6\kappa_2(\kappa_1)^2 + (\kappa_1)^4.
\end{aligned} \tag{A.1}$$

The cumulants κ_1, κ_2, κ_3 and κ_4 are the mean, variance, skewness and kurtosis of Y.

For vector Y it is better to drop the power notation used above and to adopt index notation and the summation convention. In this notation Y has components $Y^1, \ldots, Y^n$ and we write $Y^i Y^i$ and $Y^i Y^i Y^i$ for the square and cube of Y^i. The joint cumulant-generating function $K(t)$ of $Y^1, \ldots, Y^n$ is the logarithm of their joint moment-generating function,

$$\log \mathrm{E}\left(e^{t_1 Y^1 + \cdots + t_n Y^n}\right) = t_i \kappa^i + \tfrac{1}{2!} t_i t_j \kappa^{i,j} + \tfrac{1}{3!} t_i t_j t_k \kappa^{i,j,k} + \tfrac{1}{4!} t_i t_j t_k t_l \kappa^{i,j,k,l} + \cdots,$$

where summation is implied over repeated indices, so that, for example,

$$t_i \kappa^i = t_1 \kappa^1 + \cdots + t_n \kappa^n, \quad t_i t_j \kappa^{i,j} = t_1 t_1 \kappa^{1,1} + t_1 t_2 \kappa^{1,2} + \cdots + t_n t_n \kappa^{n,n}.$$

Thus the n-dimensional normal distribution with means κ^i and covariance matrix $\kappa^{i,j}$ has cumulant-generating function $t_i \kappa^i + \tfrac{1}{2} t_i t_j \kappa^{i,j}$. We sometimes write $\kappa^{i,j} = \mathrm{cum}(Y^i, Y^j)$, $\kappa^{i,j,k} = \mathrm{cum}(Y^i, Y^j, Y^k)$ and so forth for the coefficients of $t_i t_j$, $t_i t_j t_k$ in $K(t)$. The cumulant arrays $\kappa^{i,j}$, $\kappa^{i,j,k}$ etc. are invariant to index permutation, so for example $\kappa^{1,2,3} = \kappa^{2,3,1}$.

A key feature that simplifies calculations with cumulants as opposed to moments is that cumulants involving two or more independent random variables are zero: for independent variables, $\kappa^{i,j} = \kappa^{i,j,k} = \cdots = 0$ unless all the indices are equal.

The above notation extends to generalized cumulants such as

$$\mathrm{cum}(Y^i Y^j Y^k) = \mathrm{E}(Y^i Y^j Y^k) = \kappa^{ijk},$$
$$\mathrm{cum}(Y^i, Y^j Y^k) = \kappa^{i,jk}, \quad \mathrm{cum}(Y^i Y^j, Y^k, Y^l) = \kappa^{ij,k,l},$$

which can be obtained from the joint cumulant-generating functions of $Y^i Y^j Y^k$, of Y^i and $Y^j Y^k$ and of $Y^i Y^j$, Y^k, and Y^l. Note that ordinary moments can be regarded as generalized cumulants.

Generalized cumulants can be expressed in terms of ordinary cumulants by means of complementary set partitions, the most useful of which are given in Table A.1. For example, we use its second column to see that $\kappa^{ij} = \kappa^{i,j} + \kappa^i \kappa^j$, or

$$\mathrm{E}(Y^i Y^j) = \mathrm{cum}(Y^i Y^j) = \mathrm{cum}(Y^i, Y^j) + \mathrm{cum}(Y^i)\mathrm{cum}(Y^j),$$

more familiarly written $\mathrm{cov}(Y^i, Y^j) + \mathrm{E}(Y^i)\mathrm{E}(Y^j)$. The boldface **12** represents κ^{12}, while the 12 [1] and 1|2 [1] immediately below it represent $\kappa^{1,2}$ and $\kappa^1 \kappa^2$. With this understanding we use the third column to see that $\kappa^{ijk} = \kappa^{i,j,k} + \kappa^{i,j}\kappa^k[3] + \kappa^i \kappa^j \kappa^k$, where $\kappa^{i,j}\kappa^k[3]$ is shorthand for $\kappa^{i,j}\kappa^k + \kappa^{i,k}\kappa^j + \kappa^{j,k}\kappa^i$; this is the multivariate version of (A.1). Likewise $\kappa^{i,jk} = \kappa^{i,j,k} + \kappa^{i,k}\kappa^j[2]$, where the term $\kappa^{i,k}\kappa^j[2]$ on the right is understood in the context of the left-hand side to equal $\kappa^{i,k}\kappa^j + \kappa^{j,k}\kappa^i$: each index in the first block of the partition $ij \mid k$ appears once with the index in the second block. The expression 123|4 **[2][2]** in the fourth column of the table represents the partitions 123|4, 124|3, 134|2, 234|1.

To illustrate these ideas, we calculate $\mathrm{cov}\{\bar{Y}, (n-1)^{-1}\sum(Y_i - \bar{Y})^2\}$, where

$\bar{Y} = n^{-1} \sum Y_i$ is the average of the independent and identically distributed random variables $Y_1, \ldots, Y_n$. Note first that the covariance does not depend on the mean of the Y_i, so we can take $\kappa^i \equiv 0$. We then express $\bar{Y}$ and $(n-1)^{-1} \sum (Y_i - \bar{Y})^2$ in index notation as $a_i Y^i$ and $b_{ij} Y^i Y^j$, where $a_i = 1/n$ and $b_{ij} = (\delta_{ij} - 1/n)/(n-1)$, with

$$\delta_{ij} = \begin{cases} 1, & i = j, \\ 0, & \text{otherwise,} \end{cases}$$

the Kronecker delta symbol. The covariance is

$$\text{cum}(a_i Y^i, b_{jk} Y^j Y^k) = a_i b_{jk} \kappa^{i,jk} = a_i b_{jk} \kappa^{i,j,k} = n a_1 b_{11} \kappa^{1,1,1},$$

the second equality following on use of Table A.1 because $\kappa^i \equiv 0$ and the third equality following because the observations are independent and identically distributed. In power notation $\kappa^{1,1,1}$ is κ_3, the third cumulant of Y_i, so $\text{cov}\{\bar{Y}, (n-1)^{-1} \sum (Y_i - \bar{Y})^2\} = \kappa_3/n$. Similarly

$$\text{var}\{(n-1)^{-1} \sum (Y_j - \bar{Y})^2\} = \text{cum}(b_{ij} Y^i Y^j, b_{kl} Y^k Y^l) = b_{ij} b_{kl} \kappa^{ij,kl},$$

which Table A.1 shows to be equal to $b_{ij} b_{kl} (\kappa^{i,j,k,l} + \kappa^{i,k} \kappa^{j,l} + \kappa^{i,l} \kappa^{j,k})$. This reduces to

$$n b_{11} b_{11} \kappa^{1,1,1,1} + 2n b_{11} b_{11} \kappa^{1,1} \kappa^{1,1} + 2n(n-1) b_{12} b_{12} \kappa^{1,1} \kappa^{1,1},$$

which in turn is $\kappa_4/n + 2(\kappa_2)^2/(n-1)$ in power notation. To perform this calculation using moments and power notation will convince the reader of the elegance and relative simplicity of cumulants and index notation.

McCullagh (1987) makes a cogent more-extended case for these methods. His book includes more-extensive tables of complementary set partitions.

1	**2**	**3**	**4**
1	**12**	**123**	**1234**
1 [1]	12 [1]	123 [1]	1234 [1]
	1|2 [1]	12|3 [3]	123|4 [4]
		1|2|3 [1]	12|34 [3]
	1|2		12|3|4 [6]
	12 [1]	**12|3**	1|2|3|4 [1]
		123 [1]	
		13|2 [2]	**123|4**
			1234 [1]
		1|2|3|	124|3 [3]
		123 [1]	12|34 [3]
			14|2|3 [3]
			12|34
			1234 [1]
			123|4 [2] [2]
			134|2
			13|24 [2]
			13|2|4 [4]
			12|3|4
			1234 [1]
			134|2 [2]
			13|24 [2]
			1|2|3|4
			1234 [1]

Table A.1
Complementary set
partitions

Bibliography

Abelson, R. P. and Tukey, J. W. (1963) Efficient utilization of non-numerical information in quantitative analysis: general theory and the case of simple order. *Annals of Mathematical Statistics* **34**, 1347–1369.

Akaike, H. (1973) Information theory and an extension of the maximum likelihood principle. In *Second International Symposium on Information Theory*, eds B. N. Petrov and F. Czáki, pp. 267–281. Budapest: Akademiai Kiadó. Reprinted in *Breakthroughs in Statistics*, volume 1, eds S. Kotz and N. L. Johnson, pp. 610–624. New York: Springer.

Akritas, M. G. (1986) Bootstrapping the Kaplan–Meier estimator. *Journal of the American Statistical Association* **81**, 1032–1038.

Altman, D. G. and Andersen, P. K. (1989) Bootstrap investigation of the stability of a Cox regression model. *Statistics in Medicine* **8**, 771–783.

Andersen, P. K., Borgan, Ø., Gill, R. D. and Keiding, N. (1993) *Statistical Models Based on Counting Processes*. New York: Springer.

Andrews, D. F. and Herzberg, A. M. (1985) *Data: A Collection of Problems from Many Fields for the Student and Research Worker*. New York: Springer.

Appleyard, S. T., Witkowski, J. A., Ripley, B. D., Shotton, D. M. and Dubowicz, V. (1985) A novel procedure for pattern analysis of features present on freeze fractured plasma membranes. *Journal of Cell Science* **74**, 105–117.

Athreya, K. B. (1987) Bootstrap of the mean in the infinite variance case. *Annals of Statistics* **15**, 724–731.

Atkinson, A. C. (1985) *Plots, Transformations, and Regression*. Oxford: Clarendon Press.

Bai, C. and Olshen, R. A. (1988) Discussion of "Theoretical comparison of bootstrap confidence intervals", by P. Hall. *Annals of Statistics* **16**, 953–956.

Bailer, A. J. and Oris, J. T. (1994) Assessing toxicity of pollutants in aquatic systems. In *Case Studies in Biometry*, eds N. Lange, L. Ryan, L. Billard, D. R. Brillinger, L. Conquest and J. Greenhouse, pp. 25–40. New York: Wiley.

Banks, D. L. (1988) Histospline smoothing the Bayesian bootstrap. *Biometrika* **75**, 673–684.

Barbe, P. and Bertail, P. (1995) *The Weighted Bootstrap*. Volume 98 of *Lecture Notes in Statistics*. New York: Springer.

Barnard, G. A. (1963) Discussion of "The spectral analysis of point processes", by M. S. Bartlett. *Journal of the Royal Statistical Society series B* **25**, 294.

Barndorff-Nielsen, O. E. and Cox, D. R. (1989) *Asymptotic Techniques for Use in Statistics*. London: Chapman & Hall.

Barndorff-Nielsen, O. E. and Cox, D. R. (1994) *Inference and Asymptotics*. London: Chapman & Hall.

Beran, J. (1994) *Statistics for Long-Memory Processes*. London: Chapman & Hall.

Beran, R. J. (1986) Simulated power functions. *Annals of Statistics* **14**, 151–173.

Beran, R. J. (1987) Prepivoting to reduce level error of confidence sets. *Biometrika* **74**, 457–468.

Beran, R. J. (1988) Prepivoting test statistics: a bootstrap view of asymptotic refinements. *Journal of the American Statistical Association* **83**, 687–697.

Beran, R. J. (1992) Designing bootstrap prediction regions. In *Bootstrapping and Related Techniques: Proceedings, Trier, FRG, 1990*, eds K.-H. Jöckel, G. Rothe and

W. Sendler, volume 376 of *Lecture Notes in Economics and Mathematical Systems*, pp. 23–30. New York: Springer.

Beran, R. J. (1997) Diagnosing bootstrap success. *Annals of the Institute of Statistical Mathematics* **49**, to appear.

Berger, J. O. and Bernardo, J. M. (1992) On the development of reference priors (with Discussion). In *Bayesian Statistics 4*, eds J. M. Bernardo, J. O. Berger, A. P. Dawid and A. F. M. Smith, pp. 35–60. Oxford: Clarendon Press.

Besag, J. E. and Clifford, P. (1989) Generalized Monte Carlo significance tests. *Biometrika* **76**, 633–642.

Besag, J. E. and Clifford, P. (1991) Sequential Monte Carlo *p*-values. *Biometrika* **78**, 301–304.

Besag, J. E. and Diggle, P. J. (1977) Simple Monte Carlo tests for spatial pattern. *Applied Statistics* **26**, 327–333.

Bickel, P. J. and Freedman, D. A. (1981) Some asymptotic theory for the bootstrap. *Annals of Statistics* **9**, 1196–1217.

Bickel, P. J. and Freedman, D. A. (1983) Bootstrapping regression models with many parameters. In *A Festschrift for Erich L. Lehmann*, eds P. J. Bickel, K. A. Doksum and J. L. Hodges, pp. 28–48. Pacific Grove, California: Wadsworth & Brooks/Cole.

Bickel, P. J. and Freedman, D. A. (1984) Asymptotic normality and the bootstrap in stratified sampling. *Annals of Statistics* **12**, 470–482.

Bickel, P. J., Götze, F. and van Zwet, W. R. (1997) Resampling fewer than *n* observations: gains, losses, and remedies for losses. *Statistica Sinica* **7**, 1–32.

Bickel, P. J., Klassen, C. A. J., Ritov, Y. and Wellner, J. A. (1993) *Efficient and Adaptive Estimation for Semiparametric Models*. Baltimore: Johns Hopkins University Press.

Bickel, P. J. and Yahav, J. A. (1988) Richardson extrapolation and the bootstrap. *Journal of the American Statistical Association* **83**, 387–393.

Bissell, A. F. (1972) A negative binomial model with varying element sizes. *Biometrika* **59**, 435–441.

Bissell, A. F. (1990) How reliable is your capability index? *Applied Statistics* **39**, 331–340.

Bithell, J. F. and Stone, R. A. (1989) On statistical methods for analysing the geographical distribution of cancer cases near nuclear installations. *Journal of Epidemiology and Community Health* **43**, 79–85.

Bloomfield, P. (1976) *Fourier Analysis of Time Series: An Introduction*. New York: Wiley.

Boos, D. D. and Monahan, J. F. (1986) Bootstrap methods using prior information. *Biometrika* **73**, 77–83.

Booth, J. G. (1996) Bootstrap methods for generalized linear mixed models with applications to small area estimation. In *Statistical Modelling*, eds G. U. H. Seeber, B. J. Francis, R. Hatzinger and G. Steckel-Berger, volume 104 of *Lecture Notes in Statistics*, pp. 43–51. New York: Springer.

Booth, J. G. and Butler, R. W. (1990) Randomization distributions and saddlepoint approximations in generalized linear models. *Biometrika* **77**, 787–796.

Booth, J. G., Butler, R. W. and Hall, P. (1994) Bootstrap methods for finite populations. *Journal of the American Statistical Association* **89**, 1282–1289.

Booth, J. G. and Hall, P. (1994) Monte Carlo approximation and the iterated bootstrap. *Biometrika* **81**, 331–340.

Booth, J. G., Hall, P. and Wood, A. T. A. (1992) Bootstrap estimation of conditional distributions. *Annals of Statistics* **20**, 1594–1610.

Booth, J. G., Hall, P. and Wood, A. T. A. (1993) Balanced importance resampling for the bootstrap. *Annals of Statistics* **21**, 286–298.

Bose, A. (1988) Edgeworth correction by bootstrap in autoregressions. *Annals of Statistics* **16**, 1709–1722.

Box, G. E. P. and Cox, D. R. (1964) An analysis of transformations (with Discussion). *Journal of the Royal Statistical Society series B* **26**, 211–246.

Bratley, P., Fox, B. L. and Schrage, L. E. (1987) *A Guide to Simulation*. Second edition. New York: Springer.

Braun, W. J. and Kulperger, R. J. (1995) A Fourier method for bootstrapping time series. Preprint, Department of Mathematics and Statistics, University of Winnipeg.

Braun, W. J. and Kulperger, R. J. (1997) Properties of a Fourier bootstrap method for time series. *Communications in Statistics — Theory and Methods* **26**, to appear.

Breiman, L., Friedman, J. H., Olshen, R. A. and Stone, C. J. (1984) *Classification and Regression Trees*. Pacific Grove, California: Wadsworth & Brooks/Cole.

Breslow, N. (1985) Cohort analysis in epidemiology. In *A Celebration of Statistics*, eds A. C. Atkinson and S. E. Fienberg, pp. 109–143. New York: Springer.

Bretagnolle, J. (1983) Lois limites du bootstrap de certaines fonctionelles. *Annales de l'Institut Henri Poincaré, Section B* **19**, 281–296.

Brillinger, D. R. (1981) *Time Series: Data Analysis and Theory*. Expanded edition. San Francisco: Holden-Day.

Brillinger, D. R. (1988) An elementary trend analysis of Rio Negro levels at Manaus, 1903–1985. *Brazilian Journal of Probability and Statistics* **2**, 63–79.

Brillinger, D. R. (1989) Consistent detection of a monotonic trend superposed on a stationary time series. *Biometrika* **76**, 23–30.

Brockwell, P. J. and Davis, R. A. (1991) *Time Series: Theory and Methods*. Second edition. New York: Springer.

Brockwell, P. J. and Davis, R. A. (1996) *Introduction to Time Series and Forecasting*. New York: Springer.

Brown, B. W. (1980) Prediction analysis for binary data. In *Biostatistics Casebook*, eds R. G. Miller, B. Efron, B. W. Brown and L. E. Moses, pp. 3–18. New York: Wiley.

Buckland, S. T. and Garthwaite, P. H. (1990) Algorithm AS 259: estimating confidence intervals by the Robbins–Monro search process. *Applied Statistics* **39**, 413–424.

Bühlmann, P. and Künsch, H. R. (1995) The blockwise bootstrap for general parameters of a stationary time series. *Scandinavian Journal of Statistics* **22**, 35–54.

Bunke, O. and Droge, B. (1984) Bootstrap and cross-validation estimates of the prediction error for linear regression models. *Annals of Statistics* **12**, 1400–1424.

Burman, P. (1989) A comparative study of ordinary cross-validation, v-fold cross-validation and the repeated learning-testing methods. *Biometrika* **76**, 503–514.

Burr, D. (1994) A comparison of certain bootstrap confidence intervals in the Cox model. *Journal of the American Statistical Association* **89**, 1290–1302.

Burr, D. and Doss, H. (1993) Confidence bands for the median survival time as a function of covariates in the Cox model. *Journal of the American Statistical Association* **88**, 1330–1340.

Canty, A. J., Davison, A. C. and Hinkley, D. V. (1996) Reliable confidence intervals. Discussion of "Bootstrap confidence intervals", by T. J. DiCiccio and B. Efron. *Statistical Science* **11**, 214–219.

Carlstein, E. (1986) The use of subseries values for estimating the variance of a general statistic from a stationary sequence. *Annals of Statistics* **14**, 1171–1179.

Carpenter, J. R. (1996) *Simulated confidence regions for parameters in epidemiological models*. Ph.D. thesis, Department of Statistics, University of Oxford.

Chambers, J. M. and Hastie, T. J. (eds) (1992) *Statistical Models in S*. Pacific Grove, California: Wadsworth & Brooks/Cole.

Chao, M.-T. and Lo, S.-H. (1994) Maximum likelihood summary and the bootstrap method in structured finite populations. *Statistica Sinica* **4**, 389–406.

Chapman, P. and Hinkley, D. V. (1986) The double bootstrap, pivots and confidence limits. Technical Report 34, Center for Statistical Sciences, University of Texas at Austin.

Chen, C., Davis, R. A., Brockwell, P. J. and Bai, Z. D. (1993) Order determination for autoregressive processes using resampling methods. *Statistica Sinica* **3**, 481–500.

Chen, C.-H. and George, S. L. (1985) The bootstrap and identification of prognostic factors via Cox's proportional hazards regression model. *Statistics in Medicine* **4**, 39–46.

Chen, S. X. (1996) Empirical likelihood confidence intervals for nonparametric density estimation. *Biometrika* **83**, 329–341.

Chen, S. X. and Hall, P. (1993) Smoothed empirical likelihood confidence intervals for quantiles. *Annals of Statistics* **21**, 1166–1181.

Chen, Z. and Do, K.-A. (1994) The bootstrap methods with saddlepoint approximations and importance resampling. *Statistica Sinica* **4**, 407–421.

Cobb, G. W. (1978) The problem of the Nile: conditional solution to a changepoint problem. *Biometrika* **65**, 243–252.

Cochran, W. G. (1977) *Sampling Techniques*. Third edition. New York: Wiley.

Collings, B. J. and Hamilton, M. A. (1988) Estimating the power of the two-sample Wilcoxon test for location shift. *Biometrics* **44**, 847–860.

Cook, R. D., Hawkins, D. M. and Weisberg, S. (1992) Comparison of model misspecification diagnostics using residuals from least mean of squares and least median of squares fits. *Journal of the American Statistical Association* **87**, 419–424.

Cook, R. D., Tsai, C.-L. and Wei, B. C. (1986) Bias in nonlinear regression. *Biometrika* **73**, 615–623.

Cook, R. D. and Weisberg, S. (1982) *Residuals and Influence in Regression*. London: Chapman & Hall.

Cook, R. D. and Weisberg, S. (1994) Transforming a response variable for linearity. *Biometrika* **81**, 731–737.

Corcoran, S. A., Davison, A. C. and Spady, R. H. (1996) Reliable inference from empirical likelihoods. Preprint, Department of Statistics, University of Oxford.

Cowling, A., Hall, P. and Phillips, M. J. (1996) Bootstrap confidence regions for the intensity of a Poisson process. *Journal of the American Statistical Association* **91**, 1516–1524.

Cox, D. R. and Hinkley, D. V. (1974) *Theoretical Statistics*. London: Chapman & Hall.

Cox, D. R. and Isham, V. (1980) *Point Processes*. London: Chapman & Hall.

Cox, D. R. and Lewis, P. A. W. (1966) *The Statistical Analysis of Series of Events*. London: Chapman & Hall.

Cox, D. R. and Oakes, D. (1984) *Analysis of Survival Data*. London: Chapman & Hall.

Cox, D. R. and Snell, E. J. (1981) *Applied Statistics: Principles and Examples*. London: Chapman & Hall.

Cressie, N. A. C. (1982) Playing safe with misweighted means. *Journal of the American Statistical Association* **77**, 754–759.

Cressie, N. A. C. (1991) *Statistics for Spatial Data*. New York: Wiley.

Dahlhaus, R. and Janas, D. (1996) A frequency domain bootstrap for ratio statistics in time series analysis. *Annals of Statistics* **24**, to appear.

Daley, D. J. and Vere-Jones, D. (1988) *An Introduction to the Theory of Point Processes*. New York: Springer.

Daniels, H. E. (1954) Saddlepoint approximations in statistics. *Annals of Mathematical Statistics* **25**, 631–650.

Daniels, H. E. (1955) Discussion of "Permutation theory in the derivation of robust criteria and the study of departures from assumption", by G. E. P. Box and S. L. Andersen. *Journal of the Royal Statistical Society series B* **17**, 27–28.

Daniels, H. E. (1958) Discussion of "The regression analysis of binary sequences", by D. R. Cox. *Journal of the Royal Statistical Society series B* **20**, 236–238.

Daniels, H. E. and Young, G. A. (1991) Saddlepoint approximation for the studentized mean, with an application to the bootstrap. *Biometrika* **78**, 169–179.

Davison, A. C. (1988) Discussion of the Royal Statistical Society meeting on the bootstrap. *Journal of the Royal Statistical Society series B* **50**, 356–357.

Davison, A. C. and Hall, P. (1992) On the bias and variability of bootstrap and cross-validation estimates of error rate in discrimination problems. *Biometrika* **79**, 279–284.

Davison, A. C. and Hall, P. (1993) On Studentizing and blocking methods for implementing the bootstrap with dependent data. *Australian Journal of Statistics* **35**, 215–224.

Davison, A. C. and Hinkley, D. V. (1988) Saddlepoint approximations in resampling methods. *Biometrika* **75**, 417–431.

Davison, A. C., Hinkley, D. V. and Schechtman, E. (1986) Efficient bootstrap simulation. *Biometrika* **73**, 555–566.

Davison, A. C., Hinkley, D. V. and Worton, B. J. (1992) Bootstrap likelihoods. *Biometrika* **79**, 113–130.

Davison, A. C., Hinkley, D. V. and Worton, B. J. (1995) Accurate and efficient construction of bootstrap

likelihoods. *Statistics and Computing* **5**, 257–264.

Davison, A. C. and Snell, E. J. (1991) Residuals and diagnostics. In *Statistical Theory and Modelling: In Honour of Sir David Cox, FRS*, eds D. V. Hinkley, N. Reid and E. J. Snell, pp. 83–106. London: Chapman & Hall.

De Angelis, D. and Gilks, W. R. (1994) Estimating acquired immune deficiency syndrome incidence accounting for reporting delay. *Journal of the Royal Statistical Society series A* **157**, 31–40.

De Angelis, D., Hall, P. and Young, G. A. (1993) Analytical and bootstrap approximations to estimator distributions in L_1 regression. *Journal of the American Statistical Association* **88**, 1310–1316.

De Angelis, D. and Young, G. A. (1992) Smoothing the bootstrap. *International Statistical Review* **60**, 45–56.

Dempster, A. P., Laird, N. M. and Rubin, D. B. (1977) Maximum likelihood from incomplete data via the EM algorithm (with Discussion). *Journal of the Royal Statistical Society series B* **39**, 1–38.

Diaconis, P. and Holmes, S. (1994) Gray codes for randomization procedures. *Statistics and Computing* **4**, 287–302.

DiCiccio, T. J. and Efron, B. (1992) More accurate confidence intervals in exponential families. *Biometrika* **79**, 231–245.

DiCiccio, T. J. and Efron, B. (1996) Bootstrap confidence intervals (with Discussion). *Statistical Science* **11**, 189–228.

DiCiccio, T. J., Hall, P. and Romano, J. P. (1989) Comparison of parametric and empirical likelihood functions. *Biometrika* **76**, 465–476.

DiCiccio, T. J., Hall, P. and Romano, J. P. (1991) Empirical likelihood is Bartlett-correctable. *Annals of Statistics* **19**, 1053–1061.

DiCiccio, T. J., Martin, M. A. and Young, G. A. (1992a) Analytic approximations for iterated bootstrap confidence intervals. *Statistics and Computing* **2**, 161–171.

DiCiccio, T. J., Martin, M. A. and Young, G. A. (1992b) Fast and accurate approximate double bootstrap confidence intervals. *Biometrika* **79**, 285–295.

DiCiccio, T. J., Martin, M. A. and Young, G. A. (1994) Analytical approximations to bootstrap distribution functions using saddlepoint methods. *Statistica Sinica* **4**, 281–295.

DiCiccio, T. J. and Romano, J. P. (1988) A review of bootstrap confidence intervals (with Discussion). *Journal of the Royal Statistical Society series B* **50**, 338–370. Correction, volume **51**, p. 470.

DiCiccio, T. J. and Romano, J. P. (1989) On adjustments based on the signed root of the empirical likelihood ratio statistic. *Biometrika* **76**, 447–456.

DiCiccio, T. J. and Romano, J. P. (1990) Nonparametric confidence limits by resampling methods and least favorable families. *International Statistical Review* **58**, 59–76.

Diggle, P. J. (1983) *Statistical Analysis of Spatial Point Patterns.* London: Academic Press.

Diggle, P. J. (1990) *Time Series: A Biostatistical Introduction.* Oxford: Clarendon Press.

Diggle, P. J. (1993) Point process modelling in environmental epidemiology. In *Statistics for the Environment*, eds V. Barnett and K. F. Turkman, pp. 89–110. Chichester: Wiley.

Diggle, P. J., Lange, N. and Beneš, F. M. (1991) Analysis of variance for replicated spatial point patterns in clinical neuroanatomy. *Journal of the American Statistical Association* **86**, 618–625.

Diggle, P. J. and Rowlingson, B. S. (1994) A conditional approach to point process modelling of elevated risk. *Journal of the Royal Statistical Society series A* **157**, 433–440.

Do, K.-A. and Hall, P. (1991) On importance resampling for the bootstrap. *Biometrika* **78**, 161–167.

Do, K.-A. and Hall, P. (1992a) Distribution estimation using concomitants of order statistics, with application to Monte Carlo simulation for the bootstrap. *Journal of the Royal Statistical Society series B* **54**, 595–607.

Do, K.-A. and Hall, P. (1992b) Quasi-random resampling for the bootstrap. *Statistics and Computing* **1**, 13–22.

Dobson, A. J. (1990) *An Introduction to Generalized Linear Models.* London: Chapman & Hall.

Donegani, M. (1991) An adaptive and powerful randomization test. *Biometrika* **78**, 930–933.

Doss, H. and Gill, R. D. (1992) An elementary approach to weak convergence for quantile processes, with applications to censored survival data. *Journal of the American Statistical Association* **87**, 869–877.

Draper, N. R. and Smith, H. (1981) *Applied Regression Analysis.* Second edition. New York: Wiley.

Ducharme, G. R., Jhun, M., Romano, J. P. and Truong, K. N. (1985) Bootstrap confidence cones for directional data. *Biometrika* **72**, 637–645.

Easton, G. S. and Ronchetti, E. M. (1986) General saddlepoint approximations with applications to L statistics. *Journal of the American Statistical Association* **81**, 420–430.

Efron, B. (1979) Bootstrap methods: another look at the jackknife. *Annals of Statistics* **7**, 1–26.

Efron, B. (1981a) Nonparametric standard errors and confidence intervals (with Discussion). *Canadian Journal of Statistics* **9**, 139–172.

Efron, B. (1981b) Censored data and the bootstrap. *Journal of the American Statistical Association* **76**, 312–319.

Efron, B. (1982) *The Jackknife, the Bootstrap, and Other Resampling Plans.* Number 38 in CBMS-NSF Regional Conference Series in Applied Mathematics. Philadelphia: SIAM.

Efron, B. (1983) Estimating the error rate of a prediction rule: improvement on cross-validation. *Journal of the American Statistical Association* **78**, 316–331.

Efron, B. (1986) How biased is the apparent error rate of a prediction rule? *Journal of the American Statistical Association* **81**, 461–470.

Efron, B. (1987) Better bootstrap confidence intervals (with Discussion). *Journal of the American Statistical Association* **82**, 171–200.

Efron, B. (1988) Computer-intensive methods in statistical regression. *SIAM Review* **30**, 421–449.

Efron, B. (1990) More efficient bootstrap computations. *Journal of the American Statistical Association* **55**, 79–89.

Efron, B. (1992) Jackknife-after-bootstrap standard errors and influence functions (with Discussion). *Journal of the Royal Statistical Society series B* **54**, 83–127.

Efron, B. (1993) Bayes and likelihood calculations from confidence intervals. *Biometrika* **80**, 3–26.

Efron, B. (1994) Missing data, imputation, and the bootstrap (with Discussion). *Journal of the American Statistical Association* **89**, 463–479.

Efron, B., Halloran, M. E. and Holmes, S. (1996) Bootstrap confidence levels for phylogenetic trees. *Proceedings of the National Academy of Sciences, USA* **93**, 13429–13434.

Efron, B. and Stein, C. M. (1981) The jackknife estimate of variance. *Annals of Statistics* **9**, 586–596.

Efron, B. and Tibshirani, R. J. (1986) Bootstrap methods for standard errors, confidence intervals, and other measures of statistical accuracy (with Discussion). *Statistical Science* **1**, 54–96.

Efron, B. and Tibshirani, R. J. (1993) *An Introduction to the Bootstrap.* New York: Chapman & Hall.

Efron, B. and Tibshirani, R. J. (1997) Improvements on cross-validation: the .632+ bootstrap method. *Journal of the American Statistical Association* **92**, 548–560.

Fang, K. T. and Wang, Y. (1994) *Number-Theoretic Methods in Statistics.* London: Chapman & Hall.

Faraway, J. J. (1992) On the cost of data analysis. *Journal of Computational and Graphical Statistics* **1**, 213–229.

Feigl, P. and Zelen, M. (1965) Estimation of exponential survival probabilities with concomitant information. *Biometrics* **21**, 826–838.

Feller, W. (1968) *An Introduction to Probability Theory and its Applications.* Third edition, volume I. New York: Wiley.

Fernholtz, L. T. (1983) *von Mises Calculus for Statistical Functionals.* Volume 19 of *Lecture Notes in Statistics.* New York: Springer.

Ferretti, N. and Romo, J. (1996) Unit root bootstrap tests for *AR*(1) models. *Biometrika* **83**, 849–860.

Field, C. and Ronchetti, E. M. (1990) *Small Sample Asymptotics.* Volume 13 of *Lecture Notes — Monograph Series.* Hayward, California: Institute of Mathematical Statistics.

Firth, D. (1991) Generalized linear models. In *Statistical Theory and Modelling: In Honour of Sir David Cox, FRS*, eds D. V. Hinkley, N. Reid and E. J. Snell, pp. 55–82. London: Chapman & Hall.

Firth, D. (1993) Bias reduction of maximum likelihood estimates. *Biometrika* **80**, 27–38.

Firth, D., Glosup, J. and Hinkley, D. V. (1991) Model checking with nonparametric curves. *Biometrika* **78**, 245–252.

Fisher, N. I., Hall, P., Jing, B.-Y. and Wood, A. T. A. (1996) Improved pivotal methods for constructing confidence regions with directional data. *Journal of the American Statistical Association* **91**, 1062–1070.

Fisher, N. I., Lewis, T. and Embleton, B. J. J. (1987) *Statistical Analysis of Spherical Data.* Cambridge: Cambridge University Press.

Fisher, R. A. (1935) *The Design of Experiments.* Edinburgh: Oliver and Boyd.

Fisher, R. A. (1947) The analysis of covariance method for the relation between a part and the whole. *Biometrics* **3**, 65–68.

Fleming, T. R. and Harrington, D. P. (1991) *Counting Processes and Survival Analysis.* New York: Wiley.

Forster, J. J., McDonald, J. W. and Smith, P. W. F. (1996) Monte Carlo exact conditional tests for log-linear and logistic models. *Journal of the Royal Statistical Society series B* **58**, 445–453.

Franke, J. and Härdle, W. (1992) On bootstrapping kernel spectral estimates. *Annals of Statistics* **20**, 121–145.

Freedman, D. A. (1981) Bootstrapping regression models. *Annals of Statistics* **9**, 1218–1228.

Freedman, D. A. (1984) On bootstrapping two-stage least-squares estimates in stationary linear models. *Annals of Statistics* **12**, 827–842.

Freedman, D. A. and Peters, S. C. (1984a) Bootstrapping a regression equation: some empirical results. *Journal of the American Statistical Association* **79**, 97–106.

Freedman, D. A. and Peters, S. C. (1984b) Bootstrapping an econometric model: some empirical results. *Journal of Business & Economic Statistics* **2**, 150–158.

Freeman, D. H. (1987) *Applied Categorical Data Analysis.* New York: Marcel Dekker.

Frets, G. P. (1921) Heredity of head form in man. *Genetica* **3**, 193–384.

Garcia-Soidan, P. H. and Hall, P. (1997) On sample reuse methods for spatial data. *Biometrics* **53**, 273–281.

Garthwaite, P. H. and Buckland, S. T. (1992) Generating Monte Carlo confidence intervals by the Robbins–Monro process. *Applied Statistics* **41**, 159–171.

Gatto, R. (1994) *Saddlepoint methods and nonparametric approximations for econometric models.* Ph.D. thesis, Faculty of Economic and Social Sciences, University of Geneva.

Gatto, R. and Ronchetti, E. M. (1996) General saddlepoint approximations of marginal densities and tail probabilities. *Journal of the American Statistical Association* **91**, 666–673.

Geisser, S. (1975) The predictive sample reuse method with applications. *Journal of the American Statistical Association* **70**, 320–328.

Geisser, S. (1993) *Predictive Inference: An Introduction.* London: Chapman & Hall.

Geyer, C. J. (1991) Constrained maximum likelihood exemplified by isotonic convex logistic regression. *Journal of the American Statistical Association* **86**, 717–724.

Geyer, C. J. (1995) Likelihood ratio tests and inequality constraints. Technical Report 610, School of Statistics, University of Minnesota.

Gigli, A. (1994) *Contributions to importance sampling and resampling.* Ph.D. thesis, Department of Mathematics, Imperial College, London.

Gilks, W. R., Richardson, S. and Spiegelhalter, D. J. (eds) (1996) *Markov Chain Monte Carlo in Practice.* London: Chapman & Hall.

Gleason, J. R. (1988) Algorithms for balanced bootstrap simulations. *American Statistician* **42**, 263–266.

Gong, G. (1983) Cross-validation, the jackknife, and the bootstrap: excess error estimation in forward logistic regression. *Journal of the American Statistical Association* **78**, 108–113.

Götze, F. and Künsch, H. R. (1996) Second order correctness of the blockwise bootstrap for stationary observations. *Annals of Statistics* **24**, 1914–1933.

Graham, R. L., Hinkley, D. V., John, P. W. M. and Shi, S. (1990) Balanced design of bootstrap simulations. *Journal of the Royal Statistical Society series B* **52**, 185–202.

Gray, H. L. and Schucany, W. R. (1972) *The Generalized Jackknife Statistic*. New York: Marcel Dekker.

Green, P. J. and Silverman, B. W. (1994) *Nonparametric Regression and Generalized Linear Models: A Roughness Penalty Approach*. London: Chapman & Hall.

Gross, S. (1980) Median estimation in sample surveys. In *Proceedings of the Section on Survey Research Methods*, pp. 181–184. Alexandria, Virginia: American Statistical Association.

Haldane, J. B. S. (1940) The mean and variance of χ^2, when used as a test of homogeneity, when expectations are small. *Biometrika* **31**, 346–355.

Hall, P. (1985) Resampling a coverage pattern. *Stochastic Processes and their Applications* **20**, 231–246.

Hall, P. (1986) On the bootstrap and confidence intervals. *Annals of Statistics* **14**, 1431–1452.

Hall, P. (1987) On the bootstrap and likelihood-based confidence regions. *Biometrika* **74**, 481–493.

Hall, P. (1988a) Theoretical comparison of bootstrap confidence intervals (with Discussion). *Annals of Statistics* **16**, 927–985.

Hall, P. (1988b) On confidence intervals for spatial parameters estimated from nonreplicated data. *Biometrics* **44**, 271–277.

Hall, P. (1989a) Antithetic resampling for the bootstrap. *Biometrika* **76**, 713–724.

Hall, P. (1989b) Unusual properties of bootstrap confidence intervals in regression problems. *Probability Theory and Related Fields* **81**, 247–273.

Hall, P. (1990) Pseudo-likelihood theory for empirical likelihood. *Annals of Statistics* **18**, 121–140.

Hall, P. (1992a) *The Bootstrap and Edgeworth Expansion*. New York: Springer.

Hall, P. (1992b) On bootstrap confidence intervals in nonparametric regression. *Annals of Statistics* **20**, 695–711.

Hall, P. (1995) On the biases of error estimators in prediction problems. *Statistics and Probability Letters* **24**, 257–262.

Hall, P., DiCiccio, T. J. and Romano, J. P. (1989) On smoothing and the bootstrap. *Annals of Statistics* **17**, 692–704.

Hall, P. and Horowitz, J. L. (1993) Corrections and blocking rules for the block bootstrap with dependent data. Technical Report SR11–93, Centre for Mathematics and its Applications, Australian National University.

Hall, P., Horowitz, J. L. and Jing, B.-Y. (1995) On blocking rules for the bootstrap with dependent data. *Biometrika* **82**, 561–574.

Hall, P. and Jing, B.-Y. (1996) On sample reuse methods for dependent data. *Journal of the Royal Statistical Society series B* **58**, 727–737.

Hall, P. and Keenan, D. M. (1989) Bootstrap methods for constructing confidence regions for hands. *Communications in Statistics — Stochastic Models* **5**, 555–562.

Hall, P. and La Scala, B. (1990) Methodology and algorithms of empirical likelihood. *International Statistical Review* **58**, 109–28.

Hall, P. and Martin, M. A. (1988) On bootstrap resampling and iteration. *Biometrika* **75**, 661–671.

Hall, P. and Owen, A. B. (1993) Empirical likelihood confidence bands in density estimation. *Journal of Computational and Graphical Statistics* **2**, 273–289.

Hall, P. and Titterington, D. M. (1989) The effect of simulation order on level accuracy and power of Monte Carlo tests. *Journal of the Royal Statistical Society series B* **51**, 459–467.

Hall, P. and Wilson, S. R. (1991) Two guidelines for bootstrap hypothesis testing. *Biometrics* **47**, 757–762.

Hamilton, M. A. and Collings, B. J. (1991) Determining the appropriate sample size for nonparametric tests for location shift. *Technometrics* **33**, 327–337.

Hammersley, J. M. and Handscomb, D. C. (1964) *Monte Carlo Methods*. London: Methuen.

Hampel, F. R., Ronchetti, E. M., Rousseeuw, P. J. and Stahel, W. A. (1986) *Robust Statistics: The Approach Based on Influence Functions*. New York: Wiley.

Hand, D. J., Daly, F., Lunn, A. D., McConway, K. J. and Ostrowski, E. (eds) (1994) *A Handbook of Small Data Sets*. London: Chapman & Hall.

Härdle, W. (1989) Resampling for inference from curves. In *Bulletin of the 47th Session of the International Statistical Institute, Paris, August 1989*, volume 3, pp. 53–63.

Härdle, W. (1990) *Applied Nonparametric Regression*. Cambridge: Cambridge University Press.

Härdle, W. and Bowman, A. W. (1988) Bootstrapping in nonparametric regression: local adaptive smoothing and confidence bands. *Journal of the American Statistical Association* **83**, 102–110.

Härdle, W. and Marron, J. S. (1991) Bootstrap simultaneous error bars for nonparametric regression. *Annals of Statistics* **19**, 778–796.

Hartigan, J. A. (1969) Using subsample values as typical values. *Journal of the American Statistical Association* **64**, 1303–1317.

Hartigan, J. A. (1971) Error analysis by replaced samples. *Journal of the Royal Statistical Society series B* **33**, 98–110.

Hartigan, J. A. (1975) Necessary and sufficient conditions for asymptotic joint normality of a statistic and its subsample values. *Annals of Statistics* **3**, 573–580.

Hartigan, J. A. (1990) Perturbed periodogram estimates of variance. *International Statistical Review* **58**, 1–7.

Hastie, T. J. and Loader, C. (1993) Local regression: automatic kernel carpentry (with Discussion). *Statistical Science* **8**, 120–143.

Hastie, T. J. and Tibshirani, R. J. (1990) *Generalized Additive Models*. London: Chapman & Hall.

Hayes, K. G., Perl, M. L. and Efron, B. (1989) Application of the bootstrap statistical method to the tau-decay-mode problem. *Physical Review Series D* **39**, 274–279.

Heller, G. and Venkatraman, E. S. (1996) Resampling procedures to compare two survival distributions in the presence of right-censored data. *Biometrics* **52**, 1204–1213.

Hesterberg, T. C. (1988) *Advances in importance sampling*. Ph.D. thesis, Department of Statistics, Stanford University, California.

Hesterberg, T. C. (1995a) Tail-specific linear approximations for efficient bootstrap simulations. *Journal of Computational and Graphical Statistics* **4**, 113–133.

Hesterberg, T. C. (1995b) Weighted average importance sampling and defensive mixture distributions. *Technometrics* **37**, 185–194.

Hinkley, D. V. (1977) Jackknifing in unbalanced situations. *Technometrics* **19**, 285–292.

Hinkley, D. V. and Schechtman, E. (1987) Conditional bootstrap methods in the mean-shift model. *Biometrika* **74**, 85–93.

Hinkley, D. V. and Shi, S. (1989) Importance sampling and the nested bootstrap. *Biometrika* **76**, 435–446.

Hinkley, D. V. and Wang, S. (1991) Efficiency of robust standard errors for regression coefficients. *Communications in Statistics — Theory and Methods* **20**, 1–11.

Hinkley, D. V. and Wei, B. C. (1984) Improvements of

jackknife confidence limit methods. *Biometrika* **71**, 331–339.

Hirose, H. (1993) Estimation of threshold stress in accelerated life-testing. *IEEE Transactions on Reliability* **42**, 650–657.

Hjort, N. L. (1985) Bootstrapping Cox's regression model. Technical Report NSF-241, Department of Statistics, Stanford University.

Hjort, N. L. (1992) On inference in parametric survival data models. *International Statistical Review* **60**, 355–387.

Horváth, L. and Yandell, B. S. (1987) Convergence rates for the bootstrapped product-limit process. *Annals of Statistics* **15**, 1155–1173.

Hosmer, D. W. and Lemeshow, S. (1989) *Applied Logistic Regression*. New York: Wiley.

Hu, F. and Zidek, J. V. (1995) A bootstrap based on the estimating equations of the linear model. *Biometrika* **82**, 263–275.

Huet, S., Jolivet, E. and Messéan, A. (1990) Some simulations results about confidence intervals and bootstrap methods in nonlinear regression. *Statistics* **3**, 369–432.

Hyde, J. (1980) Survival analysis with incomplete observations. In *Biostatistics Casebook*, eds R. G. Miller, B. Efron, B. W. Brown and L. E. Moses, pp. 31–46. New York: Wiley.

Janas, D. (1993) *Bootstrap Procedures for Time Series*. Aachen: Verlag Shaker.

Jennison, C. (1992) Bootstrap tests and confidence intervals for a hazard ratio when the number of observed failures is small, with applications to group sequential survival studies. In *Computer Science and Statistics: Proceedings of the 22nd Symposium on the Interface*, eds C. Page and R. LePage, pp. 89–97. New York: Springer.

Jensen, J. L. (1992) The modified signed likelihood statistic and saddlepoint approximations. *Biometrika* **79**, 693–703.

Jensen, J. L. (1995) *Saddlepoint Approximations*. Oxford: Clarendon Press.

Jeong, J. and Maddala, G. S. (1993) A perspective on application of bootstrap methods in econometrics. In *Handbook of Statistics, vol. 11: Econometrics*, eds G. S. Maddala, C. R. Rao and H. D. Vinod, pp. 573–610. Amsterdam: North-Holland.

Jing, B.-Y. and Robinson, J. (1994) Saddlepoint approximations for marginal and conditional probabilities of transformed variables. *Annals of Statistics* **22**, 1115–1132.

Jing, B.-Y. and Wood, A. T. A. (1996) Exponential empirical likelihood is not Bartlett correctable. *Annals of Statistics* **24**, 365–369.

Jöckel, K.-H. (1986) Finite sample properties and asymptotic efficiency of Monte Carlo tests. *Annals of Statistics* **14**, 336–347.

Johns, M. V. (1988) Importance sampling for bootstrap confidence intervals. *Journal of the American Statistical Association* **83**, 709–714.

Journel, A. G. (1994) Resampling from stochastic simulations (with Discussion). *Environmental and Ecological Statistics* **1**, 63–91.

Kabaila, P. (1993a) Some properties of profile bootstrap confidence intervals. *Australian Journal of Statistics* **35**, 205–214.

Kabaila, P. (1993b) On bootstrap predictive inference for autoregressive processes. *Journal of Time Series Analysis* **14**, 473–484.

Kalbfleisch, J. D. and Prentice, R. L. (1980) *The Statistical Analysis of Failure Time Data.* New York: Wiley.

Kaplan, E. L. and Meier, P. (1958) Nonparametric estimation from incomplete observations. *Journal of the American Statistical Association* **53**, 457–481.

Karr, A. F. (1991) *Point Processes and their Statistical Inference.* Second edition. New York: Marcel Dekker.

Katz, R. (1995) *Spatial analysis of pore images.* Ph.D. thesis, Department of Statistics, University of Oxford.

Kendall, D. G. and Kendall, W. S. (1980) Alignments in two-dimensional random sets of points. *Advances in Applied Probability* **12**, 380–424.

Kim, J.-H. (1990) *Conditional bootstrap methods for censored data.* Ph.D. thesis, Department of Statistics, Florida State University.

Künsch, H. R. (1989) The jackknife and bootstrap for general stationary observations. *Annals of Statistics* **17**, 1217–1241.

Lahiri, S. N. (1991) Second-order optimality of stationary bootstrap. *Statistics and Probability Letters* **11**, 335–341.

Lahiri, S. N. (1995) On the asymptotic behaviour of the moving block bootstrap for normalized sums of heavy-tail random variables. *Annals of Statistics* **23**, 1331–1349.

Laird, N. M. (1978) Nonparametric maximum likelihood estimation of a mixing distribution. *Journal of the American Statistical Association* **73**, 805–811.

Laird, N. M. and Louis, T. A. (1987) Empirical Bayes confidence intervals based on bootstrap samples (with Discussion). *Journal of the American Statistical Association* **82**, 739–757.

Lawson, A. B. (1993) On the analysis of mortality events associated with a prespecified fixed point. *Journal of the Royal Statistical Society series A* **156**, 363–377.

Lee, S. M. S. and Young, G. A. (1995) Asymptotic iterated bootstrap confidence intervals. *Annals of Statistics* **23**, 1301–1330.

Léger, C., Politis, D. N. and Romano, J. P. (1992) Bootstrap technology and applications. *Technometrics* **34**, 378–398.

Léger, C. and Romano, J. P. (1990a) Bootstrap choice of tuning parameters. *Annals of the Institute of Statistical Mathematics* **42**, 709–735.

Léger, C. and Romano, J. P. (1990b) Bootstrap adaptive estimation: the trimmed mean example. *Canadian Journal of Statistics* **18**, 297–314.

Lehmann, E. L. (1986) *Testing Statistical Hypotheses.* Second edition. New York: Wiley.

Li, G. (1995) Nonparametric likelihood ratio estimation of probabilities for truncated data. *Journal of the American Statistical Association* **90**, 997–1003.

Li, H. and Maddala, G. S. (1996) Bootstrapping time series models (with Discussion). *Econometric Reviews* **15**, 115–195.

Li, K.-C. (1987) Asymptotic optimality for C_p, C_L, cross-validation and generalized cross-validation: discrete index set. *Annals of Statistics* **15**, 958–975.

Liu, R. Y. and Singh, K. (1992a) Moving blocks jackknife and bootstrap capture weak dependence. In *Exploring the Limits of Bootstrap*, eds R. LePage and L. Billard, pp. 225–248. New York: Wiley.

Liu, R. Y. and Singh, K. (1992b) Efficiency and robustness in resampling. *Annals of Statistics* **20**, 370–384.

Lloyd, C. J. (1994) Approximate pivots from M-estimators. *Statistica Sinica* **4**, 701–714.

Lo, S.-H. and Singh, K. (1986) The product-limit estimator and the bootstrap: some asymptotic representations. *Probability Theory and Related Fields* **71**, 455–465.

Loh, W.-Y. (1987) Calibrating confidence coefficients. *Journal of the American Statistical Association* **82**, 155–162.

Mallows, C. L. (1973) Some comments on C_p. *Technometrics* **15**, 661–675.

Mammen, E. (1989) Asymptotics with increasing dimension for robust regression with applications to the bootstrap. *Annals of Statistics* **17**, 382–400.

Mammen, E. (1992) *When Does Bootstrap Work? Asymptotic Results and Simulations.* Volume 77 of *Lecture Notes in Statistics.* New York: Springer.

Mammen, E. (1993) Bootstrap and wild bootstrap for high dimensional linear models. *Annals of Statistics* **21**, 255–285.

Manly, B. F. J. (1991) *Randomization and Monte Carlo Methods in Biology.* London: Chapman & Hall.

Marriott, F. H. C. (1979) Barnard's Monte Carlo tests: how many simulations? *Applied Statistics* **28**, 75–77.

McCarthy, P. J. (1969) Pseudo-replication: half samples. *Review of the International Statistical Institute* **37**, 239–264.

McCarthy, P. J. and Snowden, C. B. (1985) *The Bootstrap and Finite Population Sampling.* Vital and Public Health Statistics (Ser. 2, No. 95), Public Health Service Publication. Washington, DC: United States Government Printing Office, 85–1369.

McCullagh, P. (1987) *Tensor Methods in Statistics.* London: Chapman & Hall.

McCullagh, P. and Nelder, J. A. (1989) *Generalized Linear Models.* Second edition. London: Chapman & Hall.

McKay, M. D., Beckman, R. J. and Conover, W. J. (1979) A comparison of three methods for selecting values of input variables in the analysis of output from a computer code. *Technometrics* **21**, 239–245.

McKean, J. W., Sheather, S. J. and Hettmansperger, T. P. (1993) The use and interpretation of residuals based on robust estimation. *Journal of the American Statistical Association* **88**, 1254–1263.

McLachlan, G. J. (1992) *Discriminant Analysis and Statistical Pattern Recognition.* New York: Wiley.

Milan, L. and Whittaker, J. (1995) Application of the parametric bootstrap to models that incorporate a singular value decomposition. *Applied Statistics* **44**, 31–49.

Miller, R. G. (1974) The jackknife — a review. *Biometrika* **61**, 1–15.

Miller, R. G. (1981) *Survival Analysis.* New York: Wiley.

Monti, A. C. (1997) Empirical likelihood confidence regions in time series models. *Biometrika* **84**, 395–405.

Morgenthaler, S. and Tukey, J. W. (eds) (1991) *Configural Polysampling: A Route to Practical Robustness.* New York: Wiley.

Moulton, L. H. and Zeger, S. L. (1989) Analyzing repeated measures on generalized linear models via the bootstrap. *Biometrics* **45**, 381–394.

Moulton, L. H. and Zeger, S. L. (1991) Bootstrapping generalized linear models. *Computational Statistics and Data Analysis* **11**, 53–63.

Muirhead, C. R. and Darby, S. C. (1989) Royal Statistical Society meeting on cancer near nuclear installations.

Journal of the Royal Statistical Society series A **152**, 305–384.

Murphy, S. A. (1995) Likelihood-based confidence intervals in survival analysis. *Journal of the American Statistical Association* **90**, 1399–1405.

Mykland, P. A. (1995) Dual likelihood. *Annals of Statistics* **23**, 396–421.

Nelder, J. A. and Pregibon, D. (1987) An extended quasi-likelihood function. *Biometrika* **74**, 221–232.

Newton, M. A. and Geyer, C. J. (1994) Bootstrap recycling: a Monte Carlo alternative to the nested bootstrap. *Journal of the American Statistical Association* **89**, 905–912.

Newton, M. A. and Raftery, A. E. (1994) Approximate Bayesian inference with the weighted likelihood bootstrap (with Discussion). *Journal of the Royal Statistical Society series B* **56**, 3–48.

Niederreiter, H. (1992) *Random Number Generation and Quasi-Monte Carlo Methods.* Number 63 in CBMS-NSF Regional Conference Series in Applied Mathematics. Philadelphia: SIAM.

Nordgaard, A. (1990) *On the resampling of stochastic processes using a bootstrap approach.* Ph.D. thesis, Department of Mathematics, Linköping University, Sweden.

Noreen, E. W. (1989) *Computer Intensive Methods for Testing Hypotheses: An Introduction.* New York: Wiley.

Ogbonmwan, S.-M. (1985) *Accelerated resampling codes with application to likelihood.* Ph.D. thesis, Department of Mathematics, Imperial College, London.

Ogbonmwan, S.-M. and Wynn, H. P. (1986) Accelerated resampling codes with low discrepancy. Preprint, Department of Statistics and Actuarial Science, The City University.

Olshen, R. A., Biden, E. N., Wyatt, M. P. and Sutherland, D. H. (1989) Gait analysis and the bootstrap. *Annals of Statistics* **17**, 1419–1440.

Owen, A. B. (1988) Empirical likelihood ratio confidence intervals for a single functional. *Biometrika* **75**, 237–249.

Owen, A. B. (1990) Empirical likelihood ratio confidence regions. *Annals of Statistics* **18**, 90–120.

Owen, A. B. (1991) Empirical likelihood for linear models. *Annals of Statistics* **19**, 1725–1747.

Owen, A. B. (1992a) Empirical likelihood and small samples. In *Computer Science and Statistics: Proceedings of the 22nd Symposium on the Interface*, eds C. Page and R. LePage, pp. 79–88. New York: Springer.

Owen, A. B. (1992b) A central limit theorem for Latin hypercube sampling. *Journal of the Royal Statistical*

Society series B **54**, 541–551.

Parzen, M. I., Wei, L. J. and Ying, Z. (1994) A resampling method based on pivotal estimating functions. *Biometrika* **81**, 341–350.

Paulsen, O. and Heggelund, P. (1994) The quantal size at retinogeniculate synapses determined from spontaneous and evoked EPSCs in guinea-pig thalamic slices. *Journal of Physiology* **480**, 505–511.

Percival, D. B. and Walden, A. T. (1993) *Spectral Analysis for Physical Applications: Multitaper and Conventional Univariate Techniques.* Cambridge: Cambridge University Press.

Pitman, E. J. G. (1937a) Significance tests which may be applied to samples from any populations. *Journal of the Royal Statistical Society, Supplement* **4**, 119–130.

Pitman, E. J. G. (1937b) Significance tests which may be applied to samples from any populations: II. The correlation coefficient test. *Journal of the Royal Statistical Society, Supplement* **4**, 225–232.

Pitman, E. J. G. (1937c) Significance tests which may be applied to samples from any populations: III. The analysis of variance test. *Biometrika* **29**, 322–335.

Plackett, R. L. and Burman, J. P. (1946) The design of optimum multifactorial experiments. *Biometrika* **33**, 305–325.

Politis, D. N. and Romano, J. P. (1993) Nonparametric resampling for homogeneous strong mixing random fields. *Journal of Multivariate Analysis* **47**, 301–328.

Politis, D. N. and Romano, J. P. (1994a) The stationary bootstrap. *Journal of the American Statistical Association* **89**, 1303–1313.

Politis, D. N. and Romano, J. P. (1994b) Large sample confidence regions based on subsamples under minimal assumptions. *Annals of Statistics* **22**, 2031–2050.

Possolo, A. (1986) Subsampling a random field. Technical Report 78, Department of Statistics, University of Washington, Seattle.

Presnell, B. and Booth, J. G. (1994) Resampling methods for sample surveys. Technical Report 470, Department of Statistics, University of Florida, Gainesville.

Priestley, M. B. (1981) *Spectral Analysis and Time Series.* London: Academic Press.

Proschan, F. (1963) Theoretical explanation of observed decreasing failure rate. *Technometrics* **5**, 375–383.

Qin, J. (1993) Empirical likelihood in biased sample problems. *Annals of Statistics* **21**, 1182–1196.

Qin, J. and Lawless, J. (1994) Empirical likelihood and general estimating equations. *Annals of Statistics* **22**, 300–325.

Quenouille, M. H. (1949) Approximate tests of correlation in time-series. *Journal of the Royal Statistical Society series B* **11**, 68–84.

Rao, J. N. K. and Wu, C. F. J. (1988) Resampling inference with complex survey data. *Journal of the American Statistical Association* **83**, 231–241.

Rawlings, J. O. (1988) *Applied Regression Analysis: A Research Tool.* Pacific Grove, California: Wadsworth & Brooks/Cole.

Reid, N. (1981) Estimating the median survival time. *Biometrika* **68**, 601–608.

Reid, N. (1988) Saddlepoint methods and statistical inference (with Discussion). *Statistical Science* **3**, 213–238.

Reynolds, P. S. (1994) Time-series analyses of beaver body temperatures. In *Case Studies in Biometry*, eds N. Lange, L. Ryan, L. Billard, D. R. Brillinger, L. Conquest and J. Greenhouse, pp. 211–228. New York: Wiley.

Ripley, B. D. (1977) Modelling spatial patterns (with Discussion). *Journal of the Royal Statistical Society series B* **39**, 172–212.

Ripley, B. D. (1981) *Spatial Statistics.* New York: Wiley.

Ripley, B. D. (1987) *Stochastic Simulation.* New York: Wiley.

Ripley, B. D. (1988) *Statistical Inference for Spatial Processes.* Cambridge: Cambridge University Press.

Ripley, B. D. (1996) *Pattern Recognition and Neural Networks.* Cambridge: Cambridge University Press.

Robinson, J. (1982) Saddlepoint approximations for permutation tests and confidence intervals. *Journal of the Royal Statistical Society series B* **44**, 91–101.

Romano, J. P. (1988) Bootstrapping the mode. *Annals of the Institute of Statistical Mathematics* **40**, 565–586.

Romano, J. P. (1989) Bootstrap and randomization tests of some nonparametric hypotheses. *Annals of Statistics* **17**, 141–159.

Romano, J. P. (1990) On the behaviour of randomization tests without a group invariance assumption. *Journal of the American Statistical Association* **85**, 686–692.

Rousseeuw, P. J. and Leroy, A. M. (1987) *Robust Regression and Outlier Detection.* New York: Wiley.

Royall, R. M. (1986) Model robust confidence intervals using maximum likelihood estimators. *International Statistical Review* **54**, 221–226.

Rubin, D. B. (1981) The Bayesian bootstrap. *Annals of Statistics* **9**, 130–134.

Rubin, D. B. (1987) *Multiple Imputation for Nonresponse in Surveys.* New York: Wiley.

Rubin, D. B. and Schenker, N. (1986) Multiple imputation for interval estimation from simple random samples with ignorable nonresponse. *Journal of the American Statistical Association* **81**, 366–374.

Ruppert, D. and Carroll, R. J. (1980) Trimmed least squares estimation in the linear model. *Journal of the American Statistical Association* **75**, 828–838.

Samawi, H. M. (1994) *Power estimation for two-sample tests using importance and antithetic resampling*. Ph.D. thesis, Department of Statistics and Actuarial Science, University of Iowa, Ames.

Sauerbrei, W. and Schumacher, M. (1992) A bootstrap resampling procedure for model building: application to the Cox regression model. *Statistics in Medicine* **11**, 2093–2109.

Schenker, N. (1985) Qualms about bootstrap confidence intervals. *Journal of the American Statistical Association* **80**, 360–361.

Seber, G. A. F. (1977) *Linear Regression Analysis*. New York: Wiley.

Shao, J. (1988) On resampling methods for variance and bias estimation in linear models. *Annals of Statistics* **16**, 986–1008.

Shao, J. (1993) Linear model selection by cross-validation. *Journal of the American Statistical Association* **88**, 486–494.

Shao, J. (1996) Bootstrap model selection. *Journal of the American Statistical Association* **91**, 655–665.

Shao, J. and Tu, D. (1995) *The Jackknife and Bootstrap*. New York: Springer.

Shao, J. and Wu, C. F. J. (1989) A general theory for jackknife variance estimation. *Annals of Statistics* **17**, 1176–1197.

Shorack, G. (1982) Bootstrapping robust regression. *Communications in Statistics — Theory and Methods* **11**, 961–972.

Silverman, B. W. (1981) Using kernel density estimates to investigate multimodality. *Journal of the Royal Statistical Society series B* **43**, 97–99.

Silverman, B. W. (1985) Some aspects of the spline smoothing approach to non-parametric regression curve fitting (with Discussion). *Journal of the Royal Statistical Society series B* **47**, 1–52.

Silverman, B. W. and Young, G. A. (1987) The bootstrap: to smooth or not to smooth? *Biometrika* **74**, 469–479.

Simonoff, J. S. and Tsai, C.-L. (1994) Use of modified profile likelihood for improved tests of constancy of variance in regression. *Applied Statistics* **43**, 357–370.

Singh, K. (1981) On the asymptotic accuracy of Efron's bootstrap. *Annals of Statistics* **9**, 1187–1195.

Sitter, R. R. (1992) A resampling procedure for complex survey data. *Journal of the American Statistical Association* **87**, 755–765.

Smith, P. W. F., Forster, J. J. and McDonald, J. W. (1996) Monte Carlo exact tests for square contingency tables. *Journal of the Royal Statistical Society series A* **159**, 309–321.

Spady, R. H. (1991) Saddlepoint approximations for regression models. *Biometrika* **78**, 879–889.

St. Laurent, R. T. and Cook, R. D. (1993) Leverage, local influence, and curvature in nonlinear regression. *Biometrika* **80**, 99–106.

Stangenhaus, G. (1987) Bootstrap and inference procedures for L_1 regression. In *Statistical Data Analysis Based on the L_1-Norm and Related Methods*, ed. Y. Dodge, pp. 323–332. Amsterdam: North-Holland.

Stein, C. M. (1985) *On the coverage probability of confidence sets based on a prior distribution*. Volume 16 of *Banach Centre Publications*. Warsaw: PWN — Polish Scientific Publishers.

Stein, M. (1987) Large sample properties of simulations using Latin hypercube sampling. *Technometrics* **29**, 143–151.

Sternberg, H. O'R. (1987) Aggravation of floods in the Amazon River as a consequence of deforestation? *Geografiska Annaler* **69A**, 201–219.

Sternberg, H. O'R. (1995) Water and wetlands of Brazilian Amazonia: an uncertain future. In *The Fragile Tropics of Latin America: Sustainable Management of Changing Environments*, eds T. Nishizawa and J. I. Uitto, pp. 113–179. Tokyo: United Nations University Press.

Stine, R. A. (1985) Bootstrap prediction intervals for regression. *Journal of the American Statistical Association* **80**, 1026–1031.

Stoffer, D. S. and Wall, K. D. (1991) Bootstrapping state-space models: Gaussian maximum likelihood estimation and the Kalman filter. *Journal of the American Statistical Association* **86**, 1024–1033.

Stone, M. (1974) Cross-validatory choice and assessment of statistical predictions (with Discussion). *Journal of the Royal Statistical Society series B* **36**, 111–147.

Stone, M. (1977) An asymptotic equivalence of choice of model by cross-validation and Akaike's criterion. *Journal of the Royal Statistical Society series B* **39**, 44–47.

Swanepoel, J. W. H. and van Wyk, J. W. J. (1986) The bootstrap applied to power spectral density function estimation. *Biometrika* **73**, 135–141.

Tanner, M. A. (1996) *Tools for Statistical Inference: Methods for the Exploration of Posterior Distributions and Likelihood Functions.* Third edition. New York: Springer.

Tanner, M. A. and Wong, W. H. (1987) The calculation of posterior densities by data augmentation (with Discussion). *Journal of the American Statistical Association* **82**, 528–550.

Theiler, J., Galdrikian, B., Longtin, A., Eubank, S. and Farmer, J. D. (1992) Using surrogate data to detect nonlinearity in time series. In *Nonlinear Modeling and Forecasting*, eds M. Casdagli and S. Eubank, number XII in Santa Fe Institute Studies in the Sciences of Complexity, pp. 163–188. New York: Addison-Wesley.

Therneau, T. (1983) *Variance reduction techniques for the bootstrap.* Ph.D. thesis, Department of Statistics, Stanford University, California.

Tibshirani, R. J. (1988) Variance stabilization and the bootstrap. *Biometrika* **75**, 433–444.

Tong, H. (1990) *Non-linear Time Series: A Dynamical System Approach.* Oxford: Clarendon Press.

Tsay, R. S. (1992) Model checking via parametric bootstraps in time series. *Applied Statistics* **41**, 1–15.

Tukey, J. W. (1958) Bias and confidence in not quite large samples (Abstract). *Annals of Mathematical Statistics* **29**, 614.

Venables, W. N. and Ripley, B. D. (1994) *Modern Applied Statistics with S-Plus.* New York: Springer.

Ventura, V. (1997) *Likelihood inference by Monte Carlo methods and efficient nested bootstrapping.* D.Phil. thesis, Department of Statistics, University of Oxford.

Ventura, V., Davison, A. C. and Boniface, S. J. (1997) Statistical inference for the effect of magnetic brain stimulation on a motoneurone. *Applied Statistics* **46**, to appear.

Wahrendorf, J., Becher, H. and Brown, C. C. (1987) Bootstrap comparison of non-nested generalized linear models: applications in survival analysis and epidemiology. *Applied Statistics* **36**, 72–81.

Wand, M. P. and Jones, M. C. (1995) *Kernel Smoothing.* London: Chapman & Hall.

Wang, S. (1990) Saddlepoint approximations in resampling analysis. *Annals of the Institute of Statistical Mathematics* **42**, 115–131.

Wang, S. (1992) General saddlepoint approximations in the bootstrap. *Statistics and Probability Letters* **13**, 61–66.

Wang, S. (1993a) Saddlepoint expansions in finite population problems. *Biometrika* **80**, 583–590.

Wang, S. (1993b) Saddlepoint methods for bootstrap confidence bands in nonparametric regression. *Australian Journal of Statistics* **35**, 93–101.

Wang, S. (1995) Optimizing the smoothed bootstrap. *Annals of the Institute of Statistical Mathematics* **47**, 65–80.

Weisberg, S. (1985) *Applied Linear Regression.* Second edition. New York: Wiley.

Welch, B. L. and Peers, H. W. (1963) On formulae for confidence points based on integrals of weighted likelihoods. *Journal of the Royal Statistical Society series B* **25**, 318–329.

Welch, W. J. (1990) Construction of permutation tests. *Journal of the American Statistical Association* **85**, 693–698.

Welch, W. J. and Fahey, T. J. (1994) Correcting for covariates in permutation tests. Technical Report STAT-94-12, Department of Statistics and Actuarial Science, University of Waterloo, Waterloo, Ontario.

Westfall, P. H. and Young, S. S. (1993) *Resampling-Based Multiple Testing: Examples and Methods for p-value Adjustment.* New York: Wiley.

Woods, H., Steinour, H. H. and Starke, H. R. (1932) Effect of composition of Portland cement on heat evolved during hardening. *Industrial Engineering and Chemistry* **24**, 1207–1214.

Wu, C. J. F. (1986) Jackknife, bootstrap and other resampling methods in regression analysis (with Discussion). *Annals of Statistics* **14**, 1261–1350.

Wu, C. J. F. (1990) On the asymptotic properties of the jackknife histogram. *Annals of Statistics* **18**, 1438–1452.

Wu, C. J. F. (1991) Balanced repeated replications based on mixed orthogonal arrays. *Biometrika* **78**, 181–188.

Young, G. A. (1986) Conditioned data-based simulations: Some examples from geometrical statistics. *International Statistical Review* **54**, 1–13.

Young, G. A. (1990) Alternative smoothed bootstraps. *Journal of the Royal Statistical Society series B* **52**, 477–484.

Young, G. A. and Daniels, H. E. (1990) Bootstrap bias. *Biometrika* **77**, 179–185.

Name Index

Example index

Subject index